Multicultural Psychoeducational Assessment

Dr. Elena L. Grigorenko received her PhD in general psychology from Moscow State University, Russia, in 1990, and her PhD in developmental psychology and genetics from Yale University in 1996. Currently, Dr. Grigorenko is Associate Professor of Child Studies, Psychology, and Epidemiology and Public Health at Yale and Adjunct Professor of Psychology at Columbia University and Moscow State University (Russia). Dr. Grigorenko has published more than 200 peer-reviewed articles, book chapters, and books. She has received awards for her work from five different divisions of the American Psychological Association: the Gardner Lindzey Dissertation Award in General Psychology, Sigmund Koch Early Career Award in Theoretical and Philosophical Psychology, Berlyne Early Career Award for Creative Achievement in Psychology of the Arts, Boyd McCandless Early Career Award in Developmental Psychology, and Richard E. Snow Early Career Award in Educational Psychology. In 2004, she won the APA Distinguished Award for an Early Career Contribution to Developmental Psychology. Dr. Grigorenko's research has been funded by NIH, NSF, DOE, Cure Autism Now, the Foundation for Child Development, the American Psychological Foundation, and other federal and private sponsoring organizations.

Multicultural Psychoeducational Assessment

Edited by

ELENA L. GRIGORENKO, PhD

SPRINGER PUBLISHING COMPANY

New York

Copyright © 2009 Springer Publishing Company, LLC

Springer Publishing Company, LLC
11 West 42nd Street
New York, NY 10036
www.springerpub.com

Acquisitions Editor: Philip Laughlin
Project Manager: Julia Rosen
Cover design: Steve Pisano
Composition: Apex CoVantage, LLC

Ebook ISBN: 978-0-8261-0102-0

09 10 11 12 / 5 4 3 2 1

Library of Congress Cataloging-in-Publication Data

Grigorenko, Elena L.
    Multicultural psychoeducational assessment / edited by
Elena L. Grigorenko.
        p. cm.
    Includes bibliographical references and index.
    ISBN 978-0-8261-0101-3 (alk. paper)
    1. Psychological tests.   2. Educational tests and measurements.
3. Cultural pluralism.   I. Title.
    BF176.G75 2009
    150.28'7—dc22   2008050932

Printed in the United States of America by Hamilton Printing.

To all children growing up in the developing world, where most of the world live, but where wealth, education, and research are still scarce.

Contents

Contributors xi
Preface by Elena L. Grigorenko xv

1 How Universal Are Test Development and Use? 1
Thomas Oakland

2 Equitable Assessment Practices in Diverse Contexts 41
Elias Mpofu and Samuel O. Ortiz

3 Respecting Local, Cultural Contexts for Assessment
Practice in an Era of Globalization 77
Val Klenowski

4 Conceptualizing Developmental Assessment Within
Africa's Cultural Settings 95
A. Bame Nsamenang

5 Assessing the Environment of Children's Learning:
The Developmental Niche in Africa 133
**Sara Harkness, Charles M. Super, Oumar Barry,
Marian Zeitlin, and Jennifer Long**

6 Assessing Competencies in Reading and Mathematics
in Zambian Children 157
**Steven E. Stemler, Florence Chamvu, Hilary Chart, Linda Jarvin,
Jackie Jere, Lesley Hart, Bestern Kaani, Kalima Kalima,
Jonna Kwiatkowski, Aidan Mambwe, Sophie Kasonde-N'gandu,
Tina Newman, Robert Serpell, Sara Sparrow, Robert J. Sternberg,
and Elena L. Grigorenko**

7 Assessing Mother Tongue in the Era of Globalization: Promise and Challenge   187

Elena L. Grigorenko, Kelly Nedwick, Dinah Kwadade, Erik Boro, Lesley Hart, Tina Newman, and Linda Jarvin

8 The Logic of Confidence and the Social Economy of Assessment Reform in Singapore: A New Institutionalist Perspective   213

David Hogan, Phillip A. Towndrow, and Kim Koh

9 Instructional and Assessment Practices in Singapore   253

David Hogan, Phillip A. Towndrow, and Kim Koh

10 Considerations for Developing and Adapting Language and Literacy Assessments in Arabic-Speaking Countries   287

Saleh Shaalan

11 The Behavioral Characteristics of Kindergarten Gifted Children in Saudi Arabia: Construction and Validation of a Scale   315

Usama M. A. Ibrahim and Abdullah M. Aljughaiman

12 Developing Culture-Specific Assessments   335

Alexander G. Shmelyov and Anna S. Naumenko

13 The Use of Foreign Psychodiagnostic Inventories in Differing Methodological Contexts   351

Tatiana V. Kornilova and Sergey A. Kornilov

14 Adapting Existing Abilities and Competencies Assessment Devices to Different Cultures   375

Márcia Regina F. de Brito

15 The Challenge of Measuring Abilities and Competencies in Hispanics/Latinos   417

Antonio E. Puente and Antonio N. Puente

16 Considering Language, Culture, and Cognitive
Abilities: The International Translation and
Adaptation of the Aurora Assessment Battery   443
Mei T. Tan, Abdullah M. Aljughaiman, Julian G. Elliott,
Sergey A. Kornilov, Mercedes Ferrando-Prieto, David S. Bolden,
Karen Adams-Shearer, Hilary E. Chart, Tina Newman, Linda Jarvin,
Robert J. Sternberg, and Elena L. Grigorenko

17 Conclusions: Assessment in an Era of Globalization   469
Peter Tymms and Robert Coe

Index   487

Contributors

Karen Adams-Shearer, BA
Hartlepool Borough Council
UK

Abdullah M. Aljughaiman, PhD
King Faisal University
Saudi Arabia

Oumar Barry, PhD
University Cheikh Anta Diop of Dakar
Senegal

David S. Bolden, EdD
Durham University
UK

Erik Boro, BA
Ministry of Education
Ghana

Florence Chamvu, MA
University of Zambia
Zambia

Hilary Chart, MA
Stanford University
USA

Robert Coe, PhD
Durham University
UK

Márcia Regina F. de Brito, PhD
State University of Campinas
Brazil

Julian G. Elliott, PhD
Durham University
UK

Mercedes Ferrando-Prieto, PhD
University of Murcia
Spain

Jacquiline Folotiya-Jere, MA
University of Zambia
Zambia

Elena L. Grigorenko, PhD
Yale University
USA

Sara Harkness, PhD, MPH
University of Connecticut
USA

Lesley Hart, PhD
Yale University
USA

David Hogan, PhD
Nanyang Technological
    University
Singapore

Usama M. A. Ibrahim, PhD
King Abdulaziz and his
    Companions Foundation
    for the Gifted
Saudi Arabia

Linda Jarvin, PhD
Tufts University
USA

Bestern Kaani, PhD
University of Zambia
Zambia

Kalima Kalima, PhD
University of Zambia
Zambia

Sophie Kasonde-N'gandu, PhD
University of Zambia
Zambia

Val Klenowski, PhD
Queensland University of Technology
Australia

Kim Koh, PhD
Nanyang Technological University
Singapore

Sergey A. Kornilov, BSc/BA
Moscow State University
Russia

Tatiana V. Kornilova, PhD
Moscow State University
Russia

Dinah Kwadade, MEd
Ministry of Education
Ghana

Jonna Kwiatkowski, PhD
Emmanuel College
USA

Jennifer Long, PhD
University of Illinois at Chicago
USA

Aidan Mambwe, PhD
University of Zambia
Zambia

Elias Mpofu, PhD
University of Sydney
Australia

Anna S. Naumenko, PhD
Moscow State University
Russia

Kelly Nedwick, MA
Yale University
USA

Tina Newman, PhD
Yale University
USA

A. Bame Nsamenang, PhD
Yaounde University
Cameroon

Thomas Oakland, PhD
University of Florida
USA

Samuel O. Ortiz, PhD
St. John's University
USA

Antonio E. Puente, PhD
University of North Carolina
Wilmington
USA

Antonio N. Puente, PhD
University of North Carolina
Wilmington
USA

Robert Serpell, PhD
University of Zambia
Zambia

Saleh Shaalan, CCC-SLP
University College
London
UK

Alexander G. Shmelyov, PhD
Moscow State University
Russia

Sara Sparrow, PhD
Yale University
USA

Steven E. Stemler, PhD
Wesleyan University
USA

Robert J. Sternberg, PhD
Tufts University
USA

Charles M. Super, PhD
University of Connecticut
USA

Mei T. Tan, MA
Yale University
USA

Phillip A. Towndrow, PhD
Nanyang Technological University
Singapore

Peter Tymms, PhD
Durham University
UK

Marian Zeitlin, PhD
GENSEN EcoYoff Living & Learning
   Center
Senegal

Preface

Elena L. Grigorenko

There is always a mix of joy and sadness in completing an edited volume. It is quite delightful to realize that a large-scale project is done; yet, it is quite poignant to complete something that has taken quite a large portion of one's time, devotion, and energy and let it make its own way in the world, even though that is where, by its very nature, it belongs.

This volume is a diverse and exciting collection of contributions sampling from different theoretical perspectives on assessment, exemplifying assessments of different psychological processes and functions, and illustrating international views on assessments and the roles of assessments in different countries around the world. The issues that are raised here are complex and various, but linked together by their shared contemplations on matters integral to the meaning, validity, fairness, and interpretability of today's assessments.

The word *globalization,* although around since the 1960s, has received much attention and use only recently, within the last decade or so. These days we hear and see news of this world everywhere and virtually every day. The reason is that globalization is unfolding now. So, what is it that is happening?

There are many definitions of globalization. Palmer (2002), for example, defines it as "the diminution or elimination of state-enforced restrictions on exchanges across borders and the increasingly integrated and complex global system of production and exchange that has emerged as a result" (p. 1). Notice that what is exchanged is not specified. In the context of this book, the objects of exchange are assessments.

People have always tried to size each other up, whether in an intellectual debate (e.g., in Socrates' defiant defense during his trial by the prominent Athenians) or an armored fight (e.g., Achilles and Hector in Troy). And often the consequences of such assessments were very costly, such as in these cases. "Sizing up" became more structured and ordered when psychological and educational assessments came around in the late 19th to early 20th century. And in today's globalized (or globalizing) world, assessment still remains and will remain the main method of sizing people up. Assessment in the globalizing world assumes an agreement on the reasons, methods, and procedures for this attempt to size people up globally, that is, on a "world scale." Thus, the questions are: why, with what, and how to assess.

Answers to these questions are complex. This volume, collectively, endeavors to address all of these questions, examining assessments across the spectrum of abilities (from disabilities to giftedness), across multiple continents and cultures, across multiple languages, and across multiple domains of functioning. While the book does not offer any final or absolute conclusions, it offers a diverse collection of well-articulated approaches illustrated with data. I am profoundly thankful to the authors not only for their willingness to write for the book, but also for their patience with revisions, suggestions, and their search to find ways to express themselves in English (note that a substantial portion of the contributors to the volume are foreign-language speakers). And last but not least, I express my sincere appreciation for the support, creativity, and camaraderie I received from Springer Publishing's Senior Editor, Phil Laughlin.

But now, the book is done. And so we will wait to see how it makes its way. We hope, globally.

REFERENCE

Palmer, T. G. (2002). Globalization is grrrrreat! *Cato's Letters, 2,* 1–6.

Multicultural Psychoeducational Assessment

1

How Universal Are Test Development and Use?

THOMAS OAKLAND

This chapter discusses the status of test development and use internationally. The chapter opens with a discussion of qualities that impact test availability and then discusses the results of international surveys that provide information on the status of test development and use with children and adults. National and international technical standards and guidelines for test development and use are discussed. Guidelines for adapting tests are highlighted. Ethical issues associated with test development and use as well as national, regional, and international codes of ethics are discussed. Traditional and emerging models used to define and describe disorders are identified. The World Health Organization's International Classification of Functioning, Disability and Health is described in some detail. The impact of external and internal conditions that will influence the futures of test development and use are discussed. The chapter concludes with a description of efforts in three regions to promote test development and use that exemplify many of the themes discussed herein.

This chapter focuses on the international use of standardized tests commonly used in the behavioral sciences, industry, and education, namely those that have well-established standards for administration and scoring and generally provide scores that are interpreted normatively (e.g., comparing one person's scores to those of a norm group).

This chapter does not focus on teacher-made tests, those used exclusively in health care, the use of clinical observations, or other informal and unstandardized testing methods.

Test use is universal. Tests are used in virtually every country, with newborns through the elderly, and most commonly with students (e.g., persons engaged in formal education from preschool through graduate school). Tests are used within the behavioral sciences to describe current behaviors and other qualities, estimate future behaviors, assist guidance and counseling services, establish intervention methods, evaluate progress, screen for special needs, diagnose disabling disorders, help place persons in jobs or programs, and assist in determining whether persons should be credentialed, admitted/employed, retained, or promoted. Tests also are used widely in research and for various administrative and planning purposes. Tests may be administered to groups or individually to assess aptitudes, achievement, adaptive behavior, intelligence, language, motor, perception, personality, and other personal qualities (Oakland, 2004).

QUALITIES THAT IMPACT TEST AVAILABILITY AND USE

Although tests are widely available and enjoy widespread use in many countries, their availability and use differ considerably among the more than 220 countries. The need for tests spurs test development. Test development may occur only when a need for tests is recognized. Educational institutions and those who work in them often constitute the largest consumers of tests within a country. Thus, the development and financing of a country's educational system strongly impact test need and development. Test use and thus test development generally are stronger in countries with well-established and universally attended public education systems that include elementary, secondary, and tertiary education. Countries that lack this infrastructure or are unable to fund it adequately are less likely to need tests.

A country must have a testing industry with sufficient financial and personnel resources to support the development and use of standardized tests. Test development can be expensive, with some costing more than $500,000. Thus, companies that develop and market tests can expect a sufficient return on their investment to warrant this expense. Additionally, personnel with expertise in organizational management as well as psychometrics and test development must be available to assume leadership for developing and marketing tests.

Test development and use also assume the presence of a sufficiently large and stable market. Most tests are developed in response to requests by professionals to assist them in their work. Test consumers commonly include educators, counselors, management specialists, medical specialists, occupational therapists, physical therapists, psychologists, social workers, speech pathologists, and other professionals. An infrastructure that supports test development and use also requires the presence of a fairly large number of educational programs at the tertiary level that prepare professionals with skills associated with administering, scoring, and interpreting tests. Test development is viable only when there is a sufficiently large workforce that commonly purchases and uses tests. Thus, test development and use most commonly occur in countries that enjoy stable financial support for education, have well-developed economies that depend on test use, tertiary education programs that prepare persons for test development and use, and a large workforce that depends on test data.

A country also must display positive attitudes toward test use. Its citizens must view the use of tests and other assessment methods to be reliable, valid, efficient, humane, and address important social issues. Test development and use are based on science, and test use is a form of technology. Thus, tests are more common in countries that value science and technology.

Tests first were developed more than 3,000 years ago in China (Wang, 1993). In the 1880s tests were developed in the West to assist research efforts that examined individual differences (i.e., whether traits that distinguish people can be validly assessed). Test use assumes the presence of individual differences and the importance of identifying them. Countries differ in the value they place on individuals versus groups (e.g., families, work, and social groups) and differ in their emphasis on the importance of individuals versus groups.

Countries that place a greater emphasis on individualism (e.g., the United States and most Western European countries) expect their citizens to look after one's self and immediate family. Persons in these countries tend to be more competitive and believe their interests are more important than most others. In contrast, countries that place greater emphasis on collectivism (e.g., People's Republic of China, most Latin American countries) expect their citizens to form strong cohesive groups that protect them in exchange for their service and loyalty. Persons in these countries are more inclined to put aside their individual pursuits in favor of those important to the groups in which they are members (Hofstede, 1994).

A country's emphasis on this individualism-collectivism dimension impacts test development and use. Test development tends to occur more frequently in countries that emphasize individualism and favor meritocracy (i.e., the belief that persons should be rewarded based on their accomplishments) than collectivism and egalitarianism (i.e., the belief that all people are equal and should have equal access to resources and opportunities). Some psychologists believe this focus on individual differences may be the discipline's most enduring and unique contribution to the behavioral sciences (Benjamin, 2007).

Nationally developed tests are most common in Australia, Canada, Western Europe, and the United States. These countries generally display a stronger commitment to individualist and merit-based beliefs than to collectivist- and egalitarian-based beliefs. Collectively, they constitute about 10% of the world's population. In contrast, test development and use are lower in countries that have or had strong ties to communism or socialism or strongly value a collectivism (e.g., People's Republic of China, countries that formed the Soviet Union, as well as Mexico and those in Central and South America). Test development and use are lowest among the 55 African countries and 22 Arab countries (Hu & Oakland, 1991; Oakland & Hu, 1991, 1992, 1993).

The following 12 countries have the largest populations (e.g., in rank order: China, India, United States, Indonesia, Brazil, Pakistan, Bangladesh, Russia, Japan, Mexico, Philippines, Vietnam). Their combined population is approximately 4.2 billion. Among them, only the United States has a large number of locally developed standardized tests. An estimated 80% or more of the world's population reside in countries in which locally developed standardized tests either are somewhat uncommon or rare.

INTERNATIONAL SURVEYS ON TEST USE

Test Use With Children

Forty-four respondents with specialized knowledge of psychological and/or educational testing in their countries and who were members of the International School Psychology Association, International Council of Psychologists, or the International Test Commission completed a questionnaire through which detailed information about the status of test development and use with children and youth in their respective countries was obtained. Respondents identified 455 tests used frequently, especially measures of intelligence, personality, and achievement (Hu & Oakland, 1991; Oakland & Hu, 1991, 1992, 1993).

Among commonly used tests, 46% were developed within other countries and imported for use. Tests imported for use came mainly from one of five countries: United States (22%), United Kingdom (7%), Germany (7%), France (5%), and Sweden (5%). The 99 tests that were published in the United States were cited 301 times. Among those tests used outside their country of origin, 97% were developed in highly industrialized nations.

Foreign-developed tests were used more frequently than locally developed tests in 68% of the countries surveyed. Locally developed tests were used more frequently than foreign-developed tests in only 27% of the countries. Seven countries report no locally developed tests. Many smaller and developing countries that were not surveyed also are likely to lack locally developed tests.

Types of Tests Used

Measures of intelligence (39%), personality (24%), and achievement (10%) were cited most commonly. Measures of perceptual-motor abilities, vocational interests and aptitudes, school readiness, and social development were less common (i.e., 3% to 6% in each of the categories).

Psychometric Standards

Standardized tests can be expected to display three basic qualities: adequate, representative, and recent norms; sufficient reliability to ensure the data are stable; and sufficient validity based on both theory and empirical evidence that pertain to the ways in which tests are used. Many tests used in the more developed countries display these qualities. However, many—perhaps most—tests used in developing countries lack one or more of these basic qualities. The psychometric qualities of tests tend to be most deficient when tests are obtained from a host country (i.e., the test's country of origin) and translated for use in the target country (the location in which the translated test is used). These tests typically lack target country norms and their reliabilities and validities are unknown. As noted later in this chapter, the use of the International Test

Commission's guidelines for test adaptations helps overcome many of the problems seen in translated tests. The psychometric qualities of tests identified in Oakland and Hu's survey are summarized below.

Availability of Norms

Sound testing practices typically rely on locally developed norms. National norms were available on 80% of the achievement tests, 65% of intelligence tests, and 58% of personality tests. Thus, many tests lack local norms.

Reliability Studies

Tests must provide consistent data for them to be useful. Studies estimating internal consistency or test-retest reliability were conducted on approximately 50% to 60% of achievement, intelligence, and personality tests. Thus, the reliability of many tests is unknown.

Validity Studies

Validity (e.g., the degree to which a test accurately measures what it was designed to measure) generally constitutes a test's most valued quality. Validity studies were most common on achievement tests. Among achievement tests, concurrent validity studies were available on 71%, construct validity studies on 48%, and predictive validity studies on 43%. Among measures of intelligence, concurrent validity studies were available on 63%, predictive validity studies on 56%, and construct validity studies on 54%. Thus, the validity of many tests is unknown.

Needs for Tests

Two-thirds of the countries reported critical needs for both group and individual tests of achievement, intelligence, vocational interests and aptitudes, social development and personality as well as more moderate needs for measures of perception, motor development as well as those used for entrance into primary, secondary, and tertiary schools.

Eighty-five percent of the responding countries reported the need for tests that assess qualities important for those who are mentally retarded, blind, deaf, learning disabled, slower learners, emotionally and socially disturbed, physically impaired, and the gifted. The need for tests for those with learning disabilities was most critical.

Professionals Who Administer Tests

Sound testing practices require suitably educated professionals to correctly select, administer, score, and to wisely interpret tests and other measures. At least 16 professional groups commonly administer tests (Oakland & Hu, 1991). In many countries, school or educational psychologists assumed leadership for these activities. Other frequently cited specialists included regular or special education teachers, clinical psychologists, counselors, and professionals engaged in the health service professions.

The amount of postsecondary education found among the 16 groups ranges from a mean of 2.5 years for nurses to 6.5 years for physicians. The correlation between years of postsecondary education and the perceived adequacy of test users is significant ($r = .50$, $p < .001$). Thus, the adequacy of test users is associated with their level of education. Professionals who use both group and individually administered tests typically have more education than those who use only group tests.

Test Use With Adults

Test use with adults also is common and somewhat universal. Tests are used by tertiary institutions for entrance, retention, and graduation; by state and national boards to certify and license vocations and professions; by professionals to evaluate medical, social, and psychological problems; and in the business community to assist in selecting, training, retaining, and promoting employees as well as certifying attainment of critical abilities and skills of persons at entry and mid-management levels and above (e.g., DiMilia, Smith, & Brown, 1994; Gowing & Slivinski, 1994; Schuler, Frier, & Kauffmann, 1993; Shackleton & Newell, 1994). For example, persons seeking positions that require word and numerical processing skills increasingly are required to demonstrate competence in the use of software programs by passing tests developed for this purpose. One software company, Microsoft, administered credentialing examinations to more than 1 million persons in 15 languages and in more than 30 countries in 1997 (Fitzgerald & Ward, 1998).

The Myers-Briggs Type Indicator, commonly used in personnel selection, training, and team building, may be the most widely used measure in the world, with 2 million administrations reportedly occurring each year (Myers, McCauley, Quenk, & Hammer, 1998). It has been translated into at least 17 languages or dialects for which there is commercial distribution and another 13 languages for which there is so-called underground (e.g., noncommercial) distribution. The Minnesota Multiphasic Personality Inventory also is widely used. Cross-national research supporting the viability of the big five personality model cross-nationally has contributed to the popularity of the Revised NEO Personality Inventory and NEO Five-Factor Inventory (Costa & McCrae, 1992). Cheung's review (2004) of the uses of Western and indigenously (i.e., locally) developed personality tests in Asia underscores the growing interest in personality assessment for research and clinical use within this region.

An international survey of test-related issues in 29 countries (19 in Europe and others from Central and South America, Asia-Pacific, the Middle East, and South Africa), largely in reference to adults, also reports considerable diversity between countries in their approaches to testing, their uses of tests, and attitudes toward test user qualifications (Bartram & Coyne, 1998; Muniz, Prieto, Almeida, & Bartram, 1999). Assessment methods are more consistent within specialty areas of applied practice (e.g., within clinical, occupational, educational, or forensic practices) across countries than between specialty areas within countries.

STANDARDS AND GUIDELINES THAT MAY IMPACT TEST DEVELOPMENT AND USE

Test development and use generally are strengthened by employing standards or guidelines, including those that address legal uses of tests, standards and guidelines for test development and use, ethical issues associated with test development and use, and professional qualities needed by those who use tests. Legal issues typically differ considerably between countries. Scholarship that examines legal issues impacting test development and use internationally could not be located. Thus, the following comments address other nonlegal issues.

Technical Standards and Guidelines for Test Development and Use

Professional associations can be expected to establish and promulgate standards or guidelines that impact their professional practices. Standards define obligatory practices whereas guidelines suggest advisory practices. Standards are employed when a professional association, typically at the national level, has sufficient authority and leverage to oversee the display of practices associated with standards by its members and, when needed, can take steps to either curtail or work to improve unsuitable practices. International professional associations rarely have this authority and leverage and thus propose guidelines, not standards, for practice.

Examples of National Standards

Standards for Educational and Psychological Testing (American Educational Research Association [AERA], American Psychological Association [APA], & National Council on Measurement in Education, 1999) and its previous editions have served as the authoritative source for test development and use in the United States since 1954. The current edition discusses issues pertaining to test construction, evaluation, and documentation (e.g., validity, reliability, scales, norms, test administration and scoring), fairness in testing (e.g., rights and responsibilities of test-takers, testing persons from diverse linguistic backgrounds and those with disabilities), and testing applications (e.g., test use in psychology, education, employment, credentialing, and program evaluation). These standards and those from the Canadian Psychological Association (1987) and other sources (e.g., Joint Committee on Testing Practices, 1993; Kendall, Jenkinson, De Lemos, & Clancy, 1997; Koene, 1997; Lindsay, 1996) often find acceptance from psychologists in other countries in which national standards on test development and use have not been established.

International Guidelines

The International Test Commission (ITC, www.intestcom.org) plays a central role in addressing cross-national issues that impact test development and use. It sponsors biannual conventions, a journal (*International Journal of Testing*), a newsletter (*Testing International*), and has assumed leadership with respect to developing international guidelines for test use, adapting tests, and testing and the Internet. These guidelines are summarized below.

Guidelines for Test Use

The International Test Commission's commitment to promoting practices that can have a beneficial impact on test use is seen in its original charge. Early records reveal an uneasiness as to the presence of unqualified persons using tests, their making important decisions despite their limited preparation and experience, and their use of tests that lack suitable norms and sufficient validity (Oakland, Poortinga, Schlegel, & Hambleton, 2001). The International Guidelines for Test Use, developed under the leadership of David Bartram (past president of the International Test Commission), discuss the fair and ethical use of tests with the intent to provide an internationally agreed framework from which standards for training and test user competence and qualifications could be derived (Bartram, 1998). These guidelines were approved by the International Test Commission in 1999 and have been endorsed by the European Federation of Professional Psychologists Associations Standing Committee on Tests and Testing. A number of countries have translated and adopted these guidelines.

Guidelines on Test Adaptations

As noted above, test use in most countries is characterized by importing tests, typically from five Western countries. These tests typically are translated from the original source language to the local language. Efforts to norm these translated tests, establish their psychometric properties (e.g., reliability and validity), and determine the relevance of the test's content to the local culture are sporadic. These practices clearly are below professional standards.

The International Test Commission, under the leadership of Ronald Hambleton (past president of the International Test Commission), together with support and participation from various organizations (i.e., American Psychological Association, Canadian Nursing Association, Collegio de Psicologos, European Association for Psychological Assessment, European Test Publishers Group, International Association for the Evaluation of Educational Achievement, International Union of Psychological Sciences, National Institute for Education Measurement in the Netherlands, and the United States Department of Education) developed guidelines for adapting educational and psychological tests in an effort to overcome these deficiencies (Hambleton, 1994; Hambleton, Merenda, & Spielberger, 2005; Muniz & Hambleton, 1997; van de Vijver & Hambleton, 1996). These guidelines are discussed in some detail below, given their relevance for avoiding common problems associated with merely translating tests.

The test adaptation guidelines are intended to provide assistance to persons attempting to transform a test from one originally intended to be used with one population (the source) to one suitable for use with a different population (the target). Two examples include the transformation of a test originally developed in the United States to one revised for use in Hungary or transforming a test from one developed in Hungary designed to be used with native-born Hungarians to one revised for use in Hungary with non–native-born Hungarians from Romania. These guidelines discuss cultural and language differences, identify five technical issues and methods, and describe three conditions that possibly impact test interpretations. Each of these is reviewed below.

Measurement Error and Their Sources. Test validity constitutes a test's most important quality (AERA et al., 1999). Validity refers to the accuracy with which a test measures a construct and how the results may be used appropriately. Validity is judged in light of theory and empirical evidence that support the manner in which test data are interpreted and used. Strictly speaking, a test does not have validity.

Validity may be attenuated by various conditions. Two that are most prominent include construct underrepresentation (i.e., when a test fails to measure important aspects of the construct) and construct irrelevance (i.e., when qualities extraneous to the construct attenuate its measurement). Thus, those engaged in test development and use as well as test adaptations strive to reduce measurement error by ensuring a test measures a trait or construct adequately and consistently with the source test and that the target test does not measure extraneous qualities (e.g., that a measure of intelligence also does not measure the ability to read or to use a particular language or dialect) in order to help ensure the scores are accurate. Three broad conditions that may contribute to measurement error when adapting tests or using them are discussed below: cultural and language differences, technical issues and methods, and conditions that impact test performance.

Cultural and Language Differences. The potential for error increases as differences increase between persons who comprise the source (i.e., first) and target (i.e., the one used in the adapted test) tests in reference to languages, culture (e.g., values, dress, food, money, forms of measurement), social class, urban-rural residence, gender, and age. Four methods to address these potential problems include establishing the equivalence of the constructs for the various groups, promoting proper test administrative practices, utilizing suitable norms, and minimizing tests that rely heavily on speed.

First, establish a test's construct equivalence. Knowledge of a test's construct provides the single most important evidence of a test's validity. Construct validity is likely to be promoted when a test displays other suitable psychometric qualities (e.g., reliability, adequacy of norms) and to not be adversely impacted by unsuitable psychometric qualities. Investigations of construct equivalence consider whether the target culture has and adheres to this construct, whether the construct has a similar meaning within the two cultures, and whether the construct is displayed in a similar fashion.

Methods to investigate construct equivalence initially involve and often rely heavily on judgmental strategies (e.g., interviewing and observing persons, literature reviews, as well as consulting with cultural anthropologists and others who specialize in a region and know the culture well). These judgmental strategies are subjective and thus will benefit from input from multiple sources.

Second, promote proper test administration. For example, test directions should be understood clearly, verbal communication should be minimal, and information should be communicated consistently for source and target groups. Test administrators should be properly selected. They should be drawn from the target community(ies), familiar with the culture and with the languages (dialects), have experience administering tests, and recognize the importance of maintaining standardized methods. Their training and preparation may be needed to obtain these qualities together with ongoing supervision to ensure their presence.

Third, utilize suitable test formats. Cultures differ in their use of different test formats (e.g., multiple choice, short answer, essay). While one typically should emphasize the use of those formats with which people are familiar, the limited use of various formats may be warranted. When using tests to make cross-cultural comparisons, consider using a multiple-choice format as it can be scored more objectively. In contrast, scoring rubrics for essay exams may introduce considerable error.

Fourth, emphasize power and reduce reliance on speed. Cultures differ in reference to the importance placed on completing work, including tests, well or quickly. *Power tests* are intended to assess a person's level of mastery of a topic or trait when tested without time constraints. In contrast, *speed tests* are intended to assess the number of problems a person can complete during a predetermined and often brief time period. Power tests rather than speed tests may provide a more accurate assessment of many qualities.

Five Technical Issues and Methods. Various technical issues and methods used when adapting a test are summarized below.

Focus on the test revision process. When developing a test that is likely to be used in two or more cultures, outline a test development strategy that reflects this goal. Address issues that pertain to the choice of item formats, stimulus materials, vocabulary (e.g., unless the test assesses vocabulary, keep vocabulary simple), sentence structure (again, keep it simple), and cultural differences (e.g., seasons, time, money, weights, foods, dress, gender roles, knowledge content, writing and reading from either the right or left, as well as temperament and personality differences).

Select and prepare translators. A target test is only as good as its linguistic equivalent of the source test. Translators should include two or more persons familiar with both cultures and languages (i.e., more than a literal translation is needed), the subject matter, and with skills in test construction.

Use data analysis methods to establish equivalence and to detect bias. Ultimately data need to be collected and analyzed. The data should examine qualities at the item level (e.g., difficulty, distractibility, and discrimination), construct level (e.g., confirmatory factor analysis), together with means and standard deviations. Note that groups may differ legitimately in their means and standard deviations. Moreover, such differences may be less important when cross-cultural and cross-national comparisons are not being made.

Decenter the test. The term *decentering* refers to a process of revising a test's source language so that equivalent materials can be used in both the source and target language versions. Two typical decentering methods are used when translating tests: a forward translation or a backward translation process. A third translation process, consensus translation, is discussed later in this chapter.

Using a forward translation, a single translator or group of translators first adapts the test from the source language to the target language. Then other translators compare the equivalence of the two versions. This comparison may lead to changes in the target language version. The advantages of the forward translation are that judgments are made directly between the two versions and the process is less costly and quicker. The disadvantages of this process are that considerable inferences are required by the translators, they may be more proficient in one of the two languages, and ratings by those who are bilingual may not reflect the language abilities of those who are monolingual.

Using a backward translation, a single translator or group of translators first adapts the test from the source language to the target language.

Then another group of translators adapts the test from the target language back to the source language. Then other translators compare the equivalence of the two versions. The principal advantage of this process is that it provides a more thorough review of possible language problems. Its disadvantages are that comparisons are specific to only the source language test, the target test will contain shortcomings of the original test (e.g., problems with grammar, content), and this process is more costly in time and personnel.

Both decentering methods are far from perfect. Both methods fail to provide empirical data on the performance of actual people for whom the test is designed as well as the test's psychometric characteristics. Furthermore, the tests were not administered under testlike conditions, and limitations inherent in the scope and concept of the source test are retained by the second target test.

These guidelines propose three empirical designs to help overcome some of these limitations. Bilingual examiners can take the source and target versions. This method helps control for ability levels, is low in costs, and can be completed quickly. However, one cannot assume those who are bilingual are similar to the target group in reference to important qualities (e.g., language).

A second method employs source language monolinguals who take the original and back-translated versions. This method allows for a comparison of item characteristics. However, source language monolinguals are likely to differ from non–source language monolinguals; furthermore, taking the first test may influence performance on the second test.

A third method employs source language monolinguals who take the source language test as well as target language monolinguals who take the target language test. This provides data on both tests. However, the two groups may differ by ability.

Conditions That Possibly Impact Test Performance. Three conditions may impact test performance and thus test interpretations: assumed similarity of cultural experiences, suitable levels of motivation, and sociopolitical qualities.

One may incorrectly assume cultural experiences between the source and target groups are similar. Differences may exist in access to information, school curricula, values, attitudes, and if one reads a book from the front to the back or from the back to the front.

Test results are assumed to be valid if those who took a test displayed suitable levels of motivation. For example, cognitive measures assume those being tested are highly motivated and strive to do as well as they possibly can. However, some examinees may not strive to achieve high scores. Three test-taking qualities can adversely influence test performance: avoidance, uncooperative mood, and inattentiveness (Oakland & Glutting, 1998). The display of these qualities generally contributes to error that result in scores below one's potential. One should be alert to the presence of these and other qualities that attenuate performance. Determining whether test-takers display avoidance, an uncooperative mood, or inattentiveness is more difficult on group than individually administered tests.

Sociopolitical qualities also may influence test performance. Tests typically require an individual to perform some activity. Some persons function well when asked to perform individually. However, others seemingly do better when involved in a group. For example, those who are extroverted generally prefer group activities that involve talking while those who are introverted generally prefer individual activities that rely more heavily on writing. Orientations to life also may be influenced by many qualities, including one's religion, tribal expectations, regional differences, gender, and individual-collective values.

Ethical Issues Associated With Test Adaptation. Thirty ethical standards from the APA's Ethical Principles of Psychologists and Code of Conduct (APA, 1992) apply to ethics associated with test adaptations and use (Oakland, 2005). Among them, test plagiarism (i.e., the taking of someone's work product for personal benefit without compensating the author) as well as nonadherence to copyright provisions (i.e., when tests either are photocopied or are adapted without the consent of the test's author and publisher) are somewhat common and serious. Possible implications of six ethical principles and 30 standards from the APA Code in reference to 11 stakeholders who use adapted tests are discussed elsewhere (Oakland, 2005). Persons involved in test adaptations should be aware of the potential violation of laws and ethical principles through their work and strive to establish and maintain high standards for themselves and the profession.

International Guidelines on Computer-Based and Internet-Delivered Testing

Technology that has an international reach often requires the involvement of organizations that transcend one nation. Efforts by multinational governmental agencies, multinational companies, as well as regional and international associations often are needed to envision, revise, create, promote, regulate, and in other ways assist in forming and reforming services in light of changes due to technology. Computer use surely is a pervasive technology that has changed the ways in which we work, shop, communicate, and play.

Through computers, testing technology has acquired an international reach and is increasing. Many of the world's largest testing companies are making their tests available through the Internet. This availability invites various problems. For example, although more than 150 countries are signatures to the 1996 World Intellectual Property Organization Copyright and Performance and Phonograms Treaties, they differ considerably in their adoption and enforcement of the treaty's provisions. This is seen clearly in nonadherence to copyright protection. Encryption and enveloping technologies together with copyright management information on test products are being used to help address this growing problem (Thiemann, 1998).

The legitimate use and potential abuse of computers generally is well known. The potential for abuse warranted standards or guidelines for test administration, security of tests and test results, and control of the testing process. Therefore, the International Test Commission established international guidelines on computer-based and Internet-delivered testing in its *Computer-Based Testing and the Internet: Issues and Advances* (Bartram & Hambleton, 2005; Coyne & Bartram, 2004; http://www.intestcom.org).

The goal of these guidelines is to raise awareness among all stakeholders in the testing process of internationally recognized guidelines that highlight good practice issues in computer-based testing (CBT) and testing delivered over the Internet. The development of these guidelines drew on common themes that run through other existing guidelines, codes of practice, standards, scholarship, and other sources to create a coherent structure within which they can be used and understood. In addition, these guidelines are specific to CBT/Internet-based testing. Test developers, test publishers, and test users share responsibilities for ensuring the following four guidelines are enforced.

Attend to technological issues in CBT/Internet testing (i.e., give consideration to hardware and software requirements, ensure the robustness of the CBT/Internet test, recognize human factors issues in the presentation of material via computer or the Internet, consider reasonable adjustments to the technical features of the test for candidates with disabilities, and provide help and information, both off- and on-screen, as well as practice items within CBT/Internet tests).

Attend to quality issues in CBT/Internet testing (i.e., ensure knowledge and competence of CBT/Internet testing, consider the psychometric qualities of the CBT/Internet test, ensure that there is evidence of equivalence when the CBT/Internet test has been developed from a paper-and-pencil version, score and analyze CBT/Internet testing results accurately, interpret results appropriately, give appropriate feedback, and work to ensure equality of access for all groups).

Provide appropriate levels of control over CBT/Internet testing (i.e., ensure control over the test conditions and their supervision, consider controlling prior practice and item exposure, and ensure control over test-taker's authenticity and cheating).

Make appropriate provision for ensuring security and safeguarding privacy in CBT/Internet testing (i.e., take account of the security of test materials, ensure security of test-taker's data transferred over the Internet, and maintain the confidentiality of test-taker results).

ETHICAL ISSUES ASSOCIATED WITH TEST DEVELOPMENT AND USE

An unwritten yet generally recognized social contract binds professions and the societies in which they practice. Within this social contract, a society agrees to provide funds to help prepare professionals and to conduct research as well as allows the profession to select, prepare, and credential neophytes and to establish standards for services. This social contract also requires a profession to serve all of society well and, minimally, to do no harm.

A profession's ethics' code informs society of its commitment to serve society. Such codes are designed to protect the public by prescribing and proscribing behaviors professionals are expected to exhibit. Ethics' codes typically contain principles and standards that reflect both general virtues (e.g., beneficence, fidelity) and specific behaviors (e.g., informed consent, confidentiality).

The first known ethics' code, the Code of Hammurabi (circa 1795–1750 B.C.), reflected a desire to impose rules governing personal and vocational behaviors (Sinclair, 2005). The Hippocratic Oath (circa 400 B.C.) is the first known example of a professionally generated ethics' code. The 1953 American Psychological Association's ethics' code is the first example of one for psychologists.

Psychology is represented internationally by various associations, two of which are most prominent: the International Union of Psychological

Science (IUPsyS) and the International Association of Applied Psychologists (IAAP)—the oldest international association of psychologists. The mission of IUPsyS is to build global interaction among research communities and promote advances in psychological science and technology at the international level. Its members are national associations. The mission of IAAP is to promote the science and practice of applied psychology and to facilitate interaction and communication about applied psychology around the world. Its members are individual psychologists.

The importance of these and other international associations has increased during the last two decades, given the growing science and practices of psychology that transcend country and cultural boundaries. Thus, one may expect the emergence of international and regional codes of ethics that address cross-national practice issues, including test development and use. Such codes would promote and highlight common professional practice, thus conveying psychology's universal commitment and impact.

International Ethics Codes

Neither the IUPsyS nor the IAAP has developed ethics codes. However, they approved the Declaration of Universal Ethical Principles for Psychologists (Gauthier, 2008). Its purpose is to promote unity within the profession of psychology internationally by including ethical practices regardless of country or culture. Although this declaration is not intended to replace existing codes, it is expected to impact their revisions.

The International School Psychology Association has adopted an ethics code, applicable only to its specialty, that addresses issues associated with professional responsibilities, confidentiality, professional growth and limitations, relationships, assessment, and research (Oakland, Goldman, & Bischoff, 1997).

Regional Ethics Codes

The European Federation of Professional Psychologists Associations' (EFPA) Meta-Code of Ethics (www.efpa.be/ethics.php), adopted in 1995, is applicable to practices of members of 31 national psychology organizations. This code is one of the first regional codes to underscore the importance of principles for psychological organizations and psychologists. This brief document addresses four main principles that are applicable to practice: respect for a person's rights and dignity, competence, responsibility, and integrity. The five Nordic countries (Denmark, Finland, Iceland, Norway, and Sweden) also adopted a unified code of ethics in 1988 that was revised in 1998 to be more consistent with EFPA's meta-code (Pettifor, 2007).

International Studies of Ethics Codes That Address Test-Related Issues

Contemporary forms of tests initially were used in research, not in applied practice, and thus had limited social visibility and impact. However, both the globalization of psychology as well as an increase in test use to address important social, psychological, educational, and vocational needs have deepened their impact and broadened their visibility, resulting in questions as to whether they serve the public good. Thus, ethical and other professional standards that inform the public regarding expectations from those who develop and use tests are needed.

Separate ethical principles and standards that govern only test development and use could not be located. Ethical principles and standards governing test development and use typically are embedded within a country's broader ethics code (APA, 1992; Lindsay, 1996). Moreover, psychological tests are used broadly in some countries and narrowly in others (e.g., mainly to assess mental retardation). Scholarship that discusses ethical issues specific to tests is somewhat meager (Leach, Glosoff, & Overmier, 2001; Leach & Harbin, 1997; Leach & Oakland, 2007).

Testing standards in 31 ethics codes representing 35 countries were compared with those in the APA's 2002 Ethical Principles of Psychologists and Code of Conduct (Leach & Oakland, 2007). Codes from approximately one-third of the countries surveyed do not address test use. This finding should not be surprising in that test development and use are not prevalent in many countries. Thus, their ethics codes do not need to address these issues.

However, ethics codes in some countries with advanced test development and use do not address test issues (e.g., Canada, Switzerland). Codes from some countries emphasize broad and virtuous qualities (e.g., respect, responsibility) intended to have a pervasive impact on psychological practice and do not focus on more specific interests (e.g., clinical practice, testing, advertising). Although these codes do not address test issues directly, their virtuous-centered principles are intended to impact them.

The 20 (65%) codes that address test use included one or more specific standards that also are consistent with the 2002 APA Code of Conduct. The frequency of ethics codes, noted in the parentheses, that address these standards follows: explaining test results (15), using assessment (11), assessment by unqualified persons (11), interpreting assessment results (10), maintaining test security (10), informed consent (8), test scoring and interpretation services (7), the basis of assessment (5), test construction (5), and using obsolete tests and outdated test results (4).

Given the widespread use of imported tests (Oakland & Hambleton, 1995), one may expect standards that directly address test use cross-nationally. However, only Latvia's code explicitly addresses this issue, stating that Latvian psychologists should conduct studies ensuring suitable psychometric properties when tests have been developed elsewhere (Leach & Oakland, 2007). Other commonly endorsed standards require persons who use tests to have suitable training and experience and to ensure the test's security (Leach & Harbin, 1997; Leach et al., 2001).

Few codes address issues associated with test construction or the use of obsolete tests; two issues that often are linked. For example, when psychological tests are more likely to be imported than developed locally, the tests tend to be used for many years despite the availability of newer editions. In addition, standards that address test construction generally are not needed in countries that do not develop their own tests.

Psychologists in many countries do not honor copyright protection of test protocols, manuals, and test kits. Two examples follow. Ten or more pirated copies of the Wechsler Intelligence Scale for Children are in use globally. The Russian government has been using the 16 Personality Factor Test for decades without compensating its author or publisher.

These practices violate international copyright laws and are unethical in those countries with ethics codes that proscribe these practices. International legal agreements prevent the photocopying and reproduction of intellectual and other property, including tests. Issues concerning the protection of copyright become ethical only if they are included in a country's ethics code. Few countries address this issue in their codes.

Psychologists play a leading role in developing and using psychological tests that serve the public and professions and thus are committed to maintaining the integrity and security of test materials and other assessment methods, knowing that their unauthorized release to the public jeopardizes test integrity, results in test use by unqualified persons, and thus harms the public. Some persons are selling tests through unauthorized sources to the general public. These sales jeopardize test integrity, harm the public, and violate accepted practice as well.

The International Test Commission has urged professionals to become aware of this possible practice in their countries and to take steps to stop such unauthorized sales. Unfortunately, ethics codes typically do not address issues associated with the secondary sale or disposal of tests one no longer uses. The Commission has encouraged national psychological associations to inform their members of this problem and to take preventative measures, including the revision of their ethics codes to help prevent this and similar unauthorized releases of tests to others. National psychological associations also are encouraged to develop standards that promote the safe disposal of outdated tests.

INTERNATIONAL SOURCES USED TO DEFINE AND DESCRIBE DISORDERS

Three Commonly Used Sources to Diagnose Mental Disorders

Test data commonly are used to describe behaviors and, when working in clinical settings, to diagnose disorders. Clinicians typically use one of the following three authoritative international sources to classify mental disorders: the *Diagnostic and Statistical Manual of Mental Disorders, 4th edition, text revision* (*DSM–IV–TR;* American Psychiatric Association, 2000); its *International Version* (American Psychiatric Association, 1995); and the *International Classification of Diseases and Related Health Problems, 10th edition* (*ICD–10;* World Health Organization [WHO], 1992). The disorders identified by the *ICD–10* generally are consistent with those cited in and are cross-referenced to the *DSM's International Version*. These three diagnostic systems have been developed by the medical community and view behaviors from a medical model.

A New Model for Conceptualizing Health, Wellness, and Disability

The World Health Organization's *International Classification of Functioning, Disability and Health* (*ICF;* WHO, 2001) provides a different model for viewing disorders. Its bio-psycho-social framework views behaviors from three broad perspectives (see Figure 1.1): (1) body functions

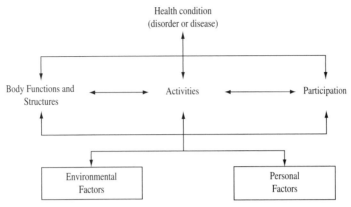

Figure 1.1 Interactions between the components of *ICF.*

From *International Classification of Functioning, Disability and Health: Children and Youth Version* (p. 17), by World Health Organization, 2007, Geneva, Switzerland: WHO. Copyright © 2007 by World Health Organization. Reprinted with permission.

and structures (e.g., physiologic, physical, and psychological functions), (2) activities (e.g., the extent to which persons engage in functional life activities), and (3) participation (e.g., their participation in social settings). A patient's health is understood from knowledge of the interaction between three broad components. Working in this model, professionals integrate medical and psychological information with knowledge of a person's social and adaptive skills (e.g., personality traits, coping abilities, stress, and social support). Professionals may use WHO's *International Classification of Diseases and Related Health Problems, 10th edition,* if a diagnosis is needed.

Thus, an understanding of a person's health requires knowledge of the dynamic nature between body functions, body structures, and activities as well as participation and environmental factors. Each can influence the others. The *ICF* emphasizes the importance of identifying possible conditions that impact activities and performance deficits. An understanding of a person's activities and performance requires knowledge of personal, social, and environmental conditions that may be impacting the person.

For example, a person's adaptive skills may be influenced adversely by his or her body functions (e.g., mental, sensory, and neuromuscu-loskeletal functions) and structures (e.g., nervous, cardiovascular, and metabolic systems). Additionally, his or her environment may not provide needed opportunities to acquire adaptive skills as well as support and reward their use. Thus, knowledge of a person's adaptive skills in conjunction with body functions, structures, and environment is important to diagnosis, if one is needed, and is essential to the design, delivery, and monitoring of services intended to have an instrumental and functional impact on a person's life.

The *ICF* places considerable emphasis on identifying functional impairments and thus emphasizes the importance of adaptive behaviors and life skills. Specifically, its activities and participation components address the execution of a task or action by an individual and his or her involvement in life situations. The term *activities* refer to tasks or actions a person is able to perform. Examples for older children and adults include writing, talking, and calculating. The term *participation* refers to activities that become integrated into one's life. Examples include regularly taking others to nearby places, talking by telephone with family and friends, and refraining from embarrassing others.

Activities and participation include the following nine domains: learning and applying knowledge (e.g., functional academics), general tasks and demands (e.g., work), communication (e.g., communication), mobility (e.g., fine and gross motor skills), self-care (e.g., self-care), domestic life (e.g., school and home living), interpersonal interactions and relationships (e.g., social skills), major life areas (e.g., health and safety, leisure skills), and community, social, and civic life (e.g., community use).

A *skill deficit* occurs when a person does not display a needed behavior. A *performance deficit* occurs when a person has displayed a needed skill yet does not use it when needed. For example, a child who does not have the ability to dress oneself displays a skill deficit. In contrast, a child who has displayed the ability to dress oneself and does not do so regularly when needed is described as having a performance deficit. If deficits in behaviors and skills have been identified and an individual is in need of services, then the *ICF* aids in describing the disability in terms of an interaction between the impairment, functioning, and the environment. Strengths or weaknesses may be identified, including the adequacy of one's adaptive skills, in light of environmental needs.

The *ICF* currently cites 10 mental and behavioral disorders: organic, including symptomatic, mental disorders; mental and behavioral disorders due to psychoactive substance use; schizophrenia, schizotypal, and delusional disorders; mood (affective) disorders; neurotic, stress-related, and somatoform disorders; behavioral syndromes associated with physiological disturbances and physical factors; disorders of adult personality and behavior; mental retardation; disorders of psychological development; and behavioral and emotional disorders with onset usually occurring in childhood and adolescence. A category for unspecified mental disorder also is provided. Other disorders have been added for children and youth in the WHO's (World Health Organization, 2007) version of the *ICF* for children and youth.

The adoption of the *ICF* will lead to various changes in health and health-related professions and thus to the tests needed to assist their work. The traditional medical model, with its emphasis on pathology, will be deemphasized in favor of a bio-psycho-social model that incorporates all components of health described at body, individual, and societal levels. Assessments will focus more on activities (i.e., tasks or actions a person is able to perform), participation (i.e., activities that become integrated into one's life), and contextual factors (i.e., the nature of one's environment together with its supports and impediments). Additionally, assessment will require the use of multidisciplinary methods.

Thus, the *ICF* encourages us to view health and disability differently. Every person, not just a few, can be expected to experience a decrement in health and thereby experience some degree of disability. Both health and disability are universal experiences. The *ICF* shifts our attention from the causes of a disorder to the disorder's functional impact on behaviors. Furthermore, the *ICF* takes into account the social aspects of disability and does not see disability only as dysfunction due to medical or biological qualities.

SOME FUTURES OF TEST DEVELOPMENT AND USE INTERNATIONALLY

The development and use of tests in the behavioral sciences may constitute psychology's most important technical contribution and is consistent with its overriding quest to understand individual growth and development. The futures of test development and use will be impacted by both external conditions—those over which psychology has little control, as well as internal conditions—those over which psychology has more control.

Conditions External to Test Development and Use

External conditions include the stability of a country's educational and political systems; a well-developed economy with financial resources that support test use and development; a testing industry that develops and markets tests for local use; public recognition that prevailing personal and social problems may be addressed through test use; and the display of positive attitudes and values toward science, technology, and individual differences. Test development and use are stronger when a country has a well-established and well-funded educational system, uses its financial capital to support the development of a testing industry, uses tests to address important personal and social problems, and has a public that holds positive views toward test use and individual differences.

Public attitudes impact test use. Some people see them as a great resource to acquire valid and unbiased information efficiently. Others are skeptical about their use. For example, people in many countries are or have been living under fear that governments could obtain various forms of test-related information to be used against them. They may oppose the use of tests, given their belief that tests are used to serve an oppressive state, not them.

The presence of these qualities will strongly impact the status of test development and use, particularly in those countries that have few test resources. Many countries lacking these desired qualities can be expected to remain underdeveloped with respect to test development and use through most of the 21st century. Thus, although qualities internal to psychology may initially promote test development and use, their continued development and use require the need for tests, a testing infrastructure that responds to this need, and the belief that test use enhances the attainment of personal and national values.

Conditions Internal to Test Development and Use

Psychology and other social sciences have control of other conditions that affect test development and use. These include preparing sufficient numbers of professionals able to develop and use tests properly, developing suitable measures that assess a broad range of important qualities, the presence of strong professional associations that support the value of assessment, standards that address issues important to test development and use, and positive attitudes toward test use held by the profession.

Competencies to develop tests require considerable graduate-level work in psychometrics as well as research design and statistics. Within the United States, the number of graduate programs that prepare persons for this work and the number of graduate students able later to replace forthcoming retirements are meager (Aiken, West, & Millsap, 2008; Rossen & Oakland, 2008). Conditions in developing countries are more dismal. For example, within the Americas, only three countries offer this graduate specialization: Canada, Brazil, and the United States. Psychology simply is not preparing sufficient numbers of graduate students to assume leadership in test development as well as to assume responsibility for preparing future generations. The discipline and profession of psychology should unite in its efforts to help ensure these vital resources are sustained.

Professionals in psychology and education are fortunate to have an abundance of standardized tests that assess a broad range of qualities important to their work. Other professions often lack this level of abundance (e.g., audiologists, occupational and physical therapists, as well as specialists in recreation and life care planning). Nevertheless, efforts are being made to help increase the number and quality of standardized tests for these and other health care specialists (Mpofu & Oakland, 2010, in press).

The infrastructure that supports test development and use within the United States is strong. For example, three professional associations directly support the value of test use: American Educational Research Association, American Psychological Association, and the National Council on Measurement in Education. Many other professional associations whose members use tests (e.g., school counselors, school psychologists, speech pathologists) also support testing practices. Additionally, a number of companies specialize in developing and marketing tests. The infrastructure that supports test development and use also is strong in Canada and Western Europe and is emerging in Brazil. However, this infrastructure generally is not found in other regions. Some of the larger test development companies have positioned themselves to market tests internationally.

Commercial firms that help support test development, marketing, and distribution are needed in most regions. Early in the 20th century three psychologists in the United States attempted to locate a publishing company willing to assist in marketing and distributing their tests. Unable to locate one, they formed their own company, one that grew into the largest test publisher in the world and was sold recently for almost $1 billion. Others within or outside of psychology need to come forward to share the risks and benefits of commercial aspects of test development, marketing, and distribution. The success of these efforts requires methods that contain costs for test development (Ilon, 1992) as well as professional associations to advocate for and respect strong laws that uphold copyright protection of intellectual property.

Professions engaged in test development and use are expected to develop and promulgate standards that address these activities. Although some national associations have developed ethics codes that address these issues, a review of codes in 31 countries in which test use occurs somewhat commonly found many did not address ethical issues associated with testing (Leach & Oakland, 2007). The *Standards for Educational and Psychological Testing* (AERA et al., 1999) provide the most thorough and authoritative standards for test development and use. The International Test Commission has provided important leadership, especially with respect to test adaptation and computer-based and Internet-delivered testing. The two major international associations of psychologists (i.e., IUPsyS and IAAP) have been somewhat silent on issues impacting testing. Thus, efforts are needed to strengthen the commitment of national and international psychological associations to address ethical issues through standards setting.

Test use is stronger when professionals see value in their use, actively support their development, and restrict their sales. Professional attitudes toward test use generally are strong in Australia, Canada, Israel, Western Europe, and the United States. However, attitudes in other regions can be less positive. For example, prevailing attitudes by psychologists in many countries favor theory over research and thus reject the belief that important personal qualities can be measured reliably and validly. The professional community has considerable control over other conditions discussed above.

The strength of national professional associations of psychology constitutes a bellwether of the strength of psychology within a country. Psychology is strong only when its professional associations are strong. More than 80 national psychological associations serve member interests. The associations vary in their support for test development and use. Conditions are more favorable when a national psychological association displays positive attitudes toward assessment, works actively to promote graduate preparation in this and related areas, and establishes high standards for test development and use. Each country needs one or more national associations dedicated to test development and use to serve as a visible and active advocate.

THREE RECENT EXAMPLES OF EXEMPLARY PROGRAMS FOR TEST DEVELOPMENT AND USE

Until recently, Brazil, Romania, the Czech Republic, Hungary, Latvia, and Slovakia lacked resources for developing and using tests. Many

Brazilian psychologists favored social psychology, theoretical orientations, and psychoanalytic orientations—conditions that did not favor the use of quantitative methods, including tests. For decades, Romania, when ruled from the late 1940s to the 1980s by communist and later another oppressive national government, displayed few positive qualities listed above under conditions external to test development and use. Both recently developed exemplary models for test development and use, ones other countries may be able to emulate.

In addition, the Czech Republic, Hungary, Latvia, and Slovakia shared a need for a quality test of intelligence yet lacked the resources to develop one. These countries are small, were caught within the clutch of communism for more than six decades, and lacked the professional resources to develop a test on their own. The efforts in these countries exemplify many of the issues discussed above. In addition, these efforts give support to the principle that a small and dedicated group of able persons who share a vision, devise a plan, and persist in its attainment can change a country and perhaps the world.

Brazil's Recent Efforts to Develop and Use Tests (Wechsler, 2007)

Efforts of Brazilian psychologists to develop and use tests underscore the importance of using their resources well. Luis Pasquali, Professor of Psychology at the University of Brasilia, assumed early leadership for test development in Brazil. He attended the 1993 International Test Commission conference in Oxford University and was introduced to various methodologies that he incorporated in his work that led to his establishing the first psychometrics laboratory in Brazil. Other laboratories were established at the University of Sao Paulo, Pontifica Catholic University of Campinas, University of San Francisco in Itativa, Federal University of Rio Grande do Sul, and the Federal University of Paravia. Other Brazilian universities are organizing similar laboratories for the development and use of psychological tests.

The national psychological association, the Federal Council of Psychologists, provided political support for forming the laboratories. Laboratory funding comes from federal and state sources as well as the private sector. The Federal Council of Psychologists also established high professional standards for test development and use. For example, in 2003, it created a national task force of researchers responsible for evaluating the psychometric qualities of all tests used in Brazil. The task force found 50% of the tests to be substandard and prohibited psychologists from using them. This decision was a shock to many engaged in test development and use and motivated them to construct and use suitably developed tests.

A professional association, the Brazilian Institute of Psychological Assessment (www.ibapnet.org.br), was founded in 1997 following the establishment of university-based laboratories and in light of growing interests in developing psychological tests and other quantitative methods in Brazil by Brazilians and for Brazilians. This institute is the only known association within the Americas south of the United States dedicated to test development and use. It publishes a journal and has well-attended biannual conferences, with approximately 1,000 persons attending.

These and other efforts by psychologists in Brazil have had a profound impact on test development and use, resulting in psychological tests being regarded more highly by professionals and the public. Tests have been developed to assess creativity, general intelligence, personality, and vocational aptitudes. The need for nationally normed achievement tests is most urgent. Thus, although test availability remains somewhat limited, a significant expansion of the number and types of tests developed in Brazil has been achieved and more are expected.

In Brazil and many other Latin American countries, individuals initiate and fund test development. Commercial firms generally only publish and/or sell tests. They rarely underwrite their development. Furthermore, test authors typically receive little if any royalties from the sale of their tests. Thus, test distributors aggressively pursue test authors, given their high profit margin. As a result, some psychologists have begun publishing their tests and contracting with commercial firms to distribute them.

Romania's Recent Efforts to Develop and Use Tests (Iliescu & Dincă, 2007)

Scientific psychology in Romania was established at the beginning of the 20th century and later was among the humanistic sciences banned by the communist regime, resulting in the virtual decapitation of this discipline. Psychology survived only by being implicitly tolerated by and embedded within other academic departments, including history, philosophy, education, as well as in some personnel departments (e.g., those with industrial and organizational orientations). Although psychology made a fresh start after 1990, it has not yet succeeded in bridging the serious professional gap (David, Moore, & Domuta, 2002).

The lack of nationally developed measures to assess psychological and educational qualities exemplifies this gap. Many of the renowned measures used internationally (e.g., 16 Personality Factors, California Psychological Inventory, NEO Personality Inventory Revised, Myers-Briggs Type Indicator, Eysenck Personality Questionnaire, State-Trait Anxiety Inventory, and State-Trait Anger Expression Inventory, 2nd edition) have been translated into the Romanian language.

On the positive side, the availability of these instruments facilitated the teaching of these instruments in academic settings and their use in research. On the negative side, the tests do not meet common professional standards. For example, test adaptations were not performed consistent with the International Test Commission guidelines on test adaptations, translations are sometimes poorly done, cultural adaptations occur marginally, tests are validated rarely, and normative samples either are too small or display seriously skewed distributions. Thus, the use of these measures when making high-stake decisions is hazardous. Additionally, copyright infringement occurs commonly by psychologists, an issue that constitutes a serious problem.

During the last four to five years a small number of Romanian test companies have formed in response to the needs of the country's 4,000 to 5,000 psychologists and others. The work of one company is described below. Its efforts can serve as a model for other countries that lack testing resources.

TestCentral™ (www.testcentral.ro) was founded in 2003 as a private initiative, forming relationships between a major local research company (D & D Research, Ltd.), many academic and professional psychologists and researchers, as well as international test companies. TestCentral has rapidly established itself as the main Romanian publisher of psychological tests. The company displays acceptable standards for adapting psychological tests in Romania that are widely regarded nationally and internationally. TestCentral publishes a variety of tests from such publishers as Psychological Assessment Resources, Sigma Assessment Systems, Mindgarden, Hogrefe, Organizzazioni Speciali, Management Research Institute, and Robertson-Cooper. Their tests assess personality, educational, clinical, and quasiclinical values and social axioms, and work/industrial/organizational qualities.

TestCentral used the University of California, Berkeley's Institute of Personality Assessment and Research efforts as a model for its work. Within this model, the company attends to financial goals and other issues keenly important to international publishers who look upon

Romania and other small national emerging markets with both interest and skepticism. The company also is committed to engaging in scholarly activities that lead to high-quality products. These activities recognize the importance of making suitable cultural adaptations, performing adequate norming, and conducting postnorming validation studies. Cultural adaptations and norming of tests at TestCentral always have been consistent with professional standards for test development and adaptation, including those from the International Test Commission (www.intestcom.org).

Test Translations/Adaptations

Translations use consecutive and back-translation methods with dyads of translators, sometimes also coupled with panels of subject matter experts. Consistent with the International Test Commission guidelines for test adaptation, the objective of this phase is to ensure the retention of the original meaning of the test items when translating them into Romanian and to work to ensure the translated items are suitable for use in the Romanian culture and reflect the same trait as that found in the culture in which the test first was developed.

Establishing Test Norms

TestCentral follows two major principles when norming tests: the sample should be nationally representative and stratified as well as sufficiently large. All normative research during the last three years has involved randomized samples of Romanians, stratified by gender, age, education, urban/rural residence, and ethnic group member in light of the most recent national census data. Additionally, the standardization samples are large. For example, the California Psychological Inventory-260 was normed on 3,200 (50% males) and a measure of children's temperament (Oakland, Glutting, & Horton, 1996) on 2,400 students (100 boys and 100 girls from each of the age groups from 7 through 18 years).

Test Validation

Romanian psychologists generally distrust tests that only have been translated. The origins of their reservations stem, in part, from copyright infringement and illegal usage, the poor quality of the translations, and the circulation of many forms of the same test. Due to these and other reservations, TestCentral was committed to the broader issue of working to ensure the tests were properly validated, not merely suitably translated and normed.

Given the limited resources of TestCentral and the relatively small market for tests, extensive validation that may have been used on tests developed in the host countries is not possible. Nevertheless, every test is subject to a thorough criterion-validation process using observer-evaluations of the targeted behavior and additional empirical research in order to determine whether the results of a test and its scales are consistent with predicted behavioral outcomes.

Extensive studies have provided strong support for many test constructs. Examples include the validity of the California Psychological Inventory (Pitariu & Iliescu, 2004; Pitariu, Pitariu, & Ali Al Mutairi, 1998), the reliability of the Nonverbal Personality Questionnaire (Iliescu, Nedelcea, & Minulescu, 2006), establishing the minimum acceptable age of administration for the measure of children's temperament (Iliescu, Dincă, & Dempsey, 2006), and the use of tests for professional selection in the military (Pitariu & Iernutan, 1984). Mountains of test data await analysis and publication.

TestCentral conceptualizes validation studies in terms of long-term perspectives. One year ago it established its own panel of subjects on whom longitudinal research is being conducted. Data from this panel of 250 individuals are used to examine the co-occurrence of personality traits assessed concurrently by two or more personality tests as well as measures of various behavioral outcomes and indicators (e.g., health and health-related behaviors such as coronary heart disease and Type A behavior pattern; smoking; medication ingestion; frequency of medical visits; frequency and duration of hospitalization and therapy, including psychotherapy and counseling); work and work-related behaviors, including tenure and work performance; family and social relationships; quality of life; and academic achievement.

Further Test Development Efforts

At times, research underscores the need to make major changes, including the development of new scales that best reflect Romanian culture and needs, not simply to adapt and norm tests. This work occurs with the permission and assistance of the original test authors. Some examples include the Romanian Anxiety Scale on the California Psychological Inventory to better fit Romanian culture (Albu & Pitariu, 1999), the revision of the Romanian Female/Male Scale of the California Psychological Inventory (Albu & Pitariu, 1991; Pitariu, 1981), amalgamating Holland's codes within the Jackson Vocational Interest Survey (Jackson, 2000), and the adaptation of the Fleishman Job Analysis Survey to become the backbone of a national occupational network, mirroring the O*Net used in the United States.

Issues Associated With Fairness

Fairness is an ongoing concern in Romania, especially given the emergence of the profession of psychology. Issues associated with fairness warrant special care when adapting tests and later when selecting and using them. For example, the California Psychological Inventory-462 has been reworked and republished in 1996 as a 434-item version because of legal pressures in light of the Americans With Disabilities Act (Gough & Bradley, 1996). However, the test infringes only marginally in light of Romanian law. Nevertheless, the 462-item version of the California Psychological Inventory was discarded even though this is the most researched version of the famous measure in Romania. The attempt to maximize fairness when using psychological and educational tests represents a main goal when adapting, developing, selecting, and using tests.

Due to the large number of the Hungarian ethnic minority within Romania (approximately 7% of the population), TestCentral has begun translating tests reports and other test materials in Hungarian. Supplementary special norms on special samples for this ethnic population are under development.

Regional Test Development: Efforts by Psychologists in the Czech Republic, Hungary, Latvia, and Slovakia to Develop a Test of Intelligence (Furman, 2007)

The need for additional high-quality psychological tests generally is most apparent in countries that are limited by their small size, those that adopted a socialist political system, established clinical service recently, and have few specialists in psychometrics. Although these countries may need tests, they often lack resources needed for their development. Thus, they are likely to rely on obtaining tests developed in other countries and either translating or adapting them for use in their countries.

In 1998, leadership within the International School Psychology Association decided to attempt to acquire a test of intelligence for use in the Czech Republic, Hungary, Latvia, and Slovakia—countries with histories characterized by the above-stated conditions that limit test development. The association leadership formed an abiding relationship with Dr. Richard Woodcock, the senior author of the Woodcock-Johnson Tests of Cognitive Abilities–3rd edition, as well as its predecessor, the Woodcock-Johnson Tests of Cognitive Abilities–revised, and Riverside Publishing Company, the test's publisher. Selected tests from this battery were offered for use. The Woodcock–Johnson battery was selected because it assesses a broad spectrum of scientifically identified intellectual abilities that compose the widely accepted Cattell-Horn-Carroll (CHC) theory of intelligence.

The Translation Process

Teams consisting of 15 to 30 psychologists from each of the four countries were formed first to become knowledgeable of CHC theory, then to assist in adapting the battery, and later to acquire standardization data. Dr. Anton Furman coordinated the work of teams in the four countries and facilitated support provided by Dr. Woodcock and his staff throughout the duration of the project. Dr. Woodcock and his staff had considerable experience translating and adapting tests.

The four country teams used consensus translation methods. They differ somewhat from the more commonly used translation/ back-translation method. Consensus translation methods rely on the development of two or more adaptations of the target test that are completed independently, typically by at least one linguist and one bilingual psychologist.

Once completed, the adaptations then were discussed and compared by the bilingual psychologists to ensure the adaptations were correct linguistically, suitable for the target culture, and measured the targeted CHC constructs accurately. Dr. Woodcock was consulted, when needed, to ensure this last goal was met. Although this adaptation process may be somewhat more complex and difficult than that commonly used in the translation/back-translation method, it helps reduce the dominant influence of one or two individual translators.

The adapted tests then were reviewed and discussed by psychologists who agreed to collect test data within each of the four countries. Issues again centered on the adequacy of the tests' linguistic translations, suitability for the target culture, and accuracy in measuring the targeted CHC construct.

Collection of Pilot Data

The examiners then were trained to administer the tests. Data on approximately 200 children and youth who varied by age, gender, education, and social class were collected in each of the four countries. These data were provided to Dr. Woodcock and his colleagues who conducted statistical analyses using item response theory and Rasch analysis. As expected, verbal ability tests exhibited the most variability compared to the item difficulty found on the original WJ-R Cognitive scale. Items that did not meet criteria were discarded.

Collection of Standardization Data

The resulting adapted scales were published in booklet form and then used to collect standardization data on 1,000 children and youth in Hungary, Latvia, and Slovakia and 500 in the Czech Republic. Again, Woodcock and his colleagues analyzed these data.

Among the seven factors, only the verbal ability factor showed differences in item difficulties between the original U.S. and target country scales. The four verbal abilities tests (i.e., Picture Vocabulary, Synonyms, Antonyms, and Verbal Analogies) were shortened. Thus, instead of providing separate scores for each of these four scales, this regional version provided one score to represent one's verbal intellectual ability.

The Resulting Test

The final version of the regional battery assesses the following seven broad cognitive abilities: crystallized, fluid, visual-spatial, speed, short-term memory, long-term retrieval, and auditory abilities. The test's factor structure is identical to that of the latest U.S. edition of the Woodcock-Johnson Tests of Cognitive Abilities. However, unlike the source test in which two or more subtests are used to assess each factor, the regional versions used one test for each of the seven broad ability factors. A computer scoring program aided the use of this battery.

This project was successful, in part, due to the abiding leadership of Dr. Anton Furman, the generosity of Dr. Woodcock, and support from the Riverside Publishing Company, Measurement Learning Consultants, and the Woodcock-Muñoz Foundation. The project's success also is due to the many dedicated psychologists in the target countries who invested their talents, time, and efforts to assist in the test's development; became trained; gathered and coded test data; and assisted in other ways. Their efforts have led to the availability of an intelligence test that meets world-class standards in Latvia, a country in which tests of intelligence were officially banned, and in Slovakia, Hungary, and the Czech Republic—countries that lacked the resources to initiate and complete the development of such a test on their own. The success of this project suggests that other similar test adaptations are possible in other countries that need such tests and lack needed resources.

CONCLUSIONS

Methods to develop and use tests have advanced considerably since their introduction in the 1880s to assist research efforts. Although test use occurs universally, its use is uneven. Test use is more common in countries that see the value of testing, are aware of its positive impact on achieving personal and professional goals and values, and in which a viable infrastructure that supports testing has been developed. Professional standards for test development and use provide direction for those engaged in these efforts.

National test publishers can and should be encouraged to assume leadership in test development within their countries. However, most countries have not established an infrastructure needed to support and sustain test development. For them, the use of adapted tests may present the most suitable immediate solution.

Although some countries may believe locally developed measures may better fit a country's culture, evidence to support this belief is sparse in countries in which test development is being born. Proof of a better fit must be based on comparisons with existing and widely used measures. Judgments as to whether new locally developed measures are superior to adaptations of widely used measures obtained from a host country should be based on research findings.

Tests that are internationally renowned constitute a resource that, when properly adapted, normed, and validated, can serve national interests (Pettifor, 2007). The development of indigenous measures at this point in many developing countries would require the advance of international perspectives and technology—qualities that may be in somewhat short supply. In addition, measures developed there are unlikely to find acceptance among the international community.

REFERENCES

Aiken, L., West, S., & Millsap, R. (2008). Doctoral training in statistics, measurement, and methodology in psychology. *American Psychologist, 63*(1), 32–50.

Albu, M., & Pitariu, H. (1991). Algoritm de construire a unei scale pentru un test psihologic: Contributii la reproiectarea scalei F/M a Inventarului Psihologic California (CPI) [An algorithm for constructing a psychological scale: Some contributions to a revision of the F/M scale of the California Psychological Inventory]. *Psychologia-Paedagogia,* Universitatea Babes-Bolyai, Cluj-Napoca, Romania, *36*(2), 30–35.

Albu, M., & Pitariu, H. D. (1999). Evaluarea anxietatii cu ajutorul Inventarului Psihologic California (CPI) [Assessment of anxiety with the California Psychological Inventory]. *Studii de Psihologie, 4,* 19–32.

American Association on Mental Retardation. (2002). *Definitions, classifications, and systems of supports* (9th ed.). Washington, DC: Author.

American Educational Research Association, American Psychological Association, & National Council on Measurement in Education. (1999). *Standards for Educational and Psychological Testing.* Washington, DC: American Psychological Association.

American Psychiatric Association. (1995). *Diagnostic and statistical manual of mental disorders* (4th ed.). *(DSM–IV: International Version with ICD-10 Codes).* Washington, DC: Author.

American Psychiatric Association. (2000). *Diagnostic and statistical manual of mental disorders* (4th ed., text revision). Washington, DC: Author.

American Psychological Association. (1992). Ethical principles of psychologists and code of conduct. *American Psychologist, 47,* 1597–1611.

Bartram, D. (1998). The need for international guidelines on standards for test use: A review of European and international initiatives. *European Psychologist, 3,* 155–162.

Bartram, D., & Coyne, I. (1998). Variations in national patterns for testing and test use: The ITC/EFPPA international survey. *European Journal of Psychological Assessment, 4,* 249–260.

Bartram, D., & Hambleton, R. (Eds.). (2005). *Computer-based testing and the Internet: Issues and advances.* New York: Wiley.

Benjamin, L. (2007). *A brief history of modern psychology.* Malden, MA: Blackwell.

Canadian Psychological Association. (1987). *Guidelines for educational and psychological testing.* Ottawa, ON: Author.

Cheung, F. (2004). Use of Western- and indigenously-developed personality tests in Asia. *Applied Psychology: International Review, 53,* 201–211.

Costa, P. T., Jr., & McCrae, R. R. (1992). *Revised NEO Personality Inventory (NEO-PI-R) and NEO Five-Factor Inventory (NEO-FFI) professional manual.* Odessa, FL: Psychological Assessment Resources.

Coyne, I., & Bartram, D. (2004). *International Test Commission computer-based and Internet delivered testing guidelines.* Draft 5, March 2002. Paper presented to the Council of the International Test Commission, Beijing, and the People's Republic of China.

David, D., Moore, M., & Domuta, A. (2002). Romanian psychology on the international psychological scene: A preliminary critical and empirical appraisal. *European Psychologist, 7*(2), 153–160.

DiMilia, L., Smith, P. A., & Brown, D. F. (1994). Management selection in Australia: A comparison with British and French findings. *International Journal of Selection and Assessment, 2,* 80–90.

Fitzgerald, C., & Ward, P. (1998). *Computer-based testing: A global perspective.* Paper presented at the International Congress of Applied Psychology, San Francisco, CA.

Furman, A. (2007). Adaptation of Woodcock-Johnson Tests of Cognitive Abilities in the European context. *World-Go-Round, 34*(5), 10–11.

Gauthier, J. (2008). Universal declaration of ethical principles for psychologists. In J. E. Hall & E. M. Altmaier (Eds.), *Global promise: Quality assurance and accountability in professional psychology* (pp. 98–105). New York: Oxford University Press.

Gough, H. G., & Bradley, P. (1996). *California Psychological Inventory manual* (3rd ed.). Palo Alto, CA: Consulting Psychologists Press.

Gowing, M. K., & Slivinski, L. W. (1994). A review of North American selection procedures: Canada and the USA. *International Journal of Selection and Assessment, 2,* 102–114.

Hambleton, R. K. (1994). Guidelines for adapting educational and psychological tests: A progress report. *European Journal of Psychological Assessment, 10,* 229–244.

Hambleton, R., Merenda, P., & Spielberger, C. (Eds.). (2005). *Adapting educational and psychological tests for cross-cultural assessment.* Mahwah, NJ: Erlbaum.

Hofstede, G. (1994). *Cultures and organizations: Intercultural cooperation and its importance for survival.* Boston: Kluwer Academic Publishers.

Hu, S., & Oakland, T. (1991). Global and regional perspectives on testing children and youth: An international survey. *International Journal of Psychology, 26*(3), 329–344.

Iliescu, D., & Dincă, M. (2007, Autumn/Winter). Current advances in test adaptations in Romania. *International Association of Applied Psychology Newsletter,* 11–12.

Iliescu, D., Dincă, M., & Dempsey, A. (2006, July). *Challenges in the Romanian indigenization and norming of the Student Style Questionnaire.* Paper presented at the Biannual Conference of the International Test Commission, Bruxelles, Belgium.

Iliescu, D., Nedelcea, C., & Minulescu, M. (2006). Noi alternative în evaluarea personalității: NPQ—Chestionarul Nonverbal de Personalitate [New alternatives in personality assessment: The Nonverbal Personality Questionnaire], Adaptare si etalonare la populatia României. *Psihologia Resurselor Umane, 11*(4), 49–61.

Ilon, L. (1992). *A framework for costing tests in Third World settings.* Washington, DC: The World Bank.

Jackson, D. (2000). *Manual for the Jackson Vocational Interest Survey.* London, ON: Sigma Assessment Systems.

Joint Committee on Testing Practices. (1993). *Responsible test use.* Washington, DC: American Psychological Association.

Kendall, I., Jenkinson, J., De Lemos, M., & Clancy, D. (1997). *Supplement to guidelines for the use of psychological tests.* Sydney: Australian Psychological Society.

Koene, C. J. (1997). Tests and professional ethics and values in European psychologists. *European Journal of Psychological Assessment, 13,* 219–228.

Leach, M. M., Glosoff, H., & Overmier, J. B. (2001). *International ethics codes: A follow-up study of previously unmatched standards and principles.* In J. B. Overmier & J. A. Overmier (Eds.), *Psychology: IUPsyS global resource* [CD-ROM]. Hove, East Sussex, UK: Psychology Press.

Leach, M. M., & Harbin, J. J. (1997). Psychological ethics codes: A comparison of twenty-four countries. *International Journal of Psychology, 32,* 181–192.

Leach, M. M., & Oakland, T. (2007). Ethics standards impacting test development and use: A review of 31 ethics codes impacting practices in 35 countries. *International Journal of Testing, 7,* 71–88.

Lindsay, G. (1996). Psychology as an ethical discipline and profession. *European Psychologist, 1,* 79–88.

Mpofu, E., & Oakland, T. (Eds.). (2010). *Assessment in rehabilitation and health.* Upper Saddle River, NJ: Merrill.

Mpofu, E., & Oakland, T. (Eds.). (in press). *Rehabilitation and health assessment.* New York: Springer Publishing.

Muniz, J., & Hambleton, R. K. (1997, August). Directions for the translation and adaptation of tests. *Papeles del Psicologo, 63*–70.

Muniz, J., Prieto, G., Almeida, L., & Bartram, D. (1999). Test use in Spain, Portugal and Latin American countries. *European Journal of Psychological Assessment, 15,* 151–157.

Myers, I. B., McCauley, M. H., Quenk, N. L., & Hammer, A. L. (1998). *MBTI manual: A guide to the development and use of the Myers-Briggs Type Indicator.* Palo Alto, CA: Consulting Psychologists Press.

Oakland, T. (2004). Use of educational and psychological tests internationally. *Applied Psychology: International Review, 53,* 157–172.

Oakland, T. (2005). Selected ethical issues relevant to test adaptations. In R. Hambleton, C. Spielberger, & P. Meranda (Eds.), *Adapting educational and psychological tests for cross-cultural assessment* (pp. 65–92). Mahwah, NJ: Erlbaum.

Oakland, T., & Glutting, J. (1998). Assessment of test behaviors with the WISC-III. In A. Prifitera & D. Saklofske (Eds.), *WISC-III: A scientist-practitioner perspective* (pp. 289–309). New York: Academic Press.

Oakland, T., Glutting, J., & Horton, C. (1996). *Manual for the Student Style Questionnaire.* San Antonio, TX: Harcourt Assessment.

Oakland, T., Goldman, S., & Bischoff, H. (1997). Code of ethics of the International School Psychology Association. *School Psychology International, 18,* 291–298.

Oakland, T., & Hambleton, R. (1995). *International perspectives on academic assessment.* Boston: Kluwer Academic Publishers.

Oakland, T., & Hu, S. (1991). Professionals who administer tests with children and youth: An international survey. *Journal of Psychoeducational Assessment, 9*(2), 108–120.

Oakland, T., & Hu, S. (1992). The top ten tests used with children and youth worldwide. *Bulletin of the International Test Commission, 19,* 99–120.

Oakland, T., & Hu, S. (1993). International perspectives on tests used with children and youth. *Journal of School Psychology, 31,* 501–517.

Oakland, T., Poortinga, Y. H., Schlegel, J., & Hambleton, R. K. (2001). International Test Commission: Its history, current status, and future directions. *International Journal of Testing, 1*(1), 3–32.

Pettifor, J. L. (2007). Toward a global professionalization of psychology. In M. J. Stevens & U. P. Gielen (Eds.), *Toward a global psychology: Theory, research, intervention, and pedagogy* (pp. 299–331). Mahwah, NJ: Erlbaum.

Pitariu, H. (1981). Validation of the CPI femininity scale in Romania. *Journal of Cross-Cultural Psychology, 12,* 111–117.

Pitariu, H. D., & Iernutan, L. (1984). Utilizarea inventarului de personalitate Freiburg (FPI) in investigarea capacitatii de adaptare la viata militara [Using the Freiburg Personality Inventory for the investigation of adaptation to the military life]. *Revista sanitara militara, 1*(1), 47–55.

Pitariu, H., & Iliescu, D. (2004). Inventarul Psihologic California—CPI260-Ro [The CPI-260 Inventory]. *Psihologia Resurselor Umane, 5*(2), 40–49.

Pitariu, H. D., Pitariu, H. A., & Ali Al Mutairi, M. (1998, August). *Psychological assessment of managers in Romania: Validation of a test battery.* Paper presented at the meeting of the American Psychological Association, San Francisco, CA.

Rossen, E., & Oakland, T. (2008). Graduate preparation in research methods: The current status of APA-accredited professional programs in psychology. *Training and Education in Professional Psychology, 27*, 42–47.

Schuler, H., Frier, D., & Kauffmann, M. (1993). *Personalauswahl, im europaischen Vergleich* [Personal comparisons in Europe.] Göttingen, Germany: Verlag fur Angewandte Psychologie.

Shackleton, V., & Newell, S. (1994). European management selection methods: A comparison of five countries. *International Journal of Selection and Assessment, 2*, 91–102.

Sinclair, C. (2005). A brief history of ethical principles in professional codes of ethics. In J. B. Overmier & J. A. Overmier (Eds.), *Psychology: IUPsyS global resource* [CD-ROM]. Hove, East Sussex, UK: Psychology Press.

Thiemann, A. (1998). *Digital publishing and test publishers' changing copyright opportunities.* Paper presented at the International Congress of Applied Psychology, San Francisco, CA.

Van de Vijver, F. J. R., & Hambleton, R. K. (1996). Translating tests: Some practical guidelines. *European Psychologist, 1*, 89–99.

Wang, Z. M. (1993). Psychology in China: A review. *Annual Review of Psychology, 44*, 87–116.

Wechsler, S. (2007, Autumn/Winter). Test standards, development, and use in Brazil. *International Association of Applied Psychology Newsletter, 12*–13.

World Health Organization. (1992). *International statistical classification of diseases and related health problems* (10th revision). *(ICD–10).* Geneva, Switzerland: Author.

World Health Organization. (2001). *International classification of functioning, disability and health (ICF).* Geneva, Switzerland: Author.

World Health Organization. (2007). *International classification of functioning, disability and health (ICF): Children and youth version.* Geneva, Switzerland: Author.

2

Equitable Assessment Practices in Diverse Contexts

ELIAS MPOFU AND SAMUEL O. ORTIZ

A priority goal in the provision of assessment services is to support decision making relative to the needs of the participant or client and produce data that might contribute important information regarding treatment, intervention, placement, selection, or other high-stakes concerns. The quality of decisions derived from assessment data depends, in part, on the fairness and equitability of assessment procedures rendered to the customer or consumer of the assessment. For example, perceived equity in assessment administration, test scoring, and interpretation may enhance the acceptance by customers of an assessment regarding a proposed treatment or intervention. Equity in assessment also depends on the appropriateness and fairness of the specific data-gathering procedures employed. For example, adherence to administration procedures for assessments that require normative interpretations is a condition of equity for standardized tests but not necessarily for other procedures, such as an intake interview. The presumption of equity in assessment, as a foundation for fair and valid decision making, permeates most assessment settings and contexts.

Although there exist ethical guidelines for working with individuals from diverse backgrounds (e.g., the American Psychological Association [APA]'s *Guidelines for Providers of Psychological Services to Ethnic, Linguistic, and Culturally Diverse Populations;* APA, 1990), there are few written prescriptions regarding specific practices designed to promote equity in assessment and evaluation. One treatise that touches upon the general issue of equity and which outlines some goals for achieving fairness in assessment is the publication *Standards for Educational and Psychological Testing* (American Educational Research Association [AERA], American Psychological Association, & National Council on Measurement in Education, 1999), known simply as "the Standards." The Standards represent a joint effort by three professional organizations to establish and codify common standards of practice regarding psychological and educational testing. Published jointly, the Standards now represent official policy of the APA and thus places responsibility on psychologists to observe and attend to them in practice. Whereas Part I of the Standards involves the expected topics regarding test construction, evaluation, and documentation, Part II is devoted entirely to the topic of fairness in testing and has considerable relevance for this chapter.

DEFINITION AND SIGNIFICANCE

Equity in assessment is a multilayered construct which includes, but is not limited to, "comparability of procedures in testing, test scoring and use of scores" for all examinees (AERA et al., 1999, p. 74). It presumes appropriate assessment conditions are employed to gather the specific information needed and affords the examinee alternative opportunities, if necessary, to demonstrate competence in any constructs of interest in the assessment. In other words, equitable assessment provides examinees an equal opportunity to display the requisite assessment processes, skills, and expectancies, as well as a fair chance to achieve the same level as others with equal ability on a given construct under measurement (AERA et al., 1999). Thus, equitable assessment is premised on both technical (e.g., comparability of assessment procedures) and socio-moral perspectives (e.g., fairness in opportunity to learn and demonstrate abilities and equivalent expectancies regarding success).

In this chapter, we discuss equitable assessment practices from both a technical efficiency and a social justice perspective. We propose that equitable assessment practices are predicated upon four main foundations: (1) from application of measures with cross-population transportability; (2) use of items that are equivalent in measuring the construct of interest; (3) knowledge of the manner in which certain variables (culture and language) affect test performance; and (4) application of a systematic approach designed to evaluate the influence of cultural and linguistic difference on the validity of obtained results. The first two are primarily concerned with the technical aspects of equitable assessment. To this end, we contrast competing measurement models to identify qualities associated with equitable measures. The latter two are primarily concerned with a social justice perspective where we consider conditions of equity in assessment, and implications for assessment for intervention with consumers who possess diverse qualities that might influence the process and outcomes of assessment (e.g., culture, language, professional socialization, and worldview). Moreover, we believe equitable assessment procedures to be obligated by ethical-moral considerations in the use of instruments and approaches that could potentially result in avoidable and undue adverse consequences on users. The importance of adverse outcomes, referred to recently as consequential validity, is emphasized in professional guidelines where fairness is defined as including not only a lack of bias and equitable treatment in the process, but also equality in outcomes. For example, according to the Standards,

> When unintended consequences result from test use, an attempt should be made to investigate whether such consequences arise from the test's sensitivity to characteristics other than those it is intended to assess or to the test's failure fully to represent the intended construct. (Standard 1.24, AERA et al., 1999, p. 23)

Accordingly, we also present here a heuristic model on conditions of equity, their sociohistorical foundations, prospective influence on assessment for intervention, and practices that are designed specifically to enhance equity in assessment.

TECHNICAL BASIS OF EQUITABLE ASSESSMENTS

Equitable assessments enable the unencumbered assessment of the constructs of interest without contamination from the specific type of measures used, consumer or provider characteristics, context of assessment, or other potentially confounding variables (Mpofu, 2004). In general, instruments used in equitable assessment are characterized by transparency and transportability. According to Smith and Taylor (2004), transparent and transportable measures are constructed to function like those for objective physical properties like temperature, volume, or length in that they "do not require the knowledge of the measuring instrument for interpretation" (p. 230). They also have comparability and transportability across samples because they are constructed to tap into the construct of interest and to yield comparable results for people of equal status on the target construct. Whereas classical test theory (CTT) has long been the major approach underlying test and scale construction, these qualities are more easily attainable with assessment instruments developed via item response theory (IRT). This occurs because CTT trades simplicity in construction for a general notion of error. In contrast, IRT may well complicate scale development but by pinpointing sources of error, it has a better capacity for the creation of tests that are independent of the test-taker and thus more transportable.

To best understand technical issues in equitable assessment it is necessary to contrast, albeit briefly, measurement from a CTT approach with that from an IRT approach. Our aim in comparing the two approaches in the development and design of scales and measures is to show why the use of an IRT approach has greater merit and potential for creating measures with technical equity or transportability across settings or samples than those constructed via approaches rooted in CTT.

Contrasting CTT and IRT Approaches to Measurement

CTT is a measurement approach in which the meaning of scores from an instrument largely depends on the specific instrument used rather than the objective qualities of the attribute the instrument is designed to measure. For example, a person's behavioral health risk status on an instrument developed using a CTT approach depends, to a significant extent, on which instruments or scales were used with the individual rather than on objective health risk. For example, depending on the samples on which these instruments were normed, an adolescent could be high-risk on one instrument and low-medium risk on a different instrument. This is because the instruments believed to measure the same construct might well display adequate reliability and validity, yet are often not actually equivalent in assessing the construct of interest. For example, an instrument might address use of mind-altering substances, but only with dependency, while another instrument measuring substance use may address amount of use (e.g., no use versus any involvement). Many adolescents with experimental use of mind-altering substances never get to regular use of substances with dependency (Kandel & Yamaguchi, 2002). Not surprisingly, an adolescent might have a high score on an instrument that measures degree of use of any substance and a low score on an instrument that measures use of substances with dependency. Use of any two instruments on substance use without the ability to calibrate them at the item level potentially results in a lack of equity in assessment of the target construct and might lead one to make inaccurate or inappropriate comparisons as a result of the failure to take into account differences in the range of the construct measured by each instrument (Kahler, Strong, Hakayi, Ramsey, & Brown, 2003; O'Neill, Sher, Jackson, & Wood, 2003; Spoth, Goldberg, Neppl, Trudeau, & Ramisetty-Mikler, 2001).

Item response theory is a method of scale or test construction that allows determination of the utility of a test item (or group of items) by the information that the item (or group of items) contributes toward estimating a person's ability (i.e., likelihood of endorsing an item) on an underlying construct (or latent trait) (Andrich, 1988; Gierl, Henderson, Jodoin, & Klinger, 2001; Rasch, 1980). The ability to estimate the latent trait is possible because with IRT, item characteristics (e.g., difficulty or endorsability) and person ability (level of status on a trait of interest) are placed on a common scale (or metric) using log-odd units or logits so that the distribution of the item parameters is independent of the estimation of the person measures, and the distribution of the person parameter is independent of the estimation of the item measures (Andrich, 2003). Person ability is estimated by the person's endorsement of a set of items that measure a single trait (e.g., a measure of substance use). A person who passes a particular item at a specified level of difficulty (e.g., endorses moderate use of substances) can be reliably said to possess a certain level of the underlying trait that the test item measures (i.e., health risk). For example, IRT/Rasch modeling is an approach that focuses exclusively on the item difficulty parameter and its relation to measuring the ability (or trait) level needed to endorse or respond correctly to an item at a given level. A conjoint analysis of person ability and test item difficulty makes it possible to create a measurement model that enables the prediction of the likelihood that a person with certain ability will answer a particular test item correctly (e.g., people with only experimental use of substances are less likely to endorse items that measure use of substances with dependency). Measures developed via IRT/Rasch methods have technical equity in that they are constructed to be either independent of each other once the effect of the latent trait is removed, or equivalent measures of the domain of interest at the instrument level (Cella & Chih-Hung, 2000; Lord, 1980).

Equitable Measures Are Sample Free and Scale Free

Measures have technical equity to the extent that their use enables the estimation of a target trait independent of the particular instrument used or the performance of the sample used to develop or norm the same instrument. Unlike instruments developed using CTT, which are sample dependent and less likely to have qualities that promote equity, measures constructed using the IRT/Rasch model enable separation of an individual's status on the construct of interest from the particular test items that are used to measure that person's status or the performance of others who took the test (Cella & Chih-Hung, 2000; Reeve & Fayers, 2005). An individual's response to an item on the target construct provides direct evidence of, for example, his or her substance use status independent of the substance use status of the sample on which the test was normed. Furthermore, an individual's status on the construct of interest can be reliably established even if he or she took different test items on different occasions or skipped some questions. This is possible because any measure developed via IRT/Rasch methods places all these substance use items on a continuum with each item maintaining its location on the hierarchy of substance use items, regardless of the distributional properties of the respondents. Thus, IRT-based measures have comparability and transportability across samples because they are constructed to tap into the construct of interest and to yield comparable results for people who have similar levels of ability on the target construct.

Many behavioral assessments share "borrowed" items that are used across settings (e.g., cultures) with the implicit assumption that items are equivalent in measuring the same construct across several settings. If this assumption were in fact false (which it often is) then use of those items is not equitable across settings and the substantive conclusions drawn from the data can be quite misleading (Embretson, 1996; Farley, Waller, & Brennan, 2000; Kang & Waller, 2005; Leigh & Stall, 1993; van de Vijver & Leung, 1997). Equitable measures are substitutable measures. That identical or similar items from different scales measure the same construct regardless of context is a significant advantage of RTI and a key limitation associated with the classical test theory (CTT) measurement approach. Use of IRT/Rasch measurement models avoids the pitfalls from this and other untenable assumptions that plague the CTT approach. Nonetheless, because a majority of behavioral measures are constructed using CTT, they potentially carry significant limitations regarding equity in measurement.

Equitable Measures Have Additivity

Assessment instruments that are equitable have equal interval properties, enabling the aggregation of data and comparison across groups and settings. Calibration of items via IRT, as previously described (see also Bond & Fox, 2001), results in interval measurement properties for otherwise ordinal scale measures (e.g., Likert scales). Measures constructed through IRT have equity in the sense that they are invariant across samples and instruments, which enables meaningful aggregation of data from multiple samples and settings for analysis. By contrast, CTT mistakenly treats the concrete counts of indicators of a construct (e.g., response choices on health risk items) as abstract or inferential measures of amount. The summative indices from adding indicator values following a CTT approach lack equity qualities and are not valid for comparisons across settings or populations since they are essentially ordinal scale measures (Velozo, 2005; Wright & Mok, 2004).

In the CTT approach, there is an assumption that the respondent group uses every scale point, and that there is a ratio (a score of "4" is twice the value of a score of "2" on a 4-point Likert scale), or an equal interval across the scale points. In real terms, when certain response options are not used for specific items in a scale, the scale is made up of items that essentially function on a different scale. This is because response categories and item scores are not necessarily the same thing; CTT analyses make little or no use of this information. IRT measurement models provide information on the frequency and monotonicity of response option use. For example, the Rasch model provides *step difficulty calibrations*, indicating how *difficult* it is to endorse *strongly agree* over *agree* (Conrad & Bezrucsko, 2004). There is an assumption that step calibrations should increase monotonically. If not, the response options are considered disordered. Infrequent and inconsistently used response options are indications that the scale is in need of revision. Essentially CTT assumes and treats responses as a ratio or interval scale when they are not. By contrast, an IRT/Rasch scaling method provides estimates for each item and for each response option. We believe that for the purposes of developing equitable measures of a behavioral or cognitive construct, the use of an IRT/Rasch probabilistic model is stronger and more valid than a CTT approach.

Most survey instruments use a Likert-type scale and provide polytomous data. Of particular pertinence to this chapter is the fact that with Likert-type measures, respondents may differ in the extent to which they use item choice categories as a function of culture (Marquis, Keininger, Acquadro, & de la Loge, 2005; Snider & Styles, 2005; van Herk, Poortinga, & Verhallen, 2004). For example, southern Europeans tend to use extreme ratings on a 5-point scale more than do northern Europeans (van Herk, Poortinga, & Verhallen, 2004). Similarly, Latinos tend to choose extremes on a 5-point rating scale more than Anglo Americans (Azocar, Arean, Miranda, & Muñoz, 2001). People with a cultural predisposition to endorse extreme choices with a polytomously scored item may be evaluated more reliably by being given fewer choices (Arce-Ferrer & Ketterer, 2003). The CTT approach typically assumes that respondents from different cultures will use a Likert scale in the same way despite the noted research that indicates they do not. Thus, cross-population comparisons predicated upon the assumption that the measures are equitable are unjustified.

Equitable Measures Allow Objective Differentiation of Groups

Item response theory incorporates a process known as differential item functioning (DIF), which is a procedure that enables a greater understanding of technical equity in assessments at the scale level (Chu & Kamata, 2005; Smith & Taylor, 2004). Differential item functioning is said to occur when conditional expected item scores vary by group membership (e.g., race, socioeconomic status, culture, gender) so that interpretation of responses is dependent, in part, on knowledge of the characteristics that may define group membership (Teresi, 2001). For example, a randomly selected person from Poland with a known, objective health risk should respond to an item in the same way as a randomly selected person from Japan who has the same objective health risk. When two people with the same objective health risk, who differ only on some category of group membership, respond to an item differently, despite possessing equivalent levels of a known health risk, then that item is said to be functioning differently across the two groups. In this manner, DIF is identified. The methodology for DIF is sound and well developed and the reader is referred to the following sources for a more detailed explanation (Mpofu & Watkins, 1994; Raju, van der Linden, & Fleer, 1995; Rudner, Getson, & Knight, 1980; Smith, 2004; Teresi, 2001; van de Vijver & Leung, 1997).

   Item characteristic curves (ICCs) are an extension of IRT techniques and are quite helpful in test development where the goal is to produce a measure that is sample independent. In general, ICCs are a relatively simple graphic depiction of various IRT parameters including difficulty, discrimination, and false positives. When the focus of IRT analysis is on level of difficulty, an ICC helps illustrate the probability that a person of a given level of ability will be successful on a test item (i.e., will pass/fail or endorse/not endorse the item). Likewise, an ICC may be developed to evaluate whether an item can discriminate successfully between a person with a specified level of ability from a person who possesses slightly less or slightly more of the ability. And last, ICCs may be evaluated to determine whether an item or group of items are overly susceptible to false positives, which is when an item indicates the presence of the latent trait or ability when in fact it is not present (e.g., when an individual simply guesses at an answer). One of the advantages of ICCs is that they are helpful for identifying items that may be potentially biased, that is, items that lack equity between groups (e.g., by type of disability, culture, socioeconomic status, gender, age). Any such items that function differently across groups (i.e., display DIF) can be isolated, and if need be, removed from the pool of items used to measure a construct. The reasons why an item may function differently across groups may be due to differences in meaning that the item has between the two groups, or items may unintentionally measure an unwanted nuisance factor or an entirely different construct in one group but not the other. Broadly speaking, the meaning of any item is rooted in one's cultural perspective and this is an important consideration in creating culturally transportable measures. Conversely, items that demonstrate DIF may be retained in a scale or measure without affecting equity if the instrument is intended for use only with the group for which DIF does not occur and where cross-population comparisons are not intended.

Equitable Measures Are Interpretable at the Individual Person Level

Quite often, assessments are carried out to inform decisions at the individual person level. With CTT approaches, person level statistics are not possible (Andrich, 1996; Bond & Fox, 2001). IRT person parameters (i.e., person ability) enable objective interpretation of performance at the person level. For example, IRT item statistics are commonly presented on an ordered hierarchy of a parameter (e.g., item difficulty, item discrimination). Fit statistics are used in IRT-based models to determine the extent to which each item and person ability are consistent with each other and the overall hierarchy of item difficulties or abilities. Infit statistics are used to identify unexpected answers close to the person's ability whereas Outfit statistics describe unexpected responses far from the person's ability. In scale and measure development, Infit and Outfit statistics are helpful in identifying poorly written items in that they reveal atypical responses relative to a person's ability or hierarchy of item difficulties (Hawley, Taylor, Hellawell, & Pentland, 1999). Infit and Outfit diagnostics are relevant to interpretation of assessments at the person level in that unexpected deviations from an individual's ability may be clinically significant. For example, if the deviation is unexpected but close to a person's ability (Infit statistics), that may indicate potential for change with treatment intervention. If the deviation is unexpected and far from the person's ability, the result may suggest that the person has specialized ability in that domain of functioning, which may in turn be a resource for supporting treatment intervention in related areas or an area on which fewer treatment resources need to be expended.

Caveats in IRT

Although use of IRT greatly assists in the development of instruments that have technical qualities that minimize or eliminate potential bias, it does not guarantee fairness in assessment. Instruments may well display the appropriate transportability properties and the ICCs may demonstrate difficulty and discrimination levels that are invariant across groups. Indeed, instruments developed via IRT might also show no evidence of DIF within or across groups, leading a developer to conclude that the instrument is suitable for use with any group. In a technical sense, particularly related to the inherent properties of the test, namely reliability, this may well be true. It does not mean, however, that construct validity is ensured even when all manner of IRT indices suggest that it is.

Consider the situation where a test of verbal ability is developed and validated via IRT methods. The test is a single scale based on verbal reasoning. As is typical for ability tests, and in keeping with IRT/Rasch principles, arrangement of the items on the instrument is done in order of difficulty from easiest to hardest. The order of items also has practical implications because it permits the establishment and use of basals and ceilings so that not every item need be administered. When arranged in order of difficulty, the items on the instrument follow and correspond to the age-based pattern of human development in verbal reasoning ability. Easy items are learned and mastered earlier by individuals at younger ages whereas harder items are learned and mastered later at older ages as verbal reasoning develops further.

The test is then normed on an English-speaking population to establish the basis for relative comparisons of performance. The test developers then decide to see if the test would be "fair" and equitable if used with bilingual populations in the United States who speak English as a second language. The test is then administered in English to a variety of individuals with limited English proficiency and the results examined for DIF. Would any be found?

The answer, perhaps surprisingly, is no. The performance of the individuals with limited English proficiency would not indicate any DIF. The easy items remain easy for both groups compared to the more difficult items, which also remain difficult for both groups. The only difference that might be found would be a lower overall average score for the bilingual group. Apart from this finding, which is often misattributed to real and inherent between-group differences in verbal reasoning ability, there would be no evidence of DIF, no unusual ICCs, and no anomalies in the technical qualities of the test. By the standards of IRT, the test would be considered fair in all respects.

Where, then, are the problems with fairness? In the example provided here, the instrument was designed to measure verbal reasoning, and in this regard, it performs very well. Whether administered to people very proficient in English (i.e., native speakers) or those with limited or no proficiency in English, the construct and its measurement are not altered. A low score indicates low verbal reasoning ability—but with two qualifications that depend on group membership. That is, first, a low score indicates low verbal reasoning ability *in English only,* not in general, and second, a low score does not indicate that the ability has a high probability of substantial change in relation to changes in another ability that is not intended to be measured by the test—English-language proficiency (Dynda, Flanagan, Chaplin, & Pope, 2008; Sotelo-Dynega, Ortiz, Flanagan, & Chaplin, 2007). Thus, English-language proficiency serves as a group characteristic that does not result in any unusual deviations when IRT methods are used in the test construction process, but does in fact result in problems with equity and fairness. Whenever native English speakers are used to establish a norm sample and set the standards for age-appropriate levels of performance on a given instrument, it puts any other linguistically different group (e.g., bilinguals or English learners) at a disadvantage because the assumption of comparability in terms of normal, age- or grade-related development in English no longer holds.

The same can be said regarding level of acculturation and knowledge of the culture that gave rise to the test. Those individuals who are not raised within the mainstream culture of the test are at a disadvantage because they will lack age-appropriate levels of cultural knowledge as compared to their same-age peers who were raised in the test's culture. For example, consider the use of a test measuring vocabulary in English (whether by asking for a verbal definition or by identification of pictures) administered to two average 10-year-olds—one a native English speaker and one who started learning English only upon school entrance at the age of 5. In both cases, the test will accurately measure the English vocabulary of each individual. If the test is carefully constructed via IRT, the native English-speaking 10-year-old will score "average" on the test, but the English learner will score lower, perhaps even below average. The obtained scores are correct in the sense they are accurate measures of actual vocabulary for both individuals.

Problems in fairness, however, arise when we attempt to ascribe clinical meaning to the observed differences. If the examiner simply accepts the fairness of the test, which has been validated by IRT methods, it may lead to the conclusion that the English learner lacks the ability to learn vocabulary words at the same rate and to the same degree as his or her English-speaking peer. But assuming both individuals are otherwise equal in all other abilities, experiences, and opportunities, is it actually fair to expect that both individuals should have the same level of English vocabulary given their differing levels of development in English? Again, the answer is obviously no. Despite the precision in measuring English vocabulary, the actual reasons why each scored how they scored are quite different in this case. The English learner scores below average not because of problems in learning per se, but because limited English proficiency inhibits verbal expression when attempting to provide oral definitions of words and limited cultural experience inhibits familiarity with English words and cultural objects and artifacts. It should be clear that fairness is not achieved solely by using a particular test, but also by considering the cultural and linguistic characteristics of the tests themselves. When differences in acculturation and linguistic history exist, the presumption of equivalence in development necessary for fairness in testing is violated. This issue is often referred to as the assumption of comparability in testing and test development (Oakland, 1977; Salvia & Ysseldyke, 1991) and will be discussed in more detail later in the chapter.

In sum, the technical adequacy of instruments derived from the application of IRT approaches addresses issues of equity in measurement from the perspective of the psychometric properties of the scales or instruments. However, to gain a comprehensive understanding of equity in measurement, consideration needs to be given to the social justice imperative for promoting the use of assessment instruments and procedures that are specifically designed to enhance fairness.

SOCIAL JUSTICE FOUNDATIONS OF EQUITABLE ASSESSMENT PRACTICES

Interest in equitable assessment is driven in part by a need to be proactive in preventing social problems and adverse consequences or decisions that might result from unfair assessment practices. For example, racial minority students in North American schools, notably Hispanics and African Americans, have been overidentified as having lower academic ability. The assessments conducted on these children, however, have been accomplished largely through the use of tests—the fairness of which have been questioned by many who believe that it is possible that they may have misrepresented the students' true ability (Ochoa, 2005; Patton, 1998; Skiba, 2001). In addition to the overrepresentation of ethnic minority students in special education, the negative consequences and potentially adverse impact from inequitable assessment are many. They can include, for example, additional strain on already tight educational budgets that must find additional funding to provide what could be inappropriate or possibly unnecessary supplemental educational programs. Students who are misidentified as having low ability may begin to withdraw from school as they find it difficult to overcome low expectations and poor academic preparation that often accompany low test scores (Kindler, 2002). Such students may also become frustrated as a result of insensitive assessments that erroneously imply low ability when in fact ability is average. Students facing these situations often drop out of school and subsequently find themselves all too frequently involved with the criminal justice system (Kindler, 2002; National Center for Educational Statistics, 2007). Equitable assessment practices are those that may prevent such problems from arising in the first place. Moreover, they might also promote societal justice by enhancing access to resources (e.g., education, employment) that may otherwise be denied populations for whom existing tests are unfair and inappropriate.

Conditions of Equity in Assessment

A condition of equity is a quality of the assessment process or context that influences an assessment outcome or the perceived fairness of assessment by consumers. As described previously, it is not sufficient to base presumptions of equity and fairness on the technical aspects of test construction alone. Technical adequacy is an important and necessary component of achieving equity in assessment but it is not sufficient. Fairness will be established only when practitioners also consider the structure of conditions of equity in assessment, their sociocultural basis, and engage in nondiscriminatory practices that enhance social justice in assessment.

The Structural Organization of Conditions of Equity

Conditions of equity may be hierarchically organized with foundational conditions supporting derived or successor conditions. For example, a belief in a condition of equity such as the "just world" philosophy (or the belief that good things happen to good people) could subsume a successor condition of subjective perceptions of equity in assessment. The perception of equity in assessment could lead to the experience of being treated equitably in assessment, which in turn may result in the interpretation of the outcomes of assessment as equitable. This could then facilitate acceptance of the outcomes of assessment and agreement with decisions that are made or adherence to psychobehavioral regimens developed from the results of the assessment. In contrast, a belief in the world as being unfair may lead to perception of an assessment situation as something potentially inequitable, which may then subsequently lead to a negative experience in assessment. This experience might then color the process and yield consistently negative interpretations of and reactions to the outcomes of the assessment. The perceptions of inequity would be maintained regardless of objective evidence that the assessment process and context were indeed equitable.

Research on stereotype threat provides an excellent example of this process. Steele and Aronson (1995) demonstrated the effect of stereotype threat with African Americans where test performance was influenced significantly as a function of the attributions made regarding the type of test being taken and its relation to race/ethnicity. Steele noted that African Americans tend to perform more poorly on tests when they are led to believe that the test measures ability or intelligence but not when they are told the test measures achievement only. They concluded that despite the fact that the tests are identical, African Americans are influenced by having internalized the stereotype that as a group, they do not perform as well on ability tests as Anglo Americans, and this belief alone threatens and reduces their performance (Steele & Aronson, 1995).

Lower-level conditions of equity may be even more malleable than higher or foundational conditions. For example, sharing information with examinees that performance on a given mathematics test was independent of gender resulted in women achieving scores comparable to those of their male peers, whereas suggesting to all examinees that women tended to perform worse than men on the test resulted in poorer achievement by the women (Spencer, Steele, & Quinn, 1999). Similarly, reversible differences in the perceived successor conditions of equity could be observed (e.g., "I could do as well on this test as anybody") but without a change in the deeper level or foundation conditions (e.g., "I remain skeptical about the purpose and fairness of assessment").

Sociocultural Influences on Conditions of Equity

The sources or causes of inequity in assessment (e.g., historical, cultural, experiential) may not be the same for assessment service providers and consumers. Providers of assessment services, which may include professional testing agencies, schools, clinics, or professionals in private practice, all aspire to provide equitable assessment for every participant, customer, or client. In educational settings, the stakeholders in assessment are primarily students and their peers, parents, and significant others who participate in assessment as respondents. They are the ones who generate the results of assessments. On the other hand, schools or educational agencies themselves may be customers in the assessment process when they have need to retain external professional assessment services or assistance in developing instruments for local use.

The complex overlap in roles related to participation for providers and consumers of assessment suggests that salience of conditions that define equity in the assessment process may vary between, as well as within, provider/consumer constituencies. For example, assessment service providers, by virtue of their formal training in assessment, may be influenced by conditions of equity prescribed by their professional codes of ethics and any that may be legally mandated, in ways that lay consumers of assessment services are not. For example, the Standards (AERA et al., 1999), cited previously, as well as this chapter, are intended to guide and influence decisions practitioners may make regarding professional practice so that they are in compliance of the profession's ethics and policies. In contrast, lay consumers of assessment services may weigh conditions of equity in assessment differently, perhaps more from sociocultural or other contextual-consequential influences. For example, they may wonder if the evaluation will result in the outcomes they desire (e.g., improved health care or accommodations on a high-stakes test). Thus, providers and lay consumers of assessment may regard an assessment process to be equitable only if they perceive in the assessment process the conditions of equity that are salient to them. We contend that extant discussions on equity in assessment have been carried out under the presumption that conditions of equity have the same meaning or significance across settings or assessment participant constituencies. This may be an erroneous view, and obscure an accurate understanding of true equity in assessment.

Assessment service providers are variously privileged by factors that include training in assessment, professional socialization, upper/middle-class affiliation, and may also share a belief in the "goodness" of the assessment process. In addition, they may have recourse to rich cannons of research findings and clinical experience to support claims regarding the equitable use of a measure with a variety of different populations. Lay customers, who may be from populations with a history of sociocultural marginalization related to inequitable assessment practices, may hold a healthy skepticism about claims of equity in assessment by service providers or test developers. Thus, the salience of a condition of equity to service providers and consumers of assessment may differ as a function of differences in socialization regarding the assessment process.

Influence of Personal Factors

Regardless of assessment constituency membership, the conditions of equity in assessment are both actual and perceived. Perceived assessment equity is what a person believes about the assessment process within a socioculturally defined performance context. Actual assessment equity is the objectively verifiable processes of and procedures in assessment that an individual potentially could experience. The degree of overlap between an individual's perceived and actual assessment equity influences the quality of the assessment process for the individual. People with a greater congruency between their perceived and actual assessment equity are more likely to experience a greater level of equity in assessment than those with less congruency. For example, if an individual believes testing to be fair, and if the test results lead to treatment decisions that are also fair, the entire experience is likely to be seen as quite equitable by the individual. However, if an individual believes testing to be unfair, perhaps because he or she sees tests as biased or the process of evaluation as unnecessary, that person may not fully participate in the process leading to results that may well not be valid or fair. Thus, the perceived lack of assessment equity may be synonymous with a real lack of actual assessment equity that results in behaviors or experiences that unfortunately devalue and potentially undermine the assessment.

Influence of Context

Opportunity structure refers to the context and processes within which people in a particular sociocultural environment (e.g., social class, ethnic group) achieve the goals to which they aspire (e.g., education, employment). The opportunity structure gives direction to goals and activities. It also provides the means or resources for achieving preferred goals (Mpofu & Wilson, 2004). Consider, for example, that opportunities to learn and practice requisite skills for assessment are often limited for people from disadvantaged backgrounds (Ortiz & Dynda, in press; Ortiz & Ochoa, 2005). As a result, they may hold perceptions and motives regarding the foundational and successor conditions of equity in assessment that are different from those of service providers.

Individuals may recognize multiple conditions of equity in assessment and selectively use them to interpret assessment situations in which they may be involved. For example, they may regard themselves to be in an inequitable assessment setting if they are evaluated by a professional from a socioculturally privileged group and if they are tested in the assessor's language instead of their own native language. For example, within the framework of psychotherapy, Sue and colleagues (1991) have found that ethnic match was a significant predictor of positive treatment outcome for clients from Mexican American backgrounds. Similarly, Sue (1998) found that clients from Asian American backgrounds tended to fare better in a therapeutic situation when they were matched to the therapist on the dimensions of ethnicity, language, or both. In contrast, within the framework of assessment, there appears to be less evidence that the ethnic match between examiner and examinee matters, although the perception that it does persists (Sattler & Gwynne, 1982). Thus, perceptions regarding conditions of equity could still undermine any objective aspects of the assessment setting, such as evidence that the social characteristics of the examiner did not influence the performance of examinee. That is, a person may appraise the equity of an assessment situation on a characteristic of the assessment process or context that is subjectively salient to him or her, or members of a culture of origin, regardless of whether there is any evidence that the characteristic negatively affected the assessment. The effect of a condition of equity on participation in assessment may not be related to the objective characteristics of the assessment process or context.

ENHANCING SOCIAL JUSTICE IN ASSESSMENT PRACTICES

Historically, scale and measure development has been the privilege of expert test constructors (who in some cases may also be service providers) rather than consumers who are generally untrained and not sophisticated in test design and construction. Consequently, there are overwhelmingly more assessment instruments that are provider oriented, in that they are administered, scored, and interpreted by service providers rather than by the end user or consumer (e.g., job applicant, therapy client, student). Consumer-oriented assessment is in its infancy (Mpofu & Oakland, 2006; Ozer & Kroll, 2002; Wright, Rudicel, & Feinstein, 1994), but holds tremendous potential for the development of measures that are more sensitive to conditions of equity that are salient to consumer constituencies (e.g., cultural, gender, linguistic, ethnic). Numerous studies have suggested that test developers and service providers were limited in their ability to reliably measure important outcomes as perceived by their customers (e.g., patients, people with disabilities, potential employees) (Heinemann, Bode, Cichowski, & Kan, 1998; Wright et al., 1994). For example, the views of significant others on issues deemed to be important for the patient were closer to those actually reported by the patient or person with a disability than were the views of the service provider (Heinemann et al., 1998). Behavioral measures could be more equitable if they were developed with knowledge of conditions of equity that are salient to the consumers and their uniquely diverse needs and perceptions.

Educational and psychological assessment service providers operate from a value system that influences the perceived equity of the measures they use. The convergence of assessment and service provider values and those of the customer is often assumed rather than actually demonstrated. For example, it was previously noted that the extant standards of educational and psychological assessment assume that all conditions of equity in assessment have the same salience to consumers of assessment instruments as they do for users of them. However, the failure to consider the various conditions or aspects of equity that are perceived to be salient for customers may influence service providers and cause them to be overly optimistic about the quality of the assessment outcomes and might misrepresent prospects for the customer and significant others. The infusion of customer-based conditions of equity into the processes and outcomes of assessment may ultimately yield a more credible assessment outcome measure.

Knowledge of the conditions of equity that are salient to consumers of educational and psychological measures is important and relevant to the quality of decisions that may ensue in an evaluation and the manner in which assessment results are used. For example, a student or parent of a student whose desired assessment outcome is increased academic competence may be less motivated to participate in assessment regimens that place emphasis on screening for disability classification purposes. Consequently, the student or parent may invest less effort or commitment to the assessment process and its targeted outcomes. Early identification of conditions of equity that are salient to customers from diverse backgrounds (e.g., those who are ethnically, culturally, or gender different) is important in helping partners in the assessment (e.g., family, peers, teachers, schools) use the results of assessment appropriately. Changes in the customer's actual or perceived conditions of equity may have important implications for adherence to assessment protocols and any decisions that may emanate from the results of the assessment. The identification of conditions of equity in assessment that are salient to consumers and from the consumers' perspectives is an important but too often neglected assessment outcome.

Cultural and Linguistic Factors in Equitable Assessment

Because equity goes hand in hand with social justice, assessment methods and procedures that promote the former necessarily promote the latter as well. Technical advances, such as the application of IRT in test development and construction, can only go so far in reaching social justice goals. As was noted previously in the chapter, IRT does not guarantee that the results obtained from a measure that satisfies all conditions for transportability, reliability, and validity will actually lead to fair or equitable outcomes. The assumption that groups are comparable in the most important fundamental ways (i.e., level of English-language proficiency and acculturation) is not always met in cases where professionals seek to evaluate the abilities of individuals from diverse cultural, ethnic, and linguistic backgrounds. Despite the fact that tests can demonstrate fairness in a technical sense, this does not mean they can be wholly relied upon to provide objective data with which to guide decisions in the assessment and intervention process. Irrespective of the methods or instruments used in assessment, it will remain the responsibility of the professional not only to ensure that the obtained results are as reliable and valid as possible but also to interpret and give meaning to the data that is not discriminatory and that leads to fair and equitable decisions and outcomes. The following discussion provides both a general heuristic as well as specific techniques for professionals that can serve to increase social justice in assessment by integrating consideration of variables that affect comparability, as well as test performance, and the meaning of any collected data.

Cultural Influences

The most common assessment context in which professionals might find themselves at risk for making discriminatory decisions that lead to inequitable outcomes occurs when the examinee is an individual who is culturally and linguistically different from the culture and language in which a given test was developed. For the purposes of this discussion, we will assume that the culture reflected in tests is mainstream United States and that the language is standard English. We wish to point out that for tests in other languages and developed in other cultures for use in other countries, the same principles discussed herein would apply and the concepts are essentially parallel and equally applicable.

Culture, or more accurately, level of acculturation, is one of the most important variables that affects test performance and which must be evaluated and understood so that results can be interpreted fairly. There has been a long-standing tendency to view culture as being equivalent to race or ethnicity. This is an unfortunate error in that it tends to highlight a variable that has nothing to do with test performance (i.e., skin color) and masks a variable that has a considerable amount to do with test performance (i.e., acculturation) (Rhodes, Ochoa, & Ortiz, 2005). All tests, regardless of the country in which they are developed, must necessarily be a reflection of the attitudes, values, and beliefs of the test developers and the culture from which the test developers emanate. What words are chosen for a vocabulary test, what tasks represent reasoning abilities, what objects are pictured and used in various illustrations, and how instructions are worded and provided are all examples of how culture becomes embedded in test design. It stands to reason that individuals who are raised completely or partly outside the culture of the test, for example, immigrants, are likely to be at a disadvantage on such a test because they lack comparable levels of acculturation. By virtue of a relatively more limited experience with and exposure to the culture in which the test was created, these individuals do not possess similar or comparable levels of acculturation as the individuals on whom the test was normed. In contrast, individuals who have been raised within the culture and who have had the opportunity and time to be exposed to the elements that are common to the culture and that may be found in various parts of a test are at a distinct advantage.

This difference in acculturation thus places some individuals (e.g., immigrants) on an unequal footing as compared to their same-age peers who were raised within the culture. This violates the assumption of comparability because the condition "that the [individual] being tested has been exposed to comparable, but not necessarily identical, acculturation patterns relative to the standardization sample" (Oakland, 1977, p. 54) is not met. It is not that the test itself is flawed or even biased, so much as it is that without equivalent levels of acculturation to same-age peers in the norm sample, measurement of abilities, skills, or knowledge in the culturally different individual is likely to result in underestimates of true functioning. This is because, despite the adequate technical properties of the test, when used with individuals who are not fully acculturated, the test becomes more a measure of that lack of acculturation and less a measure of the construct of interest.

Linguistic Influences

The other variable that may jeopardize social justice and creates significant potential for discriminatory outcomes from testing is language. In test development, careful attention is paid to wording in all aspects of the instrument, including instructions, item wording, expected verbal responses, and so forth. Unless a test is designed specifically to measure language proficiency, the language utilized by the test should not confound the skill or ability being measured. Utilization of an RTI approach in test development helps ensure that this is the case. Given the consideration regarding language in the design and construction of tests, developers often believe that as long as the individual is able to comprehend the instructions and speaks the language sufficiently well for general conversational purposes, or is dominant in the language, the test may be administered validly to linguistically different individuals (i.e., those for whom the test's language is not their native language).

Language issues in testing are not so easily resolved despite meticulous test development methods. For example, it is inappropriate to presume that having a sufficient level of proficiency in a test's language (in the present case, English) places a linguistically different individual on equal status with a native English speaker. It frequently does not (Cummins, 1984; Rhodes et al., 2005; Valdés & Figueroa, 1994). Even when an examinee is able to communicate effectively during an evaluation, there is no guarantee that his or her comprehension of the instructions, his or her ability to articulate responses, or his or her understanding of semantic nuances in the instructions (e.g., *and* vs. *or*) is equivalent to that of same-age monolingual English-speaking peers (Ortiz & Dynda, 2005). Much like acculturation, proficiency in a language is a function of when the individual first began to learn the language; how much exposure, experience with, and opportunity to learn the language he or she has been accorded; and whether the language of instruction in school matched the language of the home. These factors and others (e.g., parent's level of education, type of educational programming, current age/grade) determine whether a linguistically different individual possesses the level of *developmental* proficiency that would be typically expected and appropriate for other individuals of the same age—particularly those who constitute the norm sample. Furthermore, the type of experiences that occur during the critical period of language acquisition (birth to about 10 years of age) also has a tremendous impact on the development and degree of proficiency an individual possesses. Because English learners in the United States generally begin their learning of English after they physically immigrate, they begin this new language acquisition or learning process at some point after birth. Consequently, individuals of the same age or grade may have very different levels of proficiency or development in a language, even though both may be deemed to be "proficient."

The manner in which differences in developmental language proficiency may be manifest in testing are often subtle, but significant. For example, there may be times when an individual wishes to rely on his or her other language and in such cases its use will cause the examinee to think and respond more slowly as the translation moves from one language to the other. The additional expense of mental energy and attention draws precious cognitive resources away from tasks where their presence might enhance performance (e.g., short-term memory). In similar fashion, the drain on cognitive resources might become evident in cases where speed or completion time for a task is critical. Any developmental differences in fluency will also play a role in affecting performance, especially if an individual's cognitive efficiency is affected by the need to translate internally for better comprehension, or by difficulties in expressing responses accurately or with expected grammatical and semantic precision. In sum, the use of tests with linguistically different individuals is fraught with problems. In most cases, the lack of comparability in development (i.e., proficiency in the language) will change the nature of the test from one that is designed to measure a particular construct to one that is more a measure of proficiency in the test's language.

Language proficiency and level of acculturation should not be considered independent, uncorrelated variables. Individuals who are culturally different are invariably linguistically different and vice versa. Both are developmental processes, both create circumstances where examinee experience and exposure are not equal to same-age or grade peers in the norm sample, and both serve to inhibit performance and confound the constructs being measured by particular tests or scales. Thus, when professionals seek to evaluate individuals who are culturally and linguistically different, they must consider the combined impact of both variables, not simply one or the other. Successful nondiscriminatory assessment methods are those that recognize and evaluate the impact of cultural and linguistic differences on test performance in a systematic way. Failure to integrate these differences in the process of assessment will inevitably lead to inferences and conclusions that are not valid and largely indefensible—the result of which will likely be inequitable outcomes and this will serve to perpetuate social injustice in the process.

Approaches to Enhancing Equity in Assessment

The history of assessment is characterized by a variety of approaches that have been utilized with varying degrees of success in efforts to address the problems noted previously when evaluating the abilities of culturally and linguistically diverse learners (Ortiz, in press; Ortiz & Dynda, in press; Ortiz & Dynda, 2005; Ortiz & Ochoa, 2005). The most common approaches in current practice have largely been driven more by practitioner need in response to a glaring absence of research to guide actual evaluation procedures. These practices have persisted in part because of the lack of research into alternatives, and in this regard, their use has served the purpose of improving equity and fairness in assessment, albeit modestly. These methods include the use of nonverbal tests, use of translators/interpreters in testing, use of modified testing procedures, and development of tests in the native language. The relative advantages and disadvantages of each approach are discussed in the following section. Greater strides in fairness, however, will need to be more sophisticated and systematic and to that end, a newer approach, based on the cultural and linguistic characteristics of tests, will also be discussed as an exemplary and modern approach in nondiscriminatory assessment.

Nonverbal Testing

On the surface, development and use of nonverbal testing methods appears to be a straightforward and direct way of dealing with linguistic differences. The basic presumption is that by simply eliminating the issue of language altogether, its adverse impact on testing of individuals who do not speak the test's language is removed. Unfortunately, the issue remains rather complicated for several reasons, even for tests that are designed to be administered using no oral language whatsoever for administration and requiring no oral language from the examinee in responding.

The reality is that it is impossible to administer a test without using some form of *communication*. It may well be true that a test can be administered via pantomime or gestures and that no oral language is required on the part of the examinee. This does not mean, however, that there is no language present in the testing situation. Because a test relies on having an examinee know when to start, when to stop, what is a right answer, what is a wrong answer, when to work quickly, and so on, there must necessarily be some form of communication operating between the examiner and the examinee. Such communication may take the form of gestures or pantomime, but communication via nonverbal methods still represents a form of language. It is not an oral language, but it is a language nonetheless and the test cannot be administered without it. Moreover, it is unclear how gestures can even be taught and used in assessment without some type of instructional verbal interchange between the examiner and examinee. Therefore, even the use of an ostensibly nonverbal test remains reliant on communication and some type of language exchange between the participants even if that language is not oral. Much like with tests that utilize spoken language, problems with comprehension are not automatically obviated or facilitated as a function of using a gestural form of communication.

Another limitation to the nonverbal approach is that nonverbal tests are not entirely devoid of cultural content. In the attempt to capitalize on visual modalities, some nonverbal tests rely heavily on pictures and illustrations that may require age-appropriate cultural experiences and knowledge. For example, pictures or puzzles of an animal or a household object cannot, by definition, be culturally fair. They are and must necessarily remain culturally bound. This does not alter the technical properties of the test, but it places cultural demands on the examinee that may render their experiences or development in this regard unequal and thus inequitable.

Because of their emphasis on reducing language, nonverbal tests may also measure a narrower range of abilities than verbal tests. Tasks that measure visual processing, short-term memory, and processing speed are very common on nonverbal tests because they are easy to construct without relying on oral language. Conversely, measuring abilities such as auditory processing and crystallized intelligence (which includes language) is significantly more difficult, if not impractical to do without utilizing some aspect of language in the process. Moreover, the same problems that plague language-dependent tests with respect to the lack of equality in background and experiences between culturally and linguistically diverse individuals and the individuals on whom the test was normed also exist in a nonverbal approach. Nonverbal tests may not solve all the problems of equity in assessment with diverse populations, but they remain a reasonable choice for managing language issues in assessment. Nonverbal tests are quite popular and are certainly a viable alternative to other tests that are not language-reduced when used with culturally and linguistically diverse individuals.

Translators/Interpreters

Another common approach designed to reduce the potential discriminatory aspects of assessment involves the use of a translator/interpreter for the administration of a particular test. As with nonverbal testing, this approach is primarily in response to the language issue and is often employed in situations where communication is very difficult if not impossible due to a linguistic difference between the examinee and the examiner. Clearly, in cases where an examinee does not speak the language of the test with any degree of proficiency, the use of a translator/interpreter may well be the only option available to assist in reducing the inherent linguistic inequities in the assessment process. But there are some important cautions and drawbacks to this approach. Individuals who are used as translators/interpreters must be well trained and the examiner must also practice using them (AERA et al., 1999; Lopez, 2002, 2008). No matter how well trained a translator/interpreter or examiner might be, there is no guarantee that the test and its instructions, the items on the test, or the measurement of the intended constructs of interest will be equivalent because of the potential changes in meaning that invariably occur in translation. Results from the use of this approach are, therefore, ambiguous and often difficult to interpret fairly since it cannot be determined in what manner or to what extent translation and the use of a translator/interpreter influenced the reliability of the test. It should also be noted that tests are not often normed with the use of translators/interpreters and their use is thus a technical violation of the test's standardized administration procedures. Despite these limitations, when there are no other viable alternatives, this approach may represent the only manner in which practitioners can address some of the concerns with fairness in assessment.

Native-Language Testing

A more recent approach in response to the obstacles posed by cultural and linguistic differences has been the development of tests in languages other than English but which are meant for use with individuals in the United States. We have already discussed the technical issues that face test developers looking for cross-cultural portability in their tests. These issues are compounded when a test is designed for use on culturally and linguistically different individuals now living within the culture of the test and learning its language as well, but who may no longer be developing their native language. For these reasons, the approach remains problematic because it tends to focus on the native language at the expense of English, which is developing secondarily but quickly becoming the dominant one—especially when it is the language of instruction in school. Because language proficiency and relative language dominance are functions of usage and practice, many individuals will suffer from some degree of language loss or attrition as the second language begins to replace the native language in settings such as work, school, and in time, even the home. Thus, evaluation in the native language may not reveal actual or true levels of ability, skill, or knowledge any better than evaluation in the second language. Another limitation to this approach is that it requires a practitioner who is fluent in the language of the examinee for administration and scoring. The availability of native-language tests is still rather limited. In the United States, the most common language in which tests are available other than English is Spanish. Achieving equity through this approach is likely to require additional research regarding the manner in which bilinguals in the United States perform on native-language tests as a function of their relative proficiency in both English and the native language.

Modified Testing Procedures

Perhaps the most common approach to the evaluation of culturally and linguistically diverse individuals is one based on the use of modifications to the standardization procedures for test administration. One of the fundamental requirements for establishing and maintaining reliability and validity in assessment is to create situations where extraneous variables are controlled so that the only factor allowed to vary is the actual ability or skill being measured. Following standardized testing procedures helps ensure that no individual is given an unfair advantage or placed at a disadvantage relative to others to whom the test is given or upon whom it was normed. Thus, it would seem counterintuitive to alter procedures designed to ensure fairness in an effort to create more fairness. Nevertheless, this is the essence of this approach.

Perhaps because there has long been the perception that standardized tests were unfair to individuals who were culturally and linguistically diverse—a perception that was not entirely merited—practitioners have engaged in a variety of activities that alter standardized testing procedures in ways that at least give an impression of being more fair. Some of these procedures have been referred to as "testing the limits" because they included such changes as removal of time constraints on timed tasks, additional repetition or mediation of test instructions to ensure comprehension prior to item administration, acceptance of responses in any language rather than only in the language of the test, and administration of additional items after reaching a ceiling on a subtest, and so forth.

In and of themselves, such testing modifications may well allow individuals a better opportunity to respond correctly to any given test item and this is certainly one of the advantages of the approach. Unfortunately, one of the major drawbacks of this approach is that because it violates the standardization procedures of the test, it inadvertently introduces additional error into the testing situation. Whereas the reliability of a test is quantifiable when given in standardized manner, the same cannot be said of the test when that standardization is not followed. The degree to which the test is accurate is now unknown because there is no way of quantifying the extent to which the modifications altered the properties of the test. Likewise, the undermining of reliability also eliminates the validity of the test as no measure can be valid unless it is demonstrated to be valid. All of this effectively means that test results obtained in this manner cannot be interpreted with any manner of confidence or validity. Comparisons of performance obtained with such modifications to those who were given the test and had it scored in a standardized manner are untenable. There is simply no way to draw valid conclusions from such data. But the value of this approach may lie more in the ability to secure information about performance that is qualitative in nature rather than quantitative. Seasoned practitioners may well be able to draw upon their experience to evaluate the nature of the individual's responses and response processes such that valuable insight may be gained into why a response was or was not correct. One of the primary reasons for any evaluation is to derive information that may be useful in the design and development of interventions. As such, use of modified testing procedures and careful analysis and observation of an individual's approach to various tasks represents an ideal method for understanding and evaluating more than simply strengths and weaknesses but needs and avenues for remediation as well.

Modern Approaches

One of the curious facts regarding assessment of culturally and linguistically diverse individuals is that, as a group, they have been the subject of testing for nearly a century and from the very advent of the tests themselves (Brigham, 1923; Goddard, 1913). Consequently, there exists a small but consistent body of research demonstrating a pattern of lower performance on tests administered in English that are largely language and culture dependent and better performance on tests that are culture and language reduced (Cummins, 1984; Jensen, 1974, 1976; Mercer,

1979; Sanchez, 1934; Valdés & Figueroa, 1994; Vukovich & Figueroa, 1982). Recently, this research base was utilized as the foundation for the development of an approach to equitable assessment known as the Culture-Language Test Classifications and Interpretive Matrix (Flanagan & Ortiz, 2001; Flanagan, Ortiz, & Alfonso, 2007; Ortiz & Ochoa, 2005; Rhodes et al., 2005). Because the approach addresses directly the major obstacles in assessment (individual differences in level of acculturation and language proficiency) and because it integrates research and theory with practice, it represents the kind of practice to which practitioners involved in the evaluation of diverse populations should aspire.

At the heart of the approach are the Culture-Language Test Classifications that represent a compilation of the average performance of culturally and linguistically diverse groups on specific subtests from various intelligence, cognitive ability, and special purpose batteries. By arranging the subtests according to the degree to which they are culturally loaded and linguistically demanding (i.e., low, moderate, or high), and by assigning the respective average scores for culturally and linguistically diverse individuals culled from research, a matrix is formed in which a pattern of declining performance typical for this population is revealed. This pattern is depicted in Figure 2.1.

The arrows in Figure 2.1 represent the effect that level of acculturation and limited English proficiency have on the test performance of culturally and linguistically diverse individuals. Research has consistently demonstrated that as tests increase in their cultural content, linguistic demands, or both, the performance of culturally and linguistically diverse individuals declines proportionally. As a group, the average performance for this population on tests that are high in cultural loading and linguistic demand is about one standard deviation below the norm (Cummins, 1984; Dynda et al., 2008; Jensen, 1974, 1976; Jones & Herndon, 1992; Mercer, 1979; Sanchez, 1934; Sotelo-Dynega et al., 2007; Valdés & Figueroa, 1994; Vukovich & Figueroa, 1982). Because cultural and linguistic variables are highly correlated, as noted previously, it is the large central arrow in the figure that best reflects this typical pattern of decline in performance.

Ortiz and colleagues have subsequently developed the Culture-Language Interpretive Matrix that builds on the test classifications and permits direct examination of test scores obtained from testing culturally and linguistically diverse individuals (Flanagan et al., 2007; Ortiz & Dynda, in press; Ortiz & Ochoa, 2005). A detailed explanation of the matrix and its use is beyond the scope of this chapter and the reader

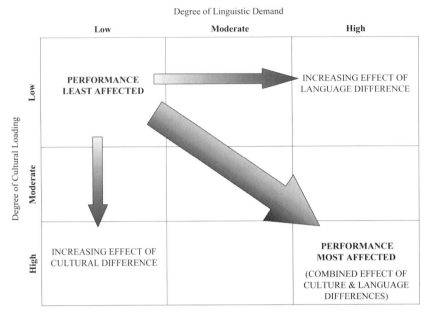

Figure 2.1 Pattern of expected test performance for culturally and linguistically diverse individuals.

From "Diversity, Fairness, Utility and Social Issues," by S. O. Ortiz and A. M. Dynda, 2009, in *Assessment in Rehabilitation and Health,* edited by T. Oakland & E. Mpofu, New York: Prentice Hall, pp. 95–141. Copyright © 2009 by S. O. Ortiz and A. M. Dynda. Reprinted with permission.

is referred to other sources for more information (e.g., Flanagan et al., 2007). The general procedure for using the matrix begins by placing an individual's test scores in the matrix and comparing the resulting pattern to the typical pattern described previously where scores for normal, nondisabled individuals from culturally and linguistically diverse backgrounds tend to decline as the tests become more culturally embedded and linguistically demanding. When the individual's pattern of scores follows the predicted pattern of decline specified in the matrix, it can be reasonably concluded that the individual's performance on the test was due primarily to cultural and linguistic differences rather than to actual ability, skill, or knowledge or lack thereof. When the individual's pattern of scores does not follow the predicted pattern of decline specified in the matrix, it can be reasonably concluded that the individual's performance on the test was due primarily to factors other than cultural and linguistic differences. If extraneous variables have been excluded as confounds on performance (e.g., fatigue, lack of motivation, emotional problems, incorrect scoring/administration), then deficiencies in performance may be defensibly attributed to actual lack of ability (i.e., disability). Because the matrix relies on scores obtained from unmodified testing, the matrix addresses directly the concerns with reliability and validity that often create difficulties in the assessment and interpretive process.

One important advantage of the Culture-Language Interpretive Matrix is that it does not require the examining professional to be proficient in the client's native language or evaluate in the native language. In addition, it places a contemporary, research-based method for enhancing equity in assessment well within the reach of any professional. However, perhaps its most significant contribution to enhancing equity in assessment is the manner in which the question of developmental equality in cultural and linguistic background and experience is managed. By providing initial comparisons of performance to the typical performance of other individuals with similar levels of acculturation and language proficiency, the matrix allows examiners to assess directly and systematically the impact of those differences on test performance. The approach is both research-based and focused on developmental inequalities that threaten the validity of obtained results. Reliability is not undermined because the matrix utilizes test scores that were obtained from standardized administration of the test. It is also systematic in the manner in which the impact of cultural and linguistic variables is considered, and this likely makes the approach more defensible in practice than other current alternatives. In short, it represents an exemplary and contemporary approach to enhancing equity in assessment that may offer a path toward greater social justice in decision making and outcomes.

SUMMARY

The significance of information derived from assessment is influenced by the many complex ways in which the conditions of equity are perceived by service providers and consumers of assessment. Conditions of equity are not only an expectation, but are also salient aspects of the process that affect participation in an assessment setting. Equitable assessment practices help reduce the potential adverse impact on consumers from confounds to the assessment process and from interactions involving the characteristics of tests, consumers, providers, and contexts. IRT methodology makes it possible to develop assessments that are largely transportable across populations and settings. This is because the items and tests map an underlying construct of interest rather than idiosyncratic sample characteristics. IRT-based measurements enhance equity in behavioral measurement in that they give consideration to a broad range of relevant indicators in the individual that characterize the construct of interest, the co-occurrence or overlap of the indicators of the construct, and their differentiation in individuals. For that reason, IRT-derived measures offer the best prospect yet in the measurement of abilities with a multiply diverse population such as that of people with disabilities and those who are culturally and linguistically diverse.

To fully achieve equity in assessment, particularly in diverse contexts, such advances in test design and construction must be accompanied by methods and procedures that are themselves designed to reduce potential inequities. Tests do not interpret themselves or make decisions; people do. Thus, it is important that professionals not rely solely on tests to eliminate every area of potential bias and to continue to utilize assessment approaches that are specifically intended to enhance fairness in the broader assessment process, such as those described in the latter part of this chapter. It is clear that attempts to comprehensively address issues of equity in assessment need to go beyond technical efficiency of items and scales to address social justice values that consumers hold and that influence their behavior in assessment. Consumers may find certain aspects of the assessment to be very salient whereas providers of assessment services may be less attentive to those same concerns. Ultimately, involving consumers as partners in the design and use of assessment instruments is perhaps the ideal manner to enhance equity in assessment and the quality of decisions from the assessment outcomes. Until then, it remains incumbent upon professionals to become well versed and understand fully the various factors that threaten fairness and equity in any assessment, to take active steps to reduce potential bias in a systematic manner, and to apply nondiscriminatory approaches designed specifically to address the known causes of inequity and lack of fairness in testing.

REFERENCES

American Educational Research Association, American Psychological Association, & National Council on Measurement in Education. (1999). *Standards for educational and psychological testing.* Washington, DC: American Educational Research Association.

American Psychological Association. (1990). *Guidelines for providers of psychological services to ethnic, linguistic, and culturally diverse populations.* Washington, DC: Author.

Andrich, D. (1988). *Rasch models for measurement.* Newbury Park, CA: Sage.

Andrich, D. (1996). Measurement criteria for choosing among models for graded responses. In A. Von Eye & C. C. Clogg (Eds.), *Analysis of categorical variables in developmental research* (pp. 3–35). Orlando, FL: Academic Press.

Andrich, D. (2003). On the distribution of measurements in units that are not arbitrary. *Social Science Information, 42,* 557–589.

Arce-Ferrer, A., & Ketterer, J. (2003). The effect of scale tailoring for cross-cultural application on scale reliability and construct validity. *Educational and Psychological Measurement, 63,* 484–501.

Azocar, F., Arean, P., Miranda, J., & Muñoz, R. F. (2001). Differential item functioning in a Spanish translation of the Beck Depression Inventory. *Journal of Clinical Psychology, 57,* 355–365.

Bond, T. G., & Fox, C. M. (2001). *Applying the Rasch model: Fundamental measurement in the human sciences.* Mahwah, NJ: Erlbaum.

Brigham, C. C. (1923). *A study of American intelligence.* Princeton, NJ: Princeton University Press.

Cella, D., & Chih-Hung, C. (2000). A discussion of item response theory and its applications in health status assessment. *Medical Care, 38,* 66–72.

Chu, K. L., & Kamata, A. (2005). Test equating in the presence of DIF items. *Journal of Applied Measurement, 6,* 342–354.

Conrad, K. J., & Bezrucsko, N. (2004, June). *Maximizing measurement precision: Fundamentals of Item-Response Theory (IRT)/Rasch measurement.* Paper presented at the Complexities of Co-Occurring Conditions Conference, Bethesda, MD.

Cummins, J. C. (1984). *Bilingual and special education: Issues in assessment and pedagogy.* Austin, TX: PRO-ED.

Dynda, A. M., Flanagan, D. P., Chaplin, W., & Pope, A. (2008). *The relations between English language proficiency and IQ test performance.* Unpublished manuscript, St. John's University, Jamaica, NY.

Embretson, S. E. (1996). Item response theory models and spurious interaction effects in factorial ANOVA designs. *Applied Psychological Measurement, 20,* 201–212.

Farley, R. C., Waller, N. G., & Brennan, K. A. (2000). An item response theory analysis of self-report measures of adult attachment. *Journal of Personality and Social Psychology, 78,* 350–365.

Flanagan, D. P., & Ortiz, S. O. (2001). *Essentials of cross-battery assessment.* New York: Wiley.

Flanagan, D. P., Ortiz, S. O., & Alfonso, V. C. (2007). *Essentials of cross-battery assessment* (2nd ed.). New York: Wiley.

Gierl, M. L., Henderson, D., Jodoin, M., & Klinger, D. (2001). Minimizing the influence of item parameter estimation errors in test development: A comparison of three selection procedures. *Journal of Experimental Education, 69,* 261–279.

Goddard, H. H. (1913). The Binet tests in relation to immigration. *Journal of Psycho-Asthenics, 18,* 105–107.

Hawley, C. A., Taylor, R., Hellawell, D. J., & Pentland, B. (1999). Use of the functional assessment measure (FIM + FAM) in head injury rehabilitation: A psychometric analysis. *Journal of Neural Psychiatry, 67,* 749–754.

Heinemann, A. W., Bode, R., Cichowski, K. C., & Kan, E. (1998). Measuring patient satisfaction with medical rehabilitation. In E. A. Dobrzykowski (Ed.), *Essential readings in rehabilitation outcomes measurement: Application, methodology, and technology* (pp. 92–103). Gaithersburg, MD: Aspen.

Jensen, A. R. (1974). How biased are culture-loaded tests? *Genetic Psychology Monographs, 90,* 185–244.

Jensen, A. R. (1976). Construct validity and test bias. *Phi Delta Kappan, 58,* 340–346.

Jones, R. T., & Herndon, C. (1992). The status of black children and adolescents in the academic setting: Assessment and treatment issues. In C. E. Walker & M. C. Roberts (Eds.), *Handbook of clinical child psychology,* Wiley Series on Personality Processes (2nd ed., pp. 901–917). New York: Wiley.

Kahler, C. W., Strong, D. R., Hakayi, J., Ramsey, S., & Brown, R. A. (2003). An item response analysis of the alcohol dependence scale in treatment-seeking alcoholics. *Journal of Studies in Alcohol, 64,* 127–136.

Kandel, D. B., & Yamaguchi, K. (2002). Stages in drug involvement in the U.S. population. In D. B. Kandel (Ed.), *Stages and pathways of drug involvement: Examining the gateway hypothesis* (pp. 65–89). New York: Cambridge University Press.

Kang, S. M., & Waller, N. G. (2005). Moderated multiple regression, spurious interaction effects, and IRT. *Applied Psychological Measurement, 29,* 87–105.

Kindler, A. L. (2002). *Survey of the states' limited English proficient students and available educational programs and services 1999–2000: Summary report.* Washington, DC: National Clearinghouse for English Acquisition and Language Instruction Educational Programs.

Leigh, B. C., & Stall, R. (1993). Substance use and risky behavior for exposure to HIV: Issues in methodology, interpretation and prevention. *American Psychologist, 48,* 1035–1045.

Lopez, E. C. (2008). Best practices in working with school interpreters. In A. Thomas & J. Grimes (Eds.), *Best practices in school psychology V* (pp. 1751–1770). Washington, DC: National Association of School Psychologists.

Lopez, E. C. (2002). Best practices in working with interpreters. In A. Thomas & J. Grimes (Eds.), *Best practices in school psychology IV* (p. 1428). Washington, DC: National Association of School Psychologists.

Lord, F. M. (1980). *Application of Item Response Theory to practical testing problems.* Hillsdale, NJ: Erlbaum.

Marquis, P., Keininger, D., Acquadro, C., & de la Loge, C. (2005). Translating and evaluating questionnaires: Cultural issues for international research. In P. Fayers & R. Hays (Eds.), *Assessing quality of life in clinical trials: Method and practice* (pp. 95–112). Oxford, UK: Oxford University Press.

Mercer, J. R. (1979). *System of multicultural pluralistic assessment: Technical manual.* New York: The Psychological Corporation.

Mpofu, E. (2004, October). *Equitable assessment practices: An African perspective.* Keynote speech presented at the International Test Commission 2004 Conference. The College of William and Mary, Williamsburg, Virginia.

Mpofu, E., & Oakland, T. (2006). Assessment of value change in adults with acquired disabilities. In M. Hersen (Ed.), *Clinician's handbook of adult behavioral assessment* (pp. 601–630). New York: Elsevier Press.

Mpofu, E., & Watkins, D. (1994). The similarities subtest of the British Ability Scales: Content and construct bias for a sample of Zimbabwe school children. *Educational and Psychological Measurement, 54,* 728–733.

Mpofu, E., & Wilson, K. B. (2004). Opportunity structure and transition practices with students with disabilities: The role of family, culture, and community. *Journal of Applied Rehabilitation Counseling, 35*(2), 9–16.

National Center for Educational Statistics. (2007). *Dropout rates in the United States: 2005.* Retrieved April 13, 2008, from http://nces.ed.gov/pubsearch/pubsinfo. asp?pubid=2007059

Oakland, T. (Ed.). (1977). *Psychological and educational assessment of minority children.* New York: Brunner/Mazel.

Ochoa, S. H. (2005). Disproportionate representation of diverse students in special education. In R. Rhodes, S. H. Ochoa, & S. O. Ortiz (Eds.), *Assessment of culturally and linguistically diverse students: A practical guide* (pp. 15–41). New York: Guilford Press.

O'Neill, S. E., Sher, K. J., Jackson, K. M., & Wood, P. K. (2003). Dimensions of alcohol dependence in young adulthood: Current versus lifetime symptomatology. *Journal of Studies on Alcohol, 64,* 495–499.

Ortiz, S. O. (in press). Best practices in nondiscriminatory assessment. In A. Thomas & J. Grimes (Eds.), *Best practices in school psychology V.* Washington, DC: National Association of School Psychologists.

Ortiz, S. O., & Dynda, A. M. (2005). The use of intelligence tests with culturally and linguistically diverse populations. In D. P. Flanagan & P. L. Harrison (Eds.), *Contemporary intellectual assessment* (2nd ed., pp. 545–556). New York: Guilford Press.

Ortiz, S. O., & Dynda, A. M. (in press). Diversity, fairness, utility and social issues. In E. Mpofu & T. Oakland (Eds.), *Assessment in rehabilitation and health.* Boston: Allyn & Bacon.

Ortiz, S. O., & Ochoa, S. H. (2005). Intellectual assessment: A nondiscriminatory interpretive approach. In D. P. Flanagan & P. L. Harrison (Eds.), *Contemporary intellectual assessment* (2nd ed., pp. 234–250). New York: Guilford Press.

Ozer, M. N., & Kroll, T. (2002). Patient centered rehabilitation: Problems and opportunities. *Critical Review in Physical and Rehabilitation Medicine, 14,* 273–289.

Patton, J. M. (1998). The disproportionate representation of African Americans in special education: Looking behind the curtain for understanding and solutions. *Journal of Special Education, 32*(1), 25–31.

Raju, N. S., van der Linden, W. J., & Fleer, P. F. (1995). IRT-based internal measures of differential functioning of items and tests. *Applied Psychological Measurement, 19,* 353–368.

Rasch, G. (1980). *Probabilistic models for some intelligence and attainment tests.* Chicago: University of Chicago Press.

Reeve, B., & Fayers, P. (2005). Applying item response theory modelling for evaluating questionnaire item and scale properties. In P. Fayers & R. Hays (Eds.), *Assessing quality of life in clinical trials: Method and practice* (pp. 95–112). Oxford, UK: Oxford University Press.

Rhodes, R., Ochoa, S. H., & Ortiz, S. O. (2005). *Assessment of culturally and linguistically diverse students: A practical guide.* New York: Guilford Press.

Rudner, L., Getson, P., & Knight, D. (1980). Item bias detection techniques. *Journal of Educational Statistics, 5,* 213–233.

Salvia, J., & Ysseldyke, J. E. (1991). *Assessment* (5th ed.). New York: Houghton Mifflin.

Sanchez, G. (1934). Bilingualism and mental measures: A word of caution. *Journal of Applied Psychology, 18,* 765–772.

Sattler, J. M., & Gwynne, J. (1982). White examiners generally do not impede the intelligence test performance of black children: To debunk a myth. *Journal of Consulting and Clinical Psychology, 50*(2), 196–208.

Skiba, R. J. (2001). When is disproportionality discrimination?: The overrepresentation of black students in school suspension. In W. Ayers, B. Dohrn, & R. Ayers (Eds.), *Zero tolerance: Resisting the drive for punishment in our schools* (pp. 176–187). New York: New Press.

Smith, R. M. (2004). Detecting item bias with the Rasch model. *Journal of Applied Measurement, 5,* 430–449.

Smith, R. M., & Taylor, P. A. (2004). Equating rehabilitation outcome scales. *Journal of Applied Measurement, 5,* 229–242.

Snider, P. D., & Styles, I. (2005). Analysis of the collectivism and individualism scale using a Rasch measurement model. In R. F. Waugh (Ed.), *Frontiers in educational psychology* (pp. 311–332). Hauppauge, NY: Nova Science.

Sotelo-Dynega, M., Ortiz, S. O., Flanagan, D. P., & Chaplin, W. (2007). *Cognitive performance and the development of English language proficiency.* Unpublished manuscript, St. John's University, Jamaica, NY.

Spencer, S. J., Steele, C. M., & Quinn, D. M. (1999). Stereotype threat and women's math performance. *Journal of Experimental Social Psychology, 35,* 4–28.

Spoth, R., Goldberg, C., Neppl, T., Trudeau, L., & Ramisetty-Mikler, S. (2001). Rural-urban differences in the distribution of parent-reported risk factors for substance use among young adolescents. *Journal of Substance Abuse, 13,* 609–623.

Steele, C. M., & Aronson, J. (1995). Stereotype threat and the intellectual test performance of African Americans. *Journal of Personality and Social Psychology, 69,* 797–811.

Sue, S. (1998). In search of cultural competence in psychotherapy and counseling. *American Psychologist, 53*(4), 440–448.

Sue, S., Fujino, D., Hu, L., Takeuchi, D., & Zane, N. (1991). Community mental health services for ethnic minority groups: A test of the cultural responsiveness hypothesis. *Journal of Clinical and Consulting Psychology, 59,* 533–540.

Teresi, J. A. (2001). Statistical methods for the examination of differential item functioning (DIF) with applications to cross-cultural measurement of functional, physical and mental health. *Journal of Mental Health and Aging, 7,* 31–40.

Valdés, G., & Figueroa, R. A. (1994). *Bilingualism and testing: A special case of bias.* Norwood, NJ: Ablex.

Van de Vijver, F., & Leung, K. (1997). *Methods and data analysis for cross-cultural research.* Thousand Oaks, CA: Sage.

Van Herk, H., Poortinga, Y. H., & Verhallen, T. M. M. (2004). Response styles in rating scales: Evidence of method bias in data from six EU countries. *Journal of Cross-Cultural Psychology, 35,* 346–360.

Velozo, C. (2005, June). *Developing measures based on the ICF.* Paper presented at the North American Collaborating Center/WHO Annual Conference, Rochester, MN.

Vukovich, D., & Figueroa, R. A. (1982). *The validation of the system of multicultural pluralistic assessment: 1980–1982.* Unpublished manuscript, University of California at Davis, Department of Education.

Wright, B. D., & Mok, M. C. (2004). An overview of the family of Rasch measurement models. In E. V. Smith, Jr., & R. M. Smith (Eds.), *Introduction to Rasch measurement* (pp. 1–14). Maple Grove, MN: JAM Press.

Wright, J. G., Rudicel, S., & Feinstein, A. R. (1994). Ask patients what they want. *Journal of Bone and Joint Surgery, 76,* 229–234.

3

Respecting Local, Cultural Contexts for Assessment Practice in an Era of Globalization

VAL KLENOWSKI

Dissatisfaction, internationally, with existing educational practices and outcomes since the early 1990s has led to increased educational reform. At the same time, there has also been a worldwide shift in control of education away from teachers toward the state for the purposes of restructuring economies. More bureaucratic forms of curriculum and assessment have resulted, with a return to the use of more techno-rational discourse in assessment and evaluation for purposes of efficiency, accountability, impact, and performance management. There has also been an increase in the use of economic and productivity models to study educational outcomes. These models fail to account for the range of outcomes achieved and fail to identify the factors responsible for such diversity in performance.

The global shift toward standards-driven reform, tied to reporting, engages directly with assessment issues related to accountability. In an accountability context standards are used as a lever to improve the reliability and consistency of teacher judgment, and classroom evidence is used by education systems internationally for reporting and tracking achievement over time. Assessment is inseparable from curriculum and has become a powerful driver for change. It is central to good education and is at the heart of the teaching-learning dynamic. The relationship between the learner, learning, and assessment, however, needs to be kept central and the idea of teacher empowerment at the local, professional level is fundamental.

This chapter will outline the different assessment regimes and associated practices for achieving accountability in the global context of standards-based reform and in so doing will highlight their value and limitations. What is apparent in this analysis is the central role of teacher empowerment at the local, cultural level in the case for "intelligent accountability" (Sahlberg, 2007) and more generative and educative forms of assessment, pedagogy, and curriculum to enhance quality and to improve equity of educational provision. This chapter argues for a central place for teacher-led culturally responsive assessment practices, for and with students. Teacher professionalism, through educative forms of school-based and teacher-led evaluation and assessment, remains vital.

GLOBAL TRENDS

Changing Curriculum Priorities

Internationally, curriculum developers have identified skills, knowledge, capabilities, or competencies that will benefit the child in the future. These predictions of what one will need have become the bases for planning of the curriculum (Kliebard, 1992) with the use of standardized testing in curriculum evaluation to check the efficacy of standardized curriculum. It has become evident from worldwide trends that despite the call for critical and creative thinking skills for the "knowledge society," this generation of students is being tested and examined more than ever before (Broadfoot, 2007).

The bureaucratization of curriculum was evident in the United Kingdom (UK) when in 1988 a national curriculum that was preoccupied with achievement in terms of student results was adopted. Evaluation and assessment took on primarily an accountability function. The national curriculum identified the content of programs, and the objectives and processes, in terms of targets or standards. The publication of league tables became a device for judgments about school performance. The costs both in human and financial terms have been huge (Broadfoot, 2007).

International Comparisons

At the same time policy makers and others have shown increased interest in international measures of educational attainment, such as the results from the Programme for International Student Assessment (PISA), developed by the Organisation for Economic Co-operation and Development (OECD), or the Third International Mathematics and Science Study (TIMSS) of the International Association for the Evaluation of Educational Achievement (IEA). These comparisons have influenced policy development, yet important questions of whether we are comparing like with like have not always been considered. The rigor of these studies, their methodologies, and the way in which the data have been interpreted and used have also been debated and critiqued by researchers such as Goldstein (2004) and Hopmann (2008). International comparisons require a common set of criteria for measuring performance, comparability between samples and the reporting of the results, a match in terms of the content of the curriculum and the approach used, and regard given to context.

Governments to justify the introduction of ongoing curriculum change have used the results from such comparisons. For example, in the UK, the then Department for Education and Employment (DfEE) commenced a National Numeracy Project to address perceived weaknesses, particularly in the teaching of mathematics at primary school level, after the publication of the results of TIMSS in 1996. This project was followed by the adoption of the National Numeracy Strategy, the National Literacy Strategy, and the Secondary National Key Stage 3 Strategy by the Department for Education and Skills (DfES). The latter strategy aims to raise standards by strengthening teaching and learning across the curriculum for all 11- to 14-year-olds. Continuing professional development for subject teachers and school managers, plus consultancy, guidance, and teaching materials, are offered.

Australia, as with other countries, has made use of international comparative data such as that of the Third International Mathematics and Science Study (TIMSS). This international comparison of achievement showed significant state and territory differences in Australia. So it is no surprise that the new Labor government in 2008 has introduced plans for a National Curriculum in Mathematics, Science, History, and English in primary and secondary schools by 2011. What has been most revealing for Australia in equity terms is that the analysis of the results of the international performance data has revealed that indigenous children have scored significantly lower than nonindigenous children (Lokan, Ford, & Greenwood, 1997). Australian schools are not adequately addressing inequalities and when compared with other developed countries, Australia is underperforming in terms of equity: "high in quality but low in equity" (McGaw, 2004). An analysis of the 2003 Programme for International Student Assessment (PISA) data suggests that Australia in general is "over-represented in the lowest categories of maths proficiency and under-represented in the highest" (Thomson, Cresswell, & De Bortoli, 2004, p. xiii). So, while the achievement of students overall is high, there are wide differences between the high- and low-achieving students. Curriculum, assessment, and pedagogic practices need to address such issues from a sociocultural perspective at the local professional level of the classroom. It is the professionalism of the teacher and trust in that professionalism by the political center that will make the difference in terms of educational change for improved learning.

Evaluation for Policy Development

In an accountability context, the need to demonstrate performance is heightened, and explicating what works is pursued. Some organizations and government agencies are reporting evidence from curriculum evaluation using a "what works" approach. The consequence of such developments for curriculum and assessment is that evaluation is little concerned with debating fundamental value issues in the curriculum program, or the assessment strategy itself, but is now incorporated into implementation. So that far from representing a relatively independent and/or predominantly professional activity, evaluation has been incorporated into the processes of policy development and system management.

The value of dialogue and deliberation with practitioners in evaluation to facilitate understanding of the challenges of diverse values in the context of practice has been recognized. However, the combination of a "what works" approach and evidence-based decision making has reinvigorated concerns relating to measurement, validity, and reliability of quantitative measurement. Some government agencies are demanding Evidence Based Policy and Practice (EBPP), derived from randomized experimental designs, as a basis for intervention and pursuit of policy agendas (see the Economic and Social Research Council's Centre for Evidence Based Policy and Practice Web site at http://www.evidencenetwork.org/cgi-win/enet.exe/pubs?QMW for examples). Although EBPP provided the research community with new opportunities, any claims regarding improvement in the conduct of public policy remain modest. In this drive for efficient use of resources with the development of guidelines and frameworks to regulate and assess evaluation practice, caution must again be taken to ensure that we are comparing like with like. It is important that in the synthesis of evaluations for EBPP that outcomes have not been simplified and contexts have not been ignored.

Despite the generation of democratic, responsive, and deliberative forms and purposes of evaluation, it would appear that evaluation for accountability and control continues to impact on current practice as is evident in the reemergence of bureaucratic forms of curriculum and assessment with the return of quantitative, reductionist approaches such as "No Child Left Behind." What also becomes apparent in the name of efficiency is a return to technological and behavioristic refinements of curriculum evaluation and a possible trivialization that threatens the richness of the intellectual activity for those involved in the discipline of curriculum evaluation.

The impact of such trends in evaluation on assessment practice is that data analyzed for a particular purpose may be used for another unintended purpose. For example, performance assessment data have been used for the development of league tables that are then used to judge the quality of schools. As Broadfoot (2007, p. 59) suggests:

> in transitions between criterion- and norm-referenced approaches and formative and summative purposes, there is considerable scope for the issue of "fitness for purpose" to be obscured. The result . . . is a number of, at best unhelpful, and at worst, downright damaging assessment practices.

For example, politicians have used league table comparisons to justify the introduction of additional testing regimes or performance targets without analyzing the national characteristics and contextual factors that might help teachers, parents, and community members understand the difference in system-level performance.

ACCOUNTABILITY

In the 1980s the discourse of markets emerged in education and the place and purpose of accountability was made explicit. At that time, particularly in England, the dangers of "raw" exam or test results for accountability purposes were identified. Accountability was dominated by inspection and standardized testing, the main criteria for judging school performance and measuring success in terms of student achievement. Schools are accountable for what they do for students; however, using assessment results in this way can lead to schools being rewarded for the "quality" of the students they can attract and enroll rather than what they actually do for students to help them achieve.

Given the current quest for consistency in education using standards-referenced assessment systems, involving student assessment and reporting against national and international benchmarks, it is important to make explicit the intended and unintended consequences of such strategies. It is useful to acknowledge the inexorable existence of the pressures to pervert. In a context that is standards-driven and values standardization, there is a great danger that technical and rationalist approaches that generalize and make superficial assessment tasks and practices will emerge. Differentials of assessments around the world and in particular cultures can be lost.

Attaining coherence between classroom assessment and system-level accountability that includes system interest in transparency of outcomes has been much debated (Fredericksen & White, 2004; Wilson, 2004). It is teachers' judgments and interpretations of assessment data in the context of social moderation that is key. For it is teachers who have direct access to the information needed for an accountability system. It is students, their teachers, and their parents, who know and work with them in different settings, who are the primary sources of information to determine what schools do for students (MacBeath, 1999).

"Intelligent accountability" policies, such as those of Finland (Sahlberg, 2007), involve trust-based professionalism. Sahlberg (2007) contrasts the Finnish system with more common systems described as "consequential accountability" where schools' efforts to raise performance and student achievement involve processes of promotion, inspection, and the use of measures such as standardized testing to evaluate success and to determine the rewards or punishments for schools or teachers. "Intelligent accountability" develops from a context that values and respects teachers' and principals' professionalism, particularly in judging what is best for students and in reporting their achievements. Finland to date has not embraced market-oriented reforms or market-oriented management models but has focused on sustainable leadership and "built upon values grounded in equity, equitable distribution of resources rather than competition, intensive early interventions for prevention and building gradual trust among education practitioners, especially teachers" (Sahlberg, 2007, pp. 152–153). In the Finnish education context, "intelligent accountability" enhances trust among teachers, students, and education authorities in the accountability processes. What is more, they are involved in the process so they develop a strong sense of professional responsibility and initiative (Fullan, 2005). The impact on teaching and student learning has been positive. Assessment of student learning is based on teacher-led assessment rather than standardized external tests, numerical grades are not used after grade five so that students are not compared with one another. Grades are prohibited by law and only descriptive assessments and feedback are used, which current research informs us will impact positively on student performance and engagement in their learning (Assessment Reform Group, 1999). Teacher-made classroom assessment is a dominant practice and is used by teachers as an opportunity for learning as much as for assessing student achievement.

There are shortcomings of such a system in that there is a reliance on teachers' and schools' abilities to judge and report on students' achievement, and there are differences among criteria that teachers use to evaluate their students, even within the same school. Issues arise when students move to a new school and experience assessment that may involve expectations that vary to those of their previous school. Despite these shortcomings, the concept of "intelligent accountability" is preferred as it enables schools to keep the focus on learning and allows more freedom in curriculum planning compared with external standardized testing contexts. This approach allows teachers to address the needs of students from particular sociocultural contexts and enables assessment practice to be responsive.

STANDARDS

The term *standards* is ubiquitous but there are no simple measuring instruments that can be used to determine an appropriate value for a student's achievement, or for that matter, of a school. There is no natural unit of measurement as there is for some physical quantities, such as weight or height. The concept of standards is elusive, and to avoid confusion, it is important to understand that the term can be used in a variety of ways.

In this chapter, the definitions of standards that are most appropriate in the context of standards-referenced assessment systems for accountability include "quality benchmarks" (i.e., what is expected) and "arbiters of performance quality" (i.e., defining success or merit) (Maxwell, 2002a).

The functions of standards as defined in this way are first to provide a common frame of reference and a shared language for communicating student achievement. They are also intended to promote teachers' professional learning, focused on good assessment practices and judgment of the quality of student achievement against system-level benchmarks. In addition, it is expected that they present more meaningful reports and engagement with assessment as a learning process.

Standards as descriptors of student achievement are used to monitor growth in student learning and provide information about the quality of student achievement. It is important to emphasize that examination or assessment standards cannot be objective in the same sense in which standards relating to physical measurements are objective. Assessment in education is intrinsically inexact and should be treated as such (Harlen, 1994).

Standards need to be described in such a way that schools can relate to them. Student work needs to be used to substantiate meaning and then the standard descriptors need to be piloted, thereby grounding them in practice. They should encompass minimum and aspirational performances and be written in positive terms in language suitable for the intended audience so that moderation can occur.

Defining examination or assessment standards requires interpretation and inference fundamentally, thus, they are subjective. The interpretation of assessment results should be in terms of being an indication of what students can do but not an exact specification (Cresswell, 2000). What should be assessed and the levels of attainment that are comparable to those represented by each grade in other examinations or assessments in the same family (Cresswell, 2000, pp. 71–72) should be defined by the standards as used in examination and assessment systems for public reporting. However, to compare attainment in different subjects, we can only use indirect bases for comparison, and for this we rely on statistics and expert judgment (Cresswell, 2000). Once again, the role of the teacher is significant, and in this context, teachers have an important role in a community of judgment practice.

STANDARDS FOR ASSESSMENT OR TEST USE

High-stakes assessments are enacted by policy makers to improve education and, setting high standards of achievement, can inspire greater effort on the part of students, teachers, and principals. The inadequacy of high-stakes assessments, or the lack of sufficient reliability or validity for their intended purposes, has the potential for unintended and harmful consequences. Policy makers can be misled by "spurious" increases in assessment results that do not relate to improved learning; students may be placed at increased risk of failure or disengagement from schooling; teachers may be blamed or punished for inequitable resources that remain beyond their control; and curriculum and teaching can become distorted if high grades or results per se, rather than learning, become the overriding goal.

The American Educational Research Association's (AERA, 2000) *Position Statement Concerning High-Stakes Testing in Pre K–12 Education* represents a professional consensus on standards concerning sound and appropriate test use in education.

Conditions for implementation of high-stakes education assessment programs include the need to provide protection against high-stakes decisions based on a single test and the provision of adequate resources and the opportunity to learn. Other conditions that apply are the need for validation for each separate intended use of the high-stakes assessment and alignment between the assessment and the curriculum. The validity of the passing scores and achievement levels and opportunities for meaningful remediation for examinees who fail high-stakes assessments are also key. Appropriate attention needs to be given to students with disabilities and to language differences among examinees. Further requirements are the careful adherence to explicit rules for determining which students are to be tested, sufficient reliability for each intended use, and the ongoing evaluation of intended and unintended effects of high-stakes testing (AERA, 2000, pp. 2–5).

Linn (n.d., p. 4) has also offered suggestions to policy makers regarding ways to improve the validity, credibility, and positive impact of assessment systems while minimizing their negative impact. He suggests that they should set standards that are high but attainable and that they should develop standards, then the assessments. Linn also believes that all students should be included in the testing programs, except those with the most severe disabilities, and that useful high-stakes accountability requires new high-quality assessments each year that are comparable to those of previous years. Policy makers are told to avoid putting all the weight on a single test when making important decisions about students and schools and to place more emphasis on comparisons of performance from year to year rather than from school to school. Long- and short-term school goals for all schools should be set and any uncertainty in any educational testing systems should be reported in all test results. Finally, both the positive effects of standards-based assessments and the unintended negative effects of the testing systems should be evaluated, and the narrowing of the achievement gap means that we must provide all children with the teachers and resources they need in order to reach our high expectations. This means improving the educational system as a whole, not just more testing or new testing systems.

QUANTITATIVE ASSESSMENTS

The last decade of the 20th century saw increased international dissatisfaction with the more quantitative, traditional forms of assessment (see Table 3.1). Much of this aversion stemmed from the view of learning on which these assessments were designed and their impacts on teaching and learning. Assessment approaches from this quantitative tradition have been challenged and alternative approaches have emerged.

The changing emphases in assessment reform include a move away from assessing knowledge and products to assessing skills, understandings, and processes. Also rather than assessment occurring at the end of a course through external means, assessment has been taking place throughout the course. A greater variety of methods and evidence has been sought to demonstrate learning instead of relying only on written methods, and this has been accompanied by a shift from norm referencing to criterion referencing with less reliance on pass or fail, summative

Table 3.1

MAJOR CRITICISMS OF QUANTITATIVE APPROACHES TO ASSESSMENT

Teachers teach to the test.

Tests have a detrimental impact on pedagogy.

External tests narrow the curriculum.

Quantitative approaches assess lower-level thinking skills only.

Emphasis is on test results.

Test results provide insufficient information for teaching purposes.

Meaningful feedback for student development is often lacking.

Quantitative approaches inhibit educational assessment.

Standards focus on products and academic purposes.

Social, affective, and physical education purposes are neglected.

assessments, and more attention on identifying strengths and weaknesses formatively and recording positive achievement (Torrance, 1997, p. 329).

TEACHER-BASED ASSESSMENT

With such shifts in assessment practice, the teacher assumes an important role and requires an understanding of the fundamental issues in assessment design that are "fit for purpose" and the need for the mode of assessment to impact positively on teaching and learning (see Table 3.2).

Assessment tasks therefore need to involve a variety of contexts, range of modes within the assessment, and range of response formats and styles. To achieve equity there is also a need to expand the range of indicators used to provide an opportunity for those who might be disadvantaged by one form of assessment to offer alternative evidence of their expertise. To achieve this form of assessment practice requires teacher-led assessment and communities of judgment practice.

Teacher-based assessment therefore offers an important alternative because in this context locally developed indicators can prove to be more effective educationally than examinations or tests administered from the center. The teacher is able to attend to the student's needs that emerge from a particular context, or sociocultural or historical background. One testing method does not fit all circumstances. Multiple judges are recommended, and Queensland's Senior Secondary System is one such example (see the Queensland Studies Authority Web site

Table 3.2

CHARACTERISTICS OF GOOD ASSESSMENT

Reliable and consistent outcomes.

Comparable judgments across assessors.

Free from bias.

Valid in terms of what is taught and learned.

Rigorous.

Supports learning and reflection.

Open and connected to criteria.

A range of assessment strategies used to appeal to all learners.

http://www.qsa.qld.edu.au/assessment/3111.html). Students' work is assessed at the local level and forms part of the state system of assessment of student performance. Assessment data are collected both formally and informally and used by teachers and administrators to set learning goals and priorities to build on what students already know.

Standard-setting and assessment are linked as teachers design assessments that are intellectually challenging for their students. Teachers set standards as they identify the tasks that they want students to complete for assessment, and they provide various opportunities for students to display thoughtful control over ideas.

AUTHENTIC ALTERNATIVE ASSESSMENTS

Alternative assessment methods have emerged in response to the dissatisfaction with quantitative systems. A catalyst for such change has been the realization that the type of assessment impacts profoundly on the learning dispositions, attitudes, strategies adopted, and learning ability. Developments in both learning theories and the theory of educational assessment (Gipps, 1994) have supported the move toward authentic, alternative assessments.

Critique of the utility of tests in measuring what students actually know inspired a move toward "alternative, authentic assessment approaches" (Newmann, 1991; Wiggins, 1989, 1991). Authentic assessment includes tasks that challenge the student's intellect and test intellectual ability in a manner that reflects probable experience for the individual in the field. Authentic assessment is connected to the curriculum and engages students, teachers, and others in assessing performance. This form of assessment goes beyond the school for models and sites of action and promotes complex thinking and problem solving, encouraging student "performance" of their learning and engages with issues of equity.

Alternative authentic assessments are varied and comprehensive, encouraging multiple methods for demonstrating learning. Problem solving in this assessment context requires students to think analytically and demonstrate their proficiency as they would in situations beyond the classroom. Such assessments encourage students to develop skills, understandings, and insights relevant to their particular needs and contexts (for examples, see the Department of Education, Training and the Arts of Queensland, Australia, Web site http://education.qld.gov.au/cor porate/newbasics/html/richtasks/richtasks.html).

These approaches attend to equity issues by making assessment fairer by reducing the dependence on performance in a single terminal examination as the only determinant of student achievement and by giving individuals the opportunity to demonstrate attainment over time and in a variety of contexts. This type of assessment is more accurate, and reflective of an individual's learning and development, by identifying the abilities being examined. This helps to encompass a wider range of abilities and facilitates the recording of achievement.

IMPLICATIONS FOR TEACHER ASSESSMENT

Teachers need the freedom to make definitive evidence-based judgments on their students' work according to established standards and a quality framework that guarantees the dependability of teacher-led assessments. The key is to use external scrutiny to maintain the quality and professionalism of teachers' own judgments.

At the upper secondary level, the assessment regime needs to reflect finer distinctions between student performance to fulfill the role of assessment for selection purposes for a wider range of destinations and progression opportunities than other levels of schooling. This is where effective and widespread use of the professional judgment of teachers is required more than ever and needs to be supported by rigorous quality assurance systems. Moderation is one such system that serves both accountability and improvement purposes. Moderation allows for comparability of standards both within, and between, schools and an audit of range and balance in curriculum coverage is part of the process. The teacher's role is fundamental in this process as from an analysis of the assessment data, teachers develop their curriculum plans and base their teaching on the learning needs of their students.

MODERATION

Moderation assists in developing coherence across the educational system. Consistency, comparability, and equity are three principles relevant to moderation practice (Maxwell, 2002b). Consistency involves constancy of judgment by the individual teacher with respect to the same evidence judged at different times and involves the equivalent application of standards across different types of evidence and opportunities for assessment. Comparability is a within-subject comparison against the performance standards for the subject. Identical aspects of knowledge, understanding, and skill are not required, but equivalence of standards in terms of knowledge, understanding, and skill is expected for that level of achievement. Students can be set different tasks but demonstrate a common standard of performance revealing equivalent levels of knowledge, understanding, and skill.

Equity involves the opportunity for every student to reach and demonstrate their current capability. Students may demonstrate their knowledge, skills, and understanding in a variety of ways so the concern should be whether they have had suitable opportunity to demonstrate what they know and can do. Moderation practice helps to ensure that these characteristics have been addressed in making judgments and that students' performances have been appropriately compared with the standard.

Moderation for accountability provides official confirmation of assessments used to report on individual students, or for cohorts of students and involves validation (Maxwell, 2002b). Validation presumes that if teachers are making appropriate judgments about a selected cross-section of student demonstrations, they will be making appropriate judgments about other student demonstrations. Moderation for accountability is designed to ensure fairness by adjusting results where there seems to be inconsistency or differences (Harlen, 1994). The moderation procedures monitor and assure comparability of the grades that are determined by this process. Important assessment data and advice are provided to teachers and schools concerning their judgments and such feedback fulfils an important quality assurance role.

Moderation for improvement involves collaborative processes promoting the professional development of teachers to undertake appropriate assessments, and to make consistent and comparable judgments (Maxwell, 2002b). It is ongoing and provides feedback for further development of comparability and may focus on both procedures and outcomes.

Research indicates that teachers who engage consistently in the moderation process are able to assess student performance more consistently, effectively, confidently, and fairly. They build common knowledge about curriculum expectations and levels of achievement and can identify strengths and areas for growth based on evidence of student learning. These teachers can adjust and acquire new learning by comparing their thinking to that of another student or teachers, and they can share effective practices to meet the needs of all students, monitor progress, and celebrate growth (Little, 2003).

In Australia, the Queensland Studies Authority (QSA) uses moderation as a quality assurance process for senior secondary studies. Moderation processes are directed at supporting and confirming understandings about judgments and performance. Teachers use assessment criteria and explicit standards to make professional judgments about performance levels demonstrated by students in the completion of assessed tasks. Teachers and assessors reach agreement about assessments through discussion, critique, and debate. They use evidence of student work to develop common understandings of the curriculum and levels of achievement to inform teaching and learning, monitoring and assessing, reporting and evaluation (Ralston & Newman, 1999).

This approach to moderation at a system level serves as vital accountability checks and balances on efforts to achieve, and demonstrate, reliability of teacher judgment in high-stakes assessment. Beyond this, however, the process of system facilitated and supported moderation provides professional development opportunities for teachers in planning teaching and learning programs, designing suitably challenging assessment tasks with accompanying statements of criteria and standards, as well as making judgments of student performance. Essentially, it is moderation that ensures that common standards are being achieved and also helps to provide comparability against benchmarks expressed as desirable features.

INCREASED TEACHER PROFESSIONALISM

Professional development occurs naturalistically through the agency of the teachers themselves as they share their knowledge and experience about working with standards in diverse school contexts and institutional settings. It is the important teacher talk and interactions during moderation meetings that impact positively on assessment practices, task design, student learning, and teaching. Teacher moderation is most effective when there is "productive conflict" embedded in the school's culture and teachers are confident to express their thinking, asking questions about the assessment data or learning after listening to others (Curriculum Services Canada, 2007). Professional learning extends beyond the time and site of the moderation meeting.

Increased professionalism, richer learning for teachers and students, and more professional conversations are some of the professional benefits achievable from moderation practice. The New Basics project schools, of Queensland Australia, require students to complete "rich tasks" that are carefully chosen to be intellectually challenging and to have real-world value. They are authentic. Performance on these tasks provides an informed and elaborate portrait of a student's achievement. The evaluation of the Consensus Based Standards Validation Process of moderation used in these primary and lower secondary levels (Klenowski, 2007) found that first teacher professionalism had grown in terms of teacher confidence, building knowledge of strategies, procedures, and systems to assess student work. Such teacher professional development is inherent in the process as teachers engage in rich learning conversations focused on student work and learning. The level of professional conversations increased and focused on improvement of current teaching and learning classroom practices. Teachers also gained creative ideas from a broader view of what other teachers used to achieve success. They also benefited from working and planning the assessment task together as there was richness in the learning experience and a collegial atmosphere developed with teams of teachers planning, sharing ideas, and demonstrating accountability. Teachers have the most direct impact on student achievement and their role during moderation practice is fundamental.

CONCLUSION

Too often, the policy context results in unintended consequences and unhelpful pressures on the development of assessment systems. The intended learning benefits of more productive assessment approaches are not brought to fruition; they are simply frustrated. Assessment has the potential to develop and sustain the teacher's engagement in judgment practice and curriculum planning. As has been illustrated in this chapter, the teacher's role is key. It is school-based and teacher-led assessment that has the potential to address equity issues together with the support from the political center.

REFERENCES

American Educational Research Association. (2000). *AERA position statement concerning high-stakes testing in pre k–12 education.* Retrieved October 25, 2007, from http://www.aera.net/policyandprograms/?id=378

Assessment Reform Group. (1999). *Assessment for learning: Beyond the black box.* Cambridge, UK: University of Cambridge, School of Education.

Broadfoot, P. (2007). *An introduction to assessment.* London: Continuum.

Cresswell, M. (2000). The role of public examinations in defining and monitoring standards. In H. Goldstein & A. Heath (Eds.), *Educational standards* (pp. 69–104). Oxford, UK: Oxford University Press.

Curriculum Services Canada. (2007). *Teacher moderation: Collaborative assessment of student work.* The Literacy and Numeracy Secretariat Capacity Building Series. Toronto, Ontario: Author.

Fredericksen, J. R., & White, B. Y. (2004). Designing assessments for instruction and accountability: An application of validity theory to assessing scientific inquiry. In M. Wilson (Ed.), *Towards coherence between classroom assessment and accountability.* The 103rd Yearbook of the National Society for the Study of Education, Part 2 (pp. 74–104). Chicago: National Society for the Study of Education.

Fullan, M. (2005). *Leadership and sustainability: System thinkers in action.* Thousand Oaks: Corwin Press.

Gipps, C. (1994). *Beyond testing: Towards a theory of educational assessment.* London: Falmer Press.

Goldstein, H. (2004). International comparisons of student attainment: Some issues arising from the PISA study. *Assessment in Education: Principles, Policy and Practice, 11,* 319–330.

Harlen, W. (1994, April). *Concepts of quality in student assessment.* Paper presented at the American Educational Research Association Conference, New Orleans, LA.

Hopmann, S. T. (2008). *No child, no school, no state left behind: Schooling in the age of accountability* (Essay). Vienna, Austria: University of Vienna, Department of Education and Human Development.

Klenowski, V. (2007). *Evaluation of the effectiveness of the consensus-based standards validation process.* Retrieved December 15, 2007, from http://education.qld.gov.au/corporate/newbasics/html/lce_eval.html

Kliebard, H. M. (1992). *Forging the American curriculum: Essays in curriculum history and theory.* New York: Routledge.

Linn, R. L. (n.d.). *Standards-based accountability: Ten suggestions* (CRESST Policy Brief). Los Angeles: University of California, National Center for Research on Evaluation, Standards and Student Testing.

Little, J. W. (2003). Inside teacher community: Representations of classroom practice. *Teachers College Record, 105*(6), 913–945.

Lokan, J., Ford, P., & Greenwood, L. (1997). *Math and science on the line: Australian middle primary students' performance in the Third International Mathematics and Science Study.* Melbourne: Australian Council for Educational Research.

MacBeath, J. (1999). *Schools must speak for themselves.* London: Routledge.

Maxwell, G. S. (2002a). *Are core learning outcomes standards?* Brisbane, Queensland, Australia: Queensland Studies Authority. Retrieved November 23, 2007, from http://www.qsa.qld.edu.au/downloads/publications/research_qscc_assess_report_1.pdf

Maxwell, G. S. (2002b). *Moderation of teacher judgments in student assessment* (Discussion Paper). Brisbane: Queensland School Curriculum Council.

McGaw, B. (2004). Australian mathematics learning in an international context. In I. Putt, R. Farragher, & M. McLean (Eds.), *Mathematics education for the third millennium: Towards 2010.* Proceedings of the 27th Annual Conference of the Mathematics Education Research Group of Australasia (p. 29). Melbourne: MERGA.

Newmann, F. (1991). Linking restructuring to authentic student achievement. *Phi Delta Kappan, 72*(6), 458–463.

Ralston, F., & Newman, H. (1999, September 29–October 2). *Towards consistency of teacher judgment: Moderation in all things.* Paper presented at Australian Curriculum Studies Association Conference, Perth.

Sahlberg, P. (2007). Education policies for raising student learning: The Finnish approach. *Journal of Education Policy, 22*(2), 147–171.

Thomson, S., Cresswell, J., & De Bortoli, L. (2004). *Facing the future: A focus on mathematical literacy among Australian 15-year-old students in PISA 2003.* Camberwell: Australian Council for Education Research.

Torrance, H. (1997). Assessment, accountability and standards: Using assessment to control the reform of schooling. In A. H. Halsey, H. Lauder, P. Brown, & A. S. Wells (Eds.), *Education, culture, economy and society* (pp. 320–331). Oxford, UK: Oxford University Press.

Wiggins, G. (1989). A true test: Toward more authentic and equitable assessment. *Phi Delta Kappan, 70*(9), 703–713.

Wiggins, G. (1991). Standards, not standardization: Evoking quality student work. *Educational Leadership, 48*(5), 18–25.

Wilson, M. (2004). Assessment, accountability and the classroom: A community of judgment. In M. Wilson (Ed.), *Towards coherence between classroom assessment and accountability.* The 103rd Yearbook of the National Society for the Study of Education, Part 2 (pp. 1–19). Chicago: National Society for the Study of Education.

4

Conceptualizing Developmental Assessment Within Africa's Cultural Settings

A. BAME NSAMENANG

This chapter is an introduction to one way of thinking about a "shape-shift" from Euro-Western hegemony in the developmental assessment of Africa's children into an African frame of reference. It is Africentric in terms of sensitizing developmental appraisers into noticing and assessing human development with strategies that are not only tuned to African life-journeys (Serpell, 1993) but also are consistent with theories of human ontogenesis in African cultural worlds (Nsamenang, 2005a). My entry point is *Human Development in Cultural Context: A Third World Perspective* (Nsamenang, 1992) that J. W. Lonner and J. W. Berry, the series editors of Sage's Cross-Cultural Research and Methodology Series, of which this is Volume 16, describe as "a comprehensive, systematic account of human development which is sensitive to the needs, interests, and ecologies of non-western cultures and individuals" (back cover). That structural systems such as political economies shape or constrain an individual's development (Nsamenang, 2008a) implies that "the sociocultural contexts from which families, communities, and organizations operate have far-reaching implications, which must be accounted for when assessing development" (Nsamenang, 1992, back cover). As Bram (1998) perceptively notes, accurate knowledge of the cultural group is an essential and salient factor not only in developing and mounting culturally sensitive early childhood services but also in testing and assessment procedures. This approach is necessary to defuse the dominant narratives of "*Western* societies that tend to lump all cultural groups from developing countries into one category" (Bram, 1998, p. 24, emphasis added), which in turn masks accurate understanding of difference and similarity in all their complexities and subtleties (Bram, 1998). To trivialize the context of assessment is to enfeeble "the impact of the nuances and details that are very important about people" (Nsamenang, 2008a, p. 74).

Accordingly, there is need for assessment procedures to "recognize and respect families' and communities' achievements and resourcefulness in raising their children, often against extraordinary odds" (Arnold, 2004, p. 25). Once we accept this fact of child development, the impact of background factors on developmental outcomes, which vary across cultures and contexts, becomes more obvious in the face of Africa's ability to raise culturally competent children within "alternative patterns of care based on different moral and practical considerations" yet to be imagined and incorporated into developmental theorizing (LeVine, 2004, p. 163). Furthermore, Serpell (1994, p. 18) judged this author's (Nsamenang, 1992) sociogenic depiction of human ontogenesis as a process that "differs in theoretical focus from the more individualistic accounts by Freud, Erikson and Piaget." But African theories of "being and development" and the assessment strategies that should follow from them, regrettably, remain unknown or at best peripheral to the developmental assessment community.

The framing of this chapter continues with a perspective on developmental assessment and transitions into the theoretical anchor and conceptual issues considered relevant to testing and assessment in sub-Saharan African cultural settings in the second section. The third segment attempts to sketch what "normative" development in Africa could look like. Part four overviews the assessment field in Africa in terms of historical and thematic perspectives and the significance of context. In the fifth part, I concentrate on various facets of the problematic of the often-invoked "best" practice in assessment. Among the key issues identified and substantiated are how to approach "best practice" through alerts to "bad practice"; how testing is rooted in shared racial beliefs; a brief review of how the UN Millennium Development Goals (MDGs) are instigating postcolonial interests in assessment in the developing world, therein implicating local and global imperatives in Africa; and an outline of forces that underlie Africa's marginality in assessment research. The sixth part is a discussion of specific challenges to assessment research in cultural context. The chapter logically terminates with a befitting conclusion.

DEVELOPMENTAL ASSESSMENT

The U.S. BabyCenter Medical Advisory Board (2008) perceives assessment as a structured evaluation of a child's development in the physical, language, intellectual, social, and emotional domains by a developmental assessment specialist, or a team of "interested" professionals. A mindset inclusive of African family and developmental realities would include the moral and spiritual facets of being human and acknowledge parents and caregivers as monitors and assessors of development. For example, the Nso of Cameroon, guided by their own ideas of development, desirable child states, and proper caregiving, "apply some unwritten, as yet unexplored, criteria" to monitor and assess child development, readily taking "action to remedy the perceived deviation from the expected developmental trajectory" (Nsamenang, 1992, pp. 149–150). It is in this light that one hopes Garrels's definition of assessment as the gathering of information about strengths and weaknesses in a child's abilities, levels of functioning, and learning characteristics (Garrels, 2006) is inclusive of what parents, caregivers, and peers as holders and potential and actual gatherers of valuable assessment data do.

It is essential to clarify that while human development professionals or experts view assessment as a well "structured" process, parental assessment is pragmatic and intrinsic to caregiving praxis, although most assessment experts, at least with reference to those in Africa, seem unaware of or sidestep parents and caregivers, including sibling and peer caregivers, as sources of assessment data. Research in low-income and culturally marginalized communities of the United States and other industrialized nations has shown that significant "funds of knowledge" (Moll & Greenberg, 1990) often exist within those communities that are either deliberately or accidentally overlooked by assessors who concentrate on preset indicators or the skills, knowledge, and values imparted by the school. Such efforts fail to recognize parents as the first to notice developmental delays because they know their children best. An assessor spends only a brief moment with the child, so it is easy for the "expert" to miss the child's subtle problems.

Developmental assessment is important if there is any sign that a child is not developing normally and at the correct pace. Early detection of problems is critical and tests may aid in this detection (McCauley, 2008). Lamentably, there is general lack of consensus on what "developing normally" means and how to monitor it across the world's diverse cultures. In this direction, Rubin (1998) alerted child development researchers not to generalize their (culture-specific) theories of normal and abnormal development to other countries. More critical is the ample controversy on procedural and ethical issues of how tests or other assessment techniques could aid detection of problems, be deployed to aid correction of perceived or detected developmental inappropriateness or developmental delays, or even be abused. The values and ethics of which and whose interpretive frame to apply to the precept and process of evaluation, which is the systematic determination of merit, worth, and significance of something or someone, heightens the confusion (Gregory, 2000; McCauley, 2008). Although assessment and evaluation are two distinct concepts, they are closely related in that judgment (evaluation), for example, about the developmental or functional status of the assessed individual tends to be made on the basis of "information" or data gathered about him or her (assessment). Evaluation often is used to characterize and apprise persons or objects of interest in a wide range of human situations, endeavors, and enterprises. This introductory part underscores the importance of imputing rights-based and ethical considerations into the "science" of assessment and wariness over whose "ultimate" interest assessment fairly and truly serves. But with what conceptual mindset and from which theoretical stance are these issues best framed?

THEORETICAL MOORINGS AND CONCEPTUAL ISSUES

The broad history of how the "current truths," our grand narratives regarding child development assessment, came to be is a larger story than this chapter ventures, but parts of that history, for example, "truth," "science," and colonialism merit passing mention here. Suffice it simply to state that "facts are not pure and unsullied bits of information, culture also influences what we see and how we see it" (Gould, 1981, p. 22). *Science* is a key term in the assessment studies, but the tenets of science, and its assumptions of "truth," have been shaken to their foundations in numerous disciplines, perhaps to good effect (Pence & Nsamenang, 2008). And as Maori scholar Linda Tuhiwai Smith reminds us, "scientific research is implicated in the worst excesses of colonialism" (2002, p. 1). The colonialism I refer to here is not just the physical colonization perpetrated by empires, but also the colonization of the idea of childhood (Cannella & Viruru, 2004; Lareau, 2003) and its monitoring devices. In this regard, we can gain from E. B. Tylor's warning to ethnologists to avoid "measuring other people's corn by one's own bushel" (Tylor, 1881, cited in Sturtevant, 1974). Malinowski also highlighted the key goal of ethnography as "to grasp the native's point of view, his [*sic*] relation to life, and his vision of the world" (Malinowski, 1922, cited in Sturtevant, 1974). Theories are not unalterable inductions from facts. "The most creative theories are often imaginative visions imposed upon facts; the source of imagination is also strongly cultural" (Gould, 1981, p. 22).

The take-home point is that context matters in developmental assessment because the developmental ecology influences developmental outcomes (Bronfenbrenner, 1979). Context and culture complement genotype to induce difference and exude diversity. Differences in the criteria for "normative" development are perceptible in the values and practices that inform and guide the nurturing of children into cultural competence throughout the globe (Nsamenang, 2008a). Bornstein and his collaborators (2004, p. 183) intimated that "there are no clear rules about how to behave as a parent." In fact, every culture offers "a framework for understanding the ways that parents think about their children, their families and themselves, and the mostly implicit choices that parents make about how to rear the next generation" (Harkness et al., 2001, p. 12). "Culture, as in social heritage and cultural tools, is a determinative complement of genotype that shapes human psychosocial differentiation in the direction of a given people's cultural meaning systems" (Nsamenang, 2008a, p. 73). The reciprocal processes by which culture and psyche co-construct one another (Shweder, 1991) result, for example, in variation in the praxes, intelligences, and desirable developmental outcomes and endstates that are valued and promoted by different peoples in different sociohistorical times.

Thus, contextualist theories envision the developmental significance of the interdependence between individuals and their societies. Such theories "share a common awareness of behavior and development as interactive elements in a fluid and changing interplay" (Pence, 1988, p. xxiii) of social and environmental factors in specific cultural contexts or communities of practice (Rogoff, 2003). Human development and being are transactional processes. The child, for example, is impacted by, and in turn influences, the nature of the caregiving and social environment (Grieve, 1992). The theories admit the primal role of genotype, but work more on the salience of the changeable conditions in which individuation occurs (Ngaujah, 2003; Nsamenang, 2006). "When that is accepted and understood, the need is to recognize the importance of cultural conceptualizations of childhood, and of the child development theories and practices that follow on from these in a given culture" (Smale, 1998, p. 3).

African culture, for example, shapes the nature of the developmental environment (Nsamenang, 1992, 2008a). Almost every aspect of development is deeply influenced by the local context, which includes affordances that promote or hinder child survival and provide protective as well as risk factors for health and thriving throughout the lifespan (Irwin, Siddiqi, & Hertzman, 2007). For instance, a child begins to evolve a sense of self from environmental cues into the visual, auditory, vestibular, and other sensory modalities (Garrels, 2006). Social context is, at a variety of levels, intrinsic to the developmental process (Richards, 1986). The assessment of African children can therefore *"be understood only in the light of the cultural practices and circumstances of their communities—which also change"* (Rogoff, 2003, p. 2).

Across the globe child development occurs in different "cultural worlds." The foremost linguist of his time, Edward Sapir, clarified that "the world in which different societies live are distinct worlds, not merely the same world with different labels attached" (Sapir, 1929, p. 209, cited in Shweder, 1991). In apparent substantiation of this conjecture, Bruner (1996) explained the ethnocentric basis of caregiving regimes with the concepts *ethnopsychology* and *ethnopedagogy* to highlight that cultures, including the African, develop their own theories of why people behave the way they do and how culture molds children into the adults they turn out to be. In this light, the parenting of African children occurs within a distinctly African way of visualizing children and their development. Africa's theory of the universe (see Nsamenang, 1992, 2004a, 2005a) that differs from that which informs contemporary assessment research and practice frames human development beliefs and caregiving praxes. Holism is intrinsic in its positing "the interplay of social, religious, and political roles, working together to ensure the well-being of the people" (Bongmba, 2001, p. 7). Callaghan (1998, p. 32) believes that if we could "listen to, and learn from, the African worldview, seeing a holistic and integrated way of looking at the family and the universe, we might see things in a new way"—we might bring a more holistic approach to developmental assessment in Africa.

The conditions of child life and the patterning of development vary because cultures premise childrearing programs on their perception of the immaturity of the child. This is because children are not born with the knowledge and skills with which to cope with life and make sense of the world (Nsamenang, 2004a), but they are born ready to learn a cultural curriculum (Rogoff, 1990). Every culture makes the learning of survival knowledge and thriving skills possible by conceiving of human nature in its own terms and organizing development and learning according to that image (Cole, 1999). For instance, "children are socialized to acquire cognitive skills or patterns of intelligence that exist already in their culture because their culture requires it; it is functional in the culture" (Ogbu, 1994, p. 366). Core elements of such learning can be achieved in the "school of life" (Moumouni, 1968, p. 29) without "the usual sense of classrooms and schools" (Bruner, 1996, p. ix). Therefore, focusing assessment on schooled knowledge and skills alone forecloses unschooled intelligences and "situated" competencies. This remark readies us to sketch what "normative" development could look like in Africa.

A GLIMPSE OF "NORMATIVE" CHILD DEVELOPMENT IN AFRICA

Context is important because development does not occur in a vacuum. Across the globe, children live in and develop into culturally competent citizens in a wide variety of ecologies and cultural circumstances (Nsamenang, 2007a). That, worldwide, different forms and styles of parenting and child care programs are framed by cultural values of desirable child states seriously subvert the notion and reality of a universal list of developmentally appropriate indicators that can apply uniformly in time and space "across multiple countries" (Bellagio Group, 2007, p. 1). The African ecoculture, for example, "brings to light the affective nature of the environment on the child's cognitive and social learning" (Ngaujah, 2003, p. 7). The evidence that African mothers and nonparental caregivers understand infant care and development in ways that contrast "sharply with expert knowledge in the child development field" (LeVine, 2004, p. 149) renders assessment practices using Euro-Western derived norms and techniques a more fraught matter than has hitherto been contemplated.

The foregoing views are plausible to the extent that various cultures, including the African, "recognize, define and assign different developmental tasks to the same biological agenda" (Nsamenang, 1992). Even with the "one child policy" in "the world's largest geopolitical community"—China (Ho, Peng, & Lai, 2001, p. 7)—early childhood care arrangements not only vary by family, but also change during the year to embrace parental employment circumstances (Yajun, Li, & Champagne, 1999). This state of the field introduces misgivings as to the applicability of universal markers of developmental appropriateness across varying cultural contexts without privileging the culture in which the indicators were developed, the context from which norms were extracted, and the value positioning of test or tools developers. African parents are not blank slates; they apply indigenous markers to monitor developmental appropriateness and to check and control child abuse. The author (Nsamenang, 1992, p. 49) recorded how African parents, at least the Nso of Cameroon, scrutinize their children's development by applying "unwritten . . . criteria to assess the extent to which children are thriving." They readily take action to correct any perceived deviation from the expected developmental trajectory.

Another important principle is agency, which is intrinsic to African childrearing practices. African parents and peer mentors use tacit cultural techniques and strategies that provoke the cognitive faculties and induce behavioral adjustment to prime children's agency, such as not providing direct answers to children's queries (Nsamenang, 2004a). For example, if a child asked for an explanation of what the parent did, a typical parental response would be: "Don't you see?" This translates into "You're expected to observe, notice, learn, and understand what and how to do what I've done." Accordingly, Africans engage children in chores and social interactions from an early age (Nsamenang, 2008b). They use social competence to assess how responsible or "intelligent" a child is maturing by keeping a mental record of tasks a child successfully completes as a marker of how *tumikila* (intelligent) the child is (Serpell, 1993). In this regard, "children's cognitive development must be understood not only as taking place with social support in interaction with others, but also as involving the development of skills with sociohistorically developed tools that mediate intellectual activity" (Rogoff, 1990, p. 35).

The foundational precept of Africentric developmental philosophy is not *educare* or *educere* but *emergence,* wherein a child is not actually "raised" but primed to emerge into maturity significantly through self-generated efforts (Nsamenang, 1992, 2004b). Indigenous African parenting practices socialize the norms that foster children's self-education in participative learning processes in their families and communities, especially in the early childhood peer cultures (Nsamenang, 2004b). One group of Africans, the Nso of Cameroon, primes its children into learning self-care and engaging in family chores; it sensitizes children from an early age to seek out others and extract skills and know-how, figuring out their way into the world from the social fields in which siblings and peers are accredited partners (Nsamenang & Lamb, 1995).

From the age of toddlerhood, most Nso children begin to "distance" themselves from their parents, increasingly coming under the sphere of influence of the peer group. In so doing, "elder peers or siblings rather than the parents or other adults readily correct, supervise and mentor them" (Nsamenang, 2005b, p. 333). Thus, the peer culture is central to African children's learning and development. Children's creations within the peer culture not only express tremendous ingenuity and recognizing them as "products" enhances their self-esteem (Nsamenang & Lamb, 1995), but also rouse and reinforce children's abstract and spatial thinking and planning skills as well as perspective taking (Segall, Dasen, Berry, & Poortinga, 1999). Interventions to improve such child-to-child spaces not only would be a transformative process but also would greatly responsibilize children and reduce the cost of child care. However, the peer culture has not been well assessed as a fundamental nonadult children's space and remains a largely uncharted developmental niche.

The child-to-child template is an important element of African developmental culture but has not received the assessment attention that matches its developmental significance. The image of the child as "agent" of her or his own development in relational interactionism necessarily obliges a shift of orientation in assessment strategies from contemporary focus on the Euro-Western ideology of liberal democracy, freedom of choice and the sovereignty of the individual, and empiricism grounded in objectivity (House, 1978). African parents also use evidence that a child has the ability to give and receive social support and to notice and attend to the needs of others as markers of mental and general development (Weisner, 1997). From this backdrop, assessment and testing in Africa are more appropriately grounded in the reality that most children's needs are best "met through everyday activities in their families, supported by communities and assisted by government [and other sources of] services" (Richter, Foster, & Sherr, 2006, p. 10), and that children are contributors to their own developmental learning (Nsamenang et al., 2008). In addition, indicators need to be teased out from the collective ethos of child care, because the "village," in spite of its waning spirit to "raise" a child (Swadener, Kabiru, & Njenga, 2000), still retains a right to monitor parental practices in order to prevent excesses, particularly child abuse or cruelty (Nsamenang, 1992). In March 2008 (personal communication, posting at Shuundzev YahooGroups.com), neighbors in Yaounde, Cameroon, reported to security agents, who promptly intervened, sinister occult practices by a teenage female student. This type of lens to testing and assessment focuses on phenomena-in-context and stands in the face of another, that systematic evaluation studies be grounded in social science research techniques (Gould, 1981), a scientific necessity hemmed in a specific set of value-laden technicalities and ways of observing that foreclose others.

Given these divergent possibilities to assessment research, and perhaps more, what is the actual state of developmental assessment in Africa?

AN OVERVIEW OF DEVELOPMENTAL ASSESSMENT IN SUB-SAHARAN AFRICA

A proper developmental assessment is an important aspect of tracking social and emotional development and the health status and well-being of children. The bulk of the so-called evidence for the developmental appraisal of children in Africa, however, exists as gray literature, that is, as unpublished, largely inaccessible academic dissertations and theses and the reports of international organizations, donor agencies, and service providers that are scattered in institutions across the continent. Nevertheless, there has been a recent upsurge in emphasis on research in child development and health care.

A Historical Perspective

In historical perspective, early attempts to assess the development of African children were those of Falade (1955), Hindley (1968), Poole (1969), Werner (1972), and Wober (1975), among others. Dicks (1991), Silvia (1994), and Aina and Morakinyo (2001) made later efforts. The most cited efforts are those of Cole and his colleagues (e.g., Cole, Gay, & Sharp, 1971; Cole & Scribner, 1974; Gay & Cole, 1967), who furnished research evidence on situated intelligences and skills sets in Liberian peasants, who had no idea of disciplinary mathematics, but were experts in endogenous calculation and measurement systems. On her part, Oloko (1994) provided data corroborating Brazilian evidence that, "despite their poor performance in school tasks," the Nigerian street trading "children were very competent at solving arithmetical problems in the context of buying and selling items of different prices" (Schliemann, 1992, p. 1). The most recent attempts are in South Africa (e.g., Dawes, Bray, & van der Merwe, 2007) and Zambia (e.g., Serpell & Jere-Folotiya, 2008).

Except perhaps for South Africa where psychological testing has a long, sustained tradition, first to serve apartheid interests and now to chart norms for a multiracial nation, systematic efforts at developmental assessment are remarkable for their paucity in sub-Saharan Africa. Moreover, it has become evident that most African researchers sparingly use instruments with rigorous psychometric properties in assessing African child development. Instead, impressionistic methods, involving questionnaires, interview techniques, and clinical observations tend to be used to outline developmental milestones, as in Nigeria (Aina & Morakinyo, 2001). The dearth of valid developmental assessment instruments for monitoring and assessing Africans implies overdependence on imported tests and other tools, a state of the field that stifles understanding of developmental trajectories as they are framed within an African cultural setting. The factors mitigating this state of the African assessment field are identified in a later section. Taken together, the evidence highlights that assessment, like much research and interventions in Africa, seldom take the African context into consideration.

A Thematic Perspective

From a brief thematic focus, we can trace the roots of developmental assessment in sub-Saharan Africa in attempts by mostly itinerant expatriate researchers to measure the apparent precocity of physical development of the African child over the Western prior to weaning (Wober, 1975). It progressed into the exploration of various aspects of Africa's developmental niches (e.g., Nsamenang, 1992; Ohuche & Otaala, 1981; Super & Harkness, 1986; Weisner, Bradley, & Kilbride, 1997) and evolved into investigation of specific topical themes, such as cognitive and social development, including a focus on African forms of intelligence (e.g., Chamvu, 2006; Kathuria & Serpell, 1999; Mpofu, 2002; Nsamenang, 2006; Serpell, 1993; Veii & Everatt, 2005). It has "advanced" into elaboration of a Development Screening Inventory for Nigeria (Aina & Morakinyo, 2001) and indicators for monitoring child and adolescent well-being in South Africa (Dawes et al., 2007), among other efforts. A 14-year trace study (Serpell, 1977, 1993) that followed the life-journeys of a cohort of 46 *A-Chewa* boys and girls in a rural Zambian community sought to understand the relations between their eco-cultural niches of development and the contemporary opportunities and demands of the national public educational system. The focal interest was to identify the psychological assessment strategies that are useful for guiding the educational process for children in a rural African community, the predictive validity of cognitive tests for a child's progress in a developmental pathway in an African rural community, and the relevant dimensions of the child to determine what to prioritize in assessment (Serpell & Jere-Folotiya, 2008).

Other efforts attempted to measure human intelligence in sub-Saharan Africa by integrating strands of relevant Western and local constructs to address local, African needs. Exemplifying this trend are studies by Serpell (1977), Dasen, Inhelder, Lavalee, and Retschitzki (1978), Dasen, (1984), Serpell (1984), Grigorenko et al. (1999), Kathuria and Serpell (1999), and Sternberg et al. (2001). The Test for Tacit Knowledge for Natural Herbs with Luo children of a rural Kenyan community by Sternberg and colleagues sampled from common illnesses in the Luo ethnic community and standard herbal treatments for those illnesses in that community.

Significance of Context in Testing and Assessment

A majority of children in rural sub-Saharan Africa are more familiar with clay or other local materials as a medium of expression than they are with pencil and paper and commercially prepared toys. Furthermore, familiarity with "intelligent behavior" in sub-Saharan Africa reveals that indigenous Africans value intelligence as having social and cognitive components, with a greater valuation of practical rather than mentalistic intelligence. Such informed awareness led Kathuria and Serpell (1999) to develop the *Panga Munthu Test* (Make-A-Person Test), which is a language-reduced test suitable for use by children in rural Zambia. The test presents children with wet clay and the children are asked to "make" a person with the clay. The children's figures are then quantitatively scored for accurate representation of human physical characteristics. It is a language-minimized test that is suitable for children in rural Africa (Serpell & Jere-Folotiya, 2008). Mpofu (2002) reported an interrater reliability index of .89 for the *Panga Muntu Test* with rural Zambian children. Given the significance of schooling and the adoption of European languages for school instruction in much of Africa (Serpell, 1993), similar interests have focused on the interfaces of African mother tongues and foreign-language acquisition in Cameroon (Fai, 1996), Namibia (Veii & Everatt, 2005), and Zambia (Chamvu, 2006; Kaani, 2006), among others.

Indeed, different cultures view concepts such as intelligence differently. Whereas Western cultures have placed much relevance on the concept of IQ, which has become a heavily coined term (McCauley, 2008), other cultures, for example, rural Africa, see intelligence not as a number on a chart but focus on the abilities to perform certain skills that are necessary for family life and growth (Mpofu, 2002; Mundy-Castle, 1975; Nsamenang, 1992, 2006; Serpell, 1993). Children's cultural experiences can, therefore, have a huge effect on the way they view and experience the assessment situation, and the way that they respond to tasks. In fact, research-based evidence (e.g., LeVine et al., 1994; Super & Harkness, 2002, 2008; Weisner, 1997) indicates that African parents cherish and promote social intelligence over paper-and-pencil tests or encyclopedic forms of intelligence. Mundy-Castle (1975) dichotomized the developed versus African worlds into *technological* versus *social intelligences*, implying that African schoolchildren acquire both intelligences. The concept of social intelligence is consistent with the participative livelihoods in agrarian activities in Africa south of the Sahara. Thus, Africans see "intelligent behavior" as unfolding not only in socio-relational and cognitive spheres, but also in participatory hands-on activities that stimulate both functional and instrumental intelligences, albeit not exactly in the proselytized Euro-Western strategies of cognitive stimulation.

Andrew Dawes and his colleagues (2007) have completed a marvelous rights-based approach to monitoring the well-being of children and adolescents in South Africa, which is practical and user-friendly. The hope is that the "friendliness" of the assessment "package" reflects the "rainbow" nature of childhood and adolescence in South Africa. That is, the development of the instruments did not only draw on international precedents and extensive peer review processes, but more so was founded on South Africa's multiracial experiences, especially its successful "childrearing within the framework of an African culture for centuries" (Callaghan, 1998, p. 31). To cite one South African icon, Nelson Mandela—"with his unparalleled profile, sterling qualities, and moral stature—grew from an indigenous African education in his early years, matured with a Euro-Western education and traumatic political experiences, but fortified himself with a lifetime commitment to his rich traditional roots" (Pence & Nsamenang, 2008, pp. 31–32). Strictly, therefore, the pertinent concern is not so much the rigor of the methodology of instrument development, but its cultural fairness to all the nation's children. The book offers the indicators as measuring the service environment as well as the developmental contexts of South Africa's children and adolescents. Another critical issue is the extent to which the measures reflect South Africa's children's rights to their cultural heritage.

Although the list is not exhaustive, the significance of the above-cited studies is that they represent growing genuine attempts to recognize and respect indigeneity, African ways of thinking and acting, and the intellectual values that follow from them by efforts to use contextually valid, local materials and strategies to assess psychosocial processes in Africa (Mpofu, 2002). They also demonstrate the appropriate application of psychometric procedures with indigenous materials and for the purpose of supporting local educational activities and practices (Serpell & Jere-Folotiya, 2008). This is a radical shape-shift from the tradition of applying mainly Western traditions of testing intelligence and educational appraisal to native Africans for the purpose of making normative comparisons. Such approaches have characteristically revealed Africans as less intelligent and backward in developmental milestones than Western children (Aina & Morakinyo, 2001). Normative methods in cross-cultural research do not seem advisable in view of the differences in cognitive values between indigenous Africa and the contents of Western tests.

Dasen (1993) interpreted research on cognitive development in Ivorian adolescents by Tape (1993) as constituting "a good beginning of the development of a truly African psychology" (p. 156), while Serpell (1994) thought this author's African social ontogeny (Nsamenang, 1992) resonated well with the cultural preoccupations expressed by parents in many an African society. Although promising beginnings have been made in Africanizing psychology and developmental assessment techniques in sub-Saharan Africa, much remains to be achieved in terms of genuine sensitivity to the cultural and contextual situativity of phenomena and sustained programmatic research.

IS THERE "BEST" PRACTICE IN DEVELOPMENTAL ASSESSMENT?

> I do not reflect on the purely abstract concepts of literacy, those divorced from the practice that informs them. Rather, I think about literacy in terms of the practice in which I am involved. (Freire & Macedo, 1987, p. 63)

How do developmental assessors think about their practice in Africa? From whose point of view should "best" or "bad" practice in developmental assessment be determined?

Approaching "Best" Practice Through "Bad" Practice

If you substitute "literacy" with "assessment" in the above quote, you may get a feel of the meaning and significance of "good" or "bad" assessment, as it would apply to you. Is there "best" testing or assessment practice? The relevant literature is replete with positioning on articulate statements on "quality" and state-of-the-art "best practices" in research and professional services. But as Chambers (1997) would query: "Whose reality counts" in testing and assessment?

Policy and mission statements, professional codes of conduct, and the ethical standards for research and services connote the reality of both malpractice and ethically apt practice that we may construe as "best practice." However, policy statements, ethical standards, and professional codes represent no more than orienting principles or practice guidelines and not actual field practices. They are "alerts" to ideals of practice on which practitioners tend to differ in interpretation and practice behaviors relating to the letter and spirit of such provisions. "Best" practice may be as elastic as the variety of practice circumstances, practitioner values and skills repertoires, and the dispositions of testees or assessees. The raison d'être of such a frame of reference is the shifting value systems and motives across cultures and disciplines and the exigencies of the assessment field in sociohistorical time. By this we mean that the professional codes and ethical principles for, say medicine or psychology, are unlikely to be appropriate for other professions, although some principles might apply across disciplines. As an abstract concept assessment, like professional attitude, is of trifling significance, but becomes cogently sensitive when we factor in the motives and competence of the assessor and the sensitivity and response tendencies of the assessee to the assessment process and experience.

The factors that determine development are cued on the developing person, but developmental assessment, except self-monitoring, first and foremost is determined by the practitioner. The implication is that the onus for professionally sound and ethically satisfactory testing and assessment practices revolves on the practitioner—a professional. Perhaps the most pervasive value of professionalism concerns measurement, about which normal professionalism regrettably creates and sustains its own reality (Chambers, 1997). It simplifies and orders existential complexes into single scales such as poverty lines and human development indices. Developmental indicators, for instance, "refer to summary measures that capture more complex manifestations of population health and child well being across a wide variety of domains (biological, social, cultural, environmental)" (Bellagio Group, 2007, p. 1). The conceptual leap from indicators of health status to socioemotional differentiation does not appear to have been charted. And "in the social sciences and policy, economics dominates, and gives primacy to mathematical analysis; what has been measured and counted becomes the reality. All this makes it hard for normal professionals to understand and serve the local, complex, diverse, dynamic, and unpredictable realities of the conditions, farming systems and livelihood struggles of poor people" (Chambers, 1997, p. 33), particularly in Africa's hybridism (Nsamenang, 2005c).

Professions and disciplines differ greatly in their standing on skilled techniques of precision measurement. Human behavior is not as easily amenable to measurement as are most physical things. As part of the practical Newtonian universe of everyday life, the physical world can be controlled, counted, compared, manipulated, and is predictable, at least to a certain extent, but not so easily with human values and behaviors. The physical sciences subject their phenomena to universal methods and norms and can easily fit data into blueprints, schedules, targets, and physical outputs to predetermined indicators. "The problem is that the idiosyncratic attributes of people are, in contrast, difficult to measure; their individual behaviour is unpredictable; and the approaches and methods for handling them are in continuous evolution and change" (Chambers, 1997, p. 39).

In brief, "best practice" is at best a fluid concept and an untidy process. Its notion presupposes bad practice. The challenge presented by this section in particular and this chapter in general is to assessors. I borrow and adapt Chambers (1997) to summarize the challenges to assessment in three dimensions, as follows:

1. Top-down or paternalistic approaches, by which the assessor pursues his or her purposes and ends (often as predetermined by sponsoring agency) with relative unconcern for the sensibilities, perspective, and participation of the assessee.
2. Behavior, attitudes, and training, referring to the assessor's mindset or disposition, expertise and competence, and rapport with the assessee. Is the assessor set on a discovery mission with a learning posture (Agar, 1986) or does he cling obsessively to a preordained attitude of certainty as to the most cost-effective ways to achieve unequivocal answers (Dahlberg & Moss, 2005)? "Learning to change, and learning to enjoy change, are fundamental" (Chambers, 1997, p. 210).

3. Field practice and ethics in contexts of certainty and handy technologies versus those of pervasive struggles with multiple realities and inexistent germane norms and tools, alongside the ethics of power relationships and commonplace errors, whose acknowledgment smacks of failure to gain insight into "progress," which erases other possibilities. Every profession has distinct ethical obligations to its clientele and public.

In the remainder of this section, I turn to specific facets of these challenges in Africa.

Assessment and Monitoring of Development Is Rooted in Shared Social Beliefs

The anchor of testing and assessment is difference and diversity. The poet Alexander Pope (1733) alluded to this in *Essay on Man* by submitting that:

Order is Heaven's first law; and, this confessed,
Some are, and must be, greater than the rest.

But who should be greater than or superior to whom and why? Are the similarities and the dissimilarities testing and assessment reveal natural, structural, or nurtured? In *Voyage of the Beagle,* Charles Darwin (1909) charged that "If the misery of our poor be caused not by the laws of nature, but by our institutions, great is our sin." What then, is, or should be the central mission or core task of developmental assessment and testing in academia?

Are the differences elicited by testing and assessment procedures induced by assessors, the mechanisms they initiate, or do assessment data reflect natural differences? Two students, for example, may earn the same score in an achievement test, but item analysis might reveal stark differences in the correct items they each scored, pointing to fundamental differences in their knowledge bases. How can assessment and testing evolve indicators to use across cultures and in ways that respect subtle differences? By developmental indicators we mean the summary of measures that capture more complex phenomena, processes, or the behaviors of the assessee in terms of health, well-being, or psychosocial functioning. Developmental trajectories emerge from unique genotypes in interaction with nurture, but their conceptual link with population level health indicators, as hinted earlier, is yet to be explicitly articulated.

In *The Mismeasure of Man*, Gould (1981) offered a mostly unspoken ethos for the assessment enterprise in the following words: "In assessing the impact of science upon eighteenth-century and nineteenth-century views on race we must first recognize the cultural milieu of a society whose leaders and intellectuals did not doubt the propriety of racial ranking—with Indian below whites, and blacks below everyone else" (p. 35). Gould did not cite racist literature "to release skeletons from ancient closets," but to point to how "white leaders of Western nations did not question the propriety of racial ranking during the eighteenth and nineteenth centuries. In this context, the pervasive assent given by scientists to conventional rankings arose from shared social belief, not from objective data gathered to test an open question" (Gould, 1981, p. 35), which in the present chapter is the monitoring of a child-in-context versus a global child (Pence & Hix-Small, 2007). Visible racism might have declined, but it is somehow veiled in the assumed neutrality of testing and assessment science. It is easily noticeable as postcolonialism, wherein the "image" of child and the monitoring tools that are found internationally are increasingly homogeneous and Western-derived (Pence & Hix-Small, 2007). Sensitive to this lopsided state of the field and its shortcomings, Swadener et al. (2000, p. 270) cogently recommended "unique local applications of nationally viable models for the care of Kenya's youngest children and support of their families." But how do local African realities face up to forces of globalization and homogenization?

Local and Global Forces: Africa's Crisis With a Variety of Models and Indicators

Africa is in crisis with its children and families (Garcia, Pence, & Evans, 2008; Weisner et al., 1997). The Millennium Development Goals (MDGs) are eight international development goals that 189 UN member states and at least 23 international organizations have agreed to achieve by the year 2015. They include reducing extreme poverty, reducing child mortality rates, fighting disease epidemics such as AIDS, and developing a global partnership for development. The MDGs aim to spur development by improving social and economic conditions in the world's poorest countries. "Substantial progress has been made globally in achieving the MDGs, and other internationally agreed development goals, but many countries remain off track to meeting them by 2015. This is particularly true in large parts of Africa, where some states are fragile or emerging from conflict. The continent as a whole is lagging behind on each Goal despite a very encouraging recent rise in the rate of economic growth, an overall improvement in the policy environment, and strong macroeconomic fundamentals" (MDG Africa Steering Group, 2008, p. 1). Africa's challenge—its children (Garcia, Pence, & Evans, 2008)—stems from both internal and exterior sources, especially the confusion that comes from a profusion of shifting models and indicators of possibility rather than reality. The eight United Nations Millennium Development Goals [MDGs], for example, have become the core indicators around which governments, relief agencies, and scholars direct their missions and resources. Gröhn's (2008) view on this matter is that while succeeding in giving detailed descriptions of both the symptoms of Africa's problem and the logical remedies to the symptoms, the MDGs seem to ignore—figuratively speaking—the actual "disease." They fail to address the underlying causes of Africa's development crisis. The point being made here is not in trivialization of the enormity of Africa's sorry state, but simply to state that the MDGs are inequitable because, setting out on a comparative mission to measure the statistical rate of change, they forget to consider the ample differences in the absolute numerical changes and subtle nuances across countries and regions. It is evident and widely acknowledged that sub-Saharan Africa does not really have a chance at achieving the MDGs by 2015 (Easterly, 2007).

The emphasis is on global indicators crafted by experts aligned to the United Nations and other international donors, led by the World Bank. In large measure, indicators mostly do not match the daily routines of the vast majority of children's circumstances. Often, for instance, there is a "rush" to obtain quantifiable outcomes in conformity to predetermined templates with mostly imported intervention models and adapted instruments of doubtful cultural relevance and "posited" indicators on slim or nonexistent for-local-needs baselines. This orientation endures in the face of evidence that the importance of successful programs is still limited in developing countries and that developing world data are just emerging (Britto, Engle, & Alderman, 2007). Double standards and mixed messages tend to blur and exacerbate trail-offs. How, for instance, has the appalling state of Africa improved since the high-profile indication by the British Prime Minister, Tony Blair, that: "There can be no excuse, no defense, no justification for the plight of millions of our fellow human beings in Africa today. And there should be nothing that stands in our way in changing it" (*New York Times*, 2005, p. 1).

Furthermore, it is baffling what lesson an African policy planner or government could take from the statement that "Africa is falling short in achieving the MDGs and empowering women to end poverty" and the indication that with the exception of maternal mortality, each individual MDG will be reached in several African countries (End Poverty 2015, 2008). Disturbed by Africa's worsening development crisis, the General Assembly of the UN on March 4, 2008, agreed to convene a high-level meeting in September 2008 on how to better meet the development needs of Africa, which is struggling with the MDGs (End Poverty 2015, 2008). Indeed, concerned by the deepening effects of the global food crisis and climate change on Africa's ability to eradicate poverty and achieve the Millennium Development Goals, world leaders attending a high-level meeting of the General Assembly on September 22, 2008, on the MDGs recommitted themselves to strengthening a "global partnership of equals," based on shared responsibility and determination to mobilize resources. They adopted a political declaration, "Africa's Development Needs: State of Implementation of Various Commitments, Challenges and the Way Forward" ("Africa's Development Needs," 2009).

The alarming condition of Africa's children is undeniable, but it is not due to lack of models and strategies, per se; these are manifold. The models and strategies tend to lose "sight of the soil out of which the existing African society has grown and the human values it has produced" (D. Westermann, as cited in Kishani, 2001, p. 37). Testing and other assessment procedures also tend to ignore that "there are in culture and human experience truths inaccessible to science" (MacGaffey, 1981, p. 229). Not only do current research tools fail to capture the bulk of the indigenous African pedagogies of developmental learning (Nsamenang et al., 2008), but the African ecoculture more so "provides opportunities for learning and development which simply do not exist in the West and therefore are not considered by the predominant theories" (Curran, 1984) and methods.

A great deal of assessment and evaluation is undertaken within the context of the school, often in disregard of evidence showing that the interface between rural African communities and schools based on the contemporary international model of Institutionalised Public Basic Schooling (Serpell & Hatano, 1997) is problematic. In spite of the benefits of Euro-Western education to Africa, Western institutionalized schooling, as it is dispensed in much of Africa today, will continue to produce dysfunctional Africans because it decontextualizes African children by not meshing their cognitive repertoires and life skills with Africa's timeless wisdom (Callaghan, 1998; Nsamenang, 2005c). This is because the curriculum of the African school tends to emphasize different values from those of the indigenous culture of the children's families, and to orient students toward an extractive definition of success (Pryor & Ampiah, 2003; Serpell, 1993; Serpell & Jere-Folotiya, 2008).

Furthermore, the instructional mode of knowledge and skills acquisition in Western-type schools diverges from Africa's largely participative curricula. Sadly, the implementation of universal primary education in most African countries "has led to declining returns in an economic sense, for example, educated Africans in agrarian economies lose their farming skills through education" only to face unprecedented rates of unemployment and inability to use school knowledge in context (Nsamenang, 2005b, p. 278). If education continues to deny the African "the opportunity to teach his children how to raise crops and animals, particularly where no alternative training or skills . . . are made available" (Ruddle & Chesterfield, 1978, p. 390), then, it can only alienate and intensify Africa's inertia and marginality in the global community (Kishani, 2001). By not seeking to capture Africa's hybridism in assessment, we are portraying only a partial picture of a complex heritage wherein Africans are navigating three major cultural worlds—the Islamic-Arabic legacies, Western Christian imperatives, and Africa's deeply ingrained indigeneity (Nsamenang, 2005b, 2008c). Assessment is also challenging because educational appraisals and psychological tests "are not impartial measuring instruments like weighing scales or measuring tapes. The estimates they provide of concepts such as intelligence, ability or aptitude are loaded with [global] evaluative meaning and thus implicitly prescribe certain courses of action" (Serpell & Jere-Folotiya, 2008, p. 94).

But how these understandings and courses of action translate or tailor into theory, research, intervention, and pedagogy of developmental assessment has yet to be framed in terms that truly reflect the circumstances and developmental trajectories in Africa, and this is a direly needed project. But how would this project fructify when emic models are so pervasive and overwhelming in Africa, although they fail to capture a holistic picture?

A Stranger Has Big Eyes But Does Not See Africa in Its Own Terms

In brief, Africa's difficulty with the ongoing monitoring and assessment pressures, such as participation in large-scale assessment studies, is lack of understanding of its children and their development in context, the application of extraverted models that pathologize Africans, and judgment and evaluation of Africa with contested Euro-Western indicators with low contextual validity in Africa's very un-Western ways. Whenever Euro-Western early childhood services, for instance, are applied as the gold standards by which to measure forms of Africa's early childhood development practices, they forcibly deny equity to and recognition of Africa's ways of provisioning for its young, thereby depriving the continent of a niche in the global knowledge waves for the early years of life (Nsamenang, 2005b).

Ongoing enthusiastic search for evaluation indicators "to compare populations as a means of identifying problems and setting priorities for types of interventions" (Bellagio Group, 2007, p. 1) to apply to child development in developing countries (Grantham-McGregor, Cheung, & Cueto, 2007) is not at all motive-neutral, and in African eyes, might be read as an exemplar of postcolonialism. Africa's "educational failure and adverse economic consequences" are more extensive than only "poor early cognitive and social development" (Black et al., 2008). But is cognitive stimulation and social development to be posited only in Euro-Western models? Africa's crisis forcefully implicates the shifting structural adjustments and comparative indices that have been applied in Africa for too long. They undermine the right of Africa's children to a social heritage and cultural identity, as enshrined in the Convention on the Rights of the Child (CRC) (Brooker, 2008; United Nations, 1989). Surprisingly, "important interest groups, nation states themselves and powerful international organizations such as OECD, UNICEF and the World Bank" (Moss & Petrie, 2002, p. 1), "including other organs of the UN system, sustain and proselytize forms of ECD that are functional in Europe and North America throughout the world as the 'right' way to make progress with young children" (Nsamenang, 2008c).

The current waves of developmental assessment and monitoring of human well-being are driven by frantic efforts to determine country positions on the league table of progress toward the MDGs, which are greatly influenced by the West. Gröhn (2008) charges that the MDGs are arbitrary and unfair to the region of sub-Saharan Africa, giving little possibility for achieving the proposed targets. The goals fail to address the underlying causes of Africa's development crisis (Gröhn, 2008, p. 6). It is an awful feeling, however, to aver that "strangers" put the MDGs together, at least with respect to their awareness of the African condition. Similarly, Reid (2006, p. 18) contends the CRC was "developed far from the lived experience of children, their families and communities." Gröhn (2008) noticed two basic problems from a sub-Saharan African standpoint with the MDGs. First, in defining what "success" or "failure" in achieving the goals are, the Millennium Project makes some rather implausible conjectures. Africa simply cannot be compared to other poor regions, as it is but obvious that emerging countries do not stand on the same platform. For one example, it is hard to figure out a moral platform and evidence-based positioning or the common criteria for any rational comparison of the developmental trajectories of poor countries that are denied $700 billion every year by unfair trade rules (Christian Aid, 2008) with those of "22 of the world's richest countries" that in 1970 "pledged to spend 0.7% of their national income on aid," but "34 years later, only 5 countries have kept that promise" (www.savethechildren.org, 2008).

As the West African proverb title of this section suggests, the expert in Africa (including the native-born scholar), like the assessor, is a stranger, who—despite her or his great observation skills and technical credentials—often does not see everything (Gröhn, 2008). Such may be the case with the MDGs. For too long, international aid organizations, relief agencies, and passionate interest groups and individuals have poured money and innovative ideas into the African continent. Analogous to the bypass of the context of childhood and MDGs are efforts to "fix" Africa's poverty with benchmarks and donor conditions that undercut perhaps more cherished African developmental values and markers. Thus, in setting out to "improve" Africa, the goals miss reaching out to Africans in their present circumstances. No doubt the 2003 UN Human Development Report explains Africa's symptoms (the "where") and the proposed remedies (the "what") in considerable detail, but it is brief, if not silent, on the root causes. Participants at the International Conference on the State of Affairs of Africa (ICSAA) (International Institute for Justice and Development [IIJD], 2006) found that Africa's debt crisis and badly managed international interventions are among the contributing factors to the current development crisis. In addition, poor education systems and the exclusion of the nonmonetarized economy and failure to factor women's input into economic analyses and productivity indices has a role to play (IIJD, 2006).

Cognizant of the foregoing, a summary statement of the root cause of Africa's crisis is trifocal: (1) "the inexplicable coercion of Africa into a Darwinian box" (Nsamenang, 2005b); (2) implementation of strategies to intervene knowledge systems and the timeless wisdom (Callaghan, 1998) on which Africa anchors into irrelevance and extinction instead of determining how to enhance them; and (3) the failure to analyze and correct why the "interventionist skin grafts onto Africa's festering sores" are shriveling off (Nsamenang, 2005b). Doubtless, then, after decades of enormous international development aid and accentuating African governmental and NGO efforts in resources and "good governance," Africa remains "caught in the spiral of pride, poverty, anger, and self-pity" (IIJD, 2006).

Factors Reinforcing Instrumentation of Low Context-Validity by Africans

The crux of the matter is that developmental assessment indicators be seen and charted as ingrained in the life-journeys (Serpell, 1993) of the children being assessed. The reason why this is not usually the case in Africa is multifaceted and several-tiered. First, most tests and techniques bear a Euro-Western cultural imprint but are translated, adapted, or imported uncritically to Africa, with only cosmetic attempts to overcome the lapses and shortcomings inherent in and incidental to these processes. Researchers tend "to prematurely attribute differences in outcomes from an original measure to cultural differences" but not to the "many sources of 'error' along the translation path" (van Wildenfelt, Treffers, de Beurs, Siebelink, & Koudijs, 2005, p. 145). Tanifum (1996) identified one source of error as the possibility of "transcreating" a new instrument whenever we translate a research tool, because no translator can reach the mindset of the creator of a test or instrument. That numerous assessment instruments are translated yearly into other languages and/or adapted for specific cultures instigates rights issues. One issue cited by Stevenson, Kochanek, and Schneider (1998) is to engage in cross-cultural research to test the limits or the generalizability of American-based research on child and adolescent adjustment rather than to evolve developmental indices for Africa. Like almost everyone else in international scholarship, most African scholars are in a rush to make "progress," partially unaware that their research and scholarship does not capture the complex reality of their people.

Second, having "received" and acquiesced to research methods and instruments as if they were neutral, most African assessment researchers fail to notice that their shapes, like forks or chopsticks, belie their cultural roots and origins (Pence & Nsamenang, 2008). Third, both overt and invisible dilemmas exist in putting into practice common indicators in a context of "inappropriate" strategies, which resemble "practices that are culturally preferred among various peoples outside the United States," and another list of "'appropriate' . . . practices preferred by contemporary upper-middle-class Americans" (LeVine, 2004, p. 152). Africa's relational developmental trajectories are oriented toward different ends than the more individualistic theories put forth by Western social scientists. Fourth, there are no universal developmental outcomes that all cultures desire; instead, there is a wide variation in desirable or cherished endstates of development (Nsamenang, 2006). Fifth, although the guidelines donors and other interest groups offer Africa are potentially uplifting recipes or "toolkits" for adept visualization of policy and program options, in much of Africa they translate, almost literally, into plain "prescriptions" due to scarcity of culture-sensitive human capacity to interpret and contextualize them (Nsamenang, 2005b). What worsens this landscape is flight of African expertise: "at least 70,000 skilled graduates leave Africa every year in search of better financial security" elsewhere (Gröhn, 2008, p. 10).

It is not an overstatement that Africa lacks the critical mass of culture-informed and context-tuned "experts," particularly with the nerve and adroitness to dare step out of the Euro-Western box to articulate their own or creatively gain from donor-posited guidelines and indicators. For instance, how can we support and upgrade the African peer culture, a potential innovative, nonadult-directed participative space, in policy research and programmatic guidelines (Nsamenang, 2008c) to actively enlist and engage children's and adolescents' voices and perspectives into testing and assessment research instead of continuing with fossilized adult-driven strategies? The peer culture offers opportunities to shift to a more radical participative approach, which empowers children and adolescents to "learn to reflect their own conditions so that they can gradually begin to take greater responsibility in creating communities different from the ones they inherited" (Hart, 2002). How would assessment in such a landscape turn out and what would it contribute to the field in policy orientation, research insights, and program visions?

Africa's marginality in psychology in general and large-scale assessment studies is conspicuous, although it has great potential to enrich and extend the field (Nsamenang, 2007b). The above-identified factors in this section only partially explain Africa's limited capacity and scholarly productivity. A more obvious constraint, of course, is Africa's low resource base in terms of meager personal means for "comfortable" commitment to scholarship without the negative consequences of extensive moonlighting. The other side of the resource-coin is institutional incapacity to sustain systematic research and innovative programming. Not so obvious is a most restrictive aspect that is complicated, but which I simplify to the human factor that tends to be experienced as an intimidating and demeaning environment (Nsamenang, 2007b). Most Africans soon learn and feel the international arena as one in which their research is "unpopular, suspect, or simply insignificant" (Staniland, 1983, p. 77). It is an awful feeling to be aware of "the low regard and little respect the West and its scholars have for Africa" (Ojiaku, 1974, p. 213) and that in the heartland of assessment research, the United States, "it is only a small minority of Americans who pay careful attention to Africa" (Ungar, 1986, p. 20). Equally disquieting are undignified experiences with research funding and paternalizing postcolonial attitudes in collaborative relationships. The scenario depicted above has instead worsened, as collaborative databases in Africa continue to be "controlled" by northern collaborators and obtaining international travel paperwork and funding traumatize and demean most African scholars (Nsamenang, 2007b).

DISCUSSION: TOWARD UNDERSTANDING SPECIFIC CHALLENGES

Kashoki (1982) rightly alluded to a huge and growing number of Africans with impressive academic and research credentials but who cannot contribute to "indigenous scholarship of a kind to be considered truly original," as efforts remain "sporadic, in relative short supply, and essentially imitative of, or largely patterned after, contributions by Western scholars" (p. 35). Africans watch in acquiescence as the continent's rich natural resources are exploited by and benefit mainly Westerners while their scholars are unable to garner the means (Nsamenang, 2007a) to participate with honor and at par in waves of testing and assessment research. Dissatisfied and voiceless, most of such scholars have had to cope with their exasperation (Murayama, 1997) and inability to influence the nature, process, and content of assessment research on their continent, even in their own countries. Is it not appropriate for Africans to accept this state of the field in the spirit of Plato's *Republic* to educate and assign citizens to roles and status positions by merit of class of superiors, inferiors, and the in-betweens?

Cole (2008) reads nuanced unfairness in assessment, in societal systems, and test motives. For almost as long as there have been IQ tests, there have been psychologists who believed that it is possible to construct "culture free" tests (Jensen, 1980). The desire for such tests springs directly out of the purposes for which tests of general intellectual ability were initiated in the first place: to offer a valid, objective, and socially unbiased measure of intellectual ability. The Western society, founded upon the principle that all people are created equal, has never lived easily with the recognition of enormous de facto social inequality. Consequently, there has been a need to explain off such inequality. From the onset of the testing movement, value orientations and traditions were strongly biased in seeking the causes of inequality in properties of the individual rather than in the structural systems of society. At the same time, we realize that social and economic conditions, by shaping people's experiences, can and do cause individual intellectual differences, as well as their consequences (Cole, 2008).

In this direction, Grieve (1992) contends that testing techniques developed for Western children do not always hold the same meaning for non-Western children. This is perhaps the case because there is no "culture free" test, making the need for the tester to be open and aware of cultural differences, but how to make this part and parcel of the assessment situation is an important challenge. To state the obvious, most items on a test imported into Africa, and this is quite frequent, are foreign to African children, and, therefore, unfair. But instruments are often presented as uninfluenced by culture. The ideal is to view and test children within their cultural context and with instruments created within that culture. When measuring cognitive abilities, for instance, the assessor needs to be keenly attentive to cultural nuances and variation in the interpretation of test items as well as the test results (Grieve, 1992). Bias comes in many forms. It can be sex, cultural, ethnic, religious, or class bias. An example of content bias against girls would be one in which students are asked to compare the weights of several objects, including a football. Since girls are less likely to have handled a football, they might find the item more difficult than boys, even though they have mastered the concept measured by the item (Scheuneman, 1982).

Young children are distractible and have a short attention span; we cannot expect them to suitably and efficiently respond to several batteries of instruments or long testing procedures with tests that consist of hundreds of items, especially if formal assessment is not in the sphere of their routines of developmental experiences. Young children are also difficult to assess accurately because of their activity level, wariness of strangers, and inconsistency in unfamiliar settings (McCauley, 2008). As the child is distracted and active, a test is not always an accurate representation of her or his ability, so the test should be used not as definitional of the child but as a clue of the child's potential ability.

The child's ability to socially interact and engage with strangers is relevant to the testing situation (Grieve, 1992). Children's social relationships can have a considerable effect on their cognitive growth and this in turn influences the assessment situation. But young children are not as able as older children to regulate their behavior, particularly their emotions, which can change from one state to another within a matter of seconds. How many testers are prepared to handle or have handled children's emotionality, and what does it mean for the assessment data? A child's temperament and affective state can influence cognitive ability. Vygotsky (1978) alerted: emotions and intellect are unified in a dynamic and meaningful system, and emotions serve as the language of the young child, where verbal skills are lacking (cited in McCauley, 2008). Do testers really focus intently on children's emotions, as they are meaningful and represent how the child is feeling, and are they to "read" this type of child language? Other important factors include cultural differences, language proficiency, and level of exposure to the testing culture. Accordingly, sensitivity to the child's background and expertise in assessing infants and young people are essential requirements (McCauley, 2008).

Children's tests should be criterion-based rather than normative, as each child develops differently and every response may have a different meaning for the child's developmental stage (Grieve, 1992). In addition, a test should allow for the fact that every child perceives the world in a unique way. The developmental stage at which a child is functioning at a given point in time influences her or his behavior in a test situation. It is thus essential for the assessor to have not only sound knowledge of developmental sequences and the culture's developmental task expectations, but also characteristics of the developmental status of the child being assessed at the point of the test and the underlying theory of the assessment instrument(s) used to explain the data. It is worth noting that comparative methodologies tend to ignore "stops" or lags along children's developmental trajectories. African parents are aware of developmental lags; they judge their children's developmental status by perceived markers while assessors judge the children by test scores or assessment data (Garrels, 2006). African parents, for example, focus on children's "emerging" abilities on awareness that a child could be "mature" in chronological age but lag behind in expected ability for a given chronological age (Nsamenang, 1992, 2005c), while assessors concentrate on predetermined age-specific milestones and indicators. Urban (2006, p. 1) cautions against assessment on the basis of "certainties and predetermined outcomes," especially in African contexts, where parents expect the unfolding of child-specific abilities, such that "the biological communality the human species shares in the genetic code plays out" (Nsamenang, 2006, p. 295) into the bewildering diversity of specific individualities in the world (Maquet, 1972).

CONCLUSION

Developmental assessment is a laborious process, a rights-imbued procedure that requires informed consent from the parents in cases where the assessees are children. The assessor has a huge responsibility to the children, the parents, and the community to make the test as fair and safe as possible. Arguments whether a culture-fair test has ever been produced and whether a test developer as a cultural agent can indeed create a culture-free test rage and are indecisive. Nevertheless, assessment is increasingly assuming significance for various forms and levels of decision points. Daunting issues of power, orientation to unequivocal answers, and missed learning opportunities in a chaotic world of considerable diversity, and field practices with error margins and tricky ethical nuances seriously and perpetually challenge and subvert the assessor's professional knowledge and expertise.

We need to rethink what it portends and entails for assessing Africa's children if the guidance of child development in sub-Saharan Africa proceeds in ways "that had not been imagined in developmental theories" (LeVine, 2004, p. 163). This evidence could serve as the impetus to look at Africa and its developmental realities as lying outside the purview of Euro-Western developmental indicators, hence, assessment strategies. Assessment, in principle, is a "good thing" for child development, but we must scrutinize the process and consequences in the wisdom of Foucault (1980) that everything is not bad but everything is potentially dangerous. Even the best of intentions researchers bring to assessment may deflect a culture's developmental markers. "Questioning the expectation that academic research can provide knowledge as base for political decision and, in consequence, administrative and managerial action does not mean, of course, to deny the importance and possibilities of research in this field in general" (Urban, 2006, p. 1).

The eight United Nations Millennium Development Goals have become the core focus around which governments and relief agencies base their missions and resources and toward which assessment researchers are tuned for funding. They, however, face one controversy in the idea and actual practice of children's participation as defined by the UN's Convention on the Rights of the Child (Morales, 2007). By bestowing on every child "a legal status on the right of one's own identity; on respect for the background of every child" (Vandenbroeck, 1999, p. 13), the CRC tacitly induces tolerance of cultural diversity. Unfortunately, "it is not difficult to perceive the prevailing attitude and orientation [in the field] as one inconsistent with and intolerant of cultural diversity" (Nsamenang, 2008b).

REFERENCES

Africa's development needs: State of implementation of various commitments, challenges, and the way forward. (2009). Retrieved May 1, 2008, from http://www.un.org/millenniumgoals/

Agar, M. H. (1986). *Speaking of ethnography.* Newbury Park, CA: Sage.

Aina, O. F., & Morakinyo, O. (2001). The validation of Developmental Screening Inventory on Nigerian children. *Journal of Tropical Pediatrics, 47,* 323–328.

Arnold, C. (2004). Positioning ECCD in the 21st century. *Coordinators' Notebook, 28,* 1–36.

BabyCenter Medical Advisory Board. (2008). *Development assessments: What you need to know.* Retrieved January 29, 2008, from http://www.babycenter.com/0_development-assessments-what-you-need-to-know_6709.bc

Bellagio Group. (2007). *Bellagio Statement on Indicators.* Bellagio, Italy: Unpublished manuscript.

Black, M. M., Walker, S. P., Wachs, T. D., Ulkuer, N., Gardner, M. G., Grantham-McGregor, S., et al. (2008, February 9). Policies to reduce undernutrition include child development. *Lancet,* 51–66.

Bongmba, E. K. (2001). *African witchcraft and otherness: A philosophical and theological critique of intersubjective relations.* New York: New York University Press.

Bornstein, M. H., Haynes, O. M., Pascual, L., & Painter, K. M. (2004). Competence and satisfaction in parenting young children: An ecological, multivariate comparison of expressions and sources of self-evaluation in the United States and Argentina. In U. P. Gielen & J. Roopnarine (Eds.), *Childhood and adolescence: Cross-cultural perspectives and applications* (pp. 166–195). Westport, CT: Praeger.

Bram, C. (1998). A culturally oriented approach for early childhood development. *Early Childhood Matters, 89,* 23–29.

Britto, P. R., Engle, P., & Alderman, H. (2007). *Early intervention and caregiving: Evidence from the Uganda nutrition and early child development program.* Unpublished manuscript.

Bronfenbrenner, U. (1979). *The ecology of human development.* Cambridge, MA: Cambridge University Press.

Brooker, L. (2008). *Supporting transitions in the early years.* London: McGraw-Hill/ Open University Press.

Bruner, J. (1996). *The culture of education.* Cambridge, MA: Harvard University Press.

Callaghan, L. (1998). Building on an African worldview. *Early Childhood Matters, 89,* 30–33.

Cannella, G. S., & Viruru, R. (2004). *Childhood and postcolonization.* New York: RoutledgeFalmer.

Chambers, R. (1997). *Whose reality counts: Putting the first last.* London: Intermediate Technology Development Group.

Chamvu, F. (2006, November). *Analysis of the psychometric properties of the Zambia Achievement Test: Reading recognition.* Poster session presented at 7th ISSBD Africa Region Workshop on Enhancing Research Capacity in Human Development, Johannesburg, South Africa.

Christian Aid. (2008). *Case study: Christian Aid—Central policy with regional implementation.* Retrieved January 29, 2008, from www.christianaid.org.uk

Cole, M. (1999). Culture in development. In M. H. Bornstein & M. E. Lamb (Eds.), *Developmental psychology: An advanced textbook* (pp. 73–123). Mahwah, NJ: Erlbaum.

Cole, M. (2008). *The illusion of culture-free intelligence testing.* Retrieved March, 16, 2008, from http://lchc.ucsd.edu/MCA/Paper/Cole/iq.html

Cole, M., Gay, J. A., & Sharp, D. W. (1971). *The cultural context of learning and thinking: An exploration in experimental anthropology.* New York: Basic Books.

Cole, M., & Scribner, S. (1974). *Culture and thought: A psychological introduction.* New York: John Wiley.

Curran, H. V. (1984). Introduction. In H. V. Curran (Ed.), *Nigerian children: Developmental perspectives.* London: Routledge and Kegan Paul.

Dahlberg, G., & Moss, P. (2005). *Ethics and politics in early childhood education.* London: Routledge Palmer.

Dasen, P. R. (1984). The cross-cultural study of intelligence: Piaget and the Baoule. *International Journal of Behavioral Development, 19,* 407–434.

Dasen, P. R. (1993). Theoretical/conceptual issues in developmental research in Africa. *Journal of Psychology in Africa, 1,* 151–158.

Dasen, P. R., Inhelder, R., Lavallee, M., & Retschitzi, J. (1978). *Naissance de l'intelligence chez l'enfant Baoule de Cote d'Ivoire* [Birth of intelligence among Baoule children of the Ivory Coast]. Berne: Hans Huber.

Dawes, A., Bray, R., & van der Merwe, A. (Eds.). (2007). *Monitoring child well-being: A South African rights-based approach.* Cape Town, South Africa: Human Sciences Research Council.

Dicks, S. A. (1991). Developmental aspects of care. *Development and Behavior: The Young Child, 12.*

Easterly, W. (2007). *How the Millennium Development Goals are unfair to Africa.* New York: Brookings Global Economy and Development.

Freire, P., & Macedo, D. (1987). *Literacy: Reading the word and the world.* South Hadley, MA: Bergin and Garvey.

End Poverty 2015. (2008). *End Poverty 2015: UN Millennium Campaign.* Retrieved March 13, 2008, from www.endpoverty2015.org

Fai, P. J. (1996). *Loan adaptations in Lamnso' and effects on the teaching of English.* Yaounde, Cameroon: DISPES II Memoir of Ecole Normale Superieure, University of Yaounde.

Falade, S. (1955). *Le developpement psycho-moteur de jeune Africain originaire du Senegal au course de sa priemiere anne* [Psycho-motor development of young Africans from Senegal during the first year of life]. Paris: Foulan.

Foucault, M. (1980). *Power/knowledge: Selected interviews and other writings.* Harvester: Brighton.

Garcia, M., Pence, A., & Evans, J. (Eds.). (2008). *Africa's future—Africa's challenge: Early childhood care and development in sub-Saharan Africa.* Washington, DC: World Bank.

Garrels, A. (2006). *Child development and assessment.* Retrieved January 29, 2008, from http://www.nfb.org/images/nfb/publications/fr/fr23/fr06fal10.htm

Gay, J., & Cole, M. (1967). *The new mathematics and an old culture.* New York: Holt, Rinehart & Winston.

Gould, S. J. (1981). *The mismeasure of man.* New York: Norton.

Grantham-McGregor, S., Cheung, Y. B., & Cueto, S., for the International Child Development Steering Group. (2007). Developmental potential in the first 5 years for children in developing countries. *Lancet, 369,* 60–70.

Gregory, R. J. (2000). *Psychological testing: History, principles, and applications* (3rd ed.). Boston: Allyn & Bacon.

Grieve, K. W. (1992). *Play based assessment of the cognitive abilities of young children* (pp. 5.6–5.21). Unpublished doctoral dissertation, University of South Africa, Pretoria.

Grigorenko, E. L., Geissler, P. W., Prince, R., Okatcha, F., Nokes, C., Kenny, D. A., et al. (1999). *The organization of Luo conceptions of intelligence: A study of implicit theories in a Kenyan village.* Manuscript submitted for publication (cited in Mpofu, 2002).

Gröhn, K. (2008, March 7). UN Millennium Development Goals merely scratch the surface of Africa's development crisis. *International Institute for Justice and Development (IIJD) Newsletter, 6*–11.

Harkness, S., Super, C. M., Axia, V., Eliasz, A., Palacios, J., & Welles-Nystrom, B. (2001). Cultural pathways to successful parenting. *International Society for the Study of Behavioral DevelopmentNewsletter, 1*(38), 9–13.

Hart, R. A. (2002). *Children's participation.* London: United Nations Children's Fund (UNICEF)/Earthscan.

Hindley, C. (1968). Growing up in five countries. *Developmental Medicine and Childhood Neuro-psychology, 10,* 1715.

Ho, D. Y. F., Peng, S.-Q., & Lai, A. C. (2001). Parenting in mainland China: Culture, ideology, and policy. *International Society for the Study of Behavioral Development Newsletter, 1*(38), 7–8.

House, E. R. (1978). Assumptions underlying evaluation models. *Educational Researcher, 7*(3), 4–12.

International Institute for Justice and Development (IIJD). (2006). *Priorities for the future: Tackling the root causes of Africa's development crisis and its persistent poverty: 2006 ICSAA Conference Report.* Boston, MA: IIJD.

Irwin, L. G., Siddiqi, A., & Hertzman, C. (2007). *Early childhood development: A powerful equalizer—Final report.* Geneva, Switzerland: WHO, Commission on Social Determinants of Health.

Jensen, A. (1980). *Bias in mental testing.* New York: Free Press.

Kaani, B. (2006, November). *Nature and prevalence of reading difficulties among school-dropouts: A case of selected areas in Chipata Distric, Zambia.* Poster session presented at the 7th ISSBD Africa Region Workshop on Enhancing Research Capacity in Human Development, Johannesburg, South Africa.

Kashoki, M. E. (1982). Indigenous scholarship in African universities: The human factor. In H. Fahim (Ed.), *Indigenous anthropology in non-Western countries* (pp. 35–51). Durham, NC: Carolina Academic Press.

Kathuria, R., & Serpell, R. (1999). Standardization of the *Panga Muntu* Test: A nonverbal cognitive test developed in Zambia. *Journal of Negro Education, 67,* 228–241.

Kishani, B. T. (2001). On the interface of philosophy and language: Some practical and theoretical considerations. *African Studies Review, 44*(3), 27–45.

Lareau, A. (2003). *Unequal childhoods: Class, race and family life.* Berkeley: University of California Press.

LeVine, R. A. (2004). Challenging expert knowledge: Findings from an African study of infant care and development. In U. P. Gielen & J. Roopnarine (Eds.), *Childhood and adolescence: Cross-cultural perspectives and applications* (pp. 149–165). Westport, CT: Praeger.

LeVine, R. A., Dixon, S., LeVine, S., Richman, A., Leiderman, P. H., Keefer, C. H., et al. (1994). *Child care and culture: Lessons from Africa.* Cambridge, MA: Cambridge University Press.

MacGaffey, W. (1981). African ideology and beliefs: A survey. *African Studies Review, 24*(2/3), 227–274.

Malinowski, B. (1922). *Argonauts of the Western Pacific.* London: Routledge & Sons.

Maquet, J. (1972). *Africanity.* New York: Oxford University Press.

McCauley, L. (2008). *The developmental assessment of young children: A practical and theoretical view.* Retrieved March 13, 2008, from http://www.priory.com/psych/assessyoung.htm

MDG Africa Steering Group. (2008). *Achieving the Millennium Development Goals in Africa: Recommendations of the MDG Africa Steering Group June 2008.* Retrieved June 1, 2008, from www.mdgafrica.org

Moll, L. C., & Greenberg, J. B. (1990). Creating zones of possibilities: Combining social contexts for instruction. In L. C. Moll (Ed.), *Vygotsky and education: Instructional implications and applications of sociohistorical psychology* (pp. 319–348). Cambridge, UK: Cambridge University Press.

Morales, J. M. (2007). Review of R. Hart (2001): *Children's participation: The theory and practice of involving young citizens in community development and environmental care.* Barcelona, Spain: UNICEF and P.A.U. Education. Retrieved March 17, 2008, from http://thunder1.cudenver.edu/cye/review.pl?n=227

Moss, P., & Petrie, P. (2002). *From children's services to children's spaces: Public policy, children and childhood.* London: Routledge.

Moumouni, A. (1968). *Education in Africa.* New York: Praeger.

Mpofu, E. (2002). Indigenization of the psychology of human intelligence in Sub-Saharan Africa. In W. J. Lonner, D. L. Dinnel, S. A. Hayes, & D. N. Sattler (Eds.), *Online readings in psychology and culture* (unit 5, chapter 2).

Mundy-Castle, A. C. (1975). Social and technological intelligence in western and non-western cultures. In I. Pilowsky (Ed.), *Culture in collision* (pp. 344–348). Adelaide: Australian National Association for Mental Health.

Murayama, M. (1997). Beyond post-modernism: Trends in 100 years. *Cybernetica, XL,* 169–178.

New York Times. (2005, 3 July). Africa at the summit. Retrieved February 17, 2009, from http://www.genocidewatch.org/images/Zimbabwe_3_Jul_05_Africa_at_the_Summit.pdf

Ngaujah, D. E. (2003, Fall). *An eco-cultural and social paradigm for understanding human development: A (West African) context.* Graduate Seminar Paper (supervised by Dr. Dennis H. Dirks), Biola University, La Mirada, CA.

Nsamenang, A. B. (1992). *Human development in cultural context: A Third World perspective.* Newbury Park, CA: Sage.

Nsamenang, A. B. (2004a). *Cultures of human development and education: Challenge to growing up African.* New York: Nova.

Nsamenang, A. B. (2004b). *The teaching-learning transaction.* Bamenda, Cameroon: Human Development Resource Centre.

Nsamenang, A. B. (2005a). African culture, human ontogenesis within. In C. Fisher & R. Lerner (Eds.), *Encyclopedia of applied developmental science* (pp. 58–61). Thousand Oaks, CA: Sage.

Nsamenang, A. B. (2005b). Educational development and knowledge flow: Local and global forces in human development in Africa. *Higher Education Policy, 18,* 275–288.

Nsamenang, A. B. (2005c). The intersection of traditional African education with school learning. In L. Swartz, C. de la Rey, & N. Duncan (Eds.), *Psychology: An introduction* (pp. 327–337). Cape Town: Oxford University Press.

Nsamenang, A. B. (2006). Human ontogenesis: An indigenous African view on development and intelligence. *International Journal of Psychology, 41,* 293–297.

Nsamenang, A. B. (2007a). A critical peek at early childhood care and education in Africa. *Child Health and Education, 1*(1), 14–26.

Nsamenang, A. B. (2007b). Origins and development of scientific psychology in *Afrique Noire.* In M. J. Stevens & D. Wedding (Eds.), *Psychology: IUPsyS global resource.* London: Psychology Press.

Nsamenang, A .B. (2008a). Culture and human development [Editorial]. *International Journal of Psychology, 43*(2), 1–5.

Nsamenang, A. B. (2008b). (Mis)understanding ECD in Africa: The force of local and global motives. In M. Garcia, A. Pence, & J. Evans (Eds.), *Africa's future—Africa's challenge: Early childhood care and development in sub-Saharan Africa.* Washington, DC: World Bank.

Nsamenang, A. B. (2008c, March 9). *Adolescent research from a global perspective: Prospect for an African input.* Inaugural Address of the Society for Research on Adolescence International Fellows Program, Chicago.

Nsamenang, A. B., Fai, P. J., Ngoran, G. N., Ngeh, M. M. Y., Forsuh, F. W., Adzemye, E. W., et al. (2008). Ethnotheories of developmental learning in the Western Grassfields of Cameroon. In P. R. Dasen & A. Akkari (Eds.), *Educational theories and practices from the "majority world"* (pp. 49–70). New Delhi, India: Sage.

Nsamenang, A. B., & Lamb, M. E. (1995). The force of beliefs: How the parental values of the Nso of Northwest Cameroon shape children's progress towards adult models. *Journal of Applied Developmental Psychology, 16*, 613–627.

Ogbu, J. U. (1994). From cultural differences to differences in cultural frames of reference. In P. M. Greenfield & R. R. Cocking (Eds.), *Cross-cultural roots of minority child development* (pp. 365–391). Hillsdale, NJ: Erlbaum.

Ohuche, R. O., & Otaala, B. (1981). *The African child in his environment.* Oxford, UK: Pergamon.

Ojiaku, M. O. (1974). Traditional African social thought and Western scholarship. *Presence Africaine, 90*(2nd Quarterly).

Oloko, A. B. (1994). Children's street work in urban Nigeria: Dilemma of modernizing tradition. In P. M. Greenfield & R. R. Cocking (Eds.), *Cross-cultural roots of minority child development* (pp. 197–224). Hillsdale, NJ: Erlbaum.

Pence, A. R. (1988). *Ecological research with children and families: From concepts to methodology.* New York: Teachers College Press.

Pence, A. R., & Hix-Small, H. (2007). Global children in the shadow of the global child. *International Journal of Educational Policy, Research, and Practice, 8*(1), 83–100.

Pence, A. R., & Nsamenang, A. B. (2008). *Respecting diversity in an age of globalization: A case for ECD in Sub-Saharan Africa.* The Hague, The Netherlands: Bernard van Leer Foundation.

Poole, E. (1969). The effect of westernization on psychomotor development of African (Yoruba) infants during the first year of life. *Journal of Tropical Pediatrics, 15*, 172–176.

Pryor, J., & Ampiah, J. G. (2003). *Understandings of education in an African village: The impact of information and communication technologies.* Report of DFID Research Project Ed2000–88. Retrieved June 13, 2007, from www.fiankoma.org/content.asp? page=papers

Reid, M. (2006). *From innocents to agents: Children and children's rights in New Zealand.* Auckland, New Zealand: Maxim Institute.

Richards, M. (1986). Introduction. In M. Richards & P. Light (Eds.), *Children's social worlds* (pp. 1–25). Cambridge, MA: Harvard University Press.

Richter, L., Foster, G., & Sherr, L. (2006). *Where the heart is: Meeting the psychosocial needs of young children in the context of HIV/AIDS.* The Hague, The Netherlands: Bernard van Leer Foundation.

Rogoff, B. (1990). *Apprenticeship in thinking: Cognitive development in social context.* New York: Oxford University Press.

Rogoff, B. (2003). *The cultural nature of human development.* Oxford, UK: Oxford University Press.

Rubin, K. H. (1998). Social and emotional development from a cultural perspective. *Developmental Psychology, 34*, 647–652.

Ruddle, K., & Chesterfield, R. (1978). Traditional skill training and labour in rural societies. *Journal of Developing Areas, 12*, 359–398.

Sapir, E. (1929). The status of linguistics as a science. *Language, 5*, 207–214.

Scheuneman, J. D. (1982). A new look at bias in aptitude tests. In P. Merrifield (Ed.), *New directions for testing and measurement: Measuring human abilities, No. 12.* San

Francisco: Jossey-Bass. Retrieved March 17, 2008, from http://pareonline.net/getvn. asp?v=4&n=6

Schlemann, A. D. (1992). Mathematical concepts in and out of school in Brazil: From developmental psychology to better teaching. *International Society for the Study of Behavioral Development Newsletter, 2*(22), 1–3.

Segall, M. H., Dasen, P. R., Berry, J. W., & Poortinga, Y. H. (1999). *Human behavior in global perspective.* Boston: Allyn & Bacon.

Serpell, R. (1977). Estimates of intelligence in a rural community in eastern Zambia. In F. M. Okatcha (Ed.), *Modern psychology and cultural adaptation* (pp. 179–216). Nairobi: Swahili Language Consultants and Publishers.

Serpell, R. (1984). Research on cognitive development in sub-Saharan Africa. *International Journal of Behavioral Development, 7,* 111–127.

Serpell, R. (1993). *The significance of schooling: Life-journeys into an African society.* Cambridge, UK: Cambridge University Press.

Serpell, R. (1994). An African social ontogeny. [Review of the book *Human development in cultural context*]. *Cross-Cultural Psychology Bulletin, 28*(1), 17–21.

Serpell, R., & Hatano, G. (1997). Education, literacy, and schooling in cross-cultural perspectives. In. J. W. Berry, P. R. Dasen, & T. M. Saraswathi (Eds.), *Handbook of cross-cultural psychology* (2nd ed., Vol. 2, pp. 345–382). Boston: Allyn & Bacon.

Serpell, R., & Jere-Folotiya, J. (2008). Developmental assessment, cultural context, gender, and schooling in Zambia. *International Journal of Psychology, 43*(2), 88–96.

Shweder, R. A. (1991). *Thinking through cultures: Expeditions in cultural psychology.* Cambridge, MA: Harvard University Press.

Shweder, R. A. (1995). Cultural psychology: What is it? In N. R. Goldberger & J. B. Veroff (Eds.), *The culture and psychology reader* (pp. 41–86). Cambridge: Cambridge University Press.

Silvia, D. (1994). School influences on children's development. *Child Psychology and Psychiatry, 35,* 135–170.

Smale, J. (1998). Culturally or contextually appropriate? *Early Childhood Matters, 90,* 3–5.

Smith, L. T. (2002). *Decolonizing methodologies: Research and indigenous peoples.* London: Zed Press.

Staniland, M. (1983). Who needs African studies? *African Studies Review, 26*(3/4), 77–98.

Stevenson, D. L., Kochanek, J., & Schneider, B. (1998). Making the transition from high school: Recent trends and practices. In K. Borman & B. Schneider (Eds.), *The adolescent years: Social influences and educational challenges* (pp. 200–216). Chicago: The University of Chicago Press.

Sternberg, R. J., Nokes, C., Geissler, P. W., Prince, R., Okatcha, F., Bundy, D. A., et al. (2001). *The relationship between academic and practical intelligence: A case study in Kenya.* Unpublished manuscript.

Sturtevant, W. C. (1974). Studies in ethnoscience. In J. W. Berry & P. R. Dasen (Eds.), *Culture and cognition: Studies in cross-cultural psychology* (pp. 39–59). London: Methuen.

Super, C. M., & Harkness, S. (1986). The developmental niche: A conceptualization at the interface of child and culture. *International Journal of Behavioral Development, 9,* 545–569.

Super, C. M., & Harkness, S. (2002). Culture structures the environment for human development. *Human Development, 45,* 270–274.

Super, C. M., & Harkness, S. (2008). Globalization and its discontents: Challenges to developmental theory and practice in Africa. *International Journal of Psychology, 43*(2), 107–113.

Swadener, B. B., Kabiru, M., & Njenga, A. (2000). *Does the village still raise the child? A collaborative study in changing child-rearing and early education in Kenya.* Albany: State University of New York Press.

Tanifum, O. (1996). Translation or transliteration: To what extent is translating creative writing a creative activity? *Epassa Moto: A Bilingual Journal of Language, Letters and Culture, 1*(3), 371–375.

Tape, G. (1993). *Milieu africain et developpement cognitive: Une etude du raisonnement experimental chez l'adolescent Ivorien* [Cognitive development in an African context: An experimental study of reasoning in Ivorian adolescents]. Paris: L'Harmattan.

Tylor, E. B. (1881). *Anthropology: An introduction to the study of man and civilization.* New York: Appleton.

Ungar, S. J. (1986). *Africa.* New York: Simon & Schuster.

United Nations. (1999). *Convention on the Rights of the Child.* Retrieved January 8, 2008, from http://www.un.org/documents/ga/res/44/a44r025.htm

Urban, M. (2006, November). *Strategies for change: Reflections from a systematic, comparative research project.* Paper presented to the Early Childhood Care and Education Policy Seminar: "A Decade of Reflection from the Introduction of the Childcare Regulations 1996 Through to Today." Dublin, Ireland.

Van Wildenfelt, B. M., Treffers, P. D. A., de Beurs, E., Siebelink, B. M., & Koudijs, E. (2005). Translation and cross-cultural adaptation of assessment instruments used in psychological research with children and families. *Clinical Child and Family Review, 8*(2), 135–147.

Vandenbroeck, M. (1999). *The view of the Yet: Bringing up children in the spirit of self-awareness and knowledge.* The Hague, The Netherlands: Bernard van Leer Foundation.

Veii, K., & Everatt, J. (2005). Predictors of reading among Herero-English bilingual Namibian school children. *Bilingualism: Language and Cognition, 8*, 239–254.

Vygotsky, L. (1978). *Mind in society: The development of higher psychological processes.* Cambridge, MA: Cambridge University Press.

Weisner, T. S. (1987). Socialization for parenthood in sibling caretaking societies. In J. B. Lancaster, J. Altman, A. S. Rossi, & L. R. Sherrod (Eds.), *Parenting across the lifespan: Biosocial dimensions* (pp. 237–270). Hawthorne, NY: Aldine de Gruyter.

Weisner, T. S. (1997). Support for children and the African family crisis. In T. S. Weisner, C. Bradley, & C. P. Kilbride (Eds.), *African families and the crisis of social change* (pp. 20–44). Westport, CT: Bergin & Garvey.

Weisner, T. S., Bradley, C., & Kilbride, C. P. (Eds.). (1997). *African families and the crisis of social change.* Westport, CT: Bergin & Garvey.

Werner, E. E. (1972). Infants around the world: Cross-cultural studies of psychomotor development from birth to two years. *Journal of Cross-Cultural Psychology, 3*, 11–134.

Wober, M. (1975). *Psychology in Africa.* London: International African Institute.

Yajun, Z., Yi, L., & Champagne, S. (1999). *Childrearing in Hubai village, China.* Working Papers in Early Childhood Development No. 25. The Hague, The Netherlands: Bernard van Leer Foundation.

5

Assessing the Environment of Children's Learning: The Developmental Niche in Africa

SARA HARKNESS, CHARLES M. SUPER, OUMAR BARRY, MARIAN ZEITLIN, JENNIFER LONG

A central challenge for assessing children's competencies in the era of globalization is how to identify both the utility and limitations of existing instruments when they are used in sociocultural contexts other than the ones for which they were created. The problem of ethnocentricity in both assessment content and procedures has been widely recognized, although it has yet to be adequately resolved. Less widely recognized, but perhaps even more important for scholars and educators interested in children's development, is that culture-bound assessments may fail to identify (and therefore to measure) abilities and competencies outside of the current Western-based repertoire. The central argument of this chapter is that in order to create appropriate assessments for children across a variety of cultural environments, we must first assess the environments themselves. What opportunities do environments offer children for learning and practicing skills and competencies? What kinds of competencies are valued in their community, and why? At what ages are children expected to master particular skills, and what are the environmentally supported motivations for doing so? What is the availability of parents, siblings, peers, and others such as teachers or coaches, to help children learn? Knowing the answers to questions like these is a necessary precursor to designing assessments meant to measure individual differences in what children have managed to learn in the context of their own culturally structured environments.

In this chapter, we discuss the theoretical framework of the "developmental niche" as it applies to assessing the environment of children's development, drawing particularly from research in sub-Saharan Africa. Our approach is based on the assumption that the actual environments children inhabit are not a random agglomeration of unrelated social customs, esthetic values, interpersonal interactions, physical situations, and beliefs about the world. Rather, these features exist in dynamically structured relationships that work together synergistically, and that can be systematically observed and described. Identifying the components of children's environments and how they work together can provide a foundation for the development of culturally informed assessments.

THE DEVELOPMENTAL NICHE

The developmental niche is a theoretical framework for the integration of concepts and findings from multiple disciplines concerned with the development of children in cultural context (Harkness & Super, 1992a; Super & Harkness, 1986). Two overarching principles reflect its origins in cultural anthropology and developmental psychology: First, that a child's environment is organized in a nonarbitrary manner as part of a cultural system; and second, that the child's own disposition, including a particular constellation of temperament, skills, and potentials, affects the process of development.

At the center of the developmental niche (see Figure 5.1) is the individual child. In one sense the niche can be described only for a single child with his or her particular set of inherited characteristics. Nevertheless, the framework is equally useful in deriving a generalized description of recurring patterns characteristic of particular cultural communities. Surrounding the child are the three major subsystems of the developmental niche.

Physical and Social Settings

The physical and social settings in which the child lives provide a scaffold upon which daily life is constructed, including where, with whom, and in what activities the child is engaged. These settings are the most evident aspect of the developmental niche, as they can be observed by a

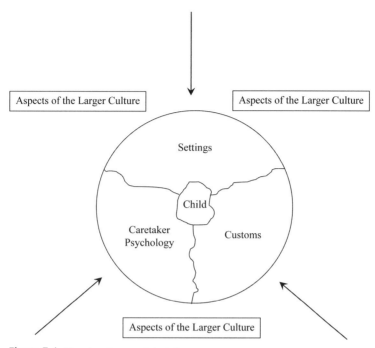

Figure 5.1 The developmental niche.

visitor or participant in the child's daily routines. For example, in North America, some young children spend their days mostly at home in the care of their parents, while others attend day-care centers for a good part of the daytime hours. In contrast, children in a Kipsigis community of Kenya studied by Super and Harkness in the 1970s spent much of the day outdoors, and much of it occupied with responsibilities for helping to collect food for the family dinner, keeping an errant calf away from the maize kernels left to dry in the sun, or tending to a younger sibling (Harkness & Super, 1985a, 1991, 1992c). The routines of daily life that make up these settings thus differ not only in terms of physical location and caretaker, but also in terms of others present, consistency of routines and types of activities, and opportunities for a variety of different kinds of developmentally relevant experiences.

Customs and Practices of Care

Culturally regulated customs and practices of child care signal particularly meaningful activities embedded in the settings of the child's life. Careful observation can lead to the discovery of such customs, or habits of care as they emerge from the ongoing flow of activities. Many customs or habits are so commonly used by members of the community and so thoroughly integrated into the larger culture that individuals need not particularly rationalize them. To members of the culture, they seem obvious and natural solutions to everyday problems, developmental requirements, or social needs: their cultural nature becomes evident only when viewed from an outsider's perspective or when challenged in practice. For example, parents' strategies for putting infants to bed vary widely even among postindustrial societies, from holding the baby until it falls asleep to simply tucking the baby into bed (Harkness, Super, et al., 2007). Often, these customs express deeply held beliefs, and related emotions, about the nature of the child and about the proper functions of a good parent.

Psychology of the Caretakers

The psychology of the caretakers can be inferred from observation of the child and family, but is best accessed through conversation with parents rather than naturalistic observation; standardized formats such as questionnaires can also be useful when empirical research with the same population has previously shown what to look for. This third subsystem includes cultural beliefs, or "parental ethnotheories," regarding children, parenting, and families (Harkness & Super, 2005, 1996). Parental ethnotheories are often implicit, taken-for-granted ideas, and they have strong motivational properties; they are related to each other both across domains and in hierarchical fashion. Linking these ideas at all levels of specificity are cultural themes, which Quinn and Holland have called "general, all-purpose cultural models that are repeatedly incorporated into other cultural models developed for special purposes" (Quinn & Holland, 1987, p. 11). For example, the theme of "emotional closeness" has been identified in multiple contexts in research with Italian parents, including ideas about family life, parental support for children's success in school, and the child's most important developmental needs (Axia & Weisner, 2002; Harkness, Blom, et al., 2007; Harkness, Super, et al., 2007). Among Swedish parents, on the other hand, the concept of "rights" appears frequently in talk about family relationships, such as in the child's "right" to have access to physical closeness with parents at any time (Harkness et al., 2006; Welles-Nyström,

2005). It is important to note that the themes of "emotional closeness" and "rights" do not necessarily conflict with each other; rather, they seem to be concerned with different culturally shared yet unspoken premises.

Three Corollaries

The three subsystems of the developmental niche—settings, customs, and caretaker psychology—share the common function of mediating the individual's developmental experience within the larger culture. Of particular significance for integrating research on these individual components are three corollaries:

1. The three components of the developmental niche operate together with powerful though incomplete coordination as a system. Thus, in an internally stable cultural environment, customs of care express or "instantiate" parental ethnotheories about the child, and they are further supported by the physical and social settings of daily life.

2. Each of the three subsystems of the niche is functionally embedded in other aspects of the human ecology in specific and unique ways; in other words, the three subsystems act as the primary channels through which the niche, as an open system, is influenced by outside forces. This corollary indicates that any one of the three components may be a primary route of influence. Economic or social change may lead to new settings for children, such as day care in the United States or a change to urban living in many developing countries; religious persuasion, scientific discovery, personal experience, or didactic instruction in "parenting" may alter caretakers' ethnotheories; and new customs of care may emerge in response to new technology or intercultural contact. Any such change will likely cause instability in the niche and activate internal adjustments as indicated in Corollary 1.

3. Each of the three subsystems of the niche is involved in a process of mutual adaptation with the individual child. Thus, the age, gender, temperament, interests, and abilities of the individual child influence parents and others in the niche, modulating cultural expectations and opportunities for the child at any given time.

Cultural Themes

The developmental niche framework makes evident the kind of systematic regularity that culture provides—environmental organization that emphasizes repeatedly or with singular salience the culture's core "messages." It is through such cultural thematicity that the environment works its most profound influences on development. This quality of the developmental niche, which we have termed *contemporary redundancy*, is important for the acquisition of skills and competencies as it offers multiple opportunities for learning the same thing, whether that "thing" is reading, sibling caretaking, or the communication of emotions (Super & Harkness, 1999). Similarly, the elaboration of themes over the course of developmental time reinforces lessons learned earlier and recasts them in a more adequate format for meeting the challenges of increasing maturity (Super & Harkness, 1999). In middle-class U.S. society, for example, the theme of "independence" is applied to the management of infant sleep, and later on to transitions to school, to parent-child relations during the teenage years, and later still in advice to parents about "letting go" of their college-bound children (Harkness, Super, & Keefer, 1992). In these and other domains, children appear effortlessly to detect, abstract, and internalize culturally based rules of performance and systems of meaning. As an organizer of the environment, thus, culture assures that key meaning systems are elaborated in appropriate ways at different stages of development, and that the learning occurs across behavioral domains and various scales of time.

THE CHALLENGE OF DEVELOPMENTAL ASSESSMENT IN SUB-SAHARAN AFRICA

The challenge of psychological or developmental assessments of African children has long been recognized, due to the fact that Western researchers have been drawn to African societies as a context for exploring the generality of their own theories. In a 1977 report, for example, Harkness and Super (1977/2008) commented that Africa had been the locus of nearly half of the then-existing cross-cultural research on children; and furthermore, that a substantial portion of this research was concerned with the performance of non-Westernized children on psychological tests. Despite considerable efforts to make the testing situation less foreign or intimidating for these children, it was frequently observed that children seemed unable to display their abilities in this context. The results were unrealistically low estimates of their competence on such apparently normal tasks as retelling a story to the experimenter. Harkness and Super (1977/2008) evoked their own experience thus:

> Consider, for example, our experience in testing children in Kokwet, a rural farming community of Kipsigis people in western Kenya. Several children—siblings or neighborhood peers—are brought to a traditional hut, where a familiar local woman administers several tests in a friendly and relaxed context. Children waiting to be tested play nearby, and because the house is used by our project staff, there is often someone making tea or doing other familiar chores. As part of the test battery the child is told a story of ten sentences about a boy who was given a special stick to help herd the family's cows. He is then asked to tell the story back to the experimenter. The chances that the child will repeat any portion of the story, no matter how short or garbled, are not great: only 10 percent of the three-year-olds say anything in this situation, and the proportion of children answering does not reach 50 percent until six or seven years. Even by age ten, a full third of the children do not give a scoreable reply. (p. 182)

The Kokwet children's responses to the experimental situation were discussed in the context of child language socialization practices in the community. As the researchers noted, young children in Kokwet typically did not participate in extended conversations with their parents or other adults; rather, they were expected to learn to understand directives (and relatedly, to carry them out). Mothers observed during naturalistic home observations spoke infrequently to their young children (an average of only 67 utterances over the course of a 2-hour recording period), and about half of their utterances were imperatives. Moreover, as the children grew older and lost their favored status as the baby of the family, their mothers' speech to them increasingly included reprimands and other negative statements. An examination of semantic contingency in the speech of these mothers (Harkness, 1988) showed that they did not generally direct their own attention to follow the child's interest, as noted among middle-class Western mothers, but rather involved the child in a joint focus of attention on tasks such as taking care of a younger sibling or sweeping the house.

Although this explanation does help to understand the Kokwet children's behavior in the particular assessment situation described, it also raises other, larger questions. Why did the Kokwet mothers speak so infrequently to their young children? Why was their speech so dominated by commands requiring a response in action, rather than questions or comments that would invite sociability through conversation? Were they not concerned about their children's development? Did the Kokwet mothers actually love their children, given the apparent absence of affectionate behavior especially to children who had acquired younger siblings? Or were the mothers too overburdened and stressed to talk with their young children, regardless of how they might feel about them? Questions such as these point to the need to understand the child's culturally structured learning environment as a basis for appropriate assessments. The developmental niche framework is helpful for identifying aspects of African children's learning environments as a first step toward a culturally informed assessment.

Parental Ethnotheories of Children's Intelligence and Personality

How parents think about their children's intelligence or competence is key to understanding their strategies for making sure that children acquire the knowledge and skills they need for success in their communities. In several studies, Harkness and Super have demonstrated broad cultural differences in parents' conceptualizations. Mothers in Kokwet identified six different groupings of words used to describe children (Harkness & Super, 1992b). The first group referred to children's helpfulness and obedience, and included phrases denoting a child who is respectful, polite, hospitable to visitors, and responsible. Particularly interesting in this group was the term *kaseit,* derived from the verb *kase,* to understand, describing a child who understands quickly what needs to be done—and does it. The second group referred specifically to cognitive qualities, including *ng'om* (intelligent), *utat* (clever, or wise and unselfish), and *kwelat* (sharp, clever, sometimes devious). The word *ng'om* was used only in describing children, and was typically used to describe intelligent behavior at home. One informant explained:

> For a girl who is *ng'om,* after eating she sweeps the house because she knows it should be done. Then she washes dishes, looks for vegetables [in the garden], and takes good care of the baby. When you come home, you feel pleased and say: "This child is *ng'om.*" Another girl may not even clean her own dishes, but just go out and play, leaving the baby to cry. For a boy, if he is *ng'om,* he will watch the cows, and take them to the river without being told. He knows to separate the calves from the cows and he will fix

the thorn fence when it is broken. The other boy will let the cows into the maize field and will be found playing while they eat the maize. (p. 377)

As the Kokwet mothers explained further, the term *ng'om* could also be applied to academic intelligence, but was accordingly elaborated: *ng'om en sukul,* or "intelligent in school." They stressed that being intelligent in school and at home were two different things: a child might do well in school despite often forgetting to be responsible and helpful at home. In summary, the Kokwet parents' concept of intelligence highlighted aspects of competence, combined with responsibility and helpfulness, that are recognizable to U.S. middle-class parents (who often bemoan the lack of such qualities in their own children), but that tend not to "count" among those qualities deemed most essential for success in American society. Instead, a study of U.S. parents' free descriptions of their children (Harkness, Super, & van Tijen, 2000) showed that the most frequent category of descriptors (amounting to about one-fifth of all descriptions) denoted cognitive intelligence. In contrast to the Kokwet parents, the U.S. parents described many aspects of their children's behavior as showing how "smart" or advanced they were, rather than contextualizing intelligence as seen in relation to the effective functioning of the household. Interestingly, however, the apparent preoccupation with cognitive excellence as expressed by the U.S. parents is not evident in the descriptions that middle-class parents from several European communities gave of their children: Dutch parents, for example, mentioned cognitive qualities only half as often as did the U.S. parents. Similarly, and in contrast to the U.S. parents, Italian, Spanish, and Swedish parents focused more on their children's social and emotional qualities when describing their children. In short, parents in each of these cultural communities expressed their own distinctive conceptualizations of children's qualities, but the current U.S. emphasis on cognitive skills appears to be a unique cultural construction (Harkness & Super, 2005).

Developmental Timetables: Parents' Expectations for Their Children's Acquisition of Competence

Given the cultural differences between the Kokwet and U.S. parents' concepts of intelligence, we might expect some related differences in "developmental timetables," or expectations about when children should achieve particular competencies. In another study (Harkness & Super, 1983), ninety-seven mothers of 179 children aged 3 to 10 years in Kokwet were asked whether they thought each of their children in that age range was old enough to carry out independent responsibilities such as carrying a message to a nearby homestead or going to the local shops to make a small purchase. In addition, the mothers were asked to judge whether each child was yet old enough for it to be evident "what kind of child" he or she was—in other words, at what age the child's personality could be reliably assessed. The Kokwet mothers' responses are here compared to responses from a sample of 66 mothers of 111 children in the town of Duxbury, Massachusetts, which at the time of the study (the late 1970s) was a quiet, well-to-do beach town and distant satellite of Boston. For children in Kokwet, going to the local shops entailed a walk of anywhere from 5 to 20 minutes each way via a dirt road used only for walking or for driving cattle, with other familiar homesteads and neighbors to be seen along the way. The shops were arranged in a short row along the main road (also unpaved), together with a bar where men from the community tended to congregate in the afternoons. In Duxbury, since shopping typically took place in malls or shopping plazas, an adapted version of this question asked mothers whether their child was yet old enough to make a small purchase independently in one store while the mother was at a different store. As shown in Figure 5.2, mothers' responses to this question are generally parallel but the Duxbury mothers show a lag at age 6, and do not reach full agreement that the child is old enough for this responsibility even at age 9. Analysis of variance shows a marginally significant overall sample difference (p = .10), but a highly significant interaction effect of age by sample (p = .01). More striking in Figure 5.2 is the cultural difference in the ages at which mothers thought that their child's personality had emerged (no statistical tests were possible due to the ceiling effect for the Duxbury mothers). Most of the Duxbury mothers responded that their child's personality was at least somewhat evident by the age of 3 years, and the trend continues to virtually full agreement by the time the child was 5. In contrast, the Kokwet mothers' judgments of when a child's personality emerges closely paralleled their expectations of when one could reliably send a child on an errand to the store. Evidently, the Kokwet and Duxbury mothers were using different kinds of criteria for judging their child's personality. For the Kokwet mothers, a child's personality could not really be judged until the child was old enough to carry out errands responsibly: at that point, some children distinguished themselves by carrying out the errand as instructed, and without getting distracted along the way. For the Duxbury mothers, in contrast, the child's personality could be known much

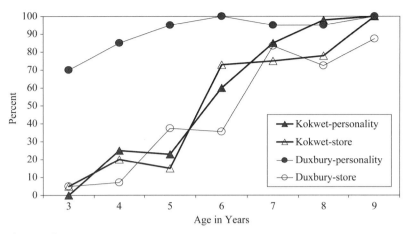

Figure 5.2 Mothers' estimates of age-based competence.

earlier as other aspects of behavior such as verbal communication were seen as relevant.

Cultural Themes and Customs of Care

The larger cultural theme that includes both child language socialization and parental ethnotheories of children's intelligence in the community of Kokwet, and others like it, is the development of helpfulness and responsibility, as has been noted by various investigators (Harkness & Super, 1983, 1991; Weisner & Gallimore, 1977; Whiting & Edwards, 1988). Whiting and Edwards (1988) characterized the sub-Saharan mothers in samples from several different ethnic groups in Kenya and Liberia as "training mothers" because their most frequent social interactions with their children involved directing the children to help out with a variety of domestic tasks. These behaviors were supported by parental ethnotheories about how children should be brought up:

> The training mothers in sub-Saharan Africa believe that responsibility and obedience can and should be taught to young children. They begin teaching household, gardening, and animal husbandry skills at a comparatively early age. The Ngeca [a Kikuyu community outside Nairobi] mothers we interviewed are typical: they believe that they should train a child to be a competent farmer, herdsman, and child nurse and that a child from age 2 on should be assigned chores that increase in complexity and arduousness

with age. They punish their children for failure to perform these tasks responsibly or for stubbornly refusing to do what their elders request of them. They allow much of their children's learning to occur through observation and imitation; only occasionally do they instruct them explicitly. Moreover, mothers seldom praise their children lest they become proud, a trait that is unacceptable. They allow the major rewards for task performance to be intrinsic. (p. 95)

Whiting and Edwards's description is particularly interesting in that it combines the idea of consciously motivated teaching with a nondidactic method, relying mainly on the child's own observation of (and participation in) a variety of tasks. As the authors also point out, the tasks that are assigned to young children in rural African communities are actually important for the successful functioning of the household, unlike "chores" such as brushing one's teeth, clearing one's plate from the table, or making one's bed that are more typically assigned to young middle-class U.S. children. It therefore makes sense that the rewards for competence in these tasks can be intrinsic rather than extrinsic: a good meal that the child helped to prepare may be a more meaningful reward than parental praise, especially when good meals cannot be taken for granted.

Cultural Agendas for Learning and Development in Nigeria

Further evidence for parental ethnotheories and practices related to children's early acquisition of competence comes from studies carried out in Nigeria by Zeitlin and her colleagues (Akinaware, Wilson-Oyelaran, Ladipo, Pierce, & Zeitlin, n.d.). A UNICEF-supported survey of child care and development in five sites in Nigeria, carried out in the late 1980s, includes data on young children from five different community samples, including rural and urban Yoruba communities as well as many other ethnic groups (e.g., Fulani, Efut, Efik, Kwa, and Terawa). Mothers in each sample were interviewed about the child's health and behavior, maternal socialization practices, and aspirations for the child's development; in addition, subsamples of children were observed at home.

Although more than a third of the children were judged to be malnourished and many suffered from illnesses such as diarrhea and malaria, they received attentive care from their mothers and other caretakers. For example, more than 90% of the mothers reported that they bathed their child at least once a day, and toilet training was accomplished early relative to current U.S. middle-class expectations, thanks to careful monitoring and encouragement. When children were afraid or unhappy, mothers typically tried to calm and comfort them. In one of the Yoruba sites, it was reported that in this situation "Most mothers treated the child's fear as real and attempted to drive away the fear-generating item even if it existed only in the child's imagination" (Akinware et al., n.d.). Likewise, in cases of aggression among children, adults assessed the situation and tried to relieve the tension by either supplying another object such as a toy or food, if the struggle was about that, or simply separating the aggressors. In general, the questionnaire responses and the observations confirmed that mothers were actively responsive to their children, and they tried as much as possible to eliminate stressful or disturbing situations while maintaining discipline and obedience. Furthermore (and in contrast to Whiting and Edwards's description above, based mainly on East African samples), mothers described reacting very positively when their child did something "good." Almost all of the mothers said that they would reward good behavior with clapping, dancing, praising, or singing for the child. It was also common for the mothers to share the good news of the child's exemplary behavior with other relatives or neighbors, thus generating more praise for the child. Undesirable behavior also elicited a response from the mother, most commonly corporal punishment using twigs or sticks, as it was believed (at least among the Yoruba) that the hand that feeds and nurtures should not be used to hit the child.

Within this context of attentive nurturance, mothers and other caretakers trained their young children to achieve culturally normative competencies including self-care skills, autonomy, providing services for others, and proficiency in social interactions. Table 5.1 shows mothers' average expectations for when their children should achieve these important competencies ($n = 1172$).

As indicated in Table 5.1, by 3 years of age most children were expected to exercise control over their bodily functions, to communicate clearly, and to feed themselves. By 5 years, the child was considered capable of dressing herself or himself, running errands, and greeting elders. Such a child would be able to interact outside the family in a social and helpful manner. The increased physical development of the 5-year-old that awarded the child greater mobility also dictated additional responsibilities: a child who was able to run down the street to play with friends would also be capable of fetching water, buying bread, and delivering messages. By 7–8 years, the child was deemed fully a member of society.

Table 5.1

MOTHERS' EXPECTATIONS FOR COMPETENCE IN EARLY CHILDHOOD IN FIVE NIGERIAN COMMUNITIES

BEHAVIOR	AVERAGE AGE (YEARS)
Feed self	2.6
Know where to defecate	2.7
Stop bed wetting	2.8
Talk clearly	3.2
Run errands	4.4
Dress without assistance	4.7
Greet elders	5.1
Care for self for 2 hrs	5.8
Obey elders	5.8
Assist with housework	6.3
Care for younger siblings	6.8
Assist with trading	7.6
Assist with farm	7.8
Think for self	8.2

Seven-year-olds were expected to obey and respect their elders, care for themselves and younger siblings, and assist in the home and in the workplace. By around 8 years, children were expected to be able to think for themselves.

As these developmental expectations indicate, social skills and task performance were important to the Nigerian mothers. The skills of knowing how to greet, how to show respect and obedience are vehicles of social acceptance and mobility throughout many Nigerian communities. A major way of demonstrating respect was through service to those in authority. When mothers were asked what their child did that made them proud, the most frequent response (more than 40%) was when the child was able and willing to help in the home, and especially to complete errands successfully. In contrast, cognitive, artistic, and other expressive skills were mentioned infrequently, if at all. Nevertheless, these children were exposed to a variety of cognitively stimulating experiences in their daily lives, as will be seen.

Physical and Social Settings of Daily Life: Children's Activities in Context

For young children in both Kokwet and the communities surveyed in Nigeria, parental ethnotheories and customs of care were reflected in the children's daily routines, an aspect of their physical and social settings of daily life. Based on "spot observations" (records of the child's location and activities in context at a given moment) of children in 54 households over the course of a year (Harkness & Super, 1983), it is clear that the amount of time that children were engaged solely in play declined rapidly from age 2 to age 6 years, at which point play amounted to less than 10% of the children's time. Children at these later ages still played, as would be natural, but their play was more often in the context of work such as caring for a younger sibling, helping their mother in the garden, or helping to watch the cows (Harkness & Super, 1985b). As such, play tended to be interrupted frequently by the demands of the immediate task (e.g., responding to a crying baby) or by directives from the mother or another older person. Time allocated to work, thus, increased dramatically from late infancy to age 7 years, after which it remained steady at about 50% of the time children were observed.

In the Nigerian survey, a content analysis of the observations suggests that the most common activity of children was playing. Play activities often involved running, jumping, rolling, and motor skill play in which children pushed and pulled various objects, including milk cans, sticks, and bottle caps. Dramatic play was observed among the older preschoolers who sold petrol, prepared and hawked food items, and flew airplanes made of string. Almost half of the observed children played with a toy, usually self-constructed. Children made play items out of unused machinery, broomsticks, bottle caps, sticks, match boxes, and discarded organic materials such as yam peelings, groundnut shells, and palm kernel pods. Manufactured toys that would have stimulated technical play were generally not available.

Music, in the forms of singing and listening and playing musical instruments, made up a large part of the preschoolers' play experiences and of their mastery of verbal skills and expressiveness. In the urban areas, the widespread availability of electricity resulted in an environment where radios and cassette players were common. Especially in markets and homes, music from such appliances provided a constant source of stimulation. Observers noted that children danced and sang to popular ethnic tunes and to religious songs and hymns. Musical activities were not done in isolation, but rather many bystanders were usually enticed to participate. It was common to see children imitate their mothers' songs. When adults were present, they were likely to praise the child for well-executed songs and dance routines.

Other times, children performed for infants or smaller children. Mothers with more education were more likely to report singing and dancing with their children. Also more grandmothers reported singing "all the time" as compared to mothers. The observers noted that women in the rural areas actually spent more time in traditional stimulation activities with their children than did the semiurban or urban mothers. More urban preschoolers were exposed to radio listening than rural or semiurban children. Generally, the radio provided background noise for market and home areas. In this case, it was not always attended to. While urban children had more passive exposure to the radio, rural children actively participated in telling stories and riddles. In rural Yoruba, storytelling, accompanied by riddles, was a prominent form of nighttime entertainment:

> The family, young and old, gathered at the close of the day to test their thought processes with riddles and to instruct the young in the preferred ways of behaving through stories and fables. Stories and riddles, in particular, provide variegated stimuli that can enrich the young child's linguistic skills and challenge his intellectual processes. They also provide a strong base for training in human relations and moral behavior. (Akinware et al., n.d.)

Generally speaking, the Nigerian communities surveyed were full of conversation, jesting, storytelling, and song. It was thus not surprising to find children with broad communication abilities. In fact, throughout the households surveyed, only a few children were described as extremely quiet. The importance of being able to communicate one's ideas and to interact socially in this environment was great, and it was through this early emphasis on verbal expression that children were prepared for their future in both school and work. Nevertheless, most writing experiences were informal and unstructured; especially in the rural samples, the most frequent medium for drawing or writing was in the sand. Even in the urban samples, less than half of the mothers reported that their children had slates to draw or write on, and even fewer had paper and pencils. Instead, much of children's learning in the study communities occurred in the context of participation in the productive life of the household.

Observations in the sampled households recorded activities that relate to language and skills development but that were not mentioned as such by the respondents, such as running errands and buying and selling. The second most frequent activities (after play) identified through content analysis involved the children helping their caregivers. Sometimes the activities were requested, while at other times children helped spontaneously when the need arose. Typically, children were asked to run errands, assist in food processing, and retrieve items such as water, bags, chairs, or foodstuffs. In most instances, the mother herself requested that the task be done and monitored its completion, which appeared to produce a sense of accomplishment for both parties. The effort and commitment that Nigerian mothers put into structuring and monitoring errands as learning experiences for their very young children became visible through the observational studies. Children were sent on many more errands if the mother was around, as older siblings and other caretakers were less likely to place this type of demand on the children. In addition, older children (e.g., 4- and 5-year-olds) who accompanied their caretakers to work were much more likely to engage in productive activities themselves when compared to their age-mates who remained at home. Caretakers other than the mother may have lacked the patience to instruct and reward the children by creating and monitoring errands that the child could perform. Also in the increasing presence of modern consumer appliances, child-care providers may not have had environments structured in ways that would permit very young children to participate in their maintenance. From a learning perspective, most errands involved the ability to remember requests or instructions, numeric proficiency in the case of purchase, motor coordination when carrying water or other items, and a sense of competence. Spontaneous helpful activities by preschool children included driving away goats or dogs from foodstuffs, adding wood to the fire, feeding domestic animals, and taking care of younger siblings in times of distress. As described by one observer:

> Self initiated activities reflected the child's knowledge of the environment. For example, they recognized that foodstuffs must be protected from household animals, and that likewise, household animals must be fed. These preschoolers had internalized social mores and conventions and, therefore, would for example carry an older person's bag without being asked to do so. (Akinware et al., n.d.)

In the process of becoming responsible members of the family, the children were attentive to the adult transactions taking place around them.

A commonly observed category of activity involved situations where the child's attention was focused on verbal interactions between adults. These interactions included conversations about foodstuffs, market prices, and the whereabouts of siblings. Mothers were generally responsive in answering questions and in engaging in conversation with an inquiring child, although they discouraged inquisitiveness beyond basic information-seeking. Several observer notations described children reminding their mothers to watch the fire, or attend to a customer, in ways that indicated considerable maturity in the child's ability to deduce cause-and-effect relationships. One little girl who was not quite 3.5 years old commented when she saw a man who worked for the national electricity company that he had probably come to turn off the electricity of a customer who had not paid the bill.

Overall, the stimulation that the rural Nigerian preschoolers received from their parents and communities was extremely interactive. Rural children appeared to have more opportunities to learn by participation in adult activities, particularly when the mother was available to structure errands as learning experiences. Rural children also engaged more actively in participatory forms of verbal entertainment, such as storytelling, singing, and oral history. Although urban children received more exposure to modern technology and architecture, their environments tended to lack the many resources for early development that were so evident in the rural settings.

A CULTURALLY GROUNDED EARLY INTERVENTION PROJECT IN SENEGAL

Based on the results of the Nigerian surveys as well as on local consultations, Zeitlin, Barry, and their colleagues developed a culturally grounded intervention program for implementation with mothers in rural communities of Senegal (Zeitlin & Barry, 2004). The program incorporated already culturally accepted tenets of positive early development, such as encouraging early motor development and the inculcation of traditional values, with the addition of culturally novel ideas about encouraging early language development and cognitive skills. For each of these domains, the program created illustrative cards to use with mothers in the context of teaching, encouraging, and assessing development in infants and young children.

Analysis of the implementation confirmed that there was wide variability in the degree to which particular caretaking practices seemed familiar and reasonable to the mothers. For example, when shown the motor development card, many parents did not need to have it explained, and just said, "Right, right. . . ." The first version of this card did not include a picture of baby massage. Parents requested that it be added, explaining that massage is the first stage of developing motor competence. The mothers also identified a stage before crawling when they would put the baby on its stomach with some objects in front of him or her in order to motivate the baby to make an effort, calling to the baby to crawl toward the mother. Likewise, walking was encouraged by standing up facing the baby and backing up as the baby approached. Parents emphasized the importance of early motor development as a practical matter: from the age of 2 years on, children should begin to care for themselves and help their parents—dressing and undressing themselves, taking care of their own belongings, helping parents with small errands, participating in domestic chores, and making small purchases at the local stores. Some parents even described training their children so that by 4 years of age, the child could herd cows alone, riding on a horse!

The language teaching card, in contrast, was not as self-evident to the mothers. One mother of a 10-day-old baby described how other members of her family made fun of her efforts to talk to her newborn. It appeared that the importance of talking to babies before they begin to talk needed to be explained very carefully, as mothers questioned the rationale of talking to a baby before the baby could respond verbally. However, the project personnel's experiences with this card brought clearly to light the importance of errands for the older child's acquisition of vocabulary. This seemed to be such a culturally self-evident practice that the mothers apparently felt no need to describe it. The baby's older brothers and sisters spontaneously demonstrated the first lesson in teaching vocabulary through errands with a 6-month-old baby by putting an object in her hands and teaching her two words: "give" and "take." The project staff found it impossible to persuade mothers to name objects for the baby without putting them into the context of an errand. The ingenuity with which the most highly motivated parents invented errands with the sole intention of teaching their children new words was impressive.

ASSESSING CULTURALLY BASED COMPETENCE

Cross-cultural or culturally informed research such as the examples described here makes it clear that there is broad variability in parental ethnotheories, practices, and settings for children's development in infancy and early childhood. Given the rich diversity of culturally constructed competencies, it seems unfortunate that assessments tend to be restricted to a relatively small repertoire of skills and abilities. For the most part, competencies emphasized in cultures other than our own have not been assessed comparatively; but when they have, the results have been instructive. Super (1976), for example, assessed motor development in infants from several different ethnic groups in Kenya, finding that motor milestones related to sitting and walking were early by comparison with a Euro-American sample, whereas crawling was not. Both trends were consistent with cultural emphases on teaching babies to sit and walk early, but not to crawl on the dirt floors of the huts. Similarly, Keller and her associates (Keller, 2007) found that children in a rural Nso community of Cameroon developed earlier competence in carrying out errands of the sort described above in Nigeria and Senegal, compared to toddlers in San Jose, Costa Rica, and Athens, Greece. Comparisons across Western countries have generally not included competencies beyond standard school-related skills of the sort that can be tested in a traditional paper-and-pencil format. We know little, therefore, about the long-term developmental significance of the differences in mothers' cultural models and practices, which are evident even in early infancy (Harkness, Super, et al., 2007; Super & Harkness, 2009). East-West comparisons have received a great deal of attention in the research community due to the generally superior performance of Asian students in the United States, especially in math and science (Fuligni, 1997; Stevenson & Lee, 1990). Even here, though, the assessments are generally limited to traditional school curriculum-based tests.

In order to broaden the base of competencies to be assessed in the context of globalization, it will be important to gain a fuller understanding of the ways that competence is understood and encouraged in various cultures. The framework of the developmental niche can be a helpful guide for this process. Documenting children's settings of daily life—where they are, with whom, and engaged in what activities—can provide basic information about the cultural curriculum for the child's development, including opportunities for learning that are not even consciously provided by parents as such. The "literacy environment" of the home (presence, accessibility, and use of written materials) has often been cited as an important way that parents can help prepare their children for school; likewise, opportunities to observe and participate in important household maintenance activities such as weaving or cooking offer the young child practice in a variety of social, cognitive, and motor skills. Customs of care highlight those activities that parents consider the most important for young children's development. In this regard, the importance of the "errand" for training young children in West African societies becomes evident as a positive strategy, not just a way for busy mothers to pass off some of their work to others (and as any parent of a 2-year-old knows, "help" from the child is not the quickest way to get something done). Understanding parental ethnotheories about children's behavior and development can help integrate these observations on settings and practices, thereby providing greater insight into their meaning and developmental consequences. In the process of taking such a structured inventory of the child's developmental niche, its characteristic *contemporary redundancy*—the ways that the same developmental themes are expressed across multiple domains and through settings, customs, and ethnotheories—becomes apparent. Children in Africa, just like children everywhere else, are best at skills and competencies learned over and over in a variety of contexts. Likewise, the elaboration of the same themes over the course of development greatly adds to their power.

Bridging the gap between cultural learning and globalized assessment will require that we assess children for the competencies that are valued in their own cultures, not just those that we (in our culture) judge a priori to be important. The process is a recursive one, of course, even for our own society, as competencies designated worthy of assessment tend to be those that parents value. With regard to competencies that are well articulated and developed in other cultures but not our own, there is the additional challenge of truly appreciating their importance. As noted above, for many years researchers have emphasized the importance of the theme of obedience and respect in traditional African societies. Even though we have known this, received wisdom, at least in middle-class U.S. culture, such qualities are not particularly interesting or important for success in modern life. In another currently popular approach, behaviors such as helpfulness, observed in traditional African cultures, among others, are perceived as a manifestation of a different kind of "culturally constructed self," as if they were an aspect of personality rather than a particular kind of competence. This is an important distinction: personality is, in theory, visible across a wide variety of contexts, whereas competence is normally displayed in the particular contexts that call for it. By learning more about how competence is developed in a variety of cultural contexts, we will be better prepared to think of new and more globally relevant ways of assessing it.

REFERENCES

Akinware, M., Wilson-Oyelaran, E. B., Ladipo, P. A., Pierce, D., & Zeitlin, M. F. (n.d.). *Child care and development in Nigeria: A profile of five UNICEF-assisted LGA's.* Unpublished report to UNICEF, Nigeria.

Axia, G., & Weisner, T. S. (2002). Infant stress reactivity and home cultural ecology of Italian infants and families. *Infant Behavior and Development, 25*(3), 255–268.

Fuligni, A. J. (1997). The academic achievement of adolescents from immigrant families: The roles of family background, attitudes, and behavior. *Child Development, 68*(2), 351–363.

Harkness, S. (1988). The cultural construction of semantic contingency in mother-child speech. *Language Sciences, 10*(1), 53–67.

Harkness, S., Blom, M. J. M., Oliva, A., Moscardino, U., Zylicz, P. O., Ríos Bermúdez, M., et al. (2007). Teachers' ethnotheories of the "ideal student" in five Western cultures. *Comparative Education, 43*(1), 113–135.

Harkness, S., Moscardino, U., Ríos Bermúdez, M., Zylicz, P. O., Welles-Nyström, B., Blom, M. J. M., et al. (2006). Mixed methods in international collaborative research: The experiences of the International Study of Parents, Children, and Schools. *Cross-Cultural Research, 40*(1), 65–82.

Harkness, S., & Super, C. M. (1977/2008). Why African children are so hard to test. In L. L. Adler (Ed.), *Cross-cultural research at issue* (pp. 145–152). New York: Academic Press. Reprinted in R. A. LeVine & R. S. New (Eds.), *Anthropology and child development: A cross-cultural reader* (pp. 182–186). Malden, MA: Blackwell.

Harkness, S., & Super, C. M. (1983). The cultural construction of child development: A framework for the socialization of affect. *Ethos, 11*(4), 221–231.

Harkness, S., & Super, C. M. (1985a). The cultural context of gender segregation in children's peer groups. *Child Development, 56,* 219–224.

Harkness, S., & Super, C. M. (1985b). The cultural structuring of children's play in a rural African community. In K. Blanchard (Ed.), *The many faces of play* (pp. 96–101). Champagne, IL: Human Kinetics.

Harkness, S., & Super, C. M. (1991). East Africa. In J. M. Hawes & R. Hiner (Eds.), *Children in comparative and international perspective: An international handbook and research guide* (pp. 217–239). New York: Greenwood.

Harkness, S., & Super, C. M. (1992a). The developmental niche: A theoretical framework for analyzing the household production of health. *Social Science and Medicine, 38*(2), 217–226.

Harkness, S., & Super, C. M. (1992b). Parental ethnotheories in action In I. Sigel, A. V. McGillicuddy-DeLisi, & J. Goodnow (Eds.), *Parental belief systems: The psychological consequences for children* (2nd ed., pp. 373–392). Hillsdale, NJ: Erlbaum.

Harkness, S., & Super, C. M. (1992c). Shared child care in East Africa: Sociocultural origins and developmental consequences. In M. E. Lamb, K. J. Sternberg, C. P. Hwang, & A. G. Broberg (Eds.), *Child care in context: Cross-cultural perspectives* (pp. 441–459). Hillsdale, NJ: Erlbaum.

Harkness, S., & Super, C. M. (2005). Themes and variations: Parental ethnotheories in western cultures. In K. H. Rubin & O.-B. Chung (Eds.), *Parental beliefs, parenting, and child development in cross-cultural perspective* (pp. 61–79). New York: Psychology Press.

Harkness, S., & Super, C. M. (Eds.). (1996). *Parents' cultural belief systems: Their origins, expressions, and consequences.* New York: Guilford Press.

Harkness, S., Super, C. M., & Keefer, C. H. (1992). Learning to be an American parent: How cultural models gain directive force. In R. G. D'Andrade & C. Strauss (Eds.), *Human motives and cultural models* (pp. 163–178). New York: Cambridge University Press.

Harkness, S., Super, C. M., Moscardino, U., Rha, J.-H., Blom, M. J. M., Huitrón, B., et al. (2007). Cultural models and developmental agendas: Implications for arousal and self-regulation in early infancy. *Journal of Developmental Processes, 2*(1), 5–39.

Harkness, S., Super, C. M., & van Tijen, N. (2000). Individualism and the "Western mind" reconsidered: American and Dutch parents' ethnotheories of children and family. In S. Harkness, C. Raeff, & C. M. Super (Eds.), *Variability in the social construction of the child.* New Directions for Child and Adolescent Development (Vol. 87, pp. 23–39). San Francisco: Jossey-Bass.

Keller, H. (2007). *Cultures of infancy.* Mahwah, NJ: Erlbaum.

Quinn, N., & Holland, D. (1987). Culture and cognition. In C. Holland & N. Quinn (Eds.), *Cultural models in language and thought* (pp. 3–42). Cambridge: Cambridge University Press.

Stevenson, H. W., & Lee, S. Y. (1990). Contexts of achievement: A study of American, Japanese, and Chinese children. *Monographs of the Society for Research in Child Development, 55*(Serial No. 221).

Super, C. M. (1976). Environmental effects on motor development: The case of African infant precocity. *Developmental Medicine and Child Neurology, 18,* 561–567.

Super, C. M., & Harkness, S. (1986). The developmental niche: A conceptualization at the interface of child and culture. *International Journal of Behavioral Development, 9,* 545–569.

Super, C. M., & Harkness, S. (1999). The environment as culture in developmental research. In T. Wachs & S. Friedman (Eds.), *Measurement of the environment in developmental research* (pp. 279–323). Washington, DC: American Psychological Association.

Super, C. M., & Harkness, S. (2009). The developmental niche of the newborn in rural Kenya. In J. K. Nugent, B. Petrauskas, & T. B. Brazelton (Eds.), *The newborn as a person: Enabling healthy infant development worldwide* (pp. 85–97). New York: Wiley.

Weisner, T. S., & Gallimore, R. (1977). My brother's keeper: Child and sibling caretaking. *Current Anthropology, 18,* 169–190.

Welles-Nyström, B. (2005). Co-sleeping as a window into Swedish culture: Considerations of gender and health care. *Scandinavian Journal of Caring Sciences, 19*(4), 354–360.

Whiting, B. B., & Edwards, C. P. (1988). *Children of different worlds: The formation of social behavior.* Cambridge, MA: Harvard University Press.

Zeitlin, M. F., & Barry, O. (2004). *Rapport intermédiaire du projet sur l'intégration des activités d'éveil et de stimulation psychosociale des jeunes enfants dans l'approche de la déviance positive mise en œuvre dans le Département de Vélingara. Deuxième partie: Les essais pratiques d'éveil améliorées à Yoff-Dakar et à Vélingara* [Progress report on the project about childrearing and psychosocial stimulation of young children in the "positive deviance" approach, carried out in the Department of Velingara. Part two: Improving childrearing practices in Yoff-Dakar and Velingara]. Dakar: Centre de Ressources pour l'Émergence Social Participative.

6

Assessing Competencies in Reading and Mathematics in Zambian Children

STEVEN E. STEMLER, FLORENCE CHAMVU,
HILARY CHART, LINDA JARVIN, JACKIE JERE,
LESLEY HART, BESTERN KAANI, KALIMA KALIMA,
JONNA KWIATKOWSKI, AIDAN MAMBWE,
SOPHIE KASONDE-N'GANDU, TINA NEWMAN,
ROBERT SERPELL, SARA SPARROW,
ROBERT J. STERNBERG, AND ELENA L. GRIGORENKO

THE IMPORTANCE OF ASSESSMENT IN THE GLOBAL ERA

The practice of educational testing is so deeply woven into the fabric of modern Western schooling that it would be almost inconceivable for a child from a Western school to imagine what school would be like without testing. Indeed, by the time a typical American public school student graduates from high school, he or she will have taken several hundred tests. Yet, much has been written recently about the potential adverse impact of this increased emphasis on educational and psychological testing. Health care providers have reported that a myopic focus on the results of educational tests may lead students to experience greater levels of psychopathology associated with stress and anxiety (Kadison & DiGeronimo, 2004), and researchers have found that the enormous pressure to do well on these tests has also led to a degradation of moral behavior (e.g., increased cheating) not only on the part of students, but also on the part of teachers and administrators (Nichols & Berliner, 2007). Against this backdrop, an objective observer might reasonably ask what advantages, if any, are there to testing?

One perceived advantage of testing from a social perspective is that tests can provide a powerful and objective tool for decision making regarding the allocation of scarce resources. In many European nations, for example, tests are used to place individuals onto different educational tracks early in their lives, which some have argued represents an egalitarian approach to the allocation of resources within the public school system. In the United States as well as in many other countries, tests are used to select which students are eligible to pursue further educational opportunities (e.g., university study) at elite institutions where the demand by students to attend far exceeds the realistic supply of resources the school has to educate all such students well. However, despite the egalitarian intentions underlying the use of tests for placement and selection, the political justice of using tests for this purpose has been a subject of intense controversy in both the United States and the United Kingdom (Lemann, 1999). Tests also serve an important credentialing function in Western societies (Labaree, 1997). They certify the knowledge of particular individuals (e.g., medical doctors with university degrees) and help everyday citizens make informed decisions about the credibility of different individuals.

A second advantage to testing is that, when done well, tests can provide important diagnostic and formative feedback to individuals regarding areas of strengths and weaknesses. Indeed, it is in this spirit that the modern IQ testing movement was born. Alfred Binet was originally commissioned by the French government in 1904 to develop ability tests capable of identifying students struggling in school so that those students could be identified for remediation and extra assistance (Birney & Stemler, 2007). Even in the modern era, one of the primary purposes of testing in the school setting is to identify students who may have specific learning disabilities (LDs) that require accommodations in order for the students to reach their full potential. The research related to LD intervention has repeatedly demonstrated that the earlier such students are identified and treated, the more the potential adverse educational impact of the LD can be mitigated (Lyon et al., 2001). At the other end of the conceptual spectrum, tests can also be used to identify areas of great potential within students and are sometimes used to determine placement into gifted/accelerated school programs.

A third advantage of testing is that it can provide an objective benchmark against which to compare the diverse educational systems of the world. Indeed, an increasing number of countries have begun to participate in large-scale comparative studies of student achievement, such as the Trends in International Mathematics and Science Study (TIMSS) (Martin, Mullis, & Foy, 2008; Mullis, Martin, & Foy, 2008) and the Programme for International Student Assessment (PISA) studies (Organisation for Economic Co-operation and Development [OECD], 2000; Programme for International Student Assessment [PISA], 2001). Participating countries benefit because they are better able to gauge the quality of their educational systems relative to static international benchmarks in a variety of content areas. Such studies have also helped to shed light on the factors associated with effective schools nationally and internationally (Stemler, 2001; Teddlie & Reynolds, 2000).

The proliferation of testing throughout the globe should not be taken lightly, however. There are several issues that researchers must confront when thinking about assessment in the era of globalization. For example, consider the fact that the majority of the world's population (approximately 70% of the general population and almost 90% of its children) lives in the developing world, yet the majority of psychological research and assessment is carried out in the developed world, and mostly in the West (especially Europe and North America). Moreover, the growth of human population has been, is now, and in the future will be almost entirely determined by the world's less developed countries (Population Reference Bureau, 2008). Ninety-nine percent (99%) of global natural increase (the difference between birth and death rates) now occurs in the developing regions of Africa, Asia, and Latin America. U.S. Census Bureau (2003) projections indicate that, for the rest of this century, the number of deaths will exceed the number of births in the world's more developed countries, and *all* of the net annual gain in global population will, in effect, come from developing countries. Thus, in the near future, many more children, proportionally as well as in absolute numbers, will be living in the developing world.

Compared with our knowledge of the development of children in the Western world, we know very little about the abilities and competencies of children in the developing world in general (Grigorenko & O'Keefe, 2004), and in Africa in particular (LeVine et al., 1994; Pritchett, 2001). There are many reasons for this asymmetry (Mpofu, Peltzer, Shumba, Serpell, & Mogaji, 2005; Nsamenang, 1997; Serpell, 1999; Sternberg, 2004; Super, 2005), but one is the lack of instruments suitable for evaluating competencies and describing relevant individual differences in children of the developing world. Many Western assessment methods do not travel well across oceans and continents, and the development of new, custom-tailored instruments is a challenging and time-consuming task for which developing countries often do not have the necessary expertise or resources (Serpell & Haynes, 2004). Correspondingly, we see an urgent need for psychologists in developed countries to collaborate with their colleagues from developing nations to construct tools that will enable everyone to better study and understand children living in the developing world. Here we exemplify one such collaboration.

The main objective of this chapter is to present an example of a collaborative effort that brought together psychologists and special education professionals in the United States and Zambia and to discuss some of the major issues and challenges facing researchers who attempt to develop assessments in a global context.

BACKGROUND

Cultural Context of the Project

Zambia is a large sub-Saharan African nation (approximately 753,000 square kilometers of land) with a population of 11.3 million people, 46.5% of whom are younger than 14 years of age (The World Fact Book, 2006). It is a low-resource developing country with an estimated gross national annual per capita income of U.S. $900 (The World Fact Book, 2006); approximately 73% of the population live below the national poverty line and 87.4% live below the international poverty line (The World Bank, 2008).

The infant mortality rate in Zambia is high (88.3 deaths/1,000 live births) (The World Fact Book, 2006), and even if Zambian children survive through preschool age (child mortality rates drop dramatically for cohorts older than 7 years of age), their developmental trajectories are typically marked by high disease burdens derived from the poor environmental conditions in which they live. These conditions are characterized by high levels of exposure to biological, chemical, and physical hazards in the environment and an often-observed lack of resources essential for human health. Malnutrition, infection, and disease are highly prevalent among the school-age population in Zambia and most of sub-Saharan Africa.

To fully appreciate the conditions in which Zambian children develop, their schooling situation must be considered as well. Currently, a major characteristic of many sub-Saharan nations is their failing educational systems. Primary education, though much more widespread than in the days before independence (the number of schools went from few to hundreds), is far from universal; the nation's literacy rate is approximately 81%, compared with approximately 99% for the United States (http://www.indexmundi.com/zambia/literacy.html). Moreover, being enrolled in school does not guarantee quality education: Classrooms are overcrowded and there are not enough teachers, textbooks, or instructional materials (Leithwood, 2000). Indeed, there is evidence that Zambian student performance is among the lowest when compared with students in other African countries. The fourth-grade Monitoring Learning Achievement (MLA) assessment (1999) and the sixth-grade Southern Africa Consortium for Monitoring Educational Quality (SACMEQ) assessment (1998) placed Zambian student performance at or near the bottom of participating nations (Kelly & Kanyika, 2000). Only a small percentage of the Zambian children assessed with the MLA-99 assessment met the requirements for the minimum performance level. Only 37.8% were minimally proficient in literacy (the second lowest achievement level; the lowest percentage was Mali at 15.3%), and only 19.9% were minimally proficient in numeracy (the second lowest, with the lowest percentage Niger's 15.3%). An even smaller percentage of Zambian children performed at the desired level (7.3% and 4.4% in literacy and numeracy, respectively). Among the children from five African countries that participated in the SACMEQ study, Zambian children showed the poorest performance, with 28% of boys and 23.1% of girls performing at the minimum level and 5.6% of boys and 4.8% of girls performing at the desired level. In addition, drop-out rates in Zambian primary school are high, driven by the economic demands on children's time (UNICEF, 1999). Finally, Zambia lacks sufficient numbers of secondary schools, which in combination with poor overall achievement, results in low (<40%) acceptance rates to such schools (Serpell, 1993); thus, secondary schools are available for less than half of those children who graduate from primary schools.

The question of why Zambian children exhibit systematically lower achievement than their peers in other African nations has several potential explanations. From the biological perspective, one possibility is that the cognitive abilities of students in Zambia are deficient. As noted above, it is entirely possible that students in this African nation are exhibiting cognitive impairments that may be associated with specific environmental factors. For example, Bellinger and Adams (2001) have shown that exposure to environmental toxins could result in significant cognitive damage to individuals.

It is possible that the depressed student achievement may also be the result of a less than optimal educational system. In order to test these hypotheses, as well as many others, researchers must have at their disposal some objective measures of student abilities and competencies. In the absence of high quality, psychometrically sound instruments to measure abilities and competencies, we will be left to speculate on the causes of depressed achievement. However, armed with validated measures of abilities and competencies, we can begin to unravel the mystery and systematically examine issues such as the prevalence of learning disabilities (at least as defined using traditional Western criteria). There is, therefore, a significant need to develop psychometrically sound instruments suitable for the Zambian environment.

Assessment From the Ground Up: What to Measure and Why

Given good reasons for wanting to assess abilities and competencies (e.g., both for the benefit of individuals and for the benefit of schools as institutions), where does one begin within the context of a culture where formal assessment is still relatively unusual? One good place to begin is with theory. The theory guiding our assumptions related to the development of assessment measures globally is Sternberg's (1998) theory of abilities as forms of developing expertise. According to this theory, everyone is born with some raw abilities that, through training and development (typically in the form of schooling), can be turned into forms of competence. Through deliberate practice (Ericsson, Krampe, & Tesch-Römer, 1993), the competence can then be developed into expertise. To make use of this model, one must first be able to identify (through assessment) different abilities possessed by diverse individuals. In the United States and other Western countries, the identification of abilities is traditionally approached via IQ and related testing. Western IQ tests typically attempt to measure cognitive processes related to memory, reasoning, and adaptive behavior. By contrast, the identification of developing and developed competencies usually is carried out via tests of achievement in specific content domains (e.g., mathematics, reading, and writing).

The assessment of both abilities and competencies is particularly important for the identification of students with learning disabilities. Although there are many models for identifying students with specific and nonspecific learning disabilities, one classic model that has been used in the West is the identification of an ability-achievement discrepancy (Individuals With Disabilities Education Act, 1997, 1999). Thus, students who have high ability but low achievement may be said to have certain types of learning disabilities (LDs). By contrast, students who have high achievement but low ability may be said to have developed coping mechanisms that they use to mask certain cognitive deficits that could potentially be remediated by enhanced education. In short, in order to help facilitate the development of expertise, we need to be able to assess both abilities and achievement (i.e., competencies). Studies in the United States also point to the fact that early intervention is critical for students with LDs (Lyon et al., 2001). Thus, it is critical to develop measures that can be administered early in a student's educational career.

Models of Assessment in the Era of Globalization

How one approaches assessment depends largely on the assumptions one makes about the nature of abilities and competencies cross-culturally. Sternberg (2004) has outlined four different models related to the assessment of abilities in different cultural contexts. In the first model, the assumption is that all human beings share a fundamental set of cognitive abilities and that cognitive ability measures developed in the Western context should be equally valid for any human population. If all individuals possess the same basic cognitive processes (e.g., problem definition, pattern recognition, reasoning, memory), any nonverbal test of these processes (e.g., Raven's Matrices, tests of reasoning) should be equally applicable to and interpretable in any culture.

In the second model, the idea is that the same tests can be used cross-culturally, but the results cannot be interpreted in quite the same light. Indeed, individuals may administer tests that are used to measure higher order thinking skills in the West, but these tests may not adequately capture these same skills in another culture because the composition of the ability itself may be fundamentally different. For example, research by Cole, Gay, Glick, and Sharp (1971) showed that the Kpelle tripe in Liberia, Africa, had a completely different approach to solving the WISC similarities test than that taken by typical Western children. Specifically, when asked to sort common items into appropriate categories, the Kpelle tended to take a functional approach to sorting (e.g., putting a knife and a potato together because a knife is used to cut a potato) rather than taxonomical categories (e.g., putting a knife and spoon together because they represent the larger category of "silverware"). It was not that the

Kpelle were unaware of the possibility of taxonomical categorization, but rather that they saw functional sorting as more "intelligent." Indeed, when asked how a fool would sort the items, the Kpelle gave taxonomical solutions. Thus, under the second model, although the same cognitive test could be used for assessment, the results must be interpreted as "correct" differentially depending on cultural modes of thought.

A third model suggests that all humans share the same fundamental cognitive processes, such as the ability to define problems, brainstorm solutions, and monitor implementation; however, the way that we assess these abilities must be culturally sensitive and emic in their development. In other words, all human beings face problems and must come up with solutions to those problems, but the nature of the problems faced in different cultural contexts may be radically different.

Finally, a fourth perspective is that the fundamental structure of human ability is different in different cultural contexts. Furthermore, we cannot even use the same methods for assessing these abilities because the assessment instruments themselves must be emic in their development. Thus, one can only truly understand abilities and competencies within a single cultural context and any attempt at cultural comparisons of cognitive processes is considered futile.

The project that we are using as an example in this chapter involved developing and adapting Western-based measures of abilities and competencies within the context of the African country of Zambia. Specifically, we administered three types of assessment: (1) traditional Western-based measures of ability, (2) African measures of ability and competency, and (3) Western-based measures of competency developed for the Zambian context.

METHODS

Testing Cognitive Ability in Zambia

To assess cognitive abilities with a population of Zambian children by means of Western standardized tests, we used nonverbal measures of reasoning and memory. We chose three subtests of the *Universal Nonverbal Intelligence Test* (UNIT) (Bracken & McCallum, 1998) and one subtest of the *Kaufman Assessment Battery for Children* (KABC-II) (Kaufman & Kaufman, 2003). All tests could be presented nonverbally to students and required no verbal responses from them.

The Universal Nonverbal Intelligence Test is an individually administered ability test that measures general intelligence and cognitive abilities of children and adolescents between the ages of 5 and 17 years. We used the Cube Design (CD), Symbolic Memory (SyM), and Spatial Memory (SpM) subtests of the *UNIT* to assess participants' nonverbal reasoning ability (CD) and nonverbal memory (SyM, SpM). The Cube Design subtest consists of 15 items in which students construct three-dimensional designs using a set of cubes. The Symbolic Memory subtest consists of 30 items and asks students to re-create a sequence of symbols they have been shown. The symbols represent a girl, boy, woman, man, and baby, in each of two colors. Finally, the Spatial Memory subtest consists of 27 items in all, in which students are shown a series of grids with chips placed in some of the squares of each grid. Each pattern is shown for 5 seconds, and then the student must re-create the pattern of chips in his or her corresponding grid. The Spatial Memory and Symbolic Memory items are shown to students for 5 seconds, and then removed. There is no time limit for responses on these subtests. Instructions were typically delivered nonverbally in each subtest through the use of gestures and demonstration items. Scoring was completed as right/wrong and partial credit was awarded on the Cube Design subtests for completing some but not all parts of the design correctly. We applied the basal and ceiling rules established by the test developers to determine at which item difficulty level to start and end administration.

The Kaufman Assessment Battery for Children-II is an individually administered assessment of intelligence and achievement. We used the Pattern Reasoning subtest of the *KABC-II* to obtain a second measure of participants' nonverbal reasoning. The Pattern Reasoning subtest consists of 36 items in which the child must perceive a pattern in a series, generate and test hypotheses about the rule used to create the pattern, and apply that rule. The student sees a row of images with one image missing and selects an image that can be placed in the missing space to complete the pattern. This task is untimed and, as with the *UNIT* subtests, can be taught through the use of sample items. Scoring was completed as right/wrong. Basal and ceiling rules established by the test developers were used for this administration.

In addition to importing Western measures of ability, we worked with our colleagues in Zambia (particularly Robert Serpell, who has developed the *Panga Munthu* Test of African intelligence) in selecting culturally relevant measures of ability. The *Panga Munthu* Test (Make-A-Person Test) (Kathuria & Serpell, 1999) is a individually administered ability test developed specifically for children in rural Zambia. The *Panga Munthu* is conceptually similar to the Goodenough-Harris Draw-A-Person (DAP) Test (Harris, 1963), which was developed in the West and was initially intended as a test of native intelligence in the United States (Goodenough, 1926). In the *Panga Munthu* Test, children are presented with wet clay and are asked to make a person. The produced clay figures are then scored by two independent raters for accuracy of representation of human physical characteristics. Wet clay is considered to be more familiar to rural Zambian children than are paper and pencil. Kathuria and Serpell (1999) cite an earlier cross-cultural study that found that Zambian children's performance on a pattern reproduction task was superior to that of English children in the medium of wire, inferior to that of English children in the medium of pencil and paper, and equal in the medium of clay. The *Panga Munthu* Test was untimed and instructions were delivered to children in English or Nyanja. Participants are instructed to "make the best model of a person you can" from a lump of modeling clay, without any example. Scoring for each physical characteristic criterion was completed as right/wrong (Kathuria & Serpell, 1999). Administration time for the *Panga Munthu* was approximately 10 to 20 minutes per student.

Testing Student Achievement in Zambia

The country of Zambia has one nationally standardized test available for Grade 5 students, the *Grade 5 National Assessment* (*NAG5*). The *NAG5* was developed by the Zambia Examinations Council (ZEC) to assess Grade 5 students' knowledge of the school curriculum in different subject areas. The number of subject areas assessed is increasing to include additional local languages, but we used two assessments that have been in use for several years. The *NAG5* in English consists of 30 multiple-choice items in which the student is asked to read three brief paragraphs and then answer 10 questions about each paragraph. A student's score is the total number of items (out of 30) answered correctly. The *NAG5* in Mathematics consists of 40 items assessing students' computation and problem-solving skills, and a student's total score is the total number of items (out of 40) answered correctly. Although the assessment was designed for Zambian students in Grade 5, children in Zambia have been underperforming on this assessment (Kelly & Kanyika, 2000), that is, less than 50% of all Grade 5 students score at or above 50% correct answers. The *NAG5* assessment items are not released by the ZEC, so we cannot provide specific examples to illustrate the pool of items on the test.

If our goal is to use assessment as a means to facilitate educational growth, the administration of the *NAG5* test comes too late, particularly for those individuals who may possess learning disabilities. Consequently, we developed the *Zambian Achievement Test (ZAT).* The ZAT is an individually administered test constructed to quantify academic achievement for the purpose of identifying academic difficulties in Zambian children in Grades 1 through 7. Two equivalent versions of the test were constructed to assess two groups of children: those who have received primarily English instruction at school and those who have received their instruction primarily in Nyanja, one of the Zambian local languages. The English version was developed first and reviewed for cultural sensitivity and familiarity of stimuli to Zambian school children (e.g., pictures of animals and types of vehicles commonly found in Zambia were used as items). The test was then translated into Nyanja by a professional translator. An independent back-translation was then conducted to assess the accuracy of the translation. Current national guidelines for Zambian education and Zambian group achievement testing were used to guide estimated item-level difficulty. This procedure for translation and cultural adaptation was inspired by the procedures used in recent large-scale, international comparative achievement studies (Chrostowski & Malak, 2004; Kelly & Malak, 2003).

The ZAT was constructed to evaluate performance in four core academic areas: (1) mathematics, (2) reading (letter and word) recognition, (3) pseudoword decoding, and (4) reading comprehension. The construction of the items was guided by Zambian school textbooks, proficiency examinations, and consultations with Zambian educators. The items were designed to cover a large range of difficulty levels, appropriate for children with 0–7 years of formal schooling in Zambia. Figure 6.1 (a–d) presents sample items from the four subtests of the ZAT.

The Mathematics subtest (see Figure 6.1a) consists of 60 items that closely mirror the progression of the content of the mathematics curriculum in Zambia. Items are presented in a four-choice response format in which the student must simply point to the correct answer. Initial items instruct students to match a stimulus number with one of four numbers presented. Later items assess knowledge of time, money, calendar skills, numeracy, calculation, and problem-solving skills. The problem-solving questions involving text were read to the students so that math scores would not be biased by reading ability.

$$1 \\ + 5$$

Point to the math problem at the top of the page.

Say: **What does 1 plus 5 equal? Find the answer to the problem—**_down here._

Point to the area with answers.

Say: **Point to it.**

Answer: **6**

A	B
C	D

4	6
10	16

Figure 6.1a Sample item from the ZAT-Mathematics subtest.

Point to the picture of the horse at the top of the page.
Say: **This is a picture of a horse.** while pointing to each of the four pictures.

Say: **Mouse, Pig, Fish, Hippopotamus.**

Say: **Which of these pictures begins with the same sound as this picture? Point to the word that begins with the same sound.**

Answer: Bottom Right

A	B
C	D

Figure 6.1b Sample item from the ZAT-Reading Recognition subtest.

Say: **I want you to read some words that are not real words. Tell me how they sound.**

Point to the first word: **How does this word sound?**

Point to the following words: **Read these words to me.**

Phonetically:
122. ig (as in p*ig*)
123. op (as in m*op*)
124. et (as in g*et*)
125. ak ('ack' as in bl*ack*)

ig

op

et

ak

ZAT-PW-English   ZAT-PW-English

Figure 6.1c Sample item from the ZAT-Pseudoword Decoding subtest.

Student Instructions: **If you are standing, please sit down; if you are sitting, please stand up.**

Examiner Instructions; Say, **Do what this says.** (Use this cue as necessary.)

Correct response: Student should stand, if he/she is sitting, sit if he/she is standing.

If you are standing, please sit down; if you are sitting, please stand up.

Figure 6.1d Sample item from the ZAT-Reading Comprehension subtest.

The Reading Recognition subtest (see Figure 6.1b) consists of 120 items and was constructed with two response types. For the first 60 items, students simply point to one of four possible responses presented in the test booklet. These items begin with letter discrimination items, progress to sound matching and sound discrimination items, and then to letter–sound matching items. The first items are letter matching: For example, students are presented with a page in which a single letter, letter combination, or short two- or three-letter word appears at the top of the page. Four possible matched options presented in isolation or embedded in words are presented below. The examiner points these out to the student as she or he delivers the instructions "Find one like this, down here" or "Find one like this hidden down here." The sound matching items are presented with a single stimulus picture and four possible answer pictures; the sound discrimination items have just four pictures. The pictures are named for the student and the student is asked to point to the one picture that begins with the same sound as the stimulus item (sound matching) (see Figure 6.1b for an example), or to point to the one picture that begins with a different sound than the other pictures (sound discrimination). The letter–sound matching items present a single stimulus picture and four words. The student is asked to point to the one word that begins with the same sound as the stimulus picture. For the next 60 items, the student must read aloud single words presented in the test book. These words, theoretically, get progressively more difficult to decode.

The Pseudoword Decoding subtest (see Figure 6.1c) consists of 38 pseudowords with phonetically regular construction. Initial items consist of simple vowel–consonant combinations (e.g., *ig*, *ak*) and become progressively more challenging in their length and phonetic construction. The student is given the instructions "I want you to read some words that are not real words. Tell me how they sound." The student must simply read the pseudowords aloud.

The Reading Comprehension subtest (see Figure 6.1d) was constructed as a performance response assessment. Students were asked to read the word, phrase, or sentence presented on each page of the stimulus book and to perform the action directed. For example, the first item is "Jump" and students are instructed, "Do what this says." There are a total of 24 items in this subtest and items become theoretically more challenging through vocabulary and sentence construction. For example, the final item is, "Acknowledge your acquaintance's arrival by gesturing with your hand rather than your voice."

The *ZAT* is presented with colorful pictures for the students and clear instructions for both the student and examiner. Children were not given time limits for responding. Students' responses were recorded by the examiner onto answer sheets. For items with four response choices, the student's response was recorded. For items in which the student had to read a word or pseudoword aloud, the examiner recorded the correctness of the response. All items were eventually scored as right/wrong.

RESULTS

Validating Adapted and Newly Developed Measures in the Zambian Context

Evaluating the validity of adapted and newly developed measures in Zambia is an important and detail-oriented exercise. Given the space limitations of the current chapter, however, we will focus this section on the conceptual questions one should ask to determine whether assessments have traveled well and will report only the major findings related to the validation of our instruments. For readers seeking more detailed technical information, we refer them to a series of Web tables found at http://sstemler.web.wesleyan.edu/stemlerlab/webtables that provide substantial technical detail regarding the results of our validations' studies.

Determining if Western Ability Tests "Work" in the Zambian Context

How does one go about determining whether Western tests travel well to other cultures? One standard psychometric approach is to evaluate the reliability and validity statistics associated with these tests. In particular, it is important to look for evidence of variation in student scores. If all students are scoring at the bottom (or the top) of the exam, then this suggests that perhaps the exam is not a good measure within the given cultural context.

We administered three subtests of the *UNIT* (Symbolic Memory, Cube Design, and Spatial Memory) and one subtest of the *KABC-II* (Pattern Reasoning) to assess the cognitive abilities of Zambian children with conventional ability tests standardized in the West. As these are all nonverbal subtests with nonverbal administration procedures, there are no comparisons of the languages of administration.

Figure 6.2 presents a box and whiskers plot of the distribution of scores on each of these tests. In essence, these boxplots show that the Western tests exhibited excellent variability. Furthermore, the three sub-tests of the *UNIT* demonstrate acceptable internal-consistency reliability coefficients. The data were analyzed using the Rasch model (Rasch, 1960/1980; Wright & Stone, 1979). The lowest person reliability estimate (conceptually equivalent to, but computationally superior to, Cronbach's alpha—see Bond & Fox, 2001) was .70, found on the Cube Design sub-test, while the Symbolic Memory subtest had person reliability estimate of .75 and the Spatial Memory subtest had a person reliability estimate of .81. The *KABC-II* Pattern Reasoning subtest also demonstrated accept-able person reliability (.81).

The item reliability estimates for each of the subscales are quite high, with no scale exhibiting reliability below .95. In addition, the item sepa-ration values, an indicator of the range of difficulty levels of items on the test, are well above the minimum requirement of 2.0, with values rang-ing from 4.45 to 6.69 (Bond & Fox, 2001). Taken together, these findings

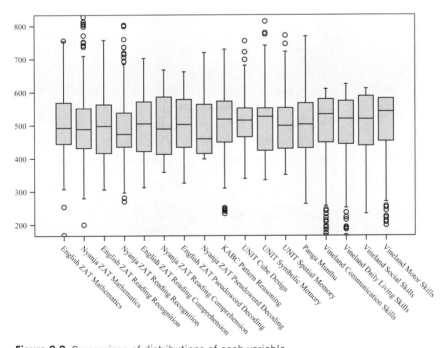

Figure 6.2 Comparison of distributions of each variable.

*Note: Each scale has been standardized with Mean = 500 and *SD* = 100.

demonstrate that the various subtests of the *UNIT* and *KABC-II* possess items that represent a broad range of difficulty levels. Furthermore, the item reliability estimates indicate that we can be quite confident that the placement of the item difficulty values along the continuum of item difficulty would be replicated if these same items were administered to another sample of test-takers from the same population. It is interesting to note that across all four of these subtests, the order of items in terms of difficulty closely approximated the order of difficulty based on U.S. norms (Bracken & McCallum, 1998; Kaufman & Kaufman, 2003).

In order to evaluate the validity of the Western ability tests, we looked at the correlations among Western tests of ability, African tests of ability, and the newly developed Zambian tests of achievement. Table 6.1 presents the criterion-related validity results of the *ZAT*. Scores on each of the four subtests of the ZAT (Mathematics, Reading Recognition, Reading Comprehension, and Pseudoword Decoding) were positively correlated with tests of reasoning (the Pattern Reasoning subtest of the *KABC-II* and the Cube Design subtest of the *UNIT*), with tests of memory skills (the Symbolic Memory and Spatial Memory subtests of the *UNIT*), with an African test of intelligence (the *Panga Munthu*), and with teachers' ratings of students on a measure of adaptive behavior (the Daily Living Skills, Socialization Skills, Motor Skills, and Communication Skills domains of the *Vineland-II*).

The results demonstrate that the measures of ability (pattern recognition and memory) are significantly correlated with one another at levels ranging from .24 to .39. Thus, these tests showed convergent validity, but they also demonstrated discriminant validity in that they exhibited slightly lower correlations with measures of achievement (described more fully in the next section) and even lower correlations with measures of adaptive behavior.

Determining if Newly Developed Achievement Tests "Work" in the Zambian Context

In order to determine whether the newly developed achievement tests "work" in the Zambian context, we must also ask questions about the reliability and validity of these tests. The data revealed that the various subscales of the *ZAT* possess items that represent a broad range of difficulty levels, which was a desirable and sought after feature of the test. In addition, the results yielded variability among test-takers (see Figure 6.2) and high levels of internal consistency among the items.

The lowest person reliability estimate was .77, found on the Nyanja version of the Mathematics subtest; however, all other person reliability estimates were more than acceptable (> .80), with the Reading Recognition and Pseudoword decoding scales reaching person reliability estimates in the high .90s. In addition, the item separation values are well above the minimum requirement of 2.0 (Bond & Fox, 2001), with values ranging from 4.13 to 7.12. Furthermore, the item reliability estimates indicate that we can be quite confident that the placement of the item difficulty values along the continuum of item difficulty would be replicated if these same items were administered to another, similar, sample of test-takers.

Overall, the Rasch analyses revealed that 46 out of the 484 items (i.e., 9.5% of the total number of items) on both the English and Nyanja versions of the ZAT exhibited infit values greater than expected (i.e., greater than 1.3), and 40 out of 484 items (8%) exhibited infit values lower than expected (i.e., less than 0.70). This general pattern of results is extremely encouraging and suggests that each of the subtests is adequately and reliably measuring a distinct, unidimensional construct, and that each of the ZAT subscales—as well as the whole ZAT—is a psychometrically sound instrument.

Furthermore, a test–retest study was conducted and the correlations, calculated using the Spearman rank coefficient, were $\rho = .56$ ($p < .001$) for Mathematics, $\rho = .90$ ($p < .001$) for Reading Recognition, $\rho = .81$ ($p < .001$) for Pseudoword Decoding, and $\rho = .82$ ($p < .001$) for Reading Comprehension. These results indicate acceptable levels of stability of the ZAT indicators over time.

The four subtests of the ZAT show internal validity in that they are significantly correlated with one another, both in English and in Nyanja. Specifically, the Pearson correlation coefficients were all statistically significant at the $p < .001$ level, with Pearson correlation values ranging from .47 to .78, with the median correlation of .62 for the English and .67 for the Nyanja versions.

In addition, for the ZAT-Nyanja, the Mathematics subtest shows statistically significant correlations ($p < .001$) with tests of reasoning ability ($r = .20$ to .40), tests of memory ($r = .32$ to .37), the *Panga Munthu* Test ($r = .30$), and assessments of adaptive behavior ($r = .17$ to .44). Each of these correlations, although statistically significant, is moderate in magnitude, suggesting that the ZAT measures a construct that shares some variance with the above constructs, but also captures unique variance explaining individual differences in students' achievement.

THE CRITERION-RELATED VALIDITY RESULTS OF THE ZAT: CORRELATION OF THE ZAT SUBTESTS WITH TESTS OF REASONING, MEMORY SKILLS, AFRICAN TEST OF INTELLIGENCE, AND ADAPTIVE BEHAVIOR

SCALE	1	2	3	4	5	6	7	8	9	10	11	12	13	14	15	16	17
1 ZAT_M_E	.73	0	107	0	94	0	99	0	100	107	94	98	56	71	71	71	63
2 ZAT_M_N	—	.77	0	497	0	162	0	359	491	501	463	440	292	373	372	368	365
3 ZAT_RR_E	.61***	—	.94	0	95	0	100	0	101	108	95	99	56	72	72	72	64
4 ZAT_RR_N	—	.57***	—	.86	0	164	0	359	491	501	463	440	292	372	371	367	364
5 ZAT_RC_E	.52***	—	.78***	—	.72	0	91	0	88	95	84	86	51	64	64	64	56
6 ZAT_RC_N	—	.47***	—	.75***	—	.70	0	159	161	165	135	143	98	134	134	134	132
7 ZAT_PW_E	.47***	—	.73***	—	.62***	—	.83	0	93	100	87	91	54	65	65	65	58
8 ZAT_PW_N	—	.60***	—	.73***	—	.75***	—	.87	354	362	329	322	218	268	267	264	261
9 KABC_PR	.41***	.40***	.36***	.41***	.25*	.33***	.26*	.34***	.53	623	571	553	359	459	458	454	442
10 UNIT_CD	.19	.20*	.20*	.21***	.15	.00	.10	.16**	.24***	.71	580	560	370	464	463	459	447

Table 6.1

	1	2	3	4	5	6	7	8	9	10	11	12	13	14	15	16	17
11 UNIT_SYM	.26*	.32***	.21*	.21***	.24*	.11	.08	.24***	.26***	.31***	.52	315	415	414	410	398	
12 UNIT_SPM	.06	.37***	.06	.29***	.04	.10	-.06	.25***	.34***	.31***	.39***	.73	327	408	407	403	391
13 Panga_Mun	.04	.30***	.02	.32***	-.03	.24*	.02	.32***	.36***	.12*	.18***	.28***	.88	279	279	279	279
14 V_T_COM	.40***	.38***	.51***	.31***	.30*	.31***	.43***	.36***	.29***	.24***	.26***	.26***	.08	—	485	489	485 / 473
15 V_T_DL	.26*	.44***	.40***	.40***	.15	.39***	.40***	.42***	.34***	.18***	.27***	.33***	.28***	.67***	—	485	473
16 V_T_SOC	.17	.21***	.25*	.19***	.15	.21*	.28*	.24***	.16***	.02	.15**	.09	.00	.54***	.59***	—	473
17 V_T_MOT	.18	.17***	.16	.07	.07	.07	.12	.08	.09	.20***	.09	.07	-.07	.42***	.42***	.49***	—

Note. Values in the lower diagonal are Pearson correlations (r). Values on the diagonals are internal consistency reliability estimates. Values in upper diagonal are sample sizes. ZAT_M_E = *ZAT* Mathematics Subtest, English; ZAT_M_N = *ZAT* Mathematics Subtest, Nyanja; ZAT_RR_E = *ZAT* Reading Recognition Subtest, English; ZAT_RR_N = *ZAT* Reading Recognition Subtest, Nyanja; ZAT_PW_E = *ZAT* Pseudoword Decoding Subtest, English; ZAT_PW_N = *ZAT* Pseudoword Decoding Subtest, Nyanja; ZAT_RC_E = *ZAT* Reading Comprehension Subtest, English; ZAT_RC_N = *ZAT* Reading Comprehension Subtest, Nyanja; KABC_PR = *KABC-II* Pattern Recognition Subtest; UNIT_SYM = *UNIT* Symbolic Memory Subtest; UNIT_SPM = *UNIT* Spatial Memory Subtest; UNIT_CD = *UNIT* Cube Design Subtest; NAG5 = *Zambian National Achievement Test*, Grade 5; PANG_MUN = *Panga Munthu* (Make-A-Person) Test; V_T_COM = *Vineland-II* Teacher Version, Communication Subscale; V_T_DL = *Vineland-II* Teacher Version, Daily Living Skills Subscale; V_T_MOT = *Vineland-II* Teacher Version, Motor Skills Subscale; V_T_SOC = *Vineland-II* Teacher Version, Social Skills Subscale; V_T_MAL = *Vineland-II* Teacher Version, Maladaptive Behaviors Subscale.

*p < .05. **p < .01. ***p < .001.

For Reading Recognition, the correlations of the scores on the *ZAT-Nyanja* were statistically significant with a variety of external criteria, with Pearson correlation values ranging from .21 to .41 ($p < .001$) with tests of reasoning ability, from .21 to .29 ($p < .001$) with tests of memory, at .32 ($p < .001$) with the African test of intelligence, and ranging from .07 (*ns*) to .40 ($p < .001$) with assessments of adaptive behavior.

The Reading Comprehension subtest showed lower correlations with the external criteria than did the Mathematics and Reading Comprehension subtests. Specifically, the Reading Comprehension subtest was significantly correlated with the Pattern Reasoning subtest of the *KABC-II* ($r = .33$, $p < .001$); however, it was not significantly related to other tests of reasoning or memory ($r = .00$ to .11). A moderate but statistically significant correlation was found with the *Panga Munthu* Test of intelligence ($r = .24$, $p < .05$), and correlations ranged from .07 (*ns*, Motor Skills subtest) to .39 ($p < .001$, Daily Living Skills domain) on indicators of adaptive behavior.

Finally, the Pseudoword Decoding subtest showed statistically significant but moderate correlations with a variety of external criteria. Correlations with reasoning tasks ranged from .16 ($p < .01$) to .34 ($p < .001$), from .24 to .25 ($p < .001$) with tests of memory, .32 ($p < .001$) with the *Panga Munthu* Test, and from .08 (*ns*) to .42 ($p < .001$) with tests of adaptive behavior.

The *ZAT-English*, taken by a much smaller sample of test-takers than those who took the *ZAT-Nyanja*, shows similar trends to the *ZAT-Nyanja*. Specifically, the Mathematics subtest of the *ZAT* shows similar correlation values with tests of reasoning ability ($r = .19$, *ns* to .41, $p < .001$), slightly lower correlations with tests of memory ($r = .06$, *ns* to .26, $p < .05$) and the *Panga Munthu* Test ($r = .04$, *ns*), and similar correlation values with tests of adaptive behavior ($r = .17$, *ns* to .40, $p < .001$—Communication domain). Again, each of the correlation values is moderate in magnitude, suggesting that the *ZAT* measures a construct that shares some variance with the above constructs, but also captures unique variance explaining individual differences in students' achievement.

In addition to the data collected during the course of the main study, we also collected data from a smaller sample of 115 students. The purpose of this sample was to evaluate the correlation between the *ZAT* and the *NAG5* in English and Mathematics. We expected to find convergent validity evidence between the relevant subtests of the *ZAT* and the two tests of the *NAG5*. Table 6.2 presents the results of this analysis.

The data reveal that the *NAG5* tests had sufficient internal-consistency reliability (Cronbach's $\alpha = .84$ for Mathematics and Cronbach's

Table 6.2

CORRELATIONS BETWEEN THE *ZAMBIAN NATIONAL ACHIEVEMENT* TEST AND THE *ZAMBIAN ACHIEVEMENT TEST*

	TEST	1	2	3	4	5	6
1	NAG5_M	–	115	92	92	92	90
2	NAG5_E	0.80***	–	91	91	91	89
3	ZAT_M_E	0.71***	0.67***	–	93	93	91
4	ZAT_RR_E	0.80***	0.79***	0.64***	–	93	91
5	ZAT_PW_E	0.63***	0.66***	0.53***	0.78***	–	91
6	ZAT_RC_E	0.69***	0.74***	0.66***	0.73***	0.68***	–

Note. NAG5_M = *Zambian National Achievement Test*, Grade 5 Mathematics; NAG5_E = *Zambian National Achievement Test,* Grade 5 English; ZAT_M_E = ZAT Mathematics Subtest, English; ZAT_RR_E = ZAT Reading Recognition Subtest, English; ZAT_PW_E = ZAT Pseudoword Decoding Subtest, English; ZAT_RC_E = ZAT Reading Comprehension Subtest, English.
*$p < .05$. **$p < .01$. ***$p < .001$.

$\alpha = .89$ for English) and that student achievement on all subtests of the *ZAT* and both tests of the *NAG5* are statistically significantly correlated. In particular, the Pearson correlation between the Mathematics subtest of the *ZAT* and the Mathematics portion of the *NAG5* was $r = .71$ ($p < .001$). In addition, the correlations were statistically significant between the *NAG5* English test and the Reading Recognition subtest of the *ZAT* ($r = .79$, $p < .001$), the Pseudoword Decoding subtest of the *ZAT* ($r = .66$, $p < .001$), and the Reading Comprehension subtest of the *ZAT* ($r = .74$, $p < .001$).

Thus, the *ZAT* exhibits excellent internal validity statistics (e.g., reliability) as well as promising evidence supporting the external validity of the measure.

DISCUSSION

Challenges in the Assessment of Abilities and Competencies in Zambia

There are a number of challenges associated with the development and adaptation of instruments in a new cultural context. Theses challenges include both technical issues and cultural issues, including but not limited to (1) ensuring accurate translation of the test items, (2) equating test difficulty when fundamental aspects of different languages vary in their complexity, (3) choosing the relevant basis for comparing students to one another (e.g., age vs. grade level), (4) differences in cultural norms that interact with test behavior, and (5) differences in student motivation that are culturally related.

With regard to the issue of translation, the first question one faces is which language(s) to use for the test. As is characteristic of the majority of African countries, Zambia has 10 languages spoken by more than 1% of the population, 7 of which are officially recognized. Current educational policy assumes that teaching in early primary grades is to be carried out in the mother tongue, with a gradual introduction of English in children's school careers. Although a given mother tongue can be predominant in a given geographical location, it is never universal because Zambia has many intertribal settlers and marriages. In such situations, English is often preferred as the communicational and instructional medium. Correspondingly, all assessments that required a student to use language were developed and administered in one of two languages, English or Nyanja, a predominant language of the Lusaka and Eastern Provinces of Zambia where this study was conducted. However, we must note right away that the diversity of tribal languages suggests that test-takers may possess higher levels of abilities and competencies than they are capable of expressing in English or even in Nyanja. Although this issue is an inherent limitation of all efforts at assessment, the issue is much more salient in the developing world and should temper our interpretation of the test results. Within the context of the current dataset, it seems that the dimension of cognition tapped by the *Panga Munthu* Test is closer to that tapped by tests in the children's indigenous language of everyday discourse than to that tapped by tests in the medium of English, which most of them only use at school.

Once the decision was made to develop the assessment instrument in two different languages (English and Nyanja), we faced the technical challenge of demonstrating that the difficulty of the test items was psychometrically equivalent across different languages. One useful approach to evaluating equivalence involves the construct plots of item difficulties across test forms (see Figure 6.3).

The Reading Recognition plot shows that students found the Nyanja items significantly easier than the English items on this subtest. This is not entirely surprising because Nyanja is a highly transparent language.

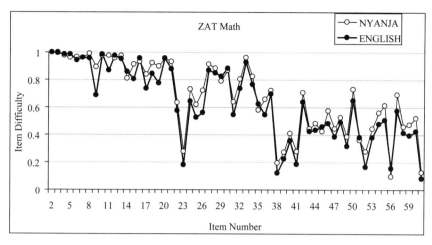

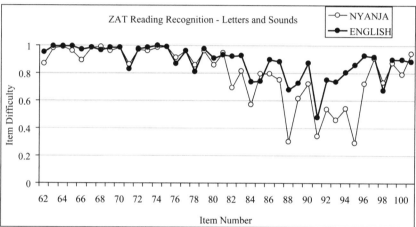

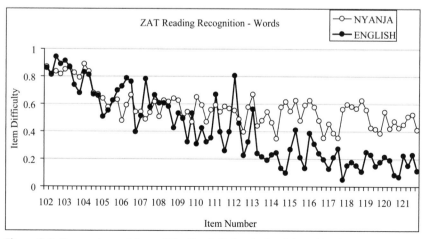

Figure 6.3 Comparison of item difficulty statistics in English v. Nyanja for the ZAT's subscales.

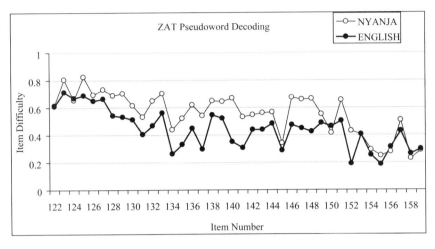

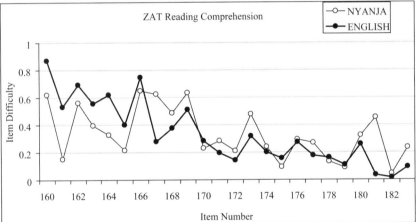

Figure 6.3 *(Continued)*

Once an individual masters the basic structure, there are few exceptions and reading/decoding becomes a fairly easy task. This explains the discrepancy in item difficulty across the tests. The encouraging news, however, is that the pattern of item difficulties remained constant across test versions. Thus, the items that were relatively more difficult in English also tended to be relatively more difficult in Nyanja (compared to easier items in the same language).

A third challenge we faced in the development of new tests in Zambia was whether to norm them on the basis of age or grade level. In contrast to Westernized countries such as the United States and United Kingdom, where age and grade level are almost perfectly correlated, age does not correlate as highly with grade level in Zambia. For our sample of 206 participants, for whom we had both age- and grade-level information, the Spearman rank correlation between age and grade was $\rho = .52$. Because the ZAT was designed as a measure of achievement that should predict school performance, we decided to norm the test on the basis of grade level.

In addition to the technical challenges associated with the development of culturally appropriate tests, there are also many cultural factors to consider that present challenges to the interpretation of test results. For example, cultures differ markedly with regard to norms of appropriate behavior. This was particularly salient to us in the development of the Reading Comprehension subtest of the ZAT. Recall that this subtest was designed as a performance assessment. The first item on the exam is "Jump" and students are instructed, "Do what this says." We realized quickly that there were certain words or commands that students in the Zambian context were simply not comfortable performing because they were outside of social norms. Furthermore, particular translation issues also became salient on this test. During the pilot testing, we discovered instances of words that could be interpreted in multiple ways, and these items had to be revised or discarded.

Finally, we noticed a marked difference in terms of the level of motivation students brought to the test. As gratitude for participation in the exams, students were offered snacks and drinks after completing the assessments. Our research team noted a few instances in which a student would attempt to take the battery of tests a second time, maybe in order to receive more snacks, or maybe because they enjoyed the novelty of the situation and the individualized attention. Because testing is relatively novel in this cultural context, most students exhibited higher levels of intrinsic motivation for the task than we have observed in some studies involving Western students, though some students may also have been made more nervous by the novelty of individual assessment.

CONCLUSIONS

Assessment is already woven into the fabric of Western schooling and is quickly gaining in importance across the globe. Yet, developing assessments of abilities and competencies cross-culturally is rarely as simple as importing currently existing Western-based tests of ability. As van de Vijver (2002) has pointed out, although Western measures may appear to measure a single invariant ability, such as memory or reasoning, differences in stimulus familiarity may call into question the precision of the cross-cultural equivalence of these constructs. Thus, the development and adaptation of tests of abilities and competencies should be solidly grounded in one's theoretical perspective about the nature of abilities and assessment cross-culturally (Sternberg, 2004).

This chapter presents the results of a collaborative study between researchers in the United States and Zambia seeking to develop culturally relevant measures of abilities and competencies. A series of Western-based tests of abilities were adapted and administered in the Zambian context and the results indicate that these measures seemed to travel reasonably well. The tests exhibited sufficient variability, strong reliability, and reasonable validity statistics when measures correlated with each other and with native tests of African intelligence.

In addition, we developed a new culturally based test of student achievement (ZAT) for use in assessing the achievement of students in Grades 1–7. Converging evidence indicates that the newly developed ZAT allows users to reliably and validly assess competencies of Zambian children in academic-related domains across a wide range of grades, ages, and number of years spent at school.

The development of psychometrically sound measures of abilities and competencies in the country of Zambia carries with it important implications for future research. Most notably, armed with psychometrically validated and culturally sensitive measures of abilities and competencies, future researchers will now be in a position to estimate the etiology of specific and nonspecific learning disabilities using the ability-achievement discrepancy. Furthermore, future researchers will be in a much better position to explore questions related to school effectiveness and student achievement.

Developing measures of abilities and competencies in the era of globalization brings with it several important challenges. Both technical and cultural factors play an important role in the quest to develop culturally sensitive measures; however, the development of psychometrically strong measures brings with it tremendous advances in our capacity to help both individuals and organizations understand how best to improve upon their strengths and remediate areas of weakness.

AUTHOR NOTE

This research was supported by a grant from the U.S. National Institutes of Health (NIH) under R21 TW006764 (PI: Grigorenko)

REFERENCES

Bellinger, D. C., & Adams, H. F. (2001). Environmental pollutant exposures and children's cognitive ability. In R. J. Sternberg & E. L. Grigorenko (Eds.), *Environmental effects on cognitive abilities* (pp. 157–188). Mahwah, NJ: Erlbaum.

Birney, D., & Stemler, S. E. (2007). Intelligence Quotient. In N. Salkind (Ed.), *Encyclopedia of measurement and statistics* (Vol. 2, pp. 473–476). Thousand Oaks, CA: Sage.

Bond, T., & Fox, C. (2001). *Applying the Rasch model.* Mahwah, NJ: Erlbaum.

Bracken, B. A., & McCallum, R. S. (1998). *The Universal Nonverbal Intelligence Test (UNIT).* Itasca, IL: Riverside Publishing.

Chrostowski, S. J., & Malak, B. (2004). Translation and cultural adaptation of the TIMSS 2003 instruments. In M. O. Martin, I. V. S. Mullis, & S. J. Chrostowski (Eds.), *TIMSS 2003 Technical Report.* Chestnut Hill, MA: Boston College.

Cole, M., Gay, J., Glick, J. A., & Sharp, D. W. (1971). *The cultural context of learning and thinking.* New York: Basic Books.

Ericsson, K. A., Krampe, R. T., & Tesch-Römer, C. (1993). The role of deliberate practice in the acquisition of expert performance. *Psychological Review, 100,* 363–406.

Goodenough, F. (1926). *Measurement of intelligence by drawings.* New York: World Book.

Grigorenko, E. L., & O'Keefe, P. (2004). What do children do when they cannot go to school? In R. J. Sternberg & E. L. Grigorenko (Eds.), *Culture and competence* (pp. 23–53). Washington, DC: American Psychological Association.

Harris, D. B. (1963). *Children's drawings as measures of intellectual maturity.* New York: Harcourt, Brace & World.

Individuals With Disabilities Education Act. (1997, 1999). 20 U.S.C. 1400 et seq. (Statute). 34 C.F.R. 300 (Regulations).

Kadison, R., & DiGeronimo, T. F. (2004). *College of the overwhelmed: The campus mental health crisis and what to do about it.* San Francisco: Jossey-Bass.

Kathuria, R., & Serpell, R. (1999). Standardization of the *Panga Munthu* test: A nonverbal cognitive test developed in Zambia. *Journal of Negro Education, 67,* 228–241.

Kaufman, A. S., & Kaufman, N. L. (2003). *Kaufman Assessment Battery for Children* (2nd ed.) *(KABC-II).* Circle Pines, MN: American Guidance Service.

Kelly, D. L., & Malak, B. (2003). Translating the PIRLS reading assessment and questionnaires. In M. O. Martin, I. V. S. Mullis, & A. M. Kennedy (Eds.), *PIRLS 2001 Technical Report.* Chestnut Hill, MA: Boston College.

Kelly, M. J., & Kanyika, J. (2000). *Learning achievement at the middle basic level: Summary report on Zambia's National Assessment Project 1999.* Lusaka, Zambia: Zambian Ministry of Education.

Labaree, D. F. (1997). *How to succeed in school without really learning.* New Haven, CT: Yale University Press.

Leithwood, K. (Ed.). (2000). *Understanding schools as intelligent systems.* Stamford, CT: JAI Press.

Lemann, N. (1999). *The big test: The secret history of the American meritocracy.* New York: Farrar, Straus, & Giroux.

LeVine, R. A., Dixon, S., LeVine, S., Richman, A., Leiderman, P. H., Keefer, C. H., et al. (1994). *Child care and culture: Lessons from Africa.* New York: Cambridge University Press.

Lyon, G. R., Fletcher, J. M., Shaywitz, S. E., Shaywitz, B. A., Torgesen, J. K., Wood, F. B., et al. (2001). Rethinking learning disabilities. In C. E. Finn, Jr., R. J. Rotherham, & C. R. Hokanson, Jr. (Eds.), *Rethinking special education for a new century* (pp. 259–287). Washington, DC: Thomas B. Fordham Foundation and Progressive Policy Institute.

Martin, M. O., Mullis, I. V. S., & Foy, P. (2008). *TIMSS 2007 international science report.* Chestnut Hill, MA: TIMSS & PIRLS International Study Center.

Mpofu, E., Peltzer, K., Shumba, A., Serpell, R., & Mogaji, A. (2005). School psychology in sub-Saharan Africa: Results and implications of a six-country survey. In C. L. Frisby & C. R. Reynolds (Eds.), *Comprehensive handbook of multicultural school psychology* (pp. 1128–1150). Hoboken, NJ: Wiley.

Mullis, I. V. S., Martin, M. O., & Foy, P. (2008). *TIMSS 2007 international mathematics report.* Chestnut Hill, MA: TIMSS & PIRLS International Study Center.

Nichols, S. L., & Berliner, D. C. (2007). *Collateral damage: How high-stakes testing corrupts American schools.* Cambridge, MA: Harvard Education Press.

Nsamenang, A. B. (1997). Towards an Afrocentric perspective in developmental psychology. *IFE Psychologia: An International Journal, 5,* 127–139.

Organisation for Economic Co-operation and Development (OECD). (2000). *Measuring student knowledge and skills: The PISA 2000 assessment of reading, mathematical, and scientific literacy.* Paris: Author.

Population Reference Bureau. (2008). *2008 world population data sheet.* Retrieved October 14, 2008, from http://www.prb.org/Publications/Datasheets/2008/2008wpds.aspx

Pritchett, L. (2001). Where has all the education gone? *The World Bank Economic Review, 15,* 367–391.

Programme for International Student Assessment (PISA). (2001). *Knowledge and skills for life: First results from PISA 2000.* Paris: OECD.

Rasch, G. (1960/1980). *Probabilistic models for some intelligence and attainment tests* (Expanded ed.). Chicago: University of Chicago Press.

Serpell, R. (1993). *The significance of schooling: Life-journeys in an African society.* New York: Cambridge University Press.

Serpell, R. (1999). Opportunities and constraints for research on education and human development in Africa: Focus on assessment and special education. *Prospects, XXIX,* 349–363.

Serpell, R., & Haynes, B. P. (2004). The cultural practice of intelligence testing: Problems of international export. In R. J. Sternberg & E. L. Grigorenko (Eds.), *Culture and competence: Contexts of life success* (pp. 163–185). Washington, DC: American Psychological Association.

Stemler, S. E. (2001). Examining school effectiveness at the fourth grade: A hierarchical analysis of the Third International Mathematics and Science Study (TIMSS). *Dissertation Abstracts International, 62*(03A), 919.

Sternberg, R. J. (1998). Abilities are forms of developing expertise. *Educational Researcher, 27*(3), 11–20.

Sternberg, R. J. (2004). Culture and intelligence. *American Psychologist,* 59(5), 325–338.

Super, C. M. (2005). The globalization of developmental psychology. In D. B. Pillemer & S. H. White (Eds.), *Developmental psychology and social change: Research, history and policy* (pp. 11–33). New York: Cambridge University Press.

Teddlie, C., & Reynolds, D. (Eds.). (2000). *The international handbook of school effectiveness research.* New York: Falmer Press.

UNICEF. (1999). *Multiple indicator cluster survey: Zambia.* Retrieved January 16, 2005, from http://www.childinfo.org/MICS2/newreports/zambia/zambiatables.pdf

U.S. Census Bureau. (2003). *International population reports.* Retrieved January 4, 2005, from http://www.census.gov/prod/www/abs/popula.html

van de Vijver, F. J. R. (2002). Inductive reasoning in Zambia, Turkey, and the Netherlands establishing cross-cultural equivalence. *Intelligence, 30,* 313–351.

The World Bank. (2008). *Key developmental data and statistics.* Retrieved from http://www.worldbank.org

The World Fact Book. (2006). *Guide to country profiles.* Retrieved January 10, 2006, from https://www.cia.gov/library/publications/the-world-factbook

Wright, B. D., & Stone, M. H. (1979). *Best test design.* Chicago: MESA.

7

Assessing Mother Tongue in the Era of Globalization: Promise and Challenge

ELENA L. GRIGORENKO, KELLY NEDWICK, DINAH KWADADE, ERIK BORO, LESLEY HART, TINA NEWMAN, AND LINDA JARVIN

As Africa struggles to fulfill the promise of the Free Primary Education (FPE) policy as a means of realizing the international targets of the 2015 Education for All and Millennium Development Goals (Inoue & Oketch, 2008; White, 2005), it faces a variety of issues that are Africa-specific. One of these issues pertains to the fact that in Africa, there are an estimated 3,000 spoken languages and as many as 8,000 dialects. These languages and dialects and their diversity are critically important for the development of many African cultures and societies (Owino, 2002).

These languages co-exist with the former colonial languages, and this co-existence generates a fair amount of both inspiration and tension. The general attitude of most African countries toward African languages was expressed in the Asmara Declaration on African Languages and Literatures (Asmara Declaration, 2000), which was generated in January 2000 in Asmara, Eretria, at the first conference on African languages and literatures ever to be held on African soil, with participants from east, west, north, and south Africa, and from the diaspora, as well as international writers and scholars.

1. African languages must take on the duty, the responsibility and the challenge of speaking for the continent.

2. The vitality and equality of African languages must be recognized as a basis for the future empowerment of African peoples.
3. The diversity of African languages reflects the rich cultural heritage of Africa and must be used as an instrument of African unity.
4. Dialogue among African languages is essential: African languages must use the instrument of translation to advance communication among all people, including the disabled.
5. All African children have the unalienable right to attend school and learn in their mother tongues. Every effort should be made to develop African languages at all levels of education.
6. Promoting research on African languages is vital for their development, while the advancement of African research and documentation will be best served by the use of African languages.
7. The effective and rapid development of science and technology in Africa depends on the use of African languages and modern technology must be used for the development of African languages.
8. Democracy is essential for the equal development of African languages and African languages are vital for the development of democracy based on equality and social justice.
9. African languages like all languages contain gender bias. The role of African languages in development must overcome this gender bias and achieve gender equality.
10. African languages are essential for the decolonization of African minds and for the African Renaissance.

Of these statements, statement 5 is of particular importance to the discussion in this chapter. Although accepted by the majority (if not all) of African countries, the realization of this statement has proven to be rather difficult. In this chapter we provide a general overview of the issues related to delivering education in mother tongues in Africa, and exemplify these issues by focusing specifically on the assessment of competencies in the mother tongues in Ghana. Our general discussion will be illustrated with specific data excerpts and conclude with some practical observations on the situation faced by the educational systems in Africa, which are striving to prepare their students for entry into the global market while recognizing the importance of preserving their ethnic, cultural, and linguistic identity.

THE CONCEPT OF MOTHER TONGUE

The concept of mother tongue is used to identify the language that is mastered naturally by members of a speaking community and utilized by them as the primary means of meaningful vocalization in their communication. Also, knowing a mother tongue often signifies an individual's belonging to a community, group, and/or family of people who share a common history, culture, and ancestry. Under typical circumstances (with the exception of multi-ethnic/cultural marriages) and in the absence of human-made (e.g., war) or natural disasters (e.g., earthquakes), the mother tongue of a child corresponds to that of his or her parents. This assumes that the mastery of a mother tongue usually coincides with an individual's socialization into cultural norms and customs and the acquisition of cognitive and social-emotional skills. Thus, acquisition of the mother tongue and the development of the corresponding vocabulary is a natural step in preparing a child for formal education (Abiri, 2003; Adetunberu & Oluwafoise, 1992; Blake, 2004; Fafunwa, 1977; Mohanlal, 2001).

In Africa, for the majority of children, formal education is delivered in a language that is foreign to the child and, in many cases, might have not been spoken by the child prior to his or her arrival at school. This approach to education has been described as a barrier to effective teaching and learning (Urevbu, 2001). Correspondingly, there is a global movement in African countries to bring mother tongues into formal education to ensure the best possible educational outcome for children of all backgrounds and languages.

However, what appears to be a good idea overall might not be (and is not) easily realized. The first problem in this idea's realization is the sheer number of mother tongues. For example, South Africa has 25 spoken languages (Lemmer, 1993). Similarly, Kenya is a linguistically heterogeneous country with more than 40 indigenous languages (Mbaabu, 1996). Nigeria is also a multilingual society, with more than 400 indigenous languages (Iyamu & Ogiegbaen, 2007). Clearly, amassing the resources required to deliver quality education in all mother tongues is simply insurmountable. Hence, countries must make choices with regard to what indigenous languages are taught at school, and they should follow through with clear and consistent policies. But this does not always happen. For example, in Kenya, 16 mother tongues are taught in school, yet the process of their language selection and the policy for teaching or dealing with the mother tongues that are not being taught are not clear (Musau, 2003).

To add to the laundry list of complications, not everyone living in Africa has a mother tongue. In fact, for the overwhelming majority of African countries, the issues of bilingualism (Banda, 1996) and multilingualism (De Klerk, 1996; Winkler, 1997) are serious ones. It is of note that those who speak at least one African language (i.e., mother/home tongue) tend to be multilingual, while those who speak the "official" language of the country and not the mother tongue tend to be either monolingual or at most bilingual (Banda, 2000). Thus, what should be expected of an African child who does not have a mother tongue or whose mother tongue is a minority/absent tongue in the particular geographical region where the child is growing up?

In short, there is an ongoing debate about the role and place of mother tongue in the development and education of a child (formal and informal [Adjei, 2007]), which is central to issues of national identity and priorities in educational programs in Africa. This debate, at this point, appears to be far from resolved (Sonaiya, 2003).

ATTEMPTS AT FINDING A SOLUTION

While there is a consensus among educators and academicians throughout the African continent that mother/home tongues should be at the core of bilingual educational programs (Alexander, 1995; Chumbow, 2005; Heugh, 1995; Luckett, 1995), this consensus is met with a certain degree of resistance from teachers (Ejieh, 2004), parents, and the general populace (Muthwii, 2004). This resistance is driven by the realization that English (or any other official language of a given country, whether it is French, Portuguese, Spanish, or Arabic) is associated with opportunities for postprimary education, the acquisition of better jobs, and better placements in society (Adegbite, 2003; Banda, 2000; De Klerk, 1996; Iyamu & Ogiegbaen, 2007; Lanham, 1996; Muthwii, 2002, 2004; Smit, 1996; Sure & Webb, 2000). Moreover, the "elite" layers of various African societies often possess and demonstrate negative attitudes toward using mother tongues as languages of school instruction or formal communication (Musau, 2003). Given these tensions, it is especially useful to review the existing policies concerning mother tongue languages that are in effect, their benefits and drawbacks, which are described within the current literature.

In Kenya, government language policy requires the use of the mother tongue as the language of instruction in primary school up to Grade

(Standard) 3. At this stage of learning, English and Kiswahili (the country's official languages) are taught as subjects, but from Grades 4–8, English is adopted as the language of instruction in all schools. The usage of the mother tongue as the school-entry medium of instruction is believed to ensure a smooth transition between the child's home and school, to connect the child's knowledge base mastered at home with the knowledge base to be mastered at school, to maintain the child's connection to the indigenous culture of his or her community in which the mother tongue is spoken, to allow the expression of early experiences of growing up, and to form the foundation for learning a second or third language (Muthwii, 2004; Parry, 2000).

Despite the many good reasons for using the mother tongue during the first years of a child's education, this policy is rather difficult to implement for a variety of reasons. Below we describe seven such reasons, although they most likely do not cover all of the related issues and concerns.

First, the variety of mother tongues that are used in Kenya requires a cadre of qualified professionals to teach in these languages. In fact, the mother tongues are so numerous that it is simply presumptuous to assume that high-quality instruction in all of them is even possible. Not all teachers are ready to teach in mother tongues (Musau, 2003). The fact that someone speaks the language does not mean that that person can teach the language or teach well in the language. Moreover, the practice on the ground shows that teacher assignments to particular geographical regions are often made irrespective of the mother tongue of the teacher himself or herself. So, there are often situations when a new teacher arrives to his or her post not speaking the language of the area in which he or she is to teach. An added complexity is that due to the increased mobility of African tribes and populations "the concept of 'mother tongue' is increasingly becoming fuzzy" (Banda, 2000, p. 59), bringing us to the concept of "regional language education" (Banda, 2000, p. 59). This separate, parallel idea proposes the harmonization of African languages by developing meta-languages from languages that show high levels of mutual intelligibility (Prah, 1998). But, however rational and appealing this idea might be, there are also serious practical obstacles to its realization regarding how the languages "to be blended" are to be selected, and whether the people who currently speak these languages will accept the idea of subsuming their own languages into a new meta-language (Musau, 2003). Remarkably enough, as a consequence of well-intentioned but poorly executed mother-tongue policies, the popular demand for education in

English has increased while the demand for education in mother tongues has plummeted to levels lower than before the policy-driven promotion of early education in local languages (Krishnamurti, 1990).

Second, there is an ongoing debate with regard to when the switch from the indigenous to "official" language of instruction should happen. For example, it was proposed (Luckett, 1995)—capitalizing on the distinction (Cummins, 1981) between basic interpersonal communicative skills, BICS, and cognitive academic language proficiency, CALP—that the transition between languages of instruction should take place only after CALP in the mother tongue has been accomplished. If otherwise (i.e., if CALP in the mother tongue has not been accomplished), it appears that the transfers between the languages either do not happen or happen in a deficient manner (Luckett, 1995). Yet, it has been argued that CALP takes 5–7 years to achieve, and waiting for it to take place might prevent the adequate development of the official language of instruction due to time constraints. Correspondingly, the literature also contains a more measured argument suggesting that instruction in both mother-tongue and the official language of instruction can start fairly early, but have to be of high quality (Muthwii & Kioko, 2003). Yet, the specifics of how this high quality can be achieved are neither demonstrated nor explicated.

A third factor impeding the use of mother tongues in early education is that, even if a consensus is reached with regard to which language needs to be used for what purpose and for how long, these general recommendations would need to be adopted at painstaking levels of detail for all of the mother tongues used in formal education. Any model of bilingual education should be adjusted for the specifics of the languages it targets, thus no single model of bilingual education is universally applicable (Tickoo, 1993). While teaching may be carried out in mother tongues, the methodologies used for teaching, for example, reading, are not mother-tongue specific, but borrowed from other linguistic and sociocultural environments (Stroud, 2003). These borrowed pedagogical approaches "based on the linguistic characteristics of European languages and ignoring the distinctiveness of African languages, only serves to further disadvantage people who are already marginalized where literacy learning is concerned" (Trudell & Schroeder, 2007, p. 166). Correspondingly, researchers (Finlayson & Slabbert, 2003; Trudell & Schroeder, 2007) argue for the importance of using pedagogical techniques that reflect the linguistic, socioeducational, and cultural realities of African communities. However, these recommendations are far from being developed and applied in the everyday reality of African schools. In fact, one stark feature of this reality is the absence of standardized literacy materials in mother-tongue languages that are suitable for the classroom. This is because, first, not all mother tongues have written orthographies. And second, when orthographies do exist, often there is a gap between the spoken and printed versions of the language because the latter may ignore significant prosodic features of the former, such as tone, vowel length, and vowel quality. These gaps might make the printed material difficult even for an experienced reader let alone a novice (Kioko, 2002). Thus, on top of preparing programs, there is also the challenge of preparing printed materials that can be used in these programs within the context of formal school instruction (Muthwii & Kioko, 2003). In other words, although in theory the argument to teach reading, at least initially, in the spoken language is based on a large body of literature demonstrating both its effectiveness (Adams, 1994) and more positive emotional outcome (Alidou et al., 2006; Dutcher, 2004), this argument is difficult to implement in practice, and the resulting difficulties, especially as they present themselves in Africa, are important to understand.

Fourth, there is also evidence that teaching other than mother-tongue subjects in the mother tongue might not be the most effective pedagogical strategy (Mooko, 2004). It appears that even when there is a majority African language in a particular African country, such as Setswana in Botswana (Bagwasi, 2003), this language might lack the vocabulary needed to teach such subjects as mathematics and sciences (Mooko, 2004). Thus, the idea of teaching all subjects in primary school in the mother tongue might not be easily implemented, even for developed indigenous languages such as Setswana.

Fifth, a number of African researchers and commentators on the mother-tongue policy have pointed out the conflict between the policy of encouraging the mother tongue as a language of instruction and the reality that English (or some other former colonial language) is the dominant language of all postprimary levels of education and all levels of the job market. Mother tongues are not used for purposes of examination at any level of postprimary education, and they are not used within any levels of societal life except those concerning immediate community and family. This lack of continuity in the usage of mother tongue and in the significance of mother tongue outside of the primary-school setting is also a challenge to the acceptance of the mother-tongue education policies by both parents and educators (Muthwii, 2004).

Sixth, overall, the system of education in Africa, at least in the majority of its countries, does not seem to be working at its optimal level; however well-defined and structured, African educational policies appear to be generally ineffective. This, in particular, is evidenced by the rather unsatisfactory levels of literacy in many African nations. Although the existing data are close to minimal, there have been some large-scale projects whose data have contributed to this assertion. For example, in collaboration with the Southern and Eastern Africa Consortium for Monitoring Educational Quality (SACMEQ[1]), the ministries responsible for primary education carried out studies designed to measure the mastery of reading in English among Standard 6 pupils in 1998 (in Kenya and Zimbabwe) and among Primary 7 pupils in 1999 (in Uganda). The levels of mastery were conceptualized at two levels, *minimum/adequate* (i.e., the mastery necessary for the recognition of basic linguistic building blocks, i.e., the alphabet and simple words) and *desirable/advanced* (i.e., the mastery necessary for successful learning within the context of the curriculum used in Standard 7). The results (as cited in Muthwii & Kioko, 2003) showed that, respectively, in Uganda, Zimbabwe, and Kenya, 35%, 54%, and 87% failed to achieve the minimum/adequate level, and 98%, 75%, and 75% failed to achieve the desirable/advanced level of competency in English. Consistently, children attending urban schools did better than children attending rural schools and boys did better than girls. Similarly, although 33% of the total population of Nigeria are reported to be literate in English, only 15% are reported as able to use English effectively in professional and administrative activities (Simire, 2003). There is also data suggesting that even at higher levels of education (e.g., university) the mastery of English remains at the nonnative level (Alimi, 2007; Kembo-Sure, 2003), with English being perceived as a foreign language, even in countries where it is the official language.

The point made above is closely related to the seventh observation that, in Africa, both former dominant (e.g., European or Arabic) and indigenous languages are undergoing constant change. Africans, whatever country they are from, seem to prefer to use the so-called official or former dominant/colonial language as a tool for socioeconomic mobility, while preserving their linguistic and cultural identity by learning and using their mother tongues or multiple African languages (Banda, 2000). In fact, those dominant languages themselves are transformed through their assimilation of indigenous African languages, while retaining enough of the former dominant languages to be understood by non-Africans (Ndebele, 1987). For example, in South Africa there are varieties of English, such as Indian English, Black English, White Afrikaans English, and White "mother-tongue" English (Schmied, 1991). Similarly, in Kenya, a number of varieties of English, for example, ethnically marked Kenyan English, standard Kenyan English, and native-speaker English (i.e., British, American, and Australian), are distinguished. It is of note that there are data suggesting that among these so-called English(es) the most preferred one by both rural and urban respondents for use in the media and education is standard Kenyan English (Kioko & Muthwii, 2003). To add to the complexity created by these developing colonial language variants, African languages themselves continue to change and evolve. This process, referred to as "effective and continuous restandardisation" (Finlayson & Slabbert, 2003, p. 165), from one point of view, reflects normal development that is characteristic of "live" languages. However, from another point of view, it simply makes the task of developing printed materials suitable for teaching and assessing in these languages difficult.

A RELATED DIFFICULTY: LINKING INSTRUCTION AND ASSESSMENT

There is rich literature that discusses the issue of language proficiency as a potential source of bias in interpreting the results of ability and achievement assessments of African children (Claassen, 1997; Foxcroft, 1997; Grieve, 2005; Owen, 1991). This issue has been empirically investigated in South Africa and it has been asserted that when a child experiences two different languages at home and at school, assessing the child's abilities and achievement in either language puts the child at a disadvantage (van den Berg, 1996).

Thus, the ideal theoretical recommendation is to carry out a bilingual assessment, that is, to test the child in the home language and the language of instruction (Foxcroft, 1997; van den Berg, 1996). However, this ideal solution is not always possible. Numerous difficulties (e.g., Wallis & Birt, 2003) prevent the implementation of this ideal solution, among which are many of the issues discussed above, specifically, the large number of languages spoken at home, the tremendous amount of variation in the usage of tribal languages as they are spoken at home, the rapid evolution of these languages over time, difficulties related to translations into and from these languages, and the dearth of professionals who can deliver assessments in multiple languages.

Consequently, because the ideal solution cannot be accomplished, a range of solutions exists where testing in a particular language is conditioned on the consideration of language proficiency (e.g., van Eeden & Mantsha, 2007). As empirical literature on assessing language proficiency in African indigenous languages is very limited, it is nearly impossible to comment on how this recommendation is or can be implemented in practice. Thus, the uneasy suspicion is that many African children are at a "double" disadvantage: first, there is a gap between home languages and the dominant language of instruction at the school (at least at postprimary levels); and second, there are no assessment materials in virtually any (or any!) African mother tongue that can be paralleled with an assessment in the dominant language.

To attempt to get a first-hand impression of the plausibility of such an assessment in a mother tongue, we undertook a study of children's expressive vocabulary in Ghana, assessing children in the language of their preference (the language they primarily use). Given the scope of the problem, we wanted to develop an instrument that would be relatively easy to generate and replicate, if needed, in other mother tongues. This is especially important in an environment where financial and human resource support for any assessment development is lacking. Specifically, in our project, an expressive vocabulary scale was developed in English and three indigenous languages of Ghana, then administered to 1,220 Ghanaian children in one out of the four languages (English, $n = 445$, Ewe, $n = 223$, Gonja, $n = 296$, and Twi, $n = 256$), 818 of whom were enrolled in schools (approximately 200 in each of the 1–4 grades) and 404 of whom were not.

Below we provide brief descriptions of the three African languages studied and compare their specific characteristics to English to illustrate their similarities and dissimilarities, and to outline the scope of our task and its degree of difficulty.

LANGUAGES STUDIED

The number of indigenous languages listed for Ghana is 79 (Gordon, 2005). The present study assessed the expressive vocabulary skills of speakers of four languages: English, Ewe, Gonja, and Twi. English is the lingua franca for Ghana, taught in local schools alongside the predominant language of the area. Since English is not a native language of Ghana, all English speakers there are bilingual. However, many are

Table 7.1

VOCABULARY EXAMPLES

ENGLISH	EWE	GONJA	TWI
Hammer	Zu	Kusɔmnyiakabilso	Hamma
Anchor	Seke	Kanyanto	Sɛkyɛ
Banana	Akɔdu	Kodu	Kwadu
Eating	Ele nu dum	Kapasojibi	ɔredidi

multilingual, speaking their home language, the regional language (Ewe, Gonja, or Twi), and English.

The three African languages of Ghana are quite distinct and mutually unintelligible; however, all being from the Kwa branch of the Niger-Congo family, they do have a lot in common. The word order in main clauses for all three African languages is Subject-Verb-Object (SVO), like English. While each language's phonetic inventory is different from that of English, they all descend from a common ancestral phonetic inventory and so share many of the same sounds. Unlike English, Ewe, Gonja, and Twi are tone languages. In this section, the available information on each of the three African languages used in this study will be highlighted. Table 7.1 gives vocabulary examples for each language.

Ewe

Ewe (sometimes written Evegbe) is classified as a Gbe language that falls under the Kwa branch of the Niger-Congo family (Gordon, 2005). It is the most prevalent of the Gbe languages, spoken by up to 3 million people in sub-Saharan Africa with the majority living in Ghana and the rest in Togo and parts of Benin (Agbedor, 1994; Ameka, Dench, & Evans, 2006). Ewe has many mutually intelligible dialects but also a standard spoken dialect based on the dialect of the coastal areas. There is also a standard written form of Ewe that was developed in the 19th century and is used in government, churches, and schools.

The first "book Ewe" developed by German missionaries was based on the Latin alphabet. Later, in the early 1930s, the African Alphabet (also based on the Latin with a mix of IPA, International Phonetic Alphabet) was adopted for many languages including Ewe (Duthie, 1996). In the 1990s a Gbe Uniform Standard Orthography (GUSO) was proposed and work was done to prepare Ewe documents in GUSO, but no final decision was ever made. There are 32 letters in the Ewe version of the African Alphabet (7 vowels, 25 consonants). Diacritics are used to mark nasality and tone. In 1996 there were reportedly more than 200 publications written originally in Ewe (Duthie, 1996). Today, there are Ewe daily newspapers, school materials, and television shows.

The number of sounds in Ewe is different from its number of letters. Ewe has 8 vowels, each of which can be long or short, nasal or open /i, e, ɛ, ə, a, ɔ, o, u/. Of the three languages studied, Ewe has the largest consonant inventory (28), with 9 sonorants including alveolar, palatal, and velar nasals and approximants as well as the bilabial nasal /m/, velar approximant /w/, and alveolar trill /r/. There are also 19 obstruents in the Ewe phonetic inventory (not all are fully contrastive). There are voiced and voiceless alveolar, velar, bilabial, and labiodental fricatives. As for plosives, there is a voiced alveolar /d/ and bilabial /b/ but no voiceless counterparts. There are both voiced and voiceless dental /t,d²/, velar /k,g/, and labial velar /kp, gb/ pairs.

Ewe has (C1)(C2)V syllables where C2 can be approximants and C1 can be all other consonants. Each syllable must bear a tone. Textbooks often gloss this as either high tone or nonhigh tone, but in reality, each syllable's tone interacts with those around it producing High, Low, Mid, Falling, and Rising tones. Only occasionally are tones marked orthographically and then only high tones (Duthie, 1996). As is common in tone languages, there is both downstep and downdrift in long utterances, which means that the high tone in the last word of an utterance will not be as high as the high tone in the first word of that same utterance.

Ewe is an isolating SVO language that relies heavily on agglutination, which means that although most morphemes are considered whole words, many words are formed by a complex concatenation of particles (morphemes that are not thought of as whole words).

While there is not a large amount of literature available, there are extensive comments on the syntax of Ewe (Aikhenvald & Dixon, 2006; Ameka, 1994).

Gonja

Gonja is an African language spoken by about 230,000 people mostly living in Ghana. Gonja is classified in the Kwa branch of the Niger-Congo language family (Gordon, 2005). The full classification is Niger-Congo, Atlantic-Congo, Volta-Congo, Kwa, Nyo, Potou-Tano, Tano, Guang, and North Guang. Literacy is reportedly very low (1%–5%), and no specific orthographic information is available, although there are several vernacular publications. Additionally, Gonja is the primary language of instruction for the Gonja district (Kluge & Hatfield, 2002), so it is likely that the alphabet issued by the Bureau of Ghana Languages that is used for Ewe and Twi has also been standardized for Gonja.

Of the three Kwa languages studied here, Gonja has the fewest number of vowels (7: /i, e, ɛ, a, ɔ, o, u/) and consonants (20). Gonja has labial, alveolar, and glottal voiceless fricatives (/f,s,h/) and stops both voiced (/b,d,g/) and voiceless (/p,t,k/), as well as the nasal stops /m,n,ŋ,nʲ,nˠ/ and the approximants /l,r,j/. Gonja also has the labial-velars /kp, gb, w/ (Casali, 1995; Painter, 1970). Like Ewe, Gonja is a tone language with two main tones, high and low. The interaction between grammatical and lexical tones can also occasionally produce rising and falling tones, and there is downdrift and downstep in long utterances.

Gonja's syllable structure is (C*)V(C). Only sonorants are acceptable as syllable final consonants, though the overwhelming majority of syllables are left open. Like Ewe, it is an isolating agglutinating SVO language.

The landmark linguistic work on Gonja is Painter's (1970) *Gonja: A Phonological and Grammatical Study*, a comprehensive account of Gonja's phonetics, phonology, morphology, and some syntax. Other works have focused on societal structure in Ghana, including sociolinguistic factors (Kluge & Hatfield, 2002).

Twi

Asante Twi (also written Ashanti) is an African language from the Kwa branch of the Niger-Congo family (Gordon, 2005). It is considered a dialect of Akan along with Akuapem Twi, Fante, and a host of others. The full genealogy is Niger-Congo, Atlantic-Congo, Volta-Congo, Kwa, Nyo, Potou-Tano, Tano, Central, and Akan. Asante Twi is spoken by about 1.9 million people in Ghana. The Asante province was historically a powerful territory, and today much of Ghanaian popular music is recorded in Asante Twi. Twi is written in the standard alphabet created by the Bureau of Ghana Languages.

Twi's consonant inventory consists of labial, alveolar, dorsal voiceless fricatives (/f,s,h/) and stops both voiced (/b,d,g/) and voiceless (/p,t,k/) as well as the nasal stops /m,n/. There is an alveolar nasal geminate /nn/, a liquid /r/, and labialized versions of each /kʷ, gʷ, hʷ, nʷ, nnʷ, w/. Additionally, Twi has 10 vowels /i, e, æ, o, u, ɪ, ɛ, ɑ, ɔ, ʊ/, which are sometimes nasalized (Dolphyne, 1988). Asante Twi, unlike Akuapem Twi, has only open syllables with optional multiple onset consonants. Twi exhibits vowel harmony (+/– ATR) (Berry, 1957), syllabic nasals (Dolphyne, 1996), palatalization, and labialization. There are three tones (high, low, mid) in Asante Twi. Initial syllables of words may not hold a mid tone. Like most tone languages, there is downstep and downdrift in long utterances.

Like Ewe and Gonja, Asante Twi is an isolating language that also employs agglutination. Twi has a default SVO word order, but OV is possible in subordinate clauses. While Asante Twi and general Akan syntax and semantics have received a fair amount of attention in recent linguistic literature (Amfo, 2005, 2007; Obeng, 1999), its morphology has received less.

Thus, the African languages Twi, Gonja, and Ewe are very similar to each other, but also share many phonological and morphological characteristics with English. As an illustration, in Table 7.1, it is clear that all three languages share a historical antecedent for the word *banana*. In each case the /k/ and /d/ sounds are retained while the vowels have changed. Yet this is not always the case, as for the word *anchor*, for which Gonja has innovated a new vocabulary item while it is clear that the Ewe and Twi vocabulary items have evolved from a common source. In the case of *hammer*, Twi has borrowed from English. Ewe and Gonja have completely different vocabulary items for this object, so it is difficult to tell if either has retained traces of the ancestral vocabulary item. Finally, for the present participle *eating*, Ewe employs a periphrastic method of conjugation, while Gonja and Twi show a suffix, /ibi/ or /idi/, which probably derives from a common source. So, while this table gives the flavor of the vocabulary for each language, it also shows some of the similarities and differences between the languages.

ASSESSING EXPRESSIVE VOCABULARY IN CHILD-PREFERRED LANGUAGE

This investigation was based on the simple idea of quantifying the knowledge of the same list of words presented in the four different languages spoken in Ghana among children enrolled in school (rural and urban schools, Grades 1–4). The words were selected in the style of existing expressive vocabulary tests, such as those on the Kaufman Assessment

Battery for Children (KABC-II) and the Clinical Evaluation of Language Fundamentals (CELF-4). The majority of the words chosen were concrete nouns, and the remainder were action verbs. They were originally ordered based on frequencies provided by Kucera and Francis via the Psycholinguistic Database (http://www.psy.uwa.edu.au/mrcdatabase/uwa_mrc.htm). Through consultation with Ghanaian colleagues, some words were replaced due to cultural inappropriateness, and some words were re-ordered to reflect the suspected frequency of use in Ghana. The final list included 47 words. Prior to the beginning of the study, all of the words were piloted with native speakers of all four languages, both adults and children. The words did not generate any difficulties and were identifiable and recognizable. A child was presented with pictures depicting an object or an action and was asked to generate an associated word. The child was either asked "What is this?" (object) or "What is he or she doing?" (action). Answers were coded according to the rubrics, with acceptable answers receiving the score of "1" and unacceptable the score of "0."

We based this assessment on the basic idea that when a list of concepts is presented to children in comparable languages (see above), each presentation will elicit comparable responses. We made sure that the samples of the children who spoke mother tongues were comparable in their demographic characteristics (e.g., rural vs. urban areas, gender, grade, and schooling status). Because English is learned in Ghana primarily in schools, all children who were selected to respond to the task in English were enrolled in school.

The results (raw percentages) of the completion of this task in the four languages investigated are shown in Table 7.2.

Four comments should be made based on the results presented here. First, it appears that words vary dramatically in their degree of familiarity to the assessed children, from being almost unknown to the majority to being known to almost all children. This indicates that a fairly simple exercise of compiling a list of words can be helpful in quantifying individual differences between children speaking in different languages.

Second, although there is much variation between items and languages, it is notable that, roughly speaking, items can be split into four categories: easy, somewhat difficult, difficult, and very difficult, and that this categorization of items appears to be consistent across the four languages (e.g., items that appear to be difficult in one language appear to be difficult in another).

FREQUENCY OF CORRECT RESPONSES

Table 7.2

ENGLISH		EWE		GONJA		TWI	
ITEM	% C(I)	ITEM	% C(I/O)	ITEM	% C(I/O)	ITEM	% C(I/O)
Fish	93.7	Tɔmelã	96.6/65.9	Kurɔtɔ	61.9/92.5	Apataa	94.9/86.5
Hen	87.4	Koklonɔ	68.2/95.2	Koshiche	91.8/88.5	Akokɔ bere	73.9/66.9
Tire/wheel	80.3	Lɔriʃɔkpo	49.7/31.8	Kɔba	63.9/47.0	Lɔri/tire	63.8/54.8
Whistle	43.9	Ekpe	49.0/38.8	Kabil	48.5/36.0	Aben	45.7/38.7
Fire	74.0	Dzo dzobibi	51.7/31.8	Adɛ	60.8/53.0	Ogya	60.1/36.3
Policeman/guard/soldier	73.5	Kpovitɔ	30.3/24.7	Chekanto	84.5/50.5	Polisini	60.9/46.0
Maize	86.5	Ebli	87.6/58.8	Aboyu	91.8/83.0	Aburow betem	83.3/54.0
Watch/wristwatch	90.4	Wɔtsi/gaf odokui	94.5/55.3	Kussscheso	86.6/82.5	Nsa wɔɔkye	86.1/52.4
Cassette/tape cassette	73.9	Haʃoka/kasete	49.7/12.8	Kashebekusɔ manyiaso	62.9/54.4	Kasɛete	61.6/32.9
Car/taxi	95.1	Evu/taxi	93.1/57.6	Akuloŋ	94.8/88.0	Torinka/taxi	90.6/55.6
Banana/plantain	91.9	Akɔdu	89.0/52.9	Kodu	86.6/80.5	Kwadu	87.0/50.0

English						
Cutting/sawing wood	72.0	Eleatidzem	78.6/45.9	Kegbanfu	44.3/38.5	Dua dwumfo/ɔretwa duam	75.4/45.3
Chair	89.0	Ablɔgɔ/zikpe	90.3/55.3	Kabɛ	64.9/55.0	Akenten-gua	84.8/54.0
Bowl	63.7	Tsikugba/agba	60.0/32.9	Chansi	41.2/30.5	Kankyee	47.1/24.2
Engine/motor	14.8	Dzonamɔ/generator	13.1/9.4	Kebilso	6.2/9.5	Afiri engyin	9.4/10.5
Photocopier/copy machine	9.6	Agbaléɔlɔmɔ/photocopier	5.5/2.4	Photocopier	4.1/2.5	Photo-copier	2.2/4.0
Needle/sewing needle	42.4	Tɔnui/abui	51.7/30.6	Kebasibi	45.5/34.5	Paane	26.8/16.1
Ball/tennis ball	80.7	Bɔɔl	82.1/44.7	Bɔl	83.5/45.0	Tɛnise bɔɔl	68.8/33.1
Toothpaste/cream/lotion/ointment	54.0	Numeklɔtike/aduklɔmi	17.6/8.2	Nku	11.7/2.5	ɛse twitwi aduru	16.7/4.0
Telephone/phone	44.8	Kaƒomɔ	12.4/8.2	Tangrafo	5.2/2.0	Tɛlefɔn	23.9/9.7
Crocodile/alligator	54.6	Elo	37.9/22.4	Lanchaŋ	54.6/38.5	ɔdenkyem	29.7/15.3
Castle/mosque/palace/fort(ress)	29.4	Mɔ/ƒiasa	28.3/8.2	Lanbu	55.7/29.5	Abankɛse	1.4/2.4
Calf/lamb	15.9	Alevi	10.3/5.6	Kebulpɔ bi	55.7/86.1	Oguan	5.1/8.3
Anchor	3.6	Seke/agblɔ	1.4/2.4	Kanyanto	2.1/2.0	Sɛkyɛ	0.7/1.6

(Continued)

Table 7.2

FREQUENCY OF CORRECT RESPONSES (*CONTINUED*)

ENGLISH		EWE		GONJA		TWI	
ITEM	% C(I)	% C(I/O)	ITEM	ITEM	% C(I/O)	ITEM	% C(I/O)
Tent	8.3	2.1/2.4	Agbadɔ	Kuyoyul	4.1/1.0	Ntamadan	1.4/1.6
Zebra	45.1	15.2/3.5	Zebra	Kucliɔŋ	12.4/6.5	Sisi	18.1/4.8
Shoe/canvas/cambuk	54.9	37.9/11.8	Afɔkpa	Asibta	52.6/28.5	Mpaboa/kambuu	19.6/4.0
Jumper/cardigan/sweater	37.7	31.0/10.6	Awulegbe/ɔ mawu	Agbada	75.3/29.5	Sweeta	7.2/1.6
Worm/earthworm	24.2	8.3/4.7	Vɔkli/vɔklui	Chɔnchɔn	41.2/11.5	Osunson	2.9/0.8
Vase/pot	54.0	34.5/9.4	Eze	Kapuliya	69.1/24.5	Ahina/ nhwiren kuruwa	18.8/3.2
Thumb	26.9	24.1/8.2	Adɛglɛfetsu	Kasilbinio	56.7/18.5	Kokurobeti	6.5/0.8
Thermometer	8.7	2.8/2.4	Dzoxɔɔkpɔmɔ/ tɛmomita	Karso	1.0/2.4	Tɛmomita	0.7/0.0
Drum	41.0	17.2/7.1	Vuʄoʄo	Kakure	17.5/7.0	Akyene	10.9/3.2
Flying	57.1	37.2/11.8	Edzodzom	Kafrigi/frigi	75.3/26.0	ɔretu	19.6/3.2
Eating/having a meal	53.6	37.2/9.4	Ele nu dum	Kapasojibi	55.7/23.0	ɔredidi	20.3/3.2
Rowing/waving/driving	25.8	17.2/7.1	Tɔdziou	Kafar	28.9/15.0	ɔrehare ɔ korow	4.3/0.8

	%C		C/O		C/O		C/O
Reading	51.3	Ele agbaléxlem/nuxlem	33.1/7.1	Kakraŋ	49.5/15.5	Ɔrekenkan	17.4/3.2
Playing a trumpet	21.7	Ele kpekum	29.7/11.8	Kafonkabil/kabil	55.7/18.5	Ɔrebɔ atentɛben/abɛn	3.6/2.4
Symbols/signs	10.3	Dzesiwo	3.4/3.5	Nkarga	16.5/4.5	Ntiamu ahorow	0.7/0.0
Money, 1,000 cedis	52.0	Ega	37.5/11.8	Amashirbi	54.6/24.5	Sika	20.3/3.2
Soccer (football) team/players	19.1	Bɔlƒolawo	6.2/4.7	Kamnyiabɔl	22.7/10.0	Bɔɔlobɔfo	3.6/0.8
Band/musicians/instrumentalists	32.6	Hadzilawo	32.4/10.6	Kashiponpo	38.1/18.0	Banbɔfo/band	5.1/2.4
Hammer	39.5	Zu/hamma	18.6/7.1	Kusɔ mnyiakabilso	46.4/19.5	Hamma	13.8/3.2
Octopus	13.0	Abosa	5.5/4.7	Octopus	3.1/2.0	Posena	3.6/0.0
Pine cone	52.8	Atimakpa	32.4/10.6	Pine cone	58.3/24.0	Nhaban ne aba	14.5/1.6
Monkey/baboon	55.4	Kese/ʃie	31.7/9.4	Lakasa	66.0/24.0	Kontrofi	15.9/3.2
Tortoise/turtle	40.1	Eklo	30.3/9.4	Sonkur	52.6/23.5	Apataa	13.8/2.4

Note. % C = % correct answers; (I) = Children in school; (O) = Children out of school.

Third, children who go to school appear to be performing, on average, better than children who are not enrolled in school. These results indicate that vocabulary acquisition, even for mother tongues, appears to be happening more effectively for children who are enrolled in school versus the children who are not.

Finally, of note is the amount of variation in the children's responses to specific items between different languages (e.g., the picture of *crocodile/alligator* was correctly named by 54.6% of the in-school children tested in English, 39.7% tested in Ewe, 54.6% tested in Gonja, and only by 29.4% tested in Twi). This variation is rather unexpected to us and needs to be investigated further. A number of possible explanations might be of interest here. First, the data for these three indigenous languages were collected in different geographical regions of Ghana. Thus, the performance might indicate specific geographic variability reflecting cultural and schooling differences. Second, as indicated above, although the three indigenous languages are similar in a number of respects, the vocabulary items investigated here are different in terms of the lengths of the words and their syllabic structure. Further studies are needed to investigate what recommendations should be provided for developing such vocabulary lists; specifically, whether such tests should focus on the comparability of the concepts tested or on the formal linguistic aspects of the words (i.e., their length and structure). Third, inevitably, because the data were collected by different local Ghanaian teams in each region (although trained specifically for the administration of the scale), there might be variation in administration and scoring procedures. Again, this concern needs to be investigated in further studies. Yet, the final conclusion is pretty obvious. The simple task of translating the same list of words into three indigenous languages and administering these lists in these three languages and in English revealed a lot of variability in the resulting data. This variability is not easy to explain and, in general, this "quick and dirty" method of language assessment without proper piloting and serious psychometric work might not be accurate. Yet, it might be more informative than assessing primary school children in the dominant language of instruction while their preferred/most frequently used language is a particular mother tongue.

CONCLUDING COMMENTS

In this chapter, we summarize the concerns that exist in a number of developing countries, in particular in countries on the African continent, where there are a large number of mother tongues that are typically acquired by children prior to the mastery of the country's official languages. This situation presents a number of issues, still unresolved, for how to educate the children who often come to school having never been exposed to the language of formal instruction. Inevitably, this situation presents a number of issues concerning assessment as well.

The literature attests to the importance of assessing in the home language because of the intimate link between the home language and the internal culture of the assessed individual (Ralston, 1995; Temu, 1992). Yet, the literature lacks practical recommendations for how such assessments can be developed in situations lacking the luxury of time, effort, and financial support for the development of different assessment devices in the West. Here we have presented an illustration of the utilization of a scale in four different languages used in Ghana—three indigenous languages and the country's official language, English. In general, we obtained comparable results across the three languages, which indicate that in situations when proper psychometric work cannot be carried out for scale development (e.g., see the steps discussed in Chapter 6 of this volume), even raw percentage data indicating the levels of difficulty of given items on vocabulary lists might be informative. Yet, we also state that these data contain a certain amount of variability that is, at least at first glance, difficult to understand. Thus, interpretations of such assessments, especially for language-comparison purposes, should be made cautiously.

Vocabulary list-making is a deceptively simple-looking exercise that can be loaded with difficulties. It is important to start with a list that is not simply borrowed from another culture, but reflects the reality of the environment in which the children live. When items are developed in a particular language within a particular culture, they might remain "culture-bound" (McCrae, 2000) and, thus, untranslatable and unadaptable. Thus, it is helpful, from the very start, to come up with lists of items that exist in all of the languages being used.

Unforeseen difficulties might arise. Specifically, there is a variety of ways in which African languages capture emotions and feelings that are quite different from English (Dimmendaal, 2002), and there is also a mismatch in the vocabulary of personality descriptors in Tshivenda and English (van Eeden & Mantsha, 2007), or even the absence of particular personality-related concepts in Xitsonga (Piedmont, Bain, McCrae, & Costa, 2002). All these (and many more!) observations demonstrate the complexities associated with translating particular concepts in African languages.

Many authors have commented on the tight links between an African culture and its language (Akinyemi, 2005). We agree with the main premise that, to understand the level of language proficiency of a child prior to his or her mastery of English, respective testing should be carried out in mother tongues or in mother tongues and English, but not in English exclusively. Here we presented an example of such assessment and discussed the numerous caveats that are associated with its creation, usage, and the interpretation of its data.

Overall, our argument is that for any pedagogical reform that involves any kind of bi- or multi-lingualism, it is important to consider not only the availability of materials for teaching in the mother tongue, but also the availability of materials for assessing in this tongue. Instruction and assessment should go hand-to-hand, and, while the debate on the issue of the role of the mother tongue in educating African children keeps unfolding, it should revolve not only around teaching, but also around assessment materials.

AUTHOR NOTE

This research was supported by funds from the United States Agency for International Development (USAID). We are thankful to Ms. Mei Tan for her editorial help and to Mr. Paa Kwesi Imbeah for his assistance with translations into local languages. We are also grateful to the Ghanaian children who participated in this research.

NOTES

1. SACMEQ (http://www.sacmeq.org/) is an international NGO dedicated to policy analysis and development with regard to issues of educational quality. The establishment of SACMEQ was initiated by the International Institute for Educational Planning (http://www.iiep.unesco.org) in 1991 and is housed in the UNESCO subregional office in Harare, Zimbabwe. SACMEQ has 15 member countries: Botswana, Kenya, Lesotho, Malawi, Mauritius, Mozambique, Namibia, Syechelles, South Africa, Swaziland, Tanzania, Uganda, Zambia, Zanzibar, and Zimbabwe.
2. While both alveolar and dental voiced plosives share the symbol /d/, they do have slightly different places of articulation.

REFERENCES

Abiri, J. O. (2003). Preparation of the secondary school mother-tongue teachers. *West African Journal of Education, 20,* 7–15.

Adams, M. J. (1994). *Beginning to read: Thinking and learning about print.* Cambridge, MA: MIT Press.

Adegbite, W. (2003). Enlightenment and attitudes of the Nigerian elite on the roles of languages in Nigeria. *Language, Culture and Curriculum, 16,* 185–196.

Adetunberu, J. O., & Oluwafoise, E. A. (1992). Implications of the teaching of social studies in the mother-tongue in the lower grades of Nigerian schools for the teacher. *Ekiadolor Journal of Education, 2,* 192–204.

Adjei, P. B. (2007). Decolonising knowledge production: The pedagogic relevance of Gandhian Satyagraha to schooling and education in Ghana. *Canadian Journal of Education, 30,* 1046–1067.

Agbedor, P. (1994). Verb serialization in Ewe. *Nordic Journal of African Studies, 3,* 115–135.

Aikhenvald, A. Y., & Dixon, R. M. W. (2006). *Serial verb constructions: A cross-linguistic typology.* New York: Oxford University Press.

Akinyemi, A. (2005). Integrating culture and second language teaching through Yoruba personal names. *Modern Language Journal, 89,* 115–126.

Alexander, N. (1995). Models of multilingual schooling in South Africa. In K. Heugh, A. Siegruhn, & P. Pluddemann (Eds.), *Multilingual education for South Africa* (pp. 79–82). Johannesburg, South Africa: Heinemann.

Alidou, H., Boly, A., Brock-Utne, B., Diallo, Y., Heugh, K., & Wolff, H. E. (2006). *Optimizing learning and education in Africa: The language factor.* Paris: ADEA.

Alimi, M. M. (2007). English articles and modals in the writing of some Botswana students. *Language, Culture and Curriculum, 20,* 209–222.

Ameka, F. K. (1994). Ewe. In C. Goddard & A. Wierzbicka (Eds.), *Semantic and lexical universals: Theory and empirical findings* (pp. 57–86). Amsterdam: John Benjamins.

Ameka, F. K., Dench, A. C., & Evans, N. (2006). *Catching language: The standing challenge of grammar writing.* New York: Mouton de Gruyter.

Amfo, N. A. A. (2005). Modal marking in Akan: The case of Anka. *Journal of Pragmatics, 37,* 997–1013.

Amfo, N. A. A. (2007). Clausal conjunction in Akan. *Lingua, 117,* 666–684.

Asmara Declaration. (2000, January). *Asmara declaration on African languages and literatures.* Presented at Against All Odds: African Languages and Literatures into the 21st Century, Asmara, Eretria.

Bagwasi, M. M. (2003). The functional distribution of Setswana and English in Botswana. *Language, Culture and Curriculum, 16,* 212–217.

Banda, F. (1996). In search of the lost tongue: Prospects for mother-tongue education in Zambia. *Language, Culture and Curriculum, 9,* 109–119.

Banda, F. (2000). The dilemma of the mother tongue: Prospects for bilingual education in South Africa. *Language, Culture and Curriculum, 13,* 51–66.

Berry, J. (1957). Vowel harmony in Twi. *Bulletin of the School of Oriental and African Studies, University of London, 19,* 124–130.

Blake, T. M. (2004). Exploring the language of schooling. *Journal of Education, 14,* 63–69.

Casali, R. F. (1995). On the reduction of vowel systems in Volta-Congo. *African Languages and Cultures, 8,* 109–121.

Chumbow, B. S. (2005). The language question and national development in Africa. In T. Mkandawire (Ed.), *African intellectuals: Rethinking politics, language, gender and development* (pp. 165–192). Dakar and London: CODE SRIA and Zed Books.

Claassen, N. C. W. (1997). Cultural differences, politics and test bias in South Africa. *European Review of Applied Psychology, 47,* 297–307.

Cummins, J. (1981). Empirical and theoretical underpinnings of bilingual education. *Journal of Education, 163,* 16–29.

De Klerk, V. (1996). Use of and attitudes to English in a multilingual university. *English World-Wide, 17,* 111–127.

Dimmendaal, G. J. (2002). Colourful psi's sleep furiously: Depicting emotional states in some African languages. *Pragmatics & Cognition, 10,* 57–83.

Dolphyne, F. A. (1988). *The Akan (Twi-Fante) language: Its sound systems and tonal structure.* Accra, Ghana: Ghana Universities Press.

Dolphyne, F. A. (1996). *A comprehensive course in Twi (Asante) for the non-Twi learner.* Accra, Ghana: Ghana Universities Press.

Dutcher, N. (2004). *Expanding educational opportunity in linguistically diverse societies* (2nd ed.). Washington, DC: Center for Applied Linguistics.

Duthie, A. S. (1996). *Introducing Ewe linguistic patterns: A textbook of phonology, grammar, and semantics.* Accra, Ghana: Ghana Universities Press.

Ejieh, M. U. C. (2004). Attitudes of student teachers towards teaching in mother tongue in Nigerian primary schools: Implications for planning. *Language, Culture and Curriculum, 17,* 73–81.

Fafunwa, B. (1977). *Introduction to language education in Nigeria.* Lagos, Nigeria: National Language Centre.

Finlayson, R., & Slabbert, S. (2003). "What turns you on!": An exploration of urban South African Xhosa and Zulu youth texts. *Language, Culture and Curriculum, 16,* 165–172.

Foxcroft, C. D. (1997). Psychological testing in South Africa: Perspectives regarding ethical and fair practices. *European Journal of Psychological Assessment, 13,* 229–235.

Gordon, R. G. J. (Ed.). (2005). *Ethnologue: Languages of the world* (15th ed.). Dallas, TX: SIL International.

Grieve, K. (2005). Factors affecting assessment results. In C. Foxcroft & G. Roodt (Eds.), *An introduction to psychological assessment in the South African context* (2nd ed., pp. 224–241). Cape Town, South Africa: Oxford University Press.

Heugh, K. (1995). The multilingual school: Modified dual medium. In K. Heugh, A. Siegruhn, & P. Pluddemann (Eds.), *Multilingual education for South Africa* (pp. 83–88). Johannesburg, South Africa: Heinemann.

Inoue, K., & Oketch, M. (2008). Implementing free primary education policy in Malawi and Ghana: Equity and efficiency analysis. *Peabody Journal of Education, 83,* 41–70.

Iyamu, E. O. S., & Ogiegbaen, S. E. A. (2007). Parents and teachers' perceptions of mother-tongue medium of instruction policy in Nigerian primary schools. *Language, Culture and Curriculum, 20,* 97–108.

Kembo-Sure, J. (2003). Establishing a national standard and English language curriculum change in Kenya. *Language, Culture and Curriculum, 16,* 197–211.

Kioko, A. N. (2002). A case for improved orthography. In F. R. Owino (Ed.), *Speaking African: African languages for education and development* (pp. 231–241). Cape Town, South Africa: CASAS.

Kioko, A. N., & Muthwii, M. J. (2003). English variety for the public domain in Kenya: Speakers' attitudes and views. *Language, Culture and Curriculum, 16,* 130–145.

Kluge, A., & Hatfield, D. H. (2002). Sociolinguistic survey of the Safaliba language area. *SIL Electronic Survey Reports, 41,* 2002–2041.

Krishnamurti, B. (1990). The regional language vis-à-vis English as the medium of instruction in higher education: The Indian dilemma. In P. Pattanayak (Ed.), *Multilingualism in India* (pp. 15–24). Clevedon, UK: Multilingual Matters.

Lanham, L. (1996). A history of English in South Africa. In V. de Klerk (Ed.), *Focus on South Africa* (pp. 19–34). Amsterdam: John Benjamins.

Lemmer, E. M. (1993). On the black child and proficiency in the medium of instruction. In J. le Roux (Ed.), *The black child in crisis* (pp. 146–170). Pretoria, South Africa: CTP.

Luckett, K. (1995). National additive bilingualism: Towards a language plan for South African education. In K. Heugh, A. Siegruhn, & P. Pluddemann (Eds.), *Multilingual education for South Africa* (pp. 73–78). Johannesburg, South Africa: Heinemann.

Mbaabu, I. (1996). *Language policy in East Africa: A dependency theory perspective.* Nairobi, Kenya: Educational Research Publications.

McCrae, R. R. (2000). Trait psychology and the revival of personality and culture studies. *American Behavioral Scientist, 44,* 10–31.

Mohanlal, S. (2001). Mother-tongue education and psycho-societal involvement in tribal communities: A case study of Paniyi tribe. *Language in India, 1,* 1–9.

Mooko, T. (2004). An investigation into the use of Setswana to teach primary school mathematics. *Language, Culture and Curriculum, 17,* 181–195.

Musau, P. M. (2003). Linguistic human rights in Africa: Challenges and prospects for indigenous languages in Kenya. *Language, Culture and Curriculum, 16,* 155–164.

Muthwii, M. J. (2002). *Language policy and practices in education in Kenya and Uganda.* Nairobi, Kenya: Phoenix.

Muthwii, M. J. (2004). Language of instruction: A qualitative analysis of the perceptions of parents, pupils and teachers among the Kalenjin in Kenya. *Language, Culture and Curriculum, 17,* 15–32.

Muthwii, M. J., & Kioko, A. N. (2003). A fresh quest for new language bearings in Africa. *Language, Culture and Curriculum, 16,* 97–105.

Ndebele, N. (1987). The English language and social change in South Africa. *English Academy Review, 4,* 1–16.

Obeng, S. G. (1999). Apologies in Akan discourse. *Journal of Pragmatics, 31,* 709–734.

Owen, K. (1991). Test bias: The validity of the Junior Aptitude Tests (JAT) for various population groups in South Africa regarding constructs measured. *South African Journal of Psychology, 21,* 112–118.

Owino, F. R. (Ed.). (2002). *Speaking African: African languages for education and development.* Cape Town, South Africa: CASAS.

Painter, C. (1970). *Gonja: A phonological and grammatical study.* Bloomington: Indiana University Press, Research Institute for Inner Asian Studies.

Parry, K. (Ed.). (2000). *Language and literacy in Uganda: Towards a sustainable reading culture.* Kampala, Uganda: Fountain.

Piedmont, R. L., Bain, E., McCrae, R. R., & Costa, P. T. (2002). The applicability of the Five-Factor Model in a sub-Saharan culture: The NEO-PI-R in Shona. In R. R. McCrae & J. Allik (Eds.), *The Five-Factor Model of personality across cultures* (pp. 155–173). New York: Kluwer Academic/Plenum.

Prah, K. K. (1998). The missing link in African education and development. In K. K. Prah (Ed.), *Between distinction and standardization of African languages* (pp. 1–15). Witwatersrand, South Africa: Witwatersrand University Press.

Ralston, D. A. (1995). Cultural accommodation: The effect of language on the response of bilingual Hong Kong Chinese managers. *Journal of Cross-Cultural Psychology, 26,* 714–727.

Schmied, J. (1991). *English in Africa.* London: Longman.

Simire, G. O. (2003). Developing and promoting multilingualism in public life and society in Nigeria. *Language, Culture and Curriculum, 16,* 231–243.

Smit, U. (1996). On the status, roles and attitudes to English in South Africa. *English World-Wide, 17,* 77–109.

Sonaiya, R. (2003). The globalisation of communication and the African foreign language user. *Language, Culture and Curriculum, 16,* 146–154.

Stroud, C. (2003). Postmodernist perspectives on local languages: African mother-tongue education in times of globalisation. *International Journal of Bilingual Education and Bilingualism, 6,* 17–36.

Sure, K., & Webb, V. (2000). Languages in competition. In V. Webb & K. Sure (Eds.), *African voices* (pp. 109–132). Oxford, UK: Oxford University Press.

Temu, M. N. (1992). African American students' self-awareness through Kiswahili language. *Journal of Black Studies, 22,* 532–545.

Tickoo, M. L. (1993). When is a language worth teaching? Native languages and English in India. *Language, Culture and Curriculum, 6,* 225–239.

Trudell, B., & Schroeder, L. (2007). Reading methodologies for African languages: Avoiding linguistic and pedagogical imperialism. *Language, Culture and Curriculum, 20,* 165–180.

Urevbu, A. O. (2001). *Curriculum studies.* Lagos, Nigeria: Juland.

Van den Berg, A. R. (1996). Intelligence tests. In K. Owen & J. J. Taljaard (Eds.), *Handbook for the use of psychological and scholastic tests of the HSRC* (2nd ed., pp. 157–190). Pretoria, South Africa: Human Sciences Research Council.

Van Eeden, R., & Mantsha, T. R. (2007). Theoretical and methodological considerations in the translation of the 16PF5 into an African language. *South African Journal of Psychology, 37,* 62–81.

Wallis, T., & Birt, M. (2003). A comparison of native and non-native English-speaking groups' understanding of the vocabulary contained within the 16PF (SA92). *South African Journal of Psychology, 33,* 182–190.

White, H. (2005). Using household survey data to measure educational performance: The case of Ghana. *Social Indicators Research, 74,* 395–422.

Winkler, G. (1997). The myth of the mother-tongue: Evidence from Maryvale College, Johannesburg. *Southern African Journal of Applied Language Studies, 5,* 29–41.

8

The Logic of Confidence and the Social Economy of Assessment Reform in Singapore: A New Institutionalist Perspective

DAVID HOGAN, PHILLIP A. TOWNDROW, AND KIM KOH

As we argue in Chapter 9, "Instructional and Assessment Practices in Singapore," Singapore has developed a highly successful system of education characterized by considerable direct teaching, rote learning, and drill and practice for high-stakes assessments. We also contend that classroom teaching is characterized by low levels of disciplinarity and minimal amount of formative assessment. Finally, we suggest that the status and influence of the national high-stakes assessment system has weakened the opportunity of schools to engage in systematic and sustainable pedagogical innovation necessary to prepare young people for the demands of 21st-century institutional environments. In this present chapter we explore this latter issue further by mapping out an assessment reform agenda that promises to support rather than hinder sustainable pedagogical innovation. In doing so, we draw extensively on contemporary organizational theory in order to identify some of the broader institutional issues that need to be addressed if pedagogical innovation, including assessment reform, is to be sustainable. In particular, we draw on new institutionalist theory and its focus on the nature of the relationship between schools and their institutional environments, specifically its focus on the importance of the logic of confidence as a key enabler of successful and sustainable innovation.

ANALYTICS: A NEO-INSTITUTIONALIST THEORY OF SCHOOLS AND THEIR ENVIRONMENTS

Since independence in 1965, school governance in Singapore has operated within an ideological and political environment that we might term post-colonial *high statism*—the exercise by the Singaporean state of substantial political, bureaucratic, and other forms of power and authority over the organization, funding, administration, and distribution of schooling and instructional practices within schools. Since the launch of the *Thinking Schools, Learning Nation (TSLN)* initiative in 1997 and the more recent *Teach Less, Learn More (TLLM)* initiative in 2005, however, the government has, cautiously and incrementally, begun to devolve prescriptive bureaucratic authority to individual schools over a range of instructional matters, including curriculum development, in the belief that instructional innovation as called for by *TSLN* requires a considerable loosening of centralized bureaucratic control over instructional practices. At the same time, the government also supported curriculum design initiatives in schools utilizing action research frameworks, expanded the opportunities for professional development (e.g., use of "white space"), supported the creation of a Teachers Network, and sponsored local postgraduate degrees in education and overseas school visits.

In short, while the state still retains considerable political and bureaucratic control over education, it has introduced some initiatives (e.g., bottom-up initiatives) that enhance the professional authority of teachers. But still, relative to the United States and the United Kingdom, the system of instructional governance in Singapore is considerably more tightly coupled in bureaucratic terms. Furthermore, the government has so far resisted pressures to weaken the exercise of more informal forms of power over instructional processes. Of these informal controls, the substantial level of *performative* control exercised by the national high-stakes assessment system over pedagogical practice is particularly notable.[1] In addition, pedagogical practice in Singapore is subject to other forms of control and these continue to remain substantial and important. Indirect and intersecting cognitive, normative, and habitual forms of power exercised through the informal production and reproduction of dominant or hegemonic categories of understanding, values, and discourses of teacher belief and pedagogical practice remain immensely powerful. Again and again we have been reminded how much pedagogical practices in Singapore are deeply responsive to cultural traditions and beliefs that are rooted in Confucian and more recent meritocratic and statist constructions of education, pedagogy, assessment, authority, and social organization. Together, these organizing beliefs constitute what we might term a *folk culture* or a *moral economy* of teaching and learning that have assumed the status of implicit "institutional rules" that profoundly shape pedagogical discourse and practices in Singapore (Cohen, 1988; Meyer, 1977; Meyer & Rowan, 1977).

From the perspective of contemporary organizational theory, the sensitivity of school practices to cultural traditions and beliefs underscores the "institutional" nature of schools as organizations. Two aspects of the institutionalist account of schooling are relevant here. The first focuses on the nature of the relationship between schools and their institutional environments. Broadly speaking, new institutionalist theories of schooling emphasize that educational systems are relatively open institutional systems "embedded" in, and "structured" by, their relevant institutional environments rather than by the nature of their core technical activities (teaching and learning), goals, size, or by the demands of bureaucratic control. As a consequence, schools have strong and continuous interactions with the many institutional environments they are embedded in—community, social-structural, political, economic, and cultural—and seek legitimacy through achievement of an "institutional isomorphism" between their organization and practices, on the one hand, and the governing institutional rules, cultural expectations, or "myths" of their relevant environments, on the other. Consequently, school organization does not so much reflect the pressure to rationalize the coordination and control of relational networks and work activity inside the organization, as we might expect from Weberian and contingency-based theoretical accounts of schooling, but reflects more the pressure on the organization to conform to environmentally generated "institutional rules" concerning the nature of education and schooling. "A school, to survive, must conform to institutional rules—including community understandings—that define teacher categories and credentials, pupil selection and definition, proper topics of instruction, and appropriate facilities. It is less essential that a school's teaching and learning activities are efficiently coordinated or even that that they are in close conformity to institutional rules" (Meyer, Scott, & Deal, 1983, p. 47). Schools require their environments not only to provide resources, but to have confidence in them. As Meyer and Rowan argue, "organisations must have the confidence of their environments, not simply be in rational exchange with them. Those that have this confidence and legitimacy receive all sorts of social resources that provide for success and stability. That is, organisations must be legitimate, and they must contain legitimate accounts or explanations for their internal order and external products" (Meyer & Rowan, 1983, p. 94).

The second aspect of new institutionalist theory that we want to emphasize focuses on cultural aspects of the processes of institutionalization and the light that these throw on the more informal aspects of the structure of instructional governance in school systems. Early expressions of institutionalist theory, following Charles Bidwell's path-breaking paper in 1965 on the organization of schooling, attributed a certain "structural looseness" to schools as organizations in that the technical core of schooling—the processes of teaching and learning—were only "loosely coupled," in Karl Weick's much-cited term, to the formal bureaucratic structure of schooling (Bidwell, 1965; Meyer, Scott, & Deal, 1983; Meyer & Rowan, 1977; Weick, 1976). But even as new institutionalists emphasized the importance of a necessary isomorphism of schools to cultural beliefs, ceremonies, rituals, ideologies, and "institutional myths," they rarely challenged the loose coupling hypothesis. But as phenomenological, symbolic interactionist and micro-ethnographic understandings of cultural aspects of the process of institutionalization, social agency, social practices, and what Michael Fullan (2007, chap. 2) terms, the "subjective meaning of educational innovation" developed during the 1980s and 1990s, a deeper understanding of the *cultural* construction and reproduction of instructional processes developed that linked the technical core of schooling to the surrounding institutional environment through cultural mechanisms as well. Broadly speaking, Powell and DiMaggio (1991, pp. 67–74) describe these kinds of processes as "mimetic" forms of institutionalization or isomorphism that they distinguish from "coercive" and "normative" forms of isomorphism. Similarly, in a 1995 overview of new institutionalist theory, Scott emphasizes that institutions "consist of cognitive, normative and regulative structures and institutions that provide stability and meaning to social behaviour" and that "institutions are transported by various carriers—cultures, structures, and routines—and they operate at multiple levels of jurisdiction" (Scott, 1995, p. 33).[2] Indeed, not long after, in a revisionist essay that acknowledges the limits of the early institutionalist work, Rowan and Miskel (1999) specifically stress a "cognitive" conception of institutionalization, focusing on the production and reproduction of tacit understandings and taken-for-granted assumptions that shape teacher and student behavior in classrooms.[3]

In short, the institutional character of schools and schooling thus highlights the manifold ways in which the technical core of schooling—teaching and learning—is not "loosely coupled" but "deeply embedded" in its institutional environment and tends toward isomorphism with it. For very good institutional reasons, then, teachers, principals, and public officials are highly sensitive and responsive to public opinion. While Singapore does not have a decentralized system of local political control exercised through democratically elected school boards as in the United States, the teachers, principals, and the Singapore Ministry of Education are highly sensitive to public opinion (particularly the views of parents) at the community and national level. This is especially evident in matters of assessment, a fact that reflects the very tight nexus between national high-stakes assessment, competitive credentialing, and social mobility in Singapore.

Within quite expansive limits, then, pedagogical practice in Singapore is subjected to what new institutionalist theories of school organization term the *logic of confidence* (Meyer & Rowan, 1977). Indeed, in the long run, given the institutional character of schooling, its responsiveness at all levels to both cultural tradition and to public opinion, and its need to secure sufficient "institutional isomorphism" to secure its legitimacy in the eye of the public, it is hard to imagine that significant pedagogical change (in terms of curriculum design, instructional practice, and above all, of assessment reform) of the kind called for by *TSLN* to meet the challenges of the 21st century can occur without a significant change in public opinion and in the dominant cultural understanding of education. This will be a huge challenge for the government, but it is not beyond its capacities to achieve and not without precedent. Moreover, it is an issue in which the professionalization of teaching looms large.

THE LOGIC OF CONFIDENCE AND PEDAGOGICAL INNOVATION IN SINGAPORE

As we have seen, for new institutionalist theorists the institutional environment is the sum of those "institutional rules" or "cultural beliefs" upon which the legitimacy and survival of the school depends. We might well then ask what are the specific "institutional rules" embedded in the "institutional environment" conformity that are essential for the legitimacy and survival of schools in Singapore? In Singapore, for example, these cultural beliefs or institutional rules have included a belief in human capital formation as the bedrock of national economic security and progress; that every child should have access to a good education and stay at school until at least the end of secondary school; that social mobility is both fair and efficient when it is based on competitive performance in national high-stakes assessments; that periodic high-stakes assessments motivate students and ensure high-quality and focused teaching; that high-stakes assessments should focus on knowledge of academic content knowledge; that knowledge is hierarchically and sequentially organized and epistemologically independent of student beliefs; that teaching is talking and learning is listening; that good teaching focuses principally on the transmission of domain-specific knowledge and skills; that teaching is a privatized social practice conducted by a single teacher in large group settings; that learning is individual and intra-subjective rather than inter-subjective and social even if it happens in large group settings; that teaching is efficient and culturally appropriate when it involves simultaneous group instruction; that poor academic performance is a function of nature ("ability"), environment ("family background"), or character ("interest"/"self-discipline") but generally not teaching itself; that ability is unidimensional and sufficiently developed and transparent to warrant the allocation of students into a differentiated whole of curriculum streams at an early age; that pedagogical authority is hierarchical and largely nonnegotiable; that the overall quality of teaching, learning, and educational administration in Singapore is very high by international standards; that high levels of investment in technology/ICT (Information and Communication Technology) can help resolve most pedagogical problems; and so on.

These institutional rules have, historically, exerted immense cultural influence—"cognitive" as well as "normative control"—over schooling and school practices in Singapore. Again and again we have been reminded how much pedagogical practices in Singapore are profoundly responsive to cultural rules and beliefs—to what David Cohen (1998) terms the *folk culture* of teaching and learning that support and legitimate traditional pedagogical practices and classroom processes.[4] However, since the Asian economic crisis of the mid to late 1990s and the announcement of the *TSLN* initiative, the Ministry of Education (MOE) in Singapore has attempted to carefully modify some, but not all, of these institutional rules in order to properly position Singapore in the changed institutional environment of the 21st-century global economy. Among the most sensitive of these efforts has been the modification of Singapore's canonical meritocratic ideology in favor of a more pluralistic, multidimensional "talentocracy"; the creation of more flexible pathways through and across streams, especially in primary schools; some devolution of pedagogical authority to schools over curriculum matters; and the limited (to this point) introduction of more open-ended assessment tasks in high-stakes assessment (e.g., Science Practical Assessment, project work) that weakens the utility of conventional forms of exam preparation. We will discuss some of these in the next section. These endeavors are delicate and complex, for they essentially involve modifying the dominant or hegemonic institutional rules in ways that could potentially weaken the historical "institutional isomorphism" between schooling and its institutional environment on which public confidence and the legitimacy of public education depends. So the institutional "cultural politics" involved are profoundly daunting, to say the least. Yet senior policy makers in the Ministry know very well that the educational system needs to change if young Singaporeans are to be adequately prepared for the challenges of the 21st century. The challenge for the government then is to find a language and a strategy of improvement that support innovation but not so fast as to get too far out of step with public opinion. In other words, long-term, sustainable, and substantial pedagogical reform depends on simultaneous change in school practices and public sentiment in order to maintain a rough "institutional isomorphism" or social contract between schools (and their attendant pedagogical practices) and their institutional environments.

The value of new institutionalist theory is that it helps conceptualize the nature of the strategic and political challenges that ministries of education in general confront in attempting to institutionalize knowledge management and innovation systems. It certainly does *not* mean that schools are locked into existing institutional rules and cultural expectations and that no long-term sustainable and substantial pedagogical reform is possible. But it does mean that fundamental long-term pedagogical innovation will depend on changes in the institutional environment as much as it will on improvements in pedagogical practice, and that the two will have to change in tandem in approximately the same direction as well as at approximately the same pace if school practices are to keep the confidence of their environments. This will not be easy, given that globalization and the pressure to create and sustain a knowledge economy demands rapid institutional innovation whereas cultural systems generally change only very slowly. Consequently, not the least of the challenges confronting policy makers in Singapore in their effort to promote institutional innovation in pedagogical practice will be the skilled management of the institutional tensions between the institutional demands of the knowledge economy, on the one hand, and the institutional rules or cultural beliefs concerning teaching and learning, on the other.

The underlying logic of "the logic of confidence" and its relationship to systemic reform and pedagogical alignment depends in large part on the degree of "institutional isomorphism" of school practices with the institutional environment. The key to achieving this, as we noted above, is a carefully targeted and very public program of professional development for teachers that focuses on developing teacher capacity in designing and implementing alternative assessments and the design of a reliable, valid, and fair system of standards-based, moderated assessment that expands the pedagogical authority of teachers in schools that function as deliberative and reflective professional learning communities. At the same time, the broader community needs to be reassured that the new order of things will modify and improve the assessment system in line with the economic well-being of the state and the demands of the global economy and that the innovations will supplement and support rather than replace the current conventional high-stakes assessment system. The task of the Ministry and local schools to engage the public, and to convince it of the need for significant pedagogical innovation, including assessment reform, would be substantially eased if the attention of the public were drawn to the changing technical and social organization of work in knowledge economies and the implications of these changes for patterns of social mobility and social stratification. In effect, policy makers and schools might well draw on the social mobility aspirations of parents and their children, in the context of dramatic changes in the organization of work and social mobility pathways, to support pedagogical innovation and realignment in the school system.

In sum, the "embeddedness" of school organizations in their institutional environments and the dependency of schools on those environments for their legitimacy promote an institutional isomorphism between school organization and its institutional environment. In Singapore, the exercise of bureaucratic control and other forms of control helps ensure institutional isomorphism, but arguably the single most important mechanism for securing it is the informal but "tight coupling" of instructional practices and national high-stakes assessment. (In the United States, on the other hand, until recently, there had been no high-stakes assessments and the "loose coupling" of administrative control and instruction provided a "buffer" between the demands of the external environment and the technical uncertainties of the teaching and learning process.) This is important because the legitimacy, and hence the survival, of the school depends on its conformity to broad institutional rules as defined by the state, the professions, or more amorphously, public opinion. Schools require their environments not only to provide resources, but to have confidence in them (Meyer & Rowan, 1983, p. 94; Scott, 1995, pp. 45–47).

THE SOCIAL ECONOMY OF ASSESSMENT REFORM IN SINGAPORE

Singapore's national high-stakes assessment system has been designed to perform a number of important institutional tasks—to motivate students to learn; to focus and drive the work of teachers and schools; to provide a reliable, valid, and politically acceptable measure of student learning and pedagogical accountability; to allocate students into different curriculum tracks and schools based on their academic performance; and to help institutionalize a meritocratic system of social order and social inequality that has substantial political legitimacy.

But while the system can fairly claim considerable success in achieving its key assessment objectives, it is not evident that the current assessment system in Singapore is the kind of assessment regime that will improve pedagogical practice and student outcomes in a way that is called for by *TSLN* and *TLLM* and that will allow young people to successfully negotiate the challenges of the changed educational and economic landscape of the 21st century. We also contend that the current assessment system is institutionally overburdened—that it attempts to do too much and to reconcile competing objectives—and requires more differentiated solutions to more effectively achieve key policy objectives. In developing our account of the challenges that confront the Singapore assessment system, we have drawn not only on the Ministry's major policy settings (*TSLN, TLLM*) and on our own empirical research as in Chapter 9, but also on neo-institutionalist theories of schooling, current models of 21st-century skills and capacities, and on current assessment research in the United States, Australia, and the United Kingdom.

Multidimensional Assessments

The first of these challenges is to broaden the range of capacities that the assessment regime measures in line with the range of understandings, skills, capacities, dispositions, and identities that government commissions, sociologists of modernity, the Organisation for Economic Cooperation and Development (OECD), international nongovernmental organizations, labor market economists, business groups, organizational researchers, and educators believe necessary for countries to be successful and thrive in 21st-century global institutional environments (Giddens, 1991; National Research Council [NRC], 1999; OECD, 1999, 2004, 2005). Schools have long assumed responsibility for promoting the well-being of young citizens and aggregate social utility. But one of the more interesting and revealing ironies of contemporary schooling is a peculiar hiatus between the breadth of the educational aspirations that systems proclaim on behalf of schools and the thinness of the measures of school outcomes that schools use to assess their performance in realizing their aspirations. While school systems have invested enormous resources in curriculum development, pedagogical reform, and assessment of traditional academic outcomes, very little time, effort, and money have been spent on developing assessment instruments, which allow for measuring the impact of schooling on broader "nonacademic" outcomes that parents, communities, schools, and governments value. In 1987, the National Academy of Education in the United States bemoaned the already high—and growing—focus on cognitive test scores in the United States in these terms:

> At root here is a fundamental dilemma. Those personal qualities that we hold dear—resilience and courage in the face of stress, a sense of craft in our work, a commitment to justice and caring in our social relationships, a dedication to advancing the public good in our communal life—are exceedingly difficult to assess. And so . . . we are apt to measure what we can, and eventually come to value what is measured over what is . . . unmeasured. The shift . . . occurs gradually . . . In neither academic nor popular discourse about schools does one find nowadays much reference to the important human qualities . . . The language of academic . . . tests has become the primary rhetoric of schooling. (quoted in Rothstein, 2004, p. 97)

And certainly, in the United States, the rhetoric of cognitive assessment has not slackened since, particularly following the passage of the No Child Left Behind legislation by the U.S. Congress in 2001.

More recently, Richard Rothstein lamented the fact that "obsessed with test scores, educators have devoted almost no effort to identifying or measuring non-cognitive skills" (Rothstein, 2004, p. 95). Nor, despite considerable attention to equity gaps in academic achievement, does anyone have any idea "how large social class gaps in non-cognitive skills—character traits like perseverance, self confidence, social responsibility, and ability to work with others and resolve conflicts" (Rothstein, 2004, p. 7) might be reduced or eased. Overall, we concur with Rothstein that these are important goals of public education, which might, in some respects, take precedence over academic outcomes.

Now, clearly Singapore is not the United States, but our sense of popular, policy, and pedagogical sentiment in Singapore is that despite the continuing institutional significance of high-stakes assessment of intellectual performance, policy makers, teachers, and parents in Singapore are committed to a broad conception of educational outcomes. Moreover, over the past 3 years, the government has edged cautiously away from the older model of meritocratic streaming introduced in the late 1970s to a more differentiated and pluralistic model of "merit" ("talent") and school organization. The new meritocratic dispensation is quite evident, for example, in a speech given on September 22, 2005, by the Minister of Education who began his speech by announcing that "we have embarked on new phase in education in recent years. We are shifting focus from quantity to quality and from efficiency to choice in learning. We have made many refinements in recent years, but they boil down to this basis shift in focus—from an efficiency-driven system to one focused on quality and choice in learning." He went on to explain:

> The changes are percolating through our schools and tertiary institutions. We are progressively shifting the balance in education, from learning content to developing a habit of inquiry. We are renewing our emphasis on an all-round education, so that we can help our young develop the strength of character that will help them ride out difficulties and live life to the fullest. And we are injecting fluidity throughout the system—recognising more talents besides academic achievements, providing more flexibility in the school curriculum and streaming system, and introducing new pathways—all to help all our students discover their interests and talents, and know that through our education system they can go as far as they can. We have to press ahead with this new strategy in education. We must give young Singaporeans a quality of education that will prepare them for life, much more than prepare them for examinations. We must give each and every student a first class education. As [the] PM [Prime Minister] put it in his National

Day Rally speech last month, we need a mountain range of different talents, each one of us being the best that we can be not just one or two peaks. (Shanmugaratnam, September 22, 2005)

And again in an interview with the editor of *Newsweek International* for publication on January 9, 2006, but published in *The Straits Times* on January 6, 2006, the Minister compared the American and Singaporean models of meritocracy in the following terms:

> Yours is a talent meritocracy, ours is an exam meritocracy. There are some parts of the intellect that we are not able to test well—like creativity, curiosity, a sense of adventure, ambition. Most of all, America has a culture of learning that challenges conventional wisdom, even if it means challenging authority. These are the areas where Singapore must learn from America. (Shanmugaratnam in Zakaria, 2006)

In recent years, therefore, the government has altered some of the key policy settings or "institutional rules" of education in Singapore without formally abandoning the particular form of meritocratic ideology that has dominated educational policy in Singapore. We welcome these changes. However, we are not convinced that the current national assessment system quite reflects either the commitment of the government to a "talentocracy" or the commitment of the larger community to a broad and generous conception of school outcomes nor, as we argue below, does it support the kind of pedagogical innovation we believe necessary to more adequately prepare young people for the institutional demands of the 21st century. In order to achieve these objectives, Singapore will need to develop a balanced and multidimensional assessment system that emphasizes the assessment of broader outcomes of schooling and does so in a way that employs a range of examinable and nonexaminable assessments that endeavors to capture and report a broad range of "academic" and "nonacademic," "cognitive" and "noncognitive," student outcomes. A balanced assessment system, in other words, will implement a multidimensional assessment regime that focuses on a broad range of student outcomes—economic, social, civic, subjective—that parents, communities, governments, and labor markets value.

Of course, whatever else they are interested in, governments and labor markets are likely to be particularly interested in economic outcomes. But it would be a mistake to construe these narrowly in terms of conventional human capital "cognitive" or "academic" outcomes that are overwhelmingly the focus of current summative assessment regimes. We say this for two reasons. First, more than 30 years of research in human capital theory, labor productivity, and income determination has clearly demonstrated that so-called noncognitive skills—personality traits, motivation, locus of control beliefs and self-management skills, and so on—are at least as important as cognitive ability as sources of labor productivity gains and lifetime income streams (Arrow, Bowles, & Durlauf, 2000; Borghans, Duckworth, Heckman, & Weel, 2008; Bowles, Gintis, & Groves, 2005; Heckman, 2004; Heckman & Rubinstein, 2001; Heckman, Stizrud, & Urzua, 2006; Jencks et al., 1972; Rothstein, 2004). And second, there is ample research evidence that knowledge economy workplaces place a premium on a whole range of economic and social skills and capacities that go well beyond conventional cognitive measures of academic achievement. For example, a 1999 study of the organization of work by the National Research Council in the United States, *The Changing Nature of Work,* suggests that Knowledge Based Economies (KBEs) are characterized by quite different forms of the technical and social organization of work and have elevated human capital formation into a matter of high state policy. Broadly speaking, KBEs place a premium on innovation, knowledge production and application, problem solving, creativity, ICT, entrepreneurship, self-regulation, lifelong learning, and a range of other skills and capacities associated with dramatic changes in the technical and social organization of work in knowledge economies. On the one hand, a new *technical organization of work,* characterized by significantly greater cognitive complexity, expanded information processing and knowledge requirements, and cross-functional, multidisciplinary task environments and project work, has generated a demand for new kinds of *cognitive and communication skills*—analytical problem solving, knowledge application, and generation of new knowledge. On the other hand, a new *social organization of work,* characterized by greater autonomy, flatter hierarchies, more team work, shared decision making, more risk taking, and more extensive oral and written communication, requires new kinds of *social understandings and skills*—a sense of agency, interpersonal problem solving, independence, collaboration, trust, and adaptability (NRC, 1999).

These changes in the demand side of the labor market and the broader institutional environment have not gone unnoticed by the international assessment community and by policy makers. Importantly, the OECD places particular emphasis on "learning how to learn" as the key capacity that young people need to successfully negotiate the new institutional environment of knowledge-based economies (OECD, 2000, p. 74). A second OECD report, prepared for the launch of the Programme for

International Student Assessment (PISA) in 2000, *Measuring Student Knowledge and Skills: A New Framework for Assessment* (OECD, 1999) makes a similar claim:

> Underlying OECD/PISA is a dynamic model of lifelong learning in which new knowledge and skills necessary for successful adaptation to changing circumstances are continuously acquired over the life cycle. Students cannot learn in school everything they will need to know in adult life. What they must acquire is the prerequisites for successful learning in future life. These prerequisites are of both a cognitive and a motivational nature. Students must become able to organise and regulate their own learning, to learn independently and in groups, and to overcome difficulties in the learning process. This requires them to be aware of their own thinking processes and learning strategies and methods. Moreover, further learning and the acquisition of additional knowledge will increasingly occur in situations in which people work together and are dependent on one another. (pp. 9–10)

In general terms, PISA defines competence as the ability to successfully meet complex demands in varied contexts through the mobilization of psychosocial resources, including knowledge and skills, motivation, attitudes, emotions, and other social and behavioral components (Schleicher, 2007). Importantly, OECD emphasizes that the reasons behind the shift from assessing whether students can reproduce what they have learned toward whether they can extrapolate from what they have learned and apply their competencies in novel situations is based on its analysis of the nature of knowledge and skills required in modern life. Schleicher (2007, p. 1) notes, for example, that "the tasks that can be solved through simple memorisation or with pre-set algorithms are those that are also easiest to digitise, automatise and offshore, and will thus be less relevant in a modern knowledge society."

PISA is undoubtedly the most conspicuous international effort to develop an expanded assessment framework that endeavors to measure 21st-century skills and capacities. It is of no small interest that Singapore has decided to join PISA from 2009. And there are compelling reasons for the government to do so. Systems want to signal to students and teachers the kinds of capacities that they believe important to develop and assess. Furthermore, labor markets and international capital markets are likely to reward governments that include broad-gauge multidimensional assessment regimes (and punish systems that don't) that clearly signal (and reward) the institutionally relevant achievements and capacities of their students since they reflect the commitment of educational systems to improve the allocative and productive efficiency of labor markets and the workforce. As we noted above, contemporary human capital research suggests that so-called noncognitive skills are at least as equally important as cognitive ability as sources of labor productivity gains and lifetime income streams. But it is also of interest that OECD has sought, through its DeSeCo Project (*The Definition and Selection of Key Competencies*) (OECD, 2005), to develop an even broader framework of 21st-century competencies than is currently captured in its PISA assessments. The DeSeCo conceptual framework classifies these competencies into three broad categories. First, individuals need to be able to use a wide range of tools for interacting effectively with the environment: both physical ones such as information technology and sociocultural ones such as the use of language. They need to understand such tools well enough to adapt them for their own purposes—to use tools interactively. Second, in an increasingly interdependent world, individuals need to engage with others, and since they will encounter people from a range of backgrounds, it is important that they are able to interact in heterogeneous groups. Third, individuals need to be able to take responsibility for managing their own lives, and situate their lives in the broader social context and act autonomously (OECD, 2005, p. 5). But "the heart" of all these key competencies, the OECD Report emphasizes, is "reflectiveness"—"the ability of individuals to think for themselves as an expression of moral and intellectual maturity, and to take responsibility for their learning and their actions" (pp. 8–9).

This is an important argument, and one that resonates with highly influential accounts of what we might term the *postmodern existential condition*. For Anthony Giddens, for example, reflexive self-understanding and agentic forms of self-formation have become ever more important in a world that is increasingly "deinstitutionalized," "detraditionalized," "de-nationalized," and "individualized" (Bauman, 2001; Beck, 1992; Beck & Beck-Gernsheim, 2002; Beck, Giddens, & Lash, 1994; Giddens, 1991; Hall, 1992, 1996; Hogan, 2006; Hogan & Chan, 2006; MacDonald, 1999). These sociological and philosophical accounts of the postmodern existential condition, we want to suggest, raise important and urgent questions about the kinds of learning opportunities, intellectual and cultural resources, and individual understandings, skills, dispositions, and identities that young people need to successfully negotiate, not just the blind contingencies of inscrutable luck and capricious fate that will be with us always, as the ancient Greeks feared, but the institutional and existential challenges of postmodernity that economists, sociologists, philosophers, and others have alerted us to (Taylor, 1989).

As we saw earlier, these concerns underlie OECD's DeSeCo Project as well. What we want to emphasize here, however, is that we have little confidence that educational systems in which the iron laws of high-stakes assessment drive classroom pedagogy day in and day out are able to provide their students with the kinds of rich pedagogical opportunities that enable them to "make meaning" that is existentially valuable by exploring, interrogating, debating, representing, dramatizing—in a word, participating—in the cultural and moral narratives of their society. In this way, through these conversations, students learn to become members of, and participate in, their own cultural traditions, and to become, therefore, cultural *citizens* of that tradition—members of a community of memory—rather than mere *subjects* of a reified and fossilized canon. In so doing, they might learn to understand themselves, their experiences, and their world all the better and thus equip themselves to reconstruct and adapt their cultural traditions in ways that serve their aspirations and values (Applebee, 1996; Bruner, 1990; Hogan, 2007; Oakeshott, 1962).

Although these subjective outcomes of schooling are not assessable in a summative sense, they are critically important normative and existential outcomes of schooling that ought to inform instruction and assessment practices. After all, this view of education has recently had the blessing of the prime minister of Singapore, Lee Hsien Loong (2004), in his National Day Address in 2004:

> The most important gift that we can give to our young and to prepare for their future is education. It's not just preparing them for a job, but learning to live a life, learning to deal with the world, learning to be a full person, what in Chinese, they say, "xue zhuo ren" (学做人). . . . We have got to teach less to our students so that they will learn more. Grades are important, don't forget to pass your exams but grades are not the only thing in life and there are other things in life which we want to learn in school.

The above view is consistent with Hall and Ames (1987), who remind us that the language of Confucian education refers to the "development of the power of 'thinking'"—*hsueh* (learning), *ssu* (reflecting), *chih* (realizing), *hsin* (living up to one's word), and *yi* (signification). Critically, learning (*hsueh*) refers to "becoming aware" and is understood to require a reflective engagement with the meanings embedded in cultural traditions to optimize the learner's capacity for intelligent and wise action in particular circumstances. Indeed, for many observers, this feature of Chinese philosophy clearly differentiates it from Western philosophy. Angus Graham (1989) suggests that Western philosophy has been preoccupied with an epistemological question ("What is the Truth?") whereas Eastern philosophy has been preoccupied with an ethical one ("Where is the Way?"). Similarly, David Wong (2005) recently observed that "Chinese philosophy is a 'wisdom' literature, composed primarily of stories and sayings designed to move the audience to adopt a way of life or to confirm its adoption of that way of life." Western philosophy, by contrast, was less driven by an ethical preoccupation than by "systematic argumentation and theory" in the search for the "truth."[5]

What, then, does this mean for contemporary educators in Singapore? At the very least, it means that Singapore can draw on a rich cultural tradition of education that is far broader than a narrowly instrumental view of education but, as the prime minister put it, *"learning to live a life, learning to deal with the world, learning to be a full person."* It also means that schooling should offer all students, and all students equally, rich opportunities to engage or participate in various disciplinary conversations that facilitate meaning making rather than information processing and permit construction of meaningful narratives about themselves, others, and the world they live in (Ford & Forman, 2006; Hogan, 2007). It certainly means that teachers need the pedagogical opportunity or space to explore issues in depth with their students, and they need to know how to construct appropriate disciplinary assessments, for both formative and summative purposes, that capture how well students are able to participate in disciplinary conversations.

A multidimensional assessment system, then, worth its salt in the contemporary world is one that captures and reports a broad array of institutional and existential capacities necessary to successfully negotiate the rapidly changing institutional and existential landscape of the 21st century. Some of these capacities are "cognitive," others "noncognitive," some "academic," others "nonacademic," some assessable, others not. Some are focused on what is necessary for economic success in the labor market, others on the kinds of capacities that can help young people lead meaningful and rewarding lives. Clearly, many of these capacities—understandings, skills, dispositions, commitments, and identities—are and should be disciplinary in character, in both the conventional and "conversational" senses of the word. Others, however, are more generic in nature. One that has received a lot of attention recently in numerous reviews and commissions is a meta-cognitive skill or disposition—the reflexive ability of students to learn how to learn.

Wynn Harlen (2007, pp. 30–31), for example, emphasizes that "an important part of preparing young people for life and work in the rapidly changing society of today and tomorrow is to help them develop awareness and understanding and the process of learning—a key aspect of meta-cognition." However, "learning how to learn is not the result of being taught to use a set of higher order skills, but rather of having used a set of effective learning practices and applied them in various contexts." In particular, learning to understand learning requires expansive opportunities for students to interact with other students and their teachers and lots of scaffolding and feedback by the teacher. In effective learning processes, "meta-cognition is embedded in the learning process and is developed, as with other learning, through interaction and discussion with other students and the teacher." A number of researchers or research groups have recently developed assessment tools and related professional development packages for teachers that focus on learning how to learn (James et al., 2006, 2007a, 2007b). More broadly, along lines similar to OECD's DeSeCo Project, Centre for Research in Pedagogy in Practice [CRPP] is currently conducting research focused on measuring and modeling a broad range of academic, economic, social, civic, and subjective student outcomes—understandings, skills, dispositions, and identities—that appear important to successfully negotiating the institutional and existential terrain of late modernity (Hogan, 2007; Hogan & Kang, 2006; Hogan, Kang, & Chan, 2007).

Partial Decoupling of High-Stakes Assessment and Classroom Instruction

A second challenge confronting Singapore is to design an assessment system that encourages teachers not just to take pedagogical risks (the system already does that through the *TSLN* and *TLLM* initiatives) but provides them with the meaningful pedagogical opportunities or white space to do so. Currently, teachers in Singapore report that they overwhelmingly teach to the test because it is their responsibility to prepare students for the *high-stakes* assessments. This is entirely understandable and reasonable under the current assessment circumstances. Moreover, parents and school principals expect them to do so for accountability purposes. Consequently, we do not fault teachers for teaching and assessing the way they do. Nor do we contest the appropriateness of systems assessing what students have been taught—that there is a relatively tight alignment between curriculum and assessment (both prescribed and enacted). Furthermore, there is substantial public support for the national assessment system that reflects a deeply institutionalized cultural belief about the nature and logic of education itself as well as dominant cultural constructions of Singapore as a "meritocratic" society that reflects the very tight nexus in Singapore between the social mobility aspirations of Singapore parents for their children and the assessment and credentialing system. Abandoning the national assessment system at this point in time or at any time in the near future, then, is not even remotely feasible if the government has any hope of retaining the confidence of the community.

Still, we remain convinced that the very tight alignment currently between the national system of summative assessment and classroom instruction constrains rather than encourages meaningful and sustainable pedagogical innovation of the kind called for by *TSLN* and *TLLM* initiatives, despite the formal permission granted schools and teachers to engage in pedagogical innovation by the Ministry's policy framework and the generous support from the Ministry for school-based curriculum development (what it terms the *white space* initiative) and "bottom-up" pedagogical initiatives at the school level with "top-down" support.[6] These are important initiatives and there has been an exponential growth in school-based or classroom-based curriculum and assessment initiatives over the past 2 years across the system that gives us hope. Yet it is still an open question whether these highly decentralized initiatives will have sufficient institutional clout to promote significant and sustainable innovation so long as the current national assessment system continues to shape the pattern of pedagogical practice in Singapore as powerfully as it currently does. In the last analysis, teacher decisions about what to teach and how to teach it are governed (although by no means wholly determined) by the social logic of the assessment system in a way that closely approximates what Bob Connell and his colleagues some years ago, writing about Australia, termed the *hegemonic curriculum*—the competitive individual appropriation in high-stakes assessments of stratified school knowledge—in a context where there is a tight nexus between academic achievement, the credentialing system, social mobility aspirations, and processes of class formation (Connell, Ashenden, Kessler, & Dowsett, 1982).

These considerations lead us to prefer a looser coupling of instruction and national summative assessment that gives teachers greater institutional space to develop instructional practices enabling students to develop the rich disciplinary understandings of content knowledge necessary to achieve Singapore's ambitions as a high-value knowledge economy and global city (Carver, 2006; Weigel, 2002). Of course, assessing these kinds of knowledge, understandings, and skills is far from easy. Indeed, in a recent review of "assessing deep understanding" in *The Cambridge Handbook of the Learning Sciences* (Sawyer, 2006), Sharon Carver (2006) highlights "the challenge of assessment . . . where the goal is for students to acquire deep understanding, the kind of knowledge experts use to accomplish meaningful tasks. Such understanding goes well beyond basic recall of facts and procedures to include the organization of concepts and strategies into a hierarchical framework that is useful for determining how and when to apply knowledge for understanding new material and solving related problems" (p. 205). Carver reminds us, if we needed reminding, that "traditional classroom tests and standards based assessments focus almost exclusively on the recognition and recall of superficial course content and are, therefore, not appropriate for assessing the thinking and problem solving that deep understanding supports" (p. 205).

How might these broader, more multidimensional assessments be undertaken? More particularly, how might they be undertaken in Singapore? One obvious possibility, despite the challenges to doing so, is to prepare an institutional environment that builds teachers' capacity in designing and implementing psychometrically sound authentic assessments. In addition, the assessments should be school-based, rubric-guided, moderated by both system officers and teams of expert teachers, and computer-assisted. All these can be developed by teachers working in distributed professional learning communities (within and across schools) to complement the school-based curriculum introduced by the Ministry of Education in 2006 (Carver, 2006; Harlen, 2007). Wynne Harlen's recent review of the research on the promise, validity, reliability, utility, and challenges of school- and rubric-based teacher assessment is especially useful in this regard (Harlen, 2007). So too is the recent work on the logic of moderation and indicators of understanding (e.g., Perkins, 1997; Pitman, O'Brien, & McCollow, 1999; Wiggins & McTighe, 2005). In addition, these assessments should also be informed by well-developed models of domain-specific or "disciplinary" and "transdisciplinary" competencies as well as by elaborated models of "evidences of understanding" rubrics and by sociocultural research on situated cognition to provide appropriate scaffolding to teachers and students in a way that allows them to explore "key topics," "essential learnings," or "generative questions" in substantial depth in conceptually driven, standards-based, well-designed, and developmentally appropriate disciplinary tasks in epistemic communities of practice or "knowledge-building" communities (e.g., Beilaczyc, 2006; Bennett, 2007; Bereiter & Scardamalia, 2006; Brown, Collins, & Duguid, 1989; Ford & Forman, 2006; Guile, 2006; Hogan, 2007; Lave & Wenger, 1991; Muller, 2000; Newmann & Associates, 1996; NRC, 2001a; Wiggins & McTighe, 2005; Wiske, 1997). For example, writing from a learning perspective that leans strongly toward a sociocultural and cognitive apprenticeship model of authentic disciplinary learning, Ford and Forman (2006, p. 3) point out that "repeatedly, for more than a century, educational reformers have reminded us that students enter and leave school with a very limited notion of what the disciplines they study are actually about . . . and that they should be engaged in the activities of historians, mathematicians, scientists or literary analysts rather than just learning about the results of those practices." In effect, learning disciplinary knowledge requires participating in those authentic, knowledge-intensive social practices in academic and nonacademic contexts that generate, evaluate, represent, communicate, report, and debate knowledge claims or aesthetic and moral judgments rather than just learning the results of these practices. Students don't learn disciplinary skills, understandings, and dispositions by learning *about* it but by *doing* it in authentic ways. "From a sociocultural perspective, teaching students about any disciplinary practice requires that they be engaged authentically in the activities of individual agents and group members that are necessary for a practice to achieve its aims" (Ford & Forman, 2006, p. 3).

A disciplinary pedagogy of this kind clearly raises important and difficult questions about assessing student participation in disciplinary and transdisciplinary practices, including, where appropriate, participation in domain-specific disciplinary processes involved in the generation or representation of knowledge claims, establishing the epistemic truth value of knowledge claims, communicating and debating knowledge claims, and reporting knowledge claims (Hogan, 2007). But these are not impossible tasks, particularly if we exploit the organizational, educational, structural, and strategic utility of developing and administering performative or authentic assessments on computers. From the perspective of assessment for learning, the value-adding benefits of digital technology are substantial and well beyond what regular print-based classroom methods are able to accomplish. For instance, when considering if students are making progress in desired directions, especially in contexts where they are engaged in group-based, community-oriented tasks (Black, 2001), in working through complex disciplinary tasks (Bennett, 2007; Carver, 2006) or "21st-century"/transdisciplinary tasks, digital technology can provide evidence—usually in the form of logs or transcripts of interactions—showing how knowledge is accessed, evaluated, managed, integrated, created, and communicated over time and distance and developed into online portfolios that map their progress in complex problem solving (Carver, 2006; Means, 2006; NRC, 2001a; Quellmalz & Kozma, 2003). In addition, digital technology supports the use of intelligent agents that can provide real-time scaffolding and feedback to students as well as foster self-assessment. The benefits of computer-assisted feedback for formative assessment practices are also well established (Hattie & Timperley, 2007).

In short, while difficult, there are no insurmountable technical obstacles to establishing a system of school-based assessment. It is important to emphasize here that that we are *not* recommending that the Ministry *replace* the current national assessment system with school-based assessments. Rather, we are suggesting that school-based summative assessments be incorporated into the national assessment system and that it be tied to the school-based curriculum development initiative. So organized, it would only account for a relatively small percentage (approximately 20%) of the total high-stakes national assessment. Further, the moderation of the school assessments by expert teachers (as in Queensland, Australia) and by officers of the Ministry would help maintain public confidence in the fairness, consistency, and reliability of school-based assessments. This in turn would do much to ensure its political legitimacy in the eyes of the community and the government.

It is important to emphasize that if a system of school-based assessments were to be adopted it would not damage or undermine the Ministry's reliance on the high-stakes assessment system to ensure quality control. After all, some 80% of the national assessment would be based on the national exams, and the moderation process would help ensure effective quality control over the remainder. In any case, as can be gleaned from Chapter 9, the recent Scottish assessment reforms remind us that it is not necessary to tie or couple quality control with the high-stakes summative assessment system since a combination of a battery of measures of pedagogical practice and assessments of student performance in a substantial and representative sample of schools would provide policy makers with a combination of input and output data to determine how well the system was performing. In other words, systems do not need to tightly couple assessment and quality control in order to ensure the former any more than they should tightly couple assessment and instruction for the same reason. Nor would school-based assessment weaken the nexus between assessment, on the one hand, and credentialing and social mobility, on the other, that is so central to public confidence in the assessment system and the fairness and legitimacy of Singapore's conception of a meritocratic social order.

In short, we have suggested that substantial and sustainable improvements in the quality of instruction and learning in Singapore in line with what the government hopes for (through its *TSLN* and *TLLM* policy initiatives) will require a recalibration or recoupling of the current alignment between assessment and instruction in order to expand the pedagogical opportunity or space teachers might have to try out new pedagogies. In a broad sense this is a matter of improved policy alignment—of making sure that the various policy settings are consistent and work together without contradiction. As it is everywhere else, this is far easier said than done. In the United States, for example, a notoriously loosely coupled system, policy makers have repeatedly sought to secure greater leverage over the pedagogical system, enhance accountability, and enhance the quality of teaching and learning through the use of high-stakes summative assessments, as Randy Bennett from the Educational Testing Service in Princeton, NJ, recently noted. Policy makers believe, he wrote, that they "can't evaluate educational effectiveness or know where education must improve" unless they have "mechanisms" available to them to identify the competencies, ages, population groups, schools, and even the individuals requiring attention (Bennett, 2007, p. 3). Assessment regimes do this. In addition, they believe that "accountability assessments can profoundly affect what teachers and students do. Policy makers know this, at least at a superficial level, and they try to use it to focus attention on achievement in particular subject areas and on the achievement of selected population groups" (Bennett, 2007, p. 3).

It is well known that the No Child Left Behind legislation in 2001, in the United States, was designed to expand centralized performative control over schools by instituting a national system of assessments in literacy and numeracy and thereby drive up the quality of classroom pedagogy. More recently, a much-discussed report by the blue ribbon panel assembled by the National Center on Education and the Economy (NCEE) in the United States entitled *Tough Choices or Tough Times* (NCEE, 2006) argued that the key to responding to alarming economic challenges from

China and India was to improve the skills and productivity of its labor force and to do so by improving the quality of teaching in American schools through improving the "quality" of teachers and by creating a "performance-based" system of education centered on a state-based exit examination at the end of 10th grade on the grounds that a national system of statewide exit examinations will lift standards, increase rigor, and enhance the quality of teaching and learning in U.S. high schools (NCEE, 2006, pp. 51–58). In effect, the NCEE panel believed that the future destiny of America resided in no small measure on a reformed assessment regime that emphasizes accountability and quality control (for a review of the NCEE report, see Hogan, 2008).

This is obviously a very large burden for any assessment system to shoulder, particularly so for a system as large and as diverse as the United States. Moreover, the research evidence gives little comfort to the architects of the No Child Left Behind (NCLB) legislation or to the blue ribbon NCEE panel, since the evidence appears to suggest that the high-stakes assessments in the United States have narrowed pedagogical practices to a conventional "teach to the test" format and made it harder and harder for teachers and schools to succeed in motivating students and improving learning. In a recent article, Grubb and Oakes (2007, pp. 19–23), for example, conclude that the U.S. evidence suggests that high-stakes summative assessments "reinforce conventional academic curriculum; they do little to enhance standards and may even undermine them; they distort curriculum and instruction; they lead to higher and more inequitable dropout rates; and, they impose substantial costs—especially on districts and schools that can least afford it—without considering alternatives." Consequently, "as a way of reforming the high school—even if reform is defined exclusively in terms of enhancing standards without consideration for alternative goals like those discussed in the final section—exit exams seem an approach that has so far failed on its own terms." Similarly, Linda Darling-Hammond, in her testimony on September 10, 2007, before the House Education and Labor Committee on the reauthorization of the NCLB legislation (Darling-Hammond, 2007, pp. 8–10), drew on extensive research by herself and others to challenge the pedagogical value of the kind of standardized assessments spawned by NCLB, including a "narrowing" and "distorting" of the curriculum, pressure on teachers "to use test formats in their instruction and to teach in ways that contradict their ideas of sound instructional practice," and, finally, a retreat from rich performative tasks and assessments to multiple-choice tests. Indeed, she concludes, "as a result of test score pressures, students are doing less extended writing, science inquiry, research in social sciences and other fields, and intensive projects that require planning, finding, analyzing, integrating, and presenting information—the skills increasingly needed in a 21st century workforce" (Darling-Hammond, 2007, p. 10).

Similar evidence and recommendations are reported for Britain by the British Assessment Reform group and others (Gardner, 2006; Harlen, 2007; James et al., 2006). Like their U.S. counterparts, British critics of high-stakes summative assessment do not dispute that summative assessments can shape instructional practices and student learning. What they question is the nature and benefits of this influence. Marshall and Drummond (2006), for example, in a major study of 1,500 teachers in 40 secondary schools across England found that teachers teach to the test, believe that they cannot responsibly do anything else, but that this "inhibits their ability to teach in a way that they understand to be good practice" (p. 147). Harlen (2007, pp. 1–2) draws on extensive research going back into the 1990s in the United States and the United Kingdom to argue that "high-stakes" assessments are not especially reliable, that they distort the curriculum and weaken classroom instruction, and all too often have a "negative impact" on student engagement and learning. Critically, Harlen emphasizes that the British accountability assessment regimes undermine rather than promote the ability of schools to prepare students for 21st-century institutions. It is clear, he argues, "that there was a mismatch between the widely recognized importance of preparing students for life in an increasingly changing and technological world and what was being taught, as dictated by tests" (p. 2). By contrast, 21st-century institutional landscapes require "a curriculum designed to develop the ability to access and evaluate information, to apply knowledge to new situations and, importantly, to acquire the prerequisites for continued learning throughout life. Using tests as measures of the outcomes of education reflects and encourages a narrow and naïve view of learning, and the more serious decisions resting on test scores (the higher the stakes) the greater the demand for 'accuracy,' with the consequence that the tests are reduced to aspects of performance that can be unambiguously marked as correct or incorrect" (p. 2). Consequently, "when national policy encourages judgment of schools and teachers on the basis of the performance of their students on such tests, 'teaching to the test' becomes even more damaging to students' learning experience in school" (p. 2).

Capacity Building and the Integration of Instruction and Assessment

The third challenge confronting system managers in Singapore is to develop teacher capacity in matters of assessment and to promote the effective integration of assessment—especially assessment *for* learning and assessment *as* learning—into the day-to-day classroom instruction. In the previous section we argued for a *looser* coupling of high-stakes summative assessment and classroom instruction; here we argue for a far *tighter* coupling of formative assessment and instruction. We recognize that this too will not be easy, and that the current tight coupling of instruction and high-stakes summative assessment limits the opportunity for a tighter coupling of formative assessment and instruction. Still, there is a considerable body of research—and some innovative practices internationally—that might be drawn on to guide the way.

The first task is to develop teacher capacity through an appropriately designed, transparent, and highly public system of professional development. This is important for both technical and political or institutional reasons, technically because teachers need high levels of assessment literacy in order to design reliable, valid, and fair authentic assessments, and politically because "the logic of confidence" requires that the public have confidence in the technical quality of the assessment data as well as fairness and professionalism of the teaching force if school-based assessments are to gain legitimacy in the eyes of the public and the government. To a very considerable extent, then, the success of assessment reform will depend on the further (and publicly transparent) professionalization of teaching. Enhancing the professional status of the profession through generous support (both in time off and financial support) for professional development workshops and postgraduate work is one means of doing so. The transfer of pedagogical authority from the center to the school through school-based curriculum development and assessment is another. Promoting action research models in schools is yet another. In Singapore, the Ministry of Education has been highly supportive on all these fronts. However, CRPP research in Singapore, and our reading of the professional development literature internationally, suggests strongly that traditional forms of professional development, focused on workshops and coursework, have a limited sustainable impact on classroom teaching over the long term. Instead, our research, and the international research literature generally, suggests that teacher learning and sustainable pedagogical innovation is optimized when it treats teachers as active learners who are engaged in concrete tasks of teaching, assessment, observation, and reflection in situ; when it is grounded in participants' questions, inquiry, and experimentation, as well as research on effective practice; when it is iterative and extended over time and supported by follow-up activities; when it is collaborative, involving sharing of knowledge among educators; when it is embedded in schools functioning as communities of learners and communities of inquiry embedded in turn in larger cluster level (9–10 schools) distributed professional communities of learning; when it is linked systematically to curriculum, assessment, and instructional innovation and cultural change at the school level; and when it is focused on developing teacher expertise in content knowledge, pedagogical content knowledge, assessment literacy, classroom inquiry, curriculum knowledge, and pedagogical judgment. As Richard Elmore (2004, pp. 73, 127) recently put it, "improvement is more a function of learning to do the right things in the setting where you work. . . . The problem is that there is almost no opportunity for teachers to engage in continuous learning about their practice in the setting in which they actually work, observing and being observed by their colleagues in their own classrooms and classrooms of other teachers in other schools confronting similar problems of practice." We agree. Again, we emphasize that professional development of this kind is important for both technical reasons—to develop, for example, high-quality assessment tasks—and politically as well in order to promote and maintain public confidence in new assessment initiatives. But focusing on developing assessment literacy by itself is not sufficient. In addition, assessment *for* learning, and indeed, assessment *as* learning, need to be fully integrated into classroom instruction and not seen as an activity that is tacked on to the end of the instructional process as in Tylerian models of curriculum, teaching, and assessment.

In a recent review of the role of technology in assessment practices, Means (2006, p. 505) maps out "two competing visions of the purpose and nature of effective classroom assessments." The first vision "calls for connecting classroom assessment to state mandated content standards and an accountability system." The second vision "drawing heavily on recent advances in the learning sciences, calls for using technology to develop and deliver assessments that are integrated into day-to-day instruction and enable teachers to gain deeper insights into their students' thinking and to adapt their instruction accordingly." While the first vision has dominated the policy-making scene in the United States and elsewhere, the second vision has slowly garnered growing support among researchers, the teaching profession, and policy makers (e.g., Black & Wiliam, 1998, 2001; Carver, 2006; Gardner, 2006; Harlen, 2007; Means, 2006; NRC, 2001a). It is important to point out that research on formative assessment has been dominated by two traditions that parallel the two visions of assessment that Means describes. In the first tradition, developed primarily within the fields of school psychology, educational psychology, and special education, formative assessments are tools "used to monitor progress and to provide feedback about the progress being made . . . In the classroom setting, formative evaluation is used to inform students and teachers about progress" (Lee, 2005, p. 209). The goal of this type of formative assessment is to determine whether specific students, groups of students, or an entire class require additional instruction. Typically, these measures are administered regularly, they are brief and efficient, and, increasingly, they use computer-assisted assessment. The second tradition, developed principally by researchers in the cognitive and learning sciences, is typified by recent publications by the National Research Council in the United States (NRC, 2000, 2001a, 2001b, 2005) and the work of Black and Wiliam (Black & Wiliam, 1998, 2001) and the Assessment Reform Group (ARG) in the United Kingdom (ARG, 2002). Donovan and Bransford (NRC, 2005, p. 16), for example, establish three goals for formative assessments: (1) to make students' thinking visible to both teachers and students, (2) to monitor student progress (in mastering concepts as well as factual information), and (3) to design instruction that is responsive to student progress.

Now, it is worth noting that both research traditions stress monitoring progress toward an instructional goal and adjusting instruction for students based on the formative measures. However, while the first tradition focuses principally on the empirical establishment of the validity and reliability of the assessment procedures, the second focuses principally on diagnosing and monitoring student errors and schematic misconceptions in order to help guide instructional practice (e.g., by pointing to the types of questions that teachers might ask) and to promote the broader integration of assessment and instruction (National Mathematics Advisory Panel, 2008, p. 187). This tradition is embodied for example, in *Adding It Up* (NRC, 2001b):

> Information about students is crucial to a teacher's ability to calibrate tasks and lessons to students' current understanding . . . In addition to tasks that reveal what students know and can do, the quality of instruction depends

on how teachers interpret and use that information. Teachers' understanding of their students' work and the progress they are making relies on . . . their ability to use that understanding to make sense of what the students are doing. (pp. 349–350)

The work of Black and Wiliam has been especially significant in this second tradition, particularly their widely cited conclusion at the end of an exhaustive review of interventions to improve student learning that "there is [a] body of firm evidence that formative assessment is an essential feature of classroom work and that development of it can raise standards. We know of no other way of raising standards for which such a strong prima facie case can be made on the basis of such learning gains" (Black & Wiliam, 2001, p. 13). Black and Wiliam, however, emphasize that these gains will not be achieved unless and until formative assessment is fully integrated into instruction and becomes the basis for evidence-based customized or differentiated instruction.

For Means, it is exactly this feature of current accountability systems of assessment that is missing and renders it difficult for them to improve the quality of teaching and learning. She continues: "Many of the systems that are designed to support classroom assessments that are linked to standards and accountability systems lack this ability to inform instructional decisions. They tend to provide information on whether a student has achieved mastery, but not provide insights into the way the student is thinking" (2006, p. 508). Similarly, in a highly influential report for the National Research Council (NRC, 2000), Bransford et al. write that "formative assessments—ongoing assessments designed to make students' thinking visible to both teachers and students—are essential [to instructional improvement]." They go on to point out that formative assessments "permit the teacher to grasp the student's preconceptions, understand where the students are in the 'developmental corridor,' from informal to formal thinking, and design instruction accordingly. In the assessment-centered, classroom environment, formative assessments help both teachers and students monitor progress" (NRC, 2000, p. 24). Furthermore, as Tomlinson (1999, p. 10) suggests, "In a differentiated classroom, assessment is ongoing and diagnostic. Its goal is to provide teachers day to day data on student readiness for particular ideas and skills, their interests and their learning profiles. These teachers don't see assessment as something that comes at the end of the unit to find out what students learned; rather, assessment is today's means of understanding how to modify tomorrow's instruction."

In a recent work, Fullan, Hill, and Crévola (2006, pp. 47–49) have sought to extend this model of instruction and assessment by adding two further elements: (1) codified expert instructional knowledge of what expert teachers know (pedagogical content knowledge or PCK), and (2) diagnostic instructional pathways that allow teachers to draw on this codified expert knowledge to inform what they do in particular learning situations. "We see classroom instruction as an activity that can be improved by making expert knowledge available to all teachers," they write. "We believe that there is such a thing as expertise in teaching: that the nature of this expertise can be made explicit, so that it is capable of being replicated and validated; and that expert teaching translates into improved learning" (Fullan, Hill, & Crévola, 2006, p. 47). Figure 8.1 is a schematic representation of their expanded model, while Figure 8.2 incorporates additional features—distributed leadership, the organization of the school as a professional learning community, and technology/ICT—into the model (Hogan, 2008).

Clearly, the ability of systems to establish integrated assessment and instruction systems like this model has been significantly enhanced by recent developments in measurement theory and methods and current computer-based technologies that allow teachers to get more or less instant real-time feedback on student performance at the individual or classroom levels, therefore permitting appropriate evidence-based individualized

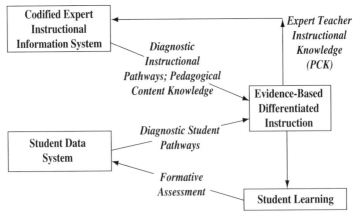

Figure 8.1 Schematic model of formative assessment, expert knowledge, and differentiated instruction.

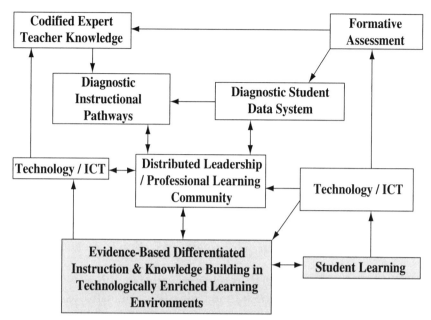

Figure 8.2 Schematic model of expert knowledge, formative assessment, professional learning communities, and differentiated instruction.

or group instruction. Indeed, appropriately used and supported, current technologies permit the full integration of formative assessment into instructional practice in classrooms, in part by eliminating large time lapses between student performance and teacher access to diagnostic data. Pellegrino (2006), for example, notes that:

> by building statistical models into technology-based learning environments for use in classrooms, teachers can assign more complex tasks, capture and replay student performances, share exemplars of competent performance, and in the process gain critical information about student competence. Without question, computer and telecommunications technologies are making it possible to create powerful learning environments and simultaneously assess what students are learning at very fine levels of detail, with vivid simulations of real world situations, and in ways that are tightly integrated with instruction. (p. 10)

Critically, a number of systems, including the Boston City School District in the United States, have developed an integrated assessment and instruction system that relies extensively on computer-based data systems (Boudett, City, & Murname, 2005).

CONCLUSIONS

To determine how a particular government might respond to the complex and extensive demands of globalization and modernization, we reviewed instructional and assessment practices in Singapore and mapped out three key challenges that need to be addressed in developing a system of assessment that will both advance the key policy objectives laid down by the government in the *TSLN* and *TLLM* initiatives as well as respond appropriately to the changed institutional landscape of the 21st century. Certainly, policy makers in Singapore have proactively sought ways to engineer more engaged and authentic learning and improved assessment practices. However, our sense is that the long-term and sustainable improvements of instructional and assessment practices require a four-part innovation strategy that:

1. *Broadens* the range of skills, understandings, and dispositions that are measured in school-based and high-stakes summative assessments;
2. *Widens* the opportunities and training available to students for personal improvement (e.g., becoming effective assessors) (cf. Boud, 2000);
3. *Loosens* the coupling of high-stakes summative assessment and instructional practice; and
4. *Tightens* the coupling of formative assessment and instructional practices through strategic assessment design that is suited to the developmental characteristics of learners (Carver, 2006).

Without these initiatives, we suspect that despite the policy settings provided by the *TSLN* and *TLLM* initiatives and the substantial "top-down" support the Ministry provides schools, the ability of teachers to develop a pedagogy that provides the cognitive depth and skills that 21st-century institutions demand and MOE policy requires will be compromised. We further contend that the current alignment (or "tight coupling") at the systemic and classroom level between curriculum, teaching, and assessment imposes significant constraints on the ability of teachers to improve the intellectual quality of assessment tasks and instructional activities at the classroom level independent of questions of teacher capacity and, therefore, inhibits rather than promotes pedagogical innovation in line with recent policy directions. In effect, we believe, for all its successes, the current assessment system extracts substantial pedagogical opportunity costs because of the institutional power and status of the high-stakes assessment system and its ability to shape teaching practices at the individual classroom level. The result of this extremely tight coupling of assessment and instruction is a pedagogy that focuses on coverage of prescribed curriculum content, the transmission of basic skills and understandings, and a pervasive culture of teacher talk, drill, and memorization. Clearly, this pedagogical arrangement has yielded any number of positive learning outcomes and national achievements, but it also entailed significant opportunity costs.

Overall, while these opportunity costs are substantial, in our view, it would be undesirable, and politically unworkable, to decouple assessment, curriculum, and pedagogy entirely, or to abandon high-stakes assessment overnight. Rather, the issue, and it is a difficult one, is how we might improve the assessment system and its alignments and couplings in a way that is educationally powerful but not contradictory—that generates desired schooling outcomes but minimizes the pedagogy and learning opportunity costs of assessment regimes focused on high-stakes assessments. These are dilemmas for all 21st-century assessment innovators to consider.

NOTES

1. Unlike the United States, national assessments in Singapore are closely aligned to curriculum content.
2. Scott goes on to emphasize that different institutions and institutional fields exhibit different mixes of regulative, normative, and cognitive elements. Regulative mechanisms—rules, sanctions, rewards, and surveillance—constrain behavior through the threat of sanctions or by prompting officials to comply with the regulations out of regard for their own interests (what Scott terms the *logic of instrumentalism*). Normative mechanisms (values, norms, standards) "introduce a prescriptive, evaluative and obligatory dimension" into the life of organizations by focusing on how role expectations (e.g., professionally based definitions of teacher responsibilities and rights) constrain and motivate behavior according to "the logic of appropriateness." Cognitive mechanisms focus on "the rules that constitute the nature of reality and the frames through which meaning is made." For those emphasizing cognitive mechanisms, "compliance occurs . . . because other types of behaviour are inconceivable; routines are followed because they are taken for granted as 'the way we do these things.'" Thus, whereas "the emphasis of normative theories is on the power of roles—normative expectations guiding behaviour—the cognitive framework stresses the importance of social identities: our conceptions of who we are and what ways of action make sense for us in a given situation" (Scott, 1995, p. 44).
3. In fact, Rowan and Miskel (1999, p. 73) openly admit that "early institutionalist theories tended to ignore the effects of institutionalized rules on the technical core of schools." See also Powell and DiMaggio (1991).

4. We might also use another term to describe the "folk culture" of teaching and learning derived from recent work on English and American social history. We have in mind the concept, to borrow from the great English social historian E. P. Thompson, of a *moral economy* (of teaching and learning). See Hogan (1989) on the moral economy of the early 19th-century English classroom. In the same way that the moral economy of 18th-century English tradesmen fueled their resistance to the normative assumptions of industrial capitalism, we can perhaps trace some of the resistance of contemporary teachers to pedagogical innovation to their "traditional" moral economy of good pedagogy.

5. Of course, this can be disputed: as Charles Taylor (1989) notes, Western philosophy, beginning with the Greeks, has long been preoccupied with deeply normative questions of practical judgment—"What is the good?" "What is a good life?" "How can I live a good life?"

6. It is important to note that while there is ample international evidence for the substantial negative effects on student motivation, participation, and self-esteem for particular student populations, there is very limited research on the relationship between high-stakes assessments and student achievement. In a recent comprehensive review of the impact of high-stakes assessment on student achievement, Stiggins (2004) could find only one research paper that explicitly addressed the question of whether high-stakes assessments in fact increased student achievement. The study, by Eric Hanushek and Margaret Reynolds, reported "tiny test score gains attributable to the presence of high stakes tests" (Stiggins, 2004, p. 23). Linn (2000) and Shepard (2000) report similar findings. Stiggins goes on to note there is considerable evidence that high-stakes assessments "are often accompanied by such negative outcomes as reduced achievement, increased drop out rates, and reduced graduation rates—especially for minority students" (Stiggins, 2004, p. 23; see also Harlen, 2007).

REFERENCES

Applebee, A. N. (1996). *Curriculum as conversation: Transforming traditions of teaching and learning.* Chicago: University of Chicago Press.

Arrow, K., Bowles, S., & Durlauf, S. (Eds.). (2000). *Meritocracy and economic inequality.* Princeton, NJ: Princeton University Press.

Assessment Reform Group. (2002). *Assessment for learning: 10 principles.* Cambridge, UK: University of Cambridge.

Bauman, Z. (2001). *The individualized society.* Cambridge, UK: Polity Press.

Beck, U. (1992). *Risk society: Towards a new modernity.* London: Sage.

Beck, U., & Beck-Gernsheim, E. (2002). *Individualization: Institutionalized individualism and its social and political consequences.* London: Sage.

Beck, U., Giddens, A., & Lash, S. (1994). *Reflexive modernization.* London: Sage.

Beilaczyc, K. (2006). Designing social infrastructure: Critical issues in creating learning environments with technology. *Journal of the Learning Sciences, 15*(3), 301–329.

Bennett, R. (2007). *Assessment of, for, and as learning: Can we have all three?* Conceptual Paper. Princeton, NJ: Educational Testing Service.

Bereiter, C., & Scardamalia, M. (2006). Education for the knowledge age: Design-centred models of teaching and instructions. In P. Alexander & P. Winne (Eds.), *Handbook of educational psychology* (2nd ed., pp. 695–714). Mahwah, NJ: Erlbaum.

Bidwell, C. (1965). The school as a formal organization. In J. G. March (Ed.), *Handbook of Organizations* (pp. 927–1022). Chicago: Rand McNally.

Black, P. (2001). Dreams, strategies and systems: Portraits as assessment past, present and future. *Assessment in Education, 8*(1), 65–85.

Black, P., & Wiliam, D. (1998). Assessment and classroom learning. *Assessment in Education, 5*(1), 7–73.

Black, P., & Wiliam, D. (2001). *Inside the black box: Raising standards through classroom assessment.* London, UK: Kings College London School of Education. Retrieved April 25, 2008, from http://ngfl.northumberland.gov.uk/keystage3ictstrategy/Assessment/blackbox.pdf

Borghans, L., Duckworth, A. L., Heckman, J., & Weel, B.-T. (2008). *The economics and psychology of personality traits.* Discussion paper No. 3333, Institute for the Study of Labor, University of Bonn. Retrieved June 2008, from http://ftp.iza.org/dp3333.pdf

Boud, D. (2000). Sustainable assessment: Rethinking assessment for the learning society. *Studies in Continuing Education, 22*(2), 151–167.

Boudett, K. P., City, E. A., & Murname, R. (2005). *Data wise: A step by step guide to using assessment results to improve teaching and learning.* Cambridge. MA: Harvard University Press.

Bowles, S., Gintis, H., & Groves, M. (2005). *Unequal chances: Family background and economic success.* Princeton, NJ: Princeton University Press.

Brown, J. S., Collins, A., & Duguid, P. (1989). Situated cognition and the culture of learning. *Educational Researcher, 18*(1), 32–41.

Bruner, J. (1990). *Acts of meaning.* Cambridge, MA: Harvard University Press.

Carver, S. M. (2006). Assessing for deep understanding. In R. K. Sawyer (Ed.), *The Cambridge handbook of the learning sciences* (pp. 205–221). Cambridge, UK: Cambridge University Press.

Cohen, D. (1988). *Teaching practice: Plus que ca change.* East Lansing: Michigan State University, National Center for Research on Teacher Education.

Connell, R. W., Ashenden, D. J., Kessler, S., & Dowsett, G. W. (1982). *Making the difference: Schools, families and social division.* Sydney: George Allen and Unwin.

Darling-Hammond, L. (2007). *Testimony before the House Education and Labor Committee on the Re-Authorization of the NCLB legislation.* Retrieved December 12, 2007, from http://edlabor.house.gov/testimony/091007LindaDarlingHammondTestimony.pdf

Donovan, M. S., & Bransford, J. D. (2005). Introduction. In the National Research Council (Ed.), *How students learn: Mathematics in the classroom* (pp. 1–26). Washington, DC: National Academy Press.

Elmore, R. F. (2004). *School reform from the inside out: Policy, practice and performance.* Cambridge, MA: Harvard Education Press.

Ford, M., & Forman, E. (2006). Redefining disciplinary learning in classroom contexts. *Review of Research in Education, 30*(1), 1–32.

Fullan, M. (2007). *The new meaning of educational change.* New York: Teachers College Press.

Fullan, M., Hill, P., & Crévola, C. (2006). *Breakthrough.* Thousand Oaks, CA: Corwin Press.

Gardner, J. (Ed.). (2006). *Assessment and learning*. London: Sage.

Giddens, A. (1991). *Modernity and self identity: Self and society in the late modern age*. Stanford, CA: Stanford University Press.

Graham, A. (1989). *Disputers of the Tao*. La Salle, IL: Open Court.

Grubb, N., & Oakes, J. (2007). *Restoring value to the high school diploma: The rhetoric and practice of higher standards*. Arizona State University, Educational Policy Research Unit. Retrieved May 2, 2008, from http://epsl.asu.edu/epru/documents/EPSL-0710–242-EPRU.pdf

Guile, D. (2006). What is distinctive about the knowledge economy: Implications for education. In H. Lauder, P. Brown, J.-A. Dillabough, & A. H. Halsey (Eds.), *Education, globalization and social change* (pp. 355–366). Oxford, UK: Oxford University Press.

Hall, D., & Ames, R. (1987). *Thinking through Confucius*. Albany: State University of New York Press.

Hall, S. (1992). The question of cultural identity. In S. Hall, D. Held, & T. McGrew (Eds.), *Modernity and its futures: Understanding modern societies* (pp. 273–326). Cambridge, UK: Polity Press.

Hall, S. (1996). Introduction: Who needs "identity"? In S. Hall & P. du Gay (Eds.), *Questions of cultural identity* (pp. 1–17). London: Sage.

Harlen, W. (2007). *Assessment of learning*. London: Sage.

Hattie, J., & Timperley, H. (2007). The power of feedback. *Review of Educational Research, 77*(1), 81–112.

Heckman, J. (2004). Lessons from the technology of human capital formation. *Annals of the New York Academy of Science, 1038*, 179–200.

Heckman, J., & Rubinstein, Y. (2001). The importance of non-cognitive skills: Lessons from the GED testing program. *American Economic Review, 91*(2), 145–159.

Heckman, J., Stizrud, J., & Urzua, S. (2006). The effects of cognitive and noncognitive abilities on the labor market. *Journal of Labor Economics, 24*(3), 411–482.

Hogan, D. (1989, Fall). The market revolution and disciplinary power: Joseph Lancaster and the psychology of the early classroom system. *History of Education Quarterly,* 381–417.

Hogan, D. (2006, July). *Education and the pursuit of happiness in Singapore*. Keynote Address to the Education Research Association of Singapore Conference, Singapore.

Hogan, D. (2007, May). *Towards "Invisible Colleges": Conversation, disciplinarity and pedagogy in Singapore*. Keynote Address to the CRPP Redesigning Pedagogies Conference, Singapore.

Hogan, D. (2008). Why no political economy? Why no pedagogy? An essay review of "Tough Choices or Tough Times." *Educational Change, 9*(1), 91–99.

Hogan, D., & Chan, M. (2006, April). *Negotiating high modernity: Life goals and aspirations of Singaporean adolescents*. Presentation at American Education Research Association Conference, San Francisco.

Hogan, D., & Kang, T. (2006). Towards talentocracy: Capital formation among young Singaporeans. In Lai Ah Eng (Ed.), *Singapore perspectives 2006: Going global: Being Singaporean in a globalized world* (pp. 31–50). Singapore: Institute of Policy Studies.

Hogan, D., Kang, T., & Chan, M. (2007). Framing lives: Longitudinal research on life planning and pathways in Singapore. In W. T. Pink & G. W. Noblitt (Eds.), *International handbook of urban education* (pp. 359–379). New York: Springer Publishing.

James, M., Black, P., McCormick, R., Pedder D., & William, D. (2006). Learning how to learn in classrooms, schools and networks: Aims, design and analysis. *Research Papers in Education, 21*(2) 101–118.

James, M., Black, P., Carmichael, P., Conner, C., Dudley, P., Fox, A., et al. (2007a). *Learning how to learn: Tools for schools.* London: Routledge.

James, M., McCormick, R., Black, P., Carmichael, P., Drummond, M.-J., Fox, A., et al. (2007b). *Improving how to learn: Classrooms, schools and networks* (3rd ed.). London: Routledge.

Jencks, C., Smith, M., Acland, H., Bane, M. J., Cohen, D., Gintis, H., et al. (1972). *Inequality: A reassessment of the effect of family and schooling in America.* New York: Basic Books.

Lave, J., & Wenger, E. (1991). *Situated learning: Legitimate peripheral participation.* Cambridge, UK: Cambridge University Press.

Lee, H. L. (2004, August 22). *National day rally speech 2004. Delivered at the university cultural centre, NUS.* Retrieved February 6, 2008, from http://stars.nhb.gov.sg/stars/public/viewHTML.jsp?pdfno=2004083101

Lee, S. W. (2005). *Encyclopedia of school psychology.* Thousand Oaks, CA: Sage.

Linn, R. L. (2000). Assessments and accountability. *Educational Researcher, 29*(2), 4–16.

MacDonald, K. (1999). *Struggles for subjectivity: Identity, agency and youth experience.* Cambridge, UK: Cambridge University Press.

Marshall, B., & Drummond, M. (2006). How teachers engage with assessment for learning: Lessons from the classroom. *Research Papers in Education, 21*(2), 133–150.

Means, B. (2006). Prospects for transforming schools with technology-supported assessment. In R. K. Sawyer (Ed.), *The Cambridge handbook of the learning sciences* (pp. 505–519). Cambridge, UK: Cambridge University Press.

Meyer, J. (1977). The effects of education as an institution. *American Journal of Sociology, 83,* 55–77.

Meyer, J., & Rowan, B. (1977). Institutionalized organization: Formal structure as myth and ceremony. *American Journal of Sociology, 83,* 340–363.

Meyer, J., & Rowan, B. (1983). The structure of educational organizations. In J. Meyer & W. R. Scott (Eds.), *Organizational environments: Ritual and rationality* (pp. 71–97). Beverly Hills, CA: Sage.

Meyer, J., Scott, W. R., & Deal, T. (1983). Institutional and technical sources of organizational structure: Explaining the structure of educational organizations. In J. Meyer & W. R. Scott (Eds.), *Organizational environments: Ritual and rationality* (pp. 45–67). Beverly Hills, CA: Sage.

Muller, J. (2000). *Reclaiming knowledge: Social theory, curriculum and educational policy.* London: Routledge.

National Mathematics Advisory Panel. (2008). *Foundations for success: The final report of the National Mathematics Advisory Panel.* Washington, DC: U.S. Department of Education.

National Center on Education and the Economy. (2006). *Tough choices or tough times: The report of the new commission on the skills of the American workforce.* Washington, DC: Author.

National Research Council. (1999). *The changing nature of work: Implications for occupational analysis.* Washington, DC: National Academy Press.

National Research Council. (2000). *How people learn: Brain, mind, experience and school.* J. Bransford, A. Brown, & R. Cocking (Eds.). Washington, DC: National Academy Press.

National Research Council. (2001a). *Knowing what students know: The science and design of educational assessment.* J. Pellegrino, N. Chudowky, & R. Glasser (Eds.). Washington, DC: National Academy Press.

National Research Council. (2001b). *Adding it up: Helping children learn mathematics.* J. Kilpatrick, J. Swafford, & B. Findell (Eds.). Washington, DC: National Academy Press.

National Research Council. (2005). *How students learn: Mathematics in the classroom.* M. S. Donovan & J. D. Bransford (Eds.). Washington, DC: National Academy Press.

Newmann, F., & Associates. (1996). *Authentic achievement: Restructuring schools for intellectual quality.* San Francisco: Jossey-Bass.

Oakeshott, M. (1962). *Rationalism in politics and other essays.* Lanham, MD: Rowman & Littlefield.

Organisation for Economic Cooperation and Development. (1999). *Measuring student knowledge and skills: A new framework for assessment.* Paris: Author.

Organisation for Economic Cooperation and Development. (2000). *Knowledge management in the learning society: Education and skills.* Paris: Author.

Organisation for Economic Cooperation and Development. (2004) *Innovation in the knowledge economy: Implications for education and learning.* Paris: Author.

Organisation for Economic Cooperation and Development. (2005). *The definition and selection of key competencies: Executive summary.* Retrieved January 1, 2008, from http://www.oecd.org/dataoecd/47/61/35070367.pdf

Pellegrino, J. W. (2006, November). *Rethinking and redesigning curriculum, instruction and assessment: What contemporary research and theory suggests.* A paper commissioned by the National Center on Education and the Economy for the New Commission on the Skills of the American Workforce. Washington, DC: NCEE.

Perkins, D. (1997). What is understanding? In M. S. Wiske (Ed.), *Teaching for understanding* (pp. 39–57). San Francisco: Jossey-Bass.

Pitman, J., O'Brien, J. E., & McCollow, J. E. (1999). *High quality assessment: We are what we believe we do.* Paper presented at the 25th Annual Conference of International Association for Educational Assessment, Bled, Slovenia.

Powell, W., & DiMaggio, P. (1991). *The new institutionalism in organizational analysis.* Chicago: University of Chicago Press.

Quellmalz, E. S., & Kozma, R. (2003). Designing assessments of learning with technology. *Assessment in Education, 10*(3), 289–407.

Rothstein, R (2004). *Class and schools: Using social, economic and educational reform to close the black-white achievement gap.* New York: Teachers College Press.

Rowan, B., & Miskel, C. (1999). Institutional theory and the study of educational organizations. In J. Murphy & K. S. Loius (Eds.), *Handbook of research on educational administration* (2nd ed., pp. 359–383). San Francisco: Jossey-Bass.

Sawyer, R. K. (Ed.). (2006). *The Cambridge handbook of the learning sciences.* New York: Cambridge University Press.

Schleicher, A. (2007). Can competencies assessed by PISA be considered the fundamental school knowledge 15 year olds should possess? *Journal of Educational Change, 8*, 349–367.

Scott, W. R. (1995). *Institutions and organizations.* London: Sage.

Shanmugaratnam, T. (2005, September 22). *Speech by Mr. Tharman Shanmugaratnam, Minister for Education, at the MOE Work Plan Seminar 2005.* The Ngee Ann Polytechnic Convention Centre, Singapore.

Shepard, L. A. (2000). The role of assessment in a learning culture. *Educational Researcher, 29*(7), 4–14.

Stiggins, R. (2004). New assessment beliefs for a new school mission. *Phi Delta Kappan, 86*(1), 22–27.

Taylor, C. (1989). *Sources of the self: The making of modern identity.* Cambridge, MA: Harvard University Press.

Tomlinson, C. A. (1999). *The differentiated classroom. Responding to the needs of all learners.* Alexandria, VA: Association for Supervision and Curriculum Development.

Weick, K. (1976). Educational systems as loosely coupled systems. *Administrative Science Quarterly, 21*(1), 1–19.

Weigel, V. B. (2002). *Deep learning for a digital age: Technology's untapped potential to enrich higher learning.* San Francisco: Jossey-Bass.

Wiggins, G., & McTighe, J. (2005). *Understanding by design* (2nd ed.). Alexandria, VA: ASCD.

Wiske, M. S. (Ed.). (1997). *Teaching for understanding.* San Francisco: Jossey-Bass.

Wong, D. (2005). *Comparative philosophy: Chinese and western.* Stanford Encyclopaedia of Philosophy. Retrieved May 1, 2008, from http://plato.stanford.edu/entries/com parphil-chiwes/

Zakaria, F. (2006, January 6). There is no textbook formula. *The Straits Times.*

9

Instructional and Assessment Practices in Singapore

DAVID HOGAN, PHILLIP A. TOWNDROW, AND KIM KOH

In the pursuit of the pedagogical Holy Grail, assessment bears an especially heavy burden in contemporary educational discourse. On the one hand, assessment is broadly viewed as a key mechanism to promote quality control and ensure accountability in teaching and learning. On the other hand, instructional reformers across the world argue that assessment reform is the key to improving teaching and learning (Black & Wiliam, 1998b, 2003; Black, Harrison, Lee, Marshall, & Wiliam, 2003; Boud, 2000; Gardner, 2006; Stiggins, 2002). Additionally, assessment issues fuel extensive debate about what reforms are needed to address contemporary stakeholder needs. Under these circumstances, what types of decisions are required and what kinds of choices are available to nations, federal agencies, teachers, and students when devising efficient and effective plans of action relating to assessment?

One response to the often competing demands bearing down on assessment systems takes a somewhat polarizing approach. Seen from one side, assessment reform agendas can be used as a lever of change by policy makers in the name of improving educational attainment levels. For example, in the United States, the federal Elementary and Secondary Education Act (ESEA), otherwise known as the No Child Left Behind Act, signed into law by George W. Bush in 2002, has the goal of 100% of students performing at grade levels and achieving state-mandated standards by the year 2014 (Cummins, Brown, & Sayers, 2007). Arguably, while the emphasis in ESEA on closing achievement gaps is praiseworthy, the high levels of accountability and the management of pedagogic practice placed on teachers and educational institutions in reaching state-set targets is a cause for concern. Chief among the issues to arise are restricting curriculum instruction to tested items (teaching to the test) and not taking into account how students feel about themselves and about their chances of being successful in the classroom (Cummins et al., 2007).

On the other hand, assessment can be viewed as a means to widen pedagogic horizons and provide ways for students and teachers to respond to the contingencies of modern life actively, account for student identity and affect, and do so productively over the long term (Black, 2001; Boud, 2000; Harlen, 2007).

Globally, issues surrounding the pace, scope, and direction of assessment policies, practices, and reforms are troublesome not least because of the uncertainty that surely exists given the dynamism, complexity, and disjunctures that are characteristic of modern life (Appadurai, 1996). Nonetheless, it seems reasonable to assume that individual nations and governmental agencies would do well to craft their particular assessment practices according to their priorities, interests, and resources (both capital and human) taking into account specific cultural, social, political, and historical factors as well as international assessment research. It would be instructive both nationally and internationally to know more about how a country's "assessment narrative" unfolds in these respects.

In this vein, this chapter builds on our previous contribution to this volume (Chapter 8) by providing a country-specific report of instructional and assessment practices in Singapore: a well-resourced nation-state that actively positions itself as a vibrant, well-governed, ambitious global city-state (Velayutham, 2007). In what follows we begin with a conceptualization of educational assessment that identifies its various purposes and then a framework is adopted showing how assessment functions at the level of the educational system. Next, we present data collected from the Core research program undertaken at the Centre for Research in Pedagogy and Practice (CRPP) in the National Institute of Education, Singapore, focusing on classroom instructional practices and how knowledge is transmitted and constructed in the classroom.[1] We also describe teachers' routines and their self-identified rationales in setting assessment tasks, using and sharing rubrics, and in giving feedback to students. Given present educational policy initiatives in Singapore, we use our findings to highlight some of the strengths in Singapore pedagogy.

Our discussion also points to areas where we consider the Singapore assessment system could be broadened and further refined.

FRAMING ASSESSMENT

We conceptualize educational assessment as any method or activity that is designed to collect data about the knowledge, skills, or dispositions of a learner or a group of learners. For example, the American Federation of Teachers (AFT), National Council on Measurement in Education (NCME), and the National Education Association (NEA) (1990, p. 1) define assessment as:

> The process of obtaining information that is used to make educational decisions about students, to give feedback to the student about his or her progress, strengths, and weaknesses, to judge instructional effectiveness and curricular adequacy, and to inform policy.

It is evident from this definition that assessment serves a variety of purposes and provides information for making educational decisions about three things: (1) students, (2) curricula and programs, and (3) policy (Nitko, 2004). Broadly conceived, the decisions made about students can be informed from the data derived from two types of assessment: summative and formative. Decisions about curricular and programs are usually based on program evaluations. Finally, in many countries, data drawn from international benchmarking exercises such as the Trends in International Mathematics and Science Study (TIMSS) and the Program for International Student Assessment (PISA) are used to make important policy decisions.

As far as educational decision making about students using assessment data is concerned—the main focus of this chapter—there is some inconsistency in the meaning and use of terms used by teachers and assessment authorities. Generally, summative assessment attempts to summarize the development of learners at a particular time and is typified by standardized tests and the assignation of scores or grades to determine which students in the class "got it and who didn't" (Tomlinson, 2001, p. 20). The term, *assessment of learning*, commonly refers to summative assessment practices.

On the other hand—although this type of contrastive analysis has its drawbacks as will become clear soon—formative assessment is linked closely to the processes of teaching and learning. According to Black and Wiliam (1998b), assessment is formative when evidence gathered is used to adapt teaching to meet students' needs. As further explained by the Assessment Reform Group (Gardner, 2006) and reinforced by Hattie and Timperley (2007), formative assessment seeks and interprets evidence for use by teachers and their students in deciding where students are in their learning (current position), where they need to go (next target), and how best to get there (strategies to bridge the gap).

Much has been made in the literature about the potential of formative assessment to raise levels of achievement (Black & Wiliam, 1998b, 2003; Black et al., 2003; Gardner, 2006; Harlen, 2007), but Stiggins (2002) points out that formative assessment is not necessarily the same as a related term, *assessment for learning*. What is distinctive about assessment for learning processes is that they crucially involve students in decision making and provide the bases for sustained learning and confidence-building over time. Not all teachers may be ready for such challenges, if only because they lack sufficient opportunities or preparation.

Another concept important to mention is *assessment as learning*. This refers to the value placed on educational experiences per se and involves practices associated with learning how to learn in terms of pupils and staff reflecting on their own evidence of learning, pupils and staff helping to set their own goals, and pupils and staff practicing self- and peer-assessment (Earl, 2003; Hayward, 2007).

When taken together, the purposes of assessment *of, for,* and *as* learning strike a common note in that they each set out to provide information about students. Given the important role assessment plays in learning (Gardner, 2006; Harlen, 2007; Shepard, 2000) and its dominating influence in characterizing an educational system overall (Rowntree, 1987), governments, through their ministries and agencies, are increasingly aware of the necessity to develop and align their assessment systems with the identified and projected needs and expectations of future employers, teachers, students, and parents. Such an enterprise requires the various strands of assessment to combine and move consistently in commonly agreed directions.

INSTRUCTIONAL AND ASSESSMENT PRACTICES

Since gaining independence in 1965, Singapore has undertaken a distinctive and remarkably successful program of national building, becoming an economic powerhouse in the Asian region and an influential, prosperous, orderly, cohesive, multiracial, global city and nation-state. In this endeavor, education has played a pivotal part. From the beginning, the government has provided a well-funded universal system of public education. For example, in 2004/2005, public expenditure on education was 3.5% of Singapore's Gross Domestic Product (GDP), or about $6 billion. Between 1970 and 2004, literacy rates jumped from 68.9% to 94.6%; during the same period, the percentage of university graduates in the population increased from 1.9% to 16.3%. These achievements are also evident in exceptional performance in international assessments in Mathematics and Science. In the Trends in International Mathematics and Science Study (TIMSS), for example, students from Singapore consistently scored in the top place in Mathematics in 1995, 1999, and again in 2003 (Table 9.1). In Science, 4th-grade students were 10th in 1995 and 1st in 2003, while 8th-grade students were 1st in 1995, 2nd in 1999, and 1st again in 2003.

The recession of the mid-1980s made it very evident that the global economy was changing rapidly and the only way for Singapore to continue growing its economy, especially under the threat of equally attractive low-cost labor in other parts of the region, was to both upgrade its existing labor force and prepare a future labor force that is well equipped to meet the challenges of a New Economy. Although the discourse around

Table 9.1

TIMSS RESULTS 2003, MATHEMATICS GRADES 4 AND 8

GRADE 4 AVERAGE SCORE			GRADE 8 AVERAGE SCORE		
COUNTRY	RANK	TIMSS 2003	COUNTRY	RANK	TIMSS 2003
Singapore	1	594	Singapore	1	605
Hong Kong SAR	2	575	Korea	2	589
Japan	3	565	Hong Kong SAR	3	586
Chinese Taipei	4	564	Chinese Taipei	4	585
Belgium-Flemish	5	551	Japan	5	570
International Average	–	495	International Average	–	467

Retrieved January 30, 2008, from http://timss.bc.edu/timss2003i/mathD.html

Knowledge-Based Economy (KBE) and globalization was not widely established then, Singapore was at the dawn of the KBE—an economy where production and services based on knowledge-intensive activities contribute to an accelerated pace of technical and scientific advancement, as well as a rapid obsolescence of knowledge (Powell & Snellman, 2004), an economy that values intellectual capital (Shapiro & Varian, 1999), where knowledge is constantly created and exchanged.

Since the influential Report of the Economic Review Committee (ERC, 1986), *The Singapore Economy: New Directions*, which highlighted the need for creativity and broad-based holistic education to provide sufficient skill base for Singapore to move up the economic ladder into higher value industries such as high technology–based manufacturing, financial, banking, and service sectors, policy makers in Singapore have wrestled with how to produce the kind of workers that would thrive in a KBE. Over the years, the accelerating pace of globalization and the criticality of graduating Singapore into a knowledge-based economy have brought together high-level committees, including the Economic Review Committee (ERC, 2003) chaired by the current prime minister, to evaluate and make recommendations on critical issues that bear on Singapore's continued economic prosperity. These issues include the organization of work associated with the knowledge economy, the changing capital formation requirements for the knowledge economy (to wit, "knowledge" capital, "imagination" capital, "emotional" capital, and "social" capital), and the growing inequality associated with the growth of such an economy. In general terms, the ERC committed Singapore to the following macroeconomic policy settings (the sloganeering tone is deliberate):

- A *globalised economy* where Singapore is the key node in the global network, linked to all the major economies;
- A *creative and entrepreneurial* nation willing to take risks to create fresh businesses and blaze new paths to success; and
- A *diversified* economy powered by the twin engines of manufacturing and services, where vibrant Singapore companies complement MNCs [multinational companies] and new start-ups co-exist with traditional businesses exploiting new and innovative ideas.

The Ministry of Education (MOE) in Singapore, too, has been strongly committed to the development of an education system that prepares young people for the worksites of the knowledge economy, promotes innovation and creativity rather than simply learning and memorization, recognizes and rewards a plurality of talents rather than a singularity of merit (namely, performance on high-stakes assessment), a broader diversity of choices and pathways for students in and through schooling, and generally prepares young people to successfully negotiate the more complex institutional demands of a rapidly globalizing and "postmodern" world, and to do so without a loss of civic attachment or a clear normative framework.

The new policy settings were initially announced at the launch of the *Thinking Schools, Learning Nation (TSLN)* initiative in 1997. Since then, educational policy in Singapore has been dominated at the broadest level by a vision of "a nation of thinking and committed citizens capable of meeting the challenges of the future, and an education system geared to the needs of the 21st century" (http://www.moe.gov.sg). Specifically, this vision has centered on the pursuit of five strategic objectives (again, the sloganeering tone is deliberate):

- Strengthening *capital formation* appropriate for a small but ambitious and highly successful knowledge economy through improved pedagogy, learning environments and student outcomes across the curriculum, but permitting greater choice and diversity and recognition of diverse "talents" without sacrificing the major gains and achievements of the past, including national performance in international assessments (e.g., TIMSS);
- Maintaining *meritocratic forms of social organisation,* including the organisation of schooling, in order to promote elite recruitment into public administration and optimal allocative and productive efficiency in the labour market;
- Supporting and maintaining *traditional social identities* but not at the cost of racial harmony through a variety of initiatives, including, in education, bilingual language policy;
- Promoting the *moral and civic development,* emotional well-being and capacity for full and effective participation by students in the institutional and community life of Singapore; and
- Preventing the growth of a permanent *underclass.*

Currently, great emphasis in Singapore is placed on developing and adopting specific educational policy initiatives that promote enrichment and engagement at the level of the school. Four high-profile drives worthy of mention are:

1. Strategies for Active and Independent Learning (SAIL) (www. moe.gov.sg:80/speeches/2004/sp20040325.htm);
2. Science Practical Assessment (SPA) (Towndrow, Tan, Venthan, & Dorairaju, 2006);
3. Project Work (PW) (www.moe.gov.sg:80/project work/); and
4. *Teach Less Learn More (TLLM)*—first mentioned by Prime Minister Lee Hsien Loong in his inaugural National Day Rally Speech of 2004 (Lee, 2004)—which seeks to improve the quality of teaching by easing linkages between assessment, curriculum, and teaching without abandoning the high-stakes assessment system.

From an assessment perspective, it is important to emphasize the critical role that the government's explicit and unapologetic commitment to a meritocratic ideology plays in its national economic strategy, its public administration and national governance, its approach to school and classroom organization, pupil management and assessment, and the extent to which it provides the *raison d'état* for a centralized national system of education that exercises tight control over the school curriculum through national examinations and strong accountability for school performance (Chua, 1997; Sharpe & Gopinathan, 2002). The four major high-stakes assessment points in the Singapore education system at the elementary and high school levels are:

■ Primary School Leaving Examination (PSLE) at Grade 5;
■ General Certificate of Education Normal Level (GCE "N") at Grade 10;
■ General Certificate of Education Ordinary Level (GCE "O") at Grade 10; and
■ General Certificate of Education Advanced Level (GCE "A") at Grade 12.

From an administrative perspective it is interesting to note that there is a purposeful institutional separation of curriculum development and educational assessment in Singapore. Established in 2004, the Singapore Examinations and Assessment Board (SEAB) is a statutory body charged with the development and administration of national examinations and offers examination and assessment services both locally and internationally. While SEAB collaborates with the Singapore Ministry of Education, its autonomy affords it operational flexibility in forming joint ventures and gives it, in its own terms, "enhanced responsiveness . . . to better respond to curricular changes when developing national examinations" (SEAB, 2005). The creation of SEAB underlines the importance, and the authority required, of an externally administered body relating to assessment and evaluation matters in Singapore. Furthermore, there is a strong sense in which SEAB reinforces the tight coupling that exists ideologically between high-stakes summative assessment and instructional practice. We pursued the implications of tightly integrating assessment and instruction in Chapter 8.

One way to develop a sense of the depth, breadth, and coherence of educational assessment in Singapore is to plot the previously mentioned functions onto a grid that makes distinctions between the formative and summative assessments that take place within local school boundaries and externally at the level of the local authority. We have adapted the Scottish government's *Assessment Is for Learning* model (http://www.ltscotland.org.uk/assess/for/index.asp, also see Hayward, 2007) to present an overview of the Singapore national assessment system as viewed from a systematic perspective and as informed by the empirical data set out in the following sections of this chapter (Figure 9.1).

As to be expected, the lower right-hand quadrant of the figure (external/ summative) lists the high-stakes examinations set and administered by

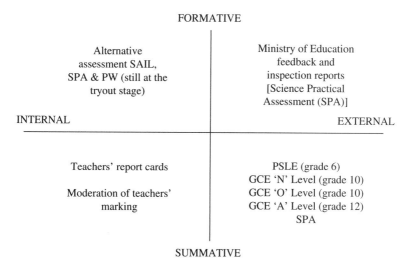

FORMATIVE

| Alternative assessment SAIL, SPA & PW (still at the tryout stage) | Ministry of Education feedback and inspection reports [Science Practical Assessment (SPA)] |

INTERNAL   EXTERNAL

| Teachers' report cards   Moderation of teachers' marking | PSLE (grade 6) GCE 'N' Level (grade 10) GCE 'O' Level (grade 10) GCE 'A' Level (grade 12) SPA |

SUMMATIVE

Figure 9.1 An overview of the Singapore national assessment system (following Hayward, 2007).

SEAB. Characteristically, teachers in Singapore also spend time completing students' progress report cards and their marking of students' work is regularly moderated in internal staff meetings (internal/summative) but it is clear that the major burden of summative assessment lies outside of schools. Furthermore, and most important, Figure 9.1 reveals that the spread of formative and summative assessment functions within the Singapore system is unequal. Clearly, there is scope for greater emphasis to be placed on the formative aspects of assessment.

Given the diversity of social, economic, and political factors influencing national contexts, there is no unproblematic route to crafting an affective assessment system that serves multiple purposes (Black & Wiliam, 2005). Even so, in the interests of emphasizing certain features and fostering the support of policy implementers in demonstrating the achievement of key objectives, educational authorities regularly publicize (and subsequently reform) their assessment practices in models or frameworks. There are strengths and weaknesses in this approach.

First, as far as continua are concerned, while the formative and summative functions of assessment are undeniably linked prototypically, Wiliam and Black (1996) question the viability of the formative-summative continuum as a whole. In practice, all evidence generated from assessments can serve summative functions, but not all evidence will serve formative functions without specific and deliberate action by teachers and students. Consequently, the formative-summative divide could be the source of tension in classrooms when the same assessments are expected to serve both formative and summative functions. This would be the case, particularly, when a teacher's instructional approaches were undifferentiated or a teacher was unclear about how and when feedback would be most effective.

A second raft of difficulties with systemic views of assessment is that they can give the impression everything contained within them is of equal value. In Bennett's (2007) estimation, the development of a comprehensive assessment system would be highly beneficial yet hugely challenging under current circumstances. He offers two reasons as to why this might be so: (1) the dominance of accountability assessment practices that make teachers and schools answerable for student achievement, and (2) the limitation of assessment carried out primarily through pencil-and-paper tests that focus on a narrow range of competencies, mostly involving candidates' interaction with language, symbols, and text (Organisation for Economic Cooperation and Development [OECD], 2005, p. 16). So, what remains?

Overall, it is not surprising that teachers and students might not always know how to balance competing demands and incorporate, especially, assessment for learning strategies (Black & Wiliam, 1998a, 1998b; Black et al., 2003; Gardner, 2006; Harlen, 2007; Hattie & Timperley, 2007; Means, 2006; Pellegrino, Chudowsky, & Glaser, 2001; Shepard, 2000; Stiggins, 2002) into their regular instructional designs. Additionally, the lack of clarity in the ways in which the various sectors of an assessment system interact leads us to ask how teachers, students, and assessment designers, in general, can:

■ Cultivate an authentic assessment culture (Wiggins, 1989);
■ Accommodate contemporary skills, competencies, and dispositions; and
■ Align assessment with curriculum and pedagogic practices.

In 2002, the Singapore Ministry of Education (MOE) decided it could improve the quality of educational practices and student outcomes to maintain Singapore's competitive advantage in a rapidly globalizing world by establishing a dedicated research center to develop baseline data and design and implement innovations in classroom practice. Since its establishment in 2003, the Centre for Research on Pedagogy and Practice (CRPP) has conducted a number of studies relating to instructional and assessment practices in Singapore. We proceed to overview one of these research studies below, a large-scale, empirical baseline analysis of pedagogical practices in Singapore schools that focused on both the enacted curriculum and on classroom assessment.

Instructional Practices

During 2004 and 2005, CRPP staff undertook a detailed observation of pedagogical practices in 1,169 Grade 5 and Grade 9 lessons in a large representative sample of schools ($n = 60$). In addition, CRPP staff surveyed almost 19,000 students and their teachers ($n = 5,269$). We report some of the findings from these studies below.

Like most East Asian societies, classroom instruction in Singapore is clearly teacher dominated. Table 9.2 gives classroom observation data for almost 1,200 lessons across all subjects that reports the distribution of classroom activities by phase within lessons (on average, each lesson had 3.5 phases). In Grade 5, almost 50% of all classroom activity involved whole class lectures, teacher monologue, IRE (initiate,

Table 9.2

PATTERN OF CLASSROOM ACTIVITY (CLASSROOM OBSERVATION DATA)

GRADE 5 (RANK ORDERED)	% OF PHASES	GRADE 9 (RANK ORDERED)	% OF PHASES
Whole Class Answer Checking/IRE	27.6	Whole Class Lecture/Monologue	32.0
Whole Class Lecture/Monologue	20.5	Whole Class Answer Checking/ IRE	22.0
Whole Class Elicitation and Discussion	6.3	Whole Class Elicitation and Discussion	6.2
Whole Class Demonstration/Activity	3.3	Whole Class Demonstration/Activity	2.7
Choral Repetition	3.0	Choral Repetition	1.4
Subtotal	*60.7*	*Subtotal*	*62.3*
Individual Seatwork	18.3	Individual Seatwork	17.6
Small Group Work	12.1	Small Group Work	10.2
Student Demonstration	5.2	Student Demonstration	5.2
Test-Taking	1.6	Test-Taking	1.6
Laboratory/Experiment	2.2	Laboratory/Experiment	1.1
Total	*100*	*Total*	*100*
N (No. of Lessons)	*591*	*N (No. of Lessons)*	*578*

response, evaluate) sequences, whole class elicitation or whole class demonstrations; just 30% of classroom activity was either small group work (12.1%) or individual seatwork (18.3%). In Grade 9, the same pattern is observed. In addition, teacher domination is also reflected in the distribution of "epistemic authority" across knowledge sources (Table 9.3). Across all subjects, the teacher was the source of epistemic authority in 76% of all lessons, varying from 90.6% in Math to 60.2% in English.

Tables 9.4, 9.5, and 9.6 report the mean scores for three different instructional strategies that teachers employ in Singapore based on teacher self-reported data for Grade 9 Math and English ($n = 3,975$): direct instruction/teaching (Table 9.4), "traditional" instruction/pedagogy (Table 9.5), and "authentic" instruction/pedagogy (Table 9.6). The items for direct instruction were derived from the secondary research

Table 9.3

DISTRIBUTION OF EPISTEMIC AUTHORITY BY SUBJECT (GRADE 9) (CLASSROOM OBSERVATION DATA)

| SOURCE | PERCENTAGE (%) OF EPISTEMIC AUTHORITY IN SUBJECT AREAS | | | | |
	SCIENCE	MATHEMATICS	ENGLISH	SOCIAL STUDIES	AVERAGE
Student	6.2	2.7	25.3	9.8	11
Teacher	86.9	90.6	60.2	66.9	76.15
Test	.0	.7	.8	.9	.6
Textbook	2.7	2.8	1.3	13.7	5.12
Internet	.0	.3	.4	2.8	.88
Data	1.6	.0	.0	.0	.4
Mass Media	.1	.2	.0	1.9	.55
Worksheet	2.5	2.1	8.0	1.8	3.6
Others	.0	.6	4.1	2.1	1.7
Total	100	100	100	100	
N (Number of Lessons)	93	129	125	101	
Total Number of Lessons: 448					

literature (Good & Brophy, 2003, chap. 9; Hattie, 2003; Purdie & Ellis, 2005; Rowe, 2003, 2006; but see also National Mathematics Advisory Panel [NMAP], 2008b, chap. 4). The items for "traditional" instruction were derived from our interviews and pilot studies with teachers. The indicators for "authentic" instruction were derived principally from Newmann's work on "authentic achievement" and Project Zero's "teaching for understanding framework" (Newmann & Associates, 1996; Wiske, 1997). The results clearly suggest that instructional practice in Singapore, contrary to common misperceptions, is far from unidimensional or monolithic. Overall, direct instruction scores the highest mean scores for both Math and English (3.79 and 3.76, respectively). Traditional instruction followed closely behind (3.69 and 3.38, respectively). Importantly, the indicators for authentic pedagogy lagged a fair way behind, but they were still moderately respectable rather than abysmally low (2.96 and 3.16, respectively) (see Table 9.7).

Table 9.4

DIRECT TEACHING (STUDENT SURVEY)

	MEAN G3 MATH	MEAN G3 ENGLISH	F-RATIO	P	$\hat{\omega}^2$
N (number of students)	4,690	4,547			
Maximizing Learning Time	4.02	4.05	.21	.65	−.003
Review	3.74	3.54	10.99	<.01	.039
Questioning	3.44	3.49	.73	.39	−.001
Structure and Clarity	3.73	3.73	.00	.98	−.004
Feedback	3.65	3.72	1.67	.20	.003
Direct Teaching (a = .92, .91)	3.79	3.76	.05	.82	−.004
Cronbach's Alpha	.92	.91			

Note. Mean scores were based on a 5-point Likert frequency scale (from 1 = Never to 5 = Always). Mean scores for individual measures are based on multiple indicators for each measure.

Table 9.5

TRADITIONAL TEACHING (STUDENT SURVEY)

	MEAN G3 MATH	MEAN G3 ENGLISH	F-RATIO	P	$\hat{\omega}^2$
N (number of students)	4,690	4,547			
Frequency of Homework	4.33	3.76	50.03	<.01	.166
Memorization	4.03	3.21	257.79	<.01	.511
Drill and Worksheets	3.84	3.48	69.24	<.01	.217
Lecture	3.61	3.78	10.80	<.01	.038
Textbook Focus	3.61	2.91	105.82	<.01	.299
Frequency of Exams	2.40	2.14	28.29	<.01	.100
Traditional Teaching	3.69	3.38	136.55	<.01	.355
Cronbach's Alpha	.76	.75			

Note. Mean scores were based on a 5-point Likert frequency scale (from 1 = Never to 5 = Always). Mean scores for individual measures are based on multiple indicators for each measure.

Table 9.6

AUTHENTIC TEACHING (STUDENT SURVEY)

	MEAN G3 MATH	MEAN G3 ENGLISH	F-RATIO	P	ω^2
N (number of students)	4,690	4,547			
Depth of Understanding	3.38	3.32	1.70	.19	.003
Quality of Homework	3.34	3.19	10.98	<.01	.039
Classroom Discussion	3.26	3.48	14.70	<.01	.053
Meta-Language	3.11	3.23	4.35	<.05	.013
Criticality and Creativity	3.11	3.20	2.87	.09	.008
Integration of Knowledge Across Disciplines	2.99	3.15	10.23	<.01	.036
Connectedness to Real World	2.97	3.22	18.75	<.01	.067
Significance and Meaningfulness	2.94	3.18	17.51	<.01	.063
Frequency of Project Work	1.14	1.54	73.77	<.01	.228
Authentic Pedagogy	2.96	3.16	10.39	<.01	.037
Cronbach's Alpha	.89	.90			

Note. Mean scores were based on a 5-point Likert frequency scale (from 1 = Never to 5 = Always). Mean scores for individual measures are based on multiple indicators for each measure.

Table 9.7

SUMMARY OF TABLES 4–6: MEAN SCORES/SD/OMEGA SQ

	G3 MATH		G3 ENGLISH		
	MEAN (1-5)	SD	MEAN (1-5)	SD	ω^2
Direct Instruction	3.79	.79	3.76	.74	−.004
Traditional Teaching	3.69	.64	3.38	.67	.355
Authentic Pedagogy	2.96	.78	3.16	.73	.037

These findings raise a number of important issues. To begin, given international research findings on the importance of direct and traditional instruction in high-achieving East Asian countries and the strong association between direct instruction in particular and various measures of student achievement (Good & Brophy, 2003, chap. 9; Hattie, 2003; NMAP, 2008b, chap. 4; Purdie & Ellis, 2005; Rowe, 2003, 2006), these results offer an explanation of the success of Singaporean schools in international assessments. But are these instructional strategies orthogonal or complementary? The correlations reported in Table 9.8 suggest that teachers in Singapore employ all three pedagogies, not just one of them. Indeed, it is particularly noticeable that the correlations between the three scales are all quite high. In Math, for example, the correlation between direct teaching and traditional instruction/pedagogy is .62; for direct instruction/teaching and authentic pedagogy, .65; between authentic pedagogy and traditional pedagogy, .59.

These are remarkably high (and statistically significant) correlations, and underscore the high degree of covariance between the three scales: teachers tend not to use one instructional strategy at the expense of the other two, but employ all three, although more of the direct and the traditional than the authentic. This suggests an important conclusion: in line with the pragmatism of the national culture, classroom instruction in Singapore is pragmatic and hybridic rather than sectarian in character. Singaporean teachers do not appear, in other words, to belong to

Table 9.8

CORRELATIONS BETWEEN THE PEDAGOGICAL APPROACHES

	G9 MATH			G9 ENGLISH		
	DIRECT TEACHING	TRADITIONAL TEACHING	AUTHENTIC PEDAGOGY	DIRECT TEACHING	TRADITIONAL TEACHING	AUTHENTIC PEDAGOGY
Direct Teaching	1	.62**	.65**	1	.58**	.68**
Traditional Teaching	.62**	1	.59**	.58**	1	.69**
Authentic Pedagogy	.65**	.59**	1	.68**	.69**	1

Note. **p <.01.

one particular pedagogical sect, or tradition, but draw on at least three pedagogical sensibilities, albeit in unequal measure. Given the extraordinary success of Singaporean schools in international assessments, such pedagogical hybridity appears to work; indeed, our multileveling modeling of the impact of instructional practices on mathematics and English achievement confirms this (Nie, Lau, & Hogan, 2008). Furthermore, it is consistent with research that recommends a variegated or differentiated pedagogy that varies according to learning objectives and teaching situation. The *Final Report* of the blue ribbon National Mathematical Advisory Panel in the United States, for example, concluded that "high-quality research does not support the contention that instruction should be either entirely 'student centered' or 'teacher directed.' Research indicates that some forms of particular instructional practices can have a positive impact under specified conditions" (NMAP, 2008a, p. xiv). We agree, but we do not at this point understand very well why and when teachers use one strategy rather than another: we are currently analyzing qualitative classroom data to find out and we plan to explore the issue further in our next round of research. We suspect, however, that Singapore's pragmatic pedagogy is very much influenced by a range of cultural and institutional factors (especially the close alignment of the high-stakes assessment system and classroom instruction) and that while it has been distinctively successful in establishing a high floor, it has also constrained the capacity for sustained pedagogical innovation and higher levels of knowledge work.

The Enacted Curriculum

As we noted earlier, one CRPP project focused on the observation of some 1,200 lessons in Singaporean schools. This project drew, in part, on Anderson and Krathwohl's (2001) influential distinction between various modes of knowledge in order to develop a coding scheme that would attempt to capture something of the *quality* of the knowledge work in Singaporean classrooms and not just the frequency of what teachers did in classroom. Specifically, Anderson and Krathwohl (2001) distinguished between four modes of knowledge:

- *Factual:* "basic propositional or declarative disciplinary knowledge that students must know in order to be acquainted with the discipline or solve problems in it";
- *Conceptual:* "interrelationships among the basic elements within a larger structure that enable them to function together";

- *Procedural:* knowledge "of how to do something, methods of inquiry, and criteria of using skills, algorithms, techniques and methods";
- *Metacognitive:* "knowledge of cognition in general as well as awareness of one's own cognition." (p. 29)

Overall, on the positive side, CRPP researchers found that Singapore has a strong, well-articulated curriculum framework and that there is a strong focus on the transmission of basic foundational knowledge and the development of basic skills in students. This helps account for why Singapore has done so well in TIMSS, for example. But we also found that across a representative sample of almost 1,200 classrooms across all subjects in Grade 5 and Grade 9 there is a limited focus on conceptual depth, knowledge manipulation/application, interpretation, problem solving and knowledge criticism, that knowledge is strongly classified into separate subjects, and that knowledge is strongly tied to the pedagogical authority of the teacher (Table 9.9). In addition, knowledge is overwhelmingly presented to students as "truth" and is strongly tied to the pedagogical authority of the teacher rather than to the epistemic deliberations and reflections of students in the classroom (although there is considerable variation by subject) (Tables 9.9 and 9.3). Finally, while there are some variations by subject, overall, there is a stable pedagogical factor structure—Basic Knowledge Transmission and Complex Knowledge Construction—across all subjects (Table 9.10). Importantly, however, the two pedagogies are not orthogonal, given the strength of the correlation between them (.378). In effect, similar to what we saw in Table 9.2, teachers do not appear to view these pedagogies as alternatives but rather simply do one a lot more than the other. Of course, why they do so is another matter altogether, although we strongly suspect that it reflects a combination of limited capacity to engage in "complex knowledge construction" and, even more important, limited opportunity to do so, given the power of the assessment system to drive classroom pedagogy across Singapore. We deal with this issue in greater depth in Chapter 8.

In broad terms, then, these results—particularly the focus on basic knowledge and skills and on the reproduction of knowledge—help explain the successes of the Singapore system. But the results also raise two important issues. One is the relationship between these results and results reported in Table 9.2. On first glance the two sets of results might appear incompatible, and raise the possibility that the findings are an artifact of the different methodologies used to collect the data (survey

Table 9.9

KNOWLEDGE PRACTICES IN GRADES 5 AND 9: MEAN SCORES (CLASSROOM OBSERVATION DATA)		
KNOWLEDGE CLASSIFICATION	**GRADE 5 (0–3)**	**GRADE 9 (0–3)**
Depth of Knowledge		
Basic/Fact/Rote	2.4	2.3
Procedural/How-To	0.7	1.1
Advanced Concept	0.1	0.2
Knowledge Manipulation		
Reproduction	2.3	2.1
Interpretation	0.6	0.7
Application	0.4	0.5
Generation of Knowledge New to Students	0.1	0.2
Knowledge Assessment		
Truth	2.6	2.5
Comparison	0.2	0.3
Critique	0.1	0.2
Number of lessons	*591*	*578*

Note. Mean scores were based on a 4-point Likert frequency scale (from 0 = Never to 4 = Almost always). Each indicator was measured in each phase in a classroom lesson (average 3.5 phases per lesson) and then aggregated for the lesson.

data vs. classroom observation) and therefore raise awkward questions about reliability and validity. But we believe that the findings are reliable, valid—and compatible. The data reported in Table 9.2 focus for the most part on teacher behaviors—or at least on what teachers *say* they do. The results reported in Tables 9.9 and 9.10 focus, on the other hand, on the *quality* of the knowledge work that teachers and students engage in classrooms. Simply because teachers in Singapore rely very much on direct instruction, for example, does not imply that the quality of the knowledge work they do is necessarily characterized by a high degree of disciplinarity. Rather, it suggests that classroom pedagogy in Singapore is preoccupied with mastery of basic knowledge and skills rather than developing a more conceptual understanding of school knowledge. Moreover, the substantially lower mean scores for authentic pedagogy (importantly, a scale

Table 9.10

TWO PEDAGOGIES: EXPLORATORY FACTOR ANALYSIS OF CLASSROOM KNOWLEDGE PRACTICES

FACTOR LOADINGS	BASIC KNOWLEDGE TRANSMISSION	COMPLEX KNOWLEDGE CONSTRUCTION
Truth	.982	
Reproduction	.945	
Single Discipline	.900	
Basic/Factual/Rote	.850	
Specialized Language	.580	
Procedural Knowledge	.425	
Critique		.817
Comparison		.750
Advanced Concept		.644
Generation of Knowledge New to Students		.620
Interpretation		.588
Application		.573
Cronbach's Alpha	*.898*	*.742*
Mean	*2.0*	*0.4*
Correlation	*.378**	
Explained Variance	58%	

that focuses much more on the quality of teaching and learning than on instructional practices) reported in Table 9.6 reinforces this conclusion.

The second issue is an extension of the first and points to the relationship between pedagogy and policy. In the context of contemporary models of 21st-century skills and understandings (OECD, 2005; Partnership for 21st Century Skills, 2007), the lack of disciplinary depth in the enacted curriculum is a significant shortfall and policy challenge. Yet the Ministry of Education is clearly cognizant of the need to improve the "quality" of teaching and learning in Singapore's schools. Indeed, this is the central thrust of its major pedagogical initiative, *Teach Less Learn More*, launched in 2005, the heart of which is "top-down support for bottom-up" pedagogical initiatives at the school level that seek to improve the *quality* of teaching and learning in Singaporean classrooms.

It is too early yet to tell whether these initiatives will have the impact the Ministry wants. We are hopeful, but we remain concerned that unless and until the current high-stakes assessment system is at least partially decoupled from classroom instruction the current high-stakes assessment system will continue to constrain the opportunity to try out and sustain significant pedagogical innovation that focuses on knowledge work with a high level of disciplinarity. We are particularly cognizant of the research findings from across the world that high-stakes assessment regimes all too often limit the capacity of systems to improve the quality of teaching and learning in their schools by driving teachers to "teach to the test" and to refrain from taking the kind of pedagogical risks necessary to improve instruction (Bennett, 2007; Darling-Hammond, 2007; Gardner, 2006; Grubb & Oakes, 2007; Harlen, 2007; James, Black, McCormick, Pedder, & Wiliam, 2006; Marshall & Drummond, 2006). In a 21st-century economic and educational context that places a premium on quite different kinds of cognitive skills than those measured in conventional forms of academic assessment or TIMSS, any policy settings or institutional practices that might constrain the ability or willingness of teachers to institute new pedagogical practices (and the ability of schools to sustain them) is a matter of considerable concern.

Assessment Practices

Over the school years 2004–2005, CRPP also collected 4,443 samples of teachers' assessment tasks (n = 346) and associated student work (n = 4,097) from Grades 5 and 9 lessons in English, Social Studies, Mathematics, and Science in 59 schools (30 elementary schools and 29 high schools); all of the teachers' assessment tasks and student work samples were embedded within the day-to-day classrooms instruction. The types of assessment tasks included daily class work, homework assignments, major assignments/projects, and teacher-made tests. From the samples, a relatively low proportion of major assignments or projects were found, indicating that teachers placed a greater emphasis on traditional class work. The samples of teacher-made tests showed that most of the tests were administered for summative purposes.

Teachers' Self-Report Data on Assessment Practices

Prior to the submission of the assessment tasks and samples of student work, teachers were asked to fill out a short questionnaire about their assessment practices in the following aspects: rationale for the assessment tasks, use of assessment rubrics, discussion of intended learning outcomes, sharing of assessment criteria with students, and giving feedback to students.

A 5-point Likert scale was used for the seven items that measured the rationale for assessment tasks. The scale ranged from 1 = strongly disagree to 5 = strongly agree. The Cronbach's alpha for the scale across subject areas and grade levels ranged from .70 to .88, indicating good reliability of the self-report data. The items for the other aspects of assessment practices were in the nominal categories of either "yes" or "no."

As can be seen in Tables 9.11 and 9.12, most of the teachers across subject areas reported that their reasons for setting assessment tasks were to prepare students for high-stakes examinations, to fulfill the

Table 9.11

TEACHERS' RATIONALES FOR SETTING ASSESSMENT TASKS AT GRADE 5 BY SUBJECT

THIS ASSESSMENT TASK ...	ENGLISH N = 66 MEAN	SOCIAL STUDIES N = 25 MEAN	MATHEMATICS N = 45 MEAN	SCIENCE N = 36 MEAN
Will prepare students for the examination	4.27	2.60	4.38	3.78
Is required by the syllabus	4.03	3.48	4.29	3.69
Is required by my department head	3.83	2.72	3.42	3.44
Gives my students something to do	3.28	3.04	3.13	3.42
Was suggested in a professional development session	3.38	2.28	2.47	3.11
Is included in the class textbook	3.09	2.80	3.29	2.78
Is not really necessary at all	1.68	1.76	1.62	1.89

Note. N = number of teachers' assessment tasks. Mean scores were based on a 5-point Likert scale (1 = Strongly disagree; 2 = Disagree; 3 = Slightly agree; 4 = Agree; and 5 = Strongly agree).

Table 9.12

TEACHERS' RATIONALES FOR SETTING ASSESSMENT TASKS AT GRADE 9 BY SUBJECT

THIS ASSESSMENT TASK ...	ENGLISH N = 32 MEAN	SOCIAL STUDIES N = 10 MEAN	MATHEMATICS N = 26 MEAN	SCIENCE N = 19 MEAN
Will prepare students for the examination	4.16	4.40	4.65	4.47
Is required by the syllabus	3.66	2.90	3.92	4.26
Is required by my department head	3.47	2.50	2.81	3.32
Gives my students something to do	4.31	3.60	4.27	3.26
Was suggested in a professional development session	2.84	3.20	1.85	2.79
Is included in the class textbook	2.53	2.00	3.15	2.74
Is not really necessary at all	1.59	1.90	1.62	1.58

Note. N = number of teachers' assessment tasks. Mean scores were based on a 5-point Likert scale (1 = Strongly disagree; 2 = Disagree; 3 = Slightly agree; 4 = Agree; and 5 = Strongly agree).

requirement of the syllabus, and to meet the demands of their heads of department. Not many teachers attributed their rationales for setting assessment tasks to the knowledge and skills that they had acquired from professional development in authentic assessment. An exceptional case was found in Grade 5 social studies where teachers rated syllabus requirements, not examination preparation, as their highest priority (in Singapore, the social studies subject is nonexaminable at elementary level).

Teachers' Use of Rubrics, Discussion of Intended Learning Outcomes, Sharing of Rubrics, and Feedback

As shown in Table 9.13, English and Social Studies teachers used rubrics more frequently. This assessment practice is not surprising because

Table 9.13

SOURCE OF RUBRICS

SOURCE	GRADE 5				GRADE 9			
	ENGLISH	SOCIAL STUDIES	MATH	SCIENCE	ENGLISH	SOCIAL STUDIES	MATH	SCIENCE
				Percent				
Self (Teacher)	39.4	56.0	11.1	25.0	18.8	30.0	26.9	10.5
Self (Teacher) & Colleagues	–	–	8.9	2.8	–	30.0	–	5.3
Self (Teacher) & Students	3.0	–	6.7	2.8	–	–	–	–
Teachers at My School	10.6	–	2.2	8.3	3.1	–	–	–
MOE Syllabus	10.6	–	6.7	–	21.9	–	–	–
Textbook	7.6	4.0	4.4	8.3	12.5	–	3.8	–
Other	12.1	–	4.4	–	3.1	–	3.8	–
No Rubrics Used	16.7	40.0	55.6	53.0	40.6	40.0	65.4	84.2

these two subject areas have more open-ended assessment tasks such as essay writing, mini projects (posters), and group work. Mathematics and Science teachers at the secondary level did not often use rubrics. In terms of the source of rubrics, most teachers reported that they developed rubrics on their own. Although the use of rubrics was not a new practice in the classrooms, the teachers were found to seldom share the assessment criteria in the rubrics with their students (Table 9.14). Hence, students often did not know how they were assessed on an assessment task. The teachers' expectations were not made explicitly to students even though a high percentage of teachers reported discussing intended learning outcomes with their students prior to assessment. Most of the teachers gave feedback on students' work but it was in the form of praise or punishment such as "excellent," "poor," or "you need to work harder."

Table 9.14

DISCUSSION OF INTENDED LEARNING OUTCOMES, SHARING OF ASSESSMENT CRITERIA, AND GIVING FEEDBACK

	GRADE 5				GRADE 9			
	ENGLISH	SOCIAL STUDIES	MATH	SCIENCE	ENGLISH	SOCIAL STUDIES	MATH	SCIENCE
				Percent				
Discussion of Intended Learning Outcomes	80.3	96.0	84.4	88.9	81.3	80.0	88.5	68.4
Sharing of Assessment Criteria	37.9	20.0	28.9	27.8	28.1	60.0	19.2	10.5
Giving Feedback	84.8	100.0	91.1	94.4	93.8	100.0	92.3	94.7

Classroom Assessment Practices

In addition to the self-report data of teachers' assessment practices, the collected samples of teachers' assessment tasks and students' work were moderated by expert teachers for their intellectual quality. Newmann and Associates (1996) contended that authentic intellectual work must consist of three essential standards: construction of knowledge, disciplined inquiry, and value beyond school. In other words, authentic intellectual work enables students to engage in higher-order thinking and real-world problem solving rather than just routine use of facts and procedures. If teachers are to aim for authentic student performance, then they need to create assessment tasks that call upon students to construct their own knowledge, through in-depth disciplined inquiry, which address real world problems. In the context of the CRPP research, the objectives were twofold: (1) how knowledge was presented by Singaporean teachers in daily classroom assessment tasks, and (2) how students' performance corresponded to the demands of the assessment tasks. As such, five intellectual quality criteria were conceptualized and used to judge the quality of the teachers' assessment tasks and associated students' work. They were *depth of knowledge, knowledge criticism, knowledge manipulation, sustained writing,* and *connections to the real world beyond the classroom.*

Under *depth of knowledge,* three types of knowledge were conceptualized based on the revised Bloom's taxonomy of knowledge (Anderson & Krathwohl, 2001): (1) factual knowledge, (2) procedural knowledge, and (3) advanced concepts. Higher-order thinking was captured by two criteria, namely *knowledge criticism* and *knowledge manipulation. Knowledge criticism* was exemplified by assessment tasks that asked students to compare and contrast different sources of information and to critique knowledge. *Knowledge manipulation* was exemplified by assessment tasks that demanded students to organize, analyze, interpret, synthesize, and evaluate information; to apply knowledge and skills; and to construct new meaning or knowledge. In line with Newmann and associates' (1996) authentic intellectual framework, *sustained writing* and *connections to the real world beyond the classroom* were also included as two of the intellectual quality criteria. The results of the quality of teachers' assessment tasks and student work are presented in Tables 9.15 and 9.16, respectively.

For all the subject areas except Grade 5 Social Studies, the intellectual quality of the teachers' assessment tasks was low. This was evidenced by higher mean scores on the elements subsumed under basic and rote knowledge, and lower-order thinking. Those elements were factual knowledge, procedural knowledge, presentation of knowledge as given/truth, and reproduction. On the contrary, the mean scores were generally low in all the elements that represented high intellectual quality. An opposite trend was observed in Grade 5 Social Studies in which teachers' assessment tasks scored higher on most of the criteria that represent high intellectual quality. The mean scores were higher for the following elements: advanced concepts; critique of knowledge; organization, interpretation, synthesis, or evaluation of information; generation/construction of knowledge new to students; sustained writing; and making connections to the real world beyond the classroom.

For both grade levels, the students' work in all subject areas except in Grade 5 Social Studies demonstrated higher levels mastery of factual and procedural knowledge but limited understanding of advanced concepts. When students moved up to Grade 9, their work tended to show even higher levels of presentation of knowledge as truth and reproduction of factual knowledge, indicating that the intellectual quality of the student work was low. The Grade 5 Social Studies work varied from traditional essay-type assignments, to visual montages of materials and news articles assembled thematically, to the worksheet responses. In this context, the worksheet lays out a strong scaffold for community problem solving and engagement. What distinguishes the students' responses in

Table 9.15

MEAN SCORE DIFFERENCES OF THE QUALITY OF TEACHERS' ASSESSMENT TASKS

CRITERIA	GRADE 5 N = 210		GRADE 9 N = 136	
	MEAN	SD	MEAN	SD
Depth of Knowledge				
Factual Knowledge	3.36	.80	3.30	.82
Procedural Knowledge	2.61	1.03	2.54	.95
Advanced Concepts	1.69	.80	1.83	.93
Knowledge Criticism				
Presentation of Knowledge as Given	3.10	.99	3.48	.81
Compare and Contrast Knowledge	1.73	.83	1.82	.88
Critique of Knowledge	1.54	.81	1.35	.77
Knowledge Manipulation				
Reproduction	2.94	1.03	3.26	.92
Organization, Interpretation, or Evaluation of Information	2.27	.83	2.35	.87
Application/Problem Solving	1.94	.90	2.04	.90
Generation/Construction of Knowledge New to Students	1.68	.91	1.50	.83
Sustained Writing	2.18	1.16	2.49	1.06
Connections to the Real World Beyond the Classroom	1.92	1.02	1.52	.86

Note. SD = standard deviation; *N* = number of teachers' assessment tasks. Mean scores were based on a 4-point rating scale (1 = no demand; 2 = low level; 3 = moderate level; and 4 = high level).

this case is that there was a broad array of possible answers at greater depth. Overall, the elementary social studies assignments allowed more student agency through the construction of texts.

In short, at the classroom level, assessment and assignment tasks are clear and well organized and have a strong focus on basic knowledge and skills. At the same time, however, they are also characterized by a limited disciplinary focus on conceptual understanding, knowledge application, and problem solving (Table 9.15). Furthermore, the disciplinary quality of the work produced by students in response to teacher assignments and

Table 9.16

MEAN SCORE DIFFERENCES OF THE QUALITY OF STUDENT WORK

CRITERIA	GRADE 5 N = 2,555		GRADE 9 N = 1,542	
	MEAN	SD	MEAN	SD
Depth of Knowledge				
Factual Knowledge	3.23	.83	2.86	.83
Procedural Knowledge	2.85	1.01	2.35	1.01
Advanced Concepts	1.65	.79	1.38	.60
Knowledge Criticism				
Presentation of Knowledge as Given	3.14	.97	3.56	.74
Compare and Contrast Knowledge	1.67	.80	1.55	.67
Critique of Knowledge	1.45	.70	1.16	.44
Knowledge Manipulation				
Reproduction	3.00	.99	3.41	.79
Organization, Interpretation, or Evaluation of Information	2.26	.76	2.03	.70
Application/Problem Solving	1.89	.82	1.74	.67
Generation/Construction of Knowledge New to Students	1.61	.87	1.31	.57
Sustained Writing	2.27	1.19	2.42	1.08
Connections to the Real World Beyond the Classroom	1.70	.94	1.55	92

Note. SD = standard deviation; *N* = number of pieces of student work. Mean scores were based on a 4-point rating scale (1 = no demonstration; 2 = low level; 3 = moderate level; and 4 = high level).

assessments has a similar profile (Table 9.16). Indeed, the correlation between what teachers ask students to do and what students produce is very high, suggesting that the intellectual quality of student work is strongly related to the intellectual quality of the teaching (Table 9.17).

CONCLUDING REMARKS

This chapter defined educational assessment as any method or activity that is designed to collect data about the knowledge, skills, or dispositions

Table 9.17

CORRELATIONS BETWEEN QUALITY OF TEACHERS' ASSESSMENT TASKS AND QUALITY OF STUDENT WORK IN GRADE 9 (FOR CORE SUBJECTS)

	STUDENT WORK QUALITY				
TASK QUALITY	DEPTH OF KNOWLEDGE	KNOWLEDGE CRITICISM	KNOWLEDGE MANIPULATION	SUSTAINED WRITING	CONNECTIONS TO THE REAL WORLD
Depth of Knowledge	.52**				
Knowledge Criticism		.65**			
Knowledge Manipulation			.62**		
Sustained Writing				.80**	
Connections to the Real World					.72**

Note. **$p < .05$.

of a learner or a group of learners. Although assessment methods vary as they attempt serve a variety of purposes—assessment *of, for,* and *as* learning—governments, through their various ministries and agencies, are keen to develop and align their assessment systems with the identified and projected needs and expectations of future employers, teachers, students, and parents. This enterprise is challenging, both in theory and practice. While conceptions of comprehensive, balanced systems of assessment might appear neat conceptually, they are difficult to implement in practice for a range of technical, cultural, and political reasons, competing demands, and the current prominence of high-accountability pencil-and-paper tests that focus characteristically on a narrow range of competencies that are commonly norm-referenced.

Singapore's high-stakes national assessment system has been designed to perform a number of important institutional tasks—to motivate students to learn; to focus and drive the work of teachers and schools; to provide a transparent, reliable, and politically acceptable measure of student learning and pedagogical accountability; to allocate students into different curriculum tracks and schools based on their academic performance; and to help institutionalize a meritocratic system of social order and social inequality that has substantial political legitimacy. In many ways, it has been a very successful system. But while the system can fairly claim considerable success in achieving its key assessment objectives, it is not evident that the current assessment system in Singapore is the kind of assessment regime that will permit or facilitate pedagogical practice and student outcomes in a way that is called for by recent educational policy initiatives, for example, *Thinking Schools, Learning Nation (TSLN)* and *Teach Less Learn More (TLLM)*.

Overall, the results reported in this chapter suggest both good news and bad news. The good news is that when teachers in Singapore design high-quality tasks and assessments for their students that are clear, well organized, and have a strong focus on basic knowledge and skills, students produce high-quality work. The bad news is that teachers do not do so very often. Moreover, they appear to do very little formative assessment–assessment for learning—in their classrooms, or integrate it into their instructional routines. Generally, teachers' assessment practices in Singapore are strongly influenced by preparation for high-stakes examinations and their near-exclusive judgments. Importantly, these practices circumscribe what counts as necessary and acceptable work that is done by students. Noticeably, the observed focus on lower-order, content and fact reproduction in the assessment tasks that teachers assign set defining thresholds for student intellectual, cognitive, and cultural engagement with the curriculum (Hogan, 2007; Luke, 2005). In response, since 2005, the Ministry has instituted a number of important assessment initiatives to improve the quality of assessment work in Singapore schools, including project work, self-assessment, and science practical assessment. These types of assessment are intended to cultivate higher-order thinking skills, communication skills, and positive habits of mind. In addition, the high-stakes summative assessments have been broadened in terms of the kind of questions that students are asked to address. Finally, the Ministry has eased the institutional pressure of the national high-stakes assessment system on classroom pedagogy in a number of top secondary schools by voiding the necessity of these schools to participate in the "O" level national assessments at the end of secondary school. All going well—and as discussed more fully in Chapter 8—these initiatives are likely to have a positive effect on classroom practice, although the challenges the system confronts are not insubstantial.

NOTE

1. This chapter makes use of data from the Core Research Program, funded by the Centre for Research in Pedagogy and Practice at National Institute of Education, Nanyang Technological University, Singapore (http://www.crpp.nie.edu.sg).

REFERENCES

American Federation of Teachers, National Council on Measurement in Education, and National Education Association. (1990). Standards for teacher competence in educational assessment of students. *Educational Measurement: Issues and Practices, 9*(4), 30–32.

Anderson, L. W., & Krathwohl, D. R. (2001). *A taxonomy for learning, teaching and assessing: A revision of Bloom's taxonomy of educational objectives.* New York: Longman.

Appadurai, A. (1996). *Modernity at large: Cultural dimensions of globalisation.* Minneapolis: University of Minnesota Press.

Bennett, R. (2007). *Assessment of, for, and as learning: Can we have all three?* Conceptual Paper. Princeton, NJ: Educational Testing Service.

Black, P. (2001). Dreams, strategies and systems: Portraits as assessment past, present and future. *Assessment in Education, 8*(1), 65–85.

Black, P., & Wiliam, D. (1998a). Assessment and classroom learning. *Assessment in Education, 5*(1), 7–73.

Black, P., & Wiliam, D. (1998b). Inside the black box: Raising standards through classroom assessment. *Phi Delta Kappan, 80*(2), 139–148.

Black, P., & Wiliam, D. (2003). "In praise of educational research": Formative assessment. *British Journal of Educational Technology, 29*(5), 623–637.

Black, P., & Wiliam, D. (2005). Lessons from around the world: How policies, politics and cultures constrain and afford assessment practices. *The Curriculum Journal, 16*(2), 249–261.

Black, P., Harrison, C., Lee, C., Marshall, B., & Wiliam, D. (2003). *Assessment for learning: Putting it into practice.* Maidenhead: Open University Press.

Boud, D. (2000). Sustainable assessment: Rethinking assessment for the learning society. *Studies in Continuing Education, 22*(2), 151–167.

Chua, B. H. (1997). *Communitarian ideology and democracy in Singapore.* London: Routledge.

Cummins, J., Brown, K., & Sayers, D. (2007). *Literacy, technology, and diversity: Teaching for success in changing times.* Boston: Pearson Education.

Darling-Hammond, L. (2007). *Testimony before the House Education and Labor Committee on the Re-Authorization of the NCLB legislation.* Retrieved December 12, 2007, from http://www.forumforeducation.org/foruminaction/index.php?page=399

Earl, L. (2003). *Assessment as learning: Using classroom assessment to maximize student learning.* Thousand Oaks, CA: Corwin Press.

Economic Review Committee. (1986). *The Singapore economy: New directions, fresh goals—towards a dynamic global city: Report of the Economic Review Committee.* Ministry of Trade and Industry, Republic of Singapore.

Economic Review Committee. (2003). *New challenges, fresh goals—towards a dynamic global city: Report of the Economic Review Committee.* Ministry of Trade and Industry, Republic of Singapore.

Gardner, J. (Ed.). (2006). *Assessment and learning.* London: Sage.

Good, T., & Brophy, J. (2003). *Looking in classrooms* (9th ed.). Boston: Allyn and Bacon.

Grubb, N., & Oakes, J. (2007). *"Restoring value" to the high school diploma: The rhetoric and practice of higher standards.* Arizona State University, Educational Policy Research Unit. Retrieved February 1, 2008, from http://epsl.asu.edu/epru/documents/EPSL-0710–242-EPRU.pdf

Harlen, W. (2007). *Assessment of learning.* London: Sage.

Hattie, J. (2003). Teachers make a difference: What is the research evidence? *Proceedings of the ACER Research Conference, 2003.* Camberwell, Victoria: Australian Council for Educational Research.

Hattie, J., & Timperley, H. (2007). The power of feedback. *Review of Educational Research, 77*(1), 81–112.

Hayward, E. L. (2007). Curriculum, pedagogies and assessment in Scotland: The quest for social justice. "Ah kent yir faither." *Assessment in Education, 14*(2), 251–268.

Hogan, D. (2007, May). *Towards "invisible colleges": Conversation, disciplinarity and pedagogy in Singapore.* Keynote Address to the CRPP Redesigning Pedagogies Conference, Singapore.

James, M., Black, P., McCormick, R., Pedder, D., & Wiliam, D. (2006). Learning how to learn in classrooms, schools and networks: Aims, design and analysis. *Research Papers in Education, 21*(2), 101–118.

Lee, H. L. (2004, August 22). *National day rally speech 2004. Delivered at the university cultural centre, NUS.* Retrieved February 6, 2008, from http://stars.nhb.gov.sg/stars/public/viewHTML.jsp?pdfno=2004083101

Luke, A. (2005). *CRPP intervention plan: Moving from the core to pedagogic practice.* Nanyang Technological University, National Institute of Education, Centre for Research in Pedagogy and Practice, Singapore.

Marshall, B., & Drummond, M. (2006). How teachers engage with assessment for learning: Lessons from the classroom. *Research Papers in Education, 21*(2), 133–150.

Means, B. (2006). Prospects for transforming schools with technology-supported assessment. In R. K. Sawyer (Ed.), *The Cambridge handbook of the learning sciences* (pp. 505–519). Cambridge, UK: Cambridge University Press.

National Mathematics Advisory Panel. (2008a). *Final report of the National Mathematics Advisory Panel.* Washington, DC: U.S. Department of Education.

National Mathematics Advisory Panel. (2008b). *Report of the Task Group on Instructional Practices to the National Mathematics Advisory Panel.* Washington, DC: U.S. Department of Education.

Newmann, F., & Associates. (1996). *Authentic achievement: Restructuring schools for intellectual quality.* San Francisco: Jossey-Bass.

Nie, Y., Lau, S., & Hogan, D. (2008). *Differential effectiveness of traditional and constructivist teaching methods on students' motivation, cognition, and achievement.* Unpublished manuscript, Nanyang Technological University, National Institute of Education, Centre for Research in Pedagogy and Practice, Singapore.

Nitko, A. J. (2004). *Educational assessment of students.* Columbus, OH: Pearson.

Organisation for Economic Cooperation and Development. (2005). *The definition and selection of key competencies: Executive summary.* Retrieved January 22, 2008, from http://www.oecd.org/dataoecd/47/61/35070367.pdf

Partnership for 21st Century Skills (2007). *Resources.* Retrieved January 22, 2008, from http://www.21stcenturyskills.org/index.php?option=com_content&task=view&id=82&Itemid=40

Pellegrino, J. W., Chudowsky, N., & Glaser, R. (2001). *Knowing what students know: The science and design of educational assessment.* Washington, DC: National Academic Press.

Powell, W. W., & Snellman, K. (2004). The knowledge economy. *Annual Review of Sociology, 30,* 199–220.

Purdie, N., & Ellis, L. (2005). *Literature review: A review of the empirical evidence identifying effective interventions and teaching practices for students with learning difficulties in years 4, 5 and 6.* Camberwell, Victoria: Australian Council for Educational Research.

Rowe, K. (2003). The importance of teacher quality as a key determinant of student experiences and outcomes of schooling. *Proceedings of the ACER Research Conference, 2003.* Camberwell, Victoria: Australian Council for Educational Research.

Rowe, K. (2006). *Effective teaching practices for students with and without learning difficulties: Constructivism as a legitimate theory of learning and teaching?* Camberwell, Victoria: Australian Council for Educational Research.

Rowntree, D. (1987). *Assessing students: How shall we know them?* London: Kogan Page.

Shapiro, C., & Varian, H. R. (1999). *Information rules: A strategic guide to the network economy.* Boston: Harvard Business School Press.

Sharpe, L., & Gopinathan, S. (2002). After effectiveness: New directions in the Singapore school system? *Journal of Education Policy, 17*(2), 151–166.

Shepard, L. A. (2000). The role of assessment in a learning culture. *Educational Researcher, 29*(7), 4–14.

Singapore Evaluation and Assessment Branch. (2005). *Frequently asked questions.* Retrieved March 28, 2008, from http://www.seab.gov.sg/SEAB/aboutUs/general.html

Stiggins, R. J. (2002). Assessment crisis: The absence of assessment for learning. *Phi Delta Kappan, 83*(10), 758–765.

Tomlinson, C. A. (2001). *How to differentiate instruction in mixed-ability classrooms* (2nd ed.). Alexandria, VA: Association for Supervision and Curriculum Development.

Towndrow, P. A., Tan, A. L., Venthan, A. M., & Gayathri, D. (2006). *Designing tasks to teach SPA skills at lower secondary level in Singapore.* Unpublished manuscript, Nanyang Technological University, National Institute of Education, Centre for Research in Pedagogy and Practice, Singapore.

Velayutham, S. (2007). *Responding to globalization: Nation, culture and identity in Singapore.* Singapore: Institute of Southeast Asian Studies.

Wiggins, G. P. (1989). A true test: Toward more authentic and equitable assessment. *Phi Delta Kappan, 70,* 703–713.

Wiliam, D., & Black, P. (1996). Meanings and consequences: A basis for distinguishing formative and summative functions of assessment? *British Educational Research Journal, 22*(5), 537–548.

Wiske, M. S. (Ed.). (1997). *Teaching for understanding: Linking research with practice.* San Francisco: Jossey-Bass.

Considerations for Developing and Adapting Language and Literacy Assessments in Arabic-Speaking Countries

SALEH SHAALAN

10

The emphasis on communication skills in new knowledge-based economies has led to an increasing interest in the assessment of speech, language, and literacy skills. While assessment of communication and reading disorders is routinely conducted in Western countries, it has gained momentum only in the last few years in developing countries, such as the Arabic-speaking Gulf Cooperation Council (GCC) countries. This poses challenges to speech and language and reading specialists working in these countries who have to develop tools to measure competencies in communication and literacy skills. This chapter discusses issues pertaining to practices of assessment of communication skills in countries known to have significant shortages in assessment tools, qualified specialists, and research in these areas. It discusses the socioeconomic and cultural contexts for the assessment processes in GCC and ways in which clinicians and researchers can meet the demands for assessment services in global and multicultural societies.

ASSESSMENT OF COMMUNICATION AND LITERACY SKILLS: THE GLOBAL REALITY

Assessment of verbal and written communication skills is indispensable in our modern societies. Communication skills, including speech, language, and literacy skills, are increasingly gaining a pivotal role as core skills in the global workplace. They are considered one of the most important of workforce readiness (employability) skills due to the nature of changing demands of employers (O'Neil, 1997). Communication skills include speaking, listening, reading, writing, and adaptability skills, such as problem solving (Bates & Phelan, 2002; Carnevale, Gainer, & Meltzer, 1990). Without these foundational skills, employees would not be able to meet the requirements of the workplace that is becoming increasingly global and reliant on knowledge-based skills.

While these workforce skills are well acknowledged in most industrialized countries, like the United States (see Bates & Phelan, 2002; Department of Labor, 1991; O'Neil, 1997), only recently have they acquired this position in Arabic-speaking countries in general, and countries of the Gulf Cooperation Council (GCC), in particular. Therefore, assessment of these communication skills is of paramount importance to both individuals and societies. Any disruption in these basic communication and literacy skills will put an individual's chance of securing a career in the highly competitive global workplace at risk.

Disorders of communication and literacy have deleterious effects on any economy. According to British statistics, it is estimated that persistent communication disorders are a contributing factor in the cost to society of young people (between 16–18 years) who are not in education, employment, or training. It is estimated that each young person in this category costs society £97,000 ($150,000) across their lifetime (Department for Education and Skills, 2002; I CAN, 2006). These disorders can affect either verbal or written communication, and they include disorders such as stuttering, where speech fluency is significantly affected; articulation and phonological disorders, where speech sounds are not produced accurately; and developmental language disorders, where children exhibit below-average performance in using and understanding linguistic structures. One common developmental language disorder is specific language impairment (SLI), which is defined as the presence of significant difficulties in the acquisition of language that are not explained by any sensory-motor, cognitive, or socio-emotional deficits (Bishop, 1997; Leonard, 1998). Moreover, speech sound disorders and language disorders tend to co-occur in many children (Leonard, 1998). Developmental dyslexia or specific learning disability is defined as the presence of poor literacy skills (reading and writing) despite adequate intelligence (Bishop & Snowling, 2004; Snowling, 2000). Speech and language pathologists are the professionals concerned with assessment of disorders in speaking, listening, prereading, and fluency skills, while reading specialists or educational psychologists typically manage children with dyslexia. Therefore, speech and language pathologists and reading specialists assess some essential parts of employability skills, that is, speech, language, and literacy skills, and endeavor to help prospective employees to meet the demands of the global workplace. This assessment and intervention is most efficient when it occurs at earlier stages of child development, that is, preschool years or the first few years of primary education.

While the profession of speech-language pathology and its role in the assessment of communication disorders is well established in most Western coun; :ies, it is still in its infancy in many developing countries, such as the GCC countries that comprise Bahrain, Kuwait, Oman, Qatar, Saudi Arabia, and the United Arab Emirates (UAE). There are only two university programs for speech-language therapy in Saudi Arabia and Kuwait, with the latter being established in 2003, and most speech-language therapy services are restricted to a few hospitals in the region. This, however, is changing rapidly with increasing numbers of speech-language pathologists entering the workforce and the rising awareness of the role of speech-language pathologists in assessment and treatment of communication disorders.

ASSESSMENT OF COMMUNICATION AND LITERACY SKILLS IN GCC COUNTRIES: RELEVANT CHARACTERISTICS

Assessments of abilities in general and assessment of communication skills in particular are naturally influenced by the ambient environment. There are societies where assessments, standardized tests, and objective measurements of abilities have a long tradition, while other societies have only recently been influenced by this emphasis on assessment of abilities. Therefore, developers of assessment tools should be heedful of the possible impacts of various factors on children's performance on communication and literacy assessments. This section outlines the major socioeconomic, cultural, educational, and linguistic characteristics that are relevant to the assessment of communication skills and literacy in the GCC countries. Furthermore, it discusses how assessment is perceived in GCC countries by referring to people's attitudes toward assessment of language and reading skills.

Socioeconomic Characteristics of GCC Countries

GCC countries have common political, economic, and social characteristics. All GCC countries are ruled by traditional sheikhdoms and monarchies and depend on oil production as their main source of income. Government is the main employer in all GCC countries, and most GCC nationals work in the public sector, while most nonnationals work for the private sector (Harry, 2007). GCC countries have many common social features, such as strong familial and tribal ties that extend beyond countries in many instances (Holes, 1989). They all underwent a very rapid process of modernization, especially since the hikes in oil prices in the 1970s.

The demographic situation in the GCC countries presents interesting challenges to the professional interested in assessment of abilities in general, and communication skills in particular. GCC countries are described as young countries with more than 40% of the population below 14-years-old (World Bank, 2003). This high proportion of young people came as a result of rapid developments following the investment of oil revenues in improving health care and social services. Another characteristic related to this rapid economic development is the presence of a large number of foreign migrants, estimated to be 10 million of the 25 million residents of the GCC countries (*Migration News*, 1995). It is estimated that the majority of the workforce in these countries consists of nonnational migrants, with an average of 1 GCC national for each 4 nonnational workers (Fasano & Iqbal, 2003). Most of this nonnational workforce is non-Arabic-speaking, with a proportion that ranges from 57% of the nonnational workforce in Kuwait to 85% in the UAE. Most of the non-Arabic-speaking workforce comes from Asia, particularly India, Pakistan, Bangladesh, Sri Lanka, and the Philippines, though there is a noticeable presence of expatriates from Europe and North America (Godfrey, Ruhs, Shah, & Smith, 2004). These large numbers of expatriates, mostly considered "temporary migrants," who exceed the number of local residents in most GCC countries, raise many issues in the assessment of communication skills in GCC countries.

This demographic situation in GCC countries, where native speakers constitute a minority that is influenced by the presence of various cultural and linguistic migrant communities, necessitates an important consideration in the types of skills an assessment professional should have. Speech and language pathologists and reading assessment professionals should have extensive training on how to assess linguistically and culturally diverse populations and be aware of the possible influence of this linguistic/cultural diversity on the language and reading skills of native speakers of Arabic in GCC countries. These professional assessors should be well versed in examining the psychometric properties of tests and the inherent problems in standardized tests. They should be able to self-assess their cross-cultural interaction skills and understand their own cultural biases. A successful cross-cultural assessor is one who tries to understand the cultural context in which each client functions and consider all cultural factors that may influence his or her client's performance on assessment of language and literacy and be willing to venture and try different methods to reach a better understanding of the client's performance.

Assessment should be informed by the government's policies regarding the labor market and localization of the workforce. Most GCC countries are trying to qualify their local citizens to run vital sectors, such as the gas and oil industry, and ensure they can replace the highly qualified foreign workers. GCC countries' main source of income is oil, and so the type of employability skills required by employers in GCC countries is related to "technology-intensive industries" or knowledge-based sectors (Harry, 2007), such as the gas and oil industry, and services sectors (e.g., telecommunication and finance). Therefore, assessment of abilities should consider these ongoing changes in the structure of the labor market and the governments' plan to increase localization, reduce dependence on the revenues of the oil industry, and to equip their citizens with knowledge-based employability skills in the era of globalization (Budhwar & Mellahi, 2007).

Another economic factor that is influencing the decision of parents of children with communication disorders to bring their children for assessment is the rising unemployment in the GCC region. It is estimated that unemployment among GCC nationals will continue to rise and reach 14% by 2010 (Girgis, 2002; *Migration News,* 1995). This awareness of looming high unemployment rates, and the competitiveness of the private sector, especially for highly skilled, knowledge-based jobs, made parents of GCC children aware of the impact of communication disorders on their children's employability skills, leading to many of them approaching speech-language pathologists and other assessment professionals to assess the speech, language, and literacy skills of their children.

Cultural Practices That Are Relevant to Assessment of Language and Literacy in GCC Countries

There could be an exhaustive list of cultural practices, beliefs, traditions, and customs that could influence the process of assessment of communication abilities; however, only two cultural practices will be discussed in this section. These were chosen due to their significant impact on the process of assessment of speech, language, and literacy skills. These practices are the widespread use of non-Arabic-speaking domestic workers and the role of family in assessment in GCC countries.

An important cultural characteristic that should be examined during the assessment of children with communication and literacy impairments in GCC countries is the influence of domestic workers on the language skills of these children. The sweeping majority of households in GCC countries have at least one domestic worker, usually a live-in maid, and it is not uncommon to find two or more domestic workers in one household. In one GCC country, it is estimated that domestic workers constitute 5% of the population (*Gulf News*, 2007). This widespread use of domestic workers in GCC countries, rarely seen at such high prevalence in other countries, is due to the affordability of foreign domestic workers and the increasing role of GCC women in the workforce (Godfrey et al., 2004; Manseau, 2006). Most of these domestic workers come from non-Arabic-speaking countries, such as India, Bangladesh, Sri Lanka, Indonesia, Ethiopia, and the Philippines. Apart from helping with domestic chores, most of them look after their employer's children when parents go to work. The language they speak at home is a pidginized form of Arabic, known as Pidgin Gulf Arabic (Smart, 1990), and few can speak English. It is not uncommon to find parents of Arabic-speaking children, especially those with communication disorders, raise some concerns about the influence of the domestic workers on the communication skills of their children. Therefore, any appropriate assessment of communication and literacy skills should consider the possible impact of having non-Arabic-speaking live-in maids on the communication and literacy abilities of Arabic-speaking children in GCC countries.

The role of family in assessment of communication skills in GCC children is different from that seen in Western cultures. In GCC countries, family is composed not only of parents and children, but it includes grandparents, maternal and paternal uncles and aunts, who might have an active role in the assessment process. Similarly to other traditional societies like India (Simmons & Johnston, 2007), important decisions in GCC families are usually collectively made. Accordingly, assessment professionals should foster a relationship of trust and mutual respect with the whole family to ease their concerns during the assessment process. This will facilitate the extended family's involvement in the assessment process and encourage other family members to seek help for their children. It is not uncommon to see several children coming from the same extended family to have their language and reading skills assessed once it is known that one of "their" children had been assessed, and the family felt comfortable with the assessment activities and the way their concerns have been dealt with.

Assessment of Language and Literacy in the Educational Context

There is an increasing demand for assessment tools and assessment professionals in the educational systems of the GCC countries. Most governments are trying to reform their educational systems to provide their students with the necessary skills for the new era. In Qatar, the government introduced reforms that saw the introduction of a new comprehensive educational system in the form of independent schools. Moreover, many GCC countries have recently introduced mainstreaming of children with special needs, which will require appropriate assessments of language and literacy skills of these children.

An important consideration when assessing language and literacy skills of children is assessing their familiarity with formal education (Carter et al., 2005). Children who have been to schools are necessarily familiar with many aspects of the assessment situation, such as the interaction with the assessor who plays the "teacher's" role, familiarity with written and pictorial material, and responding to questions of various levels of difficulty. In the GCC countries, primary education starts at the age of six and is compulsory for all children. Many children do not attend any type of formal education before the age of six, and when assessing these children, it is important to consider their subcultural background. Assessment professionals may come across children who come from households where they have not been exposed to written material or books, or who may not be familiar with the assessment tasks. Therefore, it may be necessary to modify the assessment protocols when assessing young children with no educational background.

There is a growing awareness of the importance of catering to individual needs of all children in the public education systems of most GCC countries. This will inevitably result in more interest in the assessment of both typically developing students and those with special needs. Traditionally, children with learning difficulties were not identified, and they would go to conventional public schools and not get any help. However, this is starting to change with the mounting efforts to meet the needs of all children in education and integrate them as much as possible. This tendency toward including more children with special needs, most with language and literacy impairments, in mainstream public schools is evidenced in the increasing number of students being included in the public education system. For example, in Saudi Arabia, the number of students integrated (partially or fully) in public schools has jumped from around 7,000 students in the mid-1990s to more than 34,000 in 2003 (Ministry of Education-Saudi Arabia, 2004). These large numbers of students with special needs will require proper assessment tools and qualified assessment professionals to ensure successful integration with their peers. In Qatar, new education reforms have been implemented that will see all Qatari independent schools follow curricula tied to international standards in order to facilitate the students' admission to international universities (Supreme Education Council, 2006). The Supreme Education Council of Qatar has established the Evaluation Institute, which conducts annual assessments for all children enrolled in independent schools to measure students' learning in the new education system. The new independent school system will cater to those pupils with language and learning difficulties, and a new project for children with individual needs is being piloted to ensure successful integration of these students. This emphasis on standardized testing and assessment of learning at all stages in the educational system is unprecedented in the GCC region and requires the development of assessment tools that are culturally and linguistically appropriate for their end users.

Linguistic Characteristics

The linguistic characteristics of both spoken and written languages should be considered when assessing language and reading skills of children in

GCC countries. Arabic is considered a classical example of a diglossic language, and this phenomenon of diglossia should be taken into account when conducting any assessment that involves spoken or written language. Moreover, the writing system of Arabic should be considered when assessing reading skills of Arabic-speaking children. In the following, I highlight some of the linguistic characteristics that all assessors should have in mind when dealing with children with communication and reading disorders in the GCC countries.

In his classical study of diglossia in Arabic, Ferguson (1959) defines diglossia as the existence of two varieties of the same language, "with each having a definite role to play" (p. 329). While children in GCC countries grow up speaking and listening to their spoken dialects (e.g., Gulf Arabic, Najdi Arabic, Hijazi-Arabic), they will be exposed to Modern Standard Arabic (MSA) mainly when they enter schools, although they may have been exposed to MSA from some television shows. These spoken dialects have syntactic, morphological, phonological, and lexical properties that set them apart from MSA, despite some similarities in many linguistic aspects (Holes, 1988, 2001, 2004, 2005; Ingham, 1994; Versteegh, 1997). These varieties of spoken Arabic are used in most social situations, while MSA is generally used in written media, or formal situations (i.e., formal speeches, news, television, and radio programs). Any assessment of communication skills should pay attention to the complex relationship between spoken dialects of Arabic and MSA. For example, in syntax, the basic type of word order in MSA is (V)erb (S)ubject (O)bject (VSO), while in most spoken dialects of Arabic, the basic word order is SVO (Ouhalla & Shlonsky, 2002). The phonologies of spoken dialects of Arabic are different from the phonology of MSA. For example, in Gulf Arabic most of the phonemes of MSA are pronounced in the same manner except for a few sounds, such as /dˤ/ (voiced pharyngealized dental plosive), which is substituted with /ðˤ/ (voiced pharyngealized interdental fricative) in most varieties of Gulf Arabic (Al Sulaiti, 1993; Bukshaisha, 1985). Therefore, any assessor should accept these substitutions as an indication of the local variety of Arabic, not of an error that warrants intervention. This demonstrates that an understanding of the Arabic diglossia is an integral part of the assessment of language skills of Arabic-speaking children.

Despite the fact that spoken dialects are not written and only MSA is used as the main variety for written material, appropriate assessment should be informed of the possible effects of spoken dialect on any assessment of reading or writing skills. For example, Abu-Rabia (2000) cited a common belief that younger children at preschool age should not be exposed to literary Arabic (MSA) because it is too difficult. However, he found that exposing preschool children to literary Arabic in diglossic situations had a beneficial effect on their reading comprehension in first and second grades (Abu-Rabia, 2000). Saiegh-Haddad (2003), on the other hand, found that differences between MSA and spoken Palestinian Arabic interfered with the reading processes of children of the same age and educational level. She explained that children found MSA phonemes that are distant from spoken Palestinian Arabic phonemes more difficult to isolate in tasks of phonological analysis. Moreover, she showed that children had more difficulty isolating MSA phonemes than spoken Arabic phonemes (Saiegh-Haddad, 2003, 2004). This illustrates the importance of examining the mutual effects of both MSA and spoken varieties on each other and the effect of this interaction on the performance of children on any assessment of speech, language, and reading abilities in GCC and other Arabic-speaking countries.

Orthography is another aspect of the language that should be considered when assessing the reading skills of children speaking this language. Like other Semitic languages, Arabic has a non-Latin orthography characterized by right-to-left writing and optional marking of vowels. In Arabic orthography, consonants and long vowels are represented while short vowels are optionally marked in the writing system and represented as diacritics (strokes) below, above, and beside consonants (Abu-Rabia, 2001, 2002; Saiegh-Haddad, 2005). These diacritics are frequently used with young children in early primary education and then phased out at middle primary stages. Therefore, Arabic orthography is considered transparent (regular) if vowelized, and oblique (irregular) if unvowelized (Abu-Rabia & Siegel, 2003). Readers will have to depend on context to disambiguate different words with the same spelling. Studies have shown that writing vowels on words helps facilitate reading in both typically developing and poor readers, including those at 10th grade (Abu-Rabia, 1997a, 1997b). Therefore, contextual effects play a greater role in reading skills in Arabic than they do in languages like English, and this consideration of the role of context in the reading process is essential in any adequate assessment of reading skills in Arabic-speaking children (Abu-Rabia, 1997a).

Attitudes Toward Assessment and Assessors

The attitude of Arabic-speaking people toward speech and language, and reading assessment in general, is changing toward more understanding and acceptance of assessment procedures. Their attitudes toward assessment and assessors are shaped by their understanding of the assessment process, their education and previous experience with assessment, and their relationship with assessment professionals.

One of the first and most essential considerations in assessment is people's attitudes toward language and reading impairments. It is well established that many families in GCC countries hesitate to bring their children for assessment because they do not want to "lose face" or let it be known that the family has a child with any kind of impairment. In GCC countries there are closely related networks of families where societies consist mainly of either tribes that share some common ancestors and social networks or big "urban" families that still keep close contact with each other. Therefore, news is spread very efficiently through these networks, and this makes families overconcerned about disclosing that their child has a speech-language or reading problem. It is crucial to reassure families of the confidentiality of all assessment information in order to build a relationship of trust and cooperation during the assessment process.

These "stigmatic" views toward speech, language, and reading impairments and other developmental disorders might be rooted in traditional views in the Middle East of developmental disorders as being linked to mental retardation. Many families in GCC countries, including some educated ones, fail to grasp that their children might have language and reading difficulties in the presence of normal intellectual functioning. Moreover, for those who understand this fact, they will have to face a society where many people (unfortunately, including many health professionals) still believe that all developmental disorders are linked to low cognitive abilities. Therefore, when assessing children with specific learning difficulties or language problems, where both are defined by excluding any cognitive low functioning, it is important to reassure parents that their children have average IQs and that these disorders are not necessarily correlated with cognitive abilities. In clinical practice, this has proved important in encouraging many parents to come forward and participate efficiently in the assessment and intervention processes.

Furthermore, parents' attitudes toward assessment of their children's abilities in the areas of communication skills and reading are shaped by their understanding of the role of the assessment process in the management of communication and literacy problems of their children. The professions of speech and language therapy and other related professions (e.g., clinical/educational psychology, special education specialists, etc.) are relatively new to the societies of GCC countries. There is still a severe shortage in the number of qualified specialists in these disciplines, and it is not surprising that parents of children to be assessed may not always have a proper understanding of the role of assessment of abilities in managing their children's impairments. Some parents hesitate to have their children assessed in areas of speech, language, and reading because they understand assessment as equivalent to "testing." They perceive assessment as a test that their child will either fail or pass, rather than as a tool to identify areas of strengths and weaknesses in their children's communication skills. This explains the tendency by some parents of children with communication disorders not to allow their children to be assessed because they do not want their children to "fail" these "tests." In a project that is being conducted in Qatar with children with specific language impairment (SLI), only parents of children with SLI withdrew their children after the first stage of assessment while none of the parents of typically developing children withdrew their children from assessment.

Parents' education and previous experience with assessment have a significant impact on the assessment process. Based on the clinical experience of the author in GCC countries, parents with university education or higher tend to be more concerned about the communication abilities of their children and therefore they come forward more often than less-educated parents. They are more likely to reach out for help in private or public sectors. This may be related to their increased awareness of the role of communication and reading skills in new global economies and the role of assessment in the intervention process. Experience with previous assessment professionals could have a bearing on subsequent interactions with assessment professionals. Based on reports of some parents of children with language and literacy problems in GCC countries, many were hesitant to come for assessment due to their dissatisfaction with previous interactions with other assessment professionals or based on negative feedback from other members of the extended family who were not satisfied with previous assessments of their children. Most of these unsuccessful assessment experiences were related to poor training and qualification of assessment professionals, their lack of understanding of the local GCC culture, since most of them were not GCC nationals, and sometimes due to parents' failure to grasp the main purpose of assessment, as outlined in the previous section. Therefore, it is vital that any assessment of communication and reading skills considers parents' education and their previous experience with assessment of abilities.

One of the cultural considerations is related to the family's attitudes regarding the cause of their children's language and reading problems.

Sometimes parents may have different speculations, beliefs, or theories about the cause of their child's difficulties in communication and reading. Therefore, it is important to know how the family perceives the cause of their child's difficulties as this forms an integral part of the assessment process. For example, if parents fear that they may have done something that has led to their child's developmental problem, it is important to clarify this issue in order to ensure their psychological well-being. The fact that almost every local family in the GCC countries has at least one domestic helper makes it an oft-repeated topic in many discussions of causes of speech, language, and reading disorders. Unfortunately, the impact of this foreign domestic workforce on the developing language of both typically and atypically developing children in GCC countries has not been systematically investigated and no firm conclusion should be drawn. But from studies of causalities of language impairment and dyslexia, it is safe to say that having domestic helpers does not trigger or cause language impairment per se. It is perceived that genetic factors seem to play a crucial role more than environmental factors do (SLI Consortium [SLIC], 2004; Stromswold, 1998, 2001). However, one cannot downplay the importance of input for children with language impairment during the intervention process, especially if the domestic helpers, who mostly speak pidginized Arabic, spend more time with the child than the parents do. In this case, it may be prudent to mention that having a domestic helper does not cause language impairment, but may not be a helping factor in the intervention process, especially if she is the major communication partner of the child with language or reading impairment. In a culture where awareness of language and literacy disorders is just starting to develop and mainly in the highly educated strata of the society, it is imperative to educate families of possible causes of language impairment and of factors that are less likely to be implicated in language impairment in children.

DEVELOPING ASSESSMENT TOOLS FOR LANGUAGE AND READING ABILITIES IN GCC COUNTRIES: CHALLENGES AND SUGGESTED SOLUTIONS

Current Situation and Challenges

Many countries, especially in the developing world, lack assessment tools in many areas of abilities, such as speech, language, and literacy skills.

Therefore, assessment professionals have to devise methods, tools, and procedures to deal with this lack of assessment resources. Assessment professionals resort to various methods to carry out assessments; these include developing new assessment tools, adapting existing ones, adopting nonbiased general-purpose measures, or using dynamic assessment methods. In the following section, these possible options are discussed with reference to the assessment of language and reading skills in children in GCC countries.

Research into both normal and abnormal development of language and reading skills is still in its infancy in the GCC region, and there is a limited number of studies on these topics (Abdalla, 2002; Al-Akeel, 1998; Aljenaie, 2001; Al Mannai & Everatt, 2005; Elbeheri & Everatt, 2007; Elbeheri, Everatt, Reid, & Mannai, 2006). The professions of speech-language pathology and related disciplines are not well established yet in the region. Moreover, lack of specialized child language research groups or centers has led to lack of communication among the few language and reading researchers in the region. This paucity of child language research has naturally led to a lack of appropriate assessment tools for both typically developing children and those with language and reading disorders. In a survey conducted in Saudi Arabia, speech-language pathologists showed their dissatisfaction with the tools they used to assess children with language impairment, as they had to resort to observation of children's interaction with caregivers, translating English tests, or collecting language samples (Al-Akeel, 1998). They all stressed the need to establish assessment tools based on local culture and norms of language development. Similarly, Elbeheri and colleagues (2006) found that dyslexia researchers have similar challenges, summarized in lack of epidemiological studies and assessment tools, shortage in trained professionals, and lack of validity and reliability studies of the assessment tools. Therefore, language and reading specialists and researchers working in the GCC countries have to devise short-term and long-term strategies to overcome these challenges.

Solutions

Clinicians and researchers working in the areas of language and reading disorders have attempted to overcome the dire shortage of research, normative data, and assessment tools by resorting to different strategies. Generally, researchers and clinicians tend to prefer standardized tools due to the overall acceptance of this method of assessment. In GCC countries, clinicians employ adaptations of well-established tests where standardized assessments are not available or are not appropriate for the population they deal with. Ideally, these adaptations are expected to develop into standardized tests; however, lack of resources, institutional support, and funding, and scarcity of cooperation projects between researchers and clinicians have not seen these adaptations develop into standardized tests. Apart from standardized tests and adaptations of existing tests in areas of language and reading assessment, this section introduces two other assessment measures that provide complementary and alternative procedures proved to be of great potential, namely, culture-free processing measures (e.g., nonword repetition), and the dynamic assessment (DA) methods of assessment. These are of special interest to clinicians and researchers in the GCC region because they have been proposed as potentially viable assessment tools when dealing with children belonging to various multicultural and multilinguistic backgrounds.

Developing Standardized Measures and Tests Based on Local Norms

There have been few attempts to develop standardized tests to assess speech and language skills of Arabic-speaking children in GCC countries. This is mainly due to the lack of qualified professionals and researchers, and poor research support for standardization projects, which usually require extensive resources. I am aware of one systematic attempt to create a language comprehension test for children in Saudi Arabia (Al-Akeel, 1998), though the test has not been published yet. In this doctoral dissertation, Al-Akeel explains all the steps he went through to design the test and collect data in the city of Riyadh, Saudi Arabia. The test was developed to assess language comprehension skills of Saudi children aged 3.0–6.0, and is meant to be used with children with different regional dialects of Saudi Arabia. The test was specifically designed to assess children's understanding of 24 morphosyntactic structures that he selected from three sources: spontaneous language samples of typically developing children interacting with their fathers; morphosyntactic structures that the author himself added based on his linguistic knowledge of Arabic; and some morphosyntactic structures that he modified from existing English-language tests. The test, conducted with 120 Saudi children between 3.0 and 6.0 using object manipulation and picture-pointing tasks, provides a good source of information on the order and age of acquisition of these morphosyntactic structures. The author expressed his intention to develop this criterion-referenced test into a standardized test in the future, especially with the encouraging levels of validity and reliability obtained in this study (Al-Akeel, 1998).

While Al-Akeel (1998) spent four years developing a comprehension test that taps into children's acquisition of specific morphosyntactic structures at certain levels of development, clinicians and researchers working with children with language impairment have to devise means to assess children that are logistically possible and clinically viable. One of the best means for assessing gross grammatical development in younger children with language impairments is the use of mean length of utterance (MLU) in morphemes (MLUm) or words (MLUw). The validity of spontaneous language measurements, such as MLUm or MLUw, has been reported in typically developing children (Miller, 1981; Parker, 2005) and in children with speech and language disorders (Blake, Myszczyszyn, & Jokel, 2004; Dunn, Flax, Sliwinski, & Aram, 1996). These two measurements of gross grammatical development are commonly used by clinicians along with standardized tests (Abdalla, 2002; Blake et al., 2004; Condouris, Meyer, & Tager-Flusberg, 2003) and are considered one of the cornerstones of language assessment in children with language impairment. They are relatively easy to collect and less demanding than standardized tests. Shaalan and Khater (2006) investigated the correlation between MLUw and MLUpm (mean length of utterance in productive morpheme: an adaptation of the MLUm that took into account the complex morphological structure of Arabic, which was based on Dromi and Berman [1982]) in Qatari-speaking children. Results showed that these two measures of grammatical development were highly correlated ($r = 0.98$) when examining the language sample of eight Qatari-Arabic-speaking children aged 2.6–4.5. Khater and Shaalan (2007) expanded their sample size to 40 children and the results still showed high correlation; thus they recommended the use of MLUw as an easier, and reliable, measure of gross grammatical development. MLUw shows higher interrater reliability and is less time-consuming than the more complex MLUpm where raters have to follow a long list of rules on how to count morphemes in a nonconcatenative language like Arabic. Using normative measures such as MLUw can be a robust tool to assess the grammatical development of children at risk of language disorders, especially in the preschool years.

Shaalan and van der Lely (2007) explain how they use the framework of an established vocabulary test to create a test that is linguistically and culturally appropriate for Arabic-speaking children in Qatar.

They followed the procedures used to create the Peabody Picture Vocabulary Test (PPVT) (Dunn & Dunn, 1997) to create a vocabulary test for Gulf Arabic–speaking children in Qatar. Instead of translating or adapting the English vocabulary, a new vocabulary test was developed to meet the needs of Gulf Arabic–speaking children. Vocabulary items were chosen based on familiarity ratings by native speakers, a procedure recommended to improve the psychometric properties of the instrument (Pena, 2007). Twenty-two adult speakers of Qatari Arabic were required to rate 600 words in terms of familiarity. Based on these ratings, 132 words were chosen that belonged to 20 different semantic categories (e.g., verbs, animals, occupations, adjectives, etc.) and were ranked in terms of difficulty based on their familiarity score. The criteria for choosing these words were similar to those used in the PPVT (Dunn & Dunn, 1997); therefore, the words included in the test were functional, easy to depict pictorially, and common in everyday life (except for the advanced vocabulary where some were taken from Modern Standard Arabic). Initial piloting with 10 children showed positive results; currently, validity and reliability estimates of this test are being conducted that will include a higher number of children.

Similarly, Al Mannai and Everatt (2005) designed some tests to evaluate the literacy skills of Bahraini children in Grades 1–3. The tasks included single-word reading, spelling, nonword reading, phonological awareness skills, speed of processing, and short-term memory tasks. Consistent with findings in English and other languages, Al Mannai and Everatt (2005) found that phonological processing skills, such as phonological awareness and decoding (e.g., nonword reading), were the best predictors of literacy skills in Gulf Arabic–speaking children in Bahrain. However, they found some differences between the two languages. For example, they revealed that nonverbal intelligence tasks, such as Block Design of the Wechsler Test (Wechsler, 1998), played a greater role in predicting literacy skills in Arabic compared to English, a finding consistent with that reported in Palestinian Arabic (Abu-Rabia, Share, & Mansour, 2003). Overall, the great similarities between predictors in both English and Arabic were considerable, especially since the two languages have vast differences in their linguistic features and writing systems. Al Mannai and Everatt (2005) interpreted these results to suggest that there are common limitations in phonological processes that underlie dyslexia in both languages. These tasks developed by Al Mannai and Everatt can form the foundation of a standardized assessment test, especially if they consider some language-specific characteristics of Arabic, such as the use of diacritics (Elbeheri et al., 2006).

Despite their widespread use by both clinicians and researchers of language and literacy disorders, both standardized tests and spontaneous language samples have their own limitations and it is recommended to use them along with other assessment tools (e.g., parent's questionnaires and interviews, checklists, observation of child-caregiver interaction, etc.). Standardized tests are very difficult to conduct and require extensive amounts of institutional and professional resources that may not be readily available in the GCC region. Moreover, such standardized tests and measures have their drawbacks in multicultural societies, such as those of the GCC, since they will based on the norms of the native population, while many of the clients coming for assessment may come from other linguistic and cultural communities who constitute a majority in some GCC countries. Therefore, speech-language pathologists and reading assessment professionals will have to adapt these standardized tools when using them with other non-Gulf Arabic–speaking children. However, standardized tests remain essential to establish reliable ways of comparing children with their age peers, especially in mild cases of language and reading impairments, where the deficits might be subtle and the speech-language pathologists or reading specialists need to support their clinical hypothesis with an established standardized test based on local norms.

Adapting Existing Tests to Local Populations

When adapting tests from one culture/language to another, it is important to consider methodological and cross-cultural factors. Apart from ensuring linguistic equivalence, that is, eliciting the same required linguistic structures, Pena (2007) emphasizes the importance of functional equivalence, cultural equivalence, and metric equivalence when adapting or translating tests. Functional equivalence refers to ensuring that both the instrument and the elicitations do examine the required construct, while cultural equivalence refers to how members of each culture interpret the meaning of each test structure. Metric equivalence, on the other hand, refers to equivalence in item difficulty (Pena, 2007). Therefore, Carter and colleagues (2005) recommend using the established framework or principles of standardized tests along with local, culturally appropriate materials to ensure cultural and functional equivalence. These factors along with "culture-friendly" assessment professionals can improve the adequacy of adapted assessments tools.

Appropriate adaptation of tests should be performed by assessors who are proficient in assessment procedures, rationales for testing, and have appropriate knowledge of the linguistic structures of both languages. Therefore, any adaptation of language tests from English to Arabic should consider English structures that do not have Arabic equivalents (e.g., "-ing" or auxiliaries "is," "are") and Arabic linguistic structures that do not exist in English, for example, Arabic uses different types of clitic pronouns that do not exist in English (*clitics* are accentless pronouns that attach to ends of nouns, verbs, and prepositions, such as the possessive clitic *ha* ["her"] in *Kitab-ha* ["her book"]). The assessor should be aware that many linguistic structures that exist in both languages might have different developmental trajectories. For example, though both English and Arabic have regular and irregular plurals, the English regular plural constitutes the majority of plural forms while Arabic has a majority of irregular plurals and a minority of masculine and feminine regular plurals (Plunkett & Nakisa, 1997). Moreover, assessors should be knowledgeable about the nonstandard dialects in the society concerned. For example, in the case of GCC countries, it may be necessary to adapt the test items from the "standard" dialect (usually the dialect spoken by urban people) to the dialect of some other groups (e.g., Bedouin dialects of GCC countries).

Shaalan and van der Lely (2007) reported on a battery of tests used to assess language skills of children with specific language impairment (SLI) in Qatar. The battery comprises three language tests: a sentence comprehension (SC) test, a word structure (WS) test, and a sentence repetition (SR) test. The three tests followed the rationales and framework of corresponding subtests of the *Clinical Evaluation of Language Fundamentals–3* (Semel, Wiig, & Secord, 1996), and the recommendations of Pena (2007) and Carter et al. (2005) to ensure cultural and functional equivalence. Therefore, only culturally appropriate pictures were chosen from the original tests, and some new pictures that were drawn by a local artist from the GCC were added. The preliminary results of conducting these tests with 30 typically developing Qatari children have been encouraging. All test scores were significantly correlated with chronological age and with each other, and showed normal distribution. Initial internal consistency measures showed acceptable levels of reliability. However, further testing and refinement is underway. It is expected that these adapted tests can form an adequate basis for standardized tests following further field testing and standardization studies.

In areas of reading disorders, a similar pattern of lack of standardized tests and use of adapted tests emerges. Elbeheri et al. (2006) developed tests based on adaptations of standardized tools using culturally and linguistically appropriate material. They found it was possible to use some tasks from the Wechsler scales, such as the Forward and Backward Digit Span, with minimal adaptations, such as using the more familiar Hindi numerals instead of Arabic numerals. They reported results that were consistent with English findings. However, this was not the case with the Coding subtest of the same test, where Arabic-speaking children scored in the disordered range of the scale. Therefore, they emphasized the importance of metric equivalence when adapting tests from one language to another.

While the use of standardized tests is preferable to adaptations that have the risk of not having been applied to a large population and have higher chances of giving erroneous results, it is expected that the use of adaptations in GCC countries will continue due to their clinical viability in assessing language and reading skills. However, it is essential that practitioners are aware of the pitfalls of adapting tests from another language/culture and that they try to ensure linguistic, functional, and cultural equivalences.

Using Non–Language-Specific Approaches and Processing Measures That Are Less Culturally Biased

There have been attempts to propose some general developmental stages that can be used to assess language impairment, regardless of the type of language being assessed, in bilingual or multilingual situations. Another approach is the use of some processing measures, such as nonword repetition, that were claimed to be sensitive to underlying linguistic deficits, and less influenced by extraneous variables, such as cultural or socioeconomic factors.

Hakansson and colleagues (Hakansson, Salameh, & Nettelbladt, 2003) applied a non–language-specific theory of language acquisition to analyze the performance of bilingual Arabic-Swedish children with specific language impairment in comparison with typically developing bilingual Swedish and Arabic-speaking children. The theory known as the Processability Theory (Pienemann, 1998) aims to characterize language impairment in terms of examining "the processing prerequisites that are needed for the automatization of grammatical rules on different developmental levels" (Hakansson et al., 2003, p. 259). Instead of comparing the child's performance to standardized norms, Hakansson and colleagues used some fixed developmental stages that proceed in an expected sequence, for example, in the basic level (Level 1) children use words in isolation and then proceed in higher levels to a "tighter and tighter relation between words, phrases and clauses" (Salameh, Hakansson, & Nettelbladt, 2004, p. 68). These levels of hierarchy are proposed as being uniform regardless of the language being learned. Salameh et al. (2004) used this theory to assess the grammatical development of children in both Arabic and Swedish. They found Processability Theory was capable of explaining the deficits in bilingual children with language impairments. Results showed that while bilingual children with language impairment evinced significant deficits in both Arabic and Swedish, typically developing bilingual children showed a higher level of performance in at least one language (Hakansson et al., 2003). Despite the apparent difficulties in Processability's claim that first- and second-language acquisition proceed in a similar manner and can be explained by the same mechanisms (see Bialystok, 1998), such non–language-specific accounts or similar measures that tap into general cognitive mechanisms can be useful in alleviating the common difficulties in finding assessment tools appropriate for different languages, especially those that lack normative data or standardized assessment tools.

Research on specific language impairment (SLI), which is one of the most common childhood language impairments, has suggested that studying processing-based phenotypes can lead to better understanding of the nature and characteristics of SLI (Bishop, 2004; Campbell, Dollaghan, Needleman, & Janosky, 1997). One processing-based or qualitative marker that has shown great promise for children with SLI is nonword repetition (NWR), which has a high rate of heritability and low correlation with environmental factors (Bishop, 2004; Bishop, North, & Donlan, 1996). Bishop and colleagues (Bishop et al., 1996; Barry, Yasin, & Bishop, 2007) showed that NWR provides an excellent behavioral marker due to its high sensitivity, as shown in the findings from parents of children with SLI. Moreover, Campbell and colleagues (1997) found that using this processing-dependent assessment measure reduced linguistic and cultural bias in evaluating minority children in the United States. Therefore, finding processing-dependent measures that function as clinical markers of language and reading disorders independent of cultural and socioeconomic differences in GCC countries can be a promising line of research, especially considering the multicultural composition of the GCC societies.

Using Dynamic Assessment Methods

An alternative/complementary method of assessment that has been proposed as a nonbiased method of assessment is called *dynamic assessment (DA)* (Grigorenko & Sternberg, 1998; Lidz & Pena, 1996). The DA is defined as "an assessment of thinking, perception, learning, and problem solving by an active teaching process aimed at modifying cognitive functioning" (Tzuriel, 2000, p. 387). There are different models of dynamic assessment, but most of them follow the pretest-intervention-posttest format. The intervention component of the assessment, sometimes termed the Mediated Learning Experience (MLE), is implemented in order to provide information about the child's functioning within the assessment situation (Lidz, 2002). Proponents of DA are not only interested in what the child knows but also in how he or she learns. Assessment professionals have a different role to play during the DA assessment process; they are considered "active interveners" who ensure that the child is engaged in the intervention in order to effect positive changes (Lidz & Pena, 1996). One of the basic contrastive properties of DA is that unlike conventional static tests, DA provides a good measure of modifiability, that is, the child's ability to respond to the teaching process (Tzuriel, 2000).

In the DA method of test-teach-retest, assessment professionals can evaluate children's responsiveness to intervention, and this can be a useful tool when assessing language abilities of children from culturally and linguistically different (CLD) populations, as is the case of many clients in the GCC countries. It is expected that CLD children with language impairment will respond differently from those who have lower proficiency because of not having experience with learning the language (Gutiérrez-Clellen & Pena, 2001), hence avoiding one of the common biases found in conventional standardized tests. Pena and colleagues (Pena, Quinn, & Iglesias, 1992) have adapted the use of DA to assess vocabulary abilities of Spanish-speaking children in the United States. They found that using pretest-teach-posttest not only differentiated children with language impairment from typically developing children, but it also led to significant improvement in the children's scores on the Expressive One Word Picture Vocabulary Test (Gardner, 1990). Similar improvements in children's narrative ability have been reported in a DA study by Pena and colleagues (2006).

Dynamic assessment has potential utilities in societies like GCC where native speakers are a minority and there are many large communities of people coming from various linguistic and cultural backgrounds who might approach language and literacy assessment services. Using methods like DA can reduce cultural, linguistic, and task familiarity biases. It is capable of revealing genuine differences between clients with communication and reading disorders and those typically developing children whose profiles resemble those with communication and literacy difficulties due to some inherent biases in standardized assessment tools (Gutiérrez-Clellen & Pena, 2001; Pena & Quinn, 1997; Pena et al., 1992; Pena et al., 2006; Tzuriel, 2000).

CONCLUSION

The emergence of a global workforce market, emphasis on knowledge-based employability skills, and awareness of the importance of communication and literacy skills have led to an increasing interest in assessment of language and reading abilities. The GCC countries are no exception to this global trend. This chapter discussed the challenges that face assessment professionals working in these countries who have to meet the increasing demands for communication and literacy assessments. These challenges include lack of assessment tools, paucity of research on normative data and disorders of language acquisition and literacy, assessment practices, and the need to adapt assessment activities to account for cultural, socio-economic, demographic, and linguistic factors that are specific to these societies. Faced with these challenges, clinicians working with children with disorders of language and literacy need to resort to different strategies that include the use of standardized and criterion-referenced tests; employing processing measures that tap into general processing mechanisms that are less likely to be influenced by cultural and linguistic factors, such as nonword repetition; and employing assessment methods, such as dynamic assessment, that evaluate children's responsiveness to learning situations, thus reducing cultural and linguistic biases.

AUTHOR NOTE

I would like to thank Sabah Safi for useful discussions leading to this chapter; however, all errors and mistakes remain my own.

REFERENCES

Abdalla, F. (2002). *Specific language impairment in Arabic-speaking children: Deficits in morphosyntax.* Unpublished doctoral dissertation, McGill University.

Abu-Rabia, S. (1997a). The need for cross-cultural consideration in reading theory: The effects of Arabic sentence context in skilled and poor readers. *Journal of Research in Reading, 20*(2), 137–147.

Abu-Rabia, S. (1997b). Reading in Arabic orthography: The effect of vowels and context on reading accuracy of poor and skilled native Arabic readers in reading paragraphs, sentences, and isolated words. *Journal of Psycholinguistic Research, 26*(4), 465–482.

Abu-Rabia, S. (2000). Effects of exposure to literary Arabic on reading comprehension in a diglossic situation. *Reading and Writing, 13,* 147–157.

Abu-Rabia, S. (2001). The role of vowels in reading Semitic scripts: Data from Arabic and Hebrew. *Reading and Writing, 14,* 39–51.

Abu-Rabia, S. (2002). Reading in a root-based-morphology language: The case of Arabic. *Journal of Research in Reading, 25,* 299–309.

Abu-Rabia, S., Share, D., & Mansour, M. S. (2003). Word recognition and basic cognitive processes among reading-disabled and normal readers in Arabic. *Reading and Writing, 16,* 423–442.

Abu-Rabia, S., & Siegel, L. (2003). Reading skills in three orthographies: The case of trilingual Arabic-Hebrew-English-speaking Arab children. *Reading and Writing, 16,* 611–634.

Al-Akeel, A. (1998). *The acquisition of Arabic language comprehension by Saudi children.* Unpublished doctoral dissertation, University of Newcastle upon Tyne.

Aljenaie, K. (2001). *The emergence of tense and agreement in Kuwaiti Arabic children.* Unpublished doctoral dissertation, University of Reading.

Al Mannai, H., & Everatt, J. (2005). Phonological processing skills as predictors of literacy amongst Arabic speaking Bahraini children. *Dyslexia, 11,* 269–291.

Al Sulaiti, L. M. (1993). *Some aspects of Qatari Arabic phonology and morphology.* Doctoral dissertation, Lancaster University.

Barry, J. G., Yasin, I., & Bishop, D. V. M. (2007). Heritable risk factors associated with language impairments. *Genes, Brain and Behavior, 6,* 66–76.

Bates, R. A., & Phelan, K. C. (2002). Characteristics of a globally competitive workforce. *Advances in Developing Human Resources, 4*(2), 121–132.

Bialystok, E. (1998). What's in a process? Explaining development in language acquisition. *Bilingualism: Language and Cognition, 1,* 21–22.

Bishop, D. V. M. (1997). *Uncommon understanding: Comprehension in specific language impairment.* Hove, UK: Psychology Press.

Bishop, D. V. M. (2004). Specific language impairment: Diagnostic dilemmas. In L. Verhoeven & H. van Balkom (Eds.), *Classification of developmental language disorders* (pp. 309–326). Mahwah, NJ: Erlbaum.

Bishop, D. V. M., North, T., & Donlan, C. (1996). Nonword repetition as a behavioural marker for inherited language impairment: Evidence from a twin study. *Journal of Child Psychology and Psychiatry, 37,* 391–403.

Bishop, D. V. M., & Snowling, M. J. (2004). Developmental dyslexia and specific language impairment: Same or different? *Psychological Bulletin, 130*(6), 858–886.

Blake, J., Myszczyszyn, D., & Jokel, A. (2004). Spontaneous measures of morphosyntax in children with specific language impairment. *Applied Psycholinguistics, 25,* 29–41.

Budhwar, P., & Mellahi, K. (2007). Introduction: Human resource management in the Middle East. *International Journal of Human Resource Management, 18,* 2–10.

Bukshaisha, F. (1985). *An experimental phonetic study of some aspects of Qatari Arabic.* Unpublished doctoral dissertation, University of Edinburgh.

Campbell, T., Dollaghan, C., Needleman, H., & Janosky, J. (1997). Reducing bias in language assessment: Processing-dependent measures. *Journal of Speech and Hearing Research, 40,* 519–525.

Carnevale, A. P., Gainer, L. J., & Meltzer, A. S. T. (1990). *Workplace basics: The essential skills employers want.* San Francisco: Jossey-Bass.

Carter, J. A., Lees, J. A., Murira, G. M., Gona, J., Neville, B. G. R., & Newton, C. R. J. C. (2005). Issues in the development of cross-cultural assessments of speech and language for children. *International Journal of Language and Communication Disorders, 40*(4), 385–401.

Condouris, K., Meyer, E., & Tager-Flusberg, H. (2003). The relationship between standardized measures of language and measures of spontaneous speech in children with autism. *American Journal of Speech Language Pathology, 12*(3), 349–358.

Department for Education and Skills. (2002). *Estimating the cost of being "not in education, employment, or training" at age 16–18.* London: Author.

Department of Labor. (1991). *What work requires of schools: A SCANS report for America 2000.* Springfield, VA: National Technical Information Service.

Dromi, E., & Berman, R. A. (1982). A morphemic measure of early language development: Data from modern Hebrew. *Journal of Child Language, 9,* 403–424.

Dunn, L. M., & Dunn, L. M. (1997). *Peabody Picture Vocabulary Test (PPVT–III).* Circle Pines, MN: American Guidance Service.

Dunn, M., Flax, J., Sliwinski, M., & Aram, D. (1996). The use of spontaneous language measures as criteria for identifying children with specific language impairment: An attempt to reconcile clinical and research incongruence. *Journal of Speech and Hearing Research, 39*(3), 643–654.

Elbeheri, G., & Everatt, J. (2007). Literacy ability and phonological processing skills amongst dyslexic and non-dyslexic speakers of Arabic. *Reading and Writing, 20*(3), 273–294.

Elbeheri, G., Everatt, J., Reid, G., & Mannai, H. (2006). Dyslexia assessment in Arabic. *Journal of Research in Special Educational Needs, 6*(3), 143–152.

Fasano, U., & Iqbal, Z. (2003). *GCC countries: From oil dependence to diversification.* Washington, DC: International Monetary Fund.

Ferguson, C. (1959). Diglossia. *Word, 15,* 325–340.

Gardner, M. F. (1990). *Expressive One-Word Picture Vocabulary Test.* Novato, CA: Academic Therapy.

Girgis, M. (2002). *Would nationals and Asians replace Arab workers in the GCC.* The Fourth Mediterranean Development Forum. Unpublished manuscript, Amman, Jordan.

Godfrey, M., Ruhs, M., Shah, N., & Smith, M. (2004). Migrant domestic workers in Kuwait: Findings based on a field survey and additional research. In S. Esim & M. Smith (Eds.), *Gender and migration in Arab states: The case of domestic workers* (pp. 42–63). Beirut: International Labour Organization.

Grigorenko, E. L., & Sternberg, R. J. (1998). Dynamic testing. *Psychological Bulletin, 24,* 75–111.

Gulf News. (2007, November 11). *Domestic workers form 5% of UAE's population.* Retrieved January 7, 2008, from http://archive.gulfnews.com/articles/07/11/12/10166 962.html

Gutiérrez-Clellen, V. F., & Pena, E. D. (2001). Dynamic assessment of diverse children: A tutorial. *Language, Speech, and Hearing Services in Schools, 32,* 212–224.

Hakansson, G., Salameh, E.-K., & Nettelbladt, U. (2003). Measuring language development in bilingual children: Swedish-Arabic children with and without language impairment. *Linguistics, 41*(2), 255–288.

Harry, W. (2007). Employment creation and localization: The crucial human resource issues for the GCC. *International Journal of Human Resource Management, 18*(1), 132–146.

Holes, C. (1988). *Colloquial Arabic of the Gulf and Saudi Arabia.* London: Routledge.

Holes, C. (1989). *Gulf Arabic.* London: Routledge.

Holes, C. (2001). *Dialect, culture and society in Eastern Arabia: Vol. I. Glossary.* Leiden, The Netherlands: Brill.

Holes, C. (2004). *Modern Arabic: Structures, functions, and varieties.* Washington, DC: Georgetown University Press.

Holes, C. (2005). *Dialect, culture and society in Eastern Arabia: Vol. II. Ethnographic texts.* Leiden: Brill.

I CAN. (2006). *The cost to the nation of children's poor communication.* London: Author.

Ingham, B. (1994). *Najdi Arabic: Central Arabian.* Amsterdam: John Benjamins.

Khater, M., & Shaalan, S. (2007). *Reporting norms for mean length of utterance (MLU) in words and morphemes for Qatari speaking children.* Paper presented at Linguistics in the Gulf Conference, University of Qatar, Doha.

Leonard, L. B. (1998). *Children with specific language impairment.* Cambridge, MA: MIT Press.

Lidz, C. S. (2002). Mediated Learning Experience (MLE) as a basis for an alternative approach to assessment. *School Psychology International, 23*(1), 68–84.

Lidz, C. S., & Pena, E. D. (1996). Dynamic assessment: The model, its relevance as a nonbiased approach, and its application to Latino American preschool children. *Language, Speech, and Hearing Services in Schools, 27*(4), 367–372.

Manseau, G. S. (2006). Contractual solutions for migrant labourers: The case of domestic workers in the Middle East. *Human Rights Law Commentary, 2,* 25–47.

Migration News. (1995, March). *Migration news: Middle East, 1*(4). Retrieved December 20, 2008, from http://migration.ucdavis.edu/mn/more.php?id=603_0_5_0

Miller, J. (1981). *Assessing language production in children: Experimental procedures* Austin, TX: PRO-ED.

Ministry of Education-Saudi Arabia. (2004). *The development of education.* International Conference on Education, 46th Session. Geneva, Switzerland: International Bureau of Education, UNESCO.

O'Neil, H. F. (1997). *Workforce readiness: Competencies and assessment.* Mahwah, NJ: Erlbaum.

Ouhalla, J., & Shlonsky, U. (Eds.). (2002). *Themes in Arabic and Hebrew syntax.* Dordrecht, The Netherlands: Kluwer.

Parker, M. (2005). A comparative study between mean length of utterance in morphemes (MLUm) and mean length of utterance in words (MLUw). *First Language, 25*(3), 365–376.

Pena, E. D. (2007). Lost in translation: Methodological considerations in cross-cultural research. *Child Development, 78*(4), 1255–1264.

Pena, E. D., Gillam, R. B., Malek, M., Ruiz-Felter, R., Resendiz, M., Fiestas, C., et al. (2006). Dynamic assessment of school-age children's narrative ability: An experimental investigation of classification accuracy. *Journal of Speech, Language, and Hearing Research, 49*(5), 1037–1057.

Pena, E. D., & Quinn, R. (1997). Task familiarity: Effects on the test performance of Puerto Rican and African American children. *Language, Speech, and Hearing Services in Schools, 28*(4), 323–332.

Pena, E. D., Quinn, R., & Iglesias, A. (1992). The application of dynamic assessment methods to language assessment: A non-biased procedure. *Journal of Special Education, 26,* 269–280.

Pienemann, M. (1998). Developmental dynamics in L1 and L2 acquisition: Processability Theory and generative entrenchment. *Bilingualism: Language and Cognition, 1,* 1–20.

Plunkett, K., & Nakisa, R. C. (1997). A connectionist model of the Arabic plural system. *Language and Cognitive Processes, 12*(5), 807–836.

Saiegh-Haddad, E. (2003). Linguistic distance and initial reading acquisition: The case of Arabic diglossia. *Applied Psycholinguistics, 24*(3), 431–451.

Saiegh-Haddad, E. (2004). The impact of phonemic and lexical distance on the phonological analysis of words and pseudowords in a diglossic context. *Applied Psycholinguistics, 25*(4), 495–513.

Saiegh-Haddad, E. (2005). Correlates of reading fluency in Arabic: Diglossic and orthographic factors. *Reading and Writing, 18,* 559–582.

Salameh, E.-K., Hakansson, G., & Nettelbladt, U. (2004). Developmental perspectives on bilingual Swedish-Arabic children with and without language impairment: A longitudinal study. *International Journal of Communication Disorders, 39*(1), 65–91.

Semel, E. M., Wiig, E. H., & Secord, W. (1996). *Clinical evaluation of language fundamentals-3 (CELF-3).* San Antonio, TX: The Psychological Corporation.

Shaalan, S., & Khater, M. (2006, July 19–21). *A comparison of two measures of assessing spontaneous language samples in Arabic speaking children.* Poster session presented at Child Language Seminar, University of Newcastle upon Tyne.

Shaalan, S., & van der Lely, H. K. J. (2007, March 14–15). *Characteristics of morphosyntactic deficits in Qatari children with specific language impairment (SLI).* Paper presented at Linguistics in the Gulf Conference, University of Qatar, Doha.

Simmons, N., & Johnston, J. (2007). Cross-cultural differences in beliefs and practices that affect the language spoken to children: Mothers with Indian and Western heritage. *International Journal of Language and Communication Disorders, 42*(4), 445–465.

SLI Consortium. (2004). Highly significant linkage to the SLI1 locus in an expanded sample of individuals affected by specific language impairment. *American Journal of Human Genetics, 74,* 1225–1238.

Smart, J. R. (1990). Pidginization in Gulf Arabic: A first report. *Anthropological Linguistics, 32,* 83–119.

Snowling, M. (2000). *Dyslexia* (2nd ed.). Oxford, UK: Blackwell.

Stromswold, K. (1998). Genetics of spoken language disorders. *Human Biology, 70*(2), 297–324.

Stromswold, K. (2001). The heritability of language: A review and meta-analysis of twin, adoption, and linkage studies. *Language, 77*(4), 647–724.

Supreme Education Council. (2006). *Education for a new era: A brief outline on reform policy.* Doha, Qatar: Author.

Tzuriel, D. (2000). Dynamic assessment of young children: Educational and intervention perspectives. *Educational Psychology Review, 12*(4), 386–435.

Versteegh, C. (1997). *The Arabic language.* Edinburgh: Edinburgh University Press.

Wechsler, D. (1998). *Wechsler Intelligence Scale for Children (WISC–III)* (3rd ed.). [Arabic Version]. Bahrain: The Psychological Corporation.

World Bank. (2003). *World development report 2003: Sustainable development in a dynamic world.* Washington, DC: Author.

The Behavioral Characteristics of Kindergarten Gifted Children in Saudi Arabia: Construction and Validation of a Scale

11

USAMA M. A. IBRAHIM
AND ABDULLAH M. ALJUGHAIMAN

The use of teacher nominations to identify and select gifted children to be admitted to gifted programs is an age-old practice (Hunsaker, Finley, & Frank, 1997). Teacher nomination is one of the most widely used means of identifying gifted children (McBride, 1992). The popularity of this method for identifying the gifted is attributed to the fact that gifted children possess a set of cognitive, motivational, and personal characteristics that may not be measured by intelligence or achievement tests (Gross, 1999; Renzulli, 2005). Because teachers are closely attached to their students during their years of study, they are able to recognize children who show high aptitudes at different age levels.

Although teacher nomination constitutes one of the most common methods for identifying gifted children, this method came under scrutiny by many researchers (e.g., Hadaway and Marek-Schroer, 1992; Neber, 2004). The main drawback in using teacher nomination lies in the teacher's ability to observe the gifted behavior objectively (Slabbert, 1994; Smutny, 2000; Torrance & Safter, 1986). In a meta-analysis of studies about the accuracy of teacher nomination of gifted children, Gear (1976) reported accuracy rates between 4.4% and 48%. Some of the reasons for this low accuracy rate are that teachers are not well trained and do not have enough knowledge of the characteristics of gifted children (McBride, 1992). Gross (1999) has found that female kindergarten teachers who did not receive any training in gifted education tended to exaggerate the abilities of children who show cooperation in the class and seek teachers' satisfaction.

Borland (1978) maintained that improved accuracy of teacher nominations was possible and depended on ratings based on specific characteristics of gifted students, rather than on global judgments of giftedness by teachers. Hany (1993, 1997), after reviewing recent research, also concluded that teachers were able to make adequate classification decisions regarding students, and that their judgment of whether a student was gifted or not, though biased by the heuristics of representation, confirmation, and base rate, could nevertheless be modeled using a cue utilization approach. Researchers have confirmed that in-service training for gifted education, and the provision of scales that include the characteristics that distinguish gifted children, help in increasing the teachers' competency through raising their awareness about giftedness (Hill, 1992; Pardeck, Pardeck, & Callahan, 1990; Silverman, Chitwood, & Waters, 1986).

This led many researchers to try to increase the reliability of this process by building up the scales of behavioral characteristics for the gifted, which became a common tool for nominating students to gifted programs. Therefore, researchers' concerns have been directed toward developing rating scales that include the most important behavioral characteristics that distinguish gifted students, to be used by teachers to improve the accuracy of identifying gifted children. These scales have become the most commonly used tools in the process of nominating children for gifted programs (Davis & Rimm, 2004; Feldhusen, Hoover, & Sayler, 1990; Gagné, 1999; Ma'jeeni, 1997; Renzulli et al., 1997; Silverman, 1997–2004).

Literature shows that gifted children reveal clear differences in development that parents and teachers can evidently observe (Chen, Wang, Lo, Chen, & Kuo, 2004; Liu, 1999). The early development of speech, movement, and reading are considered remarkable signs of intellectual giftedness. When these characteristics appear together at an early age they reflect an early development in intellectual ability (Jackson, 1992). Staines and Mitchell (1982) have noticed that most children vocalize their first words at the age of 12 months, while gifted children start to vocalize at the age of 10 months. At the age of 18 months, the normal child acquires about 3 to 50 words and shows attempts to connect these words together to form parts of sentences. On the other hand, gifted children start connecting words and forming sentences at the age of 11 months.

They also acquire a larger vocabulary, which helps them to form sentences that are more complicated. These differences increase noticeably at the age of 4½. The higher the level of giftedness, the more these differences increase and become easily noticed. Bryant (1989) studied the characteristics of gifted children who started reading at an early age. The findings show that they seem to be very keen to learn and to work independently. They have a good memory, a high ability for concentration, a rich vocabulary, high abilities for thinking, and a high ability to generate ideas.

This development of speech in the case of the highly gifted child may occur simultaneously with a noticeable development of movement and walking at a relatively early age in comparison with normal children. Reading at an early age is considered one of the strong signs of intellectual giftedness (Gross, 1993). Rogers and Silverman (1997) studied the behavioral characteristics of 241 highly gifted children (IQ = 160+). Results of the study indicated that at the early years of childhood, 94% of these children showed higher degrees of attention, 94% showed higher degrees of concentration, 91% showed a higher degree of linguistic development, 60% showed higher kinesthetic development, 48.9% showed prominent distinctions compared with their peers in their development, and 37% exhibited more imaginative expression. On average, highly gifted children vocalized their first words at the 9th month and were able to read well before they reached their 4th year.

These results concur with the findings of Gross's study (1993) on a number of gifted children who have a high mental ability. The findings show that they were enjoying high linguistic ability, rich vocabulary, a longer attention span, a high ability for equivoque, a high ability to grasp causative relations, and the ability to read at an early age. Moreover, Smutny (1998) has noticed a set of behavioral characteristics that are exhibited by gifted children at their 4th, 5th, and 6th years of age in response to educational activities at home or at kindergarten. These characteristics include: the desire and curiosity to know many things, asking questions that require deep thinking, having a rich and advanced language vocabulary, using complicated phrases correctly, expressing their thoughts and emotions well, solving riddles and complicated problems, having good memory, showing a high ability for imaginative expression, using previous learning experiences in new situations, exhibiting high ability to organize things logically, discussing ideas thoroughly, learning quickly and easily, taking initiative, showing keen powers of observation, making up good stories, and love for reading.

These characteristics generally concur with the results of Rogers's study (1986). Rogers conducted a comparison between gifted children and children with average intelligence. The study revealed that more than 56% of gifted children managed to know the letters of the alphabet when they reached 2 years, 31% managed to know written words when they reached the age of 2 years, 50% managed to read well when they reached the age of 4 years, 81% dealt with the games of "piecing together" in a good way when they reached the age of 3 years, 61% managed to deal with time and to tell the time exactly at the age of 5, and 2% managed to count from 1 to 10 before they reached the age of 3 years.

In view of that, many rating scales of behavioral characteristics of gifted children have been developed. For example, Renzulli and others (1997) have developed *Scales for Rating the Behavioral Characteristics of Superior Students (SRBCSS)*. These scales are used in the stages from elementary to secondary education and consist of 14 subscales to help identify student strengths in the following areas: learning, motivation, creativity, leadership, art, music, dramatics, planning, communication, mathematics, reading, science, and technology. Feldhusen and others (1990) have developed the *Purdue Academic Rating Scale,* which is used at the secondary level. Gagné (1999) has also published rating scales to identify multiple talents through ratings by peers and teachers, and self-assessment for cognitive abilities, academic talents, social skills, physical and sport abilities, and technological and artistic talent.

In Arab countries, several rating scales have been developed and/or translated into the Arabic language to be used at primary, intermediate, and secondary levels. In Jordan, Alrosan and Alsoror (1998) have developed a modified Jordanian version from *Gift Scale* for identifying gifted children at the primary level. The results of the study revealed that this scale has an acceptable degree of reliability and validity. In addition, Alrosan and others (1990, cited in Alrosan, 2006) have developed an adapted Jordanian version of the *Pride Scale* for identifying gifted children at the preschool stage. The factorial analysis revealed the existence of five main factors. These factors are the diversity of interests, constructive playing and social acceptance, imaginative thinking, independent thinking, and originality in thinking. Yet, the reliability of the scale using the internal coefficient of homogeneity of the scale was below average (.48) (Alrosan, 2006). In the Saudi environment, Aldimati (2004) has developed an arabized version of the *Gifted Classification Scale* that was developed by Johnson (1979). This scale consists of five fields. These fields are academic distinction, general mental ability, creative thinking, leadership, visual and performing arts, sport games, and psychomotor ability.

With the increasing number of enrichment programs developed for gifted and talented students in Saudi Arabia, the identification and selection of students who could potentially benefit from these provisions has become a major concern. In Saudi Arabia, gifted children are usually identified as those who are able to demonstrate high ability in one or more areas deemed necessary by the society. The most used ways of identifying gifted individuals are intelligence tests, creativity tests, and task commitment. Task commitment is measured in academic achievement. The multiple criteria identification procedure adopted by Saudi Arabia and other Arab countries is based on a number of principles similar to those advocated by Subhi and Maoz (2000, p. 746), including:

1. Gifted and talented children should be identified as early as possible in their educational careers.
2. The focus of identification is not to label students but to recognize and respond to gifted and talented students' educational needs.
3. The identification of gifted and talented students requires the utilization of formal and informal measures obtained from many resources in a wide variety of settings.
4. Identification instruments and procedures must match with the programs provided to gifted and talented children.

As there were no educational institutions specifically responsible for the identification and education of gifted individuals, the Saudi Ministry of Education established King Abdulaziz and his Companions Foundation for Giftedness and Creativity (MAWHIBA) in August, 1999. MAWHIBA is a nonprofit organization officially established with a royal decree. The main purpose of MAWHIBA is to serve as a reference authority in identifying gifted Saudi individuals and contributing to the fulfillment of their potentials and the development of their abilities, skills, and attitudes. Fulfilling their personal goals, in turn, would contribute to the comprehensive development of Saudi society.

Recently, MAWHIBA has started enrichment programs for nurturing giftedness along various stages of schooling, beginning with the elementary stage. In 2005 MAWHIBA planned for extending these programs to include kindergarten children. One of the main obstacles to such expansion was the unavailability of instruments suitable for the identification of gifted children at this early stage. The measures currently used by the

Ministry of Education to identify gifted students include the *Intellectual Abilities Test* and the Arabic version of *Wechsler's Test*. The former is suitable for individuals beyond the elementary stage. *Wechsler's Test*, on the other hand, is an individual test that is difficult to apply on a mass scale. Hence, a need was felt for an instrument suitable for the initial screening of gifted children at this age of development.

It has increasingly been recognized that teachers can provide valuable information on the giftedness of children in conjunction with standardized measures. Therefore, validity and reliability of teacher nomination can be improved when teachers are provided with objective behavioral scales to guide their nominations in the identification process. Consequently, serious attempts have been made by Arabian researchers to adapt scales to be used in the field of identifying the gifted in Saudi Arabia (e.g., Aldimati, 2004; Alfhaid, 1993; Alnafi, Alkatie, Aldobaiban, Alhazmy, & Alseleem, 2000). Yet, all these attempts focused on the stages of primary, intermediate, and secondary levels and did not touch upon kindergarten. This might be attributed to the practical perspective of those researchers, since there were no programs concerned with this age group in Saudi Arabia and most of the Arab countries. Accordingly, it has been necessary to develop a valid scale of the behavioral characteristics of preschool children that can be used by female kindergarten teachers[1] in the process of the initial screening of gifted children, in order to provide special educational services to gifted children in Saudi Arabia. The current study came as a trial to meet this need through constructing and validating a scale for defining the behavioral characteristics of gifted children at the kindergarten stage.

The age group from 3 to 6 years old has been chosen as a target group for this study for many reasons; among them are the pivotal role of the child in the first five years and its profound impacts on mental development and the readiness for learning, and the fact that identification of child giftedness during this stage helps in building up and preparing the special educational programs for this age group in a way that suits their abilities. By using the behavioral scales to identify the gifted, parents and teachers will be enlightened about the distinguishing behavioral characteristics and abilities of gifted children. In addition, to our knowledge, there is no scale of behavioral characteristics to identify gifted children in this age group in the Saudi Arabian environment.

Significance of the current study stems, first, from its ability to create a scale that contributes to the early identification of gifted children and at the same time considers the cultural and environmental features of the Saudi context. Second, there is a felt need in the Saudi society for feasible and flexible tools that enable teachers and parents to identify the characteristics of gifted students at an early age. In addition, designing a feasible scale of the behavioral characteristics of gifted children may be instrumental in activating the role of the educational institutions, especially the schools and kindergartens, in the process of identifying the gifted and utilizing the services presented to them.

Specifically, this study aims to: (a) develop a scale of behavioral characteristics for gifted children at the kindergarten stage; (b) ensure reliability and validity of the scale; (c) define differences between the means of teachers' ratings for both males and females on the different dimensions of the scale; (d) define differences between the means of teachers' ratings for the three age groups on the different dimensions of the scale; and (e) define differences between the means of teachers' ratings for gifted and nongifted on the different dimensions of the scale.

METHOD

Participants

The participants in the study included 539 kindergarten children from Riyadh, Jeddah, and the eastern province neighborhoods. Sixty children from this sample were nominated by the head teachers as gifted children according to their portfolios. The whole sample included 253 males and 286 females. Their ages ranged from 3 to 6 years. Fifty female teachers took part in the evaluation of the children, provided that each had known the child she evaluated for a period of no less than one school year. Participants who did not complete answering the scale were excluded in the analysis of the results.

Procedure

Researchers reviewed the literature in the field of behavioral characteristics of gifted children. They also reviewed a number of scales that have been developed in Arab and other environments. In the light of this, the blueprint of the scale of behavioral characteristics for gifted children from 3 to 6 years of age was formed. The blueprint of the scale included 60 items pivoted around three dimensions. These dimensions are: cognitive characteristics, personality characteristics, and motivational characteristics. The scale was shown to a jury of 18 experts in the field of gifted education. Then the researchers modified and/or deleted some items of the scales in the light of the jury members' recommendations.

The researchers conducted a pilot study to examine the clarity of the scale, and the appropriateness of its items and instructions. The pilot study aimed at knowing about the clarity of the measurements of estimation, how they were to be used, and how to deal with the scale regarding the formalities. The scale was sent to the directors of kindergartens in Riyadh, Jeddah, and the eastern province to hand over to the kindergarten teachers, after providing them with a thorough explanation about the mechanism of applying it. Then the scale was applied to 49 children in the three neighborhoods. A set of observations about the application process displayed by the teachers was documented, in addition to the observations documented through the procedures that accompanied the application process. These observations represented the difficulty of dealing with certain items that need the students' mothers' cooperation to be answered, such as the following: revealing an interest in time, managing to distinguish alphabetical characters at an early age, and counting numbers from 1 to 10 at an early age. These items need the cooperation of family, and this made the estimations of these items an obstacle to the usage of the scale. In order to make the teachers the only authority on the estimation of all the characteristics of the scale, these items have been reconsidered and subjected to modification or deletion.

In respect to scale items' ability to distinguish between children at different cognitive levels, the χ^2 equation was used to calculate the differences between children's scores at the upper and lower quartiles for each item. To do this, the children's scores on the scale were arranged in a descending order. Then mean differences between scores in the upper and lower quartiles were calculated. Selected items included those with the largest mean differences between children's scores in the two quartiles. These mean differences were statistically significant ($p < .001$).

In light of these findings, the scale was revised to include 43 items and then sent again to the directors of kindergartens in Riyadh, Jeddah, and the eastern province, who handed it over to the kindergarten teachers in these neighborhoods and explained the objectives of the scale and how to apply it. Fifty teachers from 20 kindergartens took part in the application of the scale. Each teacher evaluated between 10 and 15 male and female children from a group of children with high abilities, with the condition that she had dealt with those children for a period of no less than one school year. In addition, the head teachers of these kindergartens were asked to nominate the three kindergarten children whom they believed were most gifted in light of their portfolios, and then rate them on the behavioral characteristics scale. Then the scales were cleared out and analyzed by the Statistical Package for the Social Sciences (SPSS).

RESULTS

Validity of the Scale

The scale was sent to a jury of 18 specialists in the field of gifted education, to judge the appropriateness of each item regarding its statement, its belongingness to the field, and the appropriateness of the fields for evaluating the peculiar characteristics of gifted children. The researchers rewrote the scale in the light of the judges' recommendations. Thereby, the final version of the scale included 43 items.

Factorial Structure

A factor analysis was conducted on the scores of 539 male and female children. The principal component factoring with Varimox rotation yielded five dimensions of behavioral characteristics of gifted children. These dimensions are: motivation and the desire to learn, linguistic characteristics, learning characteristics, personality characteristics, and logical/math thinking. Eigen values were 12.76, 2.12, 2.02, 1.79, and 1.59, consecutively. These factors explained 47.36% of the total variance in scores. The five dimensions came specific with high factorial loadings, as shown in Table 11.1.

Reliability of the Scale

The reliability of the scale has been calculated through split-half coefficient for the scale items by using the Spearman–Brown formula. This yielded a reliability coefficient of .83. Also, the reliability of the scale as a whole was calculated by using Cronbach's α, which yielded a coefficient of .84. These values are high, statistically accepted, and indicate that the scale has a high degree of reliability.

Table 11.1

PRINCIPAL COMPONENT FACTORING WITH VARIMAX ROTATION OF THE SCALE ITEMS

	FACTORS/DIMENSIONS				
ITEM	FACTOR 1	FACTOR 2	FACTOR 3	FACTOR 4	FACTOR 5
Is persistent (10)	.668				
Likes collecting things (9)	.618				
Has many interests (7)	.574				
Engages in self-directed activities (16)	.571				
Has intense involvement in work (12)	.532				
Is inquisitive (11)	.529				
Enjoys learning (15)	.500				
Likes reading (17)	.499				
Has a strong desire of discovery (8)	.491				
Enjoys new things (14)	.430				
Requires little direction (20)	.400				
Has an enriched vocabulary (2)		.777			
Uses vocabularies accurately (1)		.770			
Uses complex sentences (3)		.761			
Has an ability to elaborate by using complete thoughts (4)		.738			
Explains ideas clearly (18)		.548			
Began reading at an early age (19)		.476			
Sees connections between unconnected things (5)		.473			
Raises different questions (26)			.694		
Has unusual ideas (25)			.665		
Is keenly observant 23)			.655		
Possesses an outstanding memory (27)			.647		
Learns skills rapidly and efficiently (21)			.585		
Is spontaneous (22)			.565		
Has a strong tendency for inquiry (28)			.515		

Table 11.1

PRINCIPAL COMPONENT FACTORING WITH VARIMAX ROTATION OF THE SCALE ITEMS (*CONTINUED*)

ITEM	FACTORS/DIMENSIONS				
	FACTOR 1	FACTOR 2	FACTOR 3	FACTOR 4	FACTOR 5
Has a long attention span (41)			.495		
Is able to grasp complex ideas (29)			.474		
Has multiple skills (33)				.741	
Is an independent thinker (37)				.683	
Is extremely active (40)				.628	
Has a high energy level (43)				.531	
Has leadership skills (34)				.520	
Has a keen sense of humor (6)				.511	
Is imaginative (35)				.419	
Is outspoken (36)				.410	
Prefers playing with older children (42)				.407	
Possesses good physical skills (38)				.401	
Is sensitive to critics (39)				.400	
Deals with numbers easily and accurately (31)					.760
Has a high ability to understand numeric concepts (30)					.706
Has advanced logical thinking skills (32)					.719
Has an ability to conceptualize and synthesize (13)					.575
Is able to understand abstractions (25)					.417
Eigenvalue	12.765	2.120	2.016	1.798	1.586
Percentage of variance	29.66	5.14	4.69	4.18	3.69
Total percentage					47.363

Only salient loadings of 0.40 or above are shown.

Note. The number in parentheses following each item indicates the item numbers in the scale.

In addition, the reliability coefficient for each of the five dimensions was calculated by using Cronbach's α. The reliability coefficients were as follows: motivation and the desire for learning .86, linguistic characteristics .88, learning characteristics .80, personality characteristics .81, and logical/math thinking .66. All of these values are high and statistically accepted, even though the correlation coefficient of the logical/math thinking is the least, because its items are few (five items). Moreover, the children's scores on scale dimensions were correlated with their total scores on the scale, as shown in Table 11.2.

It is clear from Table 11.2 that all the dimensions are highly correlated with the total score, and the correlation coefficients have ranged from .67 to .87. These coefficients are accepted and statistically significant. This also points to the consistency of the dimensions that the scale includes. The correlation coefficients among the five dimensions were high, but the correlation coefficients among mathematical thinking, linguistic characteristics, and personal traits were low, even though they were statistically significant.

Differences Between Males and Females in the Scale Dimensions

To examine differences between means of teachers' ratings for both males and females on the scale of the behavioral characteristics of gifted children, the *t*-test formula was run to children's scores on the five dimensions of the scale. Results are shown in Table 11.3.

Table 11.3 shows that there are no statistically significant differences between mean scores of males and females on the scale as a whole, in the learning characteristics dimension, and in the personality dimension. On the other hand, the results show that there are statistically significant differences in the dimensions of motivation and the desire to learn and the linguistics characteristics favoring females ($p < .035$ and .01 respectively), while there are significant differences favoring males in the dimension of mathematical thinking ($p < .047$). These results are in line with research results well-established in literature. They also point to the validity of the scale to diagnose characteristics of gifted children. In addition, these results document the success of female teachers in accurately deciding upon distinguishing characteristics of gifted children in kindergarten, which in turn reflects the validity of the scale in the initial screening of those children.

Table 11.2

THE CORRELATION COEFFICIENTS BETWEEN THE FIVE DIMENSIONS AND THE TOTAL SCORE OF THE SCALE

DIMENSIONS	MOTIVATION AND DESIRE FOR LEARNING	LINGUISTIC CHARACTERISTICS	LEARNING CHARACTERISTICS	PERSONAL CHARACTERISTICS	LOGICAL/MATH THINKING
Motivation and desire for learning	–				
Linguistic characteristics	.678	–			
Learning characteristics	.706	.624	–		
Personality characteristics	.607	.615	.615	–	
Logical/math thinking	.533	.485	.385	.323	–
Total Score	.868	.799	.810	.828	.672

Table 11.3

T-TEST RESULTS OF DIFFERENCES BETWEEN MALES AND FEMALES ON THE SCALE DIMENSIONS

DIMENSIONS		NO.	*M*	*SD*	*F*-VALUE	SIG. *(P)*
Total score	Males	253	182.53	27.03	1.97	.161
	Females	286	185.54	23.14		
Linguistic characteristics	Males	253	50.23	8.43	4.46	.035
	Females	286	51.65	7.22		
Learning characteristics	Males	253	28.76	5.12	6.63	.010
	Females	286	30.15	4.35		
Personality characteristics	Males	253	35.45	5.12	1.67	.196
	Females	286	36.39	4.35		
Logical/math thinking	Males	253	46.15	8.02	0.20	.652
	Females	286	45.52	7.44		
Motivation and desire for learning	Males	253	22.09	6.44	3.98	.047
	Females	286	21.82	5.52		

Differences Between Age Groups

To examine the differences between children's mean scores at the three different age groups (3–4, 4–5, and 5–6 years old) on the scale as a whole as well as on its individual dimensions, a series of analyses of variance were run on children's scores on the scale and its five dimensions. Table 11.4 shows the results of the analysis of variance for testing the significance of the differences between children's mean scores at the three age groups.

It is clear from Table 11.4 that there are statistically significant differences among the three age groups in the total score of the scale ($F[2,538] = 13,069; p < .001$). Also there are statistically significant differences among the age groups in the scale dimensions of motivation and the desire to learn ($F[2,538] = 14,55; p < .009$), linguistic characteristics ($F[2,538] = 4,789; p < .001$), characteristics of learning ($F[2,538] = 13,996; p < .001$), personality traits ($F[2.538] = 9,605; p < .001$), and logical/math thinking ($F[2,538] = 6,068; p < .002$).

To examine the source of these differences among age groups, the Scheffé Test was conducted on the total score of the scale as well as its five dimensions. Results of the Scheffé Test revealed that there were significant differences among the three age groups, favoring older children

Table 11.4

ANOVA RESULTS FOR THE DIFFERENCES AMONG THE THREE AGE GROUPS

DIMENSIONS	SOURCE OF VARIANCE	SS	df	MS	F-VALUE	SIG. (P)
Total score	Between groups	14226.53	2	7113.26		
	Within groups	291141.93	536	543.17	13.069	.001
	Totals	305368.46	538			
Motivation	Between groups	1260.378	2	630.20		
	Within groups	23202.47	536	43.29	14.558	.001
	Totals	24462.85	538			
Linguistic characteristics	Between groups	234.35	2	117.18		
	Within groups	13115.29	536	24.469	4.789	.009
	Totals	13349.64	538			
Learning characteristics	Between groups	529.588	2	264.79		
	Within groups	10140.82	536	18.92	13.996	.001
	Totals	10670.41	538			
Personality characteristics	Between groups	859.279	2	429.64		
	Within groups	239575.12	536	44.73	9.605	.001
	Totals	24834.40	538			
Logical/math thinking	Between groups	186.45	2	93.23		
	Within groups	8235.20	536	15.36	6.068	.002
	Totals	8421.64	538			

at $p < .01$. These differences were more evident in the older age group (5–6 years) compared to the younger one (3–4 years). This means that motivation, linguistic characteristics, learning characteristics, personality characteristics, and logical/math thinking improve with the advancement of children's age. This result reflects natural development along these stages of age. This also presents evidence about the validity of the scale for identifying gifted children at this age level.

Differences Between Gifted and Nongifted in the Scale Dimensions

On the differences between means of teachers' ratings for both gifted and nongifted children on the scale of the behavioral characteristics of gifted children, the t-test formula was run to children's scores on the five dimensions of the scale. Results are shown in Table 11.5. This table shows that there are statistically significant differences between mean

Table 11.5

T-TEST RESULTS OF THE DIFFERENCES BETWEEN GIFTED AND NONGIFTED CHILDREN ON THE SCALE DIMENSIONS

DIMENSIONS		NO.	M	SD	F-VALUE	SIG. (P)
Motivation and desire for learning	Gifted	60	48.4	1.69	9.05	.001
	Normal	479	41.9	5.5		
Characteristics of linguistics	Gifted	60	34.8	0.50	12.69	.001
	Normal	479	27.2	4.6		
Characteristics of learning	Gifted	60	44.4	1.02	8.6	.001
	Normal	479	38.5	5.25		
Personality characteristics	Gifted	60	52.3	2.54	10.81	.001
	Normal	479	43.3	6.43		
Logical/math thinking	Gifted	60	24.5	0.96	9.19	.001
	Normal	479	20.5	3.30		

scores of gifted and nongifted children on all the dimensions of the scale, favoring gifted children ($p < .001$). This documents success of female teachers in accurately deciding upon distinguishing characteristics of gifted children in kindergarten, which in turn reflects validity of the scale in the initial screening of those children.

DISCUSSION

This study aimed at developing a scale for identifying the behavioral characteristics of gifted children from 3 to 6 years of age in the Saudi environment, to be used by female kindergarten teachers in the process of nominating children for gifted programs.

Factor analysis has been used to examine the factorial structure of the scale. As shown in Table 11.1, the characteristics of gifted students, as perceived by their teachers, fell nicely into five domains of behavioral characteristics, namely, motivation and the desire for learning, linguistic characteristics, learning characteristics, personality characteristics, and logical/mathematical thinking. The eigenvalues for these factors were 12.76, 2.12, 2.02, 1.79, and 1.586 respectively, which explained 47.36% of the total variance in scores.

It is notable that the logical/mathematical thinking dimension delineated in the current study has not been extracted in similar research such as that of Alrosan's study (2006). The delineation of this factor can be attributed to two main reasons. On the one hand, there were differences in the age groups between the current study and that of Alrosan (2006), which in turn may have resulted in differences in behavioral characteristics. On the other hand, cultural differences may have also contributed to differences in the behavioral characteristics.

The reliability of the scale as a whole was calculated by the split-half technique. The value of the coefficient came up to .84. In addition, the reliability of the scale was calculated using Cronbach's α and the coefficient was .84. This indicates that the scale has an acceptable degree of reliability. Moreover, reliability of the scale dimensions was calculated, yielding coefficients ranging from .66 to .87, indicating an acceptable degree of reliability. The coefficient for the dimension of the logical/math thinking was the least. This may be attributed to the relatively small number of items in this dimension. Reliability of this dimension may be increased by including additional items.

The internal consistency of the scale was calculated through correlating scores on the five dimensions, and the total score resulted in values ranging from .67 to .87, which are statistically significant. In addition, the correlative relations among the five dimensions were high and accepted, even though the correlation coefficient between the mathematical thinking and the personality traits was relatively low, .32. This may denote that no logical relationship exists between personality characteristics of children and their mathematical thinking.

The differences between the mean score of males and females on the scale as a whole, and on each of the five dimensions, were calculated. Statistically significant differences were found between males and females in the two dimensions of motivation and linguistic characteristics, favoring female children. However, statistically significant differences between males and females were found in the mathematical thinking dimension, favoring male children. No statistically significant differences were found between males and females in the scale dimensions of personality characteristics and learning characteristics. These results conform to those cited in literature on gender differences that shows female supremacy in linguistic abilities and male supremacy in mathematics. This in turn confirms the validity of the scale and the ability of the female teachers to evaluate the children well.

Also, this study calculated the differences among the three age groups using the one-way analysis of variance (ANOVA), and the results revealed the existence of statistically significant differences between the mean scores of children at the three age levels ($p < .001$), favoring older ages (5–6) in comparison with younger (3–4). This indicates that motivation and linguistic characteristics, characteristics of learning, personality characteristics, and mathematical thinking for children develop with age. This presents additional evidence for the validity of the scale in the process of identifying gifted children at this stage.

Generally, the present findings supported the initial conviction that the provision of a behavioral characteristics scale of giftedness to teachers can aid teachers to make explicit their perception of giftedness in students that they nominated for participation in gifted programs in Saudi Arabia. However, for future reference, the perception of student giftedness by female Saudi Arabian teachers needs to be further explored through the same or similar procedures, but studying more representative samples.

It is worth mentioning that there are some studies that used intelligence tests to decide on the concurrent validity teacher nominations (Alnafi et al., 2000). However, it is agreed that objective data such as performance in the enrichment programs might be more appropriate criteria for the evaluation of the quality of teacher nominations (Shore, Cornell, Robinson, & Ward, 1991). This is because the fact that the teachers take into consideration the overall characteristics of gifted students in the nomination processes through students' scores in the intelligence test may not reflect such characteristics as motivational and personality traits. Therefore, further research is needed to compare students' actual performance with their scores on the current scale.

Attention must be drawn to the fact that despite the ease of administering this scale and the clear statement of its items, there is still a need for training the kindergarten teachers in using the scale. Further, more work is needed to design tools for identifying gifted children at an early age in the Arabian environment, taking into account the peculiar features of these environments.

NOTE

1. All kindergarten teachers in Saudi Arabia are females.

REFERENCES

Aldimati, A. (2004). Validating Johnson scale for identifying gifted and talented in the Saudi environment. *The Academy for the Special Education Journal, 4,* 93–158.

Alfhaid, S. (1993). *The efficiency and reliability of the teachers' estimations in identifying gifted children.* Unpublished master's thesis, King Saudi University, Riyadh, Saudi Arabia.

Alnafi, A., Alkatie, A., Aldobaiban, S., Alhazmy, M., & Alseleem, A. (2000). *The programs of identifying and nurturing the gifted.* Riyadh, Saudi Arabia: King Abdulaziz City for Science and Technology,

Alrosan, F. (2006, August). *Ways of identifying gifted at the preschool stage.* A study presented to the Regional Scientific Conference for the Gifted, Jeddah, Saudi Arabia.

Alrosan, F., & Alsoror, N. (1998). *Developing a modified Jordanian version from Gift Scale for identifying gifted at the primary stage.* Tunisia: Arabic Organization for Education, Culture and Science.

Borland, J. H. (1978). Teacher identification of the gifted: A new look. *Journal for the Education of the Gifted, 2,* 22–32.

Bryant, M. A. (1989). Challenging gifted learners through children's literature. *Gifted Child Today, 12*(4), 45–48.

Chen, E. Y., Wang, E. T., Lo, C. S., Chen, M. C., & Kuo, C. C. (2004, July 31–August 4). *See the gifted from ingenuous words and archives of gifted preschoolers.* Paper presented at the 8th Asia-Pacific Conference on Giftedness, Daejon, Korea.

Davis, A., & Rimm, B. (2004). *Education of the gifted and talented* (5th ed.). Needham Heights, MA: Allyn & Bacon.

Feldhusen, J. F., Hoover, S. M., & Sayler, M. F. (1990). *Identifying and educating gifted students at the secondary level.* Unionville, NY: Trillium Press.

Gagné, F. (1999). *Tracking talents: Examiner's manual.* Waco, TX: Prufrock Press.

Gear, G. H. (1976). Accuracy of teacher judgment in identifying intellectually gifted children: A review of the literature. *Gifted Child Quarterly, 20*(4), 478–490.

Gross, M. (1993). *Exceptionally gifted children.* London: Routledge.

Gross, M. (1999). Small poppies: Highly gifted children in early years. *Roeper Review, 21*(3), 207–214.

Hadaway, N., & Marek-Schroer, M. F. (1992). Multidimensional assessment of the gifted minority students. *Roeper Review, 15*(2), 73–77.

Hany, E. A. (1993). Methodological problems and issues concerning identification. In K. A. Heller, F. J. Monks, & A. H. Passow (Eds.), *International handbook of research and development of giftedness and talent* (pp. 209–232). Oxford, UK: Pergamon.

Hany, E. A. (1997). Modeling teachers' judgment of giftedness: A methodological inquiry of biased judgment. *High Abilities Studies, 8,* 159–178.

Hill, R. (1992, March). *Finding creativity for children.* Paper presented at the Leadership Accessing Symposium (ERIC Document Reproduction Service No. ED348169).

Hunsaker, S. L., Finley, V. S., & Frank, E. L. (1997). An analysis of teacher nominations and student performance in gifted programs. *Gifted Child Quarterly, 41,* 19–24.

Johnson, D. L. (1979). *Gifted and talented screening form: Instruction manual.* Chicago: Stroelting.

Jackson, N. E. (1992). Precocious reading of English: Origins, structure and predictive significance. In P. S. Klein & A. J. Tannenbaum (Eds.), *To be young and gifted* (pp. 171–203). Norwood, NJ: Ablex.

Liu, J. (1999). Educational innovation: A gifted program at Beijing Number 8 high school. *Journal of Secondary Gifted Education, 10*(2), 69–80.

Ma'jeeni, O. (1997). The most prominent behavioral characteristics for the preeminent students in public classes as recognized by teachers in four Gulf States. *Educational Journal of Kuwait University, 11*, 75–76.

McBride, N. (1992). Early identification of the gifted and talented students: Where do teachers stand? *Gifted Child International, 8*(1), 19–12.

Neber, H. (2004). Teacher identification of students for gifted programs: Nomination to a summer school for highly gifted programs. *Psychology Science, 46*(3), 348–362.

Pardeck, J. T., Pardeck, J. A., & Callahan, D. (1990). An exploration of an assessment instrument measuring beliefs about and understanding of gifted children. *Education, 111*, 548–552.

Renzulli, J. S. (2005). Assumptions underlying the identification of gifted and talented students. *Gifted Child Quarterly, 49*(1), 68–79.

Renzulli, J. S., Smith, L. H., White, A. J., Callahan, C. M., Hartman, R. K., & Westberg, K. L. (1997). *Scales for rating the behavioral characteristics of superior students.* Mansfield Center, CT: Creative Learning Press.

Rogers, M. T. (1986). *A comparative study of developmental traits of gifted and average children.* Unpublished PhD dissertation, University of Denver, Colorado.

Rogers, K. B., & Silverman, L. K. (1997, November). *Personal, social, medical and psychological factors in 160+ IQ children.* National Association for Gifted Children 44th Annual Convention, Little Rock, Arkansas.

Shore, B. M., Cornell, D. G., Robinson, A., & Ward, V. S. (1991). *Recommended practices in gifted education: A critical analysis.* New York: Teachers College Press.

Silverman, L. K. (1997–2004). *Characteristics of giftedness scale: A review of the literature.* Retrieved April 25, 2005, from: http://www.gifteddevelopment.com/Articles/Characteristics_Scale.htm

Silverman, L. K., Chitwood, D. G., & Waters, J. L. (1986). Young gifted children: Can parents identify giftedness? *Topics in Early Childhood Special Education, 6*(1), 23–38.

Slabbert, J. A. (1994). Creativity in education revisited: Reflection in aid of progression. *Journal of Creative Behavior, 28*(1), 60–69.

Smutny, J. F. (Ed.). (1998). *The young gifted child: Potential and promise: An anthology.* Cresskill, NJ: Hampton Press.

Smutny, J. F. (2000). *How to stand up for your gifted child: Making the most of kids' strengths at school and at home.* Minneapolis, MN: Free Spirit.

Staines, J. W., & Mitchell, M. J. (1982). *You and your toddler: The second year.* Melbourne, Australia: Oxford University Press.

Subhi, T., & Maoz, N. (2000). Middle-East region: Efforts, polices, programs and issues. In K. A. Heller, F. J. Monks, R. J. Sternberg, & R. F. Subotnik (Eds.), *International handbook of giftedness and talent* (2nd ed., pp. 743–756). Oxford, UK: Elsevier.

Torrance, E. P., & Safter, H. T. (1986). Are children becoming more creative? *Journal of Creative Behavior, 20*(1), 1–13.

12

Developing Culture-Specific Assessments

ALEXANDER G. SHMELYOV AND ANNA S. NAUMENKO

In the past three decades enormous changes have affected labor markets and the whole world of work. Among these changes we emphasize the development of information technologies and the Internet, increased personnel mobility, proliferation of global multinational and multicultural corporations, and the need of people to seek employment many times during their lives. This all makes assessment of abilities and competencies more and more important.

One of the major challenges in assessment of abilities and competencies is the need to account for cultural diversity. When living within the framework of a particular culture, most people do not become aware of its character because it comes as naturally as the air they are breathing. Indeed, sometimes the differences between cultures are extremely strong. For example, in the United States, people admire charismatic leaders and value heroism, brightness, activity, and the ability to lead, to move forward. In Chinese culture, remaining as soft as water, serene and silent, is considered as strength. The leader ought to instill in followers a sense of security and peace and should establish himself or herself by promoting the success of followers and enriching them by offering opportunities to build their careers and personality (Chin, Gu, & Tubbs, 2001). Thus, the same behaviors could be perceived and interpreted quite differently by Chinese and Americans.

In this chapter we will discuss the particularities of the assessment accounting for culture specificity. There are three principal approaches to choosing the appropriate diagnostic tools: (1) to use existing diagnostic instruments, (2) to adapt existing diagnostic instruments, and (3) to develop new diagnostic instruments. In the next few pages, we are going to discuss these three alternatives.

There are different types of psychological tools used for assessment purposes, such as psychometric tests and questionnaires, competencies models, biographical and competency-based interviews, case-tests, behavioral tests, and so forth. Some of the listed instruments (e.g., interviews and behavioral tests) require an experienced counselor to lead the assessment process. When dealing with people of different nations and ethnicities, the assessor has to be very flexible and emphatic and ought to demonstrate his or her multicultural competence. The guidelines for preparing such types of assessment and a practical framework for cross-cultural career counseling can be found in Leong and Hartung (1997), Blustein and Ellis (2000), and Flores, Spanierman, and Obasi (2003).

Other assessment tools (e.g., psychometric tests and questionnaires) are standardized and do not require an experienced practitioner to conduct the procedure. In the era of globalization, a great number of psychological tests are even administered and scored by computer. This means that multicultural competence has to be "embedded" in the instrument and that attention to it has to be paid in the development phase. In this chapter, we will discuss this type of assessment tool and focus on psychometric tests of intelligence and personality questionnaires.

USE OF EXISTING ASSESSMENT TOOLS

Ever-growing demand for assessment brings forth the development of diagnostic tools. As predicted in the late 1990s (Fouad & Zao, 2000), the new century brought an increased number of easily available (e.g., via the Internet) assessment tools with unknown validity, reliability, and standardization group information. Presumably, most such "tests" are not validated or checked for reliability at all. This means they cannot be used as an assessment tool. The requirements for test development and use in education, psychology, and employment can be found in the *Standards for Educational and Psychological Testing*, developed jointly by the American Educational Research Association (AERA), American

Psychological Association (APA), and the National Council on Measurement in Education (NCME) (1999).

Among other psychometric characteristics, such as validity and reliability, very important is the standardization sample, or for whom the test was designed. Here we are coming to an interesting, but not new, observation: Most popular assessment tools are developed within the Eurocentric perspective. It means they are standardized on the sample comprising the majority of the population (e.g., Caucasian Americans in the United States), and they are suitable only for use with this given population. However, assessment instruments are used for evaluating personality traits, abilities, or competencies of the representatives of all other ethnic and cultural groups, whereas they should be adapted for use with minority groups, or new tools, either culture-fair or culture-specific, should be developed. The extent to which "Eurocentric" assessment instruments can be transferred to non-European cultural groups should be confirmed in every case separately.

Cultural Validity of Existing Assessment Tools

A number of studies were dedicated to examining the cultural validity of popular assessment instruments. As an indicative example, we take Holland's model for assessment of career interests as it forms the basis for most of the career inventories used today. In his theory of vocational choice, John Holland (1997) proposes that people like to be around others who have similar personalities; therefore, people choose jobs where they can be around other people who are like them. Gathering together people of the same type forms appropriate work environments. Holland describes six personality types and, therefore, six work environments—Realistic (R), Investigative (I), Artistic (A), Social (S), Enterprising (E), and Conventional (C). He arranges the six types around a hexagon to represent differences and similarities between people, jobs, and environments. Types that are next to one another on the hexagon (e.g., most close to S are E and A) are most closely related. Types that are opposite one another on the hexagon are the most dissimilar (opposite to S lies R). Also, Holland hypothesizes that distances between types are equal. This model is known as RIASEC.

Much research is aimed at evaluating the cultural structural validity of the RIASEC model for assessment of career interests with different racial and ethnic samples. Examples are Chinese (Goh, Lee, & Yu, 2004; Long & Tracey, 2006; Yu & Alvi, 1996), Croatian (Sverko & Babarovic,

2006), Indian (Leong, Austin, Secaran, & Komarraju, 1998), Italian (Lent, Tracey, Brown, Soresi, & Nota, 2006), Japanese (Long, Watanabe, & Tracey, 2006), Korean (Tak, 2004), Mexican (Fouad & Dancer, 1992), Singaporean (Soh & Leong, 2001), South African (Toit & Bruin, 2002), and Spanish (Glidden-Tracey & Greenwood, 1997; Elosua, 2007).

The studies found differing fits of Holland's model for different ethnic and racial groups. Sometimes it is difficult to compare these results, because there is strong evidence that researchers used different criteria of *good* and *poor* fits. Nevertheless, we tried to sum up the results of the studies in Table 12.1. The participants of most studies were either high school or college students.

Table 12.1

VALIDITY OF RIASEC MODEL FOR DIFFERENT CULTURES

CULTURE	VALIDITY OF RIASEC MODEL	AUTHOR(S)
Asian American	The interest structures of the Asian American females were in the order RIASCE, and the interest structures of the Asian American males were in the order RISCEA. The distances between types were not uniform.	Haverkamp, Collins, & Hansen, 1994
China	Not valid	Goh, Lee, & Yu, 2004
China (Hong Kong)	The distances between types were not equal as proposed by Holland.	Farh, Leong, & Law, 1998
Croatia	Valid	Sverko & Babarovic, 2006
Japan	The validity was poorer than for the American sample. Gender differences were also found: The model seemed to fit for Japanese women much better than for Japanese men.	Tracey, Watanabe, & Schneider, 1997
Korea	Valid	Tak, 2004
Singapore	Similar structural and criterion-related validity across the Singaporean and the U.S. samples, although some culture-specific meaning was found attached to the I type.	Soh & Leong, 2001
South Africa	Not valid	Toit & Bruin, 2002
Spain (Basque)	Not valid	Elosua, 2007

In 1971 Russian psychologist Eugeny A. Klimov developed the original occupation classification, according to which all occupations could be divided into five groups on the basis of the object of work—Bionomical, Technical, Artistic, Sign Systems, and Social (Klimov, 1971). People belong to different career types according to their career interests that can be focused in one of the five named areas. Although "the directions" of Holland's (from personality to work environment) and Klimov's (from occupation type to personality) classifications are opposite, Klimov's occupation types are in general agreement with Holland's work environment types: for Artistic there is A, for Social there is S, for Technical there is R, for Sign Systems there is C, and for Bionomical there is I (this is the worst correspondence). It strikes our eye that in Klimov's classification, there is no type for Holland's E, but it is very explicable and has to do with the notorious cultural specificity. Soviet time in Russia (and that was just the time of Klimov's classification) was the era of socialism and such notions as private property, private enterprise, and an enterprising work environment did not exist at all. Thus, Holland's model was not applicable to the Russian sample of those days.

After Mikhail Gorbachev's economic reforms (also known as *Perestroika*), the Russian labor market experienced drastic changes that led to the restructuring of typical work environments. In response to these changes, one of the authors of this chapter (Professor Alexander G. Shmelyov) developed his own occupation and career interests classification in which four of Klimov's types (Bionomical, Technical, Artistic, and Social) were retained, Sign Systems type was divided into Clerical (reproductive, formal work with sign information) and Scientific (productive work with sign information, new knowledge production), and two new ones were added (Enterprising and Risk).

On the basis of his classification, Shmelyov developed the *Professional Aptitude Test (PAT)* used in career counseling in Russia. Up to the present, the data bank gathered by career counselors of the Testing Center at Moscow State University includes several tens of thousands (!) of *PAT* protocols. Confirmatory factor analysis of the test items and thousands of postdiagnostic counseling interviews provide evidence for the effectiveness of this classification for Russia of the transition period (Shmelyov & Serebryakov, 2006).

It is clear that more research is needed to evaluate the cultural validity of the various Western-based assessment instruments, but those studies still inform us only that the problem with cultural validity exists, but not why the problem exists. As Leong and Hartung (2000) have pointed out, much research is also needed to find out culture-specific factors influencing assessment tools.

ADAPTATION OF EXISTING ASSESSMENT INSTRUMENTS

Standardized testing of cognitive abilities and competencies has a far-reaching impact on the lives of individuals. For example, according to the test results, students are placed in different education programs, and the number of so-called ethnic students placed in special education programs is disproportionately high (MacMillan, Gresham, & Sipersein, 1993), whereas the number of those positioned into gifted programs is disproportionately low (Ford-Harris, 1993). Although racist theories are in the past and it is not argued anymore that one ethnicity is more intelligent than another, the measures developed for the majority sample are still used (as they are, without any adaptation) for assessing minority groups.

Of course, adaptation is needed not only when measuring IQ, but also when evaluating other abilities, competencies, and personal traits. The "translation" of a test into a foreign language requires not only item translation, but also adaptation and probably refactorization.

Adaptation of 16PF Questionnaire in Russia

In the early 1990s, Shmelyov guided the adaptation of Cattell's Sixteen Personality Factors Questionnaire in Russia. Shmelyov and Pohilko conducted an item analysis of one of the Russian translations of 16PF and indicated that for 45 of 187 items (nearly 25%) of the form A, there was either no item-scale correlation or the item's content was not applicable to the Russian realities. In order to replace unsuitable items, the researchers created 113 new items and conducted a study in which the participants answered all 300 questions (187 old and 113 new ones). As a result, 45 items that had the best correlations with the factor scales were chosen to replace the items that did not work in Russian and, thus, needed to be replaced. In 1988 the resulting test was published (Shmelyov, Pokhilko, & Soloveychik, 1988) and in 1991–1993, it was certified by the Institute for Personality and Ability Testing (IPAT) as the Russian version of 16PF.

Prior to the work with 16PF, Shmelyov and his colleagues conducted an item analysis of some other personal questionnaires' translations popular among Russian practitioners and found out that the most important was social desirability bias, or the difference between participants providing "socially desirable" answers and subjects answering more frankly. That is why in 1986 the Social Desirability Scale was developed for the computer-based version of 16PF (Gavrilina, 1988), and the whole questionnaire was named and distributed as 17PF. Later on, IPAT introduced 16PF, 5th edition, that also included some scales to control social desirability bias.

In 1990 Shmelyov conducted a study that focused on development of the form B of Russian 16PF. He added 63 new questions to the 187 items of the translated form B and hence every probationer filled in the questionnaire consisting of 437 questions (187 items of the form A and 250 items of the form B). The scales of the modified form B included only those items that correlated significantly with the appropriate factors of the form A. Out of the newly created items, 44 showed better fit with the scales than some old items and therefore replaced the old ones. Another 24 old items got new keys, because their correlations with other factor scales of the form A were higher than with the scales to which they were assigned in the American version of 16PF.

We described the story of 16PF's adaptation in Russia in so detailed a manner on purpose; we wanted the reader to have a clear idea of the adaptation process and the efforts spent on it. We suppose that these efforts could be about equal to those of a new tool development. We omitted here the financial side: An adaptation of a tool proposes payments to the copyright owners and that makes it even more expensive.

To compare the adaptation and the development processes, we discuss one Russian project devoted to the developing of a new trait-based questionnaire measuring normal personality.

DEVELOPMENT OF NEW DIAGNOSTIC TOOLS

Principally there are two possible directions in the development of new instruments for culture-specific assessment—the development of culture-specific measures and the development of culture-fair tools. In this section we discuss culture-specific tools.

Russian Thesaurus of Personality Traits

Parallel to the work on the adaptation of 16PF, in 1983 Alexander Shmelyov, Vladimir Pohilko, and Anna Kozlovskaya-Telnova started the

Russian Thesaurus of Personality Traits project (Shmelyov, 2002). The researchers have analyzed the personality trait descriptors present in the Russian language using a lexical database of 2,090 words. This work corresponded to the analysis of Allport-Odbert's list of traits made by Raymond Cattell as the initial phase of 16PF development. As a result of the Thesaurus project, came experimental reconstruction of the implicit personality theory peculiar to Russian native speakers, partly similar to those of Americans and partly very different. Expert judgments of the closeness of 2,090 trait descriptors have been factored and 15 Russian factors were derived. These factors were called Altruism/Egoism, Intellect, Actual energy, Self-control, Potential energy, Agreeableness, Pragmatism/Naiveté, Morality, Social rigidity, Haughtiness/Timidity, Formalism/Keenness, Social boldness, Ambitiousness, Civility, and Originality. The detailed discussion of similarities and differences between Cattell's and Shmelyov's factors is outside the scope of this chapter. We would like only to point out that 11 of the 15 Russian factors correspond to those of Cattell. But such scales as Social rigidity, Haughtiness/Timidity, Formalism/Keenness, and Ambitiousness do not have American analogues.

In 1994 Shmelyov created 240 original items corresponding to the 240 personality trait clusters, and then he added 10 items to control social desirability bias and 20 more items to evaluate intellectual abilities. The whole 270 items became the form A of the original 16RF questionnaire (16 Russian Factors = 15 Russian factors + Social desirability scale).

The psychometric characteristics of 16RF and the Russian version of 16PF questionnaires were compared. Cumulative percent of variance in the respondents' answers explained by Russian and American factors and the independence among Russian and American factors showed that 16RF was a more powerful tool for the Russian sample (Shmelyov, 2002). In other words, for the Russian sample, 16RF proved to be a more precise measure than 16PF. It comes as no surprise, because 16RF is initially based upon a Russian lexical database and implicit personality theory peculiar to Russian native speakers.

Of course, we need to remember that the described factor structure was obtained in the late 1980s. Since that time, dramatic changes have occurred in Russian society, politics, professional ethics, and family lives of people. Additional research is needed to refine the new structure both on the lexical base and on the questionnaire's data. Nevertheless, summing up, we suppose that developing culture-specific instruments is a more profitable and fruitful strategy than the way of adaptation.

Big Five

The "Big Five" personality traits are five independent factors of personality discovered in 1949 by Fiske (Fiske, 1949) and later replicated in numerous other empirical studies (Borgatta, 1964; Digman & Takemoto-Chock, 1981; Goldberg, 1990; Norman, 1963). These factors are most often called Surgency (Extraversion), Emotional Stability (Neuroticism), Intellect (Openness), Agreeableness, and Conscientiousness (Self-Control). In the 1960s, Cattell factored his 16 scales and also derived five *global* factors. Although the Big Five model has some opponents (e.g., Brand & Egan, 1989), most psychologists around the world tend to agree on the five-factor model, and it has become widely accepted by human resources (HR) departments and organizational users of personality tools.

The 16RF factorization conducted by Shmelyov also derived five secondary dimensions that had similar meaning to those described above. Alexander Shmelyov and Lewis Goldberg compared American and Russian factor structures and concluded that the main difference between them was in the factors' magnitude and contribution to the variance (Goldberg & Shmelyov, 1993). The first American factor (the factor having maximal variance contribution) is Surgency, or Extraversion. The first Russian factor is Agreeableness. The possible explanation of this difference is the history of Soviet time in Russia. At the time, people were evaluated more by their moral principles (altruistic–egoistic, friendly–unfriendly, collectivistic–individualistic, etc.) than by other characteristics important for the business success (confident–diffident, active–passive, bold–timid, etc.). However, in the last few years, these differences are smoothing out because of the mass and strong competition in different life spheres. Recently, Shmelyov introduced the Proverb Test as an instrument for modeling the Big Five personality traits. An exploratory factor analysis of Russian proverbs showed that the Agreeableness factor has lost in dominance since the late 1980s.

These data and explanations correspond to the recent work by Hofstede and McCrae (2004). Geert Hofstede is known as the author of the theory on interactions between national and organizational cultures. He demonstrated that there are national and regional cultural groupings that affect the behavior of societies and organizations. Hofstede has found five dimensions of culture in his studies; these are Power/Distance, Uncertainty/Avoidance, Individualism/Collectivism, Masculinity/Femininity, and Long-/Short-Term Orientation. Robert McCrae is famous for his work on the Big Five personality test. Hofstede and McCrae have analyzed data on the NEO-PI-R Test (Costa & McCrae, 1992) from 30 countries and have found relationships between Hofstede's cultural factors with the average Big Five scores in a country. When applying Hofstede's notions to the recent history of Russia, we can point out that the Individualism/Collectivism factor is changing its influence direction, thus affecting the Big Five scores of the Russian sample.

Development of Moscow Multifunctional Psychological Inventory in Russia

The first item analysis of the Russian translation of the Minnesota Multiphasic Personality Inventory (Berezin, Miroshnikov, & Rozhanets, 1976) was done by Shmelyov and Pohilko at the end of 1980s (Zabrodin, Pokhilko, & Shmelyov, 1987). It showed that the most powerful was social desirability bias, which meant that the items' content was provoked in probationers' strong defensive mechanisms. But in the time available, probationer samples were not representative—they consisted primarily of sick people and Moscow Medical Academy students.

However, in the 1990s, the confirmatory factor analysis of a big representative protocol bank verified preliminary results: Social desirability bias dominated over all other scales. Items describing medical symptoms increased the defensive settings even more. More than 30% of items had correlations with the scales other than those of original MMPI. For example, a number of items measuring Hysteria in the American version correlated with Psychasthenia, Paranoia, and Schizophrenia in the Russian one.

In the beginning of the 2000s, Shmelyov in collaboration with Lyudmila Sobchik modified the Russian version of MMPI and developed the Moscow Multifunctional Psychological Inventory. This tool consists of two parts—300 items measuring normal personality (the result is presented in terms of factors close to the Big Five personality traits) and 300 items measuring pathological tendencies that model MMPI-1 factor scales.

In many Russian organizations, exploring pathological tendencies by HR specialists can be considered as a violation of individual rights; therefore, the existing versions of MMPI raise a great hue and cry and evident or latent resistance manifesting in an increased rate of inauthentic and falsified answers. In the Moscow Multifunctional Psychological Inventory, all symptomatic questions are grouped in the second part, and before the start, the probationer receives appropriate notification and can reject filling out the second part. This forms more favorable conditions for the test administration.

Case-Tests

During the last few years, the leading author of this chapter, Alexander G. Shmelyov, has spent much effort on developing a new type of applied diagnostic instrument called *case-tests*. The case-tests are especially useful for examining personnel in particular organizations, because they capture not only the professional specific character, but also the organizational peculiarities, thus automatically taking into account the cultural context. The examinee receives descriptions of situations sometimes accompanied by visual images (portraits of the characters). The traditional educational or diagnostic cases (as they were developed and understood by Harvard Business School) propose a student to give a free answer. The case-tests offer the examinee several predefined answers describing the possible behavior in a given situation. The answers are formulated as infinitives with a more detailed parenthesized description. Examples follow:

- *To promote* (to transfer to a higher and better-paid position);
- *To give a bonus* (to assign a bonus to one's salary);
- *To have a heart-to-heart talk* (to speak with an employee about his or her problems and difficulties).

The Imitation Test of Personnel Management Brief (ITPMB, ИТУПС) that can be found on the HR-Laboratory Human Technologies Web site (http://www.ht.ru) is a good example of such a test. The case-tests are mostly developed for commercial use in a particular organization that usually prohibits distribution of cases.

The Critical Incident Technique (CIT) developed by Flanagan (1954) and the Repertory Grid technique offered by Kelly around 1955 (Kelly, 1991) are considered prototypes for the case-tests. CIT is a set of procedures used to collect direct observations of human behavior that are kept track of as incidents and used to solve practical problems. In organizational development, CIT is used as a research (interview) technique to identify organizational problems. The interviewees are asked not to express their opinions about management or business processes, but to describe particular organizational incidents. It is supposed that analysis of stories is generally a better way to assess strengths and weaknesses of the organization performance than direct answers about working procedures, psychological climate, and so forth. The Repertory Grid is an interview technique that uses factor analysis to determine an idiographic measure of personality. The interviewee is asked to list people in his or her life, such as mother, father, best friend, partner, disliked male/female, admired male/female, and so on. When possible, self-elements, such as "myself as I am now" or "myself as I would like to be," can also be included. The interviewer divides the listed people into groups of three and asks the participant to invent a criterion to distinguish one person in the group from the other two. These criteria are supposed to be the main constructs used by people to prescribe meaning to their experience. As opposed to the usual personality inventories and tests, in the repertory grid, it is not the researcher, but the interviewee, who develops the constructs.

In studies of television announcers' and realtors' professional activities conducted by Russian researchers (Mostepanova & Shmelyov, 2001; Potapkin & Shmelyov, 2004), a mixed strategy (situational operational grid) was used to develop diagnostic tools. The situational operational grid is used for replication of all possible behavioral alternatives in every case, thus giving an opportunity to conduct multidimensional data analysis (e.g., factor and cluster analysis) and reconstruction of idiographic measures of personality in the same way as it is made in the repertory grid technique.

The main idea of this approach is to develop a stimulus of specific content and form. It is impossible to develop such tests by some universal international tools.

CONCLUSION

In this chapter the authors tried to share their vision of what is seen as culturally universal and culture-specific nowadays in the field of diagnostic tools development. We wanted to avoid extreme statements such as "all tests can be used for all cultures" or "all tests have to be culture-specific." There is evidence that some tests (quite a few, actually) can work effectively with minimal cultural adaptation in different countries. These are mainly nonverbal tests developed for a broad group of participants of minimal educational level (however, another universality level is achieved among the participants of the highest educational level who speak several foreign languages, travel a lot around the world, have international work experience, etc.). Culture-specific tests are a much broader group of tools (allowing a more precise forecast for a narrower target group) developed in the very country where they are supposed to be used. From a financial point of view, the development of culture-specific tests proves to be even cheaper and more profitable for the local specialists using advanced information technologies than the psychometric adaptation of culturally universal instruments. After all, the adaptation assumes not only a statistical check of psychometric parameters, but also paying royalties to the copyright owners.

Nevertheless, the authors are aware of the globalization processes conditioned by the international financial and informational integration and technology unification. It is apparent that the increase in people working for transnational corporations will lead to increased relevance and popularity of global universal tests that have no strongly pronounced cultural-specific character. These tests will be able to help in managing migration flows and vertical mobility of transnational corporations' personnel. Development of such tests will require the integration of different countries' representatives. The faster this integration happens, the more relevant this production will be for the transnational companies.

REFERENCES

American Educational Research Association, American Psychological Association, & National Council on Measurement in Education. (1999). *Standards for Educational and Psychological Testing.* Washington, DC: American Psychological Association.

Berezin, F. B., Miroshnikov, M. P., & Rozhanets, R. V. (1976). *Method of multi-facet personality research.* Moscow: Medizina.

Blustein, D. L., & Ellis, M. V. (2000). The cultural context of career assessment. *Journal of Career Assessment, 8,* 379–390.

Borgatta, E. F. (1964). The structure of personality characteristics. *Behavior Science, 9,* 8–17.

Brand, C. R., & Egan, V. (1989). The Big Five dimensions of personality. *Personality and Individual Differences, 11,* 1165–1171.

Chin, O. C., Gu, J., & Tubbs. S. L. (2001). Developing global leadership competencies. *Journal of Leadership Studies, 4,* 20–29.

Costa, P. T., Jr., & McCrae, R. R. (1992). *Revised NEO Personality Inventory (NEO-PI-R) and NEO Five-Factor Inventory (NEO-FFI), professional manual.* Odessa, FL: Psychological Assessment Resources.

Digman, J. M., & Takemoto-Chock, N. K. (1981). Factors in the natural language of personality: Re-analysis and comparison of six major studies. *Multivariate Behavior Research, 16,* 149–170.

Elosua, P. (2007). Assessing vocational interests in the Basque Country using paired comparison design. *Journal of Vocational Behavior, 71,* 135–145.

Farh, J., Leong, F. T. L., & Law, K. S. (1998). Cross-cultural validity of Holland's model in Hong Kong. *Journal of Vocational Behavior, 52,* 425–440.

Fiske, D. W. (1949). Consistency of the factorial structures of personality ratings from different sources. *Journal of Abnormal and Social Psychology, 44,* 329–344.

Flanagan, J. C. (1954). The Critical Incident Technique. *Psychological Bulletin, 51*(4), 327–358.

Flores, L. Y., Spanierman, L. B., & Obasi, E. M. (2003). Ethical and professional issues in career assessment with diverse racial and ethnic groups. *Journal of Career Assessment, 11,* 76–95.

Ford-Harris, D. Y. (1993). The underrepresentation of minority students in gifted education: Problems and promises in recruitment and retention. *Journal of Special Education, 32,* 4–14.

Fouad, N. A., & Dancer, L. S. (1992). Cross-cultural structure of vocational interests: Mexico and the United States. *Journal of Vocational Behavior, 40,* 339–348.

Fouad, N. A., & Zao, K. E. (2000). Meeting the revolution: Future trends in vocational assessment. *Journal of Career Assessment, 8,* 403–409.

Gavrilina, O. N. (1988). *Development of social desirability scale for Russian version of 16PF questionnaire.* Diploma thesis, Moscow, Moscow State University, Department of Psychology.

Glidden-Tracey, C., & Greenwood, A. K. (1997). A validation study of the Spanish Self-Directed Search using back-translation procedures. *Journal of Career Assessment, 5,* 105–113.

Goh, D. S., Lee, J. A., & Yu, J. (2004). Factor structure of the Strong Interest Inventory with a Chinese high school sample. *Journal of Psychology: Interdisciplinary and Applied, 138,* 171–184.

Goldberg, L. R. (1990). An alternative "Description of personality": The Big Five factor structure. *Journal of Personality and Social Psychology, 59,* 1216–1229.

Goldberg, L. R., & Shmelyov, A. G. (1993). Cross-cultural research of personal traits vocabulary: Big Five in English and Russian languages. *Psikhologicheskiy Zhurnal, 4,* 32–40.

Haverkamp, B. E., Collins, R. C., & Hansen, J. I. (1994). Structure of interests of Asian-American college students. *Journal of Counseling Psychology, 41,* 256–264.

Hofstede, G., & McCrae, R. R. (2004). Personality and culture revisited: Linking traits and dimensions of culture. *Cross-Cultural Research, 1,* 52–88.

Holland, J. (1997). *Making vocational choices: A theory of vocational personalities and work environments* (3rd ed.). Odessa, FL: Psychological Assessment Resources.

Kelly, G. A. (1991). *The psychology of personal constructs* (2nd ed.). London: Routledge.

Klimov, E. A. (1971). *School . . . and then?* Leningrad: Lenizdat.

Lent, R. W., Tracey, T. J. G., Brown, S. D., Soresi, D., & Nota, L. (2006). Development of interests and competency beliefs in Italian adolescents: An exploration of circumplex structure and bidirectional relationships. *Journal of Counseling Psychology, 53,* 181–191.

Leong, F. T. L., Austin, J. T., Secaran, U., & Komarraju, M. (1998). An evaluation of the cross-cultural validity of Holland's theory: Career choices by workers in India. *Journal of Vocational Behavior, 52,* 441–455.

Leong, F. T. L., & Hartung, P. J. (1997). Career assessment with culturally different clients: Proposing an integrative-sequential conceptual framework for cross-cultural career counseling research and practice. *Journal of Career Assessment, 5,* 183–202.

Leong, F. T. L., & Hartung, P. J. (2000). Cross-cultural career assessment: Review and prospects for the new millennium. *Journal of Career Assessment, 8,* 391–401.

Long, L., & Tracey, T. J. G. (2006). Structure of RIASEC scores in China: A structural meta-analysis. *Journal of Vocational Behavior, 68,* 39–51.

Long, L., Watanabe, N., & Tracey, T. J. G. (2006). Structure of interests in Japan: Application to the Personal Globe Inventory occupational scales. *Measurement and Evaluation in Counseling and Development, 38,* 222–235.

MacMillan, D. L., Gresham, F. M., & Sipersein, G. N. (1993). Conceptual and psychometric concerns about the 1992 AAMR definition of mental retardation. *American Journal on Mental Retardation, 98,* 325–335.

Mostepanova, Y. V., & Shmelyov, A. G. (2001). Repertoire diagnostics of communicative strategies of television announcers. *Vestnik Moskovskogo Universiteta. Series 14. Psikhologia, 3,* 47–54.

Norman, W. T. (1963). Toward an adequate taxonomy of personality attributes: Replicated factor structure in peer nomination personality ratings. *Journal of Abnormal and Social Psychology, 66,* 574–583.

Potapkin, A. A., & Shmelyov, A. G. (2004). Situational operational grid as a method for professional psychological testing. *Vestnik Moskovskogo Universiteta. Series 14. Psikhologia, 2,* 50–56.

Shmelyov, A. G. (2002). *Psychological testing of personality traits.* Saint-Petersburg: Rech.

Shmelyov, A. G., Pokhilko, V. I., & Soloveychik, A. S. (1988). 16PF questionnaire: Training in psychological testing. In A. A. Bodalyov et al. (Eds.), *Psychological tests* (pp. 17–42). Moscow: Izdatelstvo MGU.

Shmelyov, A. G., & Serebryakov, A. G. (2006). Psychological testing in vocational counselling: Principles of infrastructure support of computer testing. *Psikhologicheskaya Diagnostika, 2,* 4–16.

Soh, S., & Leong, F. T. L. (2001). Cross-cultural validation of Holland's theory in Singapore: Beyond structural validity of RIASEC. *Journal of Career Assessment, 9,* 115–133.

Sverko, I., & Babarovic, T. (2006). The validity of Holland's theory in Croatia. *Journal of Career Assessment, 14,* 490–507.

Tak, J. (2004). Structure of vocational interests for Korean college students. *Journal of Career Assessment, 12,* 298–311.

Toit, R., & Bruin, G. P. (2002). The structural validity of Holland's R-I-A-S-E-C model of vocational personality types for young black South African men and women. *Journal of Career Assessment, 10,* 62–77.

Tracey, T. J. G., Watanabe, N., & Schneider, P. L. (1997). Structural invariance of vocational interests across Japanese and American cultures. *Journal of Counseling Psychology, 44,* 346–354.

Yu, J., & Alvi, S. A. (1996). A study of Holland's typology in China. *Journal of Career Assessment, 4,* 245–252.

Zabrodin, Y. M., Pokhilko, V. I., & Shmelyov, A. G. (1987). Statistical and semantic problems of development and adaptation of multi-factor personality inventories. *Psikhologicheskiy Zhurnal, 6,* 79–89.

13

The Use of Foreign Psychodiagnostic Inventories in Differing Methodological Contexts

TATIANA V. KORNILOVA AND SERGEY A. KORNILOV

THE PROBLEM OF INTERPRETING ASSESSMENT TECHNIQUES IN METHODOLOGICALLY DIFFERENT APPROACHES

The assessment of individual characteristics is based on different methods (e.g., observation, interview, individual experiment). Normative psychodiagnostic measures remain leading instruments in quick diagnostics. Both the ability and personality characteristics assessments operationalized in inventories necessarily take culture specificity and corresponding bias into account. Although this issue has been frequently addressed by psychologists, a related one has not been. The "blind spot" appears to be the possibility of theoretical reinterpretation of the inventories' basis when these inventories are used in theoretical frameworks and scientific traditions that differ from the original ones.

The use of psychodiagnostic inventories is important in the context of revealing personality factors that may influence the regulation of cognitive activity. The interpretation of the paths (or mechanisms) of the measured personality characteristics' influence on cognitive activity depends on the specificity of both the understanding of this activity and personality inventories.

The present social situation in Russia is in a stage of reorganization and transformation. The communication and experience exchange between Russian and foreign psychologists seem to be one-way with many inventories being successfully adapted to be used with Russian samples. At the same time, the development of theories and approaches presented in Russian psychology (e.g., that resulted in the idea of dynamic testing, see Sternberg & Grigorenko, 2002) have not yet received reciprocal feedback or evaluation. Theories that refer to personality in the regulation of thinking are being developed both in Russia (i.e., Tikhomirov's [1984] sense theory of thinking) and abroad (i.e., Dweck's [1999] social-cognitive theory).

There are two separate lines of discussion concerning the use of inventories that became popular and commonly accepted in different countries that have their own original theoretical frameworks. These frameworks suggest a diverse interpretational basis for both ability and personality domains.

The first and the simpler case is when psychologists accept the theoretical basis underlying the newly adapted instrument. Popular cognitive abilities assessment batteries, implicit theories questionnaires, Wason's decision-making task, as well as Eysenck's model and corresponding measures, are considered to be examples of this approach. This approach also suggests that adaptation is limited by the development of new and culture-specific norms. Cultural differences between samples are also usually discussed and explained.

However, the situation becomes more complicated when the assessment of a specific trait in another country requires a specialist to use principally diverse psychological concepts. For example, diagnostics of motivation with Edwards's (1959) EPPS (Edwards Personal Preference Schedule) questionnaire, which is based on H. Murray's theory, do not fit the framework of Leontiev's (1978) activity theory, which is widely accepted in Russia (Kornilova, 1997). One of the possible solutions here is to substantiate and perform a review of the empirical indices' content. This review can be based on hypothetical constructs that differ from the initial ones. However, there are cases (and methods) when this approach is not applicable.

Both of these approaches are used in Russia where the development of its own instruments has been halted for a long period of time. There were a few major reasons for the temporary halt of the development of psychodiagnostics in Russia in the 20th century. The first one was the Resolution of Central Committee VKP (b) 1936 "On Pedological

Distortions in the System of Narkompros" (Postanovlenie CK VKP(b) ot 4 ijulya 1936 g, 1974). This act has, in fact, forbidden the development of standardized tests as diagnostics as well as the use of instruments based on foreign theories. However, in the 1990s Russian psychology generally recovered from this temporary stop and foreign psychodiagnostic inventories have become widely used in studies, two of which will be presented in this chapter in the framework of the two approaches that we proposed earlier. The first study has allowed us to use the original interpretation of the implicit theories concept in Dweck's theory and, at the same time, to broaden the understanding of implicit theories based on Russian studies of goal orientations and goal formation. In the second study of deep motivation, we have reinterpreted motivational indices derived from the use of foreign questionnaires. Both the study of motivation and the study of goal orientations have been based on Leontiev's theory of activity.

The development of the concept of personality as an activity subject is based on Marx's methodology. Leontiev's theory is based on the same methodology. He introduced a specific understanding of a motive as an object of need. However, there were no instruments for diagnosing motives and their hierarchies developed in this theory. This is why empirical studies of Russian psychology face the problem of using personality measures, which are based on differing theoretical approaches. In our studies we have faced the same problem while using Edwards's EPPS questionnaire for diagnostics of motivational profiles of students from different professional samples.

Leontiev's book, whose title includes a reference to personality (*Activity, Consciousness, and Personality*), was published in 1978. It still remains a problem to relate the proposed methodological basis of activity mediating personality constructs to possible methods of their diagnostics. Both the level of self-consciousness and the motivation hierarchy are successfully used in theories of the personality regulation of perception, memory, thinking, and behavior. However, there is no diagnostic approach that takes the specificity of a personality concept in the activity theory framework into account. This is why psychologists accepting activity theory have to refer to methods based on differing theoretical frameworks.

Given the possible use of personality inventories that were developed in differing methodological approaches, we have conducted a number of studies on personality regulation of learning, two of which will be presented in this chapter.[1] Both of these studies were based on the use of personality inventories that originated from different methodological frameworks. They demonstrate both the theoretical implications of adapted methods and their practical implications, including those for the educational psychology domain.

SPECIFIC LEARNING MOTIVATION AND IMPLICIT THEORIES OF INTELLIGENCE AND PERSONALITY

Considering theories of personality regulation of thinking and studies of the role of implicit theories of learning, we have singled out the following research field—the study of the role of self-evaluations and goal orientations in academic achievements in university students. Studies of a layperson's beliefs' engagement in the self-regulation of learning represent a new approach to personality regulation of learning that views the self-appraisal construct as a mediating variable.

Self-consciousness is considered in activity theory as a leading level of the personality regulation of actions and decisions (Leontiev, 1978). At the same time, in the understanding of consciousness of learning, the presentation of goals to a subject includes a level of realization, whereas motivational regulation, as derived from deep motivation, is usually unconscious. The bases of a specific goal formation can be unconscious as well—even though the goal content is conscious. Tikhomirov (1969) has shown that the formation of operational senses at unconscious levels of a search process precedes the actual formation of a conscious goal of decision. The fact that implicit theories are present on both conscious and unconscious levels allows one to view this construct as containing the variable of personality regulation of goal formation and efforts allocation that may act as a link between self-evaluations and goal structures of learning.

In Bandura's (1997) theory, self-efficacy is included in goal-structures formation. Goals provide a basis for the self-regulation of efforts through implicit standards to which one compares relevant strategies and efforts. Students with higher levels of academic self-efficacy use more effective strategies in learning; they are more effective in the exploration of environment, self-control, and the self-regulation of efforts (Chemers, Hu, & Garcia, 2001). Moreover, evaluation of efforts spent on a task is where self-efficacy and academic self-concept overlap.

Neither academic self-concept nor self-efficacy concept have been widely used in Russian psychology based on activity theory. However, studies of goal formation processes in thinking and personality regulation of academic achievement became significant components of activity theory development. The leading role in regulation of thinking strategies has been studied regarding goal formation processes (Tikhomirov, 1969, 1977, 1984) and ideas based on Vygotsky's (1987) notion of thought being born not from another thought, but from the motivating sphere of consciousness. On the basis of this notion, we have developed the concept of dynamic regulative systems (Kornilova & Smirnov, 2002). Different regulative systems reveal their influence on different parameters and stages of intellectual decisions. They include both conscious and unconscious levels of psychological components, which are bootstrapped by components of integral self-regulation (Kornilova, 2007).

In this dynamic systems approach, goal achievement in learning cannot be viewed outside of the self-consciousness level that is integrative in relation to other personality (and motivational) characteristics. We suggest that diagnostics of the components of self-concept most closely related to motivation that is specific to learning can be based on the use of the concept of implicit theories.

Dweck has studied the role of lay beliefs about intelligence and personality in the context of studying subjective factors of learning regulation. These beliefs (or representations) have been referred to as implicit theories (Dweck & Leggett, 1988; Furnham, 1988). Implicit theories related to one as well as to others can focus different aspects of a self-concept's regulative function in the development of internal (specific) learning motivation on themselves. Concretization of their contribution to success in learning by Russian students has called for a discussion of the degree to which a reference to assessment techniques developed in a differing theoretical context could be applied when used on the basis of other models of learning regulation.

Dweck has studied implicit theories as factors of internal determination of students' learning for 20 years (Dweck, 1999; Good & Dweck, 2006). Dweck showed that people differ in their beliefs about intelligence, which can be defined as entity theory or incremental theory. These components of self-concept influence both the goals and the learning effectiveness. Performance goal orientation or mastery goal orientation seem to be closely related to implicit theories. Later, Dweck (2006) applied her theory to the psychology of success and demonstrated the role of implicit theories as "mindsets" in many different domains (e.g., sports, business, and everyday life).

In the study presented below, our goal was to adapt the questionnaire based on Dweck's identification of three scales reflecting implicit theories of intelligence, personality, and learning goals for Russian samples. We have added a fourth scale that measures academic self-concept. The use of this combined questionnaire has allowed us to diagnose a set of characteristics that are more or less proximal to the conscious goal regulation of students' learning. It has also made it possible to reveal the interrelations in partial systems of personality regulation, including emotional intelligence and self-estimated intelligence and to consider academic self-concept as the specific motivational predictor of academic achievements.

The practical need for such instruments' development is due to a number of reasons. The main one is that, although thorough, the analysis of the structure of learning activity in Russian psychology (e.g., Smirnov, 2001; Talyzina, 1998) has paid less attention to problems of individual differences and learning motivation influencing knowledge acquisition effectiveness and abilities to use this knowledge in job-related tasks at the university level.

Discussions of possible sources of individual differences in educational achievement usually refer to the following characteristics of a person: intelligence (the ability to acquire knowledge and skills and use them for problem solving) (e.g., Anastasi, 1996; Mackintosh, 2006; Sternberg, Grigorenko, & Bundy, 2001; Trost, 1999); metacognition (Galkina & Loarer, 1997); cognitive style (Klaus, 1987); general motivation not specific to learning activity (e.g., of achievement, dominance); specific motivation providing intense emotions when learning goals are achieved (e.g., Dweck, 1999; Good & Dweck, 2006); level and adequacy of self-esteem, self-efficacy, and self-regulation of learning (e.g., Bandura, 1997; Boekaerts, 1996).

The skills and readiness to use one's potential are one aspect of self-regulation. Individual and personality characteristics are viewed as different-level components of a student's activity in Russian psychology. Self-consciousness acts as a leading level in the activity-personality mediation of one's interaction with the world. Notions that self-consciousness structures can act as a form of self-control and motivate activity are concretized in the development of Leontiev's activity theory approach (Smirnov, 2001; Stolin, 1983). An individual's level of implicit beliefs about himself may correlate in this case with sense domain, which is only partially conscious. Sense is understood in activity theory as a relation between a motive and a goal (which is always conscious) and can regulate one's attitude toward learning. It can remain partially realized by an individual in relation to learning goals and efforts made.

The subject matter of the present study is the interrelations between specific implicit theories (representing beliefs about malleability of intelligence and personality in learning), different ability personality factors, and academic achievements.

We accept the general notion that the concept of mastery goal orientation reveals a motivational role of self-consciousness that mediates the direction of efforts made by a student, but we think that there is a missing link of self-concept components (i.e., different self-evaluations). Beliefs about one's place in the hierarchy of other students and the effectiveness and subjective value of efforts put in learning should be discussed along with the goal orientations. This allows us to take a functional role of self-concept components in goal formation and achievement into account.

One recent study (Plaks, Grant, & Dweck, 2005) shows that implicit theories as a framework are reflected in cognitive strategies in terms of less reaction time to information violating initial implicit theories. However, implicit theories act as mediators in learning by defining not only goal orientations, but learning motivation as well. We did not expect implicit theories to influence academic achievements directly.

Book and Stein (2000) discuss relations of emotional intelligence and professional career success mediated by communicative competence. In this first study we refer to the emotional intelligence measurement as described in Gardner's (1983) book, in which he includes interpersonal and intrapersonal intelligences in his concept of the multiple intelligences. Discussions about whether emotional intelligence is a trait or ability are still far from being over (Matthews, Zeidner, & Roberts, 2007; Schulze & Roberts, 2005). The idea of intellectual emotions as regulators of intellectual strategies developed in Tikhomirov's approach in Russian psychology allows us to accept the following position: Emotions are included in prognosis and decision-making processes and they execute the structuring function of decision-making strategies. This is why, although theoretical interpretations of this construct differ, one can argue that it has a regulative role in learning. This influence may be viewed as operating at the same level of unconscious regulation of goal formation as the influence of implicit theories. We followed the general assumption about the role of emotional intelligence as a possible predictor of academic achievement. Although cognitive aspects of emotional intelligence are widely discussed (e.g., see Book & Stein, 2000) and these components may be viewed as influencing academic achievement, there have been no published papers on the relations between psychometric and emotional intelligence in Russian students yet.

In Great Britain, the problem of interrelations between personality and cognitive components of achievement regulation is developed through the use of such questionnaires as NEO-FFI of Big Five and Eysenck's NEO-EPQ-R (Chamorro-Premuzic & Furnham, 2006; Chamorro-Premuzic, Furnham, & Moutafy, 2004). The group of authors listed above discovered the concept of intellectual competence that suggests the existence of an individual ability to acquire and integrate knowledge across the entire lifespan. Observed individual differences in learning depend not only on psychometric intelligence as a general cognitive ability, but on personality characteristics and self-assessed intelligence as well. Authors refer to Dweck's studies in the context of viewing implicit theories as influencing the level of achievement motivation that is leading in the differentiation of the development of intellectual skills and knowledge systems. Studying interrelations of self-estimated and measured personality and ability characteristics and discussing possible causal relations among them, Chamorro-Premuzic, Furnham, and Moutafy (2004) propose an integrative model and argue that self-evaluations of personality and intelligence are included in the single regulative profile of learning. Other studies aim at revealing psychological and socioeconomic factors that influence these self-evaluations (e.g., Rammstedt & Rammsayer [2002] have shown that the level of education can have moderating effects on self-estimated intelligence).

Conscientiousness appears to be another trait that is positively related to learning motivation, but at the same time, can be negatively related to skill acquisition, which can be explained by resource allocation with emphasis on self-regulation (Colquitt, LePine, & Noe, 2000). Personality traits in contemporary studies act as covariates rather than moderators of goal direction. On the contrary, a relationship between self-evaluations and goal orientations may be moderated by goal achievement.

Studies that attempt to reveal relations between learning motivation and learning effectiveness show that implicit theories play different roles in it and the mechanism is thought to be related to goal orientations, which (in spite of differing interpretations of the sources of goal motivation) are in turn related to the influence of personality traits (Kornilova, Smirnov, Chumakova, Kornilov, & Novototskaya-Vlasova, 2008). We accept the conclusion of Payn, Youngcourt, and Beaubien (2007) that have shown in their meta-analysis that "self-regulatory constructs and processes mediate the relationship between individual-difference variables and various outcomes" (p. 130). Self-evaluations appears in the list of antecedents of goal orientations along with implicit theories, cognitive abilities and levels of motivation, personality and general self-efficacy. These antecedents influence goal orientation dimensions and the latter influence distal consequences and outcomes (learning, academic, task and job performance) through proximal ones (state learning, specific self-efficacy, state anxiety, feedback seeking, and others).

Later models are highly integrative and expand the list of individual differences that contribute to learning and training. These include not only personality traits (as of the Big Five) and specific motivations, but also anxiety, locus of control, and intellectual engagement related to skill improvement and success that influences the feeling of self-value related to self-efficacy and career planning (Colquitt, LePine, & Noe, 2000).

In our studies we relate self-regulation of learning to a proximal construct—self-concept. Indicator variables for the possible corresponding latent variable are two types of self-evaluations: academic self-concept and subjective evaluations of intelligence in interpersonal comparisons (Smirnov, Kornilova, Kornilov, & Malakhova, 2007). We propose two corresponding different assessment procedures. The present study is aimed at verifying hypotheses of a role of self-concept components along with other individual characteristics (i.e., psychometric and emotional intelligence) as predictors of academic success in university students.

Study 1: Self-Concept Components, Psychometric, and Emotional Intelligence Predict Academic Achievement

Smirnov's Russian versions of three of Dweck's brief questionnaires (Kornilova et al., 2008) with the addition of new items measuring academic self-concept, approved on other samples, were examined anew in our study for internal validity. The questionnaire included 28 statements in its final version, producing four scales: academic self-concept (this measure represents student's beliefs about the overall effectiveness of their learning activity and subjective value of efforts put into the learning activity, and whether a student tends to think that he or she is among successful students); implicit theories of intelligence (as of a constant or malleable construct); implicit theories of personality; and goal orientations (learning/performance goals). There were 429 college students from Moscow State University who participated in this study (330 female, 99 male).

We have also developed a specific procedure called GEI (Group Estimation of Intelligence, Kornilova et al., 2008). Unlike traditional direct self-estimates of intelligence obtained through giving a numerical estimate of intelligence with reference to the normal distribution (Bennett, 1996; Furnham & Rawles, 1999) or one based on a Likert scale (Fingermann & Perlmutter, 1994; Paulus, Lysy, & Yik, 1998), the GEI procedure facilitates social comparisons within a specific reference group. We have asked 223 students from the sample described above to range themselves and their classmates by perceived "intelligence" based on the list of their class, preliminarily having written which qualities a person whom they consider to be clever should possess. A weighted mean rank of a student in a group—a variable of a peer-estimated intelligence (PEI)—is computed. A weighted rank that a student assigned to himself is used as a measure of his self-estimated intelligence (SEI).

We view self-evaluative components of a self-concept as distinct from self-efficacy. These components interact with cognitive abilities in learning and can contribute to academic success in case there is an opportunity to assess one's engagement in an activity or to compare oneself to other people. Self-evaluation of degree of engagement in learning (as academic self-concept) and self-estimated intelligence that takes feedback regarding other students' achievements into account are mediated by different process components. We assumed different relations between these variables and cognitive abilities, emotional intelligence, and actual academic achievement. In particular, academic self-concept should be more closely related to goal orientations and learning outcomes.

Discussions of a problem concerning psychometric intelligence predicting academic success (Deary, Strand, Smith, & Fernandes, 2007; Mackintosh, 2006; McGrew & Knopik, 1993; Trost, 1999; Ushakov, 2004) show that diagnostics of psychological factors of learning achievement is an independent problem in particular, due to the moderate relations between psychometric intelligence and achievement. There are a number of studies of social and emotional intelligence that refer to personality components in intellectual development (e.g., Lyusin & Ushakov, 2004). Considering intelligence as an extraneous variable, we have administered Amthauer's Intelligence Structure Test (IST-70; Amthauer, 1973; Gurevich, Akimova, Kozlova, & Loginova, 1993) to all students (even those who did not participate in the GEI procedure). IST-70 is a standardized test of cognitive abilities. The test contains abstract figural reasoning tasks as markers of fluid intelligence, and knowledge items as markers of crystallized intelligence, which form the three subscales (Verbal, Mathematical and Spatial IQ, and the General IQ scale).

We have also used the EmIn emotional intelligence questionnaire developed by Lyusin (Lyusin & Ushakov, 2004) on the basis of his mixed model in which emotional intelligence is viewed as an interaction of both cognitive and personality characteristics in processes that are crucial to identification, expression, and manipulation of emotions.

Since nonacademic intelligence (i.e., social, practical, and emotional intelligence) may affect achievement (e.g., Klaus, 1987; Lyusin & Ushakov, 2004; Sternberg, 1999), it is possible to view interpersonal and intrapersonal indices as predictors of academic success, which was computed as students' GPA for the last three semesters.

A comparison of male and female samples has revealed higher values of academic self-concept and acceptance of the implicit theory of an enriched personality in female students. Male students were more likely to accept entity theory of personality as a stable constant and assess their engagement in a learning activity as being lower whereas female students thought that personality is a developing construct and had higher academic self-concept than men. There were no significant differences in implicit theories of intelligence and goal orientations.

The unexpected result was that humanities students appeared to have a higher mastery goal orientation than natural science students. They also had higher academic self-concept. Natural science students appeared to be more pragmatic (having performance goal orientations) and tended to not overestimate their efforts in learning (probably considering their efforts as being adequate for the tasks). From our point of view, these differences come from a higher degree of uncertainty in education in humanities programs. Natural science programs have more strict control over the achievement of learning goals. Humanities programs also have less clear criteria for mastery, which makes students formulate them and put more effort into goal formation and learning activity organization, thus acting on a higher level of self-control.

A correlational analysis has revealed one significant positive relation between psychometric intelligence and self-concept component: namely, between the scales of mathematical intelligence and academic self-concept. Thus, students with higher mathematical intelligence tended to assess their academic success as being higher.

Unlike conventional intelligence measures, emotional intelligence scales correlate with many implicit theories scales: there were significant positive moderate relations between implicit theories of intelligence and indices of interpersonal and intrapersonal emotional intelligence. Significant correlations were found between implicit theories of personality and variables of intuitive understanding of others' emotions, one's emotions, emotions through expression, and control over one's emotions as well as a summary index of interpersonal emotional intelligence.

Mastery goal orientation was positively related to all emotional intelligence scales and academic self-concept positively correlated with most emotional intelligence variables.

Thus, students with a higher process motivation (efforts and engagement in learning activity) and students that adopted mastery goals showed higher emotional intelligence. Dynamics and a controllable character of understanding and manipulation of emotions (both of oneself and of other people) is not coincidentally related to the specific motivation of learning supposedly measured by the two scales of the implicit theories questionnaire—learning goal orientation and academic self-concept. Both of these scales appear to be significantly related to students' GPA in humanities and natural science students (e.g., Kornilova et al., 2008).

Taking interrelations of emotional intelligence and self-concept components into account, we have conducted a hierarchical linear regression analysis to evaluate possible contributions of each of these variables as predictors of academic achievement. However, the only variable significantly contributing to GPA was the academic self-concept, which explained 32% of variance in the GPA. Psychometric intelligence did not act as a significant predictor of students' achievement in our study.

Our data on predictive validity of the academic self-concept measure is comparable to some of the available data on predictive value of other personality measures. British psychologists cited above report about routine achievement measures (such as the degree of activity in seminars) predicting exam results and comparable, but negative, coefficients for Neuroticism as an independent variable (Chamorro-Premuzic & Furnham, 2003). They also report data on correlations between Conscientiousness, Openness (as factors of Big Five) and exam results (Chamorro-Premuzic & Furnham, 2006). According to our study, the implicit theory of incremental intelligence is positively related to academic self-concept, which in turn acts as a predictor of academic achievement. Implicit theories by themselves do not act as predictors per se.

The use of the academic self-concept measure allows us to argue that this component of self-concept has a functional role as a predictor of academic success in students. Gender differences revealed in implicit theories indices suggest that women are more ready to accept the implicit theory of enriched personality and estimate their efforts in learning as being higher. The modified version of the implicit theories questionnaire has made it possible to assess goal orientations and academic self-concept as factors that differentiate beliefs of natural science and humanities students about efforts required for successful goal achievement and orientation of this goal achievement either on pragmatic results or skill and knowledge mastery. Direct self-evaluations of intelligence are positively related to academic self-concept, which also allows us to interpret the latter as self-representation of intellectual successfulness. Academic self-concept is the strongest psychological predictor of academic success in this study. Emotional intelligence is related to all four scales of the implicit theories questionnaire, thus demonstrating its inclusiveness into the genesis of specific motivation of learning and the intensity of distant mastery goals, but it cannot be considered as a predictor of academic achievements. Thus, implicit theories, academic self-concept, goal orientations, and emotional intelligence can be viewed as different components of a personality regulation of learning. We treat them as dynamic regulative systems, which represent a hierarchy of different processes of personality regulation of learning activity.

A CROSS-CULTURAL STUDY OF THE MOTIVATION PROFILES OF RUSSIAN AND AMERICAN STUDENTS

Taking into account the difficulty of differentiating between social components as types of thinking and as types of personality profiles and the existence of multiple factors of cross-cultural differences, we have compared the motivation indices of Russian versus American students. Unlike most Russian studies in which a comparative analysis is conducted with reference to the norms for Americans published by other authors, the present one includes American and Russian samples simultaneously.

Study 2: A Comparison of the Motivational Indices of Russian Versus American Students

We have used the short modified version of EPPS (Edwards, 1959). Our sample consisted of Moscow State University students (primarily) and Saint-Petersburg State University students. The corresponding English version has been administered to students at Yale University by Elena L.

Grigorenko (Kornilova & Grigorenko, 1995). Cross-cultural design allowed us to compare the empirical indices of the students' motivational profiles in order to test hypotheses about the dominating traits in two different cultural contexts.

The study took 1 year to conduct (September 1992–October 1993). A time of changes would be the broadest definition of the situation present at that time in Russia. That situation was a socio-political background for the personal development of students in Russian universities. "What are we?" was the question associated with the public consciousness level of another one—"What would we like to be?" The analysis of a "mean" motivational profile based on consciously made personal choices (or personal preferences, as reflected by EPPS) also allowed us to take particular qualities of self-definition into account. Statements were formulated (in most cases) in the conjunctive mood ("I would like to . . . ") or suggestions about the duration and frequency of specific situations ("I like . . . "). The contexts of past and future intersected in pairs of statements, which reflected more or less significant peculiarities of the social situation in Russia. This intersection was to actualize individual preferences. The social component was taken into account, but we have suggested that it had a heterogeneous pattern of influence on self-consciousness variables.

Other authors have included different contexts characterizing social thinking during that period. For example, Abulkhanova-Slavskaya (1994) argues that usually a "developed democratic state provides a person with what, in our country, he or she has to decide/solve by him or herself" (p. 44). The controversy of self-perceptions and the ability to take responsibility for one's actions in turning points and crucial moments of public development should not be considered as culture-determined only and, thus, characterizes value beliefs about personality and Russian mentality (in its cultural understanding).

We have compared the two student samples and specified the peculiarities of Russian and American student populations concerning the intensity of particular motivational tendencies. We have relied on the identity of the statements in both the Russian and English versions: Two experienced professional psychologists that had substantial experience with communication in American culture acted as experts (according to the requirement of the adaptation procedure). For the adaptation of the full version of EPPS, we have highlighted those statements that could not be included in the initial scales in the Russian version. For example, we have dropped the "tolerance to change" or "radicalism" scale. Conceptual relations postulated by the author of the questionnaire were inapplicable to the Russian context (e.g., "the readiness to go to new restaurants" was less representative for Russian students). These culturally "inadequate" relations were excluded from the first version of the modified questionnaire to minimize the impact of the statements that differed in their connotations in the cultural contexts mentioned above.

The modified short version of the EPPS inventory consisted of the following scales: Achievement, Order, Autonomy, Intraception, Dominance, Abasement, Endurance, and Aggression.

The study included 116 Russian and 121 American students aged 19 to 29. Approximately half of the students were male and half were female.

Obtained data were analyzed with MANOVA and univariate ANOVA. The Smirnov-Kolmogorov test was used to test hypotheses concerning differences in the two samples. A multivariate analysis of variance in eight scales has revealed the main effect of cultural factor (as a complex variable).

Significant differences have been revealed for five of eight measures: American students have significantly higher values on Order, Dominance, and Aggression scales while Russian students score higher on Autonomy and Abasement scales.

Higher need for autonomy seems to be the most controversial characteristic of the Russian sample because of the fact that in real-life settings students are not economically independent yet. However, one should take into account the period of the study (1990s)—a period of transition to a more democratic lifestyle. When this notion is taken into account, this result appears to be reflecting the young generation's aspiration for independence and autonomic choices. A higher need for autonomy should be discussed along with differing cultural stereotypes in understanding of the concept. *Individualism* of American society is sometimes oversimplified and understood in terms of the absolute autonomy of a single person. One should, however, mention the extent of an individual's dependence on family and highly estimated sense of belonging to a specific social group (to a university or college in particular).

The Autonomy trait in the Russian sample was more related to the value of individual independence than would be expected of the real-life situation (ability to support oneself, take responsibilities, rationally organize one's studying and free time).

American society's urges toward rationality and orderliness are well known. Time-planning abilities, punctuality, and ability to get done what's needed in time are highly valued and rewarded. There is a great emphasis on teaching these personal traits in the educational system at both the school and college levels. Learning activities in the curriculum, including activities that require additional time, are also controlled. These activities in Russian humanities students are put under control almost entirely during examinations, and many students appear to be unprepared for the required level of self-regulation. Readiness to push one's luck in Russian culture is so strong that even students striving for high achievements tend to not relate the means for success (at the level of self-consciousness) to the need for a plan and thorough preparation. Russian students have the lowest scores on the Orderliness scale in the eight-scale profile. This scale represents an aspiration for rationality in activities. The psychological criteria for subjective rationality include not only logical competence, but following the social stereotypes in the organization of activity, behavior, and thinking as well. Striving for rationality has not become a stereotype in Russian occidentalism. Our data show that students are more likely to compensate for the lack of Orderliness with high Endurance in goal achievement.

Specificity of values in Russian students is also well characterized by high scores on Intraception and Abasement scales. Conscious recognition of specific tendencies in regulation of one's behavior is crucial to a critical attitude toward oneself.

To evaluate significant difference in Abasement scores in Russian and American students, we should take into account the following peculiarity of social thinking in the Russian student sample. Particular personal preferences in answers can be explained by the existence of a moral component in what appears to be the trivial process of analytical problem solving. This is sometimes viewed as a common feature of a "Russian national character" (Znakov, 1994). We should not forget about the interrelation between Abasement and lack of self-confidence that is highly characteristic of the personality development conditions in Russian culture.

On the contrary, conditions purposefully cultivating "individualism, uniqueness, and confidence" are characteristic of Yale students. High self-esteem is being maintained to minimize the lack of personal confidence in a person's own potential. American students are not likely to agree with sentences postulating that possible failures can be attributed to one's mistakes. A feeling of personal responsibility or guilt (and especially of "being lower than others") is not characteristic of this sample as well.

This analysis has also revealed less strong, but significant and predictable differences in Aggression scores between the two samples.

Unrewarded forms of aggressive behavior do not appear on the level of values related to Self in Russian students. We think that a discussion of this tendency should, in the first place, take into account cross-cultural differences in interpersonal communication norms. Corresponding statements in Edwards's EPPS are not characteristic of the Russian culture of an interpersonal relationship (e.g., fairly criticizing someone in public). In terms of the statements' content, the questionnaire was less likely to reflect those domains of an aggression's expression that took place in the interpersonal relationships of Russian students.

The results obtained in this study (as well as other data on the use of methods that deal with psychological reality in context of social interactions of person and environment) may be interpreted in terms of cross-cultural differences. Discussion suggests that particular cultural societies can be classified on an "individualism-collectivism" continuum (Ruzgis & Grigorenko, 1994). Classifications like this one have not been developed in Russian psychology yet. However, cross-cultural studies conducted demonstrate the need of psychologists to go beyond this univariate continuum. The results presented above allow us not only to reveal differences between "mean-statistic" motivational profiles of American and Russian student samples, but also to evaluate the quantitative predominant intensity of specific motivational tendencies. They also demonstrate the need to broaden the interpretational contexts that do not overlap completely in their content when applied to the same personality characteristics in differing cultural frameworks.

DYNAMIC REGULATIVE SYSTEMS AS SYSTEMS OF SELF-REGULATION IN THINKING AND LEARNING

The study of self-concept components in the context of academic achievement demonstrates a combination of orientation on initial theory and inclusion of the new interpretational context as well. Thus, we have used the possibility of modification of the initial Dweck's questionnaires by combining them with the addition of a new scale—of the academic self-concept. However, this study does not speak in favor of implicit theories of personality and intelligence as significant predictors of academic achievements. The academic self-concept scale has allowed us to expand the conception of personality regulation of achievements by processes of self-evaluation (and not only by goal orientations).

Referencing the emotional intelligence measurement in this study was necessary to take into account the idea of unity of intelligence and affect in Russian psychology (Vygotsky, 1987; Tikhomirov, 1984). This allowed us to find a mediating link between beliefs about goal regulation of learning from the point of personality factors at the levels of partially conscious self-evaluations, one of which was more oriented on activity structures, and the other one on self-evaluation in interpersonal comparisons (only the first one acted as a significant predictor of academic achievement).

An attitude toward a student as the subject of a learning activity in Russian psychology and transition to a competence approach in foreign theories of intellectual and personality development (Raven, 1984) calls for a rethinking of motivational and personality components of learning activity regulation. One possible solution lies in the development of the concept of implicit theories as specific personality presuppositions for learning activity success.

We have discussed the fact that implicit theories measures obtained through our modified version of the questionnaire are closely related to intuitive regulation represented by emotional intelligence scales. However, neither emotional intelligence nor implicit theories (except for self-appraisal of learning) act as significant predictors of academic achievements.

This allows us to suggest different roles of psychological characteristics such as implicit theories, emotional intelligence, academic self-concept, and subjective evaluations of intelligence in indivisible dynamic systems of regulation. These systems reveal personality and motivational influences on intellectual strategies and learning processes.

Revealed interrelations of implicit theories and emotional intelligence indices represent the importance of laypersons' beliefs about whether intelligence and personality can be developed in learning reflected in implicit theories scales and about the efforts put in learning for the achievement of different kinds of goals. However, these subjective categorizations do not directly affect learning activity effectiveness as represented in GPA (which, of course, is not and should not be treated as the only indicator of academic performance).

According to these results, we have suggested the existence of dynamic regulative systems. In these systems, influences of differently measured personality characteristics on a learning activity are being hierarchically and dynamically structured. From the point of the development of the concept of the personality regulation of thinking that is reflected in the hypothesis about the formation of dynamic regulative systems, use of foreign methods can be viewed as a way of rapprochement of different theoretical approaches.

The idea of functional structuring of the sense and cognitive components of thinking processes in comprehensive (unfolded) strategies in learning can be viewed as a substantial step toward a new understanding of the application of assessment techniques in psychological studies. Psychodiagnostic instruments can be aimed not only at the assessment as a result, but at assessment as a method of hypotheses verification that supposedly connects assessed characteristics (intelligence, personality) in new formations that have cognitive and personality components and that function in actual genesis.

The scientific goal of this approach is reflected in the verification of assumptions about processes that mediate cognitive-personality interactions and thus functionally construct dynamic regulative systems with hierarchies of psychological regulators of different types and levels.

First, components of these hypothetical and partially influencing (i.e., influencing separate goal formation stages) regulative systems are those motivational formations that represent actualization of deep types of motivation (measured by personality questionnaires, such as Edwards's EPPS). Second, they reflect components of a metacontrol level measured by variables of conscious self-regulation, less conscious self-evaluations, and implicit beliefs about intelligence and its malleability in learning.

The second study presented in this chapter suggests that, when discussing assessment techniques in the context of the measurement of specific motives or motivation type problems, consideration of specific psychological variables corresponding to these constructs or of their genesis does not determine assumptions about their functional role. One can reveal interrelations between variables even though there may be several different interpretations of these variables. In that sense, the functional role of variables is relatively independent of what underlines them whereas theoretical models are highly dependent on the way the variables (and, therefore, constructs) are understood.

A comparison of the Russian and American university students' samples in the second study allows us to reveal both commonalities and distinctions in their motivational profile. Interpretation of these commonalities and distinctions is based on an analysis of real forms of activity in learning that determine which types of motivation will be leading in the motivational profiles. However, this leaves room for additional different interpretations of motivational indices obtained through the use of the EPPS questionnaire. We suggest that possible reinterpretation of motivation indices (i.e., in Leontiev's activity theory or in Murray's theory) speaks in favor of these cross-cultural studies being open to comparing different psychological theories. This point of view would grant prospects for a rapprochement of theories of personality and motivational regulation that were initially developed on different methodological grounds.

Thus, the use of foreign experience in the development and use of assessment techniques and inventories contributes to the development of the original Russian theoretical concept of sense regulation of thinking. Studies presented in this chapter show the possibilities of mutual enrichment of scientific approaches in the contemporary context of globalization.

AUTHOR NOTE

Preparation of this chapter (and the first study described in it) was supported by Grant No. 07-06-00101a from the Russian Humanitarian Science Foundation.

We are grateful to Jodi Reich from Yale University for her invaluable help with the preparation of this chapter and her enormous editorial efforts. We would also like to thank Dr. Carol Dweck from Stanford University and Dr. Sergey Smirnov from Moscow State University for permission to use their questionnaires and obtained data in publications.

NOTE

1. Please note that this chapter only provides a brief outline of the obtained patterns of results. For more details please refer to Kornilov, Kornilova, and Chumakova (2009); Kornilova (1997); Kornilova and Grigorenko (1995); and Kornilova et al. (2008).

REFERENCES

Abulkhanova-Slavskaya, K. A. (1994). Sotsialnoe myshlenie lichnosti: problemy i strategii issledovania [Social thinking of a person: Problems and research strategies]. *Psikhologicheskiy Zhurnal, 4,* 39–55.

Anastasi, A. (1996). *Psychological testing* (7th ed.). New York: Macmillan.

Amthauer, R. (1973). I-S-T 70. *Intelligenz-Struktur-Test. Handanweisung* [Structure of Intelligence Test. Manual]. Göttingen: Hogrefe.

Bandura, A. J. (1997). *Self-efficacy: The exercise of control.* New York: Freeman.

Bennett, M. (1996). Men's and women's self-estimates of intelligence. *Journal of Social Psychology, 136*(3), 411–412.

Boekaerts, M. (1996). Self-regulated learning at the junction of cognition and motivation. *European Psychologist, 1*(2), 100–112.

Book, H. E., & Stein, S. J. (2000). *The EQ edge: Emotional intelligence and your success.* Toronto: Stoddart.

Chamorro-Premuzic, T., & Furnham, A. (2003). Personality predicts academic performance: Evidence from two longitudinal studies on British University students. *Journal of Research in Personality, 37,* 319–338.

Chamorro-Premuzic, T., & Furnham, A. (2006). Intellectual competence and the intelligent personality: A third way in differential psychology. *Review of General Psychology, 10,* 251–267.

Chamorro-Premuzic, T., Furnham, A., & Moutafy, J. (2004). The relationship between estimated and psychometric personality and intelligence scores. *Journal of Research in Personality, 38,* 505–513.

Chemers, M. M., Hu, L., & Garcia, B. (2001). Academic self-efficacy and first-year college student performance and adjustment. *Journal of Educational Psychology, 93*(1), 55–65.

Colquitt, J. A., LePine, J. A., & Noe, R. A. (2000). Toward an integrative theory of training motivation: A meta-analytic path analysis of 20 years of research. *Journal of Applied Psychology, 85*(5), 678–707.

Deary, I. J., Strand, S., Smith, P., & Fernandes, C. (2007). Intelligence and educational achievement. *Intelligence, 35,* 13–21.

Dweck, C. S. (1999). *Self-theories: Their role in motivation, personality, and development.* Philadelphia: Psychology Press.

Dweck, C. S. (2006). *Mindset: The new psychology of success.* New York: Random House.

Dweck, C. S., & Leggett, E. L. (1988). A social-cognitive approach to motivation and personality. *Psychological Review, 95*(2), 256–273.

Edwards, A. L. (1959). *Edwards Personal Preference Schedule. Manual.* New York: Psychological Corporation.

Fingermann, K. L., & Perlmutter, M. (1994). Self rating of past, present, and future cognitive performance across adulthood. *International Journal of Aging and Human Development, 38,* 303–322.

Furnham, A. (1988). *Lay theories: Everyday understanding of problems in the social sciences.* New York: Pergamon.

Furnham, A., & Rawles, R. (1999). Correlation between self-estimated and psychometrically measured IQ. *Journal of Social Psychology, 139,* 405–410.

Galkina, T., & Loarer, E. (Eds.). (1997). *Kognitivnoe obuchenie: sovremennoe sostoianie i perspectivy* [Cognitive teaching and learning: Contemporary state and perspectives]. Moscow: IP RAS.

Gardner, H. (1983). *Frames of mind.* New York: Basic Books.

Good, C., & Dweck, C. S. (2006). Motivational orientations that lead students to show deeper levels of reasoning, greater responsibility for their academic work, and greater resilience in the face of academic difficulty. In R. J. Sternberg & R. F. Subotnik (Eds.), *Optimizing student success with the other three Rs: Reasoning, resilience, and responsibility* (pp. 39–58). Charlotte, NC: Information Age.

Gurevich, K. M., Akimova, M. K., Kozlova, V. T., & Loginova, G. P. (1993). *Rukovodstvo po primeneniu testa struktury intellekta Rudolfa Amthauera* [Rudolf Amthauer's intelligence structure test manual]. Obninks, Russia: Printer.

Klaus, H. (1987). *Vvedenie v differentsialnuiu psikhologiu uchenia* [Introduction to differential psychology of learning]. Moscow: Pedagogika.

Kornilov, S. A., Kornilova, T. V., & Chumakova, M. A. (2009). *Subjective Evaluations of Intelligence and Academic Self-Concept Predict Academic Achievement: Evidence from a Selective Student Population*. Manuscript submitted for publication.

Kornilova, T. V. (1997). *Diagnostika motivatsii i gotovnosti k risku* [Diagnostics of motivation and readiness to risk]. Moscow: IP RAS.

Kornilova, T. V. (2007). Samoreguliatsia i lichnostno-motivatsionnaia reguliatsia priniatia resheniy [Self-regulation and personality-motivational regulation of decision making]. In V. I. Morosanova (Ed.), *Sub'ekt i lichnost v psikhologii samoreguliatsii* [Subject and personality in psychology of self-regulation] (pp. 181–194). Moscow: Izdatelstvo PI RAO.

Kornilova, T. V., & Grigorenko, E. L. (1995). Sravnenie lichnostnikh osobennostey rossiyskikh i amerikanskikh studentiv (po oprosniku A. Edwardsa) [Comparison of personality characteristics of Russian and American students (with A. Edwards' questionnaire)]. *Voprosy psikhologii, 5*, 108–115.

Kornilova, T. V., & Smirnov, S. D. (2002). Gruppirovki motivatsionno-lichnostnikh svoystv kak reguliativnie sistemy priniatia resheniy [Groups of motivational-personality characteristics as regulative systems of decision making]. *Voprosy psikhologii, 6*, 73–83.

Kornilova, T. V., Smirnov, S. D., Chumakova, M. V., Kornilov, S. A., & Novototskaya-Vlasova, E. V. (2008). Modifikatsiya oprosnika implitsitnikh teoriy C. Dweck (v kontekste izuchenia akademicheskikh dostizheniy studentov) [Modification of C. Dweck's implicit theories questionnaire (in context of study of students' academic achievements)]. *Psikhologisheskiy zhurnal, 29*(3), 106–120.

Leontiev, A. N. (1978). *Activity, consciousness, and personality*. Englewood Cliffs, NJ: Prentice-Hall.

Lyusin, D. V., & Ushakov, D. V. (Eds.). (2004). *Sotsialniy intellekt: Teoriya, izmerenie, issledovaniya* [Social intelligence: Theory, measurement, studies]. Moscow: IP RAS.

Mackintosh, N. J. (2006). *IQ and human intelligence*. New York: Oxford University Press.

Matthews, G., Zeidner, M., & Roberts, R. D. (Eds.). (2007). *The science of emotional intelligence: Knowns and unknowns*. New York: Oxford University Press.

McGrew, K. S., & Knopik, S. N. (1993). The relationship between the WJ-R Gf-Gc cognitive clusters and writing achievement across the life-span. *School Psychology Review, 22*, 687–695.

Paulus, D., Lysy, D., & Yik, M. (1998). Self-report measures of intelligence: Are they useful as proxy IQ tests? *Journal of Personality, 66*, 525–555.

Payn, S. C., Youngcourt, S. S., & Beaubien, J. M. (2007). A meta-analytic examination of the goal orientation nomological net. *Journal of Applied Psychology, 92*, 128–150.

Plaks, J. E., Grant, H., & Dweck, C. S. (2005). Violations of implicit theories and the sense of prediction and control: Implications for motivated person perception. *Journal of Personality and Social Psychology, 88*, 245–262.

Postanovlenie CK VKP(b) ot 4 ijulya 1936 g. (1974). "O pedologicheskih izvrashenijah v sisteme Narkomprosov" [The Resolution of Central Committee VKP (b) of 4 July 1936 "On Pedological Distortions in the System of Narkompros"]. In *Narodnoe obrazovanie v SSSR: Sbornik dokumentov.* Moscow: Yurid. Lit.

Rammstedt, B., & Rammsayer, T. H. (2002). Gender differences in self-estimated intelligence and their relation to gender-role orientation. *European Journal of Personality, 16,* 369–382.

Raven, J. (1984). *Competence in modern society: Its identification, development and release.* Oxford, England: Oxford Psychologists Press.

Ruzgis, P., & Grigorenko, E. L. (1994). Cultural meaning systems, intelligence, and personality. In R. J. Sternberg & P. Ruzgis (Eds.), *Personality and intelligence* (pp. 248–270). New York: Cambridge University Press.

Schulze, R., & Roberts, R. D. (Eds.). (2005). *Emotional intelligence: An international handbook.* Cambridge, MA: Hogrefe & Huber.

Smirnov, S. D. (2001). *Pedagogika i psihologija vysshego obrazovanija. Ot dejatel'nosti k lichnosti* [Pedagogics and psychology of higher education: From activity to personality]. Moscow: Academia.

Smirnov, S. D., Kornilova, T. V., Kornilov, S. A., & Malakhova, S. I. (2007). O svyazi intellektualnikh i lichnostnikh kharakteristic studentov s uspeshnostiu ikh obucheniya [About the relations of intellectual and personality characteristics of students with their success in learning]. *Vestnik Moskovskogo universiteta, 14*(3), 82–87.

Sternberg, R. J. (1999). The theory of successful intelligence. *Review of General Psychology, 3*(4), 292–316.

Sternberg, R. J., & Grigorenko, E. L. (2002). *Dynamic testing: The nature and measurement of learning potential.* New York: Cambridge University Press.

Sternberg, R. J., Grigorenko, E. L., & Bundy, D. A. (2001). The predictive value of IQ. *Merrill-Palmer Quarterly, 47*(1), 1–41.

Stolin, V. V. (1983). *Samosoznanie lichnosti* [The self-conscious of a person]. Moscow: Izdatelstvo MGU.

Talyzina, N. F. (1998). *Pedagogicheskaya psikhologiya* [Pedagogical psychology]. Moscow: Academia.

Tikhomirov, O. K. (1969). *Struktura myslitelnoy deiatelnosti* [Structure of thinking activity]. Moscow: Izdatelstvo MGU.

Tikhomirov, O. K. (1984). *The psychology of thinking* (N. Belskaya, Trans.). Moscow: Progress.

Tikhomirov, O. K. (Ed.). (1977). *Psikhologicheskie mekhanizmy tseleobrazovaniya* [Psychological mechanisms of goal formation]. Moscow: Nauka.

Trost, G. (1999). Vozmozhnost' predskazania vydayushiksia uspekhov v shkole, universitete, na rabote [The possibility of predicting the prominent success at school, university, work]. *Inostrannaya psikhologiya, 1,* 19–29.

Ushakov, D. V. (2004). Testy intellekta, ili gorech samopoznaniya [Intelligence tests or the bitterness of learning about self]. *Psikhologia. Zhurnal Vyshei shkoly ekonomiki, 1*(2), 76–93.

Vygotsky, L. S. (1987). Thinking and speech. In R. W. Rieber & A. S. Carton (Eds.), *The collected works of L. S. Vygotsky* (N. Minick, Trans.). New York: Plenum Press.

Znakov, V. V. (1994). *Ponimanie i obshenie* [Understanding and communication]. Moscow: IP RAS.

14

Adapting Existing Abilities and Competencies Assessment Devices to Different Cultures

MÁRCIA REGINA F. DE BRITO

Evaluation has a broad meaning and may be understood in different ways and used with different connotations: *institutional evaluation, program evaluation, student performance evaluation, evaluation of intelligence,* and *employee performance evaluation.*

Depending on the context in which it is being treated and on the people involved, be it students, teachers, administrators, or policy makers, evaluation takes on different meanings, but is almost always understood as a judgment of merit and value (which it effectively is), and subjacent to any evaluation is embedded the possibility of classification. In the course of its development as a discipline, evaluation has assumed its own characteristics and peculiarities inherent to the different contexts in which it is developed.

The term is rather broad in meaning, stretching from individual performance to large corporate evaluation, and can be used in many situations, from birth throughout life. During their childhood, individuals are compared and ranked according to previously established models; they develop conceptions and attitudes toward these procedures. The influence of this practice over their future behavior will depend on the way that the individual deals with these experiences and overcomes them.

Large-scale educational evaluation is linked to the current educational model and is almost always used to categorize schools and students and to distribute funds. It is centered basically on the idea that students can be submitted to a cultural-academic standard determined by the creators of public policies, and they must adapt to this existing standard, with few possibilities of fully developing their individual capacities. The interaction of market interests and the supposed antagonism between public and private interests ends up generating a conflictive situation that prevents effective implantation of an educational system that allows the coexistence of advances in science with the preservation of the cultural heritage of groups situated in different contexts, but subjected to the same national system.

Traditional school is seen as the provider of knowledge, and its function is to transmit the information selected by groups of specialists as being the most relevant knowledge. Although there is an emphasis nowadays on the so-called development of critical thinking, the educational system continues to work with the transmission of information that is filtered by various demands imposed by the government. School experience must give students the scientific tools needed to rethink and understand their surroundings in a broader context.

The central objective of education must not only be to present the findings of science and their usefulness, inserting the student into the scientific culture. The objective of education nowadays is not the assimilation of this scientific culture, but the reconstruction of knowledge experienced by students with the help of more than one tool to read, comprehend, and interpret the world.

School, nowadays, must be concerned with rebuilding knowledge that individuals acquire through their contextual experiences parallel to school, rather than on the transmission of information. This does not mean the exclusion of knowledge accumulated by science, but allowing other forms of education that do not focus exclusively on reproduction but on production of a new relation that allows each school in a globalized system to keep the identity of the groups that compose it, seeking education in the diversity that is completely natural, legitimate, and habitual (Besalú, 2002).

But implanting this conception of education in diversity and new forms of acting in class implies not only changes in the syllabi, but also changing attitudes, beliefs, and values. This takes time and effort from all involved: policy makers, teachers, administrators, family, students, and so forth. It also implies establishing new ways of assessing, seeking to improve the weak points and strengthening the strong ones.

This text presents a few ideas related to education and assessment, and the evolution of these themes. It deals with the assessment of abilities and competencies, how exams have begun to be structured based on these matrices, and how hard it is to conjugate the way the policy makers see assessment with actual assessment in the classroom. It shows a few numbers related to the Brazilian educational system so that we can visualize the challenges of proposing a national assessment system, as well as a few results of three of these exams and the proposal of a more formative exam that effectively assesses the progress of students in such a diversified system.

GENERAL CONSIDERATIONS FOR ASSESSMENT OF ABILITIES AND COMPETENCIES AROUND THE GLOBE TODAY

Evaluation has a long history in the field of education and, all through its trajectory, has been associated with other areas of study that have simultaneously helped to enlarge the field and to reduce it to elements that answer to immediate interests of one agency (governmental, economic, religious, etc.) or another. Usually, this influence involves interests of numerous groups, for example, when evaluation is undertaken with the sole purpose of obtaining indicators for distributing or obtaining resources. Today, economics is the main area of influence in evaluative procedures at various levels of schooling.

The development of research and studies about intelligence, as well as tests elaborated for measuring this construct, have, in some countries, been incorporated into educational evaluation. This is reflected especially in large-scale assessments, since these are strongly related to principles of psychometrics, while achievement tests prepared by teachers and applied in classrooms are more strongly linked to themes related to cognition, learning, and teaching.

Evaluation can overcome the conflict between technical knowledge and ethical values in a way that makes it possible to use the results to advance this knowledge, searching for integration between the development of professional competencies and the development of an ethical, engaged professional who is able to put these skills and competencies into action in his or her context.

Providing students with competencies needed to face the challenges of the contemporary world and to apply knowledge in a meaningful way, as opposed to memorizing and reproducing it, and providing the necessary knowledge to act in different contexts must be one of the main objectives of any educational institution. But, how is knowledge presented to students? How does the school evaluate if students have reached certain objectives? When considering the question of values related to evaluation, it is necessary to keep in mind that evaluation is not neutral. Evaluation deals with values that are not necessarily explicit.

Dias Sobrinho (2002) has addressed the question of ethics and business in terms of educational evaluation and values, discussing the radical changes that they have gone through in this time of globalization, and the excessive emphasis on economic, utilitarian, practical, and quantified aspects that dominate and control the main areas of life and shape individual professional formation. The author claims that "before, values such as good, beauty, and truth were central, and those values refer to the very essence of being, to other people, to knowledge and aesthetics. Now, however, the ideological domination of market interests confer primacy largely on competence, efficiency, and utility, that is, to utilitarian and practical values more close to 'having' than to 'being.' Such pragmatic and economic values now dominate the main aspects of life" (p. 140).

Education and the evaluation of its different components (policy makers, schools, programs, student performance, administrators, teachers, staff) are inserted in these polarities and strongly suffer their interference. The very definition of evaluation shows these divergences, and evaluation is often mistaken for only one of its core aspects.

Stufflebeam and Shinkfield (2007) have suggested that evaluation, in a broader sense, "is a systematic assessment of worth or merit of an object." According to these authors, the Joint Commission on Standards stated this definition for educational evaluation at a time when programs were the main focus of evaluation. Bonniol and Vial (2001) present the evolution of the evaluative process and point out that, etymologically, evaluation is a reflection over the relation of values. The authors go on to stress that this is a neutral definition, because specifying the type of relations, such as attributing values or formulating a judgment would mean using a model. They also present models of evaluation as a form of measurement, and others as a form of management, allowing for possible integration between them.

Evaluation has a broad meaning, and includes the idea of judgment of merit and values. Though nontechnical dictionaries often present evaluation as a close synonym to assessment, here we understand *assessment* as a general term that embraces all methods used to judge the performance of an individual, group, or organization. In this sense, assessment includes assessment of student learning, assessment of teaching, and self-assessment (López-Segrera & López, 2007). After 1970, words such as *abilities, competencies,* and later *globalization* became increasingly part of the vocabulary of education.

Most countries seek to compare tests related to verbal and mathematical knowledge, applied mostly in elementary and high school, and other more specific tests that involve cognitive abilities and professional competencies, more commonly used in the assessment of higher education, such as colleges and universities, or applied at the end of undergraduate courses.

The evaluation of students' academic progress is important and should be considered a part of public policy. However, it is important to establish the limits and the actual reach of this kind of assessment, since assessments differ considerably in conception, exam characteristics, manner of administration, and use of results (e.g., whether it will be used as a grade for students).

Educational evaluation encompasses all stages of educational life. In the last few decades, it has become common to emphasize the necessity of educational continuity and its evaluation, making it strongly linked to the world of labor. Today, different types of evaluation are undertaken with different objectives, such as evaluation of student performance by teachers and comparison between the performance of different institutions, groups of institutions, regions, countries, and so forth.

With the advance of globalization and the growth of immigration, particularly in European countries, the need for comparing educational results has been stressed in a way that allows increasing mobility (which is a component of internationalization) of students and professionals of different areas. Although some consider globalization to be the extension of a process that began many centuries ago, only very recently has this issue acquired a strong connotation, being present in many different areas, such as economics, education, sociology, and psychology.

Globalization refers to "a number of changes in the world economy, such as the increased international mobility of capital and the growing incidence of mergers and acquisitions and of strategic alliances [of companies]" (Ruigrok & van Tulder, 1995). These authors stress that one of the first people to use the term *globalization* was Theodore Levitt, a professor at Harvard Business School, in 1983. Since then, the term has become widely used and has evolved into different interpretations and a more complex meaning.

Especially in regard to evaluation, globalization takes on crucial importance when the results of international tests that compare the performance of students from different countries are analyzed and rankings are presented to the public. One example of this practice is the *Program for International Student Assessment (PISA)*. Tests such as this one are forms of assessment of abilities and competencies in different countries, with the objective of establishing comparative indicators of different educational systems.

Regarding the implications and contradictions of globalization in reference to education, and more specifically to universities, Dias Sobrinho (2005, p. 168) has noted that "globalization invades all corners of the world, from microdimensions of everyday life to large multicultural manifestations in all societies; it influences new social configurations, alters old notions of time and space in the field of communications, expands information structures, increases mobility, establishes new profiles in the world of labor, drives the exponential accumulation of knowledge, generates changes in science and technology, produces the decline of certainties, increases the complexity of human relations and in life in general."

This author also points out that globalization is a complex phenomenon tied to multiple references, and does not apply only to the increasing internalization of traditional knowledge and competencies, but brings up distinct conceptions of education, as well as differing perceptions of society and of concepts such as abilities, competencies, and professional profile demands, to the center of the debate. Business connections are a crucial characteristic of globalization that implies connection, through homogenization, of the necessary competencies to act in these contexts. A result of this is the necessity of large-scale exams applied in different countries with the support of administrative entities that guarantee and assure that the minimal competencies necessary to act in the global business world are reached.

It must be stressed that the term *competency* is not applied exclusively to higher education, but to all levels and different stages of academic life. Particularly in that which refers to professional formation, higher education institutions have adopted the concept of competency to refer to the profile of the professionals they form. Higher education's pedagogical-political project must establish the desired professional profile of graduate students based on the potential of incoming students and on the development of academic abilities, seeking to reach the professional competencies that are necessary for professional exercise in a career (Limana & Brito, 2005).

This implies that it is necessary to develop individual skills in order to achieve the desired set of professional competencies, capacitating students to reach, each in his or her own way, the maximum performance capacity and domain knowledge of the area in which they are inserted. The global economy demands increasingly complex competencies, and this reflects on the educational context, which has adopted as one of its goals endowing students with professional competencies, expressed by actions that might be available in different contexts.

Currently, higher education degrees at the undergraduate or graduate level cannot be considered the final goalposts of academic learning. With the constant advances in science, individuals need to be prepared for constant professional, as well as personal, development, seeking constant improvement. Continuous education programs are present in most countries and are generally subsidized by higher education institutions, which have the project and social mission to supply and improve continuous education programs. Thus, apart from the necessity of elaborating tests to be applied in different countries, they also need to be adequate to different stages of academic life.

Regardless of the level of education of the context in which individuals are immersed, they are submitted to different types of evaluation. While this has served as a form of disseminating and broadening evaluative culture, it has, on the other hand, served to increase the difference between those who have the means to acquire a good education and those who do not. Globalization and subsequent student mobility also bring the necessity of comparing education in different countries. Several programs such as the Global University Network (GUNI) have tried to compare different regions and to promote cooperation between developed and developing countries, seeking to construct social equality to eradicate the excluding effects of globalization and obtain lifelong quality education for all. Together with the advantages that are presented with globalization, a series of disadvantages arise, social exclusion possibly being the most serious of them all.

THE DEVELOPMENT OF ASSESSMENTS

Although only in the last century has there been an increase in the literature about evaluation and the development of psychological tests and school examinations, these evaluation tools have been in existence for quite some time, as several authors have pointed out (Madaus & Kellaghan, 1993; Urbina, 2004; Wilbrink, 1997).

Madaus and Kellaghan (1993) summarized the use of testing through history, showing that in the year 210 B.C. the first known example of the use of testing as an administrative mechanism to implement, drive, and monitor public policy was implemented in China. According to the authors, Chinese ideas about testing influenced Europe in the 16th century, when a standardized written examination was first used as a complement to oral examination. But only in the middle of the 18th century did rankings and quantified scores begin to be applied. After their implementation, there were changes in the types of exams that began to be applied in class, replacing the commonly used qualitative forms of examination. These authors pointed out that, besides these quantitative aspects, the bureaucratic potential of these tests was also perceived as a way to answer the demands of different schools and organizations, allowing them to accumulate the marks of the same student or different groups, because they could be organized, ranked, classified, averaged, and normed (Madaus & Kellaghan, 1993, pp. 7–8).

Since the establishment of these marks and rankings, there has been a refining of the conception and format of educational tests. Later, after the 1960s, policy makers started to adopt them and more and more connected them to economic interests, with the objective of answering to political and administrative goals. The construction of increasingly refined tests and their large-scale application at different levels of schooling, as well as the obtaining of indicators that allow performance comparison in different countries, has since become the main concern of many policy makers.

Because of this, there has been an improvement in static tests, which have become more sophisticated, also due to the availability and evolution of technological resources, particularly in developed countries. Besides, the emphasis on studies concerning academic abilities and professional competencies has been expanded in the last few years. Although these are concepts used commonly in different areas, their use is often closer to the commonsense definition than to an empirically built construct. Many definitions of abilities and competencies are presented, but it is important to stress a few points and concepts that are essential to the comprehension of what is measurable in large-scale national exams.

ABILITY AND COMPETENCE

Concerning the concept of *ability*, there is little disagreement about what this construct is, but it is important to establish two meanings to skill: *trace ability* and *academic ability*. *Trace ability* relates to the potential that individuals dispose of and is closer to the definition offered by Krutetskii (1976), based on a longitudinal study undertaken with the objective to verify the components of mathematical ability. According to this author, "ability is an individual psychological characteristic, primarily mental, that responds to the requirements of a given activity and, given equal conditions, influences the success in the creative domain of this activity—in particular a relatively fast, easy, and full mastery of knowledge, skills, and habits related to a given activity" (pp. 74–75).

The conventional view of abilities is that they "represent relatively stable attributes of individuals and are developed through the interaction between heredity and environment," measurable by intelligence tests and factorial analysis (Sternberg & Grigorenko, 2002, p. 3).

However, it is possible to say that these attributes, when already developed and established as academic abilities, may be accessed through conventional educational evaluations. In this sense, ability is more closely related to capacities, and the construction of an assessment would emphasize goals such as the verification of reading capacities and text interpretation that allow students to understand what is being asked in a certain question; the capacity to critically analyze given information; the drawing of conclusions through induction and/or deduction; the establishment of relations, comparisons, and contrasts in different situations; the detection of contradictions; the making of choices involving values and evaluating consequences; the questioning of reality; and the capacity of coherent use of consistent arguments in open-ended questions.

Such capacities are developed throughout an individual's life, and school is a very influential factor in this process. From the beginning of schooling, children foster these capacities, making them fit their own needs and those of the context in which they are inserted, transforming them into competencies that enable them to act in an ever-changing world. Thus, it is not only capability or initial potential that is being treated, but the development and enhancement of such primary capacities, and given the schools' influence over them, it is more fitting to call them *academic abilities,* since they refer more closely to the cognitive development and the acquisition of expertise in order to act in specific situations.

Competency, on the other hand, is more closely related to the mastery of specific areas, and an exam could be constructed in a way to lead students to show competency in projecting intervention actions, proposing solutions to problems, constructing integrating perspectives, elaborating syntheses, and administrating conflicts. Goals such as these are linked to competencies related to higher education, but competencies are developed throughout life.

Concerning the assessment of abilities and competencies related to exams, it is more suitable to refer to academic abilities, in a sense of developed capacities, and professional competencies, in a sense of expertise development. Sternberg, Torff, and Grigorenko (1998) and Sternberg (1999) defined expertise development, or competency, as a continuous process of acquisition and consolidation of a set of components required for a high level of expertise in one or more areas related or not to the educational context.

Limana and Brito (2005) defined competency as a reflexive and efficient action, in a certain type of situation, supported by an articulate and dynamic set of knowledge, abilities, and attitudes. Competency is associated with the effective execution of an action and refers to the capacity of fulfilling a certain task.

Competency can also be understood as the expected level for the accomplishment of a task (Munhoz, 2004). This idea, developed by cognitive research on learning, indicates that development of a certain competency is linked to three essential aspects: (1) individuals must have the ability (or potential) to perform the activity, (2) individuals must have adequate learning experiences, and (3) individuals must dedicate considerable effort to tasks required for the acquisition of competencies.

When referring to competencies developed in higher education institutions, which are essentially professional competencies, it is necessary to establish a set of criteria relative to the desired graduate student profile, as described by pedagogical projects. Internally, each institution possesses criteria that form the basis for judging competencies, which, in turn, are analyzed through individual or collective student academic performance. Competencies at a higher education level are related to students' required performances and actions, and should guarantee that the professionals have a basic mastery of knowledge and the capacity to use it in different contexts that demand investigation, analysis, evaluation, prevention, and action in defined situations and in the promotion of well-being.

The development of professional competency transcends the mere accumulation of knowledge, memorization of facts, and definition of concepts. It is much more important than the knowledge accumulated throughout a course. Professional competency involves the capability to mobilize, articulate, and put into action knowledge, abilities, attitudes, and values necessary for the efficient and effective performance of activities required by the nature of work and technological development. Competency is associated with the effective accomplishment of an action and is related to the capacity to successfully achieve a given task.

ADAPTING ASSESSMENT DEVICES TO DIFFERENT CULTURES

Teaching and, consequently, evaluation need to be updated in a way so that they can answer to the new demands of the global world. The development of competencies is not restricted exclusively to academic activities. Individuals develop abilities and acquire competencies regardless of scholarship, according to the context in which they are inserted (Acioly & Schiliemann, 1987; Brito, 2000; Carraher, Carraher, & Schliemann, 1995; Grigorenko & O'Keefe, 2004; Scandiuzzi, 1996). The biggest dilemma is that school works in a dynamic that is sometimes quite detached from students' real life, and assessments and large-scale examination are planned, elaborated, and applied mostly to verify if students are acquiring academic abilities (which, in the educational sense, almost always means cognitive abilities) and competencies that are planned for them by policy makers, not taking into consideration their real core of abilities and competencies.

To illustrate this point, we can analyze the differences between effective competencies and what is expected from the student in a large-scale examination. Scandiuzzi (1996) described the way *apás* (a type of sieve with no holes, used as lids or wall decoration by the native *kayabi*) are handcrafted and then painted. The *apás* are built by apprentices following progressive levels of difficulty, showing the historical sequence of their people. Only men can learn the art of making these *apás*. These men are considered individuals of great wisdom and are the ones who act as teachers in the oral transmission of this knowledge. When teaching the young, the elder retells the history of their people, using each of the 14 types of figures to show a greater degree of complexity, symmetry, and elaboration.

How to evaluate this cultural richness in a test that, although it attempts to capture the essential elements of that which the student is capable of doing with what the school has given him, presents questions with four or five alternatives from which he must choose the one that seems the most correct? Since national exams are applied to all the students chosen, these competencies can be incorporated into the tests not only of indigenous professors, but of any professor in the area, leading them to broaden the horizons of knowledge and bringing them closer to diversity in education.

From the beginning of schooling, the acquisition and mastery of basic academic competencies is demanded. These competencies are analyzed by national and international large-scale exams that seek to measure and compare the performance of students, assessing their mathematical and reading literacy, relating this to variables such as social and economic level, possession of goods, household characteristics, media access, and so forth.

Different exams are also applied to older students, and since the 1990s there has been a significant increase of these large-scale exams to high school students. These exams present differences and specificities according to each country, but are generally used to regulate the educational system and to allow access to higher education. Policy makers have been seeking to match policies especially to the economic factor, controlling previously defined goals, emphasizing results in a way that befits the global system.

Brito et al. (2000) pointed out that, in the last decades of the 20th century, these exams have gained strength around the world, and many sophisticated standardized evaluation methods have been developed. In many countries, different examinations were developed in order to manage access to universities and to verify the efficacy of high school education. These authors have researched existing exams for high school level students and have verified that France is potentially the pioneer in this new concept, having introduced the *baccalauréat* in 1808 into the regular educational system. In the United States, the *Scholastic Aptitude Test* (SAT) was first applied in 1926, undergoing several modifications over time. However, it is still used by almost all universities, especially those with more competitive admissions. Sweden instituted the *SweSAT* in the 1970s with the objective of allowing adults lacking high school education admission to higher education. In Portugal, selection to higher education institutions is made at the end of high school, through the *provas globais finais*. In Israel, the *Bagrut Certificate* is used to allow admission to universities through a national exam. In Brazil there is a somewhat similar examination for high school students called the National Examination of High School (in Portuguese, *Exame Nacional do Ensino Médio*—ENEM).

Exams directed to high school students and applied in different countries with different concepts and forms actually share a common goal, which is to manage access to higher education and, in a way, establish a minimum standard of competencies that students must achieve in order to be considered ready for a higher level of education. Despite the fact that most of these exams claim to be able to deal with abilities and competencies, they are generally tied to disciplinary high school concepts and seek to answer to the demands of the professional world, which are strongly linked to higher education and technological development, often leaving aside desirable social values.

Teachers should not see themselves as mere diffusers of knowledge, dealing only with declarative knowledge, concepts, and facts. They must act in a way that motivates students to seek knowledge and to direct it toward building a better society. Their main concern should be forming conscientious citizens who are able to act in the global world. This teaching must be directed toward current needs, based on past experiences and concerned with the future. It is no longer about teaching the "whats" and the "hows," but how to ethically and competently apply that which is learned. In this teaching proposal, assessment cannot be restricted to the knowledge of facts and concepts and the use of rules and principles. The ideal would be that students learn how to work with these elements in a way that would expand the horizon of knowledge. Furthermore, all evaluation must be guided by the need to assess the capacities subjacent to the more obvious facts and concepts.

In this context, the role of student performance evaluation changes, because it is no longer about the evaluation "of learning," but about the evaluation "to learn," thus becoming a component of the process of development of all students toward their professional future.

In this sense, all curriculums must be strongly linked to the local social context, since formative models for all professionals must be conceived as an important element of the broader context. When competencies involved in different course proposals are analyzed, it can be verified that certain academic competencies are common to all courses in a specific area. For instance, there are certain broader competencies that are necessary for engineers, followed by specific ones (such as chemical engineering, mechanical engineering, etc.), according to the emphasis given by each institution on certain areas of specialization with the objective of allowing continuous professional development.

However, the broader sense of the role of education must not be lost, although education and evaluation are not terms with equal meanings to all segments of society. To allow abilities and competencies to become the only core elements of a curriculum is to replace emphasis on the acquisition of finished, complete knowledge for another kind of knowledge that merely presents this same process in a different way, one that emphasizes the acquisition of competencies but that continues dealing with accumulated knowledge, not allowing students to produce new ideas and seek true emancipation.

Dias Sobrinho (2002), discussing relativity of values and the different values related to "being" and "having" has pointed out that knowledge, "now dressed in a suit of competencies and abilities adequate to the imperative of the marketplace, is no longer a reference for truth as a fundamental value and has lost its central sense of construction and emancipation of mankind and humanity. Now, being the main basis for generating resources, it no longer has value for the sake of truth, but for what it represents in terms of utility for economic performance" (p. 140). This author also argues that curriculum is now being conceived according to these demands and that education, and consequently curriculum, is now led by an emphasis on the development of professional competencies, leaving aside greater humanistic goals.

In this sense, evaluation would be a form of control over what is learned. Only abilities and competencies with immediate utility would be learned and evaluated, which means education ends up losing its broader character. Dias Sobrinho (2002) also stresses that the idea of placing individual efficiency, technical competency, and entrepreneurial spirit on one side and solidarity, sociability, and cooperative spirit on another as strictly antagonistic elements is false, for they can work together, allowing the integration and complexity necessary to forming individuals.

CLASSROOM ASSESSMENT AND LARGE-SCALE ASSESSMENT

The result of students' academic performance evaluation must be seen from two different possibilities: the meaning and use of evaluation as understood by teachers (results can be discussed with students in a way that they may perceive possibilities for improvement, and can be shared with their families and other teachers and used for course adjustments by the teachers); and the view of policy makers and their use of the results (shared among other institutions). Furthermore, the effect of evaluation in each of these situations must be also considered.

Classroom assessment is generally prepared by teachers based on themes related to the course and considered to be necessary to be learned and incorporated into the cognitive structure of students. These tests and/or exams are conceived and analyzed as a reference for teachers, parents, and school administrators.

Assessment in the classroom allows teachers to evaluate the learning process and discuss it with the students, propose new ideas, search for new solutions, and so forth. They can change ideas and elaborate alternative situations that lead students to make changes in the course of their activities and to share expectations with their families, which is an important factor in the development of their abilities and in overcoming obstacles.

Achievement test construction requires certain types of knowledge from teachers so that the instrument can adequately reach its intended goals. Classroom tests may present different forms and types of questions, such as paper and pencil or case studies, and may or may not include problem solving that allows students to apply what they have learned. Complementarily, teachers may require students to read and write about a text, formulate questions during lessons, assign homework, or observe student participation in the classroom, among others (Anastasi & Urbina, 2000).

The outcomes of multiple classroom assessments provide information to teachers, students, parents, and school staff (principal, educational adviser, psychologist, etc.), and teachers can use different outcomes to improve their teaching methods and to promote changes in their method of evaluating students' learning and performance. On the other hand, in large-scale evaluation these results are used in different decisions than the ones used by teachers, because it serves for policy makers to inform the public about how students are performing, allows ranking for establishing a comparison between schools, states, and countries, thus enabling a more efficient allocation of resources.

Differently from large-scale evaluation, classroom evaluations are more diverse and allow teachers to follow individual student progress. Though their focus is also on the product, it is possible to evaluate the process, which is actually what most teachers seek to assess, although many of them are unsure of how to achieve this.

In research in which, among other aspects, the meaning of evaluation for higher education level teachers and students was analyzed, Brito (1984) verified that this concern about students' learning process is present in most teachers, as stated in the following text, extracted from the protocol of a biology teacher with more than 15 years of university teaching experience:

> evaluation is the "assimilation" or not of that which has been taught. This "assimilation" does not mean a mere return by students of the subject matter taught in class, but the acknowledgement that mental operations (analysis, synthesis, comparisons, classification, establishing relations, rankings, conceptualizations, induction, deduction, etc.) are used by students. (p. 112)

On the other hand, to students, evaluation may mean simply a grade or mark, and these concepts are often taken as synonyms. This grade or mark is strongly linked to the punitive power exercised by teachers.

Some large-scale exams are not linked to a mark, which means that the result obtained does not necessarily imply that students can move on to the next grade, or that it has any influence whatsoever on students' activities. Because it is unrelated to any effect on students' performance, the students do not feel committed to doing well in the exam in a way that shows the actual effect that school is having on their performance and that which needs to be improved, whether they are achieving the proposed learning goals and, particularly in higher education, whether they are acquiring the competencies necessary for future professional action.

In addition, since many large-scale examinations are made through sampling and with no concrete incentive to participate, students often feel unmotivated to take the tests, negatively influencing their performance. However, when large-scale examinations are done as a means of access to higher education, for example, they acquire larger importance and students are more driven to try to perform better.

Another point to consider is the different views that teachers and policy makers have about assessment. Centralized assessment is related to policy and policy makers, while classroom assessments are more related to teaching and instruction.

The differences between classroom and large-scale examinations include underlying assumptions, uses, and activities, as well as what is assessed, how it is assessed, and the manner of treating and reporting the results. The main differences are in conception, since large-scale assessment seeks to verify and compare marks obtained by students from different schools and the focus lies on obtaining and showing high marks, which are seen as a high indicator of productivity. Considering the differences between the two examinations, Stiggins (1993) points out that large-scale assessment is more related to psychometrics, while classroom assessment is related to learning and teaching.

Educational large-scale evaluation is applied to a vast number of students from the same school, county, state, or country and is applied to students at different educational levels. It differs from classroom assessment in terms of conception, format, application, and use of results. It generally consists of paper-and-pencil or computer-based tests and may contain objective and/or open-ended questions with different levels of difficulty and complexity. This type of evaluation is often accompanied by a socioeconomic questionnaire containing questions about the student, teachers, teaching methods generally employed, how the students' achievement is evaluated, and so forth. Sometimes questionnaires are also submitted to family members or school administrators, course coordinators, or other educational authorities that can provide more information about legal aspects related to the school, college, or university.

A crucial aspect of such differences seems to reside in the different paths assumed by each of these forms of evaluation. A good example is the emphasis recently given by mathematical education to classroom problem solving. Teachers have been systematically trained to deal with students in a way that they can perceive the representations used by students and lead them to develop flexibility in their thinking, which is one of the components of mathematical ability. In the tests, students are compelled to show how they are reasoning about the task and how they can apply the content learned. How can these aspects be perceived in a multiple-choice question that is not the same for all students?

Another concern is that neither policy makers nor administrators have the necessary preparation to use evaluative procedures in the educational context. On the other hand, in-service and pre-service teachers do not receive any training in the construction and elaboration of tests that are really effective as resources of learning. Few make use of research that shows that it is possible to assess, in a single achievement test, both declarative and procedural knowledge.

Methods of construction and application of tests and exams are also different, since in the case of large-scale exams, applications are usually annual or biennial, generally involving samples of students and dealing only with more general aspects of knowledge that is common to all students, thus being a bit restricted. On the other hand, in the classroom, teachers utilize several forms of evaluation at different moments; they can elaborate comprehensive questions and spend more time discussing the results with the students, improving the learning and teaching process.

The dialog between these two types of exams is something to be considered. How can a teacher use the results of large-scale exams inside the classroom? These exams signal the desired orientation to be given to education. If it proposes to be increasingly inclusive and participative, schools must be provided with resources that allow them to form conscientious and competent citizens, individuals that are able to formulate adequate analyses about the context in which they live, and to seek solutions to particular problems. However, if teachers intend to form this type of citizen, they cannot dedicate their time solely to the training of their students to adequately answer questions proposed by large-scale examinations.

Classroom assessment and large-scale assessment could work together conceptually and operationally, and the two systems may be combined into an integrated set. In the construction of an integrated system, it will be necessary to allocate time and effort to change attitudes and conceptions of policy makers as well as classroom teachers. In this sense, large-scale examinations will be a resource for teachers in the classroom; as part of the process, policy makers need to search for alternative means of making these tests as close to the actual classroom settings as possible.

With globalization and the increasing appeal for internationalization and accreditation, these exams have become widespread. The results of these exams are made available for research on the Web sites of their respective funding organizations, such as the United Nations Educational, Scientific and Cultural Organization (UNESCO, 2008) and the Organization for Economic Cooperation and Development (OECD, 2008).

LARGE-SCALE ASSESSMENT IN BRAZIL

When a large-scale exam is planned, all the population of students of that grade or level are taken into consideration. But how can one keep, within a single test, elements that show the fundamental differences between the participating groups? In a country of continental dimensions such as Brazil, there is an inherent difficulty in working this dimension in a measurement instrument applied every year or every other year.

In Brazil, until the 1980s, there were no profound studies regarding the theories of educational measures. The Bowles report, elaborated in 1963 for UNESCO (see Vianna, 1989), indicated that there was the intention, in Brazil, of adopting an aptitude exam, in the mold of the SAT, for admission to higher education. This exam would complement academic knowledge tests that were applied as forms of selection. However, since the construction and application of admission exams followed their own dynamics, no evaluation theories were developed on a large scale. Furthermore, there was very little interest, among researchers, in developing studies about educational measures.

With the linking of funding to performance on exams and the emergence of themes related to evaluation around 1990, papers on these exams started to appear without a solid background in the theory of measures and without making clear the theoretical origins of the models used. However, the exams were applied and, to the present date, the federal government is responsible for the following: (1) ENCEJA: *Exame Nacional de Certificação de Competências de Jovens e Adultos* (National Examination for Certification of Competencies of Youth and Adults), for individuals that did not have the opportunity of a regular basic education; (2) ENEM: *Exame Nacional do Ensino Médio* (National Examination of High School); (3) SAEB: *Sistema de Avaliação da Educação Básica* (Elementary Education Evaluation System); (4) *Prova Brasil:* Brazilian Examination; and in the elementary level (5) *Provinha Brasil* (Brazilian Test of Literacy in Language and Mathematics), to evaluate pupils in Grades 1 and 2, available on the Internet, making it possible for any school or teacher to download and apply to their students; and (6) ENADE: *Exame Nacional de Desempenho dos Estudantes* (National Examination of Students' Performance) for universities and colleges. Some of these exams and their results will be presented next.

The Numbers of Education in Brazil

To give an idea of the number of students involved in large-scale exams in Brazil, a few numbers comparing Brazil and Mercosul are presented. From the global indicators presented by *Mercado Comun del Sur* (Mercosul) in 2005 comes Table 14.1, which brings an approximate idea of the demographic and educational data of the countries involved.

Aside from many other indicators, this reference presents the sources of the data and the calculation methods used. The first line indicates the total population of each country, and the second, the percentage of that population living in urban areas. The total enrollment numbers indicate

Table 14.1

POPULATION AND ILLITERACY RATES IN MERCOSUR[a] (2005)

POPULATION	ARGENTINA	BOLIVIA	BRAZIL	CHILE	PARAGUAY	URUGUAY	VENEZUELA
				COUNTRY			
Total	38,592,150	9,427,219	184,388,620	16,267,278	5,898,650	3,305,723	26,577,423
Urban (%)	91.8	64.2	82.8	86.8	56.7	93.5	88.3
Illiteracy Rate (%)	2.6	13.0	11.1	3.4	5.1	2.2	5.0
Total Enrollment	12,166,833	3,090,031	58,514,435	4,625,110	1,898,517	905,101	11,604,503

[a]MERCOSUL = *Mercado Comum do Sul* (Southern Common Market).

From *Indicadores Estadísticos del sistema educativo del Mercosur* [Statistical Indicators of Mercosul's Educational System], by Mercado Común del Sur, 2005. Retrieved February 16, 2008, from http://www.mercosur.int/msweb/portal%20intermediario/es/index.htm

the number of students enrolled, starting from elementary school up to higher education.

Since 2007, Brazil's Census of Basic Education (*Censo da Educação Básica*) has changed its focus from the schools to the students and has started to work with more detailed information on the schools, each of their students and teachers, and the classes students were enrolled in. This allowed the Ministry of Education to refine the information, which, up to then, was sent in globally, covering the entire school. This caused duplication of information. The new information system, linked to the student, is done over the Internet and makes it possible to obtain information such as the student's full name, address, ethnic background, parents' names, date of birth, among others; it is also possible to watch his or her progress. When data are compared year by year, a drop in enrollment numbers can be seen, but that occurs because of the deletion of duplicated data, which was inflating the numbers. According to Ministério da Educação (2008), this will allow better distribution of resources.

The 2007 Census of Basic Education carried out in Brazil showed that 52,969,456 students were enrolled in elementary school, of which 46,610,710 were in public schools (24,516,221 of these in municipal schools) and 6,358,746 in private schools (see Table 14.2).

Of the 27 states of the federation, São Paulo showed the highest enrollment numbers, with more than 10 million students in elementary school (10,629,102 students), while Roraima, in the northern region,

Table 14.2

EVOLUTION OF ENROLLMENT, BY ADMINISTRATIVE DEPENDENCY, IN THE PAST 4 YEARS

ADMINISTRATIVE DEPENDENCY	YEAR			
	2004	2005	2006	2007
State	24,351,782	23,571,777	23,175,567	21,914,653
Municipal	24,949,623	25,286,425	25,243,156	24,516,221
Federal	178,380	182,499	177,121	179,836
Private	7,371,305	7,431,103	7,346,203	6,358,746
Total	56,851,090	56,471,804	55,942,047	52,969,456

From *Assessoria de Comunicação Social—ACS,* by Ministério da Educação, 2008. Retrieved June 18, 2008, from http://portal.mec.gov.br/arquivos/pdf/saeb_tabelas.pdf

Table 14.3

ENROLLMENT DISTRIBUTION IN THE DIFFERENT EDUCATIONAL LEVELS

EDUCATIONAL LEVEL	ENROLLMENTS (YEARS)				DIFFERENCE 2006–2007	VARIATION % 2006–2007
	2004	2005	2006	2007		
Kindergarten	6,903,763	7,205,039	7,016,095	6,494,878	–521,479	–7.43
Elementary School	34,012,434	33,534,700	33,282,663	32,102,787	–1,196,475	–3.59
High School	9,169,357	9,031,302	8,906,820	8,362,994	–546,156	–6.13
EJA[a]	5,718,061	5,615,426	5,616,291	4,983,060	–635,464	–11.31
Special Education	371,382	378,074	375,488	337,089	–38,786	–10.33
Professional Education	676,093	707,263	744,690	688,648	–56,042	–7.53
Total	56,861,090	56,471,804	55,942,047	52,969,456	–2,994,402	–5.35

[a]EJA = *Educação de Jovens e Adultos* (Youth and Adult Education).

From *Assessoria de Comunicação Social—ACS*, by Ministério da Educação, 2008. Retrieved June 20, 2008, from http://portal.mec.gov.br/arquivos/pdf/saeb_tabelas.pdf

shows only 136,148. When the Brazilian regions are put side by side for comparison, the southeastern region clearly has the highest number of enrollments (20,550,441 students) and the midwestern region has the lowest (3,675,676 students).

Student distribution over the years in the different levels of elementary school shows the variation suggested by the Ministry in the enrollment numbers, where, in the education of youth and adults, the variation is of –11.31% (see Table 14.3).

SAEB

SAEB was created in 1988 and first applied in 1990, being gradually enhanced in terms of data methodology, operation, and analysis. Beginning in 1995, in an attempt to enhance the comparability of the data, the exam began to be applied to students in the final grades of each cycle of elementary (4th and 8th grade) and on the third and last year of high school. The item response theory (IRT) and matrices sampling of items began to be utilized in the analysis. From limited sampling broadness, it went to full public and private application, and began including the end of high school. The number of assessed areas was also increased, for besides language and math for the elementary level, science was added; and for high school science it encompasses physics, chemistry, and biology (see Table 14.4).

Table 14.4

SAEB'S SAMPLING BROADNESS, 1995–2005

YEAR	NUMBER OF SCHOOLS	PUPILS			
		4TH ELEMENTARY GRADE	8TH ELEMENTARY GRADE	3RD HIGH SCHOOL	TOTAL
1995	2,839	30,749	39,482	26,432	96,663
1997	1,933	70,445	56,490	40,261	167,196
1999	6,798	107,657	89,671	82,436	279,764
2001	6,935	114,512	100,792	72,415	287,719
2003	5,598	92,198	73,917	52,406	218,521
2005	5,940	83,929	66,353	44,540	194,822

SAEB–2005. *Primeiros Resultados: Médias de desempenho do SAEB/2005 em perspectiva comparada*, 2007, p. 2. Retrieved February 20, 2008, from http://www.inep.gov.br/salas/download/prova_brasil/Resultados/Saeb_resultados95_05_UF.pdf

Since 1997, a national calibrated and validated database has been organized, and it is from this database that the questions presented to the students are chosen.

The exam is applied every 2 years, and the participants are selected through random, probabilistic sampling to represent the 27 states of the federation and the country as a whole. Alongside the exam, questionnaires are also applied. They aim to determine the infrastructure and contextualize the school (school questionnaire), the dean's profile and the mechanisms of school management (deans' questionnaire), the profile and procedures of teachers (teachers' questionnaire), and the social and cultural characteristics and habits of the students (students' questionnaire).

It is a pencil-and-paper type of exam, with multiple-choice questions, except for the language exam, which also contains open-ended questions. The exam is based on all the subject matter that the students are supposed to have acquired by the end of a determined cycle and is always elaborated based on the Brazilian National Curricular Standards, with grades ranging from zero to 500.

As seen in Figure 14.1 and Table 14.5, the average scores are very low, being that in the elementary 8th grade the average has decreased year after year, especially in math. After the presentation of the last SAEB exam, measures were taken to improve the performance of the schools, but it is always convenient to ask if the competencies and abilities the test proposes to measure are being measured effectively.

Figure 14.1 shows that there has been a slight improvement in language performance in the 4th grade, the 8th grade has stayed practically unaltered, and a decline occurs in high school performance.

Regarding math, as shown in Figure 14.2, in 2005, there was a decrease in the grades of the 8th grade and the 3rd grade of high school, while the

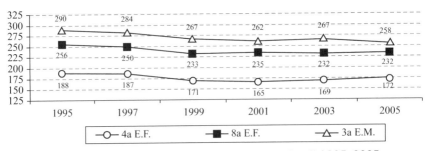

Figure 14.1 Portuguese-language proficiency averages in Brazil 1995–2005.
From *Assessoria de Comunicação Social—ACS*, by Ministério da Educação, 2008. Retrieved January 24, 2008, from http://portal.mec.gov.br/arquivos/pdf/saeb_tabelas.pdf

Table 14.5

SAEB PROFICIENCY, 1995–2005

GRADE	SUBJECT	1995	1997	1999	2001	2003	2005
4th Elementary[a]	Portuguese	188.3	186.5	170.7	165.1	169.4	172.3
	Mathematics	190.6	190.8	181.0	176.3	177.1	182.4
8th Elementary[b]	Portuguese	256.1	250.0	232.9	235.2	232.0	231.9
	Mathematics	253.2	250.0	246.4	243.4	245.0	239.5
3rd High[b]	Portuguese	290.0	283.9	266.6	262.3	266.7	257.6
	Mathematics	281.9	288.7	280.3	276.7	278.7	271.3

[a]Includes rural (in 1997 the northern region was not included, and in 1999 and 2001, only the states in the northeastern region plus Minas Gerais and Mato Grosso) and federal schools (only in 1995, 2003, and 2005).
[b]Does not include rural schools, but includes federal schools in 1995, 2003, and 2005. SAEB–2005. *Primeiros Resultados: Médias de desempenho do SAEB/2005 em perspectiva comparada*, 2007, p. 6. Retrieved February 20, 2008, from http://www.inep. gov.br/salas/download/prova_brasil/Resultados/Saeb_resultados95_05_UF.pdf

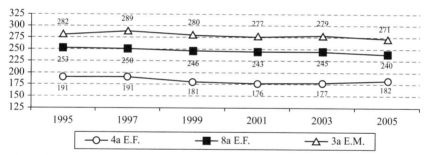

Figure 14.2 Averages of proficiency in mathematics in Brazil 1995–2005.
From *Assessoria de Comunicação Social—ACS*, by Ministério da Educação, 2008.
Retrieved February 8, 2008, from http://portal.mec.gov.br/arquivos/pdf/saeb_tabelas.pdf

average in mathematics does not reach 200 points in any year the exam was applied, which indicates that the goals regarding insertion of these students into the system are not being reached.

Just like any large-scale exam, SAEB has advantages and disadvantages, and emphasis is often placed on the exam as a highly efficient indicator of student performance, leaving aside the competencies that come from the social context and that are important in successful living. Many Brazilian children go to school for 4 hours a day, after which they are involved in various types of activities depending on the context in which they find themselves. For instance, children living in big seaside cities sell seafood, coconut water, and so forth, to help with the household budget.

In Brazil, many children better fit the category of *street children,* and according to the review of various definitions presented by Grigorenko and O'Keefe (2004), this category can be defined as "children who live with their families and may attend school but spend all or part of their time on the streets, trying to make money for themselves or their families" (p. 36). In the past 10–12 years, public policies aiming to keep children in schools have been enhanced, including giving financial support to low-income families. But since the majority of public schools in Brazil do not work with a full-time schedule, this allows children to divide their time between school and the streets.

Therefore, this exam is designed to assess competencies and academic abilities often already related to the next level in the educational system, seeking to register the existence of desired cognitive skills in the continuation of studies, leaving aside the competencies that are inherent to the context in which the children are inserted and in which they need to survive and establish connections. Since these exams also seek to predict success or failure, they can become the main element that will definitely deny some children the opportunity to fully develop their potential, according to their needs.

In 2005, Brazil's Ministry of Education established a new large-scale examination named *Prova Brasil.* It proposes to evaluate abilities and competencies in language (Portuguese) and mathematics. According to Instituto Nacional de Estudos e Pesquisas Educacionais Anísio Teixeira— INEP [National Institute of Studies and Educational Researches Anísio Teixeira] (2008), it has a broad effect, since each school and municipality presents its respective data. This examination includes all students from public schools in urban and rural areas.

Both assessments (SAEB and *Prova Brasil*) are paper-and-pencil tests developed with the main objective of evaluating abilities in the Portuguese language, with a focus on reading, and mathematics, with a focus on problem solving. Although the policy makers use the term *abilities,* in general what is actually assessed are academic abilities and capacities to read and solve problems. These exams are similar to the models applied in other countries, focusing on the product instead of the process, and most of them refer to abilities and competencies, and are more attached to the quantity of knowledge that is retained by students than meaningful learning that will help them in life beyond school.

In these examinations, students do not necessarily answer the same questions, and it becomes a problem when comparing results, because different tests are not comparable; this principle is valid for psychological tests and educational examinations. In addition, even with the use of socioeconomic questionnaires, it is impossible to measure all the complex components of school settings and to compare performance in culturally different groups of students.

These two large-scale examinations are linked to economic aspects and funding issues, since, according to INEP (2008), the average obtained by a school is used to calculate an indicator named Development of Basic Education Index—IDEB (*Índice de Desenvolvimento da Educação Básica*) that is central to the federal government's educational program. Thus, evaluation becomes the main concrete action toward adhering to the goals of the funding program.

Regarding state intervention, incentives, and educational performance, Morduchowicz (2002, p. 108) argues that these studies used the same tools that

> were once applied to the analysis of production functions, especially in the manufacturing industry. A production function is a mathematical relation that describes how resources may be transformed into goods. Applied to education, production functions encompass the analysis of the existing relation between school input and educational outcomes, generally measured by the results of standardized learning tests.

This condition is the same one underlying similar examinations around the world and establishes the main difference between classroom assessment, which is planned, developed, and applied by teachers to support learning, and large-scale assessment, which is planned and reported by policy makers.

ENEM

In Brazil, the *Exame Nacional do Ensino Médio* (ENEM) has been applied since 1997. It is a voluntary test and it has been improved in recent years. Many higher education institutions use the results of this exam, adding them to the results of their own selection tests, as a criterion for admission.

In 1997, 157,221 students enrolled for the test, of which 115,575 actually took it. In 2007, 14,529,686 students were enrolled and 10,646,597 took the test (ENEM, 2007, p. 6). As part of the educational policy of inclusion, this exam can be used for access to universities and colleges, as well as for the attribution of scholarship subsidies to students coming from public schools and from native communities. With the expansion of schools in these communities, there has been an increase of local students taking the ENEM (see Table 14.6).

According to an official publication, ENEM is applied to all public high schools in native communities in Brazil and

> In contrast to other schools dedicated to this stage of education, in which the exam is only undertaken where there are more than one thousand students, its application is a rule for native and *quilombola* institutions (quilombola are communities of Brazilian descendants of slaves). The increase in the number of native youths undertaking the test is strongly related to the increase of the number of higher education institutes dedicated to these communities. (ENEM, 2007, p. 31)

The results from ENEM are used for university and college admissions and, in some cases, the exam is the only requirement to admit a student. Grades are between 0–100 and, as seen in Table 14.7, the grades are very poor; the southeast and south regions presented better results, but in multiple-choice questions, the results indicate a high level of difficulty and show that students are concluding high school with

Table 14.6

NUMBER OF STUDENTS ENROLLED AND PARTICIPANTS IN ENEM 2006 BY REGION

REGION	ENROLLED[a]	PARTICIPANTS[b]
North	257,299	183,913
Northeast	939,700	683,274
Southeast	1,825,071	1,370,349
South	433,298	334,882
Midwest	286,778	210,583
Brazil	3,742,146	2,783,001

Source: MEC/INEP, 2008, p. 101. Retrieved January 10, 2008, from http://www.inep.gov.br/download/enem/Relatorio/ENEM_2006.pdf
[a]Of the 3,743,370 enrolled in ENEM 2006, 1,224 did not inform their region.
[b]Of the 2,784,192 participants, 1,197 did not inform their region.

Table 14.7

GRADE AVERAGE IN MULTIPLE-CHOICE AND OPEN-ENDED QUESTIONS (ENEM 2006) BY REGION

REGION	GRADE AVERAGE	
	MULTIPLE-CHOICE	OPEN-ENDED
North	32.17	49.05
Northeast	33.83	50.92
Southeast	38.85	52.44
South	38.73	55.29
Midwest	35.45	50.96
Brazil	36.90	52.08

Table 14.8

GRADE AVERAGE IN OPEN-ENDED QUESTIONS (ENEM 2006) BY TYPE OF SCHOOL AND BY REGION

REGION	TOTAL	ONLY IN PUBLIC	MOSTLY IN PUBLIC	ONLY IN PRIVATE	MOSTLY IN PRIVATE
North	49.05	48.65	49.54	58.00	54.33
Northeast	50.92	50.16	49.87	59.49	54.88
Southeast	52.44	51.52	51.27	59.88	55.36
South	**55.29**	54.72	54.86	**60.59**	56.67
Midwest	50.96	50.04	50.63	59.55	54.77
Brazil	52.08	51.23	51.16	59.77	55.27

Adapted from ENEM, 2006, p. 102. Retrieved Januray 20, 2008, from http://www.inep.gov.br/download/enem/Relatorio/ENEM_2006.pdf

very poor performance. This is an examination that students take when they are leaving high school, and there is no chance to use the results to improve student performance.

The type of school that the students attended is a noteworthy aspect. By 1970, public schools began to decrease in quality, which can be attributed to several factors, and noted as a crucial turning point in the Brazilian educational system. Table 14.8 shows a recently confirmed

Table 14.9

GRADE AVERAGE IN MULTIPLE-CHOICE QUESTIONS (ENEM 2006) BY TYPE OF SCHOOL AND BY REGION

REGION	TOTAL	ONLY IN PUBLIC	MOSTLY IN PUBLIC	ONLY IN PRIVATE	MOSTLY IN PRIVATE
North	32.17	31.48	33.03	42.79	36.96
Northeast	33.83	32.39	33.50	46.44	37.94
Southeast	38.85	36.35	38.70	52.75	44.20
South	38.73	37.41	39.74	49.85	42.54
Midwest	35.45	33.97	35.96	48.47	39.67
Brazil	36.90	34.94	36.84	50.57	41.75

Adapted from ENEM: Relatório Pedagógico, 2006, http://www.inep.gov.br/download/enem/Relatorio/ENEM_2006.pdf. Retrieved February 16, 2008.

fact, that the results of private schools, both in open-ended as well as in multiple-choice questions, are well above the results of public schools. The results from ENEM 2007 indicate that among the best 20 schools, only 2 were public. Given that the scores are less than 60 on average, what does this mean in terms of competencies? Besides the fact that students are only being prepared to be admitted to a university or college, high school seems to have a small effect on students' performance.

When the focus is on questions that include multiple-choice questions and deal with abilities and competencies in science and mathematics, the results are complicated further because the average grade in Brazil in 2006 was 36.90, and even in private schools, the results indicate that students are not developing competencies that allow them to obtain a satisfactory performance on the exam (see Table 14.9).

ENADE and Dynamic Evaluation

ENADE is a large-scale Brazilian examination, applied to a sample of undergraduate students when they are beginning and finishing university-level education, which has been undertaken annually since 2004. It represents an intermediate stage between the old *Exame Nacional de Cursos*—ENC (National Examination of Undergraduate Courses), and a new system for the future that is still in development. In the last few years, this examination has been improved, although it cannot yet be considered a finished, closed model of large-scale student performance evaluation.

ENADE verifies students' learning potential upon admission to higher education and later compares it to the results of a second test taken when the students are at the end of their undergraduate studies. It is thus considered to be a form of dynamic assessment that collects information on the progress of students' performance throughout their higher education; the core idea of the exam is the concept of value-added.

Different from most similar tests, ENADE is directed to the measurement of the process (students' progress), not the product (students' level upon completing higher education). This type of testing allows a more complete understanding of the student-environment-educational context, based on the idea of value-added.

Some researchers criticize exams such as ENADE for their alleged inability to assess a whole course through students' performance on the test. Many authors have shown that a test is only an indication of declarative knowledge memorized throughout the course. Like classroom assessments, there are well-elaborated and poorly elaborated tests, and these are suitable to rate specific matters, but they are limited and are not sufficient to tell us about all the complexity of a school system.

The test rates students' performance and shows if they have or have not presented some progress in terms of abilities (here understood as capacities). The objective of ENADE is to verify what the student is able to do with the knowledge acquired rather than "what" and "how much" he or she has learned. It is an examination whose main objective is to help universities and colleges better understand which improvements are possible for all students. It is planned and developed to help students and professors at the university level; it is an evaluation to improve learning and not about memorized facts and concepts learned.

Putting ENADE into practice is very complex because it is taken by students around the country at the same time; it is applied to a large array of courses encompassing all areas of knowledge. The students' questionnaire in its latest version (version 2007) was composed of 113 questions, previously sent to the selected students. Furthermore, the courses' coordinators receive another questionnaire with questions that are similar to those sent to students so the results can be compared.

The examination comprises 40 questions, divided as follows: 10 general formation questions common to all areas, and 30 specific component questions. The questions may be open-ended or multiple-choice, both in the common part and in the specific part. The questions are elaborated as multiple-choice, case studies, situations, and problematic alternatives, among others. In relation to the degree of difficulty, the questions should be distributed into questions of low difficulty, intermediate difficulty, and high difficulty.

Following current legislation, the test is composed of two parts: the first part is common to all areas and the second part is specific to each area. The first part considers the same set of questions for all courses that participate in the ENADE with the objective of rating the "acquisition of competencies, the development of abilities, and the knowledge considered essential in the formation of any higher education student, thus allowing comparability between courses from different institutions."

The common part of the test deals with tacit knowledge, which is the "hidden" basis that subsidizes intelligent action (Polanyi, 1962), aimed at the acquisition of practical ability related to the development of knowledge useful to reach objectives valued by the subject or by his or her culture, but whose transmission is not generally maintained by the environment. It deals with the knowledge the individual needs to be successful, but that is not taught and frequently not even verbalized (Sternberg, 1999; Sternberg, 2008; Sternberg & Grigorenko, 2002; Sternberg et al., 1998). In the second part, the 30 specific content questions aim to verify the student's mastery of the subject matter, rating the learning potential of the first-year students and the competencies the last-year students have developed along their trajectory in the higher learning institute.

These questions must take into consideration the specificities of each area and its modalities, both in the realm of knowledge and in the abilities expected of the professional, investigating what the student is able to perform based on the activities and knowledge acquired during the course; in other words, performed through the exploration of several levels of complexity.

The students' sample is selected from a list, provided by the higher education institutions, of all enrolled students that fulfill the required prerequisites for the test. The list is then sampled and the names of all selected students are passed on to their respective institutions.

When a given course presents a low number of students, all are included. Students not selected or out of the sample for any reason may participate in ENADE as well, but their results will not be accounted with the group. This means that the student receives the grade report but this grade is not part of the various analyses to which the results are submitted, thus avoiding the inclusion of students who did not participate in the sampling process. The main advantage of sampling is that it allows a higher number of students to be submitted to the test within a shorter period of time.

As basic criteria, students who have fulfilled 7% to 22% of the minimum course load of the course's curriculum until the initial registration date are considered first-year students, and those who have fulfilled at least 80% of the minimum course load of the curriculum are considered last-year students. The areas analyzed were health and agriculture in 2004, engineering and teacher preparation in 2005, technology and human sciences in 2006, and health and agriculture again in 2007, and so on.

Students considered first-year students in 2004 were last-year students in 2007, and part of them were subjects in 2004 and again in 2007. Thus, comparisons on the progress of the same student, as well as the group, can be established.

These results are made available to institutions and researchers, and each institution can analyze the performance of its students. Since the government provides only two exams (at the beginning and at the end of the undergraduate level), the institutions can provide similar examinations every year or semester, then compare results and improve issues that need to be perfected. Studies on ENADE in specific areas like medicine (Perin, 2007), computer engineering (Souza, 2007), mathematics (Lara, 2007), and teacher-training programs (Brito, 2007) are improving information about higher education in general and in particular institutions. The grades in general formation can be compared because beginners and graduates answer the same 10 questions.

Here are presented some results from 2004, 2005, 2006, and 2007 (2007 students were from the population that was starting higher education in 2004). The year 2008 is not available yet, but students were from the population that was starting higher education in 2005. Tables 14.10, 14.11, 14.12, and 14.13 show the average on the first part of the examination, that is, the part that considers the same set of questions for all students that participate in ENADE with the objective of rating the acquisition of competencies, the development of abilities, and the knowledge considered essential in the formation of any university student, thus allowing comparability between courses from different institutions. General Formation is the common part of the test that deals with knowledge that is subjacent to any action and acquisition of competencies related to the development of knowledge that is useful to reach objectives valued by the subject or by his or her culture, but whose transmission is not generally maintained by the environment. This type of knowledge is not part of a specific course but is necessary throughout life.

Table 14.10

GRADE AVERAGE IN GENERAL FORMATION BY REGION (ENADE 2004)

| | REGION | | | | | |
AREA	NORTH	NORTHEAST	SOUTHEAST	SOUTH	MIDWEST	TOTAL
Agronomy	33.6	32.8	38.0	38.8	33.8	36.3
Physical Education	30.6	30.6	31.3	32.7	26.7	31.2
Nursing	34.3	37.5	34.6	35.0	34.4	35.0
Pharmacy	33.6	41.5	37.8	38.4	38.1	38.1
Physiotherapy	39.2	41.0	39.5	42.3	38.7	40.1
Speech Therapy	38.5	37.6	42.2	40.9	35.0	40.2
Medicine	47.3	47.4	55.7	58.6	57.1	54.7
Veterinary Medicine	34.2	37.3	38.3	39.5	39.2	38.5
Nutrition	31.2	29.4	34.8	36.5	36.6	34.8
Dentistry	33.3	44.8	42.0	44.9	42.5	42.7
Social Service	22.0	21.3	26.9	28.2	31.7	25.9
Occupational Therapy	5.6	39.3	40.6	41.5	32.8	38.7
Zootechnology	37.3	37.3	42.0	43.6	35.4	39.7
Total	33.6	37.1	36.9	38.2	36.0	36.5

From INEP. Retrieved February 20, 2008, from http://www.inep.gov.br/superior/enade/2004/relatorios.htm

The results obtained in 2004 in the General Formation component are shown in Table 14.10, and the south region obtained the best results in 2004. Among all the areas, medicine was the one that always had the highest grade, independent of region. This is due to the fact that medicine has a high candidate/vacancy relation, leading to a more competitive admissions process and, therefore, a high level is demanded from the candidates.

In 2005, 525,685 students were examined and the grades are again very close and too low. The best result is engineering—Group V, but in general students did not present good grades and three of them (social sciences, teacher-training, and engineering—Group VIII) are under 50 (see Table 14.11).

It might be expected that, in 2006, when the areas examined were closer to the issues presented in the General Formation questions, students would have a better grade average, but in 2006, the grade average was again very poor (see Table 14.12).

Table 14.11

GRADE AVERAGE IN GENERAL FORMATION BY REGION (ENADE 2005)

AREA	NORTH	NORTHEAST	SOUTHEAST	SOUTH	MIDWEST	TOTAL
Architecture and Urbanism	48.1	52.7	49.6	51.4	54.2	50.9
Biology	58.4	56.9	60.6	57.4	55.5	58.7
Social Sciences	59.7	51.2	40.8	41.2	48.3	45.7
Computer	54.0	54.9	55.1	53.5	53.3	54.6
Engineering— Group I	52.3	54.7	54.8	54.3	55.9	54.7
Engineering— Group II	50.3	55.7	54.1	53.6	55.5	54.2
Engineering— Group III	34.4	56.3	57.6	56.6	46.2	56.5
Engineering— Group IV	63.2	57.3	62.7	57.9	59.8	60.1
Engineering— Group V	—	63.8	64.2	59.6	—	62.5
Engineering— Group VI	57.4	56.8	59.3	58.3	58.9	58.8
Engineering— Group VII	61.5	59.0	59.6	57.5	59.6	59.2
Engineering— Group VIII	51.0	39.8	54.3	50.9	41.5	48.1
Philosophy	38.1	50.8	55.7	57.6	53.2	54.4
Physics	50.2	52.7	59.9	49.4	49.2	54.2
Geography	53.3	56.8	61.9	58.9	62.4	59.6
History	54.9	53.7	53.9	52.9	50.6	53.4
Portuguese Language	53.3	55.0	58.6	56.9	54.6	56.9
Mathematics	54.3	53.8	54.4	53.1	53.7	54.0
Teacher Training	48.4	48.0	50.5	49.0	46.3	49.2
Chemistry	51.5	52.6	52.0	51.6	56.1	52.4
Total	52.1	53.1	55.0	53.6	52.1	54.0

Adapted from INEP. Retrieved February 10, 2008, from http://www.inep.gov.br/superior/enade/2005/relatorios.htm

Table 14.12

GRADE AVERAGE IN GENERAL FORMATION BY REGION (ENADE 2006)

| | REGION | | | | | |
AREA	NORTH	NORTHEAST	SOUTHEAST	SOUTH	MIDWEST	TOTAL
Business Administration	40.1	43.0	42.0	42.8	40.8	42.1
Archival Science	–	55.5	48.5	52.0	53.4	50.7
Library Science	36.2	49.2	49.9	41.1	48.5	47.4
Biomedicine	50.6	44.9	47.2	46.0	45.4	46.8
Accounting Science	42.6	43.7	44.6	44.4	43.5	44.1
Economic Sciences	43.0	45.2	46.1	44.8	46.4	45.4
Media	45.0	45.3	48.4	48.1	44.7	47.6
Design	46.9	47.5	48.3	47.8	49.3	48.1
Law	46.5	49.2	47.9	48.3	48.9	48.2
Teacher Preparation	44.1	43.5	47.4	47.5	45.2	46.2
Music	42.8	47.7	48.3	47.4	48.8	47.8
Psychology	40.7	46.9	44.7	46.1	48.4	45.4
Executive Secretariat	44.0	46.4	43.8	45.0	41.3	44.4
Theater	–	40.6	49.7	48.1	37.8	46.7
Tourism	40.3	50.0	50.5	50.6	48.5	49.7
Total	42.8	45.6	45.5	45.7	45.2	45.4

From INEP. Retrieved February 22, 2008, from http://www.inep.gov.br/superior/enade/2006/relatorios.htm

In 2007 some of the last-year students are those that were starting higher education in 2004. The 10 questios of the general formation test are not the same, but they were equivalent. Comparing the average in this part of the examination in 2004 and in 2007 it is possible to detect an increment (Table 14.13).

Table 14.13 shows the average on the first part of the examination comparing two groups of students when they were beginning the higher education (in 2004) and when they were graduating (in 2007). While

Table 14.13

GRADE AVERAGE BY AREA IN GENERAL FORMATION IN TWO SUCCESSIVE EXAMINATIONS

AREA	AGRONOMY	PHYSICAL EDUCATION	NURSERY	PHARMACY	PHYSIO-THERAPY	SPEECH THERAPY	MEDICINE	VETERINARY MEDICINE	NUTRITION	DENTISTRY	SOCIAL SERVICE	OCCUPATIONAL THERAPY	ZOO TECHNOLOGY
2004[a]	36.3	31.2	35.0	38.1	40.1	40.2	54.7	38.5	34.8	42.7	25.9	38.7	39.7
2007[b]	51.8	44.4	43.0	49.2	47.9	48.2	64.6	50.3	47.7	54.7	44.1	46.1	52.6
2004[c]	33.6	29.4	33.5	35.4	37.8	37.3	53.5	36.0	32.8	39.8	24.7	37.4	37.7
2007[d]	56.1	46.3	45.7	52.6	51.0	49.2	69.0	54.5	48.8	57.9	42.5	45.2	59.4

Adapted from INEP. Retrieved January 5, 2008, from http://www.inep.gov.br/superior/enade/relatorios.htm
[a]Grade average for first-year students and last-year students (ENADE 2004–General formation).
[b]Grade average for first-year students and last-year students (ENADE 2007–General formation).
[c]Grade average for students in the first year (ENADE 2004–General formation).
[d]Grade average for students in the last year (ENADE 2007–General formation).

the examination is held every 3 years and the questions are different, the issues are similar. In this way, it can provide some comparisons and see how students are progressing along the time spent in the university. Comparing the scores of students from each of the two tests, it can be verified that there was an increase in this first part about general formation.

In a dynamic evaluation perspective, subjects learn both during the interval between tests and in sucessive evaluations. The construction of the test is of fundamental importance in this model. If an item is answered incorrectly the school, administrators, teachers, and the students will have feedback, helping students to solve the item, control the learning process, and improve this content.

Dynamic evaluation is interested in how the knowledge is learned and how it is used. The primary interest is in the process because in a world in constant transformation, knowledge should be a useful tool for the student; he or she must become able to have a domain of the knowledge and transfer the learned information to new situations. The increase in grades from 2004 to 2007 may be attributed to several factors, among them the understanding and acceptanceof the test by universities, college administrators, and students.

It is possible to work with a conception of dynamic evaluation underlying a large-scale assessment in the same way as classroom assessment: it depends on the dialog between the people who build the tests in both contexts. If the large-scale examination and classroom assessment are planned to assess the potential of students and how they progress during their trajectory, how they acquire expertise and master knowledge, it will improve learning and help teaching.

When the same conception of dynamic evaluation underlies a system that includes large-scale and classroom assessment, new advantages will be brought to the system. In this sense, following the concept of dynamic evaluation, it is expected that changes will occur also in the format of the test and what is assessed, how it is assessed, and the use of the results; the emphasis is that results are meant more to be useful to schools than to build indicators.

Dynamic evaluation can be planned and applied in classrooms (Sternberg, 2008; Sternberg & Grigorenko, 2002, 2004), as well as in the broader context of schools and groups of schools. It can be adopted by elementary students and by higher education students alike. In the first case, classrooms, it refers more closely to the work of teachers and is linked to evaluation as a process.

In the second case, it is related to the broader context, for instance, the progress of students through their academic lives, and, in this sense, assessment would offer some indicators of the "school effect" on the students' performance. There are certain longitudinal evaluations (tracking the same students through their whole process of education) and transversal evaluations that allow comparison of performances of different students at the same moment.

REFERENCES

Acioly, N. M., & Schliemann, A. L. (1987). Escolarização e conhecimento de matemática desenvolvido no contexto do jogo do bicho [Schooling and mathematical knowledge developed in the context of a betting game]. *Cadernos de Pesquisa, 61*, 42–57.

Anastasi, A., & Urbina, S. (2000). *Testagem Psicológica* [Psychological testing]. (7th ed.). Porto Alegre, RS: Artmed Editora.

Besalú, X. (2002). *Diversidad cultural y educación* [Cultural diversity and education]. Madrid: Editorial Síntesis.

Bonniol, J. J., & Vial, M. (2001). *Modelos de Avaliação: Textos fundamentais* [Evaluation models: Fundamental texts]. Porto Alegre, RS: Artmed Editora.

Brito, M. R. F. (1984). *Uma análise fenomenológica da avaliação* [A phenomenological analysis of evaluation]. Unpublished doctoral dissertation, Pontifícia Universidade Católica de São Paulo, São Paulo, Brasil.

Brito, M. R. F. (2000). Este problema é difícil porque não é de escola: A compreensão e a solução de problemas aritméticos verbais por crianças da escola fundamental [This problem is difficult because it's not a school problem: Comprehension and solution of verbal arithmetic problems by elementary schoolchildren]. *Temas em Psicologia, 8*(1), 93–109.

Brito, M. R. F. (2007). ENADE 2005: Perfil, desempenho e razão da opção dos estudantes pelas Licenciaturas [ENADE 2005: Profile, performance and reason for choice of the students going through teacher preparation]. *Revista Avaliação, 12*(3), 401–443.

Brito, M. R. F., Munhoz, A. M. H., Primi, R., Gonçalez, M. H., Rezi, V., Neves, L., et al. (2000). Exames Nacionais: Uma análise do ENEM aplicado à matemática [National Examinations: An analysis of ENEM applied to mathematics]. *Revista Avaliação, 5*(4), 45–53.

Carraher, T., Carraher, D., & Schliemann, A. L. (1995). *Na vida dez, na escola zero* [A+ in life, F at school]. (10th ed.). São Paulo: Cortez Editora. (Original work published 1988)

Dias Sobrinho, J. (2002). *Universidade e avaliação. Entre a ética e o mercado* [University and evaluation: Between ethics and the marketplace]. Florianópolis, SC: Editora Insular.

Dias Sobrinho, J. (2005). Educação Superior, globalização e democratização; Qual universidade? [Higher education, globalization and democratization: Which university?]. *Revista Brasileira de Educação, 28*, 164–173.

ENEM. (2007). *Revista do ENEM 2007*. Exame Nacional do Ensino Médio. Retrieved February 3, 2008, from http://www.enem.inep.gov.br/arquivos/enem_revista2007.pdf

Grigorenko, E. L., & O'Keefe, P. (2004). What do children do when they cannot go to school? In R. J. Sternberg & E. L. Grigorenko (Eds.), *Culture and competence: Contexts of life success* (pp. 23–54). Washington, DC: America Psychological Association.

Instituto Nacional de Estudos e Pesquisas Educacionais Anísio Teixeira (INEP). (2008). *Prova Brasil*. Retrieved February, 8, 2008, from http://provabrasil.inep.gov.br/

Krutetskii, V. A. (1976). *The psychology of mathematical abilities in schoolchildren*. Chicago: University of Chicago Press.

Lara, I. C. M. (2007). *Exames Nacionais e as verdades sobre a produção do professor de Matemática* [National Exams and the truth about the production of the mathematics teacher]. Unpublished doctoral dissertation, Universidade Federal do Rio Grande do Sul, Porto Alegre, Brasil.

Limana, A., & Brito, M. R. F. (2005). O modelo de avaliação dinâmica e o desenvolvimento de competências: Algumas considerações a respeito do ENADE [The model of dynamic evaluation and the development of competencies: Some considerations on ENADE]. *Revista Avaliação, 10*(2), 9–32.

López-Segrera, F., & López, Y. C. (2007). Glossary. In *Higher education in the world 2007*. GUNI Series (Vol. 2, pp. 403–407). New York: Palgrave Macmillan.

Madaus, G. F., & Kellaghan, T. (1993). Testing as a mechanism of public policy: A brief history and description. *Measurement and Evaluation in Counseling and Development, 26*(1), 6–10.

Mercado Común del Sur—MERCOSUR. (2005). *Indicadores Estadísticos del sistema educativo del Mercosur* [Statistical Indicators of Mercosul's educational system]. Retrieved February 16, 2008, from http://www.mercosur.int/msweb/portal%20intermediario/es/index.htm

Ministério da Educação. (2008). *Assessoria de Comunicação Social—ACS*. Retrieved January 15, 2008, from http://portal.mec.gov.br/arquivos/pdf/saeb_tabelas.pdf

Morduchowicz, A. (2002). Intervenção Estatal, Incentivos e Desempenho Educacional [State intervention, incentives and educational performance]. In A. Morduchowicz (Ed.), *Equidade e Financiamento da Educação na América Latina* [Equity and financing in education in Latin America] (pp. 101–134). Brasília: UNESCO.

Munhoz, M. A. (2004). *Uma análise multidimensional da relação entre a inteligência e o desempenho de estudantes universitários* [A multidimensional analysis of the relation between intelligence and university student performance]. Unpublished doctoral dissertation, Universidade Estadual de Campinas, Campinas, São Paulo, Brasil.

Organization for Economic Co-Operation and Development. (2008). Retrieved January 13, 2008, from http://www.oecd.org/home/

Perin, G. L. (2007). *Avaliação da Educação Superior: Uma realidade da educação médica* [Evaluation of higher education: A portrait of medical education]. Unpublished doctoral dissertation, Universidade Estadual de Campinas, Campinas, São Paulo, Brasil.

Polanyi, M. (1962). *Personal knowledge: Towards a post-critical philosophy*. Chicago: University of Chicago Press.

Ruigrok, W., & van Tulder, R. (1995). *The logic of international restructuring*. New York: Routledge.

Scandiuzzi, P. P. (1996). Apás Kayabi e simetria [Kayabi Apás and symmetry]. *Zetetiké, 4*(6), 107–122.

Souza, M. A. V. (2007). *Solução de problemas: Relações entre a habilidade matemática, representação mental, desempenho e raciocínio dedutivo* [Problem solving: Relations between mathematical ability, mental representation, performance and deductive reasoning]. Unpublished doctoral dissertation, Universidade Estadual de Campinas, Campinas, São Paulo, Brasil.

Sternberg, R. J. (1999). Intelligence as developing expertise. *Contemporary Educational Psychology, 24,* 359–375.

Sternberg, R. (2008). Assessing what matters. *Educational Leadership, 26*(4), 20–26.

Sternberg, R. J., & Grigorenko, E. L. (2002). *Dynamic testing. The nature and measurement of learning potential.* New York: Cambridge University Press.

Sternberg, R., & Grigorenko, E. (2004). Successful intelligence in the classroom. *Theory Into Practice, 43*(4), 274–280. Retrieved January 13, 2008, from http://ejs.ebsco.com/Article.asp?ContributionID=6627811

Sternberg, R. J., Torff, B., & Grigorenko, E. L. (1998). Teaching triarchically improves school achievement. *Journal of Educational Psychology, 90*(3), 374–384.

Stiggins, R. (1993). Two disciplines of educational assessment. *Measurement and Evaluation in Counseling and Development, 26*(1), 93–104.

Stufflebeam, D. L., & Shinkfield, A. J. (2007). *Evaluation: Theory, models and applications.* San Francisco: Jossey-Bass.

United Nations Educational, Scientific and Cultural Organization. (2008). *Assessoria de Comunicação Social.* Retrieved February 16, 2009, from http://www.brasilia.unesco.org/estatistica

Urbina, S. (2004). *Fundamentos da testagem Psicológica* [Foundations of psychological testing]. Porto Alegre: Artmed Editora SA.

Vianna, H. M. (1989). Introdução à avaliação educacional [Introduction to educational evaluation]. First Edition. São Paulo: IBRASA.

Wilbrink, B. (1997). *Assessment in historical perspective* (pp. 1–26). Retrieved February 3, 2008, from www.benwilbrink.nl/publicaties/97AssessmentStEE.htm

15

The Challenge of Measuring Abilities and Competencies in Hispanics/Latinos

ANTONIO E. PUENTE AND ANTONIO N. PUENTE

GENERAL CONSIDERATIONS

A fundamental assumption within psychology is that the information gathered as part of experimental and clinical studies is representative and, therefore, generalizable to the population psychology seeks to understand and serve. Alternatively, if the information is limited to a small or limited group of individuals, its applicability and universality is diminished. The end result is the potential development of individual conclusions and conceptual frameworks that are not universal. If a discipline is populated by a narrow slice of the larger constituency and if the tools used to decipher the riddles of mind are narrow in scope, the end result is error prone and, consequently, of limited utility and eventual acceptance.

This chapter addresses the challenge of understanding how to measure abilities and competencies in Hispanic/Latino populations, especially in the United States. The assumption is how the psychological community addresses the issue of assessment of Hispanics in the United States, then, serves as a template for how the assessment of Spanish-speakers worldwide is being attended to. Further, the underlying question is simple: Do we have the tools available and the conceptual framework used to understand people in general to apply with equal rigor and robustness to individuals that do not (at least at present) represent the majority group in numbers, in educational attainment, in socioeconomic status, and in positions of power? If the answer is yes, the current tools and frameworks are adequate, then the field should proceed to adapt as much as and as fast as possible to address issues of the measurement of the abilities and competencies of Spanish speakers. If, in contrast, those tools and frameworks do not match the clinical or scientific criteria, alternative approaches and paradigms should be considered.

The chapter seeks to understand one ethnic-minority group in the United States, Hispanic/Latinos, for two reasons. First, this is the fastest-growing and possibly the most disfranchised group in the United States today. Second, considering the differences in a variety of variables, ranging from language to social structure, the understanding of this group and their assessment may help establish a strong paradigm for the assessment of mental functions in other ethnic-minority groups both in the United States and abroad. This is critical in that regardless of settings, Russia, South Africa, or the United States, certain groups, because of socioeconomic, educational, and cultural factors, will by design be outside the majority group and, thus, potentially disenfranchised, marginalized, and misunderstood.

DEFINING HISPANIC AND LATINO/A DEMOGRAPHICS AND HETEROGENEITY

Defining Hispanic and Latino/a

More specific than culture is that of Hispanic/Latino/a culture. However, a definition of *Hispanic/Latino/a* must first be addressed. Even though there are reasons to consider Hispanic and Latino/a as distinct, for the purposes of this chapter, they will be considered as similar and the *Hispanic* term will be used instead of *Latino/a.* The word *Latino* has historically been attached to Mexico and has not always included other Central and South American as well as Caribbean countries.

According to Puente and Ardila (2000), *Hispanic* is usually defined in the United States as a person whose primary (or, in some cases, secondary) language is Spanish. The U.S. Census Bureau (2008) reports that about 66% of Hispanics living in the United States are of Mexican origin, 14.4% are of Central or South American origin, 10.6% are

Puerto Rican, 4.2% Cuban, and 7.4% are classified as being of "Other origin." Another way to define Hispanics is to determine the country of origin, within one, possibly two, generations. If the individual has roots to either Latin America and/or Spain, then that person could be considered Hispanic.

Then there is the question of Hispanic or Latino. *Hispanic* refers to the origin from the Iberian Peninsula, but those that have been "colonized." *Latino* refers more to those residing in "Latin America," which includes all countries south of the United States, including but not limited to Brazil. The confusion is furthered by the fact that in the United States, Latinos are often associated with those individuals of Mexican heritage, just like the group "La Raza" that purports to reflect all individuals of Hispanic heritage is heavily focused on issues associated with individuals with Mexican cultural ancestry. Thus, neither word nor phrase correctly captures what the underlying concept is about. This group does not consider itself "colonized" just as much as they do not consider themselves directly intertwined with Brazil. In summary, no clear resolution to this problem is evident and, hence, the words *Hispanic* and *Latino/a* (male/female) will be used interchangeably.

Demographics

As of 2001, the U.S. Census reports that Hispanics comprise about 12.5% of the entire U.S. population. This figure does not include the high number of Hispanics who are in the United States illegally. In California alone, Hispanics account for 32.4% of the population. The U.S. Census Bureau (2008) has recently reported that Hispanics have surpassed African Americans as the largest minority in the United States. Gonzalez (2008) has provided critical information regarding such demographics including educational, vocational, and economic parameters that make this minority group quite different than others residing in the United States. Further, by the year 2050, Hispanics will comprise 25% of the entire population in the United States (54 million). In fact, the nation's Hispanic population continues to grow at a much faster rate than the population as a whole. Additionally, the population of Hispanics (who may be of any race) reached 39.9 million on July 1, 2003, accounting for about one-half of the 9.4 million residents added to the nation's population since Census 2000. Its growth rate of 13.0% over the last 3 years was almost four times that of the total population (3.3%).

According to recently published findings by the Pew Hispanic Center (Gonzalez, 2008), a combination of trends is occurring; one trend is the rapidly growing and shifting demographics and the second is how poorly this group is fairing overall. There are more than 44,300,000 million Hispanics in the United States. From 2000 to 2005, there was a shift to the Hispanic population, where they used to comprise 12.5% of the population, now they made up 14.8% of the population. Of these, 8.9% represents native-born Hispanics whereas 5.9% represents foreign-born. The top three countries with the largest foreign-born population are, in order from highest to lowest, Uruguay, Venezuela, and Argentina. Approximately 40% of those of Mexican identity are foreign-born. From 2000 to 2005, there was a 21.5% increase in population growth with native-born outpacing foreign-born approximately two to one.

Mexico represents the largest group of individuals by an extremely wide margin with 63.9% of the population of Hispanics in the United States. Puerto Rico represents 9.1%, followed by Cuba at 3.5%. Spaniards, in contrast, represent less than 1% of the total Hispanic population in the Unites States. On average, the average age of males is 35 and for females, 37. Native-born Hispanics tend to be much younger, 16 for males and 18 for females, whereas foreign-born Hispanics are much older and more similar to the U.S. population at large, with males being on average 34 years of age and females, 36. Though traditionally located in states such as California, New Mexico, Texas, and New York, each of those states has experienced significant losses in their total Hispanic population.

In terms of education, foreign-born Hispanics are more poorly educated than native-born Hispanics who, in turn, are the worst educated group in the United States. This is particularly concerning in that many tests, except possibly excluding intellectual ones, are problematic in their sensitivity and specificity with individuals with limited or no education. In Ardila, Rosselli, and Puente (1994), the authors show how brain-damaged and educated individuals appear quite similar in neuropsychological tests to nonbrain-damaged but noneducated individuals.

Regardless of origin of birth, Hispanics are the most poorly educated ethnic-minority group in the United States. Further, they tend to speak English poorly, in general, as well as relative to other foreign-born ethnic groups. Hispanics who are foreign-born and less than 18 indicate that they speak English less than well 46% of the time compared to close to 73% for foreign-born Hispanics older than 18. Native-born individuals still do not fare particularly well with approximately 15% reporting not being able to speak English very well. Besides being poorly educated, Hispanics tend to earn less than all other ethnic-minority counterparts. Approximately 11% made more than $50,000 with native-born being twice as likely as foreign-born to reach this standard of living. This percentage was the lowest of any other group tabulated by Pew. In contrast, Hispanics similarly tend to have the largest percentage of poorly paid workers with 50% receiving less than $20,000 per annum in salary.

Within-Group Heterogeneity

Hispanics are a heterogeneous group. Each group (e.g., Cuban, Mexican, and Puerto Rican) has its own distinct cultural characteristics, heritage, and behavioral patterns. Further, Hispanics living in the United States and Canada are more likely to know some English and the American way of life. This could include an understanding of standardized testing, the importance of time and time-based productivity, and competition in academic situations (Puente & Ardila, 2000). It is also noted by these authors that Hispanics from the United States are more likely to appear similar to North Americans on standardized tests than would Hispanics from Mexico, Central or South America, and so on, although there is very little data in this area. Padilla (1999) concurs and suggests that within-group comparisons should be considered due to the fact that Hispanics are often considered unidimensional.

Acculturation

The role of acculturation provides a critical variable in the neuropsychological evaluation of Hispanics. Berry (1997) defines acculturation as the individual's ability to understand and maneuver outside of the culture they were raised in and most familiar with. Berry further states that acculturation is a process in which both psychological and behavioral changes occur as a result of long-term contact with another culture. If this is the case, how can acculturation be measured? As culture can be considered dynamic in nature, this task is difficult. Zea, Asner-Self, Birman, and Buki (2003) have suggested that many individuals are affected by several cultures at once, and the mix and interactions are always changing. Although there are many tests of acculturation, it is difficult to isolate highly specific variables that address all subgroups of Hispanics. However, one example would be to give a Hispanic a timed test. If the patient understands the value of time, then the person should be able to perform the task. However, if they do not understand that they must respond as quickly as possible (this is the case with many Hispanics as the concept of time may be different for them), they will not perform as well and possibly present themselves as brain-damaged (Ardila et al., 1994). According to Shorris (1992), the degree of acculturation among Hispanics varies. As time goes by, patterns of behavior, beliefs, and values become similar to those of Americans. Thus, as a rule, Hispanics living in the United States eventually integrate their values with American values. In many ways, the faster the individual assimilates, the faster there is upward mobility across socioeconomic stages.

TRADITIONAL APPROACH TO THE ASSESSMENT OF ABILITIES AND COMPETENCIES OF SPANISH-SPEAKERS

Testing Spanish-speaking individuals, both in the United States and abroad, has lagged behind the testing of English-speaking individuals as well as those from other countries, including Russia and European nations. Historically, the greatest efforts have been linked to research and practice in the United States, to a degree Puerto Rico, and Spain. However, the efforts extended in any of the preceding cases have spanned less than 50 years and often research and practice of assessing Hispanics is no more than a couple of decades old. This section addresses the traditional efforts that have been used and the problems that arise with such efforts.

Translating Tests and Responses

Psychological assessment of Hispanics has typically taken place by adapting standard measures into adaptive situations. In some cases, the tests are used directly since the tests are nonverbal. In other cases, the tests are "translated." However, many of these translations have little or no research backing the validity (Fernandez, Boccaccini, & Noland, 2007). Some tests, such as the Wechsler Intelligence Tests for Children (WISC), have been translated and standardized (Wechsler, 2004), but others have no research and far-reaching implications. Specifically, most tests that are published in the United States have no Spanish translations. When Hispanics are sampled for standardization purposes, test authors often use Census Bureau statistics. However, as a rule, best practices (such as those used by the Wechsler tests) oversample underrepresented populations. Thus, the standard for benchmark tests is to extend the sampling numbers to beyond the proportion indicated by Census Bureau statistics.

Using two companies as examples, Pearson and Multi-Health Systems, we find that most of the tests are not translated into Spanish. The Profile of Mood States, from Multi-Health, is a well-regarded and frequently used test of mood status, but the test is not available in Spanish and the sampling does not appear to oversample Hispanics. For Pearson, the Millon scales are excellent examples of robust and sophisticated measures of psychopathology and health behaviors. Again, the lack of oversampling applies here together with a lack of a Spanish translation.

For Psychological Corporation, the story is essentially the same. Only one set of tests of psychopathology that has been published has been adequately researched and translated—the Beck Tests. Western Psychological Services publishes Katz Adjustment Scale-Revised and Substance Abuse Subtle Screening Inventory, neither of which have been confirmed by research as valid tests for Spanish-speaking Hispanics in the United States (Fernandez et al., 2007). But things are not as simple as the tests being not available. For example, Western Psychological Services publishes the Luria-Nebraska Neuropsychological Battery, which was very popular during the 1980s. The senior author worked on a carefully designed translation and study, with colleagues from the Universidad Complutense de Madrid and the Universidad de Granada (both in Spain). That series of investigations were not published largely because of copyright problems. The Spanish translation used the stimulus cards developed by Alexander Luria in Russia, approximately half a century ago. The cards have been adapted and copyrighted by one of Luria's students in Denmark. Further, those cards are now sold by a close-to-defunct company in Spain at a cost equaling the cost of the test in the United States. This snafu essentially made the publication of the Luria-Nebraska economically unfeasible, a decision made by the Spanish test publisher TEA who has the primary distribution agreement of Western Psychological Services products in Spain.

In other words, the tests are difficult to translate due to the fact that cognitive equivalence is more complicated than language equivalence. And if they are adequately translated, then it is difficult and expensive to standardize those tests with Spanish-speaking populations. Finally, if all the previous concerns are addressed, then there are economic and copyright concerns. This combination makes it scientifically and economically challenging for test publishers to address this growing population in the United States.

In addition to translated tests with no research confirming the validity of the tests, there are numerous tests that have only been confirmed as valid through research conducted in Spain. It has been argued that studies conducted in Spain are to be instrumental for practitioners and clients in the United States; most Spanish people living in the United States are from Latin America and both the culture and language of people from Latin America differ substantially from the culture and language of people from Spain (Fernandez et al., 2007). In other words, tests from Spain may actually introduce error in the testing procedure that may be subtle. That is, the tests may be in Spanish but the cognitive equivalence may not be and, thus, one may end up measuring quite different things.

Mixing and Matching Origins, Languages, and Norms

The first individual trained in psychology to win a Nobel Prize, Roger Sperry (personal communication, April 1994), once suggested to the senior author that culture was of little, if any, value to brain function. And for many neuropsychologists, including the more classical ones, that concept has remained true. For example, there have been few, if any, references to the concept of culture in Lezak's *Neuropsychological Assessment* books. That relaxed approach translates to psychologists who assume, as previously discussed, that all Hispanics are similar, that all forms of Spanish are similar, and that norms from one country (namely the United States) are applicable to those individuals from other cultures.

Of course, the situation is much more complicated than that. As an example, the word *bus* is very different in Spanish-speaking countries. In Spain and in many South American countries such as Uruguay and Chile, *bus* is *bus* but it could be *autobus, omnibus,* or even *micro.* For Caribbean countries like Cuba, Puerto Rico, and the Dominican Republic, the word *bus* is called *guagua.* In other words, subcultures of Hispanic heritage may be as dissimilar with each other as they are to the U.S. culture. There is little, if any, empirical data that address this. What data exist do reflect an entirely different perspective. Recently, Bure-Reyes, Puente, Gontier, and Sanchez (in press) tested different Hispanic subsamples, including samples from Chile, the Dominican Republic, Puerto Rico, and Spain. And, indeed, all Hispanics were not similar across a number of neuropsychological tests when several factors such as gender, education, and age were held constant. In this study, a series of commonly used tests were administered, including FAS Fluency, Stroop, Trail Making Part A and B,

Rey Osterreich Complex Figure Text, and Verbal Serial Learning Curve. Whereas the differences were subtle, all tests did not yield similar results and the time values across subsamples were also dissimilar.

CURRENT CHALLENGES AND TRAJECTORIES IN ASSESSMENT OF SPANISH-SPEAKERS

There is little question that problems currently exist with regard to the assessment of Hispanic individuals residing in both the United States as well as other countries. However, the problems are even more complex than previously outlined. Thus far, major concerns have been raised about the challenges associated with test development. For example, a "good" translation goes well beyond adequate literal translation; it should capture the cognitively equivalent translation. Using the number 8 as an illustration, *eight* is a two-syllable word in Spanish but one syllable in English. The FAS Fluency Test is often used to determine verbal fluency but it turns out that the letters *F, A,* and *S* are used with different frequency in the English and Spanish languages. Beyond these problems, there are more complex issues facing the task at hand. This section addresses the limited number of personnel in the field as well as the scientific challenges associated with development of appropriately sensitive tests for Spanish-speakers.

Personnel Problems

The assumption that psychology represents the discipline that seeks to serve is a fallacy. A review of the American Psychological Association as well as the National Academy of Neuropsychology, as examples, reveals the paucity of professionals who are Hispanics. The Hispanic Neuropsychological Society has approximately 50 dues-paying members in contrast to the more than 4,000 members of NAN (and the Division of Clinical Neuropsychology of APA). Anecdotal evidence also supports the notion that those that are in the field either do not know Spanish or have, at best, a rudimentary appreciation of the language. When studies have been done to address whether the typical practitioner is trained and prepared to address clients who are Hispanics, many believe that they are indeed prepared though they report little, if any, formal training as well as knowledge of either the language and/or the culture (Echemendia, Harris, Congett, Diaz, & Puente, 1997).

Limited Tests

Camara, Nathan, and Puente (2000) surveyed both clinical and neuropsychologists in an effort to determine the most commonly used tests. Of the top 100, none were in Spanish and only a handful (e.g., WAIS and Beck Depression Scale) are available in Spanish. Some, such as the WAIS, have different translations, such as Mexican, Chilean, Argentinean, and Spanish. Most of these versions have adequate norms, though, at times limited. For example, the Mexican WAIS is normed on individuals who live in urban settings and apparently no rural-dwelling adults were used in the normative sample. Other tests, such as the Minnesota Multiphasic Personality Inventory (MMPI), do not appear to have norms for Spanish-speakers. And, others such as the Beta III, an intelligence test, not only has a normative sample that includes an oversampling of U.S.-residing Hispanics but the instructions are actually printed in Spanish in the test booklet. In Spain, the publishing house TEA has a number of tests that are available (see www.tea.es and Salazar, Perez-Garcia, & Puente, 2007), but, unfortunately, the translations are more geared toward Iberian Spanish and, in many cases, norms are not only not available from Spain but certainly not from the United States.

Translations

Translating a test is more complicated than one would anticipate. As other sections of this chapter address, equivalency is a challenging task. Beyond the careful translation and back-translation, several other steps could be taken. They include, but are not limited to, internal analysis of the validity of each item, external analyses of subtest and global scores, and comparisons of alternative forms. The Hispanic Neuropsychological Society has been working on addressing the problems with translators and translating with the hope that a position paper will eventually be published on these complex topics. The article "Professional Consideration for Improving the Neuropsychological Evaluation of Hispanics" (Judd et al., in press) provides numerous suggestions on how to avoid literal translations. One classic example is the translation into Spanish of Luria's approach to neuropsychological assessment. Ardila (1999), who obtained his doctorate training with Luria, completed a conceptually equivalent translation of that approach to the evaluation. Nevertheless, a true cognitive equivalence is very hard to complete. In this case, some of the stimuli and questions appear more relevant to Russian populations than Spanish-speaking ones.

Copyright

For many psychologists, the "correct" translation of a test is sufficient (whatever correct might be). However, copyright law prevents the unauthorized translation of a test, even if it is meant for the most humane reasons possible. What is typically done is that the test is translated for "local" use and not for widespread distribution and application. However, if a researcher decides to translate the test, getting copyright permission is difficult and sometimes extremely slow. In some cases, for example, Luria's visual stimuli, the copyright is complicated. One author, but not the developer of the stimuli (Luria), holds the copyright. The question arises to whom do you ask permission, especially if the author is deceased and lived in a country where copyright laws did not exist during the development of the test materials. The senior author has finished collaborating on a series of studies focusing on testing effort in neuropsychological evaluations with Spanish-speaking individuals. Unfortunately, the studies were done with verbal consent of the test's author. Once the studies proved a useful addition to the literature, the author was contacted and an e-mail was forwarded from the author indicating that he was supportive of having the translated test instructions and stimuli published. We had requested authorship but no royalties. But the author died unexpectedly and discussions with the test publisher have gone astray. There is good likelihood that this individual test will not become available to the general public. These two tests provide an example of the difficulties associated with copyright of tests and testing materials.

Normative Samples

Next is the question of what the reference sample should be. Should a 25-year-old Mexican national living in the United States for a few months be compared to Anglos? The answer is probably not. Should that Mexican national living in the United States for 20 years be compared to Anglos? Maybe this should be the case. However, the situation is not so simple. If the purpose is to determine ability and competency, probably comparing to the sample reflecting origin or where the greatest acculturation has occurred would be the most appropriate. If the purposes are to determine achievement, then probably comparing to the reference sample that reflects the problem in question would be most appropriate. An example may be in order. If the question is whether the person has a cognitive problem or a learning disability, the country of origin or acculturated country should produce the reference sample. If the question is whether that person has the capacity to perform a specific task required of a particular sample, then the population from which that criterion is based on should probably be the reference sample.

Another problem is that of educational equivalence and, for that matter, records. Individuals whose native language is not English may either have attended a low-income neighborhood school or school in Latin America. Either situation would call into question whether the total number of grades completed would be equivalent in different schools. A high school education in Latin America sometimes is more comprehensive than the equivalent in the United States. College is typically 5 years compared to the typical 4 in the United States.

Another question involves whether a variety of normative samples should be used. Specifically, the question should focus on what is the intended use of the testing data obtained. In other words, if the idea is to determine how the client fares to the population in which the individual resides, then the normative reference from the majority population would be most applicable. Examples of this situation might be determining whether the client is able to return to gainful employment in the community of residence (e.g., Mexican living in the United States), a child who is being placed in a specific grade, or even a non-U.S. citizen and nondocumented individual charged with a crime who is being judged by a "jury of their peers" (i.e., presumably U.S. citizens). If in contrast, the question becomes what capacity or what change has occurred as a function of an injury or trauma, then using demographically corrected norms appear to make more sense. The decision of which norms to be used then rests on the question to be answered. If the question is one of relative comparison or between subjects, then nondemographically corrected norms appear most applicable. If in contrast, the question is whether the change is absolute (e.g., within subject), the demographically corrected norms would appear to be best.

In essence, sampling issues and challenges make the adaptation of these tests for Spanish-speakers quite complicated. What is required is both knowledge of the client's history as well as of the referral question. Matching both of these critical variables provides guidance as to addressing questions of normative or reference samples.

Development of New Instruments

In the development of culture-specific or culturally unbiased (if that is possible) instruments, the overall focus should be the criterion. In other words, developing a concept that is the focus of measurement is a very difficult task. For example, if intelligence is the construct, then adding a significant number (whatever that may be) of items that are timed is tantamount to developing a test that is full of measurement error. Further, what on the surface may appear similar in reality is not. Not all things are similarly equivalent in terms of more "pure" cognition. Take the case of proverbs. When the senior author was developing a Spanish version of the Wechsler Intelligence Scale for children, the working group consisted of an American-born Mexican American, a Cuban, a Puerto Rican, a Mexican, and a South American. The group could not arrive at an equally acceptable proverb to insert in one of the subtests. A final example is that of the FAS Test, the most commonly used test of verbal fluency in North American neuropsychology (Camara et al., 2000). Here, the goal is simply not to translate a test but to develop a clearly defined criterion. The standard is not the original test, if one is used as the basis for the current test but, instead, the standard is to use a clearly defined concept that is being measured.

According to Helms (1997), several steps should be used in the development of tests in order to reduce potential cultural bias and, in turn, increase fidelity of the concept being measured:

1. Functional equivalence: Do the scores have the same meaning across different cultural groups? Though superficially similar, different tasks mean different things across cultures. For example, time is a most valuable commodity in the United States, but it is less important than other things (e.g., social value) in Hispanic cultures.
2. Conceptual equivalence: Do the items have similar meaning or value across different groups? In other words, does a "correct" translation adequately capture the meaning involved? The concept trumps the wording in this context.
3. Linguistic equivalence: Are the words, phrases, and grammar similar in nature? Literal equivalence may violate linguistic equivalence. Proverbs from different Hispanic cultures are rarely the same.

4. Psychometric equivalence: Are we measuring the same thing in different contexts? If time comprises one of the major variables in measuring intelligence in American contexts and if time is not as valued by Hispanics, would it mean that Hispanics are not as fast and, therefore, not as intelligent as Americans?

5. Condition equivalence: Are individuals equally comfortable and understandable of the manners in which the concepts are being tested? Residents of the United States begin with testing at birth as every child is given an APGAR test to rate their status and function. That testing is part of the American educational, vocational, and social life. This is not the case for Hispanics where testing is often limited in scope and found primarily in schools.

6. Context equivalence: Like #4, are the concepts equal across different contexts? Contexts are often assumed to be equal. For example, a test administered by a stranger means the same thing. In Hispanic cultures, strangers, even professionals, are not viewed as individuals with whom one would want to share intimate aspects of one's lives.

7. Sampling equivalence: Are the normative samples equally comparable? Sometimes the assumption in sampling is that if there are enough Hispanics or all subjects are Spanish-speakers, that would be suitable. However, using the WAIS sampling in the United States and Mexico as an example, sampling equivalence does not hold true. The American WAIS samples extremely carefully (both authors have participated in the standardization of the WAIS IV), where the Mexican WAIS does not stratify among a variety of variables. For example, all subjects for the standardization are city dwellers.

Puente and Agranovich (2004) have elaborated on some of the preceding issues, specifically as to how they apply to neuropsychological testing. The factors include time, attitudes toward testing, values and meanings, modes of knowing, and patterns of abilities.

1. Time. In 1996, Perez-Arce and Puente suggested that ecological validity may be assumed but not realized in testing situations. They suggested that Hispanics use different problem-solving strategies compared to Anglo-Americans. Slowed performance could be equivalent to prolonged enjoyment of an activity.

2. Attitude toward testing. Puente and Perez-Garcia (2000) and Ardila (2001) have indicated that Hispanics approach testing in quite a different way than Anglos. Suspiciousness and lack of rapport could result in altered test results.
3. Values and meanings. Ardila (2001) has pointed out that questions on some tests have different meaning for Hispanics. One example is that snow is used in some intellectual tests, such as the WAIS. With most Hispanics not living in temperate climates, the item would have less value or understanding for a Spanish-speaker.
4. Modes of knowing. The process of knowing and the object of knowledge are not universal (Ardila, 1999; Luria, 1999). In some societies, opinion equals facts and vice versa.
5. Patterns of abilities. Cognitive abilities measured by neuropsychological tests represent culturally learned abilities, and therefore, they are being affected by different environmental and cultural contexts (Ardila, 1995, 2001; Nell, 2000; Puente & Perez-Garcia, 2000).

From the perspective of test publishers, the view appears quite different. Having helped in the standardization of several tests as well as translation and standardization projects, the authors note that the concerns of test publishers are, at times, diametrically opposed to researchers and clinicians and often not well understood by the consumers of test products. Some problems include:

1. The economic viability of the translated product.
2. The costs and complications associated with multicultural or multinational group studies.
3. Representation of subjects used in normative studies.
4. Selection, training, and participation of qualified standardization personnel.
5. Marketing and eventual acceptability/use of the developed product.

Criterion-Based Testing and Hispanics in North America

The possibility exists that what is actually being measured is relatively simple. Society determines, sometimes implicitly, what is important to serve the needs of its members. For example, in North America, time is considered a valuable, if not the most valuable, commodity. In contrast, in Latin America, time is not something meant to be conquered, instead it is meant to be enjoyed and savored. Thus, using time as a critical criterion for the measurement of a concept, such as intelligence, means it would be interpreted quite differently. For example, in the United States, the faster one completes a task (at least most tasks, as some are biologically impossible to do simply fast), the more intelligent that person would be. In Latin America, the opposite might actually be true. A fast person might be perceived as anxiety-ridden, uncomfortable, and unconfident and, thus, a "slower" person may be perceived as somebody that understands the task at hand and moves through it slowly as a means to experience all aspects of that situation.

The possibility then metamorphoses further in that the better one understands the criteria that society thinks are important and that, in turn, are often reflected in the tests that are developed, the greater the likelihood that those individuals would be labeled as successful, normal, and adapted and, in turn, be able to have greater access to the opportunities that arise with the conquering of the tests that reflect society's criteria of success. As an example, if a student works fast (and accurately, of course), then he or she would obtain a greater SAT or GRE score, which, in turn, would provide greater educational opportunity, which, in the long run, would provide greater economic and social gains. In essence, society rewards those that conquer its criteria and provides the spoils to the winner. One could easily argue that the measurement of abilities and competencies is nothing more than measuring what society considers important and generously rewarding those that measure well. Simply put, the measurement of abilities and competencies is a sophisticated way to preserve society's goals and maintain its intellectual control on the trajectory chosen.

If this approach is then adapted, especially poorly, to other cultural contexts, such as to ethnic minorities and to individuals residing in other countries, what transpires is nothing short of intellectual imperialism. The goal of society in power is to define constructs that help the societal trajectory. If the societal trajectory is narrowly defined or overly nationalistic, then intellectual imperialism ensues. If, in contrast, the measurement of ability and competency reflects a more universal concept, which is something that has rarely been attempted or accomplished, then the winner tends to be the larger group, and a more universal construct is developed.

However, there is a downside to this approach. One, there is an assumption that there are universally accepted or desired constructs for abilities and competencies. Thus far, the history of measurement has tended to be strongly culturally bound and, in some cases, nationally bound (see Puente, 1995). As long as those boundaries exist, there is a serious limit to the application of universal concepts of abilities and competencies. Second, if indeed universal concepts arise (e.g., intelligence should simply measure problem solving à la Thorndike [1904]), then one could argue that the ethnic-specific adaptive behaviors (e.g., the limited concern for completing tasks quickly in Latin cultures) may erode the beauty and unique qualities associated with that culture. Third, in some cases, what could happen is that what a society considers important at one stage eventually erodes and an alternative concept replaces it. With Hispanics, by the year 2040, this group may represent the largest single group of individuals in the United States. Does that mean that Spanish will replace English as the language of choice? Does that mean that intelligence tests will have few, if any, timed items? Does that mean that individual accomplishment and independence would be replaced with social interaction and group cohesion as the primary criteria of success?

Whatever the case, it is clear that the current concepts of measurement of ability and competency in North America appear biased, incomplete, and not easily (if entirely) transferable to those whose heritage is Hispanic. Alternatives need to be developed and to be developed quickly. If the current paradigm exists and Hispanics become the majority group in the United States but remain the most poorly acculturated and educated with the lowest earnings, the largest families, and the most fertile, what is bound to occur is a modern-day South Africa and instead of being racial discrimination, it will be discrimination of a group based on the assessment and utility of abilities and competencies.

PSYCHOMETRIC ASSESSMENT

Psychometric assessment of Hispanics has typically fallen under three areas:

Emotional

Neuropsychological

Intellectual

For better or worse, an assumption is made regarding the origins of psychopathology. If the etiology of psychopathology is functional (e.g., the patient is exhibiting a personality disorder because of an extensive history of abuse), then it is considered emotional. Tests such as the MMPI are excellent examples of this type of instrument. If the origin is physical, physiological, or neurological, then the psychopathology is considered to be organic. For these problems, neuropsychological tests are used to measure the extent of the deficits. Tests such as the ones captured by the Halstead-Reitan Neuropsychological Battery are good illustrations. The final category is tests of intelligence. These tests are broadly defined as tests that measure intellectual abilities (often in a wide scope such as the WAIS, KABC, and the Stanford-Binet) using statistical deviations referred to as an intelligence quotient or an IQ. However, these categories are, by definition, artificial. They assume, for example, that emotional problems are not products of physical origins, which is a faulty assumption. The opposite is also true in that neuro-psychological tests are meant for "organic" problems, which is similarly a faulty assumption. Finally, it should be said that intellectual tests are looking more like neuropsychological tests. Using the WAIS as an example, the group of advisory experts were all neuropsychologists.

Emotional Assessment

Emotional psychometric assessment has many different testing materials in the process of assessment. One method that is still used widely today is projective tests with the Rorschach index. Hispanic results may be skewed due to the fact that the color responses, modulated by culture, can influence affective ratio (Cuellar, 1998). Furthermore, Latinos who are assessed by the Rorschach sometimes are considered to have more psychopathology than they should because of abnormally high scores on specific measures (Dana, 1998).

Neuropsychological Assessment

According to Cuellar (2004a, 2004b), the field of neuropsychological testing has ignored the role of important variables such as ethnicity, culture, language, and education. Significant measurement error in individuals from disenfranchised groups occurs when one incorrectly assumes that cultural and language variables have little if anything to do with physiological functioning. There are many important variables that involve physiological functioning but some of the most important are ethno cultural and educational (Cuellar, 1998). Furthermore, in a study conducted by Mungas, Reed, Haan, and Gonzalez, there were noted differences in Hispanics compared to Caucasians. Caucasians performed better on all measures except for Word List Learning-II, where there was no difference observed (Mungas, Reed, Haan, & Gonzalez, 2005). The 13 different neuropsychological measures are:

Non Verbal Conceptual Thinking

Verbal Conceptual Thinking

Object Naming

Picture Association

Verbal Attention Span

Visual Attention Span

Pattern Recognition

Spatial Localization

Verbal Comprehension

Verbal Expression

Spatial Configuration Learning

Word List Learning-I

Word List Learning-II

All tests were properly translated from English to Spanish by "standard back-translation methods." The translation was performed by bicultural Mexican Americans, and fully bilingual individuals who have bachelor degrees in Spanish. Furthermore, most of the translators were psychometrists as well. They concluded that even if the neuropsychological test was properly translated into Spanish, the monolingual Spanish-speaker will perform worse than a monolingual English-speaker on most if not all measures. This could be attributed to the fact that monolingual Spanish-speakers in the United States have a correlation between high Spanish use, low English use, little education, and little or no acculturation (Mungas et al., 2005).

Cognitive Assessment

Currently, there are many cognitive tests available to assess cognitive function. Unfortunately, many of these cognitive tests have a cultural bias that reduces their effectiveness for individuals from different cultures, especially Hispanics. There is a general understanding that, although translated versions can sometimes produce results without cultural bias, translated tests still maintain cultural bias. Furthermore, these cognitive tests misidentify Hispanics as "cognitively impaired" (Marshall, Mungas, Weldon, Reed, & Haan, 1997). The Mini-Mental Examination is an easy and short test that examines overall cognitive functioning. It is widely used in a clinical evaluation of individuals who might be demented. Others have suggested that such variables as ethnic origin negatively affect the scores on the Mini-Mental Status Examination (Marshall et al., 1997). A more efficient way of cognitively assessing a Hispanic who is not able to speak English fluently is through a nonverbal test, which is very valuable in the evaluation of diverse populations. Naglieri, Booth, and Winsler (2004) discovered that the nonverbal assessment of Hispanics with limited English proficiency is the most accurate way of detecting intelligence. It is noted that intelligence tests show a large difference between children with limited English proficiency and those who are proficient. This can lead to misdiagnoses of a Hispanic child as being mentally impaired. In addition, research has provided data to suggest that Hispanic and White children are equally gifted, concluding that when dealing with intelligence and cognitive assessment, it is vital that the practitioner use proper instrument selection (Ardila, 1995, 2001).

No matter what kind of assessment is being carried out on the Hispanic, it is necessary to utilize valid cultural indices to be able to evaluate cultural variables. In order to conduct a proper assessment, it is necessary to see where a Hispanic is due to the variability between nationalities and Hispanics in the United States. Cultural variables include:

Linguistic abilities, such as verbal fluency

Ethnic identity measures (i.e., ethnic distance, ethnic affirmation, and ethnic loyalty)

Behavioral acculturation

Cognitive acculturation (familism)

Bicultural typologies

Ethnic-specific status variables (i.e., Hispanic stress)

Cultural Assessment

Different cultural variables are measured through the use of different measurements. For example, ethnic identity can be measured using the Multigroup Ethnic Identity Measure (MEIM). In addition, behavioral acculturation and cognitive acculturation can be measured by the Multi-dimensional Measure of Cultural Identity for Latino and Latina Adolescents (MMCILLA). Depending on the nationality of the Hispanic, there are various acculturation measures specifically developed for that nationality. For example, Cuellar (1998) notes that for Mexican Americans, the acculturation scale that would be most appropriate is the Acculturation Rating Scale for Mexican Americans.

Other measurements can also be used in measuring cultural variables. There is a strong correlation between all types of acculturation and intelligence scores, health status, alcohol and drug abuse, low-birth weight, and consumption of cigarettes (Cuellar, 1998).

SUMMARY AND CONCLUSIONS

Shifting demographics in the United States reflect a major problem for society in general, and psychology in particular. If society measures what is most valuable, but the demographics either do not acculturate, appreciate, or adapt to those standards, social unrest and intellectual apartheid may occur. This chapter outlines the shifting demographics, the current state of the assessment of abilities and competencies, and potential solutions to the situation. At best, psychology has a decade, possibly two, before critical problems in social functioning occur.

Though the United States is a country of immigrants, most have either spoken English before arriving or quickly learned English and acculturated. The current immigration pattern in the United States has set precedents in a number of ways. First, the sheer number of individuals arriving in the United States is unexpected and large. Second, these individuals not only speak a different language, but they have not acculturated at the rate of prior immigration groups. Third, Hispanics disproportionately represent the largest group in terms of less education, economic measures, and engagement with health insurance programs. Hispanics are, by default, becoming economic and social failures to a highly competitive and fast-evolving system. This situation is bound to produce greater representation of patients requiring psychological diagnostic services, and eventually, treatment. For example, a disproportionate number of Spanish-speaking children will become part of disenfranchised groups in the educational system. The likelihood of Spanish-speakers becoming the largest percentage of learning disabled children, for example, is good. Another challenge is that Hispanics are heterogeneous and, in many ways, their heterogeneity may exceed between-group differences. That is, differences between different Hispanic subgroups, for example, Mexicans and South Americans, may exceed the differences between Hispanics and other comparison groups such as Anglo-Saxons.

This situation is particularly problematic considering not only that Hispanics now represent the largest ethnic-minority group in the United States, but that they will most likely become the largest social group in this country (exceeding Anglo-Saxons). That is, the largest social group in this country will be the poorest, least educated, and less likely to be covered by health and social programs.

Just because psychology has not historically had the necessary science, instruments, and personnel to evaluate Spanish-speakers has not resulted in a lack of attempting to evaluate them. However, it is important to note that traditional approaches are full of failed attempts with large error variances. These problems include, but are not limited to, lack of adequately translated tests, limited normative and standardization samples, limited scientific and clinical literature, as well as limited personnel. In addition, economic problems facing test publishers have sometimes resulted in limited efforts in the evolution of appropriately conceived and developed test instruments.

One way to summarize the situation has been indicated by Mungas and colleagues (2005). They have stated that sensitivity and specificity are both needed, but at the same time, how far one can deviate from the original construct for concepts to be equivalent becomes a challenging question. A particular challenge is that the development of a test originates and captures the "spirit" of that culture and then that is applied to a completely different one, often without much understanding of the culture for which the test has been generalized to.

When all is said and done, the underlying and fundamental question is whether culture should be integrated and held to the same standards as, for example, age and education. Roger Sperry has said that culture is irrelevant when it comes to brain function. What is absolute is underlying brain function and, in many ways, variables such as culture are artificial and should be construed as superfluous to understanding the underlying functional concept—What is the status of the individual? No more, no less.

REFERENCES

Ardila, A. (1995). Directions of research in cross-cultural neuropsychology. *Journal of Clinical and Experimental Neuropsychology, 17,* 143–150.

Ardila, A. (1999). Spanish applications of Luria's assessment methods. *Neuropsychology Review, 9,* 63–71.

Ardila, A. (2001). Acquired language disorders. In M. O. Ponton & J. Leon-Carrion (Eds.), *Neuropsychology and the Hispanic patient: A clinical handbook* (pp. 87–103). Mahwah, NJ: Lawrence Erlbaum.

Ardila, A., Rosselli, M., & Puente, A. E. (1994). *Neuropsychological evaluation of the Spanish-speaker.* New York: Plenum Press.

Berry, S. (1997). Personal report of intercultural communication apprehension. In R. Reynolds, R. Woods, & J. Baker (Eds.), *Handbook of research on electronic surveys and measurements* (pp. 364–366). Hershey, PA: Idea Group Reference/ IGI Global.

Bure-Reyes, A., Puente, A. E., Gontier, J., & Sanchez, L. (in press). Neuropsychological test performance of Spanish speakers: Is performance similar across subgroups? *The Clinical Neuropsychologist.*

Camara, W. J., Nathan, J. S., & Puente, A. E. (2000). Psychological test usage: Implications in professional psychology. *Professional Psychology, 32,* 141–154.

Capetillo, C., Carion-Baralt, J., Marmol, L., San Miguel Montes, L., Navarrette, N., et al. (in press). NAN Education Paper: Professional consideration for improving the neuropsychological evaluation of Hispanics. *Archives of Clinical Neuropsychology.*

Cuellar, I. (1998). Cross-cultural clinical psychological assessment of Hispanic Americans. *Journal of Personality Assessment, 70,* 71–86.

Cuellar, I. (2004a). Latinos and Latino cultures in America: An exploration of cognitive, affective, and behavioral referents. *PsycCRITIQUES, 49,* 61–63.

Cuellar, I. (2004b). Acculturation and cognitive science from theory to measurement to application. *PsycCRITIQUES, 49,* 311–314.

Dana, R. H. (1998). Projective assessment of Latinos in the United States: Current realities, problems, and prospects. *Cultural Diversity and Mental Health, 4,* 165–184.

Echemendia, R. J., Harris, J. G., Congett, S. M., Diaz, M. L., & Puente, A. E. (1997). Neuropsychological training and practices with Hispanics: A national survey. *Clinical Neuropsychologist, 11,* 229–243.

Fernandez, K., Boccaccini, M. T., & Noland, R. M. (2007). Professionally responsible test selection for Spanish-speaking clients: A four-step approach for identifying and selecting translated tests. *Professional Psychology: Research and Practice, 38,* 363–374.

Gonzalez, F. (2008, January 23). *Statistical portrait of Hispanics in the United States, 2006.* Retrieved February 2, 2008, from http://pewhispanic.org/factsheets

Helms, J. E. (1997). The triple quandary of race, culture, and social class in standardized cognitive ability testing. In D. Flanagan, J. Genshaft, & P. Harrison (Eds.), *Contemporary intellectual assessment: Theories, tests, and issues* (pp. 517–532). New York: Guilford Press.

Luria, A. R. (1999). Outline for the neuropsychological examination of patients with local brain lesions. *Neuropsychology Review, 9,* 9–23.

Marshall, S. C., Mungas, D., Weldon, M., Reed, B., & Haan, M. (1997). Differential item functioning in the Mini-Mental State Examination in English- and Spanish-speaking older adults. *Psychology and Aging, 12,* 718–725.

Mungas, D., Reed, B. R., Haan, M. N., & Gonzalez, H. (2005). Spanish and English neuropsychological assessment scales: Relationship to demographics, language, cognition, and independent function. *Neuropsychology, 19,* 466–475.

Naglieri, J. A., Booth, A. L., & Winsler, A. (2004). Comparison of Hispanic children with and without limited English proficiency on the Naglieri non-verbal ability test. *Psychological Assessment, 16,* 81–84.

Nell, V. (2000). *Cross-cultural neuropsychological assessment: Theory and practice.* Mahwah, NJ: Erlbaum.

Padilla, A. M. (1999). Hispanic psychology: A 25-year retrospective look. In W. J. Lonner, D. L. Dinnel, D. K. Forgays, & S. A. Hayes (Eds.), *Merging past, present, and future in cross-cultural psychology: Selected papers from the Fourteenth International Congress of the International Association for Cross-Cultural Psychology* (pp. 73–81). Lisse, Netherlands: Swets & Zeitlinger Publishers.

Perez-Arce, P., & Puente, A. E. (1996). Neuropsychological assessment of ethnic-minorities: The case of assessing Hispanics living in North America. In R. Sbordoen & C. Long (Eds.), *Ecological validity of neuropsychological testing* (pp. 283–300). Delray Beach, FL: GR Press.

Puente, A. E. (1995). Intellectual perestroika and Russian neuropsychology. *Journal of the International Neuropsychological Society, 1,* 510.

Puente, A. E., & Agranovich, A. V. (2004). The cultural in cross-cultural neuropsychology. In G. Goldstein, S. Beers, & M. Hersen (Eds.), *Comprehensive handbook of psychological assessment: Vol. 1. Intellectual and neuropsychological assessment* (pp. 321–332). Hoboken, NJ: Wiley.

Puente, A. E., & Ardila, A. (2000). Neuropsychological assessment of Hispanics. In E. Fletcher-Janzen, T. Strickland, & C. Reynolds (Eds.), *Handbook of cross-cultural neuropsychology* (pp. 87–104). Dordrecht, Netherlands: Kluwer Academic Publishers.

Puente, A. E., & Perez-Garcia, M. (2000). Neuropsychological assessment of ethnic minorities: Clinical issues. In I. Cuellar & F. Paniagua (Eds.), *Handbook of multicultural mental health* (pp. 419–435). San Diego, CA: Academic Press.

Salazar, G. D., Perez-Garcia, M., & Puente, A. E. (2007). Clinical neuropsychology of Spanish speakers: The challenge and pitfalls of a neuropsychology of heterogeneous population. In B. Uzzel (Ed.), *International handbook of cross-cultural neuropsychology* (pp. 283–302). Mahwah, NJ: LEA.

Shorris, E. (1992). *Latinos: A biography of the people.* New York: Norton.

Thorndike, E. L. (1904). *Introduction to the theory of mental and social measurement.* New York: Science Press.

U.S. Census Bureau. (2008). Retrieved February 18, 2008, from http://www.census.gov/population/www/popdata.html

Wechsler, D. (2004). *Finally . . . A True Spanish Version of WISC-IV!* Pearsonassess. com. Retrieved January 10, 2008, from http://pearsonassess.com/HAIWEB/Cultures/en-us/Productde tail.htm?Pid=015-8978-846

Zea, M. C., Asner-Self, K. K., Birman, D., & Buki, L. P. (2003). The Abbreviated Multidimensional Acculturation Scale: Empirical validation with two Latino/Latina samples. *Cultural Diversity and Ethnic Minority Psychology, 9,* 107–126.

Considering Language, Culture, and Cognitive Abilities: The International Translation and Adaptation of the Aurora Assessment Battery

MEI T. TAN, ABDULLAH M. ALJUGHAIMAN, JULIAN G. ELLIOTT, SERGEY A. KORNILOV, MERCEDES FERRANDO-PRIETO, DAVID S. BOLDEN, KAREN ADAMS-SHEARER, HILARY E. CHART, TINA NEWMAN, LINDA JARVIN, ROBERT J. STERNBERG, AND ELENA L. GRIGORENKO

This chapter is about the translation and cultural adaptation of a new psychological assessment for intellectual ability, the Aurora Battery, which is currently being developed in the United States, for use in the United States but also around the world. This international aspect of Aurora came about when interest in and inquiries about the project reached the authors from educators and researchers in England, Spain, Saudi Arabia, Russia, Holland, India, Israel, and elsewhere, in addition to those from school districts in various parts of the United States. Collectively, this attention reflects a general, globally occurring need for alternative methods of assessing and understanding children's abilities, and addressing them in educational settings now and into the future. But this common need has also brought forth some interesting questions about language and culture, for although Aurora was developed with a close eye to any potential cultural bias within the United States, such global interest was not fully anticipated. Do most children in Russia know what a treehouse is? Does the Spanish language contain many common homophones, as English does? Will Saudi Arabian children understand the meaning of "raining cats and dogs" when the phrase is presented to them in Arabic? As it turns out, a phrase such as "it's raining cats and dogs" can neither be translated literally nor adapted culturally in any meaningful way in Arabic because it has no real equivalent in the Arabic language or the Arab culture.

These kinds of considerations of language and culture have directed the translations and adaptations of Aurora. By *translation* we refer to the linguistic transformation of one language to another; *adaptation* refers to the adjustments in style, presentation, and content that are made to try to eliminate cultural bias and ensure that the assessment is measuring the same construct across cultures (as per Fons van de Vijver's definitions of bias and equivalence; van de Vijver, 2004). These processes are ongoing in the four countries from which researchers have contributed to this chapter. Their accounts are illustrative of the variations and difficulties of linguistic translation and cultural adaptation.

WHAT IS AURORA AND WHY?

The Aurora Battery is based upon Robert Sternberg's theory of successful intelligence, which defines intelligence as the collective and balanced ability to adapt to, shape, and select environments so as to accomplish one's goals, as well as the goals of one's culture or society (Sternberg, 1999). According to this conception of intelligence, memory, analytical, creative, and practical abilities are equally important to intellectual functioning and successful outcomes in life. Aurora attempts to measure these types of cognitive abilities, additionally looking at strengths in verbal, visual/spatial, and numerical content domains within each class of ability as well as across abilities.

Aurora was conceived in 2004 as an alternative or a supplement to the current methods of gifted identification generally applied to school children in the United States, which traditionally have consisted largely of IQ-based measures. It is designed to address the identification and development of intellectually gifted children roughly between 9 and 12 years of age. It may also be used for more highly gifted children who are younger, or for less gifted youths who are older. Measuring a variety of intellectual abilities, it is designed to assess patterns of abilities broader than those assessed by more traditional identification instruments (Chart, Grigorenko, & Sternberg, 2008). The value in this is twofold: First, its broad scope can provide a larger picture of a child's abilities; and second, it focuses attention on abilities that, as suggested by the theory's name, when actively and mindfully practiced, can lead to success in one's academic as well as personal endeavors.

In its entirety, Aurora is a comprehensive evaluation battery. It includes a group-administered paper-and-pencil portion, a parent interview, a teacher rating scale, and an observation schedule. These various tools were developed to allow the most comprehensive possible examination of an individual's abilities, with the understanding that a paper-and-pencil test provides only one view of a child's range of ability. The teacher rating scale asks a teacher to examine a child's abilities as they are exhibited in how the child functions in the classroom setting (including social skills and the acquisition or display of tacit knowledge); the parent interview explores how children display their abilities in their normal everyday life activities outside of the classroom; and the observation schedule is a set of tasks to be done individually with a child to gauge his or her particular abilities in depth. This chapter will concern only the paper-and-pencil module (Aurora-*a*), which is intended to be group-administered in school or other classroom-like settings and, to date, has been the tool most often translated for use in other countries as it is the most developed and the one that lends itself most readily to translation at this point.

The implications of Aurora and its translations are significant, as it has the potential to exert effects on students' self-concepts and worldviews of education. Group-administered paper-and-pencil tests are generally seen as efficient instruments for use in schools, where the identification of skills and abilities most commonly takes place. The results of such school-administered tests frequently influence important decisions about children's academic futures, as well as students' own self-conceptions (Amrein & Berliner, 2003; Barksdale-Ladd & Thomas, 2000). In addition, the broad acceptance of a new form of assessment can have more general effects by implying new values in education; the use of specific assessments defines the skills and abilities that are considered important and worth examining in school, and hence, naturally affects what is taught in schools and how. It is therefore important that the device be based on a sound and rigorously tested theory of abilities.

In the following pages, Aurora-*a* and its theoretical bases and development will be described; the international rules of translation that serve as guidelines for the translation and adaptation of assessments in general will be considered. We will examine a few prominent examples of assessments that have been translated, then accounts from principal investigators in England, Spain, Russia, and Saudi Arabia concerning their ongoing translations of Aurora-*a* will be presented.

Of foremost importance is to consider that a test of intelligence developed and validated in one culture may or may not be valid in another culture (Sternberg, 2004). However, unlike the work done with conceptions of intelligence in indigenous cultures (Grigorenko et al., 2001, 2004; Sternberg et al., 2001), in which cultural differences clearly stand out before all language considerations, the work described here is by international researchers who have chosen to work with Aurora because of their familiarity with the theory of successful intelligence and their belief in it as a valid and useful construct for understanding human abilities within their own cultures. For the most part, each of them has already used some Western assessment tools (such as the Wechsler Intelligence Scales for Children, WISC), but feel the need to explore other forms of assessment. However, although they accept that the components of Sternberg's conception of intelligence and the mental representations on which they act are universal, they also must consider the outward manifestations of these components, how they are exercised within a particular culture (both through language and culture or behavior), and therefore the different ways in which they may be measured. The same construct may require different measurement tools in one culture versus another. And so, although each country began with translation (van de Vijver's "application"; van de Vijver, 2004), some subtests have been discovered to require adaptation; in others, new assembly (adaptation to such a degree that practically a new instrument is assembled; van de Vijver, 2004) might be needed. In some sense, the translation and adaptation of Aurora's paper-and-pencil test has thus far constituted an examination of the subtleties of cultural differences in conceptions and expressions of intelligence.

THE PRIMARY TRANSLATION: THEORY TO ASSESSMENT—AURORA'S PSYCHOMETRIC BASES

The first level of translation is that of concept to instrument. Sternberg's theory of successful intelligence (Sternberg, 1999; Sternberg, 2004) equally emphasizes the roles of analytical, creative, and practical thinking in the accomplishment of one's goals within one's given environment. According to the theory, each of these types of thinking is important because each can have a powerful effect on the extent to which one succeeds in life. The theory also holds that each of the three abilities is, to a substantial extent, teachable and learnable. Therefore, examining all three in individuals can usefully inform teaching approaches and direct efforts toward identifying cognitive strengths and weaknesses.

Analytical intelligence is involved in analyzing, evaluating, judging, and comparing and contrasting. Analytical abilities are exhibited in or recruited by reasoning and logical thinking, as exercised in activities such as persuasive writing, debating, research, and mathematical problem solving. Creative abilities are reflected in the capacity to generate new ideas, and to create and design in activities like writing, drawing, building, and imaginative play. Creative intelligence is particularly well measured by problems assessing how well an individual copes with relative novelty. Practical intelligence is involved when individuals apply their abilities to the kinds of problems that confront them in daily life, such as on the job or in the home. Practical abilities are exercised in leadership and other social interactions, as well as in the adaptation and application of knowledge in real-world problem solving.

To match the paper-and-pencil assessment tasks to the theory, an organizational grid was established. This grid is shown in Table 16.1.

Contained within the grid are the 17 subtests, briefly described, that currently constitute Aurora-*a*. Titles or title words that are in parentheses indicate original subtest names that have since been altered to be more student-friendly. The number of items is shown, as well as the format of each subtest—open-ended (free response), right or wrong (short answers that are scored as correct or incorrect), and multiple-choice. Although the grid in Table 16.1 shows clear lines of demarcation, there are no clear lines separating human cognitive abilities and no pure tests for segregating these abilities into specific content domains. Therefore, although each subtest's primary designation is shown by its place in the grid, these placements are by no means "pure."

RULES AND GUIDELINES FOR INTERNATIONAL TRANSLATION

Previous attempts at assessment translation and adaptation have yielded useful guidelines. A set of these has been published by the International Tests Commission (International Test Commission [ITC], 2001) to ensure conceptual equivalence between different language/culture versions and

Table 16.1

AURORA-*a* GRID: THE AURORA SUBTESTS GROUPED BY TARGET ABILITY AND DOMAIN

	ANALYTICAL	CREATIVE	PRACTICAL
Images (visual/ spatial)	Shapes (Abstract Tangrams): complete shapes with missing pieces. (10 items) (MC) Floating Boats: identify matching patterns among connected boats. (5 items) (MC)	Book Covers: interpret an abstract picture and invent a story to accompany it. (5 items) (OE) Multiple Uses: devise three new uses for each of several household items. (5 items) (OE)	Paper Cutting: identify the proper unfolded version of a cut piece of paper. (10 items) (MC) Toy Shadows: identify the shadow that will be cast by a toy in a specific orientation. (8 items) (MC)
Words (verbal)	Words That Sound the Same (Homophone Blanks): complete a sentence with two missing words using homophones. (20 items) (RW) (Limited) Metaphors: explain how two somewhat unrelated things are alike. (10 items) (OE)	(Inanimate) Conversations: create dialogues between objects that cannot typically talk. (10 items) (OE) Interesting (Figurative) Language: interpret what sentence logically comes next after one containing figurative language. (12 items) (MC)	(Silly) Headlines: identify and explain an alternative "silly" meaning of actual headlines. (11 items) (RW) Decisions: list elements given in a scenario on either "good" or "bad" side of a list in order to make a decision. (3 items) (RW)
Numbers (numerical)	Number Cards (Letter Math): find the single-digit number that letters represent in equations. (5 items) (RW) Story Problems (Algebra): (before any algebra training) devise ways to solve logical math problems with two or more missing variables. (5 items) (RW)	Number Talk: imagine reasons for various described social interactions between numbers. (7 items) (OE)	Maps (Logistics Mapping): trace the best carpooling routes to take between friends' houses and destinations. (10 items) (RW) Money (Exchange): divide complicated "bills" appropriately between friends. (5 items) (RW)

Note. MC = multiple choice; OE = open-ended items that need to be scored by an individual using a rating scale; RW = answers are either right or wrong; ( ) in subtest titles = subtest titles or portions of titles no longer in use.

their original instrument. Sireci (2007) summarizes the most critical steps that should be followed to produce high-quality alternate-language versions of tests as follows: (1) know the culture as well as the language; (2) select translators carefully; (3) involve as many people in the adaptation process as possible; (4) pilot-test the adapted examination; (5) conduct statistical analyses of test quality and comparability; and (6) document the adaptation process. This procedural map establishes standards and guidelines but is not strictly prescriptive. Adaptations of individual tests are somewhat individualized processes, depending upon the type of test, the purposes of the translation, and the nature of the project. In general, though, translation might be described as a procedure of self-checking through various means while engaging in an iterative process of refinement.

Two major examples of cognitive or academic tests and assessments that have been translated internationally are the WISC-III (Wechsler, 1991, 3rd edition; now replaced by the WISC-IV, Wechsler, 2003) and the assessment for the Progress in International Reading Literacy Study (PIRLS; International Association of the Evaluation of Education Achievement, 2001). In both cases, several versions of the original test have been published and the translation and adaptation processes have been refined and improved over the years.

The WISC is an assessment for general mental ability (g), involving both verbal and nonverbal tasks, which is designed to be administered to individuals. To translate the WISC-III, each participating country carried out its own particular process for the translation and adaptation of the test. In general, however, as for the adaptation of the earlier WISC-R (Revised, norms published in 1974, precursor to the WISC-III), each country examined the items of the test for cultural bias with respect to gender, racial/ethnic group, region, and religion of the country. Panels of experts and focus groups of examiners targeted items for revision (Weiss, 2003). The aim in each case was to preserve the item's effectiveness as an indicator for the target construct (van de Vijver, 2003); that is, modifications for various cultural understandings were made while attempting to maintain the integrity of the measure. (For more details, consult Georgas, Weiss, van de Vijver, & Saklofske, 2003.)

The PIRLS assessment focuses on the reading achievement and reading behaviors and attitudes of U.S. 4th-graders and their international equivalents. Its translation may be viewed as an example of how complex and intricate the process may be for an assessment whose main intention involves language directly (in this case, the skill of reading). For the translation and adaptation of the PIRLS items, specific guidelines and procedures were established by the PIRLS International Study Center (ISC) for translating the tests into the national language and cultural context of each target population (Martin, Mullis, & Chrostowski, 2004; Martin, Mullis, & Kennedy, 2007). An English international version was developed first, then each participating country translated all of the materials into the target language(s) and adapted them to the cultural context. The primary focus of each translation was the comparability of reading difficulty and accessibility across the different countries. After the initial translation, each piece was reviewed, with particular attention paid to the readability of the texts for the target population. Cultural adaptations were kept to a minimum, to maintain the readers' understanding without altering the level of difficulty or the intention of the text. All parts of the test were then submitted to two independent translation companies who verified that the meaning of the original test had been maintained. It should be noted, though, that despite this detailed process, some doubts remain as to the validity of the resulting PIRLS translations because of the complexity of accounting for the subtleties of language and comprehension across cultures (Hilton, 2006).

TRANSLATING AURORA ACROSS LANGUAGES AND CULTURES

At this time, Aurora-*a*'s subtests have undergone extensive item-testing, during which different students were administered different subtests and the results were examined for the internal consistency and range of difficulty of items within each subtest. Where item-correlation was below .7, items were discarded and/or added and item-correlation was improved. This was carried out with approximately 1,300 students in the 4th–6th grades. Aurora is currently undergoing validation studies in the United States with small samples in each for Connecticut, New York, and Illinois. Correlations between subtests of the same type (testing for analytical, creative, or practical abilities) thus far have been explored but with only a limited number of such tests; thus, final conclusions are still pending. However, at this point, numerous countries have opted to translate the instrument to explore its possible usefulness in their own cultures.

Following are accounts from England, Spain, Russia, and Saudi Arabia that outline their educational contexts for Aurora and describe their teams' efforts thus far toward adaptation and translation. Despite the historical differences of their countries, the investigators from all four

countries began with an interest in the identification of the gifted population, starting with the acceptance of broader notions of intelligence
and a subsequent search for better identification tools. And although
each country is at a different stage of Aurora's translation and adaptation (presented in order of later stages of work to early), their common
experiences reflect a pattern in the particular challenges and benefits of
working with Aurora cross-culturally.

THE USE OF AURORA IN DIVERSE CULTURES

England

It is now more than 80 years since Charles Spearman (1927) wrote his
seminal text highlighting his view of the nature of general intelligence,
or *g*. Perhaps surprisingly, this view has resisted the challenge of more
recent and broader conceptions of intelligence and continues to pervade
thinking concerning intelligence and how it should be assessed. Some
might argue that it is time the English education system adopted a rather
broader notion of what constitutes intelligence and, by implication, what
it means to be a gifted student.

As in France, intelligence testing in England was spurred by the introduction of compulsory education at the end of the 19th century. Schools
were rapidly populated by large numbers of children whose needs were
often poorly understood. Such diversity, in needs and aptitudes, led to
the introduction of special schooling, which required appropriate means
of assessment. In 1913, Cyril Burt was appointed by the London County
Council to be Britain's first professional educational psychologist and
from this step eventually grew a massive Child Guidance network in
which IQ testing was core to the psychologist's role (Burt, 1957).

For most of the first half of the 20th century, intelligence testing
in English educational contexts was largely reserved for identified individuals with special needs. However, the introduction of a selective tri-
partite system in 1944, with academic, technical, and functional types
of schools for children aged 11 and above, necessitated a new form of
assessment. The resultant tool, the 11 plus examination, was used to
determine the most appropriate type of school for each child. It originally assessed general reasoning skills and mathematical ability but was
criticized for having a strong class bias with many more children from
middle-class backgrounds achieving success. As a result, it gradually

evolved into a test with less emphasis on curriculum-based knowledge. With the advent of comprehensive schooling in the 1960s, the 11 plus is now used in relatively few geographical areas within England.

A significant transformation in educational assessment practices in England resulted from the introduction of a National Curriculum in 1989. Over the next two decades, teachers became increasingly skilled in undertaking curriculum-based classroom assessments that were complemented by National tests in English, Mathematics, and Science at ages 7, 11, and 14. However, many believe that these statutory assessments, which carry with them high stakes for teachers and schools and encourage teachers under stress to work toward test outcomes, fail to adequately identify giftedness. Segmented into eight levels, each child's academic progress can be monitored by reference to his or her performance in various curricular areas. As a result, judgments about a child's abilities have increasingly been determined by the child's academic performance rather than by tests of underlying intellectual processes.

The identification of gifted and talented students in England during the past decade has been subject to significant Government involvement. As a result, it became policy through the introduction of the Gifted and Talented Strand, which was part of the Excellence in Cities initiative (1999), to identify a 10% cohort of gifted (7%) and talented (3%) children within each school. The term *gifted* refers to those students who are capable of excelling in academic subjects such as English or History. *Talented* refers to those students who may excel in areas traditionally viewed as non-academic, such as music and those requiring visual/spatial skills, such as those having particular abilities in games, physical education, drama, or art; or to those students who are vocationally skilled.

In England, the responsibility for formally identifying the gifted or talented student rests primarily with the child's school, although a significant minority (6% of secondary and 24% of primary) of schools have failed to comply with this task (Department for Children, Schools and Families, 2008). Government guidelines suggest that identification of gifted and talented students should be a continual, whole-school process that is fair and nondiscriminatory, making use of a wide range of assessment sources, both quantitative (e.g., test scores) and qualitative (e.g., teacher observations). The importance of not making judgments on the basis of the child's performance at a single point in time is stressed. Evaluators are also supposed to take into account the child's rate of progress.

The need for a tool like Aurora is reflected in the fact that most English schools will identify gifted students primarily on the basis of their performance on the statutory tests in the "core" academic subjects of English, Mathematics, and Science. This is hardly surprising as not only is there a sound infrastructure in England for curricular assessment, based upon the National Curriculum, but also the best predictor of future academic performance is usually the individual's prior performance. Thus, this approach would appear, in the first instance, to be both sound and fair.

However, there are flaws with the use of curriculum-based assessment that mirror those of traditional intelligence testing (Elliott, 2000). First, this approach is of little value in identifying those gifted children who, for whatever reason, have failed to show their underlying potential. Indeed, as it taps directly into ongoing classroom performance, it is, for this particular purpose, likely to be even less valuable than traditional IQ tests, which, on occasion, can reveal intellectual ability not manifested in school. Second, curricular success in England largely involves analytical processing and memorization. Children with particular creative or practical strengths may be identified by their teachers in relation to arts subjects such as drama, ceramics, or photography, but such subjects continue to have low status in schools. Furthermore, without the focused teaching that seeks to apply these abilities to learning in other areas of the curriculum (Sternberg & Grigorenko, 2004), their potential will continue to be marginal. As has been described in previous sections of this chapter, Aurora attempts to compensate for these weaknesses and assess a much wider range of abilities, making it an attractive possible alternative to the current methods of identification.

Prior to the initial testing in England with Aurora, some Anglicization was necessary. In producing the first Anglicized version, a postgraduate research assistant who is an English-language specialist checked all of the items. As a result, a significant number of words and phrases were altered. These included the replacement of words with linguistic equivalents, such as *popsicle* to *ice lolly*, *mail* to *post*, *vacation* to *holiday*, *candy* to *sweets*, and *soccer* to *football*. But it also included replacing terms that would be culturally unfamiliar (or less familiar) to English students, such as *goldfish crackers* to *fish fingers*, *orchid* to *gladiola*, *state* to *county*, *skittles* to *smarties*, and *elk* to *moose*. In addition, all spellings had to be Anglicized, for example, *color* to *colour*.

Initial testing with Aurora began in January 2007 in Hartlepool, a town situated on the northeast coast of England within the Tees Valley subregion. It is a relatively densely populated town, with a largely mono-cultural, White population of 90,000 inhabitants, and is characterized by relatively high levels of social deprivation: It is the 23rd most disad-vantaged area in the country (out of 354 areas); unemployment is above both the regional and national average; and life expectancy is below the national average. It is served by 30 primary schools, 6 secondary schools, and 4 further-education providers. Only 5.9% of students leaving school at age 16 enter employment, and post-16 education participation rates remain low by national standards.

Schools in Hartlepool previously identified gifted students using both qualitative and quantitative data but, for expediency, relied largely on the results from the National Curriculum tests already discussed. Senior managers from Hartlepool Children's Services were dissatisfied with this form of identification and recognized the potential offered by Aurora for identifying a more diverse cohort of gifted students. Con-sequently, in January 2007, all 1,200 Year 7 students (age 11–12 years) across the town took Aurora's paper-and-pencil test.

Subsequent to this initial testing, more modifications were introduced to further improve Aurora's design and formatting, and to make it bet-ter fit English students' expectations of test appearance. To do this, team members, in conjunction with a panel of local schoolteachers and a School Improvement Adviser from Hartlepool Children's Services, provided a number of suggestions. The Aurora test papers were then redesigned by a professional graphic artist to streamline and unify the test's appearance. The tests were adjusted to look more like the National Curriculum tests in English, Mathematics, and Science that would be familiar to all children in England; for example, items were boxed, a pencil icon was added to indi-cate where answers should be written, and answer boxes were added. They also underwent general editing to simplify and shorten the instructions, and the titles of the subtests were changed to be more student-friendly.

In addition to these alterations to the subtests themselves, it was realized that, despite the common language, it was preferable if the open-ended subtests were marked by English markers who would be more likely to understand and appropriately judge the idiomatic use of creative language and cultural references in the students' answers. A new set of examples for scoring was compiled for Number Talk, using all English examples as opposed to American ones.

A second round of testing took place in Hartlepool in November 2007 with all Year 6 students (aged 10–11 years) and a selection of Year 5 students (aged 9–10 years). Preliminary feedback from teachers and senior managers involved in the improvement process was largely positive but no data are yet available on how beneficial the modifications to the tests have proven to be. Once the test data have been fully analyzed, we will have a clearer picture as to whether further modifications are necessary, and a stronger grasp of Aurora's capacity for identifying children whose potential would otherwise be left unrecognized.

Spain

Historically, in Spain, educational policy has focused on students with special needs, such as learning difficulties and attention deficit, and on those who have experienced academic failure. Relatively little effort and attention have been dedicated to the study of giftedness. In the 1980s, García Yagüe directed the first research carried out in Spain on the nature and identification of giftedness in students (García Yagüe, Gil, De Pablo, & Lázaro, 1986). Since then, Candido Genovard initiated a scientific study of giftedness in Spain with a double aim: to design identification measures and to propose intervention strategies (Genovard, 1990; Genovard & Castelló, 1990). Later on, in Murcia, Lola (Maria Dolores) Prieto (1997) began research directed toward (1) teacher training; (2) the identification of high-ability students; and (3) intervention strategies and the design of programs.

Since the 1990s, different models and theories of giftedness (e.g., triarchic and multiple-intelligences theories) have been examined and employed (Genovard, 1990; Genovard & Castelló, 1990) in the development of research as well as programs for gifted students. Javier Tourón carried out studies concerning the identification of giftedness using a number of different tools, including the Raven's Progressive Matrices (SPM; Raven, 1938), the Renzulli Scales for Rating Behavioral Characteristics of Superior Students (SRBCSS; Renzulli et al., 2002), and the WISC-R (Tourón, Reparaz, & Peralta, 1999). His Center for Talented Youth (CTY) at the University of Navarra, dedicated to the identification of and programming for gifted and talented students, is a notable accomplishment. In addition, in Canarias (Artiles, Álvarez, & Jiménez, 2002) and Madrid (Casanova, 2002), there are now programs for the identification and nurturing of students with diverse high abilities, based on the identification model proposed by Antoni Castelló and Concepció Batlle (1998), which differentiates between giftedness and different talent types (academic talent, verbal talent, special talent, creative talent, logical-mathematical talent).

This same model is also being used in the autonomous region of Murcia, where a research group based at the University of Murcia, supported by the Murcia regional educational ministry and the Fundación Seneca, is applying the Castelló and Batlle model to identify gifted and talented elementary and high school students (Ferrando, 2006; Sánchez, 2006). In addition, they also plan to use the Aurora Battery, with which they hope to broaden the spectrum of examined abilities and to explore the mechanisms of both general and triarchic intelligences.

In the summer of 2007, this team translated Aurora's paper-and-pencil test. Initial changes were made regarding the terms and concepts that would be unintelligible within the Spanish context. Further review by other members of the team polished this initial translation so that all terms and concepts were made appropriate for Spain. Later, external reviews were also solicited as part of the piloting process.

To collect pilot data on the initial translation of Aurora-*a*, the team in Murcia decided to use only those subtests concerning creative abilities, namely, (1) Book Covers, (2) Multiple Uses, (3) Conversations, (4) Interesting Language, and (5) Number Talk. Therefore, the adaptation of these subtests was their primary focus.

A group of 40 Murcia University psychology students were asked to serve as an expert panel to review the translation. These students had experience working in schools; 25%–30% of them were elementary school teachers, and the rest had experience working in other areas of education. Several modifications resulted from this process. For example, the word *kids* was changed to *youths* in the Book Covers example, as it was thought to be more appropriate for an application with 12- to 14-year-olds; in Multiple Uses, the name for item three was changed from *blue glass bowl* to *blue fruit bowl*; and the instructions given for the Number Talk and Conversations tasks were shortened, making them more direct and easy to understand in Spanish. In addition, more text was introduced in the "Tree House and Tree" example in Conversations to more fully express the substance of the English-version example.

In Interesting Language, several changes were introduced. In fact, this subtest required the most work and was, according to the panel, the most complicated to adapt because of the cultural differences in phrases of figurative language. For instance, in the example given at the beginning of the subtest, the figurative phrase used was replaced by a more commonly used Spanish expression.

Following this phase of adaptation, two teachers from the expert panel volunteered to try out the translation in their schools. The first sample was composed of 24 children ages 7 to 9 years old, from very diverse multicultural backgrounds. The sample from the second school was composed of 22 children aged 8 to 11 years old. Both were public schools serving medium-low income populations. The students were asked to read each item carefully and answer it; this procedure allowed an understanding of how a small sample of 25 boys and 21 girls might interpret and respond to the test items.

In addition, teachers' comments were collected. These comments generally concerned the length of the tasks, even though two sessions had been used to administer them. But teachers also commented on how the children seemed to enjoy the tasks, showing interest and motivation, and that this was especially true of children with special learning needs. Children asked to repeat this kind of activity in the classroom more often.

After this first application of Aurora, it was concluded that the translated language was comprehensible to students and the instructions generally clearly understood by students. Only the instructions for Number Talk seemed problematic, particularly to the 8-year-olds, who needed them to be repeated several times in order to understand them.

Next, data collection began in earnest with two samples of students who were tested using the Aurora creative set. The students in both samples were identified as high-ability students. The first sample was composed of 38 students attending a High School in Yecla (Murcia) from 13 to 15 years old (25 males and 13 females). Gifted and talented identification had been made based on the following measurements: (1) teacher, parent, and peer observation scales based on multiple-intelligences theory; (2) the Differential Aptitude Test (DAT; Bennett, Seashore, & Wesman, 1986), an instrument aimed at measuring IQ and different abilities such as spatial, verbal, reasoning, and so on; (3) the Baron Emotional Intelligence Questionnaire (EQ-i: YV; Bar-On, 1997, 2004), a 60-item self-report that measures five scales—an intrapersonal scale, an interpersonal scale, a stress-management scale, an adaptability scale, and general mood; (4) the NEO Big Five (McCrae & Costa, 2003), a personality questionnaire for ages 8–15 years old; and (5) subtest three of the Torrance Tests of Creative Thinking (TTCT; Torrance, 1966) figural version.

The second sample was composed of 40 primary-level students attending a special weekend program for gifted and talented students. These students had been identified either as gifted or talented using the Castelló and Batlle (1998) model. In general, they showed verbal, academic, mathematical, spatial, or creative talents. They came from a middle socioeconomic level background (i.e., their parents were generally professionals, such as teachers, doctors, architects, or workers in the service sector). The measures used in their identification were (1) teacher screening, teacher nomination; (2) an IQ test; (3) the TTCT; (4) the Cattell Personality Test (Early School Personality Questionnaire [ESPQ] or Children's Personality Questionnaire [CPQ] was used, depending on the student's age), which targets 14 dimensions of personality taken from a factor analysis of personality performed by Porter and Cattell (1963); and (5) Bar-On's EQ-i: YV.

Currently, Murcia's research team is engaged in the initial translation of the rubrics, which will allow for the scoring of all the collected data. In the next step, while applying these rubrics, the further adaptations that will be necessary to effectively use Aurora in the Spanish culture will be determined.

Russia

To begin to understand how a test battery such as Aurora might fit into Russia's current philosophy concerning education, one must begin with the relatively recent changes in Russia's educational system on the national level. One of the national projects currently being realized in Russia, whose main goals involve innovative education and, therefore, receptivity to new ideas, is called *Education* (Prioritetnyj nacional'nyj proekt "Obrazovanie," 2007). This project is supported by government officials working in the Intellectual Potential Department and its workgroup called *Gifted Generation* (Maksimov & Chernenko, 2007), which focuses on the need to identify gifted children and realize their potential in Russia.

Russia's current interest in innovative approaches to the measurement and understanding of intellectual potential is great. Naturally, then, the question of how this potential is reflected in science and measured in practice has arisen. Because of Russia's social and political history, the process of answering it has necessarily involved looking outward to the international community.

Russia's long history of "testing" being prohibited by law started in the 1930s, when the development of psychometrics and research on assessment in Russia were put on hold (Postanovlenie, 1974; Shmelyov, 2004) because of both ideological issues and the objective misuses of existing tests (e.g., the Binet-Berit). Although many studies on how different abilities are related to academic success, life achievement, and salaries have been conducted by cognitive and educational psychologists (and psychometricians), such research programs have only recently been developed in Russia and most of them are based on methods developed by foreign psychologists. This is primarily because Russian psychologists have only a handful of psychometric instruments available. Three of the most popular and well-known are the WISC-III, Raven's Progressive Matrices, and Amthauer's IST[1] (1973). However, these tests went through revalidation, restandardization, and renormalization procedures more than 15 years ago, during socioeconomic and cultural conditions that differed significantly from present conditions. In addition, because of the prohibition on testing, there is no "tradition" of testing in Russia and the criticism of testing is still influential.

It was not until the early 1990s, when the Soviet Union ceased to exist and the prohibition on testing was lifted, that Russian psychologists began substantially to increase their exchange of ideas with foreign colleagues to develop new approaches to intelligence and giftedness. Three main approaches have recently appeared and are being developed at the present time. One regards intelligence as a range of ability based on an individual's IQ, level of motivation, and level of special knowledge (or "crystallized intelligence") (Druzhinin, 1999). The second one focuses on intellectual behavior as the product of an ongoing development process (Ushakov, 2003). The third proposes a model of "mental experience" as the basis of intellectual activity, describing it in such terms as mental structures, mental space, and mental representations that underlie individuals' attitudes toward the world itself and that determine the specific attributes of intellectual activity (Kholodnaya, 2002). However, these approaches, as well as Talyzina's (Talyzina & Karpov, 1987) attempt to implement activity theory categories into intelligence testing, did not result in any real assessment inventories that could make individual and group diagnostics possible.

Aurora-*a* is currently undergoing translation and adaptation in Russia because it provides a fundamental, validated basis for the assessment of three kinds of abilities in a single battery. For example, the idea of practical thinking has been developed more theoretically than practically in Russia (Teplov, 1985; Zavalishina, 2005), but current implementations of Sternberg's theory reveal that it is extremely important to include different abilities and domains in assessment inventories. This complex approach to intelligence, as proposed by Sternberg and illustrated by several corresponding methods, has recently shown high predictive validity in terms of academic achievement in Russian student samples as well (Grigorenko & Kornilov, 2007). This predictive quality is of interest to Russian educators. However, in addition to this achievement-related function, it is also important to recognize that compared with the existing individually and group-administered test batteries, Aurora provides the opportunity to assess a broader range of abilities (analytical, creative, practical), and this tested range can serve the goal of identifying gifted individuals, their cognitive strengths and weaknesses, and specific abilities profiles. It is hoped that Aurora may help bridge the gap between the theories, practice, and specialists in different settings (e.g., clinical, psychological, and educational). These professionals might then gain access to an instrument that can help them explore individuals' potentials, and then make corresponding decisions based on reliable, comprehensive, and complex assessment results.

The translation and adaptation of Aurora's paper-and-pencil test into Russian is being realized by a team from the Department of Psychology at Moscow State University (also referred to as MGU or Lomonosov University). The main issues that the Russian Aurora Team faces are both linguistic and cultural.

Linguistically, as expected, the numerical and figural subtests of Aurora did not require much adaptation, whereas the verbal ones did. The main problem was finding linguistic alternatives for particular items that would translate properly the structure and psychometric intention of a subtest or item "idea." The Russian language has a few peculiarities that made these problems even more challenging: specific phonological patterns, word endings, sentences that lack main parts of a sentence, and optional order of words in sentences.

The cultural issues for translation and adaptation are more various. The main problems concern the difficulty of translating conceptions, and therefore, measurements of practical intelligence and tacit knowledge that may be specific for particular occupational settings and cultures. The "practical" subtests of Aurora were adapted to reflect the present socioeconomic and cultural situations in Russia. For example, in the Decisions subtest, the story problems requiring children to make decisions based on different facts had to be adjusted to reflect the Russian social values involved in the process of acquisition and to take into account the cultural norms and the behavioral patterns invoked by these different situations. For example, when test-takers are asked to provide reasons for and against the idea of buying an old bicycle now versus a new one later, Russian children might be confused, as buying an old bicycle does not correspond with their social reality. That in turn is because the idea of buying an old bicycle in the post-Soviet culture is strongly associated with poverty and such beliefs can affect reasoning and decision making.

Second, there are numerous issues concerning both cultural and linguistic differences in metaphorical and creative thinking among American children as compared with Russian children. As a result, subtests that include metaphorical thinking (e.g., Interesting Language) had to be rewritten. Subtests measuring creative abilities (Book Covers, Multiple Uses, Conversations, and Number Talk) will also require rubrics that remain true to the theoretical framework but that adjust for different types of responses because, for example, creativity measurement that takes into account originality and novelty is in part culture-dependent (Lubart, 1990; Rudowicz, 2003).

Finally, there is a cultural issue beyond the test structure or content: the introduction of Aurora into the educational culture of Russia. This introduction will require us to find a way to recruit schools in the standardization program, train administration and scoring personnel, and adapt testing packets to the length of the classes. By addressing all of these various elements, it is hoped that Aurora may be successfully adapted to the present cultural and socioeconomic environment in Russia for use by a broad range of professionals.

Saudi Arabia

The interest in identifying gifted children and nurturing their abilities in the Kingdom of Saudi Arabia (KSA) and other Arab countries started roughly in the last quarter of the last century. But this interest did not crystallize into a methodological and academic endeavor in the KSA before 1990, when the findings of the first study ever in the KSA, entitled "The National Program of Identifying and Nurturing Gifted Children," were published. This study was sponsored by the King Abdul-Aziz City for Sciences and Technology. It officially adopted and Arabized the WISC-R and the figural battery of the Torrance Tests of Creative Thinking. It also developed the General Aptitudes Scale-Group Test (a scholastic aptitude scale). Since then, the scales used in identifying gifted children have been limited to the WISC-R, the General Aptitudes Scale and, though infrequently, the TTCT.

The increasing concentration on the usage of these largely traditional intelligence scales in identifying gifted children has suffered a great deal of criticism from scholars in the KSA and in the Arab world in general. Though educationalists working in the field of nurturing gifted children have censured these traditional scales for their inability to recognize the multifaceted nature of children's intellectual gifts, and a great number of researchers have called for the importance of incorporating into such traditional scales the recognition of creative skills and personal skills—on the understanding that giftedness is not a linear but a multifaceted concept that is affected by and affects the individual's personal and emotional traits—such studies have not resulted in any academic scale dealing with the main multifarious issues of giftedness in one unified scale.

These criticisms of the use of the WISC-R and other traditional tests do not refer to any weakness of the scales either in structure or objectivity. On the contrary, these tests exhibit a great deal of objectivity and credibility, a fact that has helped them stand the test of time over a whole century. However, their weak point lies in their inability to tap the various aspects of giftedness identified by modern international research (Coleman & Cross, 2005; Gagne, 1995; Gardner, 1999; Renzulli, 1978; Sternberg & Grigorenko, 2002; Tannenbaum, 1983; Ziegler, 2005). These scales, both individual and group, rely on the primacy of so-called general abilities (g, as measured more broadly by IQ), a notion that has become outdated by current research (Chart et al., 2008; Guilford, 1967; Hadaway & Marek-Schroer, 1992). Therefore, the process of recognizing the gifted through such scales can never fulfill the vision upheld by the academic and vocational authorities that are interested in nurturing gifted children in the KSA.

Additionally, the General Aptitudes Scale, which was developed by the King Abdul-Aziz City for Sciences and Technology, and which is commonly used in the KSA today, has lost its effectiveness because its contents have not been updated since its establishment in the mid-1990s. Accordingly, there is an urgent need to have a set of modern, authentic tools—an individual scale, a group scale, a teacher rating scale, and an observation tool—which collectively can serve to identify gifted children in the Arab world in general and in the KSA in particular so that appropriate educational services for the gifted can be developed. The Aurora Battery is considered a significant qualitative transition in the field of measuring cognitive abilities, as it has broken the traditional limitations of most well-known scales that focus only on memory and analytical thinking skills. To our knowledge, there is no comparable battery available in the field right now.

In the Saudi Arabian team's ongoing efforts to adapt the Aurora Battery Scale to the Arab culture, they have recognized certain factors that require specific attention. First, the instrument is not culturally neutral, as it is mainly based on Western culture. Such a feature is quite a serious challenge, as it could certainly negatively influence student performance, especially in the Saudi environment. For example, in the subtest that employs figurative language (Interesting Language, Creative-Verbal), one finds phrases and concepts like "it's raining cats and dogs," which are hard to translate into Arabic. That is, they are very easy to translate literally, but the purely literal translation is meaningless in the Arabic language and culture.

Second, those who translate the instrument need to make sure that the items used to test specific psychological traits and features maintain their psychometric qualities through the translation. Such a goal cannot be realized by those who have only linguistic competence; translators must also have a good background in the philosophy and the dimensions of the scale itself.

Third, it is necessary to follow rigorous research procedures that will eventually lead to valid and stable results. The Saudi team intends to create Arabic norms for the Aurora Battery using the following procedure: (1) translating the battery; (2) modifying it to the Arabic culture; (3) comparing the translated version with the modified one; (4) forming a reviewers' committee and a language and culture editing committee for the Arabic draft of the battery; (5) applying the tools on a small pilot sample; and (6) administering the battery to many representative samples of Saudi society, which will allow meaningful statistical analyses to be carried out on the collected data. In this step, the internal consistency and cross-time stability will be assessed through reapplication of the tool, if possible. It is expected that the sample for this study will consist of 1,000–1,500 participants. The final step will be the translation of the instruction manual and the directory for using the tools of the scale. The accumulation of data will be ongoing and further revisions will be made, if necessary, at different stages of the usage of the battery in the Arab countries.

In this mission, the Saudi team has chosen to use the term *test adaptation* rather than *test translation* to indicate that the mission is not simply to replace words in one language with words of a different language. Instead, the mission is to go beyond the literal translation and to take into consideration aspects of the Arabic culture as well as language; this procedure will then result in an assessment that will provide a high degree of reliability, validity, and practical usability in the Arabic context. It is believed that this battery is a real qualitative transition in the field of identifying gifted children.

CONCLUSIONS

As these various countries illustrate individually, Aurora is timely, emerging as many nations are reevaluating their current notions of giftedness and intelligence and searching for new or modified ones. However, obstacles do exist in the translation and adaptation process, particularly concerning different cultural notions of practical and creative thinking, and concerning those subtests that use particular forms of language (e.g., figures of speech, homophones, ambiguous "headlines"). The complexities of maintaining equivalencies cross-culturally with respect to meaning, psychometric construct measurement, and item difficulty present daunting challenges, and each country's challenges will differ from the others'. Saudi Arabia's adaptations for cultural context will most likely be greater than England's; both Spain and Russia may need to pay greater attention to linguistic equivalencies; and in Russia, administration processes may prove more perplexing than in other countries as the culture emerges from a period of no testing. However, the nature of the necessary adjustments in all four countries remains to be determined as they work their way through the process of translating, piloting, and revision. Only subsequent thorough data analyses can inform the proper evaluation of these translations.

In conclusion, as these various countries illustrate, collectively, the process of translation and adaptation of assessments is intricate and lengthy, and becomes more so as we try to globalize more complicated measures. Tests for academic achievement or knowledge are less complicated than those for cognitive abilities; tests for more narrow conceptions of cognitive abilities (analytical only) are less complicated than those for broader, multifaceted conceptions of intelligence. What is *global*? It is a term that seems to make the world smaller but cannot cure the world's complexity. However, these countries' dedication to this investment reinforces the promise of Aurora and the hope that the battery can eventually work with integrity internationally.

AUTHOR NOTE

The authors wish to thank Karen Jensen Neff and Charlie Neff for their generous support of this project. Correspondence regarding this chapter should be sent to Elena L. Grigorenko at the Child Study Center, Yale University, 230 South Frontage Road, New Haven, CT 06519–1124 (elena.grigorenko@yale.edu).

NOTE

1. The IST-70 (Intelligence Structure Test) is a group-administered intelligence test developed by Rudolf Amthauer (1973). It is based on the general-factor concept and gives a general IQ score as well as memory, spatial, verbal, and mathematical abilities scores. IST-70 for ages 13 to 60 is one of the best-known and commonly used psychodiagnostic instruments in Russia.

REFERENCES

Amrein, A. L., & Berliner, D. C. (2003). The effects of high-stakes testing on motivation and learning. *Educational Leadership, 60,* 32–38.

Amthauer, R. (1973). I-S-T 70. *Intelligenz-Struktur-Test. Handanweisung* [Structure of Intelligence Test. Manual]. Gottingen: Hogrefe.

Artiles, C., Álvarez, J., & Jiménez, J. E. (2002). *Orientaciones para conocer y atender al alumnado con altas capacidades, guía para las familias* [Guidelines for knowing and responding to students with high potential: a guide for families]. Tenerife: Consejería de Educación Cultura y Deportes del Gobierno de Canarias, Dirección General de Ordenación e Innovación Educativa.

Barksdale-Ladd, M., & Thomas, K. F. (2000). What's at stake in high-stakes testing: Teachers and parents speak out. *Journal of Teacher Education, 50,* 384–397.

Bar-On, R. (1997). *The Emotional Quotient Inventory (EQ-i): A test of emotional intelligence*. Toronto, Canada: Multi-Health Systems, Inc.

Bar-On, R. (2004). The Bar-On Emotional Quotient Inventory (EQ-i): Rationale, description, and summary of psychometric properties. In G. Geher (Ed.), *Measuring emotional intelligence: Common ground and controversy* (pp. 115–146). Hauppauge, NY: Nova Science.

Bennett, G. K., Seashore, H. G., & Wesman, A. G. (1986). *Differential Aptitude Tests for Guidance*. Oxford: The Psychological Corporation. (Spanish adaptation 1992, Buenos Aires: Paidós)

Burt, C. (1957). *The causes and treatment of backwardness* (4th ed.). London: University of London Press.

Casanova, M. A. (2002). La atención del alumnado con altas capacidades en la Comunidad de Madrid [Attention to students with high abilities in Madrid]. *Bordón, 54,* 457–461.

Castelló, A., & Batlle, C. (1998). Aspectos teóricos e instrumentales en la identificación del alumno superdotado y talentoso: propuesta de un protocolo [Theoretical and instrumental aspects of gifted and talented identification: a proposal for a protocol]. *FAISCA, 6,* 26–66.

Chart, H., Grigorenko, E. L., & Sternberg, R. J. (2008). Identification: The Aurora Battery. In J. A. Plucker & C. M. Callahan (Eds.), *Critical issues and practice in gifted identification* (pp. 345–365). Waco, TX: Prufrock Press.

Coleman, L. J., & Cross, T. L. (2005). *Being gifted in school: An introduction to development, guidance, and teaching* (2nd ed.). Waco, TX: Prufrock Press.

Department for Children, Schools and Families. (2008). *Pupil level annual school census.* London: Author.

Druzhinin, V. N. (1999). Struktura psihometricheskogo intellekta i prognoz individualnyh dostizheniy [Structure of psychometric intelligence and prognosis of individual achievements]. In A. N. Voronin (Ed.), *Intellekt i tvorchestvo* (pp. 5–29). Moscow: IP RAN.

Elliott, J. G. (2000). The psychological assessment of children with learning difficulties. *British Journal of Special Education, 27,* 59–66.

Excellence in Cities Initiative. Retrieved November 30, 2008, from http://www. standards.dfes.gov.uk/sie/eic/

Ferrando, M. (2006). *Creatividad e inteligencia emocional: un estudio empirico en alumnos con altas habilidades, tesis doctoral* [Creativity and emotional intelligence: an empirical study with high ability students, a doctoral thesis]. Murcia, Spain: Universidad de Murcia.

Gagne, F. (1995). The differentiated nature of giftedness and talent: A model and its impact on the technical vocabulary of gifted and talented education. *Roeper Review, 18*(2), 103–111.

García Yagüe, J., Gil, C., De Pablo, C., & Lázaro, A. (1986). *El niño bien dotado y sus problemas* [Gifted children and their problems]. Madrid, Spain: Cepe.

Gardner, H. (1999). *Intelligence reframed: Multiple intelligences for the 21st century.* New York: Basic Books.

Genovard, C. (1990). *Estudio preliminar sobre la identificación del alumno superdotado.* [Preliminary study on gifted student identification]. Madrid: Fundación Juan March, Serie Universitaria 250.

Genovard, C., & Castelló, A. (1990). *El límite superior. Aspectos psicopedagógicos de la excepcionalidad intelectual* [The upper limit: Psychopedagogical aspects of intellectual exceptionalism]. Madrid, Spain: Ed. Pirámide.

Georgas, J., Weiss, L. G., van de Vijver, F. J. R., & Saklofske, D. (Eds.). (2003). *Culture and children's intelligence: Cross-cultural analysis of the WISC-III.* San Diego: Academic Press.

Grigorenko, E. L., Geissler, P. W., Prince, R., Okatcha, F., Nokes, C., Kenny, D. A., et al. (2001). The organisation of Luo conceptions of intelligence: A study of implicit theories in a Kenyan village. *International Journal of Behavioral Development, 25*(4), 367–378.

Grigorenko, E. L., & Kornilov, S. A. (2007). *Akademicheskiy i prakticheskiy intellekt kak faktory uspeshnosti obuchenija v vuze* [Academic and practical intelligence as factors of successful learning in university]. In S. D. Smirnov (Ed.), *Kognitivnye i lichnostnye faktory uchebnoj dejatelnosti: Sbornik nauchnyh statey* (pp. 34–48). Moscow: Izd-vo SGU.

Grigorenko, E. L., Meier, E., Lipka, J., Mohatt, G., Yanez, E., & Sternberg, R. J. (2004). Academic and practical intelligence: A case study of the Yup'ik in Alaska. *Learning and Individual Differences, 14,* 183–207.

Guilford, J. P. (1967). *The nature of human intelligence.* New York: McGraw-Hill.

Hadaway, N., & Marek-Schroer, M. F. (1992). Multidimensional assessment of the gifted minority student. *Roeper Review, 15*(2), 73–77.

Hilton, M. (2006). Measuring standards in primary English: Issues of validity and accountability with respect to PIRLS and National Curriculum test scores. *British Educational Research Journal, 32,* 817–837.

International Test Commission (ITC). (2001). International guidelines for test use. *International Journal of Testing, 1,* 93–114.

Kholodnaya, M. A. (2002). *Psikhologia intellekta: paradoksy issledovaniya* [Psychology of intelligence: Paradoxes of research]. Moscow: Piter.

Lubart, T. I. (1990). Creativity and cross-cultural variation. *International Journal of Psychology, 25,* 39–59.

Maksimov, N., & Chernenko, E. (2007). Vunderkindy: Uznat' genija [Child prodigies: To recognize the genius]. *Russkiy Newsweek, 22*(147). Retrieved November 30, 2007, from http://www.runewsweek.ru/theme/?tid=118&rid=1872

Martin, M. O., Mullis, I. V. S., & Chrostowski, S. J. (Eds.). (2004). *TIMSS 2003 Technical Report.* Chestnut Hill, MA: Boston College.

Martin, M. O., Mullis, I. V. S., & Kennedy, A. M. (Eds.). (2007). *Progress in International Reading Literacy Study (PIRLS): PIRLS 2006 Technical Report.* Chestnut Hill, MA: Boston College.

McCrae, R. R., & Costa, P. T. (2003). *Personality in adulthood: A five-factor theory perspective.* New York: Guilford Press.

Porter, R. B., & Cattell R. B. (1963). *The Children's Personality Questionnaire.* Champaign, IL: Institute of Personality and Abilities Testing. (Spanish adaptation 1990, Madrid: TEA editions)

Postanovlenie CK VKP(b) ot 4 ijulya 1936 g. (1974). "O pedologicheskih izvrashenijah v sisteme Narkomprosov" [The Resolution of Central Committee VKP (b) of 4 July 1936 "On Pedological Distortions in the System of Narkompros"]. In *Narodnoe obrazovanie v SSSR: Sbornik dokumentov.* Moscow: Yurid. Lit.

Prieto, M. D. (Ed.). (1997). *Identificación, evaluación y atención a la diversidad del superdotado* [Identification, evaluation and attention to the diversity of the gifted]. Málaga, Spain: Aljibe.

Prioritetnyj nacional'nyj proekt "Obrazovanie" [Priority National Project "Education"]. (2007). Retrieved from http://www.rost.ru/projects/education/education_main.shtml

Raven, J. C. (1938). *Standard Progressive Matrices, Sets A, B, C D and E.* London: H. K. Lewis & Co.

Renzulli, J. S. (1978). What makes giftedness? Re-examining a definition. *Phi Delta Kappan, 60,* 180–181.

Renzulli, J. S., Smith, L. H., White, A. J., Callahan, C. M., Hartman, R. K., & Westberg, K. L. (2002). *Scales for rating the behavioral characteristics of superior students, technical and administration manual* (Rev Ed.). Mansfield Center, CT: Creative Learning Press.

Rudowicz, E. (2003). Creativity and culture: A two way interaction. *Scandinavian Journal of Educational Research, 47,* 273–290.

Sánchez, C. (2006). *Configuración cognitivo-emocional en alumnos de altas habilidades: tesis doctoral* [High ability students' cognitive-emotional configuration, a doctoral thesis]. Murcia, Spain: Universidad de Murcia.

Shmelyov, A. G. (2004). Test kak oruzhie [Test as a weapon]. *Psihologija. Zhurnal Vysshej Shkoly Ekonomiki, 1,* 40–54.

Sireci, S. G. (2007). *Guidelines for adapting certification tests for use across multiple languages.* Retrieved November 15, 2007, from http://www.cesb.org/Guidelines%2 0for%20Adapting.html

Smirnov, S. D. (2007). *Pedagogika i psihologija vysshego obrazovanija. Ot dejatel'nosti k lichnosti* [Pedagogics and psychology of higher education: From activity to personality]. Moscow: Academia.

Spearman, C. (1927). *The abilities of man.* London: Macmillan.

Sternberg, R. J. (1999). The theory of successful intelligence. *Review of General Psychology, 3,* 292–316.

Sternberg, R. J. (2004). Culture and intelligence. *American Psychologist, 59,* 325–338.

Sternberg, R. J., & Grigorenko, E. L. (2002). Difference scores in the identification of children with learning disabilities: It's time to use a different method. *Journal of School Psychology, 40*(1), 65–83.

Sternberg, R. J., & Grigorenko, E. L. (2004). Successful intelligence in the classroom. *Theory Into Practice, 43,* 274–289.

Sternberg, R. J., Nokes, C., Geissler, P. W., Prince, R., Okatcha, F., Bundy, D. A., et al. (2001). The relationship between academic and practical intelligence: A case study in Kenya. *Intelligence, 29,* 401–418.

Sternberg, R. J., The Rainbow Project Collaborators, and the University of Michigan Business School Project Collaborators. (2004). Theory-based university admissions testing for a new millennium. *Educational Psychologist, 39,* 185–198.

Talyzina, N. F., & Karpov, Y. V. (1987). *Pedagogicheskaja psihologija: psihologija intellekta* [Educational psychology: Psychology of intelligence]. Moscow: Izd-vo MGU.

Tannenbaum, A. J. (1983). *Gifted children: Psychological and educational perspectives.* New York: Macmillan.

Teplov, B. M. (1985). *Um polkovodtsa* [Mind of a commander]. Moscow: Pedagogika.

Tikhomirov, O. K. (1984). *Psihologija myshleniya* [Psychology of thinking]. Moscow: Izd-vo MGU.

Tikhomirov, O. K. (2006). *Psihologija: Uchebnik* [Psychology: Textbook]. Moscow: Vysshee obrazovanie.

Torrance, E. P. (1966) *The Torrance Tests of Creative Thinking: Norms-Technical Manual Research Edition—Verbal Tests, Forms A and B, Figural Tests, Forms A and B.* Princeton, NJ: Personnel Press.

Tourón, J., Reparaz, C., & Peralta, F. (1999). The identification of high ability students: Results of a detection process in Navarra (Spain). *High Ability Studies, 10,* 163–181.

Ushakov, D. V. (2003). *Intellekt: strukturno-dinamicheskaja teoriya* [Intelligence: Structural-dynamical theory]. Moscow: IP RAN.

Van de Vijver, F. J. R. (2003). Principles of adaptation of intelligence tests to other cultures. In J. Georgas, L. Weisss, F. J. R. van de Vijver, & D. Saklofske (Eds.), *Culture and children's intelligence: Cross-cultural analysis of the WISC-III* (pp. 255–273). San Deigo: Academic Press.

Van de Vijver, F. J. R. (2004). Bias and equivalence in cross-cultural assessment: An overview. *Revue européenne de psychologie appliquée, 54,* 119–135.

Wechsler, D. (1991). *Wechsler Intelligence Scales for Children* (3rd ed.). New York: Psychological Corporation.

Wechsler, D. (2003). *Wechsler Intelligence Scales for Children* (4th ed.). San Antonio, TX: Harcourt Assessment.

Weiss, L. (2003). United States. In J. Georgas, F. J. R. van de Vijver, & D. Saklofske (Eds.), *Culture and children's intelligence: Cross-cultural analysis of the WISC-III* (pp. 41–53). San Diego: Academic Press.

Zavalishina, D. N. (2005). *Prakticheskoe myshlenie: specifika i problemy razvitija* [Practical thinking: Specificity and problems of development]. Moscow: IP RAN.

Ziegler, A. (2005). The Actiotope Model of Giftedness. In R. J. Sternberg & J. Davidson (Eds.), *Conceptions of giftedness* (2nd ed., pp. 411–436). New York: Cambridge University Press.

Conclusions: Assessment in an Era of Globalization

PETER TYMMS AND ROBERT COE

This volume presents a diverse range of perspectives on assessment and the implications of attempts to make it global. A number of important issues are raised and some valuable insights offered. Of course, there can be no real conclusions to this work, but a number of general themes have struck us as arising from the forgoing chapters. We focus on three of these themes.

The first is that for any assessment, validity is fundamental, and validity must be established within a particular cultural context. The second is that different kinds of assessments have very different purposes and that a consideration of these purposes is vital to understanding how they may work in a particular context. The third is that many of the issues in the globalization of assessment reflect similar issues in other areas of globalization, such as the relationships between rich and poor, problems of limited capacity and resources, and the persistent challenge of facilitating real and sustainable development. We therefore direct our thoughts to these three issues.

ASSESSMENT VALIDITY AND CULTURE

The problem of validating an assessment for cross-cultural use at first sight seems very different from the standard process of validation with homogeneous populations. However, the process is—or should be—essentially the same. In fact, there are no homogeneous populations and one of the standard ways to detect unwanted bias in an assessment is to conduct the kind of differential item functioning (DIF) analysis with different groups described by Mpofu and Ortiz in chapter 2. Cultural diversity within countries can be very much an issue for validity, as Klenowski's example in chapter 3 of the underperformance of indigenous children in Australia illustrates. Validating an assessment for international use may typically be more of a challenge than validation within a country, but it is not fundamentally different. In both cases, one needs to show that the assessment as a whole, and individual items within it, performs sufficiently similarly for groups with different characteristics. As Puente and Puente illustrate in chapter 15, different cultural groups within the same country may approach assessment situations very differently and even the fact that they speak a common minority language (e.g., Spanish) does not necessarily imply a common culture.

The fact that the process of validation may be the same whether an assessment is national or international does not imply that the results of that process will be the same. An assessment may be valid in one context but not in another. Modern conceptions of validity embrace all aspects of assessment construction, administration, scoring, generalization, extrapolation, and decision making (Kane, 2006). Assessment developers must be clear how test scores will be interpreted and used, what assumptions and properties of the assessment underpin such interpretations and uses, and what evidence supports them. With the emphasis on assessment use, and in particular, the consequences of use (Messick, 1989), it is clear that the context in which an assessment is taken, interpreted, and used may matter a good deal. Simply to take an assessment that has been developed and validated in one country, translate or adapt it for use in another, and assume that the validity argument automatically transfers would be to misunderstand the nature of validity. As Shmelyov and Naumenko state in chapter 12, "the extent to which 'Eurocentric' assessment instruments can be transferred to non-European cultural groups should be confirmed in every case separately."

For these reasons, it may be that the process of proper translation and adaptation of an existing assessment is no less demanding than development of a new assessment. Much of the thinking behind the development of interpretive and validity arguments (Kane, 2006) must be redone, and the evidence required to support these arguments is likely to be different in the new context. If population norms are to be provided, there is no substitute for new standardization studies, which are expensive. Given this, it perhaps seems surprising that, as Oakland demonstrates in chapter 1, there is already very widespread use of Western tests across cultures. However, his advice that where local infrastructure is inadequate to support test development, "the use of adapted tests may present the most suitable immediate solution," may not solve as many problems as it creates.

For instance, the examples given by Harkness et al. in chapter 5 of cultural differences in the values and "ethnotheories" held by parents in different countries illustrate how problematic it would be to draw the same conclusions from applying an adaptation of the same assessment in different contexts. They summarize the results of attempts to adapt Western psychological assessments for use with non-Westernized children: "Despite considerable efforts to make the testing situation less foreign or intimidating for these children, it was frequently observed that children seemed unable to display their abilities in this context. The results included unrealistically low estimates of their competence on such apparently normal tasks as retelling a story to the experimenter."

It is also clear from the work reported in chapter 7 by Grigorenko et al. that many apparently simple words like *calf, shoe, thumb,* or *money* can have quite different rates of understanding in different languages, even where the languages themselves and the cultures of the people who speak them may be quite similar.

Brain Function, Culture, and Assessment Performance

Puente and Puente quote the Nobel Laureate Roger Sperry as saying that "culture is irrelevant when it comes to brain function." If brain function is indeed the same across cultures, then assessments can and should be equitably developed to tap into the fundamental features of brain function. But it is clear that cultures do differ. Indeed the word *culture* would have no meaning if there were no variation. Differences are very apparent when individuals learn different languages, interact according to different social norms, eat different foods, and so on. It follows that the brains within different cultures have learned to respond to the various manifestations of culture differently. This indicates that a nuanced insight into a brain would give indications of its cultural origin. It may not be possible to do this in practice but in principle systematic cultural differences must be embedded in brains, at least functionally if not structurally.

Moreover, most assessments do not observe brain function directly, but collect information through characterizing behavioral responses to particular stimuli. Inevitably, the ways in which those stimuli are interpreted by individuals will be influenced by their understandings, values, and experiences, and their choices of behavioral responses are a function of the contexts in which they are asked to respond. Even when the underlying construct appears or intends to relate directly to some aspect of brain functioning, any attempt to operationalize it in an assessment must be subject to cultural influences.

It may be helpful to view this as a continuum, with variation according to the degree of cultural influence on the outcomes of an assessment. Shmelyov and Naumenko use the distinction between "culturally universal and culture-specific." At one end, we have assessments that measure in relatively direct ways the deep functioning of the brain. Examples might include assessments of short-term memory or reaction times. At the other end of our continuum would be assessments of developed competencies such as the skills and knowledge taught within the school curriculum or personality characteristics developed as part of societal norms (see Figure 17.1).

Some measures bridge the divide between fundamental psychological measures that may be adapted for use across cultures and those such as language assessments that are culture-specific. Shaalan's chapter 10, looking at the development of communication skills in Arabic-speaking countries, perfectly illustrates the issues. On the one hand, it is easy to accept that there are general language processing measures that can be picked up with well-validated tools that cross national boundaries. But when dealing with literacy, the issue of whether one assesses the same thing with apparently equated reading assessments in different languages and scripts comes to the fore. The well-known problems that some children have in learning to read alphabetic scripts are more prevalent in some languages/scripts than others. These differences are explored in

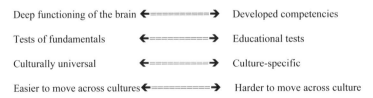

Figure 17.1 The continua associated with test uses.

Ziegler and Goswami's (2005) paper "Reading Acquisition, Developmental Dyslexia, and Skilled Reading Across Languages: A Psycholinguistic Grain Size Theory," in which they seek to explain the differences in terms of the relationships between phonology and orthography. Differences between alphabetic scripts are clear and largely explicable but in nonalphabetic scripts the situation is more complex since children must learn characters one by one rather than learn a limited number of letters and build from them. This illustrates a construct (reading) that is, from a simplistic point of view, the same across cultures but can, in practice, be very different. As a result, assessments that seek to assess reading in different scripts in the same scale, such as PIRLS (Mullis, Martin, Gonzalez, & Kennedy, 2001), must be interpreted with great care. Differences between individuals or countries may be due to education or could also be due to script and language. This raises the broader issue of the meaning of constructs in different cultures.

What Do We Mean by the "Same" Construct in Different Contexts?

A number of writers emphasize the need to establish validity across cultures to show that the assessment measures the same construct in different contexts. However, this appears to beg the question of whether we can even talk about the same construct when the culture differs. For example, in chapter 16, Tan et al. cite Sternberg's definition of successful intelligence as "the ability to adapt to, shape, and select environments so as to accomplish one's goals and those of one's society and culture." This definition is clear, but likely to vary in its operationalization in different cultures, as indeed they show. The range of opportunities for adaptation, shaping, and selection, as well as the types of individual, social, and cultural goals, may well differ appreciably in different contexts. Indeed, Sternberg (2004) (as summarized in chapter 6 by Stemler et al.) provides a useful discussion of the different ways in which a construct that has been developed in one culture can be operationalized in another. A specific example of this is cited by Sternberg (from Cole, Gay, Glick, & Sharp, 1971) to illustrate that the criteria by which a sorting task would be judged to be "intelligent" would be somewhat different among the Kpelle people of Liberia than for Western psychologists.

Also notable from the study reported by Stemler et al. is that despite their considerable and appropriate efforts to produce valid and reliable measures of ability for Zambian children, some of the correlations achieved (internal consistency estimates, correlations among different ability scales and between these and the measures of achievement) are fairly modest. It seems likely that as more work is done in contexts similar to the one studied here, the quality of available instruments will gradually improve, but it is clear that the process of developing assessments in such circumstances is far from straightforward. Whether the relationship between ability and achievement is different in Zambia from other countries and whether that implies that one or other of these constructs is not quite the same in different countries is open to question.

How Can Cross-Cultural Assessments Be Developed and Validated?

Mpofu and Ortiz in chapter 2 discuss a number of possible approaches to the problems of using an assessment in a culture that is different from the one in which it was developed. They demonstrate that conventional approaches, such as the use of language-free nonverbal assessments, use of translators or interpreters, testing in a child's native language, and modifying testing procedures all suffer from a range of limitations. Instead they advocate "modern" approaches that seek to identify when underperformance may be due to cultural or linguistic differences and make appropriate adjustments. They also point out an important distinction between *culture, acculturation, ethnicity,* and *language proficiency.* These ideas bring a useful perspective and experience to the problems of assessment adaptation.

Oakland in chapter 1 discusses characteristics that may make adaptation of an assessment from one culture to another more or less easy, though some of these seem questionable (e.g., that use of multiple-choice formats are most appropriate to reduce error). What he does not say, however, is that if translation and adaptation are intended from the start of the process of assessment development, there is more chance that it will be successful. The kinds of processes now well-established in the development of international surveys such as PISA and TIMSS, where all participating countries have an opportunity to contribute to the development, are much to be preferred to the unilateral development of an assessment in one country without regard to its use in other locations and subsequent adaptation. The examples of collaboration between people with different combinations of expertise in assessment development and knowledge of local culture described in this volume by

Stemler et al. in chapter 6 and by Tan et al. in chapter 16 also seem to provide good models for cross-cultural development.

Mpofu and Ortiz in chapter 2 argue strongly for the use of item response theory (IRT). They state that "IRT methodology makes it possible to develop assessments that are largely transportable across populations and settings." However, we should remember that IRT is not a panacea for assessment validity. Although the appropriate use of this technique may help to identify misfitting items, or differences in difficulty for the same item across groups (differential item functioning, or DIF), it is still possible for bias to remain. Indeed, it is inevitable. The example they give of the effects on the performance of African American test-takers of describing the same test as of "ability" versus "achievement" provides a nice illustration of this. Their discussion of the problems of trying to remove the effects of language competence from "nonverbal" tests is also sobering.

In this context, *bias* is not just a difference between the performance of different groups, but an unwanted difference. Whether a particular difference constitutes "bias" or not is often a value judgment and depends on the purpose of the assessment. For example, if an assessment of mathematical ability showed a correlation with reading ability, that would not necessarily imply bias, since we might expect a tendency for the two kinds of ability to go together. However, if we found that the relative difficulty of some mathematics items was different for strong and weak readers (i.e., DIF), then this would suggest that the items that were relatively hard for weak readers were at least partially measuring reading rather than mathematical ability, and hence, we might conclude that these items were biased against weak readers. On the other hand, we might want our test of mathematical ability to be a good predictor of performance in some existing mathematics assessment that required high levels of reading competence. In this case, the other items, those that did not advantage those whose reading level was high, would be identified as "biased." Of course, if we did not find such DIF, that would not necessarily indicate lack of bias, but only that all items exhibited the same amount of bias in relation to reading.

DIFFERENT PURPOSES OF TESTING

In the face of criticism of tests Stemler et al. (chapter 6) make a good case for the need for good assessments, particularly in large and growing poor countries whose populations dominate the world's statistics. As we have already pointed out, validity depends very much on how an assessment is to be interpreted and used. Assessments are used for many different purposes, some of them quite culturally specific, and it is important to distinguish the various uses that are made of them. For this discussion we separate three broad types of use: for selection, accountability, and diagnosis.

Selection

The use of assessments to select candidates for employment or further education is common in many countries. Where opportunities are limited and highly desired, as will often be the case in poorer countries, this may be an efficient and fair way to make hard decisions. For example, Mutumbuka (2006) notes that the average cost per student in a secondary school in Lesotho is 3.8 times that of a student in primary school. It is quite legitimate for a poor country to aim for universal primary education but to ration secondary education and to use testing to select students who might receive financial help to go to secondary schools. This is, for example, the model adopted by Zambia in the years of educational expansion following independence in 1964 (Mwanakatwe, 1968).

Where resources are scarce, the use of assessments to make selection decisions may be efficient and fair, though, this will depend on the capacity to create, administer, and use such assessments appropriately. Once again, the need for fairness returns us to questions of validity. Inevitably, high-stakes assessments suffer particular problems with validity, since people are strongly motivated to achieve better scores than they deserve. Cultural bias can also be a problem since many existing or adapted assessments may advantage dominant groups over those who are already disadvantaged politically, economically, and culturally. Grigorenko et al.'s discussion in chapter 7 of the difficulties of assessing children in their mother tongue and the pressures to educate and assess in an international language such as English illustrate the complexities of this issue.

Accountability

There is a need for certifying competence and for accountability. The accreditation of professionals is well established across the world in many areas, and the use of testing for accountability seems to grow year on year. But whether it is always cost-effective to employ universal testing as an accountability mechanism for schooling has yet to be demonstrated. England, for example, has seen a severe and expensive accountability system imposed on its schools since 1990 and yet the evidence for improved standards of the kind that was anticipated is simply not there (Coe & Tymms, 2008; Tymms, Coe, & Merrell, 2005; Tymms & Merrell, 2007). Although scores on high-stakes assessments have increased, performance on parallel but low-stakes assessments shows much more modest, or even zero, growth. It has also been shown that the standard-setting procedure for national tests were faulty in the early days. Again, this illustrates the pressure that attaching high stakes to an assessment puts on its validity.

Klenowski (chapter 3) deals specifically with the issues associated with testing for accountability purposes within education. She lists problems identified across the world that have been associated with such assessments. Her solution is to involve teachers more and to move toward the kind of system adopted in Queensland, Australia. This has apparently resulted in rich authentic assessment where the teacher has a key developmental role to play. There may also be advantages in terms of teacher motivation in involving teachers directly in assessment. She does acknowledge the shortcomings of teacher judgment: "There are differences among criteria that teachers use to evaluate their students, even within the same school." But she seems persuaded that moderation can deal with the problems. However, a systematic review of the literature (Harlen, 2005) showed that: "The findings of the review by no means constitute a ringing endorsement of teachers' judgments made in certain circumstances." A similar finding is reported by Aljughaiman and Abdelmajeed in chapter 11 for the low accuracy of identification of gifted children by teachers.

Klenowski (chapter 3) further claims that: "To achieve equity there is also a need to expand the range of indicators used to provide an opportunity for those who might be disadvantaged by one form of assessment to offer alternative evidence of their expertise." But simply allowing multiple forms of assessment does not necessarily remove bias, since the same individuals may still be disadvantaged by multiple indicators. For sure, we should aim to recognize individuals' success in different fields but bias within teacher judgment tends to be carried over from one assessment to the next (the "halo" effect, where learners with desirable characteristics such as good behavior are seen as more able, and its opposite, the "horns" effect). If we need diversity to maintain equity, that diversity must include assessments that specifically do not involve teacher judgment!

Further, if we want reform, we need to do so from a research base. Exhortations that appeal to associations, such as copying what is done in countries that are apparently successful, are a recipe for enthusiastic change followed by disenchantment. We need to think in terms of the careful trialing of new policies on increasingly large scales (e.g., see Campbell, 1969; Fitz-Gibbon, 2004; Slavin, 2008; Tymms, Merrell, & Coe, 2008).

Clearly, not all cultures will want to follow the Queensland path as perceived by Klenowski. Writing from Singapore, Hogan, Towndrow, and Koh (Chapter 8) refer to direct teaching, rote learning, drill, and practice in high-stakes assessments and claim that Singapore has developed a "highly successful system of education." They paint a quite different picture from Queensland, though not without the possibility of improvement. They argue that the influence of high-stakes testing has been both beneficial and constraining, and they look for ways in which the assessment system can be improved. They do not want to abandon high-stakes testing but they do want some realignment. Pragmatically, they could not see any possibility of the removal of such assessments. In chapter 9, they refer to the skill with which teachers can work on developing new material and point to projects that may show a new way.

Diagnostic and Formative Feedback

Interest in the use of assessment for diagnostic and formative feedback has also grown dramatically around the world, and we distinguish between the use of assessments to provide information about individuals and about organizations.

For Individuals

As noted by Stemler et al. (chapter 6), one of the first uses of testing in modern times was to identify able children using a method that would bypass teachers' judgments which, it was felt, might be unduly influenced by the trouble that individuals caused. The work was carried out in France by Alfred Binet around the start of the 20th century and was the first of many tests of intelligence. Since then numerous assessments have been developed to diagnose specific strengths and difficulties and programs created to help remediate problems. Definitions of "special needs" or learning "disabilities" are inevitably culturally specific, so we must be careful about applying assessments from one context to another.

We must also remember that diagnosing a problem is not the same as solving it; many strategies for addressing these "deficits" have very little evidence of efficacy, despite being widely advocated.

Assessments can also be used more widely to inform teaching and learning. Hogan (chapter 8) pays considerable attention to the concept of Assessment for Learning in thinking about education in Singapore and more widely. Klenowski (chapter 3) also refers to these ideas. The basic research has profound implications for much educational practice, so it is worth illustrating it with a key example (Black & Wiliam, 1998). Imagine a teacher testing a class and returning the marked work. To some she gives grades, to others she gives grades and comments, and to a third group she gives comments only. The meta-analysis of experiments indicates that the giving of grades alone has no impact on the child's future performance but that comments alone are of positive benefit. No surprise here one might think, but what might be less expected is that a combination of grades and comments is as of little use as grades alone. It is as though the grades obscure the comments. This finding is of major importance for the use of assessments internationally, as it suggests that much educational practice is in need of major reform.

For Organizations: Monitoring With Feedback

National testing programs are often employed as accountability mechanisms. But they also have the potential to generate feedback for self-improvement. Some might argue that they can and are used for both, but it is at least possible that the accountability agenda dominates and detracts from the potential use of data for self-improvement. It is therefore interesting to note that there is one very large-scale unit devoted to providing feedback to schools for improvement and specifically *not* for accountability purposes. The Centre for Evaluation and Monitoring (CEM) in Durham University in the UK runs monitoring projects designed for feedback. The projects operate on a large scale, processing data from more than 1 million students every year from thousands of schools. It started with a school effectiveness research project known as COMBSE (Confidential Measurement Based Self-Evaluation) but spread widely as schools and colleges saw its potential (Fitz-Gibbon, 1996). This project, which was designed for pre-university courses, provided a blueprint for other projects (Fitz-Gibbon & Tymms, 2002) for children and young people aged 3–18. That schools and colleges value such systems cannot be doubted—they pay to be monitored. There are also persuasive arguments and some evidence to suggest that school performance feedback systems can have a positive impact on a range of outcomes of education (Visscher & Coe, 2002). But more rigorous work is needed before definitive statements can be made (Coe, 2002).

GLOBAL ISSUES IN ASSESSMENT

Our third main issue relates to concerns about the globalization of assessment. We have already shown how this volume holds a very diverse set of chapters, bringing together the experience of many writers within individual countries and across countries. It contains much intelligent thought and takes us forward in thinking about assessment in the global arena. We concur with Shmelyov and Naumenko's position in chapter 12, in which they note that the globalization process will impact on the use of assessments around the world and that this is inevitable. In chapter 14, de Brito also makes strong points about globalization and states that "curriculums must be strongly linked to the local social context." We need to guard against the possibility that the assessments of the rich and powerful do not dictate the curriculum of the poor and weak. We would like to see as much as possible done to ensure that the good intentions of assessment developers in the rich and powerful countries at least do no harm to those in the poorer and weaker countries.

An example of this can be found in Grigorenko et al.'s chapter 7. They discuss the advantages of educating African children in their mother tongue, but also the many difficulties of this, including the large number, and ever-changing nature, of different languages, together with the different models of bilingual education they entail; the difficulties of finding qualified teachers and resources in those languages; lack of written orthographies for some languages; unsuitability of many languages for teaching technical subjects; tensions between needing to teach long enough in the mother tongue to reach proficiency, but not so long as to miss out on development in the official language; lack of value placed on mother tongue proficiency by both parents and teachers; and the disappointing levels of literacy in any language that are often achieved in African countries. Given such a long and daunting list of difficulties, it might seem to be an attractive solution from the perspectives of an outsider simply to abandon efforts to provide mother-tongue education. This, however, would be to deny the cultural, political, and educational importance of African languages. As the Asmara Declaration on

African Languages and Literatures (Asmara Declaration, 2000) states, "All African children have the unalienable right to attend school and learn in their mother tongues. Every effort should be made to develop African languages at all levels of education."

We are also worried about the diagnosis of special needs. If we are to identify children with dyslexia or autism or who have some other special need, then this needs to be followed up with action. It is not sufficient simply to identify. We must therefore be concerned, as Shaalan is in chapter 10, about the capacity within countries that may be less experienced with assessment development to develop new assessments or adapt existing ones, to administer those assessments on a large and consistent scale, to interpret the results, and to take action. Further, we need to note that there is always migration from poorer to richer countries and that, as a result, many countries are short of the very expertise that they themselves have developed. For example, nurses from India and the Philippines have increasingly found work in the European Union (Troy, Wyness, & McAuliffe, 2007). Similar patterns can be found in other skilled areas. The efforts of schools, universities, and the state have generally produced those highly qualified people in the poorer countries only to see them be lost elsewhere. Could it be that efforts to enhance the assessment expertise in poorer countries will result in increased migration of the more able?

Cultural Sensitivity

In chapter 4, Nsamenang quotes Bram as stating that "western societies tend to lump all developing countries in to one category." We need to accept that some individuals see the rest of the world as variations on their own country and seem to find it difficult to get in to the minds of others whom they would aspire to help. This is not a new phenomenon but one that we should be ever alert to. For example, Oakland in chapter 1 claims that "Tests first were developed in the 1880s." He is apparently unaware, as de Brito in chapter 14 reminds us, of France introducing the baccalauréat into the regular educational system in 1808, or of the competitive examinations used from 1836 for entrance to the University of London (Tattersall, 2007), or of the Imperial Examination used in China for selection of the civil servants for 1,300 years (e.g., see Niu, 2007).

Oakland states that national test publishers can and should be encouraged to assume leadership in test development within their countries. He quotes a figure of up to $500,000 for the possible costs of test development and points out the need for commercial test developers to perceive a good chance of getting a return on their investment from future sales. This, however, seems to overlook the economic and skill resources of many poor countries and of the test publishing facilities available to them. Moreover, the claim that "the development of indigenous measures would require the development of international perspectives" and the objection that they would be "unlikely to find acceptance in the international community" seem to imply a global perspective that is monolithic rather than plural. Surely, the availability of appropriate assessments to people in those countries should matter more than publication in high-status journals?

Differing Perspectives

The second major point concerns different theoretical positions. In chapter 13, Kornilova and Kornilov refer to a "blind spot" when inventories "are used in theoretical frameworks and scientific traditions that differ from the original ones." Ultimately, one might suppose that different theoretical positions can always be tested and distinguished from one another to produce a consensus provided there are enough data, but we posit that that may not be the case given a sufficiently complex situation. It may be that there are different theories that can "explain" and predict all that can be seen. Kornilova and Kornilov write of "different countries that have their own original theoretical frameworks."

These differences are well summarized by Nsamenang in chapter 4 who challenges our thinking, quoting LeVine (2004) and reminding us of "Africa's ability to raise culturally competent children within 'alternative patterns of care based on different moral and practical considerations' yet to be imagined and incorporated into developmental theorizing."

CONCLUSIONS

It seems unlikely that anyone who begins to read this book thinking that the problems of assessment in the era of globalization are simple, well-defined, and tractable could possibly retain that view by the time they reach the end. Many of the challenges seem immensely complex and hard to define, let alone address. Some of the strategies that have been tried are reported here, but the results are not always as expected or hoped. What is clear is that despite good intentions, considerable effort, and impressive insights, these problems are not about to be solved any time soon.

Of course, it is impossible to summarize in a few words such a wealth of experience, expertise, and insight as can be found in this volume. The reader, even the lazy reader, must read the forgoing chapters in full to get a full appreciation of their message. Nevertheless, we must attempt to provide some kind of conclusion.

It may seem to be a tautology to say that if we are to understand assessment in an era of globalization, then we must understand both the nature of assessment and the nature of globalization. In thinking about assessment, our focus must be on validity, for which we must begin with a clear idea of the purpose of any assessment; if we know how we want to use and interpret the results of an assessment, then we can begin to evaluate its fitness for that purpose. Thinking about the purposes of assessment will lead us to issues of context and culture, about which so much of the discussion has revolved. Attempts to understand the nature of globalization will raise some of the same issues, along with the challenges created by economic and political inequality, constraints of limited capacity and resources, and the persistent problems of facilitating real and sustainable development.

Ultimately, we are left with the impossibility of thinking otherwise, of seeing the world in the same way as a person whose language, culture, and experiences are not ours. Only by making strenuous efforts can we remember that our view is not the only one. Nevertheless, and paradoxically, it is clear that the principles of developing, administering, interpreting, and using assessments are fundamentally the same, whether in a global, national, or local context. Despite important differences of detail, the characteristics of valid assessment are universal.

REFERENCES

Asmara Declaration. (2000). Agreed statement by participants at the conference entitled *Against All Odds: African Languages and Literatures into the 21st Century,* held at Asmara, Eritrea, January 11 to 17, 2000. Retrieved December 19, 2008, from http://www.outreach.psu.edu/programs/allodds/declaration.html

Black, P., & Wiliam, D. (1998). Inside the black box: Raising standards through classroom assessment. *Phi Delta Kappan, 80*(2), 139–148.

Campbell, D. T. (1969). Reforms as experiments. *American Psychologist, 24,* 409–429.

Coe, R. (2002). Evidence on the role and impact of performance feedback in schools. In A. J. Visscher & R. Coe (Eds.), *School improvement through performance feedback* (pp. 3–26). Lisse/Abingdon/Exton, PA/Tokyo: Swets & Zeitlinger.

Coe, R., & Tymms, P. (2008). Summary of research on changes in educational standards in the UK. In M. Harris (Ed.), *Education briefing book 2008: IoD Policy Paper* (pp. 86–109). London: Institute of Directors.

Cole, M., Gay, J., Glick, J. A., & Sharp, D. W. (1971). *The cultural context of learning and thinking.* New York: Basic Books.

Fitz-Gibbon, C. T. (1996). *Monitoring education: Indicators, quality and effectiveness.* London: Cassell.

Fitz-Gibbon, C. (2004). Editorial: The need for randomized trials in social research. *Journal of the Royal Statistical Society Series A, 167*(1), 1–4.

Fitz-Gibbon, C. T., & Tymms, P. B. (2002). Technical and ethical issues in indicator systems: Doing things right and doing wrong things. *Education Policy Analysis Archives, 10*(6). Retrieved April 8, 2008, from http://epaa.asu.edu/epaa/v10n6/

Harlen, W. (2005). Trusting teachers' judgements: Research evidence of the reliability and validity of teachers' assessments for summative purposes. *Research Papers in Education, 20*(3), 245–270.

Kane, M. T. (2006). Validation. In R. L. Brennan (Ed.), *Educational measurement* (4th ed., pp. 18–64). Westport, CT: American Council on Education and Praeger.

LeVine, R. A. (2004). Challenging expert knowledge: Findings from an African study of infant care and development. In U. P. Gielen & J. Roopnarine (Eds.), *Childhood and adolescence: Cross-cultural perspectives and applications* (pp. 149–165). Westport, CT: Praeger.

Messick, S. (1989). Meaning and values in test validation: The science and ethics of assessment. *Educational Researcher, 18*(2), 5–11.

Mullis, I. V. S., Martin, M. O., Gonzalez, E. J., & Kennedy, A. M. (2001). *PIRLS 2001 international report: IEA's study of reading literacy achievement in primary school in 35 countries.* Boston: Boston College, Lynch School of Education, International Study Center.

Mutumbuka, D. (2006). The World Bank and secondary education in Africa. In R. L. Smith et al. (Eds.), *Norwegian Post-Primary Education Fund for Africa* (pp. 7–8). Oslo: University College, Centre for International Education.

Mwanakatwe, J. M. (1968). *The growth of education in Zambia since independence.* Oxford, UK: Oxford University Press.

Niu, W. (2007). Western influences on Chinese educational testing. *Comparative Education, 43*(1), 71–91.

Slavin, R. E. (2008). What works? Issues in synthesizing educational program evaluations. *Educational Researcher, 37*(1), 5–14.

Sternberg, R. J. (2004). Culture and intelligence. *American Psychologist, 59*(5), 325–338.

Tattersall, K. (2007). A brief history of policies, practices and issues relating to comparability. In P. Newton, J.-A. Baird, H. Goldstein, H. Patrick, & P. Tymms (Eds.), *Techniques for monitoring the comparability of examination standards* (pp. 324–328). London: Qualifications and Curriculum Authority.

Troy, P. H., Wyness, L. A., & McAuliffe, E. (2007). Nurses' experiences of recruitment and migration from developing countries: A phenomenological approach. *Health Resources for Health, 5*(15). Retrieved April 8, 2008, from http://www.human-resources-health.com/content/5/1/15

Tymms, P., Coe, R., & Merrell, C. (2005). *Standards in English schools: Changes since 1997 and the impact of government policies and initiatives: A report for the* Sunday Times. Durham, UK: Durham University, CEM Centre.

Tymms, P., & Merrell, C. (2007). *Standards and quality in English primary schools over time: The national evidence: Primary Review Research Survey 4/1.* Cambridge, UK: University of Cambridge, Faculty of Education.

Tymms, P. B., Merrell, C., & Coe, R. (2008, September). Educational policies and randomized controlled trials. *The Psychology of Education Review, 32*(2), 3–7.

Visscher, A. J., & Coe, R. (Eds.). (2002). *School improvement through performance feedback.* Lisse/Abingdon/Exton, PA/Tokyo: Swets & Zeitlinger.

Ziegler, J. C., & Goswami, U. (2005). Reading acquisition, developmental dyslexia, and skilled reading across languages: A psycholinguistic grain size theory. *Psychological Bulletin, 131*(1), 3–29.

Index

Abasement scores, 366
Abilities, 405
  academic, 383
  cognitive, in Zambia, 164–166
  creative, 447
  Institute of Personality and Ability
    Testing, 340
  Intellectual Abilities Test, 320
  language/reading, in GCC countries,
    299–309
  patterns of, 431
  person, 45
  practical, 447
  trace, 383
  Western ability tests, 170–177
  Woodcock-Johnson Tests of Cognitive
    Abilities, 34–35
Abulkhanova-Slavskaya, K. A., 364
Academic self-concept, 354, 362–363, 367
Academic success, 363
Accountability, 77, 80
  "consequential accountability," 82
  "intelligent accountability," 82–83
  moderation for, 90
  as purpose for testing, 476–478
  standardized testing driving, 81
  systems for, 241
Acculturation, 52
  culture and, 474
  equity and, 60–61
  of Hispanics, 421–422
  language proficiency and, 63
  levels of, influencing test performance,
    60–61
  test performance and, 60–61, 69–71

Achievement, 5. *See also* Student
    achievement
  academic, 359–363
  International Association for the
    Evaluation of Educational
    Achievement, 79
  Monitoring Learning Achievement,
    161
  testing for, 162
Achievement tests, 162. *See also Zambian
    Achievement Test*
Achilles, xv
Acquisition of competencies, 406
Activities, 23
Activity, Consciousness and Personality
    (Leontiev), 353
Activity theory, 356
Adaptation
  of 16PF Questionnaire, 340–341
  defined, 444
  ethical issues associated with, 15
  international guidelines for, 9–10
  for local GCC populations,
    304–306
  in Romania, 30–31
  standardized testing and, 306
  translation and, 446
Adaptive behaviors, 23
Adding It Up (NRC), 240–241
Additivity, 47
Administrators, 7, 25, 391
Adults, 7–8
Advanced concepts, 278–280
AERA. *See* American Educational
    Research Association

489

Africa
  "Africa's Development Needs," 114
  bilingual challenges in, 195
  child development in, 101–102, 116, 152
  children as challenge of, 113
  developmental assessment in, 100, 104–116, 138
  foreign languages used for formal education in, 189
  gender bias in language of, 188
  hybridism of, 115
  ineffectiveness of educational system in, 194
  Kashoki on assessment research in, 120
  language issues in, 140–141, 150, 178–180, 187–191, 207–208
  literacy at unsatisfactory levels in, 194
  low regard from international community for, 120
  normative development in, 96
  peer culture in, 103
  regional language education in, 191
  rural v. urban mothers in, 148
  schools in, emphasizing different values from indigenous culture, 115
  search for evaluation indicators in, 116
  testing in mother tongue recommended in, 208
  translation of test instruments in, 118
African Americans, 53
African children
  bilingualism challenges of, 195
  challenge of developmental assessments for, 138
  developmental assessment of, 100, 104–116, 138
  developmental issues for, 96, 141–142, 144–145
  differences in response to languages from, 200–206
  double disadvantage of, 196
  "emergence" in, 102
  lack of understanding of, 116
  mother tongue and, 206, 480
  musical activities of, 147

  performances by, for smaller children, 148
  physical/social setting for, in Kokwet, Kenya, 147–150
  responses by, in Ghana, 202–205
  rights of, to learn mother tongue, 188
  self-initiated activities of, in Nigeria, 149
  as subject of cross-cultural research, 138–139
  Super on motor competence in, 152
African expertise, 119
African parenting, 101, 123, 139–140
  agency in, 102
  expanded concept of intelligence in, 140–141
  Harkness and Super on, 140–141
  in Nigeria, 144–145
African pedagogies, 114
"Africa's Development Needs," 114
AFT. *See* American Federation of Teachers
Age-based competence, 142–143, 146
Age groups, 328–329
Agency, 102
Al-Akeel, A., 301–302
Al Mannai, H., 303
Alternative assessments. *See* Authentic alternative assessments
American culture, 335
American Educational Research Association (AERA), 26, 42, 85, 336
American Federation of Teachers (AFT), 255
American Psychological Association (APA), 17, 26, 42, 336–337
American students, 363–364, 366
Americans With Disabilities Act, 33
Ames, R., 228
Analysis of variance (ANOVA), 331, 365
Analytical intelligence, 447
Anderson, L. W., 269–270
ANOVA. *See* Analysis of variance
APA. *See* American Psychological Association
APA Code of Conduct, 19–20

Apás, 385
Apprentices, 385
Arabic, 292, 299
    dialects of, 295
    MSA as formal version of, 295
    Palestinian Arabic, 296
    Qatari Arabic, 303
    transparency/obliqueness in, 296
"arbiters of performance quality," 83
Aronson, J., 54–55
Artistic type, 337, 339
Ashanti. *See* Twi
Asmara Declaration on African
        Languages and Literatures,
        187–188
Assessment(s), xv, 276, 281. *See also*
        Developmental assessment;
        Equity/Equitable assessments;
        Formative assessment;
        High-stakes assessments;
        Multidimensional assessments;
        Programme for International
        Student Assessment; Summative
        assessment
    Assessment Is for Learning, 261
    Assessment Reform Group, 240
    attitudes toward, in GCC countries,
        296–299
    authentic alternative, 88–89
    Bennett on challenge of comprehensive
        assessment system, 262
    bilingual, 195
    Brazilian Institute of Psychological
        Assessment, 29
    British Assessment Reform group,
        237
    centralized v. classroom, 390
    challenges of bilingual, 195
    challenges/trajectories in, of Spanish
        speakers, 425–428
    characteristics of good, 87
    classroom, 277–280, 389–392, 412
    cognitive, 436
    of communication/literacy skills, 288–290
    conditions of equity in, 59
    criteria, 277
    cross-cultural, 474–475
    cultural, 437
    culture of, 263
    curriculum-based, 77, 453
    defined, 255
    educational, 452
    emotional, 434
    ethnocentricity in, 133
    Eurocentric perspective in, 337
    evaluation and, 98
    in GCC countries, 288–290, 296–309
    Ghana study of, in mother tongue, 196
    globalization and, 153, 163–164, 469,
        480, 483
    initiatives by MOE, 282
    Institute of Personality Assessment and
        Research, 30
    instruction going hand in hand with, 208
    Kashoki on research on, in Africa, 120
    knowledge, 271
    large-scale, 389–413
    limits on, in mother tongue, 207
    as means to widen pedagogic horizons,
        254
    *Measuring Student Knowledge and
        Skills: A New Framework for
        Assessment*, 225–226
    multicultural, xvi
    NEO Five-Factor Inventory, 8, 358
    neuropsychological, 434–435
    "of," "for," and "as" learning, 255–256,
        479
    pedagogy and, 254
    personality, 30
    psychological, 29
    psychometric, 433–434
    purpose of, 469
    quality of Singaporean teachers, 279
    quantitative, 86–87
    for reading, 291
    reform, 220–221, 237
    shared social beliefs as root of, 111
    Singaporean teachers and, 273–275
    Singapore Examinations and
        Assessment Board, 260–261
    for SLI avoided by GCC parents, 298
    social justice enhanced through
        practices of, 58–71

Assessment(s) (*continued*)
  Spanish speakers and, 425–428
  standards for, 84–86
  Sternberg on, 163–164
  teacher-based, 87–89
  technology in, 239
Assessors
  behavior/attitudes/training of, 110
  field practice of, 111
  responsibility to parents of, 123
Attention span, 317
Attitudes, 110, 431
  of assessors, 110
  in GCC countries, 296–299
  public, 25
Aurora-*a* (paper-and-pencil module of
    Aurora Battery), 445, 447–448,
    450, 456
Aurora Battery
  as comprehensive evaluation battery,
    445
  for identification of gifted students in
    England, 454
  international aspect of, 443
  for KSA, not culturally neutral, 463
  psychometric bases of, 446–447
  for Russia, 458–461
  for Saudi Arabia, 461–464
  for Spain, 455–458
  Sternberg's theory as basis for, 444
  translation of, across languages/
    cultures, 450–451, 460
  in England, 451–455
Australia, 79–80, 91, 477
Authentic alternative assessments, 88–89
Authentic instruction, 265, 267–268
Autonomy, 365
Avoidance, 15
Aysenck's model, 352

Baby massage, 151
Baccalauréat, 386
Bahraini children, 303
Bandura, A. J., 354
Basic interpersonal communicative skills
    (BICS), 192
Basic Knowledge Transmission, 270, 272

Behavior, 110
Bennett, Randy, 235, 262
Berry, J. W., 95
Best practice, 108–116
Bias, 48, 60–61, 188, 306–307, 344, 433,
    436, 475
BICS. *See* Basic interpersonal
    communicative skills
Bidwell, Charles, 216
Big Five personality traits, 343
Bilingual assessment, 195
Bilingualism, 195
Binet, Alfred, 158
Bionomical type, 339
Black, P.
  on formative assessment, 240–241
  formative/summative assessment
    continuum questioned by, 262
Blustein, D. L., 336
Book, H. E., 357
Borland, J. H., 316
Boston City School District, 243
Botswana, 193
Brain function, 472
Bram, C., 95–96
Bransford, J. D., 240
Brazil, 27–29
  competencies tested in, 406
  enrollment in schools, 395–396
  large-scale assessment in, 392–413
  Mercosul and, 393
  Portuguese language proficiency
    averages in, 398
Brazilian Institute of Psychological
    Assessment, 29
Brazilian National Curricular Standards,
    398
British Assessment Reform group, 237
Brito, M. R. F., 384, 390
Broadfoot, P., 81
Bruner, J., 100
Bureaucratization, 78
Bush, George, 253
Business connections, 380

California Psychological Inventory, 32–33
Callaghan, L., 100

CALP. *See* Cognitive academic language proficiency
The Cambridge Handbook of the Learning Sciences (Carver), 232
Capacity building, 238–243
Capital
  emotional, 258
  formation of, 259
  human, 218, 225, 227
  imagination, 258
  knowledge, 258
  social, 258
Capital formation, 259
Caretaker psychology, 135–137
Carver, Sharon, 232
Case-tests, 345
Catell, Raymond, 342
Catell-Horn-Caroll (CHC) theory of intelligence, 34
CBT. *See* Computer-based testing
CD. *See* Cube Design
CELF-4. *See* Clinical Evaluation of Language Fundamentals
CEM. *See* Centre for Evaluation and Monitoring
Census of Basic Education, 395
Centralized assessment, 390
Centre for Evaluation and Monitoring (CEM), 479
Centre for Research in Pedagogy in Practice (CRPP), 230, 254, 263, 270
Chambers, R., 109
The Changing Nature of Work (NRC), 225
CHC. *See* Catell-Horn-Caroll theory of intelligence
χ^2 equation, 322
Chih (realizing), 228
Child development. *See also* Developmental assessment; Developmental niche
  in Africa, 101–102, 116, 152
  environment of, 134
  Keller on, 152
Child language research, 300
Children. *See also* African children; Gifted children
  as Africa's challenge, 113

Bahraini, 303
  as contributors to their own developmental learning, 103
  daily routines of, 135
  indigenous v. nonindigenous, 79
  interaction with strangers as factor in testing process, 122
  of Nso learning self-care, 102–103
  peer culture empowering, 119
  play activities of, in Nigeria/Kenya, 147
  responses by, in language study, 202–205
  socialization of, 101
  testing for, criterion-based v. normative, 122
  test use with, 4–7
  Wechsler Intelligence Scale for Children, 20
China, 235–236, 382
Chinese culture, 335
Choral repetition, 264
CIT. *See* Critical Incident Technique (CIT)
Civic development, 259
Classical test theory (CTT), 44, 46
Classroom. *See also* Connections to world beyond classroom
  assessment practices in, 277–280, 389–392, 412
  discussion, 267
  expert knowledge/instruction and, 242
  high-stakes assessments, instruction in, 230–237
  pattern of instruction in, 264
CLD. *See* Culturally/linguistically different populations
Clinical Evaluation of Language Fundamentals (CELF-4), 201
Clitic pronouns, 305
Code of Hammurabai, 17
Codes of conduct, 109
Cognitive ability, 164–166
Cognitive academic language proficiency (CALP), 192
Cognitive assessment, 436
Cognitive components, 369

Cognitive development/growth, 108, 122
Cognitive-personality interactions, 369
Cognitive processes, 162
Cognitive resources, 63
Cognitive skills, 146, 150
Cognitive test scores, 222
Cohen, David, 218
Cole, M., 121
Collaboration, 160
Collectivism, 3–4
Colonialism, 98, 188
Colonial language variants, 194–195
Communication, 64
Communication disorders, 288
Communication skills, 287–290, 472
Communism, 4, 29
Comparability, 89–90
Competence/competencies, 133,
    227–228, 383
  achievement tests measuring, 162
  acquisition of, tested in Brazil, 406
  age-based, 142–143, 146
  baby massage for motor, 151
  bias in concept of, 433
  culturally based, 151–153
  higher education and, 380
  at higher education level, 384
  mastery and, 384
  personality and, 153
  technical, 388
  in various languages of Zambia, 178–180
Complex Knowledge Construction, 270,
    272
Comprehensive evaluation battery, 445
Computer-based testing (CBT), 15–17
*Computer-based Testing and the Internet:
    Issues and Advances* (ITC), 16
Conceptual depth, 270
Conceptual knowledge, 269
Condition equivalence, 430
Conditions of equity, 54–58
  assessment decisions/results and, 59
  context influencing, 57–58
  participation influenced by, 71
  personal factors influencing, 56–57
  sociocultural influences on, 55–56
  structural organization of, 54

Confidentiality, 297
Connections to world beyond classroom,
    277–280
Connell, Bob, 231
Conscientiousness, 358
Consensus Based Standards Validation
    Process, 92
"Consequential accountability," 82
Consequential validity, 43
Consistency, 89–90
Construct, 473–474
Construct equivalence, 11–12
Construct irrelevance, 11
Construct underrepresentation,
    11
Construct validity, 12
Contemporary redundancy, 153
Context, 57–58, 473–474
Context equivalence, 430
Contextualist theories, 99
Context-validity, 118–120
Continuous education programs, 381
Conventional type, 337
Convention on the Rights of the Child
    (CRC), 116, 124
Cooperative spirit, 388
Copyright protection, 20, 427
Correction coefficients, 327
CRC. *See* Convention on the Rights of
    the Child
Creative abilities, 447
Credibility, 85
Crévola, C., 242
Criterion-based testing, 122, 431–433
Critical Incident Technique (CIT), 345
Critical thinking, 376
Cross-cultural issues, 336
  assessments, 474–475
  career counseling, 336
  Cross-Cultural Research and
    Methodology Series, 95
  portability, 66
  research, 138–139
CRPP. *See* Centre for Research in
    Pedagogy in Practice
Crystallized intelligence, 459
CTT. *See* Classical test theory

Cubans, 419, 420
Cube Design (CD), 165
Cue utilization approach, 316
Cultural assessment, 437
Cultural bias, 436
Cultural context, 469
Cultural diversity, 335
Cultural equivalence, 304
Cultural indices, 436
Cultural-Language Test Classifications
    and Interpretive Matrix, 69–71
Culturally based competence, 151–153
Culturally/linguistically different (CLD)
    populations, 308
Cultural sensitivity, 481–482
Culture/cultural traditions/cultural
    practices. *See also* Acculturation;
    Folk culture; Indigenous culture;
    Peer culture
  acculturation and, 474
  African language tightly linked with,
    208
  in Africa's hybridism, 115
  American/Chinese, 335
  Aurora Battery and, 450–451, 460, 463
  bias, 48, 60–61, 306–307
  Bram on, 95–96
  child's environment as part of cultural
    system, 134
  Chinese, 335
  competencies with, 151–153
  cross-cultural portability, 66
  Cultural-Language Test Classifications
    and Interpretive Matrix, 69–71
  in developmental assessment of African
    children, 100
  developmental niche/themes of, 138
  differences, 11–12
  environments of children as part of,
    134
  in equitable assessments, 59–63
  evaluation as part of, 381
  fairness and, 52, 64
  in GCC countries, 291–293, 298–299
  *Human Development in Cultural
    Context: A Third World
    Perspective*, 95

  in institutionalist theories, 216–217
  in interpretation of Zambian test
    results, 181
  intolerance of diversity, 124
  for KSA, in adapting Aurora Battery,
    463
  learning based on, 153
  measures, 52
  mother tongue preferred due to, 207
  multicultural assessments, xvi
  Multidimensional Measure of Cultural
    Identity for Latino and Latina
    Adolescents, 437
  in parenting, 99
  questions about, in Aurora
    development, 443
  sociocultural influences on conditions
    of equity, 55–56
  Sperry on irrelevance of, 471
  students as members of community of,
    228
  in testing, 121, 123, 181
  test performance for individuals of
    diverse, 70
  themes in developmental niche, 138
  translation of Aurora Battery across
    language, 450–451
  universal markers in child development
    and, 101
  validity of RIASEC Model for
    different, 338
  validity within context of, 469
  Zambia testing considering, 181
Culture-free processing measures, 301
Curriculum
  assessment as driver for, 77
  bureaucratization of, 78
  changing priorities in, 78
  CRPP researchers finding strong
    framework for, 270
  distortion of, through high-stakes
    assessments, 236–237
  hegemonic, 231
  local social context and, 387
Curriculum-based assessment, 77, 453
Customs, 135–137
Czech Republic, 28, 33–36

Daily routines, 135
Darling-Hammond, Linda, 236
Darwin, Charles, 111
Dasen, P. R., 108
Data analysis, 13
Decentering, 13–14
Declaration of Universal Ethical
    Principles for Psychologists, 18
Declarative knowledge, 387, 405
*The Definition and Selection of Key
    Competencies* (DeSeCo Project),
    227–228
Democratic state, 364
Demographics
    of GCC countries, 290
    of Hispanic/Latino populations,
        417–421
    of Zambia, 160
Department for Education and
    Employment (DfEE), 79
Department for Education and Skills
    (DfES), 79
Depth of knowledge, 277–280
DeSeCo Project. *See The Definition and
    Selection of Key Competencies*
Developing countries
    collaboration of psychologists needed
        in, 160
    majority of world population living in,
        159
Developmental assessment, 97–98, 138
    of African children, 100
    best practice in, 108–116
    as laborious process, 123
    in Sub-Saharan Africa, 104–108
Developmental niche
    cultural themes in, 138
    defined, 134
    physical/social setting as part of,
        134–135
    three corollaries in, 137
Developmental proficiency, 62
Developmental timetables
    for children in Nigeria, 144–145
    Harkness and Super on, 141–142
Development of Basic Education Index
    (IDEB), 401

DfEE. *See* Department for Education
    and Employment
DfES. *See* Department for Education
    and Skills
Diacritics, 198
Diagnosis, 478–480
*Diagnostic and Statistical Manual of
    Mental Disorders* (DSM), 21
Diagnostic instructional pathways, 242
Diagnostic tools, 341–346
Dialects
    of Arabic, 295
    GCC countries issues with, 305
    important role of, in Africa, 187
DIF. *See* Differential item functioning
Differential item functioning (DIF),
    48–51, 475
Differentiated instruction, 242–243
Digital technology, 234
Diglossia, 295
DiMaggio, P., 216
Direct teaching, 213, 266, 267, 268, 271,
    478
Disability, 21–22
Discipline, 213
Disease, 160
Disposition, 134
Distributions, 171
Domestic workers
    influence of, in GCC countries, 292
    SLI and, 299
Donovan, M. S., 240
DSM. *See Diagnostic and Statistical
    Manual of Mental Disorders*
DSM International Version, 21
Durham University, 479
Duxbury, MA, 142
Dweck, C. S., 352–353, 355
Dynamic assessment (DA), 301, 308–309
Dynamic evaluation, 412
Dynamic regulative systems, 355, 363,
    367
Dyslexia, 289, 300, 481

Early childhood development (ECD), 116
EBPP. *See* Evidence Based Policy and
    Practice

ECD. *See* Early childhood development
Economic Review Committee (ERC), 258
Economics, 2, 224
Economy, 258. *See also* Knowledge Based Economies
  globalized, 258
  moral, 215, 246
  National Center on Education and the Economy, 235
  The Singapore Economy: New Directions, 258
Education
  formal, delivered in foreign language in Africa, 189
  formal, in GCC countries, 293–294
  higher, conflict with mother tongue, 193
  questions surrounding bilingual/ multilingual, 191–192
  regional language, 191
  standardized tests in, 26
Education (Russia), 458
Educational assessment, 452
Educational equivalence, 428
Educational institutions, 2
Educational pathologists, 289
Educational policies, 223–224
Educational system(s)
  of GCC countries, 293–294
  ineffectiveness of African, 194
  MOE commitment to, for KBE, 258–259
  OECD concerns about, 228
  test use impact of, 24–25
  as transmission system for government, 376
Educational Testing Service, 235
Edwards, C. P., 143, 352
Edwards Personal Preference Schedule (EPPS), 352
EFPA. *See* European Federation of Professional Psychologists Associations
EFPA Meta-code of Ethics, 18–19
Egalitarianism, 4
Elbeheri, G., 300

Elementary and Secondary Education Act (ESEA), 253
Elicitation/discussion, 264
Ellis, M. V., 336
Elmore, Richard, 239
Embeddedness, 220
Emergence
  in African children, 123
  child development in Africa through, 102
Emotional assessment, 434
Emotional capital, 258
Emotional closeness, 136–137
Emotional intelligence, 357, 368
  academic achievement predicted by, 359–363
  self-concept and, 362
Emotions, 207
Employability skills, 309
Employee performance evaluation, 375
ENADE. *See Exame Nacional de Desempheno dos Estudantes*
ENEM. *See Exame Nacional do Ensino Médio*
England. *See* United Kingdom
English language, 207
Enrollment, evolution of, in Brazil, 395
Enrollment distribution, in Brazil, 396
Enterprising type, 337
Entity theory, 355, 361
Entrepreneurial spirit, 388
Environments
  of child development, 134
  of children as part of cultural system, 134
  for learning, 133
Epistemic authority, 265
EPPS. *See* Edwards Personal Preference Schedule
Equitable measures
  additivity of, 47–48
  individual person level interpretability of, 49–50
  objective differentiation of groups allowed by, 48–49
  sample free/scale free property of, 46

Equity/equitable assessments, 41
  acculturation and, 60–61
  approaches to enhancing, 63–71
  conditions of, 54–58
  CTT v. IRT approaches to, 47
  Cultural-Language Test Classifications
    and Interpretive Matrix for, 69–71
  cultural/linguistic factors in, 59–63
  definition/significance, 42–43
  Hispanics/African Americans and, 53
  in moderation practice, 89–90
  social justice foundations of, 53, 72
  technical basis of, 43
ERC. *See* Economic Review Committee
Errands
  Keller on child development through,
    152
  as learning experiences, in Nigeria, 149
  as learning experiences, in Senegal, 151
Essay on Man (Pope), 111
Ethical issues
  EFPA Meta-Code of Ethics, 18–19
  international ethics codes, 18
  international studies on ethics codes,
    19–21
  regional ethics codes, 18–19
  test adaptation and, 15
  with test development/use, 17–21
Ethical standards, 109
Ethical values, 377
Ethics, 98
Ethnicity, 474
Ethnocentricity, 133
Ethnopedagogy, 100
Ethnopsychology, 100
Ethnotheories, 140–143
Eurocentricity, 337, 470
European Federation of Professional
    Psychologists Associations (EFPA),
    18–19
Evaluation
  assessment and, 98
  Aurora Battery as comprehensive tool
    for, 445
  Brito on, 390
  Centre for Evaluation and Monitoring,
    479

Clinical Evaluation of Language
    Fundamentals, 201
  culture and, 381
  dynamic, 412
  Evaluation Institute, 294
  globalization and, 378
  history of, 377
  institutional, 375
  of intelligence, 375
  International Association for the
    Evaluation of Educational
    Achievement, 79
  for policy development, 80–81
  program, 375
  research and, 377
  search for indicators in Africa, 116
  student performance, 375
Evaluation Institute, 294
Evaluation of intelligence, 375
Evaluative culture, 381
Everatt, J., 303
Evidence Based Policy and Practice
    (EBPP), 80–81
Ewe, 197–198, 206
*Exame Nacional de Desempenho
    dos Estudantes* (ENADE), 393,
    404–406, 408–411
Exame Nacional do Ensino Médio
    (ENEM), 386, 401–404
Expectations, 276
Expert knowledge
  classroom instruction and, 242
  schematic model for, 242–243
Expert panel, 457
Expressive One Word Picture Vocabulary
    Test, 308

Factor analysis, 323, 330
Factor structure, 342
Factual knowledge, 269, 278–280
Fairness, 33, 41–43, 50–51. *See also*
    Equitable measures; Equity/
    Equitable assessments
  cultural/linguistic considerations, 52, 64
  nonverbal testing limitions of, 65
Family role, 293, 297
Federal Council of Psychologists, 28

Feedback, 266, 276
Ferguson, C., 295
Field practice, of assessors, 111
Figurative language, 463
Figures of speech, 464
Finland, 82
"Fitness for purpose," 81
Flores, L. Y., 336
Folk culture, 215
  Cohen on, 218
  as moral economy, 246
Ford, M., 233
Forman, E., 233
Formative assessment, 213
  Black on, 240–241
  NRC on, 241
  research dominated by two traditions,
    240
  schematic model for, 242–243
  Singapore educational system lacking,
    282
  summative assessment and, in
    Singapore, 261
  tighter coupling for, 238, 244
  Wiliam and Black questioning
    continuum of divide between/
    continuum with, 262
  Wiliam on, 240–241
Formative feedback, 478–480
Forward and Backward Digit Span, 306
FPE. *See* Free Primary Education
Free Primary Education (FPE), 187
Fricatives, 198
  in Gonja, 199
  in Twi, 199–200
Fullan, Michael, 216, 242
Functional equivalence, 304
"Funds of knowledge," 97
Furman, Anton, 34–35

Garrel, A., 97
GCC. *See* Gulf Cooperation Council
GCC countries, 288, 290, 295
  assessment of communication/literacy
    skills in, 289
  attitudes toward assessments in,
    296–299

confidentiality importance in, 297
cultural considerations, 298–299
cultural practices relevant to language/
  literacy in, 292–293
demographics of, 290
developing assessment tools for
  language/reading abilities in,
  299–309
dialect issues in, 305
domestic workers influence in, 292
educational system of, 293–294
family role in, 293
learning disabilities growing
  recognition in, 294
parenting in, 297–298
parents in, avoiding assessment for
  SLI, 298
paucity of child language research in,
  300
reading assessment professionals in,
  291
socioeconomic characteristics
  of, 290
solutions to assessment challenges in,
  300–309
speech/language pathologists in, 291
speech/language pathologists not well
  established in, 300
test adaptation in, 304–306
translation of tests for, 305
Gender bias, 188
General Aptitudes Scale, 462
General intelligence, 451
Genotype, 99
Ghana
  KABC-II studied in, 200–201
  languages collected in different regions
    of, 206
  languages studies in, 196–200
  language study in, 196
  methodology of study of language in,
    201
  responses by children of, in language
    study, 202–205
  vocabulary in mother tongues of,
    197
Giddens, Anthony, 227–228

Gifted children, 315. *See also* Gifted
  students
  characteristics of, 316–317
  identification procedure for, 319
  KSA and, 461
  methodology of study on gifted
    children in Saudi Arabia, 321–323
Gifted Classification Scale, 318
Gifted Generation (Russia), 458
Giftedness. *See* Gifted children; Gifted
  students; Theories of giftedness
Gifted students, 454
Gift Scale, 318
Globalised economy, 258
Globalization, 112
  assessment based on, 153, 480
  assessment issues in, reflecting other
    issues in, 469
  business connections and, 380
  defined, xv, 379
  immigration and, 379
  models of assessment in era of,
    163–164
  nature of assessment and nature of, 483
  radical changes of educational
    evaluation through, 378
  Sobrinho on, 380
  testing in era of, 159
Global trends
  changing curriculum priorities, 78
  international comparisons, 78–80
Global University Network (GUNI), 381
Global workplace, 288, 309
Goldberg, Lewis, 343
Gonja, 197–199, 206
*Gonja: A Phonological and Grammatical
  Study* (Painter), 199
Goswami, U., 473
Gould, S. J., 112
Government
  economic outcomes fostered by, 224
  educational systems transmitting
    information flitered by, 376
  role of, in educational system of
    Singapore, 214
  Singapore, changing institutional rules,
    224

Grade 5 National Assessment (NAG5),
  166
Graham, Angus, 229
Grieve, K. W., 121
Gröhn, K., 113, 117
Gross, M., 317
Grubb, N., 236
Guidelines, 8. *See also* Standards
  international, 9–17
  technical, 8–9
Gulf Cooperation Council (GCC), 287.
  See also GCC countries
GUNI. *See* Global University Network

Hakansson, G., 307
Hall, D., 228
Hany, E. A., 316
Harkness, Sara, 138–139
  on African parenting, 140–141
  on challenges of foreign testing, 471
Harlen, Wynne, 230, 232
Hartlepool, England, 454
Hartung, P. J., 336
Harvard Business School, 379
Health, 21–22
Hector, xv
Hegemonic curriculum, 231
Helpfulness, 143
Higher education, 380, 384, 405
Higher education degrees, 381
High-stakes assessments
  decoupling, from classroom instruction,
    230–237
  distortion of curriculum through,
    236–237
  for quality control, 234
  Singapore's system of, 218, 221, 260,
    281
  student achievement and, 246
High-statism, 214
Hill, P., 242
Hippocratic Oath, 17
Hispanics/Latinos
  acculturation of, 421–422
  challenges of addressing measurement
    of, 417
  copyright issues with testing for, 427

criterion-based testing and, 431–433
cultural assessment for, 437
defined, 417–418
demographics of, 417–421
development of new instruments for, 429–431
as economic/social failures, 438
educational equivalence in sampling, 428
emotional assessment of, 434
equitable assessment and, 53
future questions for, 433
as largest minority in United States, 419
limited tests available for, 426
neuropsychological assessment of, 434–435
normative samples for, 427–428
psychometric assessment of, 433–434
traditional approach to testing of, 422
translation of standardized tests for, 422–424
translation of tests as challenge for, 426–427
within-group heterogeneity of, 421
Hofstede, Geert, 343–344
Holland, John, 337
Homework, 266
Homogenization, 112
Homophones, 464
House Education and Labor Committee, 236
Hsin (living up to one's word), 228
Hsueh (learning), 228
Human behavior, 110
Human capital
    formation of, 218
    research, noncognitive skills and, 227
    theory, noncognitive skills and, 225
Human Development in Cultural Context: A Third World Perspective (Lonner and Berry), 95
Humanities students, 361
Human ontogenesis, 96
Hungary, 28, 33–36
Hybridism, 115

IAAP. *See* International Association of Applied Psychologists
ICC. *See* Item characteristic curve
ICF. *See International Classification of Diseases and Related Health Problems*
ICSAA. *See* International Conference on the State of Affairs of Africa
IDEB. *See* Development of Basic Education Index
Illiteracy, 394
Imagination capital, 258
Imitation Test of Personnel Management Brief (ITPMB), 345
Immigrants, 60–61
Immigration, 379
Implicit theories
    of intelligence, 359
    intuitive regulation and, 368
    of learning, 354–355, 358, 362
    of personality, 359
Inattentiveness, 15
India, 235–236
Indicators, 113, 116
Indigeneity, 108
Indigenous culture, 115
Individual efficiency, 388
Individual experiment, 351
Individualism, 3–4, 365
Individualism-collectivism continuum, 367
Individual person level, 49–50
Individual seatwork, 264
Infit statistics, 50
Innovation, 213, 220
Institute of Personality and Ability Testing (IPAT), 340
Institute of Personality Assessment and Research, 30
Institutional evaluation, 375
Institutional isomorphism, 215, 217
    embeddedness and, 220
    logic of confidence and, 220
    reforms potentially weakening, 219
Institutionalist theories, 215
    cultural factors in, 216–217
    rules in, 217
    value of new, 219

Institutionalized Public Basic Schooling, 114
Institutional rules, 217–218, 224
Instituto Nacional de Estudos e Pesquisas Educacionais Anísio Teixeira (INEP), 400
Instruction, 208
Intellectual Abilities Test, 320
Intellectual imperialism, 432
Intellectual Potential Department (Russia), 458
Intellectual property, 16
Intelligence, 5, 102
  African language to describe, 140–141
  analytical, 447
  Catell-Horn-Caroll (CHC) theory of intelligence, 34
  crystallized, 459
  emotional intelligence, 357, 359–363, 368, 375
  evaluation of, 375
  expanded concept of, in African parenting, 140–141
  general, 451
  implicit theories of, 359
  Panga Manthu Test of African Intelligence, 165–166
  peer-estimated intelligence (PEI), 360
  practical, 460
  psychometric intelligence, 358–363
  self-estimated intelligence, 360
  Sternberg's theory of successful, 162, 444
  Universal Nonverbal Intelligence Test, 164–165, 172
  Wechsler Intelligence Scale for Children, 20, 429, 449, 462
"Intelligent accountability," 82–83
Internal consistency, 331
International Association for the Evaluation of Educational Achievement (IEA), 79
International Association of Applied Psychologists (IAAP), 18, 27
International Classification of Diseases and Related Health Problems (ICF), 21–24

International Classification of Functioning, Disability and Health, 1
International Conference on the State of Affairs of Africa (ICSAA), 117
International guidelines
  on computer-based/Internet-delivered testing, 15–17
  International Test Commission, 9
  for test adaptation/use, 9–10
International School Psychology Association, 33–34
International surveys, 1, 4–8
International Test Commission (ITC), 9–10, 16
  leadership of, 27
  unauthorized sales of tests monitored by, 20–21
International Union of Psychological Science (IUPsyS), 17–18, 27
Internet, 265
Interrelations, 369
Interval measurement properties, 47
Interview, 351
Intuitive regulation, 368
IPAT. *See* Institute of Personality and Ability Testing
IQ tests, 121, 158, 162
IRT methodology, 475
IRT/Rasch modeling, 45, 46
ISC. *See* PIRLS International Study Center
Isomorphism
  institutional, 215, 217, 219–220
  mimetic v. coercive/normative, 216
Italian parenting, 136
ITC. *See* International Test Commission
Item characteristic curve (ICC), 48–49
Item characteristics, 45
Item choices, 48
Item difficulty statistics, 179–180
Item reliability estimates, 171
Item response theory (IRT), 44–47, 397
  caveats in, 50–53
  DIF and, 50–51
  ICCs and, 48–49
  transportability improved by, 71–72

Item translation, 340
ITPMB. *See* Imitation Test of Personnel
    Management Brief
IUPsyS. *See* International Union of
    Psychological Science (IUPsyS)
Ivorian adolescents, 108

Job market, 193
"Just world" philosophy, 54

KABC-II. *See The Kaufman Assessment
    Battery for Children-II*
Kashoki, M. E., 120
*The Kaufman Assessment Battery for
    Children-II* (KABC-II), 165
    broad range of difficulty levels in, 172
    in study of languages of Ghana,
        200–201
KBE. *See* Knowledge Based Economies
Kellaghan, T., 382
Keller, H., 152
Kenya, 139, 152
    developmental timetables in, 142
    indigenous languages of, 189
    mothers in, describing parenting
        practices, 140–141
    physical/social settings for children in,
        147–150
    school policies on language in, 190–191
Kindergarten, 320
Kinesthetic development, 317
King Abdulaziz and his Companions
    Foundation for Giftedness and
    Creativity (MAWHIBA), 319
Kingdom of Saudi Arabia (KSA), 301, 461
    Aurora Battery for, 461–464
    methodology of study in, on gifted
        children, 321–323
    no programs concerned with
        kindergartners in, 320
Kipsigis community, 135, 139
Klenowski, Val, 477
Klimov, Eugeny, 339
Knowledge
    assessments of, 271
    Basic Knowledge Transmission, 270,
        272
    capital, 258
    Complex Knowledge Construction,
        270, 272
    conceptual, 269
    criticism, 277–280
    declarative, 387, 405
    depth of knowledge, 277–280
    expert, 242–243
    factual, 269, 278–280
    "funds of knowledge," 97
    manipulation, 271, 277–280
    *Measuring Student Knowledge and
        Skills: A New Framework for
        Assessment*, 225–226
    metacognitive, 270
    modes of, 269–270
    pedagogical content knowledge, 242
    practices, 271
    procedural, 278–280
    tacit, 406, 445, 460
    technical, 377
Knowledge assessment, 271
Knowledge Based Economies (KBE), 225
    emphasis on communication skills in,
        287
    Singapore at the dawn of, 258
    social stratification and, 220
Koh, Kim, 478
Kornilova, T. V., 482
Kpelle tribe, 163–164
Krathwohl, D. R., 269–270
KSA. *See* Kingdom of Saudi Arabia
Kwa, 198–199

Language(s). *See also* Speech; Speech/
    language pathologists; Specific
    language impairment (SLI)
    abilities, in GCC countries, 299–309
    acculturation and proficiency in, 63
    acquisition, 62
    in Africa, 140–141, 150, 178–180,
        187–191, 195, 200–208
    Aurora Battery translation across
        diverse, 450–451, 460
    BICS/CALP, 192
    child language research, 300
    children's responses with, 202–205

Language(s) (*continued*)
Clinical Evaluation of Language Fundamentals, 201
Cognitive academic language proficiency, 192
cognitive resources used in, 63
colonial language variants, 194–195
comprehension skills, 301
cultural factors and, tightly linked in Africa, 208
Cultural-Language Test Classifications and Interpretive Matrix, 69–71
differences, 11–12
English, 207
Ewe as SVO, 198
fairness in, 52, 64
figurative, 463
in GCC countries, 291–293, 299–309
gender bias in, 188
Gonja as SVO, 199
impairment, 299
issues in test development, 62
for KBE, 287
linguistic factors in equitable assessments, 59–63
for mathematics, 193
meta-language, 267
mixing/matching, 424–425
mother tongue, 189–190, 206
native-language testing, 66–67
Portuguese, 398
questions about, in Aurora development, 443
regional language education, 191
research on, 188, 202–206
Spanish speakers, 425–428
spontaneous language samples, 304
Subject-Verb-Object, 197–198
teaching, with cards, 151
test performance for individuals of diverse, 70
Language assessment, 292–293
Large-scale assessment, 389–413
Latinos, 417–418
Latvia, 20, 28, 33–36
LD. *See* Learning disabilities

Learning, 214, 221, 228
Assessment Is for Learning, 261
assessment "of," "for," and "as," 255–256, 479
children as contributors to their own developmental, 103
communities, 243
errands for, 149, 151
implicit theories of, 354–355, 358, 362
Measurement Learning Consultants, 35
Mediated Learning Experience, 308
Monitoring Learning Achievement, 161
outcomes, discussion of intended, 277
rote, 213, 478
self-care, 102–103
special learning needs, 457
Strategies for Active and Independent Learning, 260
summative assessment and, 255
technology-based environments for, 243
Learning disabilities (LD), 158, 163
recognition growing for, in GCC countries, 294
stigmatic view in GCC countries, 297
Lecture/monologue, 264
Leong, F. T. L., 336
Leontiev, A. N., 353, 356
LeVine, R. A., 482
Levitt, Theodore, 379
Lezak, M. D., 424
Limana, A., 384
Linguistic characteristics, 294–296
Linguistic equivalencies, 464
Linn, R. L., 85
Literacy, 108–109, 288–289, 394
in KBE, 287
mother tongue and, 193
unsatisfactory levels of, in Africa, 194
in Zambia, 161
Literacy assessment, 292–293
Literacy skills
assessment of, in GCC countries, 289–290
of Bahraini children, 303
Living up to one's word (*hsin*), 228

Locally developed indicators, 87
Logic of confidence, 217, 220, 238
Logic of instrumentalism, 245
Lonner, J. W., 95
Loong, Lee Hsien, 228, 260
Loose coupling, 216
    for summative assessment, 238, 244
    tight coupling, 220
    in the United States, 221

Madaus, G. F., 382
Malinowski, B., 99
Maoz, N., 319
Mass media, 265
Mastery, 384
Mastery goal orientation, 357, 361
Mathematics, 167
    question of most effective language for
        teaching of, 193
    students in Singapore scoring top place
        in, 257
    testing in, 168
MAWHIBA. *See* King Abdulaziz and
    his Companions Foundation for
    Giftedness and Creativity
McCrae, Robert, 343–344
MDGs. *See* Millennium Development
    Goals
Means, B., 239, 241
Means length of utterance (MLU), 302
Measure development, 58
Measurement. *See also* Equitable
    measures
    bias in, 433
    challenges of, for Hispanic/Latino
        populations, 417
    challenges to, of human behavior, 110
    CTT v. IRT, 44–45
    error in, 11, 429
    interval measurement properties, 47
    professionalism in, 109
Measurement Learning Consultants, 35
*Measuring Student Knowledge and Skills:
    A New Framework for Assessment*
    (OECD), 225–226
Mediated Learning Experience (MLE),
    308

Medicine, 408
MEIM. *See* Multigroup Ethnic Identity
    Measure
Memorization, 266
Mental disorders, 21–24
Mercado Comun del Sur, 393
Mercosul, 393–394
Meritocracy, 4, 224
Metacognition, 230
Metacognitive knowledge, 270
Meta-language, 267
Methodology
    of Ghana language study, 201
    of Saudi study on gifted children,
        321–323
Metric equivalence, 304
Mexican Americans, 57
Mexico, 420
Meyer, J., 215–216
Millennium Development Goals (MDGs),
    96, 112–114, 187
    CRC and, 124
    Gröhn on, 117
Mini-Mental Examination, 436
Minister of Education, 223–224
Ministry of Education (MOE), 217–218
    assessment initiatives by, 282
    commitment of, to development
        of educational system for KBE,
        258–259
Minnesota Multiphasic Personality
    Inventory (MMPI), 8, 344
Miskel, C., 216
The Mismeasure of Man (Gould), 112
Mission statements, 109
MLA. *See* Monitoring Learning
    Achievement
MLE. *See* Mediated Learning Experience
    (MLE)
MLU. *See* Means length of utterance
MLUw. *See* Words
MMCILLA. *See* Multidimensional
    Measure of Cultural Identity for
    Latino and Latina Adolescents
MMPI. *See* Minnesota Multiphasic
    Personality Inventory
MNCs. *See* Multinational companies

Moderation, 89–91
Modernity, 68–71
Modern Standard Arabic (MSA), 295
Modified procedures, 67
MOE. *See* Ministry of Education
Monitoring Learning Achievement
    (MLA), 161
Monolinguals, 14
Mood, 15
Moral behavior, 157
Moral development, 259
Moral economy, 215, 246
Morphemes, 198, 302
Morphosyntactic structures, 301–302
Moscow Multifunctional Psychology
    Inventory, 344
Moscow State University, 363, 460
Mothers
    African v. U.S., 140–143
    errands structured as learning
        experiences by Nigerian, 149
    expectations of, for competence in
        early childhood in Nigeria, 146
    in Nigeria, 144–145
    rural v. urban, in Africa, 148
    "training mothers," 143–144
Mother tongue(s)
    absence of standard literacy materials
        in, 188, 193
    African children educated in, 480
    concept of, 189–190
    conflict with, in higher education/job
        market, 193
    cultural factors creating preference for,
        207
    debate over official language and,
        190
    difficulty of implementing school
        policies on, 191
    dominant language as compared to, for
        African children, 206
    factors impeding use of, 191–195
    in Ghana, 196–200
    socialization coincident with, 189
    testing carried out in, 208
Motivation indices, 370
Motivation profiles, 363

Motor competence
    baby massage as first stage of
        developing, 151
    Super on, in Kenya, 152
Movement, 317
MSA. *See* Modern Standard Arabic
Multidimensional assessments, 222–230,
    232
Multidimensional Measure of Cultural
    Identity for Latino and Latina
    Adolescents (MMCILLA), 437
Multigroup Ethnic Identity Measure
    (MEIM), 437
Multi-Health Systems Test, 423
Multinational companies (MNCs), 258
Mungas, D., 438
Murcia University, 456
Music, 147
Myers-Briggs Type Indicator, 7–8

NAG5. See Grade 5 National Assessment
Nasality, 198
National Academy of Education, 222
National Center on Education and the
    Economy (NCEE), 235
National Council on Measurement in
    Education (NCME), 26, 42, 255,
    337
National Curriculum, 452–453
National Education Association (NEA),
    255
National examinations, 386
National exams, 234
National Institute of Education, 254
National Mathematical Advisory Panel
    (NMAP), 269
National Research Council (NRC), 225,
    240–241
National standards, 9
Native-language testing, 66–67
Natural science students, 361
NCEE. *See* National Center on
    Education and the Economy
NCLB. *See* No Child Left Behind
    (NCLB)
NEA. *See* National Education
    Association

NEO Five-Factor Inventory, 8, 358.
See also Revised NEO Personality
Inventory
Neuropsychological assessment,
434–435
Neuropsychological Assessment (Lezak),
424
Newmann, F., 265
Ngeca tribe, 143
Ng'om (intelligent), 140–141
Nigeria, 144–145
Mothers in, structuring errands as
learning experiences, 149
stimulation/interaction for preschoolers
in, 150
verbal expression developed early in,
148
NMAP. *See* National Mathematical
Advisory Panel
No Child Left Behind (NCLB), 81, 222,
235–236, 253
Noncognitive skills, 223, 225
Non–language-specific approaches,
306–307
Nonverbal Personality Questionnaire,
32
Nonverbal testing, 64–65, 436
Nonword repetition (NWR), 307
Normative psychodiagnostic measures,
351
Normative samples, 427–428
Normative scoring, 1
availability of, 6
in Romania, 31
NRC. *See* National Research Council
Nsamenang, A. B., 482
Nso of Cameroon, 97, 102–103
Nyanja, 178–180

Oakes, J., 236
Obasi, E. M., 336
Obedience, 146
Objective differentiation, 48–49
Obliqueness, 296
Observation, 351
Obsolete tests, 20
Obstruents, 198

OECD. *See* Organization for
Economic Co-operation and
Development
"On Pedagogical Distortions in the
System of Narkompros," 352–353
Opportunity structure, 57
Orderliness scale, 366
Organizational theory, 215
Organization for Economic Co-operation
and Development (OECD), 79, 222,
225–226
concerns of, for educational systems,
228
reflectiveness as key priority of,
227
Orthography, 296
Outfit statistics, 50

Painter, C., 199
Palmer, T. G., xv
Panga Manthu Test of African
Intelligence, 165–166
Parenting. *See also* African parenting
conceptions of children's intelligence
in, 140–141
contrasting styles of U.S. v. African,
140–141
cultural factors in, 99
emotional closeness as theme of Italian,
136
ethnotheories of, 140–143
European, 142
in GCC countries, 297–298
Italian, 136
SLI and, 298
Swedish, 136
Participation, 23
Pasquali, Luis, 28
PAT. See Professional Aptitude Test
Paternalistic approach, 110
Patterns of abilities, 431
PCK. *See* Pedagogical content knowledge
Peabody Picture Vocabulary Test (PPVT),
303
Pearson Tests, 423
Pedagogical content knowledge (PCK),
242

Pedagogical innovation, 213, 220
  assessment reform and, 220
  current alignment in Singapore
    inhibiting, 244
  question of whether Singapore
    educational system supports
    enough, 224
  tight alignment between summative
    assessment and classroom
    instruction constraining, 231
Pedagogical practices
  authentic instruction, 265, 267–268
  Basic Knowledge Transmission, 272
  classroom activity, 264
  Complex Knowledge Construction, 272
  direct teaching, 213, 266–268, 271
  in Singapore, 263–269
  traditional teaching, 266–268
Pedagogies. *See also* African pedagogies
  assessments widening horizons of, 254
  innovation in, 213
Peer culture, 103, 119
Peer-estimated intelligence (PEI), 360
PEI. *See* Peer-estimated intelligence
Pellegrino, J. W., 243
Pena, E. D., 304
Performance deficit, 23
Performative control, 214
Person ability, 45
Personal factors, 56–57
Personality, 5, 359
  characteristics, 351, 356, 358
  competence and, 153
  descriptors, 207
  development of concept of, 353
Personnel problems, 425
Physical setting, 134–135, 147–150
Pictures, 65
Pidgin Gulf Arabic, 292, 299
Pilot data, 35
PIRLS. *See* Progress in International
  Reading Literacy Study
PIRLS International Study Center (ISC),
  450
PISA. *See* Programme for International
  Student Assessment
Play, 147

Plosives, 198
Policy development, 80–81
Policy makers, 391
Policy statements, 109
Political systems, 24–25
Pope, Alexander, 111
Population, 394
Portuguese language, 398
*Position Statement Concerning High-
  Stakes Testing in Pre K-12
  Education* (AERA), 85
Postmodern existential condition,
  227–228
Powell, W. W., 216
Power tests, 12
PPVT. *See* Peabody Picture Vocabulary
  Test
Practical abilities, 447
Practical intelligence, 460
Practices of care, 135–137
Predictors, 362
Pride Scale, 318
Principal component factoring, 324–325
Private interests, 376
Procedural knowledge, 278–280
Processability Theory, 307
Process motivation, 362
"Productive conflict," 91
Professional Aptitude Test (PAT), 339
Professional development, 238–239
Professionalism, 91–92, 109
Professionalization, 238–239
Program evaluation, 375
Programme for International Student
  Assessment (PISA), 79, 159, 255
  globalization taking on crucial
    importance through results from
    tests like, 380
  as most conspicuous international
    effort to measure 21st-century skills,
    225–226
Progress in International Reading
  Literacy Study (PIRLS), 449
Project Work (PW), 260, 267
Prova Brasil, 400
Provas globais finais, 386
Pseudoword decoding, 167, 169, 176

Psychodiagnostic inventories, 351
Psychological assessment, 29
Psychological characteristics, 368
Psychological Corporation, 423
Psychology/psychologists, 160
    American Psychological Association,
        17, 26, 42, 336–337
    assessments in, 29
    Brazilian Institute of Psychological
        Assessment, 29
    California Psychological Inventory,
        32–33
    caretaker, 135–137
    characteristics of, 368
    collaboration in developing countries
        needed, 160
    Declaration of Universal Ethical
        Principles for Psychologists, 18
    ethnopsychology, 100
    European Federation of Professional
        Psychologists Associations, 18–19
    Federal Council of Psychologists, 28
    International Association of Applied
        Psychologists, 18, 27
    International Union of Psychological
        Science, 17–18
    Moscow Multifunctional Psychology
        Inventory, 344
    Neuropsychological Assessment, 424
    neuropsychological assessment for
        Hispanics, 434–435
    Psychological Corporation, 423
    Russian, 368, 459
    standardized testing for, 26
    *Standards for Educational and
        Psychological Testing*, 9, 27, 42
    studies in, generalized to larger
        populations, 417
Psychometric(s), 25
    bases, 446–447
    equivalence, 430
    intelligence, 358–363
    standards, 5–6
Psychometric assessment, 433–434
Public attitudes, 25
Public interests, 376
Puerto Ricans, 419, 420

Purdue Academic Rating Scale, 318
Purpose, 469, 476
Puzzles, 65
PW. *See* Project Work

Qatar, 293–294
Qatari Arabic, 303
QSA. *See* Queensland Studies Authority
"Quality benchmarks," 83
Quality control, 234
Quantitative assessments, 86–87
Queensland, Australia, 477
Queensland Studies Authority (QSA), 91
Questioning, 266

Racism, 112
Rasch analyses, 173
Rationality, 365
Reading, 317
"Reading Acquisition, Developmental
    Dyslexia, and Skilled
    Reading Across Languages:
    A Psycholinguistic Grain Size
    Theory" (Zeigler and Goswami),
    473
Reading assessment, 291
Reading comprehension, 167, 169, 176
Reading disorders, 306
Reading recognition, 167, 169
Realistic type, 337
Realizing *(chich)*, 228
Reasoning, 391
Refactorization, 340
Reflecting *(ssu)*, 228
Reflectiveness, 227
Reform
    assessment, 220–221, 237
    Assessment Reform Group, 240
    British Assessment Reform group, 237
    global shift toward, driven by
        standards, 77
    institutional isomorphism weakened
        by, 219
    for Singapore, 244
"Regional language education," 191
Regulative mechanisms, 245
Reid, M., 117

Relativity of values, 388
Reliability, 6
  Cultural-Language Interpretive Matrix
    and, 71
  of scale in Saudi study on gifted
    children, 323
  of Zambian tests, 172–177
Repertory Grid technique, 345–346
Responses, 202–205
Responsibility, 143
Results, 407
Revised NEO Personality Inventory, 8. *See
  also* NEO Five-Factor Inventory
Revision, 13
RIASEC Model, 337–338
"Rich tasks," 92
Riddles, 148
Rights, 136–137, 188
Riverside Publishing Company,
  35
Riyadh, Saudi Arabia, 301
Rogers, M. T., 318
Romania, 29–33
Romanian Anxiety Scale, 32
Rote learning, 213, 478
Rothstein, Richard, 223
Rowan, B., 215–216
Rubrics, 275–276
Russia, 443
  Aurora Battery for, 458–461
  social situation in, 352
  in time of change, 364
Russian mentality, 364
Russian psychology, 368, 459
Russian students, 363–364, 366
Russian Thesaurus of Personality Traits,
  341–342

SACMEQ. *See* Southern Africa
  Consortium for Monitoring
  Education Quality
SAEB. *See* Sistema de Avalia-cão da
  Educação Básica
SAEB proficiency, 399
Saiegh-Haddad, E., 296
SAIL. *See* Strategies for Active and
  Independent Learning

Saint-Petersburg State University, 363
Samples, 46
Sampling, 390
Sampling broadness, 397
Sapir, Edward, 100
SAT. *See Scholastic Aptitude Test*
Saudi study on gifted children
  ANOVA results in, 329
  correction coefficients in, 327
  differences between age groups in, 328
  differences between gifted/nongifted in
    scale dimensions of, 329–330
  factorial structure of, 323
  male/female differences in, 326–328
  participants in, 321
  pilot study examinations, 322
  principal component factoring with
    varimox rotation of scale items,
    324–325
  procedure for, 321–322
  reliability of scale for, 323
  results of, 323
  t-test results, 328, 330
  validity of scale, 323
Saudi teachers, 322
Scale development, 58
Scale dimensions, 326–328
*Scales for Rating the Behavioral
  Characteristics of Superior Students
  (SRBCSS)*, 318
Scales of behavioral characteristics, 316,
  320, 332
Scandiuzzi, P. P., 385
Scheffé Test, 328
Schliecher, A., 226
Scholastic Aptitude Test (SAT), 386
Schools
  in Africa, emphasizing different values
    from indigenous culture, 115
  limited conceptual depth in Singapore,
    270
  policies on language in African,
    190–191
  poor condition of, in Zambia, 161
Science, 98, 193
Science Practical Assessment (SPA), 260
Scotland, 261

Scott, W. R., 245
SEAB. *See* Singapore Examinations and
    Assessment Board
Security, 17
SEI. *See* Self-estimated intelligence
Selection, 476
Self-concept, 361
    academic, 354, 362–363, 367
    emotional intelligence and, 362
Self-concept components, 357–358, 360,
    367
Self-consciousness, 354, 356–357
Self-efficacy concept, 354, 360
Self-esteem, 366
Self-estimated intelligence (SEI), 360
Self-regulation, 356
Senegal, 150–151
Sense components, 369
Sense regulation of thinking, 370
Serpell, R., 96
Setswana, 193
Shared social belief, 111–112
Shinkfield, J. A., 378
Shmelyov, Alexander, 339, 343
    on Eurocentricity of assessment
        instruments, 470
    Russian Thesaurus of Personality
        Traits, 341–342
    16PF Questionnaire adaptation led by,
        340–341
Signification *(yi)*, 228
Sign systems, 339
Singapore
    assessment reform in, 221
    as economic powerhouse, 256–257
    government role in educational system
        in, 214
    KBE and, 258
    Minister of Education of, 223–224
    Ministry of Education, 217–218
    overview of, 213
    reform plan for, 244
    as well-resourced nation-state, 254
Singaporean students, 257
    expectations of teachers not clear to,
        276
    quality of work of, 280–281

Singaporean teachers
    assessment practices among, 273
    direct teaching by, 271
    expectations of, 276
    quality of work, 281
    rationales of, 274–275
    relying on direct teaching, 271
    rubrics used by, 275–276
    self-report data of, on assessment
        practices, 273–275
The Singapore Economy: New Directions
    (ERC), 258
Singapore educational system, 213
    conceptual depth focus lacking
        in, 270
    formative/summative assessment in,
        261, 282
    high-stakes assessments, 218, 221, 260,
        281
    pedagogical innovation in, 224, 244
    pedagogical practices in, 263–269
    role of government in, 214
    shift in policy focus of, 223–224
Singapore Examinations and Assessment
    Board (SEAB), 260–261
Sistema de Avalia-cão da Educação Básica
    (SAEB), 393
    advantages/disadvantages of, 399–400
    frequency of, 398
    sampling broadness of, 397
Situational operational grid, 346
16PF Questionnaire. *See* Sixteen
    Personality Factors Questionnaire
Sixteen Personality Factors Questionnaire
    (16PF Questionnaire), 340–341
Skill(s)
    basic interpersonal communicative
        skills, 192
    cognitive, 146, 150
    communication, 287, 288–289
    core, in global workplace, 288
    deficit in, 23
    Department for Education and Skills,
        79
    employability, 309
    language comprehension, 301
    literacy, 303

Skill(s) (*continued*)
  Measuring Student Knowledge and Skills: A New Framework for Assessment, 225–226
  noncognitive, 223, 225
  PISA as most conspicuous international effort to measure 21st-century, 225–226
  social, 146
  social understandings and, 225
  two meanings to, 383
SLI. *See* Specific language impairment
Slovakia, 28, 33–36
Smirnov-Kolmogorov test, 365
Smith, Linda Tuhiwai, 98
Smutny, J. F., 317
Sobrinho, Dias, 378
  on globalization, 380
  on relativity of values, 388
Sociability, 388
Social beliefs. *See* Shared social belief
Social capital, 258
Social context, local, 387
Social desirability bias, 344
Social Desirability Scale, 341
Social identities, 259
Social inequality, 121
Socialism, 4
Socialization, 101, 189
Social justice, 53, 58–72
Social organization, 225, 259
Social relationships, 122
Social setting, 134–135, 147–150
Social situation, 352
Social skills, 146, 445
Social stratification, 220
Social type, 337, 339
Sociocultural influences, 55–56
Socrates, xv
Solidarity, 388
Sonorants, 198
South Africa, 189, 433
Southern Africa Consortium for Monitoring Education Quality (SACMEQ), 161, 194
Soviet Union, 459
SPA. *See* Science Practical Assessment

Spain, 455–458
Spanierman, L. B., 336
Spanish speakers, 425–428
Spatial Memory (SpM), 165
Spearman, Charles, 451
Special learning needs, 457
Special needs, 481
Specific language impairment (SLI), 288
  domestic workers and, 299
  GCC cultural considerations surrounding, 298–299
  NWR and, 307
  parental apprehension about assessments for, 298
Speech, 287, 316
Speech/language pathologists, 289
  extensive training for culturally diverse populations required of GCC countries by, 291
  GCC region lacking in, 300
Speed tests, 12
Sperry, Roger, 424
  on irrelevance of culture, 471
Split-half technique, 331
SpM. *See* Spatial Memory
Spontaneous language samples, limitations of, 304
SRBCSS. *See* Scales for Rating the Behavioral Characteristics of Superior Students
Ssu (reflecting), 228
"Standard back-translation methods," 435
Standardization data, 35
Standardized testing
  accountability driven by, 81
  in GCC countries, 300–301
  limitations of, 304
  origin of, 382
  test adaptations compared to, 306
  testing limits of, 67
  translation of, for Hispanics, 422–424
Standards, 8, 83–84. *See also* Guidelines
  "arbiters of performance quality," 83
  for assessment/test use, 84–86
  global shift toward reform driven by, 77
  national, 9
  "quality benchmarks," 83

role of teachers in interpretation of, 84

Standards for Educational and Psychological Testing, 9, 27, 42

technical, 8–9

The Standards. *See Standards for Educational and Psychological Testing*

Standards-driven reform, 77

Standards for Educational and Psychological Testing (The Standards), 9, 27, 42, 336

Statistics, 50

Steele, C. M., 54–55

Stein, S. J., 357

Step difficulty calibrations, 47

Stereotype threat, 54–55

Sternberg, R. J., 163–164, 444

Sternberg's theory of successful intelligence, 162, 444

Storytelling, 148

Strangers, 122

Strategies for Active and Independent Learning (SAIL), 260

Stress, 157

Student achievement
high-stakes assessments and, 246
Measuring Student Knowledge and Skills: A New Framework for Assessment, 225–226
testing, in Zambia, 166–170

Student performance evaluation, 375, 387

Students
American, 363–364, 366
gifted, 454
humanities, 361
as members of community of cultural traditions, 228
natural science, 361
reasoning and, 391
Russian, 363–364, 366
Scales for Rating the Behavioral Characteristics of Superior Students, 318
in Singapore, 257, 276, 280–281

stress experienced by, from overemphasis on testing, 157
in Zambia, 178

Stufflebeam, D. L., 378

Subhi, T., 319

Subject-Verb-Object language (SVO), 197–198

Successful intelligence. *See* Sternberg's theory of successful intelligence

Sue, S., 57

Summative assessment
as assessment of learning, 255
Black on, 262
debate over benefits of, in England, 237
formative assessment and, in Singapore, 261
looser coupling for, 238, 244
pedagogical innovation and, 231
recommendations for, 234
Wiliam and Black questioning continuum of divide between/continuum with, 262

Super, C. M., 138–139
on African parenting, 140–141
on developmental timetable of African v. U.S. children, 141–142
on motor development in infants in Kenya, 152

Supreme Education Council of Qatar, 294

Sustained writing, 277–280

SVO. *See* Subject-Verb-Object language

Swedish parenting, 136

SweSAT, 386

SyM. *See* Symbolic Memory

Symbolic Memory (SyM), 165

Syntax, 199–200

Tacit knowledge, 406, 445, 460

Task performance, 146

Teacher nomination
accuracy of, in question, 315–316
scales of behavioral characteristics and, 320, 332

Teachers. *See also* Saudi teachers; Singaporean teachers
assessments based on, 87–89
comments, 457

Teachers (*continued*)
  professional development for, 238–239
  professionalism in, 91–92
  rating scale, 445
  role of, in interpretation of standards,
    84
Teaching, 238–239
Teach Less, Learn More (TLLM)
  initiative, 214, 221, 260
Technical competency, 388
Technical knowledge, ethical values and,
  377
Technical organization of work, 225
Technical type, 339
Technology
  in assessment practices, 239
  learning environments based on, 243
tertiary education programs, 3
Test administration, 12, 64
TestCentral, 30–32
Test construction, 20
Test consumers, 3
Test development, 1
  APA supporting, 26
  conditions external to, 24–25
  conditions internal to, 25–27
  economics of, 2
  ethical issues with, 17–21
  exemplary programs for, 27–36
  future of, 24–27
  in individualist v. collectivist countries, 4
  language issues in, 62
  market for, 3
  in Romania, 32–33
Testing. *See also* Standardized testing
  for achievement/competencies, 162
  for children, criterion-based v.
    normative, 122
  children's interaction with strangers as
    factor in process of, 122
  Chinese ideas of, 382
  for cognitive ability in Zambia,
    164–166
  computer-based, 15–17
  conditions of equity influencing, 71
  copyright issues with, 427
  credentialing function of, 158

criteria-based, 122, 431–433
  cultural factors in, 121
  cultural traditions as factor in, 121, 123,
    181
  debate over culture-free, 123
  as diagnostic tool, 158
  different purposes of, 475–480
  educational institutions as largest
    consumers of, 2
  Educational Testing Service, 235
  formats, 12
  globalization issues of, 159
  Harkness on, 471
  Institute of Personality and Ability
    Testing, 340
  instruments for, in Africa, 118
  Internet-delivered, 15–17
  limits of standardized, 67
  in mathematics, 168
  modern approaches to, 68–71
  modified procedures for, 67
  in mother tongue, 208
  in native language, 66–67
  needs for, 6–7
  nonverbal, 64–65, 436
  obsolete, 20
  origin of, 3
  power tests, 12
  professional administration of, 7
  results of, in Zambia, 170–178
  revision of, 13
  speed tests, 12
  standardized, driving accountability, 81
  standardized, in psychology/education,
    26
  for student achievement in Zambia,
    166–170
  students feeling stress/anxiety from,
    157
  test-retest study, 173
  as tool for decision making, 158
  traditional approach to, 422
  unauthorized sales of, 20–21
  various uses of, 2
Test performance
  acculturation influencing, 60–61,
    69–71

conditions that impact, 14–15
pattern of expected, for culturally/
    linguistically diverse individuals, 70
Test-retest study, 173
Test use
    with adults, 7–8
    with children, 4–7
    educational systems impact on,
        24–25
    ethical issues with, 17–21
    international guidelines for, 9–10
    international surveys on, 4–8
    political systems impact on, 24–25
    public attitudes impact on, 25
    standards for, 84–86
    types of, 5
Test validity, 11. *See also* Validity studies
    construct equivalence, 11–12
    construct validity, 12
    in Romania, 31
Textbook, 265
Theories of giftedness, 455
Thinking Schools, Learning Nation
    (TSLN) initiative, 214, 221, 259
Third International Mathematics and
    Science Study (TIMSS), 79
Thompson, E. P., 246
Tight coupling, 220, 238, 244
Tikhomirov, O. K., 354
TIMSS. *See* Third International
    Mathematics and Science Study;
    Trends in International Mathematics
    and Science Study (TIMSS)
TLLM. *See Teach Less, Learn More*
    initiative
Tomlinson, C. A., 241–242
Tough Choices or Tough Times (NCEE),
    235
Towndrow, P. A., 478
Trace ability, 383
Traditional teaching, 266–268
Training, 110
"Transcreation," 118
Transformation, 452
Translation, 13–14
    of achievement tests in Zambia, 167
    adaptation and, 446

of Aurora Battery across languages/
    cultures, 450–451
challenges in, for Zambian testing,
    178
challenges of, for Hispanics, 426–427
in Czech Republic/Hungary/Latvia/
    Slovakia project, 34
defined, 444
monolinguals, 14
in Romania, 31
rules/guidelines for international,
    447–450
"standard back-translation methods," 435
of standardized tests for Hispanics,
    422–424
of test instruments in Africa, 118
of test instruments in GCC countries,
    305
variability in data as result of, 206
Translators/interpreters, 65–66
Transparency, 43–44, 296
Transportability, 43–44, 71–72
Trends in International Mathematics and
    Science Study (TIMSS), 159, 255
Tshivenda, 207
TSLN. *See Thinking Schools, Learning
    Nation* initiative
Tumikila (intelligent), 102
Twi (Ashanti), 197, 199–200, 206
2003 UN Human Development Report,
    117
Tylor, E. B., 98

UNESCO. *See* United Nations
    Educational Scientific and Cultural
    Organization
United Kingdom (UK), 79, 451–455
    National Curriculum in, 452–453
    NEO-FFI of Big Five used in, 358
    summative assessments questioned in,
        237
    transformation of educational
        assessment practices in, 452
United Nations, 113, 116
United Nations Educational Scientific
    and Cultural Organization
    (UNESCO), 392

United States, 221
United States Agency for International Development (USAID), 208
Universal markers, 101–102
Universal Nonverbal Intelligence Test (UNIT), 164–165, 172
University of California, Berkeley, 30
USAID. *See* United States Agency for International Development
U.S. BabyCenter Medical Advisory Board, 97

Validation, 90
Validity. *See also* Test validity
    consequential, 43
    construct, 12
    context, 118–120
    within cultural context, 469
    Linn on, 85
    in modified approaches, 68
    national v. international, 470
    of scale in Saudi study on gifted children, 323
    of Western ability tests, 170–177
    of Zambian tests, 172–177
Validity studies, 6
Values, 98, 431
van de Vijver, F. J. R., 182, 446
Variables, 369
Varimox rotation of scale items, 324–325
Verbal expression, 148
Vocabulary
    African languages differing from English, 200
    list-making of, loaded with difficulties, 207
    mismatch in, of personality descriptors in Tshivenda/English, 207
    in mother tongues of Ghana, 197
Voyage of the Beagle (Darwin), 111

Wason's decision-making task, 352
Wechsler Intelligence Scale for Children, 20, 429, 449, 462
Weick, Karl, 216
Wellness, 21–22
Western ability tests, 170–177

White space initiative, 231
Whiting, B. B., 143
WHO. *See* World Health Organization
Wiliam, D., 240–241, 262
Wong, David, 229
Woodcock-Johnson Tests of Cognitive Abilities, 34–35
Woodcock-Muñoz Foundation, 35
Woodcock, Richard, 34
Words (MLUw), 302
Work, 225
World Bank, 113
World Health Organization (WHO), 1
World Intellectual Property Organization Copyright and Performance and Phonograms Treaties, 16

Yagüe, García, 455
Yale University, 363
Yi (signification), 228
Yoruba community, 144–145
    storytelling/riddles in, 148

Zambia, 179–180, 476
    challenges in translation of testing of students in, 178
    cultural factors in interpretation of testing in, 181
    demographics of, 160
    literacy rate in, 161
    results of testing in, 170–177
    testing cognitive ability in, 164–166
    testing for student achievement in, 166–170
Zambian Achievement Test (ZAT), 167, 181
    sample items from, 168
    validity results of, 172–177
    Zambian National Achievement Test correlations with, 177
Zambian children
    disease burdens on, 160
    at educational disadvantage, 161
ZAT. See Zambian Achievement Test
Zeitlin, Marian, 144–145, 150–151
Ziegler, J. C., 473